Step-by-Step
Functional Verification
with SystemVerilog
and OVM

Step-by-Step Functional Verification with SystemVerilog and OVM

by

Sasan Iman

SiMantis Inc.
Santa Clara, CA
Spring 2008

Sasan Iman
SiMantis, Inc.
900 Lafayette St. Suite 707
Santa Clara, CA 95050
iman@simantis.com

Step-by-Step Functional Verification with SystemVerilog and OVM

ISBN-10: 0-9816562-1-8
ISBN-13: 978-0-9816562-1-2

Printed on acid-free paper.

Printed in the United States of America

9 8 7 6 5 4 3 2 1

Hansen Brown Publishing Company
San Francisco, CA
info@hansenbrown.com

Foreword

By now, the metaphor of "the perfect storm" is in danger of becoming a cliché to describe the forces causing rapid evolution in some aspect of the electronics industry. Nevertheless, the term is entirely applicable to the current evolution—arguably even a revolution—in functional verification for chip designs. Three converging forces are at work today: complexity, language, and methodology.

The challenges posed in the verification of today's large, complex chips is well known. Far too many chips do not ship on first silicon due to functional bugs that should have been caught before tapeout. Hand-written simulation tests are being almost entirely replaced by constrained-random verification environments using functional coverage metrics to determine when to tape out. Specification of assertions, constraints, and coverage points has become an essential part of the development process.

The SystemVerilog language has been a major driver in the adoption of these advanced verification techniques. SystemVerilog provides constructs for assertions, constraints, and coverage along with powerful object-oriented capabilities that foster reusable testbenches and verification components. The broad vendor support and wide industry adoption of SystemVerilog have directly led to mainstream use of constrained-random, coverage-driven verification environments.

However, a language alone cannot guarantee successful verification. SystemVerilog is a huge language with many ways to accomplish similar tasks, and it doesn't directly address such essential areas as verification planning, common testbench building blocks, and communication between verification components. Such topics require a comprehensive verification methodology to tie together the advanced techniques and the features of the language in a systematic approach.

Fortunately, the Open Verification Methodology (OVM) recently arrived to address this critical need. Developed by Cadence Design Systems and Mentor Graphics, the OVM is completely open (freely downloadable from ovmworld.org) and guaranteed to run on the simulation products from both companies. The OVM leverages many years of verification experience from many of the world's experts. It was greeted with enormous enthusiasm by the industry and is used today on countless chip projects.

Thus, the timing of this book could not be better. It provides thorough coverage of all three forces at work. The complexity challenge is addressed by timely advice on verification planning and coherent descriptions of advanced verification techniques. Many aspects of the SystemVerilog language, including its assertion and testbench constructs, are covered in detail. Finally, this book embraces the OVM as the guide for verification success, providing a real-world example deploying this methodology.

Functional verification has never been easy, but it has become an overwhelming problem for many chip development teams. This book should be a great comfort for both design and verification engineers. Perhaps, like *The Hitchhiker's Guide to the Galaxy*, it should have "DON'T PANIC!" on its cover. So grab a beverage of your choice and curl up in a comfortable chair to learn how to get started on your toughest verification problems.

Michael McNamara
Past Chairman of the Verilog Standards Committee.
Former VP of Engineering of Chronologic Simulation (creator of VCS).
Currently Vice President and General Manager, Cadence Design Systems.
Spring 2008

Table of Contents

Preface

Functional verification has been a major focus of product development for more than a decade now. This period has witnessed the introduction of new tools, methodologies, languages, planning approaches, and management philosophies, all sharply focused on addressing this very visible, and increasingly difficult, aspect of product development. Significant progress has been made during this period, culminating, in recent years, in the emergence and maturity of best-in-class tools and practices. These maturing technologies not only allow the functional verification challenge to be addressed today, but also provide a foundation on which much-needed future innovations will be based. This means that having a deep understanding of, and hands-on skills in applying, these maturing technologies is mandatory for all engineers and technologists whose task is to address the current and future functional verification challenges.

A hallmark of maturing technologies is the emergence of multi-vendor supported and standardized verification languages and libraries. The SystemVerilog hardware design and verification language (IEEE standard 1800), and the SystemVerilog-based Open Verification Methodology (OVM) provide a powerful solution for addressing the functional verification challenge. SystemVerilog is an extension of Verilog-2005 (IEEE Standard 1364-2005), and enhances features of Verilog by introducing new data types, constrained randomization, object-oriented programming, assertion constructs, and coverage constructs. OVM, in turn, provides the methodology and the class library that enable the implementation of a verification environment according to best-in-class verification practices.

This book is intended for a wide range of readers. It can be used to learn functional verification methodology, the SystemVerilog language, and the OVM class library and its methodology. This book can also be used as a step-by-step guide for implementing a verification environment. In addition, the source code for the full implementation of the XBar verification environment can be used as a template for starting a new project. As such, this book can be used by engineers starting to learn the SystemVerilog language concepts and syntax, as well as advanced readers looking to achieve better verification quality in their next verification project. This book can also be used as a reference for the SystemVerilog language and the OVM class library. All examples provided in this book are fully compliant with SystemVerilog IEEE 1800 standard and should compile and run on any IEEE 1800-compliant simulator.

Acknowledgements

The creation of this book would not have been possible without the generous support of many individuals. I am especially grateful to David Tokic and Luis Morales for helping turn this book from a nascent idea into a viable target, to Susan Peterson for getting this project off the ground and for her infectious positive energy, and to Tom Anderson for his continued technical and logistical guidance and support throughout the life of this effort. Special thanks also go to Sarah Cooper Lundell and Adam Sherer for valuable planning and technical discussions, and to Ben Kauffman, the technical editor.

The examples included in this book were developed and verified using the Incisive Functional Verification Platform® developed by Cadence Design Systems, and obtained through Cadence's Verification Alliance program. I would like to thank Cadence Design Systems and the Verification Alliance program for their generous support of this effort.

The technical content of this book has benefited greatly from feedback by great engineers and technologists. Special thanks go to David Pena and Zeev Kirshenbaum for in-depth discussions on many parts of this book. In addition, technical feedback and discussions by individuals from a diverse set of companies have contributed significantly to improving the technical content of this book. I am especially grateful to these individuals whose names and affiliations are listed below.

Sasan Iman
Santa Clara, CA
Spring 2008

Adiel Khan	Cadence Design Systems
Abhijit Sinha	SiMantis Inc.
Anup Sharma	Azul Systems
Chuck Chiang	Cisco Systems
Dave Pena	Cadence Design Systems
Firooz Massoudi	Maxim Integrated Products
Gabi Leshem	Cadence Design Systems
Gerard Ventura	Cadence Design Systems
James Baldwin	Qualcomm
Jayavel Sabapathy	SiMantis Inc.
Jenny Zhang	Cadence Design Systems
Phu Huynh	Cadence Design Systems
Poornachandra Rao	Analog Devices
Richard Miller	Cisco Systems
Syed Mahmud	Maxim Integrated Products
Tim Pylant	Cadence Design Systems
Umer Yousafzai	Cadence Design Systems
Vincent Huang	AMD
Virendra Jaiswal	SiMantis Inc.
Warren Stapleton	Montalvo Systems
Yahya Khateeb	PLX Technology
Zeev Kirshenbaum	Cadence Design Systems

Online Resources

SystemVerilog

To learn more about the SystemVerilog language, and to keep up with the latest updates to the SystemVerilog LRM, visit:

http://www.SystemVerilog.org/
http://www.EDA-stds.org/sv/

OVM

This book is based on OVM release 1.0.1. To download the latest version of the OVM class library, to participate in OVM user forums, to learn about the latest related news and seminars, and to contribute to the OVM community, visit:

http://www.OVMWorld.org/

Book Examples and Updates

To download the full implementation of the XBar design and its verification environment, examples used in this book, and for any updates and/or errata released for this book, visit:

http://www.SiMantis.com/

Feedback

We welcome your feedback on this book. Please email your feedback to:

fvsvovm@simantis.com

Book Structure

This book provides a complete guide and reference for functional verification methodology, learning the SystemVerilog language, and for building a verification environment using SystemVerilog and the OVM class library. Given the range of material covered in this book, it is expected that the focus of any one reader may be on one specific topic, or that any one reader may prefer to bypass familiar content. To better support the range of readers who can benefit from this book, its content is grouped into parts. These parts are ordered so that the prerequisite knowledge required for any topic is covered in the parts appearing before that topic. This means that this book can be studied in a linear fashion, but the clear breakdown of topics into these parts facilitates selective focus on any one topic. This book consists of the following parts:

- Part 1: Verification Methodologies, Planning, and Architecture
  This part focuses on the functional verification problem, its relation to the product development flow, challenges that it raises, available tools, and metrics that are used for evaluating the effectiveness of a functional verification approach (chapter 1). This part also provides a detailed description of verification planning for a coverage-driven verification flow (chapter 2). The architectural view of a verification environment is also described in this part of the book (chapter 3).
  The discussion in this part of the book is implementation independent, and provides the background that is necessary before a verification solution can be implemented.
- Part 2: All about SystemVerilog
  This part provides a detailed introduction to the SystemVerilog language by describing its programming (chapter 4) and verification related features (chapter 5). This part can be used to learn the syntax and semantics of the SystemVerilog language, and to also learn its verification related features. In addition to chapter 4, randomization features are described in chapter 10, assertion features are described in chapter 15, and coverage features are described in chapter 17. The content in this part is organized through tables and examples so it can also be used as a desk reference for the SystemVerilog language.

- Part 3: <u>Open Verification Methodology</u>
  This part provides an in-depth description of OVM features, and gives examples of
  using these features to implement the different pieces of a verification environment. Chapter 6 describes the infrastructure and the core utilities of the OVM class
  library. Chapter 7 describes OVM features for building a verification environment
  hierarchy and support for modeling simulation phases. Chapter 8 describes transaction sequence (i.e., scenario) generation architecture of the OVM, and the utilities available for implementing this architecture. Chapter 9 describes transaction
  and channel interfaces, and their implementation using the predefined classes of
  the OVM class library.
  The discussions in this part describe the architectural view of verification environment elements based on OVM constructs, and illustrate the implementation of
  these elements through small and self-contained examples. The use of OVM constructs described in this part of the book for implementing a full-scale verification
  environment is described in part 5 of this book.
- Part 4: <u>Randomization and Data Modeling</u>
  This part provides an in-depth look at the randomization feature of SystemVerilog
  by describing how the randomization engine operates, constructs provided by SystemVerilog, and issues that must be considered when using randomization (chapter
  10). This part also describes techniques and the relevant issues for building a data
  model using the SystemVerilog language constructs (chapter 11). A data model
  implemented using the guidelines described in this chapter is used to represent a
  transaction that is exchanged between verification environment components.
- Part 5: <u>Verification Environment Implementation and Scenario Generation</u>
  This part describes the implementation of a verification environment using a module-based (chapter 12) and a class-based (chapter 13) approach. It also describes
  the implementation of transaction sequences for modeling verification scenarios
  (chapter 14). The description in this part is based on the XBar design, a cross-bar
  switch (section 12.2). The discussions on class-based implementation of the verification environment for the Xbar design (chapter 13) and the generation of its transaction sequences (chapter 14) provide a complete example of a verification
  environment implementation using the OVM class library and its recommended
  guidelines.
- Part 6: <u>Assertion-Based Verification</u>
  This part provides an in-depth description of the sequence and property specification constructs of SystemVerilog (chapter 15), and describes the recommended
  methodology for assertion-based verification (chapter 16). A good understanding
  of the material in this part is needed for having the ability to write concise and
  complex properties, and to make effective use of assertions in reaching verification
  closure.
- Part 7: <u>Coverage Modeling and Measurement</u>
  This part provides an in-depth description of the coverage constructs of the SystemVerilog language (chapter 17). The definition of a coverage plan, implementation of a coverage plan using the constructs provided by SystemVerilog, and the
  flow for carrying out a coverage-driven verification flow is described (chapter 18)

PART 1

Verification Methodologies, Planning, and Architecture

CHAPTER 1

Verification Tools and Methodologies

The introduction of SystemVerilog as a new hardware design and verification language is motivated by the need for a powerful tool that can facilitate the implementation of the latest verification methodologies. As such, having intimate knowledge of the challenge posed by functional verification, the latest verification methodologies, and the way in which design and verification flow fit together is a first step in the successful use of SystemVerilog in completing a verification project.

This chapter brings functional verification into focus by describing its context, the challenges it raises, and the approaches that best address these challenges. Section 1.1 sets the stage by describing the background against which a verification project is executed, the meaning of functional verification within this context, and the challenges faced in successful execution of a verification project. The execution of a verification project cannot be improved without tangible metrics for evaluating its quality. Section 1.2 introduces metrics that collectively define the execution quality of a verification project. Section 1.3 summarizes the interaction between design and verification, and in doing so, highlights the natural order of verification project execution imposed by design activities. Section 1.4 describes the different technologies that are available for verification and discusses where in the verification flow they best fit. Finally, section 1.5 describes best-in-class verification methodologies that leverage the available technologies to address verification challenges while adhering to restrictions inherent in its order of execution.

1.1 Setting the Stage

A functional verification project plays against the backdrop of a product development flow. The following subsections describe the product design flow, the meaning of functional verification and challenges that must be met to successfully and efficiently execute a verification project.

1.1.1 Design Flow: From Intent to Product

Good knowledge of the design process is needed for effective management of verification project complexity. This knowledge is also necessary for understanding the effect of local verification decisions on the overall progress and effectiveness of verification. This section provides an overview of the design flow.

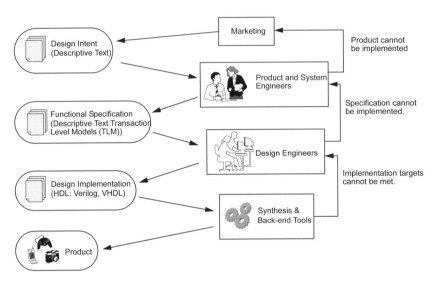

Figure 1.1 Product Development Flow

Product development flows are as varied as the products they produce. Most flows, however, can be described in terms of abstract phases corresponding to product idea development and design and implementation stages. Figure 1.1 shows an overview of one such design flow, from intent to final product. A product is usually scoped by a marketing team as an opportunity to satisfy a demand in the marketplace. The initial description of a product must be described with careful consideration of the overall abilities and limitations of the underlying technologies. This consideration is essential for delivering the product with good confidence, on target, and with the desired functionality. The initial product intent is turned into a functional description through discussions between the marketing team and product and system engineers. These discussions are geared towards solidifying the general features of the product (e.g., user level features available to consumer, the number and types of required interfaces) and identifying the architecture that is best suited for delivering the desired functionality. An important part of this architectural exploration stage is to perform analysis sufficient for confirming that the required features are practical and can be supported by the suggested architecture (e.g., that the proposed bandwidth of the internal bus of a multi-interface device can support the expected traffic between all interfaces).

Transaction level models (TLM) are used at the architectural level of abstraction to model the blocks identified in the early stages of architectural exploration and analysis. In general, transaction level models allow designers to specify block behaviors at a high level of abstraction where the focus is on the system level behavior of blocks and interaction between blocks, and not on low-level implementation and cycle accurate behaviors.

Once the architectural model of a design is finalized, design engineers take this functional specification and create an implementation in a target language (e.g., Verilog, System-Verilog, VHDL). This functional specification is then translated into a final implementation through a series of steps in which appropriate tools and techniques are used to create the design implementation. Once the design implementation is produced, the final product is created by using the synthesis and back-end tools to build the chips and boards that will comprise the final product.

Transaction level models play an important role in the design and verification process in that they provide an early model of the design that can be used for architectural evaluation and whose verification must be considered in the verification flow. An overview of transaction level models and the design flow is described in the following subsections.

1.1.1.1 Transaction Level Modeling and Design Abstraction Levels

Different levels of abstraction are used in taking a design through stages of implementation. These abstraction levels are:

- Transaction level models (TLM)
- Register transfer level models (RTL)
- Netlist of gates

Unlike a register transfer level description (which requires that a design be described in terms of registers, combinational blocks, and their interconnections), and netlist of gates (which requires that a design be described in terms of gates in a target library and their interconnections), transaction level models are not an abstraction level in the strict sense of the term. This is because transaction level modeling allows models to contain a range of detail all the way from algorithmic description down to cycle accurate models.

Modeling a design at the transaction level has multiple benefits. It allows a system to be modeled when there is very little detail available about the internal implementation of its blocks. Also, given the low-level of detail in a transaction level model, it is possible to create fast simulation models of the system that can be used by software developers to work on software applications that will eventually run on the completed system. Given that the focus in transaction level modeling is more on inter-block communication, these models are ideal for doing system performance analysis and verifying that a system can meet the expected performance requirements.

A transaction level model can be developed at the following levels of detail:

- Architectural view (AV)
- Programmer's view (PV)
- Programmer's view plus timing (PVT)
- Cycle callable (CC)

Architectural view models a timeless communication mechanism between modules where the focus is on the fact that a transaction is moved between blocks and not on how or in what exact timeline the transfer takes place.

Programmer's view models inter-module communication explicitly using blocking transactions between modules where a module waits for the other module to complete the transaction before continuing with its operation. This approach, through its blocking mechanism, provides a means of ordering module executions based on their communication requirements.

Programmer's view with timing model improves programmer's view by modeling inter-module communication using blocking and non-blocking interactions where exchange of transactions include an estimate of transaction time. As such, in this model, module execution ordering is controlled by the timing estimates for transactions.

Cycle callable view further enhances programmer's view with timing with accurate cycle level timing behavior. Beyond cycle callable view, a bus functional model is used to model the interaction between modules.

A model developed at the transaction level can be improved as more detail about the implementation of a block becomes available. As such, a transaction level model provides a path to continually improving the system level model of a design.

The use of transaction level models in system modeling is an important concept from a verification perspective. The reason is that these transaction level models are used for system level modeling and as such, their implementation must also be verified in the same sense that RTL descriptions of the design must be verified. In addition, transaction level models can be leveraged during chip and system level verification to improve verification speed. Also, concepts from transaction level modeling can be used for communication between verification environment blocks.

OSCI[1] has standardized an API that describes predefined transactions that can be used for TLM based interactions. These standard transaction types can be modeled in SystemVerilog and for inter-module communication. The SystemVerilog implementation of this API is described in chapter 9.

1.1.1.2 Design Implementation Flow

The goal of functional verification is to verify correct implementation of the design produced by design engineers from the design specification. This step corresponds to the third step in figure 1.1.

Figure 1.2 shows details of a typical flow used by designers to turn a functional specification into a design implementation. This flow consists of the following steps:

- Architectural design
- Block design

---

[1] The ideas and general guidelines of transaction level modeling have been standardized by the Open SystemC Initiative (OSCI) (http://www.systemc.org) who at the time of this writing, provides TLM 2.0 as a standard API for developing transaction level models using SystemC.

- Module design
- Chip/System design

The very first step is to create the design architecture. This step identifies the individual modules and blocks in the system and describes the functionality for each block. Only after this architecture is decided can the design of these individual blocks get started. The next step is to design the individual blocks identified during the architectural design stage. Blocks are implemented as RTL descriptions, and then grouped together to form design modules. Modules may optionally contain blocks described at the transaction level that model non-digital parts of the system (e.g., analog parts, RF blocks, etc.). Modules are combined to form the full-chip design, which is then combined to form the implementation description of the entire system.

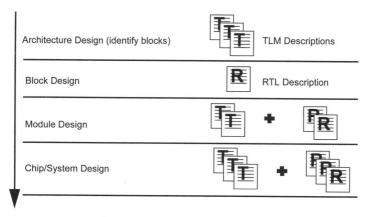

Figure 1.2 Design Implementation Flow

This breakdown of the design implementation flow hints at the way verification activity dovetails with design activity. The interaction between design and verification flows is described in more detail in the next section.

1.1.2 Functional Verification: Gaining Closure

Product design flow, as shown in figure 1.1, points at two stages which fundamentally lead to functional errors and malfunctions in the final product:

- Translating the product intent into a functional specification
- Translating the functional specification into a design implementation.

These steps require manual processing of at times vaguely described ideas and goals in non-exact natural languages by engineers and operators who can be prone to misunderstanding descriptions and making errors in following well defined procedures. The error-prone nature of this step is in contrast with the automated translation of design implementation into a netlist of gates. This step is performed by using synthesis and physical design tools which are less prone to errors because of their high degree of automation and tool maturity.

The main source of functional errors in a design can be attributed to the following:

- Ambiguities in product intent
- Ambiguities in the functional specification
- Misunderstandings by designers even when the specification is clear
- Implementation errors by designers even when the understanding is correct

The primary goal of *functional verification* is to verify that the initial design implementation is functionally equivalent to product intent. Or alternatively, proving the convergence of product intent, functional specification, and design implementation.

Figure 1.3 shows a pictorial view of this concept. The process of functional verification facilitates the convergence of product intent, functional specification, and design implementation, by identifying any differences between the three and giving the system and design engineers the opportunity to eliminate this difference by appropriately modifying one, two, or all three descriptions so the difference is eliminated. Verification closure is gained when this convergence is proved with a high degree of confidence.

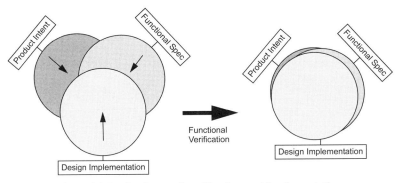

Figure 1.3 Design Intent, Specification, and Implementation

1.1.2.1 Black-Box, White-Box, and Gray-Box Verification

The ultimate goal of functional verification is to verify that a design works as expected when stimulated on its boundary. As such, any errors in the design that cannot be detected by stimulating and observing its boundary can effectively be ignored. Such errors include:

- Errors that will never be activated
- Errors that can be activated but will never be propagated to design outputs
- Multiple errors that can potentially hide one another

Black-box verification refers to verifying a block or design functionality only through its boundary signals. Figure 1.4 shows the general architecture for performing black-box verification. In this approach, stimulus is applied to both the design under verification (DUV) and a reference model (i.e., golden model). Outputs produced by the DUV and the golden model are then checked to be equivalent within the abstraction level (e.g., transaction accurate, instruction accurate, cycle accurate, etc.).

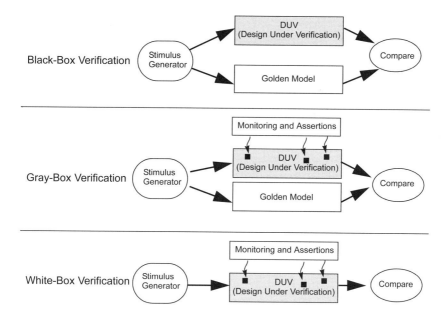

Figure 1.4 Black-Box, Gray-Box, and White-Box Verification Approaches

Black-box verification suffers from the following major drawbacks:

• Difficult to verify features related to design decisions
• Difficult to debug errors
• Requires an accurate reference model

All implementations of the same design specification are not created equal. Each implementation contains many design decisions that give it the performance or efficiency that make it different from other implementations. A CPU instruction pipeline is an example of this type of design implementation feature. A CPU may appear to be working even if its instruction pipeline is not working as expected, or not working at all. The performance of such a crippled design will, however, be negatively affected. Other examples of such features include the threshold settings for FIFO read/write operations or details of bus arbiter scheduling. It is very difficult to verify correct implementation of such features using the black-box verification approach.

An added complication in using black-box verification is that depending on the complexity of the DUV, it may take many cycles for the effect of an internal error to appear on the design outputs, therefore requiring much longer simulation traces to expose an error.

Even when an error is detected on the output, it is usually very difficult to trace the problem to its root cause.

An added difficulty in using black-box verification is that it requires a reference model implemented with enough accuracy to detect any and all internal bugs. Given that a model with such strict accuracy requirements (e.g., cycle accurate) may not be available or perhaps as difficult to build as the design itself, it is not always possible to rely completely on this verification approach.

White-box and gray-box verification provide alternative approaches for addressing the limitations of black-box verification. In _white-box verification_, no reference model is needed, because correct design operation is verified by placing monitors and assertions on internal and output signals of the DUV. _Gray-box verification_ is a combination of white-box and black-box verification approaches, where monitors and assertions on internal design signals are used along with a reference model. The use of monitors and assertions reduces the accuracy requirements of the reference model and also reduces debugging effort when bugs are found. These architecture used for white-box and gray-box verification approaches are also shown in figure 1.4.

Table 1.1 lists challenges inherent in completing a verification project, and also lists the degree of effort required to address these challenges when each of the verification approaches discussed in this section are used. As shown, gray-box verification provides the best balance of effort required to address these different challenges. As such, gray-box verification is the approach intuitively chosen most often by verification engineers to carry out their tasks. It should be emphasized that there are many shades of gray in gray-box verification, where these shades refer to the balance of effort dedicated to reference model development and monitor/assertion development. The exact shade of gray-box verification will ultimately depend on the specific requirements of a verification project and the verification engineer's experience from previous projects.

Verification Challenges	**Verification Approach**		
	Black-Box	**White-Box**	**Gray-Box**
Effort to create reference model	High	None	Medium
Effort to add monitors and assertions	None	High	Low
Effort to trace bug on output to its source	High	Low	Low
Effort to verify implementation related features	High	Low	Low

Table 1.1: Verification Approaches and Effort Needed to Create Verification Implementation

1.1.3 The Verification Challenge

Functional verification is a simple problem to state but a challenging one to address. The increasing size and complexity of designs and shortening time-to-market windows mean that verification engineers must verify larger and more complex designs in a shorter time than in previous projects. An effective solution to meeting this increased demand for achieving verification closure must address the following _verification challenges_:

- Completeness
- Reusability
- Efficiency
- Productivity
- Code performance

The challenge in _verification completeness_ is to maximize the part of design behavior that is verified. The major challenge in improving verification completeness is in capturing all of the scenarios that must be verified. This, however, is a manual, error-prone, and omission-prone process. Significant improvements in this area have been made by moving to coverage-driven verification methodologies. Coverage-driven verification approaches require a quantitative measure of completeness whose calculation requires strict planning, tracking, and organization of the verification plan. This strict requirement on verification plans naturally leads to exposing the relevant scenarios that may be missing. Fine-tuned verification planning and management methods have been developed to help with the planning and tracking of verification plans.

The challenge in _verification reusability_ is to increase portions of the verification environment infrastructure that can be reused in the next generations of the same project or in a completely different project, sharing features that are similar with those in the current project. A high degree of reuse can be achieved for standardized interfaces or functions. Blocks can be reused in any project that make use of the same standardized interface. Beyond standardized interfaces, identifying common functionality in the verification environment planning stage can lead to further reuse of verification infrastructure.

The challenge in _verification efficiency_ is to minimize the amount of manual effort required for completing a verification project. Clearly, manual efforts are error-prone, omission-prone, and time consuming. In contrast, automated systems can complete a significant amount of work in a short time. Automated systems must, however, be built manually. As such, improvements in efficiency must be made through careful analysis of the trade-off between the extra effort required for building an automated system and the gains it affords. Coverage-driven pseudo-random verification methodology is an example of a methodology where making the effort to build an automated system for stimulus generation and automated checking leads to significant improvements in verification efficiency, and hence productivity. An important consideration in deciding the feasibility of building an automated system is that such automation requires a consistent infrastructure on which it can be developed, and also imposes a use model on how engineers interact with it. As such, deployment of an automated system requires consistency both in infrastructure and engineering approach, both of which take time and targeted effort to achieve.

The challenge in _verification productivity_ is to maximize work produced manually by verification engineers in a given amount of time (e.g., number of failed scenarios debugged, verification environment blocks implemented, etc.). Achieving higher productivity has become a major challenge in functional verification. Significant improvements in the design flow have afforded design engineers with much higher productivity. Improvements in verification productivity have, however, lagged those on the design side, making functional verification the bottleneck in completing a design. Effective functional verification requires that this productivity gap between design and verification be closed. Productivity gains in verification can be obtained by moving to higher levels of abstraction and leveraging reuse concepts.

The challenge in *verification code performance* is to maximize the efficiency of verification programs. This consideration is in contrast with verification productivity, which deals with how efficiently verification engineers build the verification environment and verify the verification plan. The time spent on a verification project is usually dominated by the manual work performed by verification engineers. As such, verification performance has usually been a secondary consideration in designing and building verification environments. An important area in which verification performance becomes a primary consideration is in running regression suites where the turnaround times are dominated by how efficiently verification programs operate. Expert knowledge of tools and languages used for implementing the environment is a mandatory requirement for improving verification performance.

The methodologies and topics discussed in this book aim to address these verification challenges through the following topics:

- Best-in-class verification methodologies
- Improved verification planning processes
- Best use of SystemVerilog features and constructs
- Reuse considerations

1.2 Verification Metrics

Deciding which verification methodology is best suited for a given application should be based on a set of well defined metrics. Such metrics relate directly or indirectly to verification challenges discussed in section 1.1.3. The following *verification metrics* are used to facilitate this type of comparative analysis:

- Granularity
- Manual effort
- Effectiveness
- Completeness
- Correctness
- Reuse of verification environment
- Reuse of simulation data

Verification quality is the collective result of these individual metrics. These metrics are used to compare and contrast the verification methodologies discussed later in this chapter. The following subsections further discuss each metric.

1.2.1 Granularity

Verification granularity is a qualitative measure of the amount of detail that must be specified in describing and implementing a verification scenario. Granularity directly affects verification productivity by considering the effort required by verification engineers to deal with verification objects.

Verification granularity is different from design granularity. Design granularity refers to the abstraction level used at different stages of the design flow. For example, a transaction level model is described in terms of transactions and, therefore, verification scenarios described for such a model are also described at the transaction level. Verification granularity refers to using a higher level granularity than design granularity in describing verification scenarios. For example, for a USB port design described at the register transfer level (i.e., in terms of registers, combinational operators, and wires and buses), a verification scenario can be described in terms of sending a bulk transfer instead of specifying the individual signals that must be assigned in doing such a transfer. Describing scenarios at a higher level of abstraction than the design abstraction requires an automated method of translating a higher level statement (e.g., sending a bulk transfer) into signal activity at the USB port. In a verification environment, a driver (section 3.2.2) is used to facilitate this type of translation.

Verification granularity can be increased by:

- Describing scenarios at a higher level of abstraction
- Implementing scenarios using higher level language constructs

By describing scenarios at a higher level of abstraction, a verification engineer is able to focus on verification scenarios and not on low-level details of how that scenario is carried out.

A verification engineer can produce and debug only a limited amount of verification code in a day. Allowing verification engineers to implement a feature using higher level language constructs leads directly to higher productivity in building the verification environment. SystemVerilog provides a number of language constructs (e.g., randomization, coverage collection, property specification) aimed directly at allowing verification engineers to describe higher level intent with fewer lines of code.

1.2.2 Manual Effort

Verification manual effort is a measure of time spent by engineers in completing the verification project. Sources of manual effort are:

- Writing the verification plan
- Building the verification environment
- Executing verification scenarios
- Debugging failed scenarios

Some verification activities must be carried out by engineers. For example, extracting the verification plan from the design specification and design implementation has to be done manually and cannot be automated (at least not yet). Debugging also has to be done manually. It is, however, possible to make trade-offs in carrying out some tasks manually versus building an automated program for executing that task. For example, random generation of stimulus requires that coverage be collected in order to measure verification progress. Extra effort is required in building the infrastructure necessary to apply random stimulus and collect coverage, but the degree of automation obtained through such initial effort makes this a good strategy to follow. Note that such a trade-off may not exist for a very small verification project where the manual effort for building an automated system is greater than the effort required for completing the verification using directed-tests. In general, a trade-off analysis should be done to decide how much and what parts of the verification environment should be automated. Given the complexity of today's projects, more automation generally leads to less overall manual effort and, therefore, more productivity.

1.2.3 Effectiveness

Executing a verification plan usually consists of multiple simulation runs, each consisting of different verification scenarios. In general, not every simulation cycle contributes to verifying a new scenario and not all simulation runs execute unique scenarios. *Verification effectiveness* is a measure of how much of the simulation time contributes directly to covering more scenarios. All simulation runs that only verify previously verified scenarios should be removed from the simulation regression.

1.2.4 Completeness

Verification completeness is a measure of how much of the relevant design functionality is verified. *Verification plan completeness* refers to how much of the relevant functionality of the design is included in the verification plan. Ideally, a verification plan should be complete in that it should include all relevant scenarios. Verification plans are, however, rarely complete, since it is not possible to enumerate all corner cases of a complex design. Verifications plans may also be incomplete because of poor verification management processes or lack of time.

Verification methodology affects verification completeness. For example, if all scenarios are verified using directed testcases, then verification completeness is only as much as the directed scenarios that have been verified. In a methodology where stimulus is randomly generated, scenarios that are not specified in the verification plan may be generated as a by-product of the random generation process. In this sense, a random generation approach provides better verification completeness than directed—test–based verification.

1.2.5 Verification Environment Reusability

Verification environment reusability is a measure of how much of the verification environment is reused in subsequent verification activities. Possibilities include:

- Reuse of environment across design generations
- Reuse of environment blocks across design stages (block to system level)

Changes to a design across successive generations includes the addition of new features or changes in architecture. Such changes appear in two flavors: 1) those requiring architectural changes in the verification environment, and 2) those requiring additional scenarios to be verified using the same verification architecture. Verification environment reuse possibilities based on these two flavors should be identified before the environment is built, by identifying design and architectural features that are expected to remain the same and those that are expected to change. The architectural design of a verification environment should include clear boundaries between these features so that the verification environment and its blocks can be leveraged for verifying future generations of the design.

The more compelling motivation for reuse is leveraging verification pieces across the design flow as the design integration is moved from block to module and to system level. Verification infrastructure for blocks at the boundary of the system level design can directly be reused in the verification environment for the next level of integration. After integration, the verification focus for internal blocks moves from stimulus generation and collection to monitoring and checking. As such, a general guideline for making reuse possible is to separate stimulus generation functionality from checking and monitoring functionality.

1.2.6 Simulation Result Reusability

Simulation result reusability is a measure of whether data produced during design simulation can be reused to answer questions raised about conditions that occurred during that simulation run. In the extreme, any and all questions about a simulation run can be answered if a global dump of all signal changes in the design is stored. This approach, however, is not feasible for a real design with even moderate complexity. As such, simulation result reusability must be considered as a factor when deciding how to track a simulation run.

Simulation result reusability is a factor that should be considered in coverage modeling. A good strategy is to anticipate the types of questions that may be raised after simulation is completed and to collect enough data during simulation so that answers to such questions can be provided from the collected data. For example, a coverage collection model may collect only information on what bus transaction types were observed during the simulation process. After simulation is completed, a question may be raised about how many transactions types were repeated back-to-back at least once.

1.3 Interaction between Design and Verification

Verification engineers depend on designers to provide them with the design implementation. Design engineers in turn depend on verification engineers to provide them with the verification environment they need to verify their blocks and clusters as they make progress in completing the design. As such, successful completion of a design project requires careful orchestration of the interaction between system, design, and verification engineers.

Figure 1.5 shows an overview of design flow and each engineer's responsibilities as the design is carried out to completion. Initially, all engineers participate in preparing a verification plan. Once the verification plan is available, verification engineers first prepare the interface verification components that will be used to interact with design boundary modules. Such interface verification components are readily available for standardized protocols. The verification engineers will then prepare the module level testbench and the system level testbench. While verification engineers are preparing the module level testbench, design engineers implement system blocks and verify these blocks by writing assertions that are checked using a formal verification tool. These blocks are then combined to form design modules. At this point, the module testbench developed by the verification engineers is used by the design engineers to verify design modules. Modules are then combined by design engineers to create the complete system. At this time, the system testbench created by the verification engineers is used to verify the system level design. The system is modeled by the system engineers at the architectural levels and using transaction level models. Architecture verification continues by system engineers as work progresses on module and system test-bench development where these testbenches are used by system engineers to further verify architectural assumptions and performance.

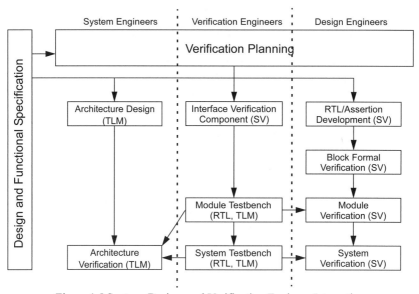

Figure 1.5 System, Design, and Verification Engineer Interactions

1.4 Verification Technologies

Technologies available for performing functional verification fall into three categories:

- Formal verification
- Simulation-based verification
- Acceleration/Emulation-based verification

The following sections provide an overview of these approaches.

1.4.1 Formal Verification

Formal verification uses logical and mathematical formulas and approaches to prove or disprove a given property of a hardware implementation. It is important to emphasize that since formal verification operates on equations describing the system and not on test vectors, any property proved by a formal verification tool holds for all possible test vectors applied to that behavior.

Formal verification has two major advantages over other verification technologies:

- Formal verification techniques are able to make universal statements about a property of a design implementation holding for all possible input streams
- Formal verification techniques do not require test vectors to be applied

These advantages of formal verification make this verification approach suitable for gaining full confidence that a design property holds for all cases. Also, the second advantage allows formal methods to be applied when a testbench and test vectors are not yet available.

Formal verification techniques fall into two major categories

- Equivalence checking
- Property checking

These approaches are discussed in the following subsections.

1.4.1.1 Equivalence Checking

In this approach, the *equivalence checking* formal verification tool proves that two hardware implementations are functionally equivalent under all possible input combinations and sequences. This means that, for example, a finite state machine will produce the exact same output sequence under all possible input sequences and same initial conditions.

The input to an equivalence checking tool is two formal representations of a design implementation before and after a given transformation. The equivalence checking tool creates a canonical model[2] of each implementation. Every Boolean function has a unique canonical representation under an assumed set of conditions (e.g., variable ordering). As such, once the canonical representation of the implementation before and after the transformation is available, then under ideal conditions, proving the equivalency of the two representations is straightforward.

In practice, however, building an equivalence checking tool for real sized designs and for transformations occurring in the design process is a difficult task. First of all, an equivalence checking tool requires that a formal model of the implementation before and after a transformation be available. Looking at the product design flow in figure 1.2, such models are available only before and after the synthesis process where RTL descriptions are translated into a netlist of gates. The equivalence checking between an RTL and the netlist of gates is, in fact, the most common application of equivalence checking tools.

[2.] A Canonical model of a Boolean function is a representation of that function that is unique under a given ordering of its variables. A Binary Decision Diagram is one such canonical representation for Boolean functions and is used extensively in tools for formal verification of digital systems.

Other challenges exist in building an equivalence checking tool. Building canonical representations of a design is not practical for very large systems. This means that special tricks must be deployed or manual intervention may be required to reduce the size of blocks that will be formally checked. One technique for reducing block sizes is to identify intermediate signals that are common between the before and after representations. Also, some transformations such as re-timing (i.e., moving combinational logic across registers during technology mapping and timing optimization) cannot be easily handled by implementations of the straightforward equivalence checking approach explained above.

These challenges have been addressed by new tools targeting equivalence checking, making them a required utility for synthesis and back-end flow. However, the need for formal representation of before and after transfer—and the fact that such complete representations are usually not available before the RTL design stage—mean that equivalence checking approaches cannot make a large contribution to the main challenge of functional verification and are best suited for later stages of product design flow. A property checking approach to formal verification, however, provides a very powerful technique for addressing the functional verification challenge. This approach is described in the following section.

1.4.1.2 Formal Property (Assertion) Checking

Given a formal description of a design implementation (e.g., an RTL description), *property checking* verifies that a given property described in a temporal logic[3] holds for the given implementation.

Figure 1.6 shows an example of how property checking is used to prove or disprove that a given implementation meets an expected property. The property to be checked is summarized in the top section of this figure. As shown, the described property can be reformulated as an equation that should always evaluate to true when considering the relationship between property variables imposed by the design (i.e., the equation describing the design). In this example, the relationship between variables in the good design does, in fact, lead to the property equation always evaluating to true. The same cannot, however, be shown for the bad design, leading to the conclusion that the bad design does not meet the property required in this example.

Other factors that make property checking a powerful and naturally suitable technique for functional verification include:

- Properties can be described at any stage of product specification and design creation. This includes properties defined at the system design stage all the way down to properties specified for micro-architecture design of blocks.
- Properties can be collected incrementally as specification and development proceeds.
- Properties can be used with formal property checking tools in the beginning stages of the design process when a verification environment is not available to provide test vectors.
- Properties can be used with simulation-based and acceleration-based verification.

[3.] A Temporal Logic represents a system of rules and symbols for representing and reasoning about relationships between logical variables in terms of time. For example, a temporal logic expression can state the expected relationship between two A and B variables in different clock cycles.

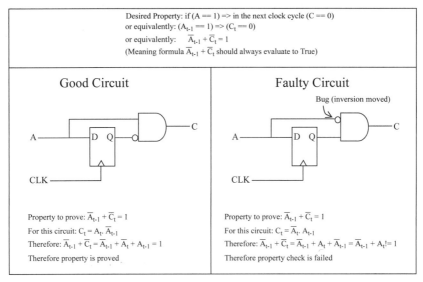

Figure 1.6 Formal Property (Assertion) Checking Example

- Properties indirectly define coverage collection metrics that will be needed to check verification progress.

Multiple languages have been developed to facilitate effective and powerful property descriptions. Property Specification Language (PSL) is one such standard language. System-Verilog also provides its own syntax for defining properties in the form of assertions.

1.4.2 Simulation-Based Verification

The fundamental step in simulation-based verification is the process of evaluating the next state values of design signals given its current state and input values, and to schedule future value assignments to design signals while considering signal delays. In a simulation tool, each evaluation of the next state is referred to as a delta cycle. Simulation consists of continuing delta-cycle evaluations at the next immediate time for which a signal assignment is scheduled. Simulation is completed when there is no future value assignment scheduled (i.e., no more changes in design signals are expected). Simulation can also be stopped explicitly through program or tool control mechanisms.

A verification environment consists of a testbench and a design. The fundamental operation in simulation-based verification is to use the testbench to apply input values to the design, compute the next state values of the design, and check to see if the next state is indeed the expected state for that design. A verification scenario is then the process of consecutively taking the design through different states where the sequence of observed design states corresponds to a verification scenario listed in the verification plan.

Figure 1.7 shows a representation of this process. The total state space of the design in shown in the figure. A simulation run starts at an initial state where the next state is identified by the current state and input values to the design. A *simulation trace* corresponds to the set of design values observed as a given path in the state space is traversed. A traversed path in the state space is identified by the verification scenario carried out by the simulator.

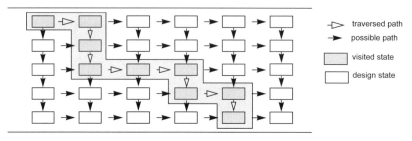

Figure 1.7 Simulation-Based Verification Flow

SystemVerilog provides a comprehensive set of constructs for modeling both the design and the verification environment. As such, both the design and the verification environment can be implemented completely using SystemVerilog. It is, however, important to note that in general, the distinction between a testbench and a design is a logical distinction, and the simulator is oblivious to the boundary between the code implementing the design and the code implementing the testbench. The equal treatment of design and testbench programs by the simulator can lead to race conditions between the design and the testbench. As such, SystemVerilog provides explicit means of separating the testbench from the design by introducing a ***program*** block (section 5.3).

1.4.3 Acceleration and Emulation

Formal and simulation-based verification techniques provide many benefits in the early to middle stages of the design flow. The speed of these techniques, however, falls far short of the simulation speed that is needed towards the end of the flow, when the entire system, along with its application software, must be verified. In addition to the larger design that must be simulated, system level simulations also need to run for many thousands or millions of instructions so that the macro behavior of the application software can be verified. Acceleration and emulation techniques are developed to satisfy these requirements.

The fundamental idea behind acceleration and emulation is to map the design into a configurable platform (e.g., FPGAs) so that the digital portion of the design can be simulated at close to final product clock rates.

Hardware acceleration refers to the idea of using a configurable platform to simulate the DUV. In hardware acceleration, the testbench program is running on a host computer. In *hardware emulation*, however, the stimulus to the design is provided by real world interfaces and verification is in general, limited to monitoring the verification progress and debugging through software and hardware observation mechanisms.

In using a hardware acceleration platform, the maximum acceleration is limited by the runtime of the testbench on the host computer and the speed of the communication channel between the host computer and the acceleration platform. As such, it is important to consider hardware acceleration requirements when architecting a verification environment. To achieve this end:

- Make the time consuming part of the testbench (usually the drivers) synthesizable so that they can be placed on the acceleration platform as well.
- Use transaction level models to communicate between parts of the verification environment that are on the host and the acceleration platform in order to minimize communication overhead.

1.5 Verification Methodologies

Verification activities permeate throughout the design process. As such, multiple technologies and multiple facilities are used by those involved in the verification activities. Different methodologies are, therefore, required to bring together these tools and facilities and to produce a predictable outcome for the project. Assertion-based verification and coverage-driven verification are two such methodologies. Assertion-based verification focuses on how assertions can be used consistently across the design flow and across multiple tools. Coverage-driven verification is concerned with best approach for architecting and completing the verification project. These methodologies overlap since assertions can be considered as coverage points that are used as part of coverage analysis.

These methodologies are discussed in the following subsections.

1.5.1 Assertion-Based Verification

Assertion-based verification is the practice of using assertions as an integral part of functional verification flow. The main components of this methodology are:

- Identifying properties to be asserted
- Deciding when these properties must be asserted
- The verification tools used to confirm asserted properties

Properties that must be verified consist of these main categories:

- Operating environment assumptions
- Verification related assumptions
- Design specifications
- Design and implementation decisions

Environment assumptions specify the conditions that must be present in the verification environment in which this design must operate. Some obvious operating environment assumptions are that, for example, the traffic at an Ethernet port of a design must adhere fully to the Ethernet protocol, or that reset conditions must be present before the device can be put in the correct operating mode.

Verification related assumptions refer to properties that must be maintained as part of a constrained test in which a device is operated in only one or two of its possible modes. As such, a verification related property for the test might be that the device mode is limited to modes specified for this testcase.

Design specification properties refer to how the design is expected to react to stimulus from its environment.

Design and implementation decision properties relate to specific implementation decisions that have been made in the design process which are not necessarily present in the design specification but must be satisfied during device operation (e.g., only one bit of a one-hot state machine should be active at any given cycle).

Not all properties must be satisfied at all times during a device operation. For example, some device properties may fail during the reset sequence and, therefore, it is not necessary to assert such properties during the reset sequence. The same applies for verification related assumptions. Verification related assumptions hold for specific scenarios only, and as such, must be enabled only during the relevant scenarios.

1.5.1.1 Assertion Evaluation and Tool Flow

Assertions can be evaluated using a variety of verification tools and technologies. These include:

- Formal analysis
- Simulation
- Acceleration
- Emulation

A simulation-based approach has the advantage of being able to verify all assertions that can be specified using SystemVerilog's assertion language. It does, however, have the disadvantage of verifying an assertion only for simulation traces that occurred during a simulation run. As such, complementary approaches such as coverage collection are needed to confirm that an assertion is in fact verified for all relevant simulation traces. As an example, consider the following assertion:

```
env_prop: assert property (@(posedge clk) a ##1 (a || b) |=> c);
```

This property requires signal **c** to be active in the cycle after either trace **(a a)** or trace **(a b)**. This assertion will pass even if only one of these two traces occurs during simulation. As such, assuming this property to have been satisfied simply because it passed for one of the possible traces leaves some scenarios unverified. A more important observation is that if neither trace **(a a)** nor trace **(a b)** occur, then this assertion will never have an opportunity to fail. As such, it is necessary for simulation-based assertions to include a coverage collection mechanism to confirm scenarios that such a property must verify did indeed occur.

Formal verification has the advantage that it provides universal pass or fail confirmations for a given property. Formal verification does, however, have limited application since it cannot be applied to large designs or very complex properties, and it also requires that assumptions about that property are fully described (see section 1.4.1). A major advantage of formal methods, however, is that it does not require any stimulus. As such, formal methods are ideal for early stages of the design where small blocks are being created and no verification environment is yet available. Assertions defined at this stage are usually related to design decisions.

In addition to simulation and formal methods, assertions can also be evaluated using acceleration and emulation systems. Vendors for such systems provide tools that allow such assertions to be compiled and placed on the acceleration platform along with the design. As part of the tool selection process for a project, it is important to evaluate assertion acceleration capabilities and limitations of prospective tools so that assertions can be used seamlessly with those tools.

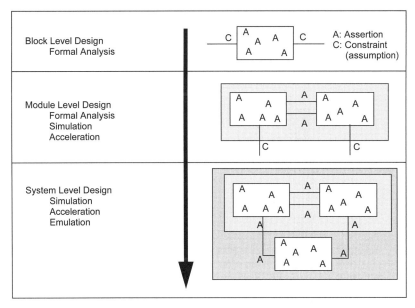

Figure 1.8 Assertion Evaluation and Verification Tools

Figure 1.8 shows stages of the design process and the tools that are used at each stage to verify assertions. During block level design, assertions are specified by designers to identify properties that must be maintained because of design implementation decisions and assumptions made about the boundary conditions of blocks. At this stage of design, there is usually very little stimulus generation capability available, and blocks are small. As such, this stage is ideally suited for using formal verification methods. In the next phase, blocks are grouped to create modules. Assertions defined by block designers are carried along with the block to this stage and aid in making sure that expected boundary conditions for each block are satisfied when blocks are connected, and that properties related to design decisions are maintained. Any failure of block level assertions aids in debugging by quickly pointing to the source of the unsatisfied property. Additional assertions are added to the design when modules are created. These assertions relate to the end-to-end properties of the module. Modules, along with their assertions, are then combined to form a system. At this level, new end-to-end assertions are added and assertions inherited from lower design levels (i.e., block and module) are leveraged to identify and quickly locate the source of any problems.

1.5.1.2 White-Box vs. Black-Box Assertions

Concepts of white-box and black-box verification also apply to assertion-based verification. White-box assertions are placed on properties that depend on internal signals of a block. White-box assertions aid in debugging by locating a potential problem in its source without the need for this error to be propagated to the design boundary. Additionally, assertions placed on internal signals help in making sure low-level implementation features of the design are working as expected. Black-box assertions are placed on the boundary signals of a block. Black-box assertions are usually specified to check for protocols at the block boundary or to make sure assumptions made by the designer are satisfied at its boundary. Figure 1.9 shows a pictorial view of white-box and black-box assertions.

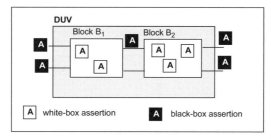

Figure 1.9 White-Box vs. Black-Box Assertions

1.5.2 Coverage-Driven Verification

Coverage-driven verification is a simulation-based verification approach specifically developed to address the productivity and efficiency challenges faced in functional verification projects (see section 1.1.3). The productivity and efficiency gains achieved by using a coverage-driven verification approach leads directly to improvements in verification completeness and correctness since these gains allow verification engineers to spend more time completing the project, and they verify scenarios at a faster pace.

The centerpiece of a coverage-driven verification approach is the random generation of stimulus. This random generation is the main source of productivity gained by following this methodology. Coverage collection becomes mandatory only when stimulus generation is randomized. The reason is that in the absence of coverage collection, no information is available about scenarios covered during random generation.

Coverage-driven verification methodology brings together the following verification concepts and approaches:

- Transaction-driven verification
- Constrained random stimulus generation

- Automatic result checking
- Coverage collection
- Directed-test–based verification

Transaction-driven verification allows scenarios to be specified at a higher level of abstraction. Constrained random generation leads to productivity gains in generating the scenarios, and automatic result checking provides confidence that the design works for all randomly generated scenarios. Coverage collection is mandatory, since without coverage collection it is not clear which scenarios have been randomly generated. A directed-test–based approach is also necessary since ultimately, not all scenarios can be generated efficiently using random generation techniques. These topics are discussed in the following subsections.

1.5.2.1 Transaction-Driven Verification

During simulation, all traffic in the design exists in terms of low-level signals of bit and bit vectors. Dealing with verification scenarios at this level of detail leads to major inefficiencies. In *Transaction-driven verification*, low-level signal activity is abstracted into atomic operations so that scenarios can be described using these higher level atomic operations. Drivers are used to translate these abstracted activities in the verification environment into low-level signal activity that can be understood by the DUV (see figure 1.10).

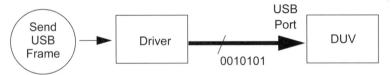

Figure 1.10 Transaction-Driven Verification

Transaction-driven verification follows these guidelines:

- Data and traffic are specified at a higher level of abstraction (e.g., frames, packets).
- Verification scenarios are described at a higher level of abstraction (e.g., write to memory, execute instruction).
- *Transaction drivers* are used to translate these abstracted data and activity into low-level operations and signal values that the design can understand. Within the verification context, transaction drivers are referred to as *bus drivers*, interface drivers, or simply as *drivers*.

Transaction-driven verification improves verification productivity by allowing verification engineers to deal with more abstracted items. It also facilitates interaction with architectural models of the design developed at the transaction level, and provides for efficient communication between verification environment components residing on the emulation/acceleration and host computer platforms.

1.5.2.2 Constrained Random Generation

A verification scenario is composed of a sequence of transactions where each transaction requires data and parameter values to achieve the desired effect. For example, in verifying that an Ethernet packet is routed correctly through an Ethernet switch, transactions consist of sending and receiving Ethernet packets, where each transaction is identified by its data and parameters, which include the destination address and the payload content of the packet.

Random stimulus generation refers to using random generation techniques for generating both the data content of a transaction as well as sequences of transactions that form a given verification scenario. In its most complete form, random generation is used to generate both data and scenarios. Random data generation (e.g., randomizing the source and destination addresses of an Ethernet packet) is simple to implement since it requires only data values to be generated randomly and it usually does not affect the scenario that is being carried out. Random scenario generation, however, requires that the verification environment support the scenarios that are being randomly generated in both checking and coverage collection. As such, random scenario generation not only requires more effort to be implemented, but also requires that necessary infrastructure for supporting its verification be available.

Random generation improves verification productivity because a single simulation run can verify multiple scenarios and data value combinations, therefore reducing the time it takes for a verification engineer to build, execute, and verify each scenario.

Figure 1.11 compares verification progress between directed-test–based verification and random generation techniques. Each verification step in this figure corresponds to the time it takes to complete that step versus the contribution made by that step to overall verification completion. In a directed-test–based approach, verification progress is made almost linearly throughout the project since every new directed test contributes to the overall verification progress. A random generation based approach, however, has an initial lead time, since it takes longer to build a randomized environment.

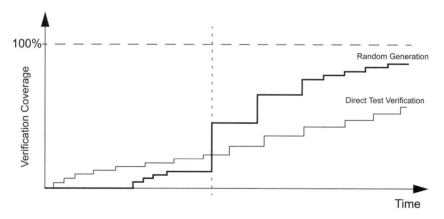

Figure 1.11 Directed Test Based Verification vs. Random Generation

An added advantage of a randomized environment is that scenarios that were not specified in the verification plan may also be generated because of the combination of random activity across the verification environment. As such, a random generation environment not only improves verification productivity, but also helps with verification completeness, since given extra time or computing cycles, further running of a randomized environment leads to more unspecified scenarios to be generated.

A randomized environment is not completely random, since generated data and parameters must remain within the legal set of values. Also, random scenario generation requires that each simulation run eventually be guided towards scenarios that are not yet generated. As such, constraint definition is an important part of random generation utilities.

Building a randomly generated environment is not a trivial task and requires significant changes over traditional directed-test verification techniques. Random generation of verification scenarios requires each randomly generated scenario to be automatically verified. As such, automatic checking must be an integral part of any randomly generated environment. This means that a randomly generated environment requires a reference model so that the result of each randomly generated scenario can be predicted at simulation runtime. In addition, a randomized verification environment should be able to handle all types of behaviors that may be generated by the random generation of scenarios. These behaviors include special handling of error conditions in addition to normal operation of the design. Random generation of scenarios also means that verification progress must be measured automatically through coverage collection mechanisms. This is because the exact scenario being generated is not known before a simulation run is started. And different simulation runs of the same test may create different scenarios and data combinations. In summary, a verification environment that contains random stimulus generation must also be a self checking environment and must also include coverage collection.

Random stimulus generation is ideally suited to verifying a finite state machine. As an example, random generation, automatic checking, coverage collection, and coverage analysis for an FSM can be summarized as follows:

- Random generation:
  - Initially, put the state machine in a random legal state.
  - Generate random inputs.
- Automatic checking
  - Check that the next state produced by simulation is the same as that specified.
  - Check that the output produced by simulation is the same as that specified.
- Coverage collection
  - Collect all states reached.
  - Collect state transitions.
  - Collect inputs applied in each state.
- Analysis
  - Check that all valid states have been reached.
  - Check that all state transitions have been made.

It is tempting to try to build a single verification environment that randomly generates all possible verification scenarios. For a number of reasons, however, this is not a practical goal for real designs. These reasons include:

- A design usually has multiple modes and use models that require different verification environment topology and configuration.
- Some corner cases have an extremely low probability of occurring under normal design operations, so a special verification environment is required for generating such scenarios.
- Running a single environment and a single test for a long time leads to many duplicated scenarios.

Even the best designed verification environment architecture and generator is limited in the types of scenarios that it can generate because the effort required for adding the missing scenarios to the same environment is prohibitively expensive. Additionally, given the number of parameters and states in a large design, it is practically impossible to reach all corner cases using a single randomized test and a single environment. In such cases, it is best to create a specially constrained version of the environment and/or the randomized testcase focused on the missing scenarios so that these scenarios occur with high likelihood.

Because of these limitations in covering all scenarios using a single test, a randomized verification environment will usually have a number of randomized testcases that cover a large part of the verification plan. The next set of randomized testcases will cover a smaller set of scenarios, and ultimately, some testcases will be direct testcases that focus on only one or two specific scenarios.

1.5.2.3 Automatic Result Checking

As mentioned in the previous section, automatic result checking is a requirement for a randomized verification environment.

Automatic result checking is performed using monitors and scoreboarding techniques. Monitors are mostly used for protocol checking and collecting design traffic while scoreboarding techniques are used for end-to-end behaviors or data transfer checks.

1.5.2.4 Coverage Collection

Random stimulus generation has the potential to provide significant improvement in verification productivity and efficiency. However, without a clear strategy to measure verification progress, these gains may be difficult to realize. Accurate measurement of verification progress requires that the following analysis be made for each randomized simulation run:

- What scenarios included in the verification plan were generated in a simulation run
- What interesting scenarios not included in the verification plan were generated
- The contribution of each run to the overall verification progress
- Constraints modifications that are necessary for generating the missing scenarios

Coverage information collected during each randomized simulation run is used to decide the contribution of each simulation run to the overall verification progress. Additional modifications in the simulation environment or new testcases are required when running further cycles of existing testcases does not make any further contribution to the overall progress (see section 18.4).

Coverage results for each simulation run can also be used to rank testcases for the purpose of regression suite creation or ordering. Testcases with high contribution to overall progress take priority in the regression environment.

1.5.2.5 Directed Tests

Not all verification scenarios can be created using a single randomized environment. As such, multiple environment and/or testcase variations are usually created, with each new variation focused on creating scenarios not covered previously. Ultimately, the last remaining scenarios must be covered using directed testcases where either a very specialized environment or a fully constrained testcase is created.

Adding a directed test, specifically one that requires a customized environment, causes difficulties in managing the verification project. Such testcases require manual interaction to create and verify, therefore, degrading overall productivity. In addition, such special testcases are difficult to use, to maintain, and to reuse across projects. As such, a verification environment should be architected to minimize the number of such specially designed directed testcases.

1.5.2.6 Coverage-Driven Verification Project Life Cycle

The life cycle of a coverage-driven verification project (see figure 1.12) consists of the following stages:

- Developing the verification plan
- Building the verification environment
- Bringing up the verification environment
- Running randomized testcases
- Creating directed tests for corner-case scenarios

In the first stage, the verification plan is developed according to the design specification and appropriate feedback from system engineers, design engineers, and verification engineers. The verification plan will be extended and completed throughout the verification life cycle. Therefore, the main goal at this stage should be to have enough detail in the plan so that a stable verification environment architecture can be created.

In the second stage, the verification environment is designed and implemented according to the requirements identified from the verification plan. In stage three, tightly constrained verification scenarios are carried out in order to check for correct operation of the verification environment and to debug and fix any existing problems. The goal in this stage is to gain confidence in the correct operation of the verification environment, and verification progress at this stage is of secondary concern. Multiple passes through stages two and three may be needed before the environment is stable enough to be used in the next stage.

The goal in stage four is to cover as much of the verification plan as possible with each simulation run. Coverage results are used to decide if consecutive runs of a testcase contribute to the overall verification progress. A new testcase, and potentially a variation of the environment is then created to target verification scenarios that remain to be generated. This stage is completed when the remaining scenarios must be considered individually and through highly customized environments or testcases.

In stage five, the remaining verification scenarios are generated through directed testcases. As mentioned previously, the goal should be to minimize the number of scenarios requiring a customized test.

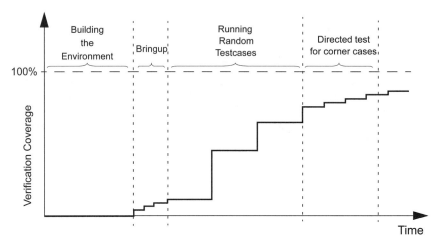

Figure 1.12 Coverage-Driven Verification Methodology Stages

1.5.3 Metric-Driven Verification

Metric-driven verification (or *specification-driven verification*) refers to a coverage-driven verification approach where the verification plan is in an executable format. This means that the verification plan can be used directly to drive verification scenarios and the verification environment can back-annotate the verification plan in order to measure verification progress and identify verification closure.

A metric-driven verification approach can further improve verification quality and productivity by:

- Removing manual interventions that are inherently slow and error-prone
- Improving regression management environments through automatic sorting of simulation run contribution to overall coverage and ordering regression priorities

CHAPTER 2

Verification Planning

The terms testplan and verification plan have historically been used interchangeably to refer to a list of scenarios that must be verified in order to complete a verification project. But given the increasing complexity of designs, and the increasing number of abstractions, actors, and technologies involved, the term verification plan is increasingly used to describe the planning that goes into completing a verification project.

This chapter describes the motivation and the need for creating holistic verification plans that act as the centerpiece and driving point of a verification project. This chapter also describes the flow for creating such a verification plan. This flow takes into consideration factors such as who must be involved in the creation of this plan, what content should be included, what format should be used, how this content is used to guide the design of the verification and coverage plan, and finally, how it should be used to iteratively improve the verification plan and arrive at verification closure.

2.1 The Modern Verification Plan

Historically, verification was an organically grown activity where a bottom-up approach was used to verify pieces of hardware until enough confidence was gained in correct operation of the whole system. The popularity of coverage-driven verification methodologies, facilitated by hardware verification languages, has motivated a shift to up-front planning of the verification requirement, albeit mostly for the portion that lies within the scope of individual or groups of verification engineers using the same verification technology (i.e., formal, simulation-based, acceleration). *Holistic planning* of a verification project, however, requires that this up-front planning be extended to all verification aspects of the design flow. The general flow of a design life cycle (see figure 1.1) consists of different levels of abstraction, different verification technologies, and different types of engineers who collectively produce the final product. As such, up-front verification planning should be extended to include all aspects of a design flow.

The verification planning methodology described in this chapter promotes a more elaborate up-front planning process that requires involvement by all decision makers in the design and verification flow, and one whose result is intended to drive and manage verification activity across the whole project life cycle. In this context, *verification project management* refers to guiding a verification project through all of its distinct phases, including planning, implementation of verification infrastructure, measuring verification progress in a quantitative manner, and directions for how to react to these measured metrics. Additionally, verification management includes guidance on resource allocation, anticipating project slips and reporting progress in reference to given milestones.

In addition to acting as a project management baseline, the comprehensive nature of this upfront planning process leads to further benefits in improving other aspects of product development flow. These benefits include:

- Alignment of product functionality interpretations by the various actors
- Development of a common description of the desired functionality
- Capturing and/or definition of project milestones
- Definition of the engineering view of the plan, assigning resources to features
- Common understanding of project tasks, goals, and complexity by all actors
- Refinement of existing specifications (concept and design) due to identification of holes, ambiguities, or misinterpretations
- Definition of verification approaches to tackle all, or a subset, of product features

Effective verification planning requires careful consideration of all factors that impact this planning process or are affected by it. These factors include:

- Work of multiple specialists has to be tracked and merged
- Thousands of tests have to be managed and processed
- Multiple verification technologies have to be managed in the flow
- Planning changes, being costly in both time and resources, have to be minimized
- Multiple teams at multiple sites have to be coordinated
- Status must be collected and reported from across the design flow
- The inherent inefficiencies and unpredictability in project resources (tools and engineers) must be managed

A verification plan is the natural place to centralize verification related procedures and management related activities. In this sense, the verification plan should be developed with the end in mind and as a document that is able to guide the verification project throughout its lifetime. Verification planning challenges, goals, content, and life cycle are discussed in the following subsections.

2.1.1 Verification Planning Challenges

The first step in developing a powerful verification plan is to understand the factors involved in taking a design through the design flow. The main challenge in effective verification planning is to create a flow that addresses all of these factors. These factors include:

- Multiple actors are involved
- Multiple verification technologies are used
- Multiple DUVs must be verified

- Multiple documents must be created, tracked, and updated, including:
  - Descriptions of concept
  - Requirements
  - Verification scenarios
  - Implementation
- Multiple dependencies on other teams must be managed

Multiple actors influence the final content and form of product specification, functional specification, and design implementation. These actors include concept, design, verification, and software engineers. In fact, verification closure is defined as the convergence of these three views of the product (figure 1.3). A verification plan must reflect the collective opinion of all these actors as to what must be verified and how. Capturing this collective opinion in one centralized place also helps in gaining verification closure by highlighting any differences that may exist between these actors. The interaction between these actors is explained in section 2.2.3.

A holistic verification plan should also consider the different verification technologies that are used throughout the design and verification flow. These include:

- System level simulation
- Formal verification methods
- Simulation-based verification
- Acceleration and emulation-based verification

The benefits of each verification technology must be leveraged to further improve verification quality (section 1.4).

Even though the final system will consist of one DUV, multiple intermediate DUVs must be created in order to manage project complexity and to also allow for a hierarchical design flow. In addition, each DUV must be verified with and without the target software (i.e., either drivers or the application software). As such, the verification plan must consider the existence of multiple DUVs, how each DUV is verified, and the contribution of verification results for each DUV to the overall verification progress.

A verification project depends on other teams for input and feedback. In addition, the results produced throughout a verification project are usually used to support other teams in their activities. Teams that a verification project interacts with include:

- Marketing team for feature requirements
- Software team for early validation, and tapeout
- IP providers
- Updates throughout the project from customers

A verification plan must consider interaction between multiple teams and how the results produced or needed by other teams affect the overall schedule and ordering of priorities.

Verification planning goals are decided to best address the challenges described in this section. These goals are described in the next section.

2.1.2 Verification Planning Goals

The design of a verification plan should both guide the technical aspects of the verification activity (e.g., what scenario with what verification technology) as well as provide guidance for project management. The following goals must be achieved when creating a verification plan:

- Maximize quality and quantity of completed verification
- Mitigate project risks
- Forecast and track verification resource requirements
- Transparency of verification progress
- Early warning of slippages and issues

The first goal of maximizing quality and quantity of completed verification is the standard target for all verification plans. The remaining targets are meant to facilitate project management aspects of the verification plan where project progress can be measured and slippages can be countered by judicious use of resources and by shifting priorities. Methods for achieving these targets are described while describing the flow for building a verification plan (section 2.2).

2.1.3 Verification Plan Contents

To achieve the targets of a verification project, a verification plan should include the following content:

- Features, including:
  - Product features
  - Implementation-specific features
  - Use-cases and system level scenarios that the product must support correctly
- Verification technology used to verify features
- Milestones (what features/scenarios by what time?)

Product features refer to features that are defined in the functional specification of the product. These constitute the low-level features of the device (i.e., data traffic format, register bank structure, effect of read/write to these registers, etc.). Implementation-specific features are decided by designers and reflect designer's knowledge about verifying performance related features of the design and also low-level behaviors that expose the root cause of system level failures.

Use-cases and system level scenarios refer to how software programmers and system users view the design. Under ideal conditions where 100% of device features are verified, this type of use-case analysis and verification is not necessary, but knowing that 100% of device features cannot even be enumerated, let alone verified, it becomes necessary to verify these larger scale use-cases.

Different verification technologies are used to verify different features enumerated in the verification plan. For example, low-level design implementation features are verified in the block design phase using formal methods, while a use case scenario requiring many tens of thousands of simulation cycles may need to be verified using acceleration or emulation technologies.

Milestones should also be included in the verification plan so that a timeline is given for verifying different features. This description of milestones will be needed in identifying project slippages and how resources can be shifted to remedy the situation.

2.1.4 Verification Project Cycle: Gaining Closure

The ultimate goal of a verification project is to achieve complete verification of all design features in as short a time as possible and within the applicable resource limitations. Given the competing nature of these requirements, it is clear that a verification plan must strike a balance between these goals. The situation is made even more difficult as parameters of this problem may change throughout the flow. For example, features may be redefined or changed, project deadlines may be shortened, or resources' availability may change. As with all practical solutions to optimization problems, reaching this balance will require an iterative process to reach a viable solution.

Figure 2.1 shows the steps involved in creating and executing a verification plan. These steps are:

1. Build Plan
2. Build Environment
3. Execute
4. Measure
5. React to Measurements

Verification completion is checked within each iteration of this cycle and verification closure is decided when the achieved verification progress reaches the expected guidelines. These topics are discussed in the following sections.

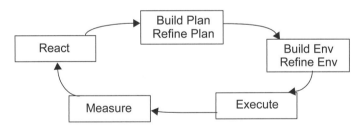

Figure 2.1 Verification Execution Cycle

2.2 Building the Verification Plan

Careful planning and execution places a verification project on very strong footing. Given that the verification plan is used as the central repository for all verification plans, activities, updates, and schedules, obtaining this strong footing is not possible without the creation of a solid verification plan.

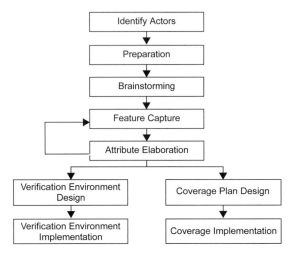

Figure 2.2 Verification Plan Development Cycle

Figure 2.2 shows the flow for creating a verification plan and the coverage plan derived from that verification. The following steps must be completed when building a verification plan:

- Identify all actors concerned with project execution
- Prepare for the planning sessions and planning document
- Brainstorm the product functionality
- Structure the verification plan, keeping in mind the necessary views and reuse
- Capture features and attributes
- Formulate the verification environments and coverage implementations

These steps are described in the following subsections.

2.2.1 Identify Actors

A holistic verification plan should take into account all decision makers at all levels of authority (from overall product features to micro-architecture decisions) and at all stages of the design and verification process. In this regard, everybody's opinion is important, since verification plan thoroughness will depend on the collective knowledge of team members on every aspect of the design.

The list of all actors in a project includes:

- Project managers
- Design architects
- Software/Firmware engineers

- Verification engineers
- Design engineers

Project managers will ultimately use the verification plan for tracking and resource allocation. As such, their involvement in specifying project deadlines and milestones is needed. Architects must confirm that product intent is indeed realized in the functional specification and design implementation (e.g., latency, bandwidth targets are met, FIFO size, arbitration algorithms implemented as specified). Software and firmware engineers must comment on their view of the hardware and the support they need to verify the software even before the final hardware is ready. Verification engineers are ultimately responsible for the quality of sign-off and as such, are owners of the verification plan. Design engineers must comment on implementation specific verification requirements. Table 2.1 shows a summary of verification planning participants, input each is expected to provide, and benefits each will gain.

Actor	Provides	Expects
Project Manager/ Marketing	Schedules and priorities	Verification plan for tracking status and aiding management
Design Architects	Architectural requirements such as latency and bandwidth	Ensure design intent is realized in the implementation
Concept Engineers System Engineers	Conceptual Scenarios, implementation guidelines	Ensure scenarios and use-cases are captured in verification effort
Design Engineers	Design Intent (assumptions about specified features, design details	Ensure implementation is in line with original intent and verification plan sections that focus on design details
Software Engineers	Software view of the system	Ensure software scenarios are captured in the plan
Verification Engineers	Verification approaches (intent), experience in how to verify features	Agreement from all actors on the verification plan. Common status reporting language across all actors

Table 2.1: Project Actors and Participation in Verification Planning

Even though the completed verification plan will require feedback from all project actors, initial meetings should be limited to those who can define the structure of the verification plan and top level features that must be verified. This initial limit is necessary, since reaching consensus becomes more difficult as the number of participants grows. As such, it is better to create the first version of the verification plan with only the most relevant stakeholders present, and then follow up in other meetings where everyone can comment and extend the content of the verification plan. One example would be to first make a verification plan that contains only the product intent, and then complement this plan by bringing in hardware and software engineers, and project managers.

2.2.2 Preparing to Start the Brainstorming Session

Before a brainstorming session can be held, the verification plan owner must prepare for the meeting. The following issues must be decided before starting a brainstorming session:

- Verification plan format
- Overall verification plan structure
- Verification plan naming conventions

Verification plan format and structure and naming conventions ultimately will be decided by the actual contents of the verification plan. It is, however, useful for the verification plan owner to finalize on a general format and prepare templates that can be used as the starting point.

2.2.3 Brainstorm about the Content

Discussions on functional verification can easily turn into engaging conversations about how the product could have been, or things that could still be done, or changes that could be made to make the design better. It is important to walk into such sessions focused only on what is decided and to proceed to gain consensus over these finalized topics. The primary objective of a brainstorming session is to identify all features that must be verified from all stakeholders' perspectives.

The following guidelines help in improving the efficiency of an initial brainstorming session:

- There are always more features than can be discussed in the allotted time for such a session. Therefore, maximize the benefit derived from time spent.
- All stakeholders are born equal and their comments are relevant to the final quality of the product.
- Do not discard any feature discussed at this stage.
- Do not discuss how to verify a feature, rather what features to verify.
- Identify product features.
- Identify system level scenarios and use-cases.
- Discuss what views should be included in the plan.
- Discuss what metrics should be collected during verification.

Once all features of interest are identified in the brainstorming sessions, they can be prioritized and redundant or unfeasible scenarios removed. The focus at this stage again is to identify all features and not how they will be verified. These decisions will be made at a later time when the structure of the verification environment is decided.

2.2.4 Verification Plan Structure

Verification plan structure is identified by the following features:

- Verification plan outline
- Planning views
- Verification scenarios
- Verification build and run infrastructure

These topics are described in the following subsections.

2.2.4.1 Verification Plan Outline

Figure 2.3 shows a typical outline of a verification plan. In this outline, the verification plan is divided into two main categories for functional requirements versus design requirements, and interface versus core features. Functional requirements include features that are derived from the functional specification of the design. Design requirements include features that relate to how the design is implemented.

```
1. Introduction
2. Functional Requirements
        2.1 Functional Interfaces
        2.2 Core Features
3. Design Requirements
        3.1 Design Interfaces
        3.2 Design Cores
4. Verification Views
5. Verification Environment Design
```

Figure 2.3 Verification Plan Outline

Verification environment design relates to what stimulus and checking is required for carrying out the features listed in this verification plan.

2.2.4.2 Verification Views

A verification plan should be useful to all actors in the verification project. Clearly, not all actors view the plan in the same light. Design engineers are more interested in viewing scenarios listed for their blocks, a system level engineer is more interested in end-to-end scenarios, a verification manager is more interested in a view of what part of the verification project has been completed, and a CAD tool manager is more concerned about when the tools should be available so that the verification technology listed for each scenario (e.g., formal, emulation) is available when needed.

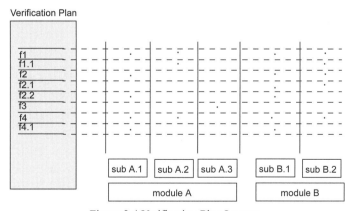

Figure 2.4 Verification Plan Layout

As such, it is important to decide up front what views of the verification plan will be needed by different actors. This information will be useful in that it highlights any missing information that should be included in the verification plan.

Figure 2.4 shows a verification plan view that correlates each feature with modules in the design. The organization in this figure shows the verification plan organized by features, where each feature contains sub-features. It is possible to organize the verification plan so that features are listed by the module that implements their functionality. A feature based view is recommended since it allows features to be verified without the main focus being on what module contains the logic for these features.

2.2.4.3 Verification Scenario Details

In general, a verification plan lists scenarios that must be verified about a design. More details about each scenario should be included in the verification plan in order to make it useful for all actors involved in the project. In general, the following information should be included in a verification plan:

- Scenarios to be verified
- Design feature verified by each scenario
- Design blocks/clusters that are activated by each scenario
- Verification mode that is used for verifying scenarios (e.g., formal or simulation)

At an abstract level, designs are better described by summarizing their features than listing scenarios that must be verified. In addition, verification priorities are more naturally decided for design features than design scenarios. As such, organizing a verification plan by the features provides a better view into the overall progress of verification.

In addition, in a large design, not all design blocks and/or clusters are available at the same time. Clearly, for an end-to-end feature, most blocks in the design will be needed while more local features are based on a few modules or blocks. As such, a verification plan should include information about how to schedule the verification of scenarios listed in the plan. By listing the modules needed for verifying each scenario, it becomes easier to synchronize the verification activity with the design activity as new blocks become available.

Verification scenarios ultimately are verified using different verification technologies. A block level feature is usually verified using formal techniques, while a system level end-to-end feature is best verified in an emulation environment. As such, listing the verification technology used for verifying a scenario makes it easier for that scenario to be scheduled and assigned to engineers.

2.2.4.4 Verification Build and Run Infrastructure

A verification environment consists of many types of design, data, configuration, and script files in different languages that must be brought together to start even the most simple of simulations. Files in a verification environment include design files for the DUV and the verification environment, configuration files describing DUV initial conditions and verification environment settings such as random seed values, data files such as initial contents of memory blocks, and program files such as assembly programs to be loaded into processor instruction memory and c/c++ programs describing golden models.

The running of the simulation is usually automated by using scripts that perform all of the necessary tasks required for starting the simulation. Given the complexity of verification environments consisting of different tools and languages, there are usually a number of different such scripts, each with different configuration switches. A verification plan should clearly describe methods available for building and running the verification environment. Consequently, each scenario should clearly indicate the build and run mechanism used for that scenario.

The inclusion of build and run procedures in the verification plan provides two benefits. First, it helps guide new engineers joining the project on how to get started with the verification activity. And second, it helps as a central location for documenting the build and run infrastructure for the verification environment.

2.2.5 Capturing Features

Two types of features must be identified in the verification plan:

- Product features
- System use-cases

The question to answer during this stage is "What is the product expected to do?" Engineers naturally talk about verification in terms of how it is done and not what the target feature is. For example, a statement such as "Verify that the MAC state machine goes into state **5** if the packet is less than **48** bytes" should be turned into "Short packets must be dropped by the interface." Concept engineers also tend to speak about the features at a very high level. These statements should also be turned into statements more relevant to architecture of the design. For example, a statement such as "The hard drive must be hot-swappable" should be turned into "The SATA interface should initialize during system runtime within the tolerance defined for the SATA interface initialization process."

Verifying system use-case scenarios would not be needed under ideal conditions where a design is fully verified. The reality, however, is that not all scenarios can even be enumerated for a reasonably sized design. As such, verifying system level use-cases allows for confidence to be gained in the overall operation of the design.

2.2.6 Capturing Attributes

Features of a design can be divided into two views:

- Port-based view
- Function-based view

In port-based view, operation of the design is described from its interface perspective. As such, the design is viewed as a black-box for the purpose of features that relate to its interface behavior. The features listed for this view are extracted from the protocol that is implemented by design interfaces. For example, for a USB module, the port-based feature listing will include behavior of USB traffic as described in its documentation. The following attributes must be listed for features described in this view:

- Attributes that are defined by pin values at a given time
- Attributes defined by data structures that pass through design pins across multiple cycles

- The interaction between such attributes

Attributes defined by design pin values consist of design attributes that are controlled by design pin values. Examples include command value for a bus interaction, the reset pin value, and interrupt pins being active or inactive. Attributes that are defined by data structures passing through design pins include design attributes that are extracted from such data structures. For example, the destination address of an Ethernet packet arriving on a serial pin of an Ethernet module and the type of memory access requested in a PCI-express transfer.

In function-based view, design features are extracted from internal functionality of design blocks, design specifications, and design decisions. Attributes relating to function-based view are extracted from internal state of the design for each of the features identified in this view. For example, states of a state machine, and register values controlling design operation.

2.3 From Plan to Environment

The verification plan is used to derive the stimulus needed to carry out the verification steps for each feature. In addition, the plan is used to identify the checks that must be made for the stimulus applied.

2.3.1 Identifying Required Stimulus

A carefully designed and described verification plan points directly at the stimulus needed to verify scenarios in the verification plan. Scenarios in the verification plan identify stimulus sequences that must be generated, while attributes for these scenarios identify the valid range of values for the generated stimulus sequences.

Stimulus generation affects two aspects of the verification environment:

- Drivers
- Scenario generators (i.e., sequencers)

Drivers used for verification purposes have two specific purposes: first they must support interactions defined by the given interface, and second, they must be able to inject errors that the design is expected to detect or recover from. As such, the scenarios described in the verification plan should clearly indicate what error conditions should be injected at the design interface which should necessarily be supported by the driver. Additionally, not all modes of a design interface may be needed in a project. As such, the implementation of a driver can be simplified by excluding such unused modes of operation.

Scenario generators are developed to directly support the generation of scenarios listed in the verification plan. As such, the examination of the verification plan should immediately lead to the types of sequences that must be generated in the verification environment.

2.3.2 Identifying Required Checkers and Collectors

Scenarios in a verification plan should list the checks that must be made to verify each scenario. These checks can be divided into protocol checks and data checks. Protocol checks are used to confirm adherence of design signals to specific timing requirements of the specification (e.g., correct timing of bus handshaking signals). Data checks, however, verify correct transfer or modification of data values by the design (e.g., correct transfer of Ethernet packet payload from one switch port to another). Protocol checks are made using monitors, while data checks are made using collectors and scoreboards.

When deciding where to perform a check identified by the verification plan, an effort should be made to make this check as close to its source as possible, or in multiple places if the problem can occur due to multiple failures. This approach improves design debugability where bugs are identified as close to their source as possible.

2.4 Measuring Progress

Progress of a verification project is defined as the portion of features that are already covered compared to featured that must be covered for the current target milestone. Metrics to collect for this purpose are:

- Code coverage
- Assertion coverage (for formal tools)
- Assertion coverage (for simulation/acceleration/emulation tools)
- Functional coverage

Code coverage is collected by the simulation tool. Assertion coverage is collected from the results of formal verification used most often by designers during module and block design. Assertion coverage is also collected during simulation and acceleration/emulation-based verification, and is automatically collected once the assertions are built into the environment. Functional coverage is collected during simulation-based verification and the necessary infrastructure must be developed in the verification environment to collect this information.

2.5 Reacting to Results

The results collected during the execution of a verification plan must be used to bring the project closer to completion and decide on whether or not closure has been reached. Steps to take based on execution results include:

- Milestone charting
- Simulation failure analysis
- Coverage hole analysis
- Regression ranking

Milestone charting is used to measure milestone definitions (features that must be completed to reach specific milestones) against actual timelines. This analysis is used to adjust resources and anticipate slippages, based on the amount of progress being made.

Simulation failure analysis is used to debug, identify, and fix problems that have led to a failed scenario. The failure may be in either the verification environment or the DUV. As such, this analysis leads both to maturity of the verification environment as well as design stability and correctness.

Coverage hole analysis provides information about what scenarios have not yet been exercised. This information is used in milestone charting to understand how the verification environment must be extended in order to fill the coverage holes that must be met by the given milestones.

Regression ranking is used to identify verification runs in the regression suite that contribute the most to the coverage metrics. This ranking allows a few regression runs to be selected that lead to most confidence about the design after any modifications. It also allows designers and verification engineers to choose simulation runs that best target features about which they are concerned in their current work.

CHAPTER 3

Verification Environment Architecture

The architecture of a verification environment should allow all scenarios in the verification plan to be verified according to the guidelines of the target verification methodology. In general, this target can be achieved through different verification environment architectures. However, experience shows that as these seemingly different architectures mature into their final form, common structures and features start to take shape. Advance knowledge of these best-in-class structures and features is essential for building a verification environment that can handle today's complex designs.

This chapter describes an overview of a verification environment architecture that facilitates the application of coverage-driven and assertion-based verification methodologies. The discussion in this chapter is focused on the architectural blocks of the verification environment, and the general use model and features that should be supported by each block. This discussion is independent of any implementation tool or language and describes each block at an abstract level.

3.1 Abstract View of a Verification Environment

A verification environment connects to a DUV through that DUV's boundary signals. These boundary signals can be grouped into interfaces, with each port representing interrelated signals that collectively describe an interface protocol supported by the DUV. This conceptual grouping of signals into interfaces can be applied to any size design, from a simple block to complex systems, with ports representing complex protocols such as a parallel bus (e.g., PCI) or a serial interface (e.g., PCI-Express), or even trivial behaviors such as a single wire used for resetting the device. The discussion in this chapter views a DUV as a block with a number of abstract interfaces.

This interface-based view of a DUV suggests a layered architecture for its verification environment. In this architecture, shown in figure 3.1, the lowest layer components interact directly with DUV interfaces, while each higher layer component deals with increasingly higher levels of verification abstraction. These higher levels of abstraction correspond to more complex verification scenarios composed of more complex atomic objects. This layered architecture leads to an intuitive path for extending a verification environment, as the design flow moves from block to system level. In this flow, additional verification component layers are added to the verification environment as design integration moves to the next step.

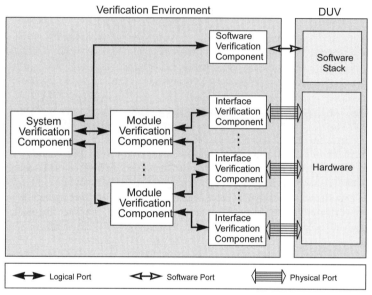

Figure 3.1 Complete Architecture of a Verification Environment

Structurally, this verification environment is composed of interface and module/system verification components. *Interface verification components* provide an abstraction for the physical ports with which they interact. This feature allows higher layer verification components to interact with the DUV at the abstraction level provided by the interface verification component. Interface verification components also contain additional features to monitor and collect coverage information for the physical port they interact with. Software verification components are a specialized type of interface verification components that interact with the software stack of a system level DUV (section 3.3).

Module/system verification components contain module/system level scenario generation functionality and carry out end-to-end data checking. It should be noted that the internal architecture of module and system verification components are similar since they both interact with higher and lower layer verification components. As such, the distinction between module and system verification components is intended to reflect the level of abstraction each component deals with. Interface verification components have a different architecture since they interact directly with DUV ports.

Verification components can operate in two modes:

• Active mode

- Passive mode

An *active verification component* generates traffic for lower layer verification components, or at DUV ports in the case of interface verification components. A *passive verification component* monitors only verification environment traffic and as such, does not contain any stimulus generation capability. Reuse of a verification component when moving to the next design integration step depends on correct implementation of these modes. As such, careful attention should be paid to features that should be supported in each mode. These features are discussed in the following sections.

Interface, software, and system verification components are described in the following sections.

3.2 Interface Verification Components

An interface verification component is used to interact with one or more DUV ports that support the same protocol. Given that in general, carrying out verification scenarios requires simultaneous interaction with multiple ports, the architecture of an interface verification component is geared less towards generating full verification scenarios and more towards providing an abstracted view of DUV ports to higher layer verification components and also monitoring DUV port traffic through protocol checking and coverage collection.

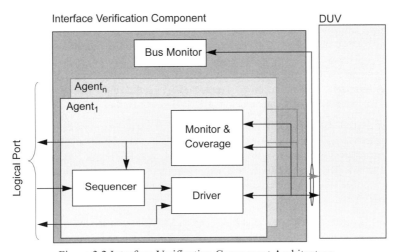

Figure 3.2 Interface Verification Component Architecture

The architecture of an interface verification component is shown in figure 3.2. An interface verification component can interact with multiple DUV ports that follow the same protocol. Each interaction of an interface verification component with a DUV port is carried out using an agent. The implementation of an interface verification environment must support the creation, connection to DUV port, and management of one or more agents. Each agent contains the following blocks:

- Driver
- Sequencer
- Agent and bus monitors

The driver block interacts with DUV ports to create the abstraction provided by the verification component. This block also provides additional verification related features which are usually not defined as part of the protocol supported by the DUV port (e.g., injecting errors). The agent monitor block provides the information that is required by protocol checker blocks to verify that DUV port properties are satisfied during simulation runtime. The information detected by a monitor block is also used by sequencer blocks when generating reactive sequences. The properties checked by this block are protocol related properties that do not require global view and can be checked by observing only local port signals. Coverage collector records information about the types of activities that are observed at DUV ports. The bus monitor tracks activities that are common across all agents placed inside an interface verification component. As an example, in a bus type connection where all agents connect to the same DUV bus, most of the monitoring is done in the bus monitor, while in a point-to-point type connection where each agent is connected to a separate DUV interface, most of the monitoring is done in the agent monitor. The sequencer block is used to generate multi-transaction behaviors at the DUV port where each transaction is defined at the level of abstraction provided by the driver.

As an example, consider the interface verification component for an Ethernet port. The driver block would provide atomic operations for transmitting an Ethernet packet to a given destination address and receiving packets. The monitor block checks that each packet received at DUV ports is a valid Ethernet packet. For scoreboarding purposes, the monitor also collects packets received and transmitted at this port. The coverage collector records information on what size data payloads, how many packets, and to what source and destination addresses were sent and received. The sequencer block is used to send a group of Ethernet packets that collectively correspond to a TCP/IP data transfer.

The logical view of a DUV port, as presented by an interface verification component to higher layer verification components, consists of a set of software-oriented constructs. These constructs allow higher layer verification components to access status collected by the monitor, and to interact with the driver and sequencer in the interface verification component. This logical view is formed by combining the views provided by the monitor, driver, and sequencer blocks.

Details of the logical view and blocks in an interface verification component are discussed in the following subsections.

3.2.1 Logical View

The logical view of an interface verification component provides the following:

- Sequencer interaction and customization
- Driver interaction and customization
- Monitor status

The sequencer in an interface verification component provides a set of default and commonly used sequences. These sequences are used when the interface verification component is used to generate random traffic with only a local view of the DUV port it is attached to. An interface verification component should provide a view of its predefined sequences, how these sequences can be customized, and how new sequences can be added to the sequencer. During module and system level verification, the sequencer in the interface verification component interacts with the higher layer verification components to drive the intended traffic into the DUV port. This interaction may be driven from higher layers or initiated by the local sequencer. The logical view of a sequencer should provide a view of how this interaction can take place and be customized for any specific application.

The driver in an interface verification environment is used mostly by the sequencer in that interface verification component. In some cases, however, it may be necessary to drive or configure this driver from outside the verification component. Additionally, when creating new sequences for the sequencer in the interface verification component, detailed knowledge of driver control and the configuration mechanism is required. An interface verification component should, therefore, provide a detailed view of the mechanisms used for interacting with its driver.

Monitors in higher layer verification components rely on information provided by the monitors in lower layer verification components. As such, developing monitors in the higher layer verification components requires detailed knowledge of the status information made available by lower layer monitors. An interface verification component should, therefore, provide a detailed view of conditions detected by its monitor during the simulation process and how this information can be accessed. This view is also necessary when adding sequences to the sequencer in an interface verification component.

3.2.2 Driver

A design communicates with the outside environment through its ports. The exact form of this communication is decided by the protocol implemented by that port. A protocol usually provides a set of high level atomic operations (e.g., send a packet, send a datagram) that in reality are carried out through many cycles of complex handshaking procedures across multiple design pins. An important observation is that the detailed steps of how each protocol operation is carried out is not really relevant in any part of the verification environment except that port. As such, it is possible to localize all low-level protocol related activities to the block that interacts with that port. A driver implements the functionality that hides this detail and provides an abstract view of the protocol at the logical port of the interface verification component.

A driver used for verification purposes is more complex than a driver that just supports the operations defined in a protocol. The reason is that a verification driver should not only be able to produce and understand correct protocol behavior, but it should also be able to produce invalid traffic that the design is expected to detect, and also identify invalid behavior that the design might produce at its port. The exact form and extent of invalid conditions that should be detected and generated by a verification driver is defined by the verification plan. Such extra requirements, however, can usually be derived by analyzing what protocol errors can occur (e.g., CRC errors).

A driver block should provide the following:

- A logical view of the physical port to higher layer verification components
- Ability to produce and understand all valid physical traffic at the DUV ports
- Ability to generate protocol errors that the DUV is expected to handle
- Ability to recover gracefully from incorrect DUV behavior
- A configuration interface

The logical view provided by the driver, should be complete to the degree that it is no longer necessary to interact with the physical interface. Additionally, a verification driver should be able to recover gracefully from errors on the physical interface, report the detected failure in its status reporting mechanisms, and synchronize with the next valid behavior. The types of error conditions injected by the driver should be the kind that relate to low-level signal activity of the protocol and not the types of errors that can be injected through interaction with the logical port of the driver. For example, in sending an Ethernet packet, the driver need not have a feature to insert a wrong tag in an Ethernet packet, since this can be set when specifying a packet content through its logical port. The driver should, however, include features for injecting a wrong preamble and set an invalid CRC before sending a packet.

A driver is identified by its feature set and user interface. These topics are covered in the following subsections.

3.2.2.1 Feature Set

The features supported by a driver should be derived from the verification plan for the interface protocol such that all scenarios can be implemented through the driver and without interacting directly with the physical port.

The following guidelines should be followed when deciding driver features:

- Define a set of atomic operations for the driver that can be combined in different ways to create any desired behavior at that physical port.
- In the logical port of the driver, include physical port timing information that may be useful to control or know about (e.g., idle cycles before an Ethernet packet).
- Define driver operations for injecting errors and driver status fields for recording observed error conditions.
- Choose a parameterized operation over multiple operations that essentially create the same behavior with minor modifications.

The set of atomic operations defined for a port is usually in direct correspondence with the logical view of the protocol implemented at that port. For example, if a protocol is defined in terms of different types of packets, then the atomic operations for the driver will include sending packets of different types where the details of packet transmission is handled by the driver.

The physical implementation of a protocol often includes detailed timing and handshaking mechanisms. For example, an abstract operation of writing a block of data to memory is carried out through many cycles of finely orchestrated signal transitions. In general, this detailed timing information is not relevant at the higher levels of abstraction. Sometimes, however, it may be useful to include such information in the abstract definition of the logical port of the driver. For example, in sending an Ethernet packet, the abstract operation is defined by the contents of the packet that must be sent or the contents of the packet that was received. A useful addition to this interface is to also specify the number of cycles to wait before the packet is sent. In the receive direction, it is useful to include in the received packet the number of idle cycles that were detected before the preamble of the received packet was detected.

The logical port of a driver should provide the ability to inject errors at the physical port and provide information about erroneous conditions caused by the DUV and detected by the driver. As an example, the Ethernet protocol requires that packet preamble to be at least **56** bits of alternating zeros and ones. In defining the operation to send a packet, it is useful to define the length of the preamble as a parameter to the logical port so that this size can be randomized to values smaller, the same, or larger than **56** bits. In the receive direction, a collected Ethernet packet should also include a field that stores the number of preamble bits that were detected before the collected packet was started. The inclusion of such features depends on a careful analysis of what can go wrong at the physical port that is not considered in the logical description of the protocol.

The features provided by the driver should be rich and comprehensive so that direct interaction with DUV physical port is not required. This set of features should, however, be well organized and grouped. As such, it is a good practice to define parameters at the logical port in cases where groupings of different features as a parameter makes sense.

3.2.2.2 User Interface

The user interface for a driver block should allow other blocks to interact procedurally with the driver. The procedural interface should include the following types of interactions:

- Transaction processing methods
- Configuration methods

Transaction processing is used for passing a transaction to the driver to be processed. These methods are used in cases where a transaction is intended to be transmitted to the DUV. This is in contrast with configuration steps that control driver behavior and do not immediately result in activity at the DUV port.

Configuration methods for a driver are identified by the set of parameters that must be set before the driver can interact with the physical port or accept transactions from its logical port. For example, in a UART driver, the number of data bits and stop bits should be specified before the driver can receive a frame from the physical interface. The configuration methods also control settings for transaction parameters that rarely change across multiple transactions. For example, in a system bus driver, the burst size for writing to the bus may be fixed across many bus transactions. Such parameters should also be included in the configuration space. Configuration methods provides a mechanism for assigning and querying the settings of these configuration space parameters.

Note that methods for accessing the internal status of a driver are not listed as a requirement and in fact, should not be provided. The reason is that when an interface verification component is put in passive mode, the driver block is removed. As such, no other block should depend on status detected by the driver block. Instead, all such status should be detected independently by the monitor block, which is always present in passive or active modes. An example of a user interface is shown in figure 3.3.

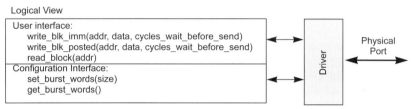

Figure 3.3 Driver Logical View

3.2.3 Sequencer

A sequencer is an intelligent block that generates random transaction sequences. Such sequences should be created dynamically during simulation runtime and according to randomizable parameters so that scenarios can be generated randomly during simulation runtime. The detailed architecture of the sequencer and its use in generating scenarios is described in detail in chapter 14.

The sequencer in an interface verification component generates a sequence of transactions that collectively form a scenario described for the protocol supported by the design port. The important observation about this sequencer is that, conceptually, it is not aware of conditions at other DUV ports. Given that a meaningful scenario is usually defined in terms of traffic through multiple DUV ports, this means that the types of scenarios generated by the sequencer inside an interface verification block is limited in extent to scenarios that require only local visibility. The task of creating scenarios that require interaction with multiple DUV ports is assigned to module/system verification components that interact with multiple interface verification components. The types of traffic generated by the sequencer in an interface verification block is, therefore, limited to the following:

- Atomic operations defined at the abstraction level of the DUV port protocol
- A composite operation at the DUV port
- Responses to requests received from the design that do not require global view

Activity at a design port is usually abstracted into atomic operations that reflect the logical view of the protocol implemented by that interface. For example, for a memory interface, atomic operations include memory read/write operations and at an Ethernet port, atomic operations consist of Ethernet packet receive and transmit operations. Composite operations at a port refer to a sequence of atomic operations that collectively form an atomic operation at a higher level of abstraction. For example, individual memory write operations can be combined to write an arbitrary size block of data to memory, or multiple Ethernet packets can be sent in order to transfer a large block of data. The composite operations generated by the sequencer in an interface verification component usually correspond to how that interface is used at the system level and, therefore, the composite operations correspond to atomic operations at the system level.

The sequencer in an interface verification component can also provide responses to requests received from the design. These requests are at the abstraction level of DUV port protocol (e.g., memory read request from DUV with the interface verification component pretending to be the memory subsystem). The types of responses generated by the sequencer are limited to replies that do not require knowledge of events or conditions at other DUV ports.

Note that the limitations imposed on the sequencer in an interface verification component, as described in this section, are a consequence of separating interface verification components from module/system verification components. This separation requires that interface verification components interact solely with the DUV port, and the features provided by this interface verification component should be used by module/system verification components to generate system-wide scenarios requiring interaction with multiple DUV ports. From an implementation point of view, system level scenarios can be generated by the sequencer inside an interface verification component if the effort is made to make system-wide information available inside this block, but this approach would go against the logical separation made between an interface verification component and a module/system verification component.

3.2.4 Agent and Bus Monitors

Agent and bus monitor blocks in an interface verification component are used to collect the information necessary by other blocks in the environment. These blocks include sequencers, requiring port traffic information when generating reactive sequences, and protocol checkers requiring port activity information for verifying protocol compliance at the port.

Monitors are passive components. This means that a monitor does not drive any port signals and only monitors them. As such, a monitor block is present in both active and passive modes of a verification component. This means that data and status collected by monitors in an active verification component can be used for data checking even when that verification component is reused in passive mode in the next design integration step. This approach is shown in figure 3.4. This example shows a DUV that interacts with two drivers on its two physical ports. The drivers both drive and collect traffic from the interface so they can pass the collected traffic to higher layer verification components. Data checking across this DUV is, however, implemented by using traffic collected by the monitors. Given this architecture, it is possible to migrate the same data checking implementation to the next design integration steps, where DRIVER$_1$ and DRIVER$_2$ are replaced by actual design blocks. The availability of block level data checking at higher levels of design integration leads to more visibility into any design problems that may come up at this block boundary. Note that the actual implementation of a scoreboard will be a part of the module/system verification component that interacts with both interface verification components. In this case, the module/system verification component implements the scoreboard by waiting on monitor events provided at the logical ports of these interface verification components to grab the collected packet and use it in the scoreboarding check.

Monitors check for two types of signal attributes:

- Syntax checks
- Timing checks

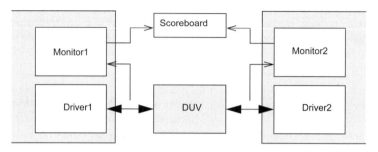

Figure 3.4 Data Checking Using Monitors

Syntax checks verify that all signals at DUV port have valid values. Syntax checks are easy to implement and define since they do not depend on timing information (e.g., burst size should always be a valid burst size value). Identifying and implementing timing checks is more involved, since such properties are defined across multiple signals and multiple time cycles.

Similar to the sequencer, the monitor in an interface verification component tracks only activities that can be extracted from the DUV port it monitors. As such, the monitor in an interface verification component tracks protocol compliance at the port and collects atomic operations at the abstraction level of the design port (e.g., memory write transaction for a memory interface).

The coverage collector in an interface verification component mirrors closely the conditions that the monitor tracks and the atomic transactions that the monitor extracts from the DUV port. In general, coverage should be collected on any check that the monitor makes, since such checks must have been a part of the verification plan or may be needed to be implemented in the monitor. In addition, the coverage collector should track the types of transactions collected by the monitor from the DUV port and all attributes of such transactions. For example, for an Ethernet interface, the coverage collector should track Ethernet packets collected from the interface, and for each packet it should track the source address, destination address, packet type, data size, and whether the packet was corrupt or not.

Coverage should be collected for traffic initiated by both the DUV and the interface verification component. Traffic initiated by the DUV is used for identifying what design traffic was checked by the monitor, and traffic initiated by the interface verification component is used to identify what scenarios or sub-scenarios were generated at that interface.

3.3 Software Verification Components

Software verification components are necessary when verifying system level designs that include the software stack. Figure 3.5 shows an example of such a system. In this view, a software verification component provides an abstraction of the software interface to the verification environment so that the module/system verification components can treat the software port in the same manner as that of a physical port.

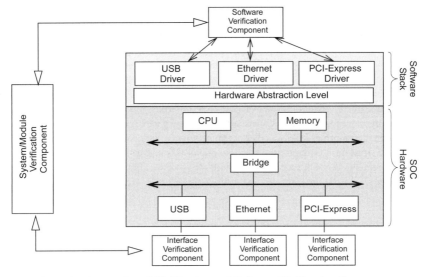

Figure 3.5 System Level Verification and Software Verification Components

A software verification component is an abstraction level that is traditionally provided through hardware-software co-verification tools, such as Seamless from Mentor Graphics and Incisive Software Extension (ISX) from Cadence Design Systems. Simulation tool vendors provide custom solutions that can be used with SystemVerilog.

The exact method by which a software verification component interacts with a DUV is beyond the scope of this discussion. What is important is that once this interface is in place, a module/system verification component can use the software verification component to configure, drive, and collect traffic through the software port in real time during simulation runtime while interacting with the physical ports, thereby enabling it to carry out system level verification scenarios through the software and physical ports.

3.4 Module/System Verification Components

Figure 3.1 shows a three layer verification environment composed of interface, module, and system verification components. In practice, however, a verification environment may consist of more layers, each corresponding to a new design integration step (e.g., module, cluster, chip, system, etc.). Each design integration step may also require the addition of more than one layer of verification components, thereby adding to the overall number of layers. The number of layers added in each integration step depends on the complexity of the newly integrated DUV. Other than interface verification components, all other components have a similar architecture in that they interact with verification components at higher and lower layers to create the desired scenarios and track DUV behavior. These components differ only in that they operate on different size DUVs. In this section, the term "system verification component" is used generically to refer to all such verification components.

The focus of a system verification component is generally on end-to-end behavior of the DUV and not on individual blocks composing that DUV. This approach is based on the implicit assumption that in a layered verification environment, smaller blocks have already been verified to some degree and the focus of verification is on the current DUV (e.g., when verifying a module, blocks are assumed to be verified). This assumption holds throughout the design life cycle, as modules are created by combining blocks, and later when systems are created by combining modules. This approach allows verification environment complexity to be managed more efficiently where each new layer can deal with only the new features added in the latest design integration step. In spite of this end-to-end focus of a system verification component, this approach also provides further verification of features in smaller blocks, since system-wide scenarios will ultimately result in activation of individual blocks and modules.

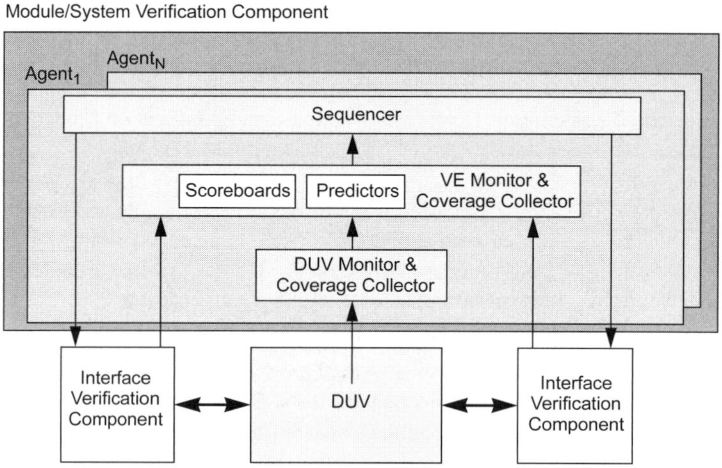

Module/System Verification Component

Figure 3.6 Module/System Verification Component Architecture

Behaviors that a system verification component is focused on include:

- Bugs in modules that could be verified only as part of the overall system
- Wrong assumptions by designer about module operation
- Wrong wiring between system modules
- Problems with module interactions arising from protocol mismatches

The architecture of a system verification component is shown in figure 3.6. This component contains multiple agents where each agent provides the same functionality while interacting with a different set of lower layer verification components. Each agent in a system verification component contains the following blocks:

- Sequencer
- Verification environment (VE) monitor and coverage collector
- DUV monitor and coverage collector

The VE monitor interacts with monitors in lower layer verification components (e.g., system monitors track monitors in interface and module verification components) to provide information about the current state of DUV as observed by lower layer verification components. The DUV monitor tracks DUV internal signals since these signals cannot be tracked through monitors attached to DUV ports. The combination of VE monitor and DUV monitor allows a gray-box verification approach (see section 1.1.2.1) to be leveraged in this architecture. Information provided by these monitors is further used by the sequencer to create end-to-end scenarios.

These blocks are discussed in the following subsections.

3.4.1 Sequencer

Generally, the sequencer in a system verification component is responsible for the following operations:

- Initializing DUV and verification environment
- Configuring DUV and verification environment
- DUV end-to-end scenario generation

These activities are discussed in the following subsections.

3.4.1.1 Initialization

Initialization refers to setting DUV and verification environment conditions that must be set before simulation is started. Initialization settings include the following:

- DUV pins that must be set before a design can be activated
- DUV register settings that cannot be changed during device operation
- Memory pre-loading
- Verification component settings that must be made before simulation is started

The motivation for placing initialization steps in the sequencer is that such initialization can be changed as part of scenarios and even randomized if necessary. If design and environment initialization is not done in the sequencer, then it becomes a part of the environment. This means that running a scenario requiring a different set of initialization settings will require not only a change in the scenario but the environment as well.

As mentioned previously, a sequencer generates scenarios through dynamic generation of sequences during simulation runtime. This means that a scenario may be created only after design initialization is completed at time zero and, therefore, not all initialization actions can be performed within the sequencer. The goal, however, should be to do as much of the initialization in the sequencer to avoid having to change the environment for scenarios requiring different initialization settings.

3.4.1.2 Configuration

Verification environment configuration refers to settings in DUV and verification environment that can be changed during simulation runtime or as specified by design specification. As such, resetting a design can be considered a configuration setting, since a device can be reset at any time during the simulation runtime. In fact, resetting a design in mid-operation is a required scenario that must be included in any verification plan.

The important consideration in building the configuration infrastructure is that often, the state of the verification environment at the time of such reconfiguration becomes invalid since normal device operation is interrupted. For example, upon reset of a design, all scoreboard contents, monitor observed condition flags, etc. will have to be initialized to match the design state right after reset.

Configuration may be needed as part of verification scenario execution (e.g., resetting the device, or changing device register settings), or used to simulate multiple scenarios requiring different configurations during the same simulation run. In either case, special care should be taken to update the state of the environment if a configuration step affects the state of DUV such that such changes are not automatically detected by the environment.

3.4.1.3 Scenario Generation and Driving

The sequencer in a system verification component is concerned with creating end-to-end scenarios. At this level of abstraction, the sequencer deals with atomic operations defined at the abstraction level of the design ports provided by interface verification components (e.g., packets, transactions, etc.). As such, the sequencer should generally describe its scenarios by using the facilities provided by the sequencer in interface verification components. This means that system level scenarios are created by appropriately timed and constrained execution of smaller sequences provided by the sequencer in interface verification components. The sequencer uses status information provided by its monitors to synchronize the sequence of activities that it produces.

It is important to note that a sequencer does not participate directly in data checking and scoreboarding. This activity is delegated to the monitor that collects traffic flowing through the environment. It is at times tempting to use the generator to inject expected values into a scoreboard, since data to be injected is readily available. Doing so, however, limits the reusability of the scoreboarding implementation when the DUV in this verification step is used as a block in a larger system. Given that the sequencer will be removed in that environment, any scoreboarding that depends on this sequencer will also become unusable. On the other hand, since monitors stay in place as the DUV is placed inside a larger system, any scoreboarding based solely on monitor collection can be reused (section 3.5).

3.4.2 VE Monitor

The VE monitor for a system verification component serves these purposes:

- Providing a pointer to lower layer monitors (e.g., interface monitors)
- Verifying DUV end-to-end behavior
- Scoreboarding

Blocks in a system verification component must have access to events, status, and objects collected by monitors in all lower layer verification components. This information is necessary for generating scenarios that depend on careful timing of activities generated and tracked across the verification environment. As such, the VE monitor in a system verification component should act as a central place for providing a link to monitors in lower layer verification components.

End-to-end behaviors add semantics beyond those defined at DUV ports. These semantics relate to behavior defined for the current level of design integration. Such behaviors cannot be checked at the interface level or at levels of abstraction below the one for the current DUV. As such, VE monitor for a system verification component should include checks for all such new end-to-end behaviors.

The VE monitor in a system verification component is also the ideal place for scoreboarding, since this monitor has access to all lower layer verification components where data objects are collected from the environment. Including the scoreboard in the monitor also allows for easy reuse of the scoreboard when the DUV verified at this stage is integrated into a larger system. More details on scoreboarding is provided in section 3.4.4.

3.4.3 DUV Monitor and Assertion Checker

Any new design integration step produces new end-to-end behaviors. These new behaviors attach new meanings to signal values and conditions in internal DUV blocks. In addition, a new DUV usually contains new internal blocks that have not been verified as part of any previous verification steps. The DUV monitor provides the following facilities to account for these considerations:

- Information about internal state of DUV
- Protocol checks across signals spanning multiple internal blocks
- Central placeholder for internal block assertions

The sequencer in a system verification component may require information about the internal state of the DUV in order to successfully generate a corner-case condition. All such information should be provided in the DUV monitor. This approach centralizes all interaction between the verification environment and DUV internal signals in DUV monitors allowing for easier design change management.

Many bugs viewed on the boundary of a design originate deep within the DUV and many cycles before such problem is observed at DUV ports. As such, it is necessary to provide early visibility into internal DUV problems that can be identified through checks made across internal blocks interfaces. This approach improves verification debugging through the visibility provided by this white-box verification approach. These types of check should be added by system integrator.

Internal blocks should come with assertions that were defined and used by block designer in the formal verification flow. The DUV monitor can be a central placeholder for all such assertion packages that are not included in DUV monitor of any lower layer verification component.

3.4.4 Scoreboarding

Scoreboarding is used to check for the following potential problems as data objects are produced, consumed, and moved across a design:

- Data values being different than expected
- A packet being received when one is not expected
- A packet not received when one is expected

The monitors in interface verification components verify that all signal timings at DUV ports match the specification. As such, data checking does not need to consider signal timing and is done at the transaction level where all signal and transfer timing information has already been removed from the collected data object or transaction. For example, when scoreboarding an Ethernet packet injected and expected to be received at a switch port, the exact signal timings of the packet traveling through design interfaces is assumed to be correct and only packet content as abstracted by the Ethernet format is scoreboarded.

Scoreboarding requires a reference model so that the expected outcome of an activity can be predicted. The general architecture of scoreboarding is shown in figure 3.7. In this view, the monitor on the input side collects a data object moving into the DUV. It then computes the expected output of the DUV based on that input and inserts the expected result in the scoreboard. The output monitor then checks every data object collected at the output against those already in the scoreboard.

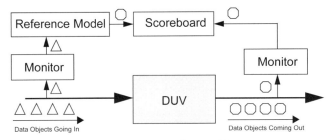

Figure 3.7 Scoreboarding Architecture

A scoreboard is essentially composed of a list of expected data objects where every data object collected at the DUV output is compared against the next expected data object. The matching of an actual object against an expected data object depends on a number of design dependent factors. A generic scoreboard implementation should, however, provide the following functionality:

- Support ordered checks where order of expected and actual data objects should be the same
- Support unordered checks where the collected data object may arrive out of order
- Allow for initial mismatches to be ignored since many designs may take some cycles to synchronize
- Perform end-of-simulation checks to make sure the scoreboard is empty and all expected data objects have been matched against an actual collected object

3.4.5 Coverage Collector

Coverage information is collected as part of monitor implementations. Coverage collection in a system verification component focuses on the following types of information:

- Basic traffic for each of the interfaces
- Combined effect of traffic at all interfaces
- Internal design states
- Sequences generated
- Delay and throughput information (performance information)
- Configuration modes
- Resets and restarts
- Errors observed and errors injected

Each system verification component should collect coverage information for the abstraction level of its sequencer, monitors, and scoreboard. This information includes scenarios that are verified by its VE monitor and scoreboard and also internal design conditions tracked by its DUV monitor. Once a verification component is made passive and reused in the next design integration step, it will continue to collect the same coverage information since its monitors and scoreboarding utilities are still operating even in passive mode. Using this approach, coverage information in the final verification environment is collected in a distributed fashion across all active and passive verification components.

3.5 Verification Component Reuse

The architecture of a module/system verification component, as described in this chapter, facilitates direct reuse of a verification component in the next design integration step. The only change required before this reuse is to change from active to passive all verification components that are no longer needed for stimulus generation. Making an interface verification component passive means taking out the driver and the sequencer. A module/system verification component does not contain a driver, and as such, making a module/system verification component passive only that its sequencer be disabled.

The composition of a module level verification environment is shown in figure 3.8. This figure shows a module **DUV₁** that is connected to two interface verification components **IVC₁** and **IVC₂**, and to module verification component **MVC** through these interface verification components. All verification components in this structure are active and contain sequencers, with interface verification components **IVC₁** and **IVC₂** also containing drivers.

The reuse of module level verification components at the system level is shown in figure 3.9. This figure shows module **DUV₂** which is constructed by combining module **DUV₁** and blocks **Block₁** and **Block₂**. The verification environment for **DUV₂** is very similar in structure to the one shown for **DUV₁** in figure 3.8, and consists of active interface verification components **IVC₃** and **IVC₄** and system verification component **SVC**. In addition, this system level verification environment include the entire verification environment for **DUV₁**, with the following modifications:

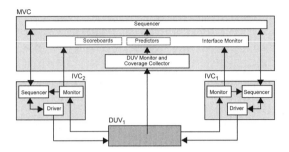

Figure 3.8 Module Level Verification Environment Integration

- The sequencer in verification component **MVC** is removed
- The sequencer and driver in verification components **IVC₁** and **IVC₂** are removed

Given the monitoring, scoreboarding, and coverage collection strategies described in this chapter, all of these activities transfer directly from the verification environment for **DUV₁** to the verification environment for **DUV₂**. While end-to-end behavior is being checked by scoreboards in the verification environment for **DUV₂**, end-to-end checks are being performed for **DUV₁** as well. In addition, coverage is also collected by the monitors in all passive verification components allowing for distributed collection of coverage as design integration moves to the next step.

The reuse of verification environment for **DUV₁** in making the verification environment for **DUV₂** can be repeated recursively, as design moves to the higher levels of integration.

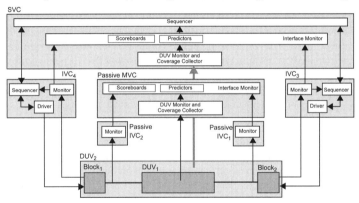

Figure 3.9 System Level Verification Environment Integration

PART 2

All about SystemVerilog

CHAPTER 4

SystemVerilog as a Programming Language

SystemVerilog features and constructs have been defined because of the specific requirements of the latest design and verification methodologies. As such, learning SystemVerilog syntax and programming without intimate knowledge of the methodology behind its inception would be as unrewarding as flying a supersonic jet with the piloting skills of a glider pilot. Familiarity with the verification methodology and architecture described in part one of this book is a first step in understanding the motivation behind the introduction of new SystemVerilog constructs. With this methodology in mind, features of SystemVerilog discussed henceforth will present themselves not as mundane details of a programming language, but as facilitating constructs for the implementation of a modern verification environment.

This chapter discusses SystemVerilog syntax, flow, and structure. In doing so, this chapter provides an overview on how to write simple programs in SystemVerilog. Chapter 5 describes SystemVerilog features that are specially introduced or used to better facilitate functional verification.

4.1 The Generalized Model of a Digital System

Digital systems are created by essentially interconnecting individual blocks, each represented by a core functionality and input/output ports. This model of a digital system persists at all levels of abstraction where at the highest level, blocks represent complex system level functionality and at the lowest level, blocks represent transistors. Given that each block in such a representation can be modeled as a single or the interaction of multiple threads of execution (i.e., processes) that act on the internal state of the block (i.e., data values), then it can be seen that any digital system can be modeled by defining the following:

- Internal state of the block
- Threads of execution and their programs operating on the internal state of the block (i.e., processes)
- Interconnection between these threads of execution
- Synchronization between these threads of execution

A block's internal state is represented by data values that the block holds; its functionality is represented by threads of execution that manipulate these internal data values; its dependence on other blocks is represented by its interconnection information; and its order of execution, with respect to other blocks needed for deciding the order of execution for its threads, is represented by its synchronization information.

Hardware description languages are essentially created to implement this generalized view of a digital system. For example, in Verilog, threads of exception include *always* and *initial* blocks, data interconnection (i.e., dependence) between processes are either explicitly defined (i.e., using sensitivity lists) or implicitly derived by deciding what variables from outside a process are used in its description, and synchronization information is either derived implicitly (by propagating value changes as events) or explicitly by using wait statements based on events or absolute time values.

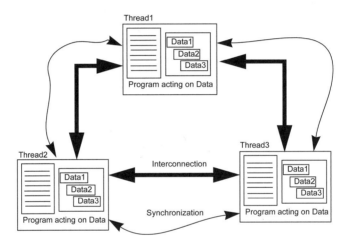

Figure 4.1 Generalized Model of a Digital System

The power of a modeling language to represent complex systems using this generalized model and the productivity it affords is directly proportional to the following elements:

- Ability to represent complex and user defined data types
- Ability to represent interconnections at different levels of abstraction
- Expressiveness of the procedural language used to model the program executed in each thread and the interaction between threads
- Ease of building a hierarchical model

Even though Verilog is a good language for modeling a digital system consisting of wires, registers, and modules that are connected through ports, it quickly runs out of steam when more abstract models must be built. Specifically, Verilog lacks the ability to specify abstract data types, interconnection between modules represented as anything but bits and bytes, and higher level software programming techniques that facilitate better modeling of each thread of execution, and the synchronization between concurrent threads.

The usefulness of a modeling language in building a complex verification environment depends not only on the above factors, but verification constructs provided in the language to facilitate verification activities such as:

- Constrained random stimulus generation
- Coverage collection
- Property checking

Verilog also lacks the support for carrying out these verification related activities.

SystemVerilog has been defined in order to address these limitations of Verilog. To that end, SystemVerilog provides the following broad enhancements beyond what Verilog offers:

- The ability to model systems at a higher level of abstraction by providing complex and user defined data types and interfaces
- The ability to use software programming techniques such as recursive function calls and pointer-based programming, leading to better programming expressiveness
- An object-oriented programming paradigm through introduction of classes and its related semantics
- Verification related utilities such as constrained random generation, coverage collection, and property specification and checking

In the remainder of this chapter, a general view of the SystemVerilog language is presented. SystemVerilog's verification related features are discussed in the chapter 5.

4.2 Structure of a SystemVerilog Program

Even though SystemVerilog adds many new features to Verilog, the structure of a System-Verilog program remains essentially the same as that of a Verilog program. A SystemVerilog program hierarchy consists of three fundamental entities:

- Module blocks
- Program blocks
- Procedural blocks (i.e., processes)
- Data objects

Module Blocks are used to model structural hierarchy of the design. In module-based verification environments, module blocks are also used to model the hierarchy of the verification environment (section 12.1). Module blocks can contain module blocks, procedural blocks, and data objects. Program blocks are used to define a clear boundary between the verification environment and the DUV (section 5.3). Program blocks can contain only type and variable declarations and one or more initial blocks. Procedural blocks can contain procedural blocks and data objects. Data Objects can contain only data objects[1].

The following program shows examples of these relationships:

[1.] Classes are special types of objects that combine related data values and procedural blocks. Classes will be discussed in section 4.7.

```
Program 4.1: SystemVerilog program structure
1   :    typedef struct {int ii; int jj;} twoval_t;
2   :
3   :    module leaf (input int aa, output int bb);
4   :        int cc=5;
5   :        assign bb = aa * cc;
6   :    endmodule
7   :
8   :    module mytop;
9   :        twoval_t tv;
10  :
11  :        function int decrement (input int a);
12  :            int decval;
13  :            decval = 2;
14  :            decrement = a - decval;
15  :        endfunction
16  :
17  :        leaf leaf_i (.aa(tv.ii),.bb(tv.jj));
18  :
19  :        initial begin
20  :            int yy;
21  :            yy = 10;
22  :            tv.ii = 100;
23  :            #1 $display(tv.jj, decrement(yy));
24  :            $finish;
25  :        end
26  :    endmodule
```

The new user defined type **twoval_t** (line 1) is an example of a data object containing (or being composed of) other data objects. Module **mytop** includes data objects (e.g., **tv** of type **twoval_t**), modules (e.g., **leaf_i**, an instance of module **leaf**), and procedural code in the form of an *initial* block. Figure 4.2 shows a pictorial view of block relationships in this program sample.

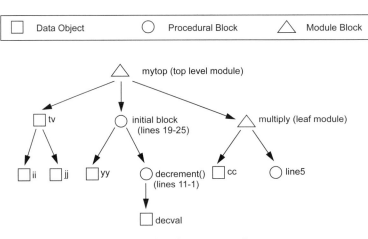

Figure 4.2 Hierarchy of a SystemVerilog Program

4.2.1 Hierarchies of Different Types

Note that in the generalized view shown in figure 4.2, three types of hierarchies can be identified:

- Module hierarchy
- Procedural (i.e., function call) hierarchy
- Data object hierarchy

It is very important to have a clear understanding of, and the differences among, these types of hierarchies when programming in SystemVerilog, since these hierarchies correspond to ideas in different domains, consisting of hardware design (module hierarchies reflecting design architecture) and software design (procedural and data object hierarchies, and eventually class-based hierarchies reflecting software organization).

A *Module Hierarchy* corresponds to how modules are instantiated in other modules. It is possible to have multiple module hierarchies if multiple top level modules exist. Top level modules are defined as modules that are not instantiated in any other module. Figure 4.2 has only one module hierarchy rooted at module **mytop**. Module hierarchies are used for providing a structured programming environment by grouping closely related procedural blocks in modules. The process of elaboration which takes place before simulation starts, removes the module hierarchy and produces a set of interconnected procedural blocks similar to the one shown in figure 4.1. Simulation is actually performed on this elaborated view of a SystemVerilog program.

Procedural Hierarchy corresponds to how procedural blocks call functions or tasks. Figure 4.2 shows two procedural hierarchies: one rooted at the ***initial*** block (lines 19–25); and the second rooted at the procedural block created because of the continuous assignment statement (line 5), which makes no other procedure calls and as such, has no sub-hierarchy.

Data Object Hierarchy describes the composition of complex data types. Four data object hierarchies in figure 4.2 are those rooted respectively at **tv, yy, decval,** and **cc**.

SystemVerilog provides powerful constructs for specifying these hierarchies. The remainder of this chapter describes these constructs. Section 4.3 describes data modeling and manipulation. Section 4.4 describes procedural blocks composed of data objects and procedural statements. Section 4.5 describes the use of procedural blocks and instantiation to create module hierarchies. Synchronization between concurrently running threads of execution is described in section 4.6. Object-oriented programming—which is the preferred programming paradigm for building scalable and highly complex programs while maintaining high productivity—is described in section 4.7.

4.3 Data Types and Objects in SystemVerilog

SystemVerilog defines the following forms of data:

- Literals
- Parameters

- Constants
- Variables
- Nets
- Attributes

Literals refer to explicit representation of a value in program code such as integer literal **1** or string literal **"Arbiter"**. *Parameters* are values that can be individually assigned for different instances of a module and as such, allow for customization of different instances when building the module hierarchy. Parameters are taken into consideration during program elaboration (creation of the module hierarchy) before simulation starts, and as such cannot be changed during simulation runtime. *Constants* are represented by named objects whose values don't change throughout the simulation runtime. *Variables* are named data objects whose values can change during simulation runtime. *Nets* are similar to variables, but more closely model a physical wire, since the new value of a net data object is decided by resolving the newly assigned value with the previous value of the net (this is in contrast with variables where last assignment always prevails). *Attributes* are used to attach properties to objects (i.e., modules, instances, wires, etc.) for later retrieval.

A data object can be fully described by the following properties:

- Lifetime: When it is created and when it is destroyed
- Update mechanism: How its value is changed
- Type: The type of data it holds

These aspects are discussed in the following subsections.

4.3.1 Data Lifetime

SystemVerilog defines two types of data lifetime:

- Static
- Automatic

An *automatic variables* is created when program execution enters the scope[2] in which that variable is declared. For example an automatic variable inside a function call is created when program execution enters that function and is destroyed when program execution returns from that function call. *Static variables* are created at the beginning of program execution and hold their value throughout program execution until they are assigned a new value. The major implication of this difference is that a static variable defined in a method (i.e., function or task) will hold its value across multiple calls to that method, even when that method is called from different places in the program flow. As such, static variables in a function or task can be used to share data between consecutive invocations of that function or task.

Variables declared inside functions and tasks are by default automatic variables. However, SystemVerilog provides the necessary syntax to mark all variables declared inside a

---

[2] A scope defines an enclosing context within which a data object is visible and can be used in expressions.

program, module, function, or task as either automatic or static by appending the appropriate keyword to that procedural block (see section 4.4).

4.3.2 Update Mechanisms

Update mechanism refers to how the value of a data object is changed when a new value is assigned to it. The following data types each use a different update mechanism:

- Constants
- Variables
- Nets

The value of a *constant* data object cannot change throughout the program lifetime. The value of a *variable* is updated to be the last value assigned to it. The value of a *net* is updated according to a resolution function that takes into account the value of the net before the last assignment and the last value assigned to it. Nets are meant to model physical wires in a design while variables are meant for storing program data.

The update mechanisms for variables and nets, as described above and defined in the Verilog language, impose restrictions on how values can be assigned to these data objects. Assignments in Verilog are one of:

- Procedural assignments
- Continuous assignments

A *procedural assignment* is a one time action of putting a value into a data object. In a *continuous assignment*, the assigned value is imagined to be continuously driving the data object. In Verilog, a variable can be assigned only through procedural assignments and a net can be assigned only through continuous assignments or module ports (which indirectly imply continuous assignments). The reason for this restriction is that the effect of a continuous assignment to a data object should be taken into account when computing its value after any new assignment. This calculation requires a resolution function which is available only for net type data objects. SystemVerilog relaxes this requirement slightly by allowing a variable to be assigned by only a single continuous assignment. This flexibility does not violate the overall assumption about needing a resolution function in handling continuous assignments. The reason is that if a data object is driven with only one continuous assignment throughout the simulation runtime, then it does not need a resolution function, and hence that data object can be a variable.

4.3.3 Data Types

SystemVerilog extends the built-in data types defined in Verilog in the following ways:

- Introduces new built-in types
- Allows any number of unpacked dimensions for each variable
- Introduces enumerated data types
- Introduces user defined data types
- Introduces composite data types
- Introduces classes and object-oriented programming constructs

Classes and object-oriented programming is discussed in section 4.7. Other topics are discussed in the following subsections.

4.3.3.1 Built-In Data Types

Table 4.2 shows a summary of syntax used for writing SystemVerilog constant values. The following observations apply to these constants:

- Integer constants can be specified as either sized or unsized.
- A sized integer constant is sign extended to fill all of its bits (e.g., **-4'b1** is sign extended to fill four bits).
- A negative integer constant behaves differently when it includes a base specifier (e.g., **-'d12** or **-4'd12**). Without a base specifier, the constant is assumed to be a signed value when used in evaluating an expression. For example, expression (**-2/2 = -1**), since constant **-2** is considered a negative value when evaluating the expression. With a base specifier, however, the 2's complement value of the integer constant is assumed to represent an unsigned value when used in evaluating the expression. For example, expression (**-'d2/2=2147483647**), since constant (**-'d2**) is first sign extended to fill a 32-bit holder, producing value of **4294967294**, and then used as an unsigned value in evaluating the expression. Special care should, therefore, be applied when using negative integer constants with a base specifier (either sized or unsized).

Constant Type	Notation	Examples
Integer	Unsized	19813 (decimal, no x or z allowed) 'b10z10x10 (binary including x, z) 'o7z1x (octal including x, z) 'd192 (decimal) 'h1zfaxfa (hex including x, z) -'h1fbca (negative hex)
	Sized	8'b10z10x10 (binary including x, z) 12'o7z1x (octal including x, z) -10'd192 (decimal sign extended to 10 bits) 28'h1zfaxfa (hex including x, z) -24'h1fbca (negative hex sign extended to 24 bits)
Real	Decimal	14.55 0.45
	Scientific	1.4e13 (exponent must be an integer) 0.55e-4 (exponent must be an integer)
String	Quoted	"this is a text" "\n" (a new line character) "\t" (a tab character) "\\" (a \ character) "\"" (a quote character) "\ddd" (an octal digit for a character d<8)

Table 4.1: SystemVerilog Constant Types and Syntax

Table 4.2 shows a summary of built-in data types available in SystemVerilog. The following observations apply to data types shown in this table:

- Types **reg** and **logic** are exactly the same. Type **logic** is introduced in SystemVerilog in order to better reflect the usage of this data type.

Form	Type	Signed (default)	Values	Packed Size	New in SV
Variables	byte	yes (signed)	0,1	8 bits	yes
	shortint	yes (signed)	0,1	16 bits	yes
	int	yes (signed)	0,1	32 bits	yes
	longint	yes (signed)	0,1	64 bits	yes
	integer	yes (signed)	0,1,x,z	32 bits	
	bit	yes (unsigned)	0,1	User Defined	yes
	logic	yes (unsigned)	0,1,x,z	User Defined	yes
	reg	yes (unsigned)	0,1,x,z	User Defined	
	time	no	0,1,x,z	64 bits	
	shortreal	always signed		float	yes
	real	always signed		double	
	realtime	no			
	String	NA			
	void	NA			yes
	event	NA			
	chandle	NA			yes
Nets	supply0	no	0,1,x,z, 7 strengths	User Defined	
	supply1	no	0,1,x,z, 7 strengths	User Defined	
	tri	no	0,1,x,z, 7 strengths	User Defined	
	triand	no	0,1,x,z, 7 strengths	User Defined	
	trior	no	0,1,x,z, 7 strengths	User Defined	
	tri0	no	0,1,x,z, 7 strengths	User Defined	
	tri1	no	0,1,x,z, 7 strengths	User Defined	
	wire	no	0,1,x,z, 7 strengths	User Defined	
	wand	no	0,1,x,z, 7 strengths	User Defined	
	wor	no	0,1,x,z, 7 strengths	User Defined	

Table 4.2: SystemVerilog Built-In Data Types

- Types *bit*, *logic*, and *reg* can have packed sizes of any dimension (see section 4.3.3.3.1).
- Types *byte*, *shortint*, *int*, *longint*, and *integer* are signed by default but types *bit*, *logic*, and *reg* are unsigned by default. To change from the default, keyword *signed* or *unsigned* must be used when declaring variables of this type.
- Some built-in data types can be described by using other data types. For example, *byte* is the same as "**bit [7:0]**" and *integer* is the same as "**logic signed [31:0]**".

The following program shows example declarations for these data types.

```
Program 4.2: SystemVerilog example data type declarations
1  :   module top;
2  :       byte unsigned b1, b2;
3  :       shortint unsigned si1, si2;
4  :       int unsigned i1, i2;
5  :       longint unsigned li1, li2;
6  :       integer unsigned ir1, ir2;
7  :       bit signed [10:1][10:1] bt1, bt2;
8  :       logic signed [10:1][10:1] lg1, lg2;
```

```
9   :          reg signed [10:1][10:1] rg1, rg2;
10  :          time t1;
11  :          shortreal sr1, sr2;
12  :          real r1, r2;
13  :          realtime rt1, rt2;
14  :          string str;
15  :  endmodule
```

4.3.3.2 Enumerated Data Types

An enumerated data type is represented by a set of named constants and a data type for the values represented by these named constants. A variable declared to have an enumerated data type is strongly typed and can only take values from the set of named constants included in the enumerated type declaration.

An enumerated type is represented by the following elements:

- Data type for values represented by named constants
- Name and value assigned to each named constant

The syntax for an enumerated type is as follows:

enum [data_type] {$name_1$=$value_1$, $name_2$=$value_2$,...,$name_N$=$value_N$} var_name

The following rules apply to the above syntax:

- Names for the named constants (e.g., **$name_1$**, **$name_2$**, etc.) must be unique.
- If **data_type** is omitted, it is assumed by default to be of type *int*.
- Values assigned to named constants (e.g **$value_1$**, **$value_2$**, etc.) must be valid values for type **data_type**. For example, if **data_type** is *bit*, then valid values are **0** and **1**.
- Two named constants cannot have the same value.
- If the value for a named constant is omitted, it is assumed to be the next value after the value for the previous named constant.

SystemVerilog provides a shorthand notation for declaring an enumerated type where names for a group of named constants can be represented as a range and values assigned to a named constant can be assigned automatically. The syntax for shorthand representation of a named constant or a group of named constants is:

$syntax_1$: enumName[$index_1$:$index_2$]=enumValue
$syntax_2$: enumName[Number]=enumValue

In **$syntax_1$**, one named constant is assumed for each value in the range **[$index_1$:$index_2$]** where each named constant is assigned consecutive values starting from **enumValue**. In **$syntax_2$**, the range is assumed to **[0:Number-1]**. For example:

enum int {red[1:3]=1, green[2:3]=5} colors;
is equivalent to:
enum int {red1=1, red2=2, red3=3, green2=5, green3=6} colors;

The following rules apply to this shorthand notation:

- Either the range **[$index_1$:$index_2$]** or **enumValue** can be omitted.
- If range **[$index_1$:$index_2$]** is omitted, then only one named constant **enumName** is assumed.
- If **enumValue** is omitted, then its value is taken from the last enum value assigned to

the preceding named constant, with **0** assumed if it is the first named constant in the list.

- Values *x* and *z* can be assigned to named constants if data type is four-valued (e.g., *integer*). In this case, the value for the named constant immediately following this named constant must be explicitly specified.

SystemVerilog provides methods for iterating over the named constants of an enumerated type. These methods are:

```
function enum first();
function enum last();
function enum next(int unsigned N = 1);
function enum prev(int unsigned N = 1);
function int num();
function string name();
```

Function *first()* returns the first named constant in the enumerated type declaration, *last()* returns the last named constant, *next()* and *previous()* return the next and previous named constants respectively, *num()* returns the number of named constants, *name()* returns a string containing the name of a named constant.

An example of using enumerated type and its functions is shown below.

```
Program 4.3: Declaring and using enumerated types
1    module top;
2        initial begin
3            enum {asia=1, europe, africa=8, america, australia=44} location;
4            location = location.first();
5            for (int i = 0; i< location.num(); i++) begin
6                $display("%s:%d", location.name(), location);
7                location = location.next();
8            end
9        end
10   endmodule
```

The output produced by the above example is shown below:

```
asia:        1
europe:      2
africa:      8
america:     9
australia:   44
```

As shown in the output, the constant value assigned to **europe** is **2**, which is the next value to that assigned to the previous named constant **asia**. Similarly, the constant value assigned to **america** is **9**.

4.3.3.3 Arrays

SystemVerilog provides the following types of array data types:

- Static arrays
- Dynamic arrays
- Associative arrays
- Queues

Static arrays are multidimensional arrays whose size is explicitly specified when declaring the array. Dynamic arrays have one or more dimensions with one dimension whose size is undefined during declaration and is decided when creating the array. Associative arrays allow access to array elements using a key that can have any data type. Queues are used to model an ordered set of elements. These array types are described in the following subsections.

4.3.3.3.1 Static Arrays

A *static array* is a multidimensional array whose number of dimensions and width for each dimension is specified in its declaration. SystemVerilog static arrays can have any number of dimensions and can be operated on as whole arrays, slices, or individual elements.

SystemVerilog extends the classic notion of arrays by allowing the programmer to define how each dimension of an array is stored in memory. This decision provides a trade-off between storage efficiency and access flexibility. Members of a *packed dimension* of an array are grouped into memory words before being stored in memory. As such, a packed array dimension provides good storage efficiency. Members of an *unpacked dimension* of an array are stored in individual memory locations. As such, an unpacked array dimension can be accessed with great flexibility.

The syntax for a static array declaration is as follows:

element_data_type [PRange$_1$]...[PRange$_N$] array_name [URange$_1$]...[URange$_M$];

Dimensions specified before **array_name** are packed dimensions, while dimension specified after **array_name** are unpacked dimensions. The following guidelines apply to static arrays:

- A single packed word is used to store all packed dimensions of an array.
- Array elements are accessed as shown below. As such, packed dimensions change more frequently than unpacked dimensions.
    array_name [URange1]...[URangeM][PRange1]...[PRangeN]
- An array dimension range can be specified as [index$_1$:index$_2$] or as **[Number]**, where **[Number]** is equivalent to **[0:Number-1]**.
- If an array is declared as signed, then the memory word containing all of the packed dimensions is assumed to be a signed value. A slice of a packed dimension is not a signed value.
- Packed dimensions can only be specified for arrays of type *bit*, *logic*, *reg*, and *wire*. Unpacked dimensions can be specified from any type.

Arrays can be accessed using the following mechanisms:

- Reading and writing the whole array
- Reading and writing a slice of array
- Reading and writing a variable slice of array (identified by another variable)
- Reading and writing an array element
- Equality operations on array or slice of array

It is important to note that dimension part-selects (slice spanning multiple elements of a dimension) can be used only with packed dimensions. Examples of these access types are shown below:

```
      ┌─────────────────────────────────────────
      │ Program 4.4: Array access types
      ├─────────────────────────────────────────
 1    :   module top;
 2    :       initial begin
 3    :           //   dimension numbers
 4    :           //   3    4      1    2
 5    :           bit [4:0][3:0] arr1 [2:0][1:0];
 6    :           bit [4:0][3:0] arr2 [2:0][1:0];
 7    :           int index;
 8    :           index = 1;
 9    :
10    :           arr1 = arr2;
11    :           if (arr1!= arr2)
12    :               $display ("Arrays are not equal");
13    :           arr1[1][1] = arr2[2][0];
14    :           if (arr1[1][1]!= arr2[2][0])
15    :               $display ("Arrays are not equal");
16    :           arr1[1][1][1][2:1] = arr2[2][0][0][1:0];
17    :           if (arr1[1][1][1][2:1]!= arr2[2][0][0][1:0])
18    :               $display ("Array slices are not equal");
19    :           arr1[1][1][1][index +:2] = arr2[2][0][0][(index-1) +:2];
20    :       end
21    :   endmodule
      └─────────────────────────────────────────
```

The above program shows examples of a whole array assignment (line 10), array slice assignment (lines 13, 16), array variable slice assignment (line 19), and array compare operations (lines 11, 14, and 17). Dimension order for array element access is shown on lines 3 and 4.

SystemVerilog provides the following system defined methods for accessing array elements: *$left()*, *$right()*, *$low()*, *$high()*, *$increment()*, *$size()*, and *$dimensions()*. See the SystemVerilog reference manual for details of these functions.

4.3.3.3.2 Dynamic Arrays

Dynamic arrays are similar to static arrays except that they can have one unpacked array dimension whose size can be decided during simulation runtime. Memory for a dynamic array is allocated during simulation runtime. A consequence of this runtime allocation is that the memory for dynamic arrays is not part of the program memory space.

The syntax for a dynamic array declaration is as follows:

element_data_type [PRange$_1$]...[PRange$_N$] array_name [];

SystemVerilog provides the following operators and methods for creating and interacting with the dynamic arrays:

- Operator *new*
- Function *size()*
- Function *delete()*

Operator *new* is used to allocate a dynamic array. Accessing a dynamic array before memory is allocated results in a runtime error. Function *size()* returns the size of the unpacked dimension of the array, which is the size specified when the array was allocated. Function *delete()* is used to reset the array size to **0**.

The rules of access for dynamic arrays (i.e., reading and writing slices, etc.) are the same as those for static arrays once the size of a dynamic array is known. Since this size is only decided at program runtime, dynamic array access can lead to a runtime error message while the same error types are checked at compile time for static arrays.

The following program code shows an example of dynamic arrays:

```
Program 4.5: Dynamic array declaration and allocation
1  :   module top;
2  :       bit [4:0][3:0] arr1 [], arr2[];
3  :       int count = 10;
4  :       initial begin
5  :           arr1 = new[count];
6  :           $display(arr1.size());        // displays 10;
7  :           arr2 = new[20](arr1);
8  :           $display(arr2.size());        // displays 20;
9  :           arr1.delete();
10 :           $display(arr1.size());        // displays 0;
11 :       end
12 :   endmodule
```

Operator *new* is used (lines 5, 7) to allocate dynamic arrays of size **10** and **20** for arr$_1$ and arr$_2$. Operator *new* allows an array to be specified for initializing the allocated array. This is shown on line 7 where elements of arr$_1$ (**10** elements) are used to initialize the first **10** elements of arr$_2$.

4.3.3.3.3 Associative Arrays

In *associative arrays*, array elements are identified by a key value. This identification mechanism is in contrast with static and dynamic arrays where array elements are identified by their position within a linear memory space. Associative arrays are ideally suited for sparse linear arrays where not all array positions contain relevant values, or in cases where array elements must be identified by a key and not by their position in the array.

Associative arrays are declared using the following syntax:

data_type array_name[key_type];

In this syntax, **data_type** is the type of each array element which can be any type allowed for static and dynamic arrays, **array_name** is the name of the associative array being declared, and **key_type** gives the data type for keys used to access array element.

Examples of associative array declaration, assignment, and usage is shown in the following program:

```
Program 4.6: Associative array declaration and access
1  :   module test;
2  :       class profile;
3  :           int id_num;
4  :           string first_name;
5  :           string last_name;
6  :           function new(int id, string fn, string ln);
7  :               id_num = id; first_name = fn; last_name = ln;
8  :           endfunction
9  :       endclass
10 :
```

```
11  :         typedef bit signed [3:0] signed_nibble;
12  :         typedef bit [3:0] unsigned_nibble;
13  :         integer a_arr0[integer];
14  :         integer a_arr1[string];
15  :         integer a_arr2[profile];
16  :         integer a_arr3[signed_nibble];
17  :
18  :         initial begin
19  :             profile prof1;
20  :
21  :             a_arr1["jack"] = 1414;
22  :             a_arr1[""] = 2424;
23  :
24  :             prof1 = new(0, "FirstName", "LastName");
25  :             $display(a_arr2[prof1]);
26  :             a_arr2[prof1] = 123;
27  :             a_arr2[null] = 234;
28  :             $display(a_arr2[prof1]);
29  :         end
30  :     endmodule
```

The following comments apply to this example:

- Associative array **a_arr$_0$** uses predefined type *integer* as its key type (line 13).
- Associative array **a_arr$_1$** is declared to have a key of type string (line 14). This array can be accessed by using string keys (lines 21–22). The empty string is a valid key for an associative array (line 22).
- Associative array **a_arr$_2$** is declared to have a key type of user defined class **profile**. Class **profile** is defined to hold fields of different data types (lines 3–5). The above example shows the creation of data object **prof$_1$** (line 24) which is used as a key for associative array **a_arr$_2$** (line 26). *Null* is a valid key for associative arrays having a class key type (line 27).
- Reading an associative array element that is not yet initialized returns the default value for the array element type. For example, reading array element **a_arr$_2$[prof$_1$]** (line 25) returns an empty string since no value is assigned to **a_arr$_2$[prof$_1$]** previously.
- Associative array keys can be a user defined type. The declaration of associative array **a_arr$_3$** is defined to have user defined type **signed_nibble** (line 11) as its key type (line 16).

SystemVerilog defines a set of predefined methods for accessing associative arrays. The function prototype for these methods are:

```
function int num();                      // return number of elements in array
function void delete([input k]);         //delete element at key k (key is optional, delete all if not given)
function int exists(input k);            //return 1 if element at key k exists
function int first(ref k);               //return 1 if first key exists, assign k to first key
function int last(ref k);                //return 1 if last key exists, assign k to last key
function int next(ref k);                //return 1 if key next to k exists, replace k with key next to k
function int prev(ref k);                //return 1 if key prev to k exists, replace k with key prev to k
```

Examples of associative array method usage is shown in the following example:

Program 4.7: Associative array method usage

```
1  :    module test;
2  :        integer aa5[integer];
3  :
4  :        initial begin
5  :            integer aakey;
```

```
6   :              for (int i = 0; i < 5; i++) aa5[i] = 10*i;
7   :              $display(aa5.num());
8   :              aa5.delete(3);
9   :              $display(aa5.num());
10  :              $display(aa5.exists(3));
11  :              if (aa5.first(aakey)) $display("First key is: ", aakey);
12  :              while (aa5.next(aakey)) $display("next key is: ", aakey);
13  :              if (aa5.last(aakey)) $display("Last key is: ", aakey);
14  :              while (aa5.prev(aakey)) $display("Prev key is: ", aakey);
15  :              aa5.delete();
16  :              $display(aa5.num());
17  :          end
18  :      endmodule
```

First, associative array **aa5** is initialized with **5** members (line 6). Function ***num()*** is used to print the number of elements in this array, yielding a value of **5** (line 7). Function ***delete()*** is used to delete array member stored at key **3** (line 8), after which, function ***num()*** returns a value of **4** (line 9), and function call **aa5.exists(3)** returns a value of **0** (line 10). Function *first()* is used to place the first key of **aa5** (value **0**) into variable **aakey** (line 11). Function ***next()*** is used iteratively to print consecutive keys for array **aa5** which prints a sequence of (**1, 2, 4**) (line 12). Function ***last()*** is used to assign the last key for array **aa5** (value **4**) into variable **aakey** (line 13). Function ***prev()*** is then used iteratively to continuously assign the previous key to the key stored in variable **aakey** back into variable **aakey** and print the result, producing output (**2,1,0**). Function ***delete()*** is used to delete all elements of array **aa5** (line 15).

An associative arrays can only be assigned to another associative array having the same key and member data types.

4.3.3.3.4 Queues

A *queue* is an ordered collection of homogeneous (i.e., all having the same data type) elements. Queue elements can be accessed in constant time[3]. In addition, a queue can be grown or shrunk on both ends in constant time. A SystemVerilog queue construct is suitable for implementing FIFO (first-in-first-out) and stack (first-in-last-out) data structures.

Queues are declared using the following syntax:

```
data_type queue_name[$];
data_type queue_name[$:max_size]
```

In this syntax, **data_type** is the type of each queue element which can be any type allowed for static and dynamic arrays, **queue_name** is the name of the queue being declared, and **max_size** (if provided) gives the maximum number of elements allowed in the queue.

SystemVerilog defines a set of predefined methods for manipulating and accessing queues. The function prototype for these methods are:

```
function int size();                      //returns number of elements in queue
function void insert(int index, queue_type item);// inserts elements at position index
```

---

[3] In this context, constant time refers to the computation effort required to process an entry. For example, accessing an element in a linked-list may in the worst case require that all linked-list elements be traversed. Meanwhile, an array element can be accessed using its index. Therefore, accessing array elements can be done in constant time but access time for linked-list elements is proportional to the size of the linked-list.

```
function void delete(int index);              //deletes elements at position index
function queue_type pop_front();              //removes element at head of queue
function queue_type pop_back();               //removes element at tail of queue
function void push_front(queue_type item);    //adds element to head of queue
function void push_back(queue_type item);     //adds element to tail of queue
```

Examples of queue declaration, assignment, and usage is shown in the following:

```
     Program 4.8: Queue declaration, access, and manipulation
 1   :   module test;
 2   :       int intq[$];
 3   :       int bounded_intq[$:2];
 4   :
 5   :       initial begin
 6   :           int val, size;
 7   :           size = intq.size();          // size=0, intq={}
 8   :           intq.push_back(10);          // intq={10}
 9   :           intq.push_back(20);          // intq={10,20}
10   :           intq.push_front(30);         // intq={30,10,20}
11   :           intq.push_front(40);         // intq={40,30,10,20}
12   :           intq.insert(1, 50);          // intq={40,50,30,10,20}
13   :           intq.insert(3, 60);          // intq={40,50,30,60,10,20}
14   :           val = intq.pop_back();       // val=20, intq={40,50,30,60,10}
15   :           val = intq.pop_front();      // val=40, intq={50,30,60,10}
16   :           intq.delete(2);              // intq={50,30,10}
17   :           val = intq[1];               // val = 30
18   :           val = intq[100];             // val = 0;
19   :           size = intq.size();          // size = 3
20   :       end
21   :   endmodule
```

This example, shows the declaration of unbounded queue **intq** and bounded queue **unbounded_intq** (lines 2–3). Predefined queue functions are then used to add, remove, and access queue elements (lines 7–19). The contents of queue after each operation is shown as a comment on each line. Note that the first element shown in the contents of the queue is at index **0**. Accessing a queue element at a non-existing index (line 18) returns the default value for the type of queue element. Using function *delete()* to delete a member at a non-existing index results in a runtime warning message. Using function *insert()* to insert a value at a negative index or beyond the last element of the queue also results in a runtime warning message.

4.3.3.4 Composite Data Types

SystemVerilog provides the *struct* and *union* constructs for declaring composite data types. Members of a *struct* construct are stored in consecutive memory locations, while members of a union share the same memory space whose size is the size of the largest member of the union.

A *struct* composite data can be declared as a *packed* struct. In this case, the memory used to store the contents of this struct are packed into memory words (similar to packed array dimensions). Packed *structs* can be accessed as a packed one-dimensional array whose most significant bit contains the most significant bit of the first member of *struct*.

A *union* can also be declared as a packed union. In this case, all members of the union must have the same size.

A packed struct that has any four-state member is stored in a four-state memory word. Otherwise, the packed struct is stored in a two-state memory word.

Use of packed structs is shown in the following example:

```
Program 4.9: Packed struct declaration and assignment
1  :    module top;
2  :        initial begin
3  :            typedef enum [3:0] {READ, WRITE, IDLE} opcode_t;
4  :            struct packed {
5  :                opcode_t opcode1;
6  :                opcode_t opcode2;
7  :                bit [7:0] data;
8  :            } IR;
9  :            // IR as a packed word: opcode1[3:0]opcode2[3:0]data[7:0]
10 :            IR.opcode1 = READ;
11 :            if (IR[15:12]!= READ) $display ("Assignment Failed");
12 :        end
13 :    endmodule
```

This example shows a packed struct declaration that defines instruction **IR**. Each opcode is four bits (line 3). The packed struct, therefore, is **16** bits. Members of a packed struct can be accessed either through member names or their relative position in the packed memory word storing the struct data. As shown, **IR.opcode1** is assigned on line 10 and then **IR[15:12]** is checked for correct assignment on line 11. Variable **IR** is stored as 2-valued data. If, however, one of struct members (lines 5–7) were 4-valued, then **IR** would be stored as 4-valued data.

4.3.3.5 User Defined Data Types

A user can define a new type by using the *typedef* construct. Defining a new type can greatly increase code readability as complex data types and array sizes can be defined as a new data types with an easily understood name.

Defining a new data type is at times necessary since casting in SystemVerilog only allows simple names to be specified for the type to be cast into. As such, a type whose description consists of more than simple names must be defined as a new type before it can be used in casting.

Some examples of new data types include:

```
typedef int my_favorite_type;
typedef enum bit [3:0] {READ, WRITE, IDLE} opcode_t;
typedef struct packed {byte opcode1; byte data;} instruction;
typedef bit [3:0][3:0] my_2packed_1unpacked_array [1:0];
typedef my_2packed_1unpacked_array my_2packed_2unpacked_array [1:0];
my_2packed_1unpacked_array arr_2_1;
my_2packed_2unpacked_array arr_2_2;
```

Data types **my_favorite_type, opcode_t, instruction, my_2packed_1unpacked_array**, and **my_2packed_2unpacked_array** are declared in the above examples. Note that in the above examples, **arr_2_1** is a three-dimensional array with two packed dimensions and one unpacked dimension, and **arr_2_2** is a four-dimensional array with two packed dimensions and two unpacked dimensions.

4.3.4 Operators

SystemVerilog provides operators from both Verilog and C. SystemVerilog operators follow the semantics of operators in Verilog. SystemVerilog operators are shown in table 4.3. The following notes apply to operators listed in this table:

	Operation	Syntax	Notes			Operation	Syntax	Notes
Logical	NOT	! E			**Arithmetic**	Negation	- E	
	AND	E_1 && E_2				Add	$E_1 + E_2$	
	OR	$E_1 \| \| E_2$				Subtract	$E_1 - E_2$	
	Equality	$E_1 == E_2$	2			Multiply	$E_1 * E_2$	
	Inequality	$E_1 != E_2$	2			Divide	E_1 / E_2	
	Case equality	$I_1 === I_2$	3			Modulo	$S_1 \% S_2$	
	Case inequality	$I_1 !== I_2$	3			Power	$E_1 ** E_2$	
	Wild equality	$I_1 ==? I_2$	1,4			Increment	++ J	
	Wild inequality	$I_1 !=? I_2$	1,4			Decrement	-- J	
Bitwise	NOT	~ I	5		**Shift**	Unsigned left	$I_1 << I_2$	
	AND	I_1 & I_2	5			Unsigned right	$I_1 >> I_2$	
	OR	$I_1 \| I_2$	5			Signed left	S <<< I	1
	XOR	$I_1 \wedge I_2$	5			Signed right	S >>> I	1
	XNOR	$I_1 \sim\wedge I_2$ $I_1 \wedge\sim I_2$	5		**Concat.**	Non-repeating	$\{I_1,...,I_n\}$	
Reduction	AND	& I	6			Repeating	$\{C\{I_1,...,I_n\}\}$	
	NAND	~& I	6		**Part Select**	Member	[C]	
	OR	| I	6			Fixed part	$[C_1:C_2]$	
	NOR	~| I	6			Variable right	[I+:C]	1
	XOR	$\wedge$ I	6			Variable left	[I-:C]	1
	XNOR	$\sim\wedge$ I $\wedge\sim$ I	6		**Cnd**	Conditional Select	$I ? E_1 : E_2$	7
Relational	Less than	$E_1 < E_2$			**Assignments**	Blocking	V = E	
	Less or equal	$E_1 <= E_2$				Non-blocking	V <= E	
	Greater than	$E_1 > E_2$				Operators	+= -= *= /= %= &= |= ^= <<= >>= <<<= >>>=	
	Greater or equal	$E_1 >= E_2$						

I: An expression producing an unsigned integer   J: A variable of integral data type
S: An expression producing a signed integer   V: A variable of any type
R: An expression producing a real value   C: An unsigned integer constant
E: One of I,S,R

Table 4.3: SystemVerilog Operators

- Note$_1$: New operators introduced by SystemVerilog.
- Note$_2$: Equality operators return a **0** or a **1** depending on the values of their arguments. If any of the arguments contains an *x* or a *z* in any bit position, then the result is an *x*.
- Note$_3$: Case equality operators compare *x* or *z* values in any bit position of their arguments. As such, these operators only return a value of **0** or **1**.
- Note$_4$: Wild equality operators treat *x* or *z* values in any bit position of their argu-

ments as don't care values. These operators only return a value of **0** or **1**.

- Note$_5$: If the arguments to the bitwise operators are not the same size, then the shorter argument is zero-filled in the most significant bit positions.
- Note$_6$: Reduction operators return a **0**, **1**, or x depending on the individual bit values of its argument. Value z is treated the same as x when combining individual bit values.
- Note$_7$: If the condition expression for a conditional select operator evaluates to an x, then the result is computed by bitwise combination of both its arguments, with the exception that a value of **0** is returned if any of its arguments have a real data type. The bitwise combination returns an x for any bit position if the values of arguments in that bit position are different or a z.

4.4 Procedural Statements and Blocks

A _procedural block_ has its own thread of execution where the statements inside the block are executed sequentially, similar to that of a C or C++ program. Procedural blocks are composed of procedural statements. SystemVerilog allows the following types of _procedural statements_ to appear in a procedural block:

- Assignment Statements
- Subroutine Calls
- Selection Statements
- Loop Statements
- Jump Statements
- Event Control Statements

These procedural statements are described in the following subsections.

4.4.1 Assignment Statements

Assignment statements are used to update data values in the program. SystemVerilog provides the following assignment statements.

- Blocking Assignments
- Non-Blocking Assignments
- Increment/Decrement Statements
- Procedural Continuous Assignments

The following program shows an example of these assignment statements:

Program 4.10: SystemVerilog assignment statements

```
1  :   module top;
2  :       wire [9:0] net_data;
3  :       initial begin
4  :           logic [9:0] data [10:0];
5  .           logic [9:0] val_data;
6  :
7  :           data[0] <= 'x;              // non-blocking assignment
```

```
8    :              data[1] = 'z;              // blocking assignment
9    :
10   :              data[2] = 7;
11   :              data[2] ++;               // increment variable
12   :              data[2] --;               // decrement variable
13   :
14   :              assign var_data = data[2];  // continuously assign value 7 to var_data
15   :              var_data = 4;             // will not change var_data
16   :              deassign var_data;        // remove continuous assignment
17   :              var_data = 5;             // now var_data will change
18   :
19   :              force var_data = data[1];
20   :              release var_data;
21   :
22   :              force net_data = data[1];
23   :              release net_data;
24   :        end
25   :  endmodule
```

Lines 7 and 8 show examples of non-blocking and blocking assignments. These types of assignments have been covered extensively in introductory books on Verilog. SystemVerilog introduces *increment* and *decrement* operators which assign the current value plus one and current value minus one onto itself respectively.

Procedural continuous assignments include *assign*, *deassign* of variables and *force* and *release* of variable and net data types. The procedural continuous assignment has been placed on the deprecated list in SystemVerilog and is expected to be removed from the language in future releases.

4.4.2 Subroutine Calls

SystemVerilog provides the following two subroutine call methods:

- Functions
- Tasks

These methods are described in the following subsections.

4.4.2.1 Functions

Functions have a list of arguments and return a value. Functions execute in zero simulation time, which means that time control statements cannot be used inside a function.

Function arguments can be one of:

- *input*
- *output*
- *inout*
- *ref*

The semantics of each argument type is as follows: For *input* argument types, the value of the argument is copied from the caller's context upon entering the function. The value of an *output* argument type is copied upon completion of the function from inside of the function to the actual variable specified in the caller's context. The value of an *inout* argument type is copied twice once upon entering the function and once upon leaving. No value is copied when using a *ref* argument type, and both the function and its caller use a reference to data object passed in the argument. Therefore, any change that a function makes to the value of a *ref* type argument is immediately visible outside the function. Both *inout* and *ref* qualifiers result in changes to the argument value made inside the function to become visible in the caller's context, with the difference that changes made inside a function to a *ref* type argument are immediately visible in the caller's context but changes made inside a function to an *inout* type argument become visible only after the function returns.

A function can be declared as *automatic* or *static*. All variables local to an automatic function are assumed to be automatic variables unless explicitly changed for each variable in its declaration. All variables inside a static function are assumed to be static variables unless explicitly changed for each variable in its declaration. The value of static variables are maintained across calls to the same function. SystemVerilog allows individual variables declared inside a static function to be marked as automatic. It also allows individual variables declared inside an automatic function to be marked as static variables.

The following program shows an example of a function declaration and its usage.

```
Program 4.11: Declaring and calling functions
1   :   typedef struct {int ii; int jj;} twoval_t;
2   :
3   :   module top;
4   :       function automatic twoval_t twoval_increment (
5   :                           twoval_t data,
6   :                           ref twoval_t increment,
7   :                           inout bit er,
8   :                           output bit ol);
9   :           static int local_int;
10  :           twoval_increment.ii = data.ii + increment.ii;
11  :           twoval_increment.jj = data.jj + increment.jj;
12  :           er = er || 0;
13  :           ol = twoval_increment.ii > 20 || twoval_increment.jj > 20;
14  :       endfunction
15  :
16  :       function automatic int increment;
17  :           input int data=0;
18  :           const ref int incr;
19  :
20  :           int local_val;
21  :           local_val = data + incr;
22  :           return local_val;
23  :       endfunction
24  :
25  :       initial
26  :       begin
27  :           twoval_t A;
28  :           twoval_t incr;
29  :           bit err,overload;
30  :           int i;
31  :
32  :           A.ii =1; A.jj=2;
33  :           incr.ii =10; incr.jj=21;
34  :           A = twoval_increment(A, incr, err, overload);
35  :           $display(A.ii, A.jj, err, overload);
36  :           i = 4;
37  :           $display(increment(3,i));
38  :           $display(increment(,i));
```

```
39  :        end
40  :    endmodule
```

The following properties apply to functions:

- Function declarations can follow an ANSI[4] format (lines 4–8) or Verilog style format (lines 16–18).
- A function argument without a direction specifier is assumed to have the same direction as the last argument that had a direction specifier. In the absence of any such previous direction specifier, direction defaults to *input* (line 5).
- Argument default data type, if not specified, is *logic*.
- Arrays can be formal arguments to a function.
- A function can be defined as either static or automatic (lines 4, 16) but variables local to a function can be assigned a different lifetime (line 9).
- Functions do not need to be inside a begin-end block.
- A return statement can be used to return from a function (line 22).
- The return value of a function can be ignored by casting it to a void, as in "**void'(myfunc())**"
- A function having arguments of type *inout*, *output*, or *ref* cannot be used in event expressions, in an expression within a procedural continuous assignment, or in an expression that is not within a procedural statement.
- The return value of a function can be a composite data type (lines 10, 11).
- Only variables can be passed as *ref* type arguments. Nets cannot be used as *ref* type arguments.
- The *const* keyword can be used to prevent a function from changing the value of a variables passed to it as a *ref* type argument (line 18). This is useful when a large data structure must be shared with a function as a *ref* so that the entire structure does not need to be copied but any changes to that data structure from inside the function must be prevented.
- Arguments with default values can be omitted when calling a function (line 38).

4.4.2.2 Tasks

Tasks and functions are very similar, except in the following ways:

- A task does not return a value
- A task may have time consuming statements

The following program sample highlights these differences.

```
   Program 4.12: Declaring and calling tasks
1  :    typedef struct {int ii; int jj;} twoval_t;
2  :
3  :    module top;
4  :        task automatic twoval_increment (
5  :                         twoval_t data,
6  :                         ref twoval_t increment,
7  :                         inout bit er,
8  :                         output twoval_t out);
```

[4.] ANSI: American National Standards Institute: http://www.ansi.org/

```
9   :                 #14ns out.ii = data.ii + increment.ii;
10  :                 #33ns out.jj = data.jj + increment.jj;
11  :                 er = er || 0;
12  :            endtask
13  :
14  :            initial begin
15  :                twoval_t A, B, incr;
16  :
17  :                A.ii =1; A.jj=2;
18  :                incr.ii =10; incr.jj=21;
19  :                twoval_increment(A, incr, err, B);    //task is called
20  :                $display(B.ii, B.jj, err);            // prints "11 23 0" at time 47.
21  :            end
22  :      endmodule
```

In this example, task **twoval_increment** (lines 2–12) does not have a return value and assignments performed inside the task have an associated delay value (lines 9, 10). Other than return value behaviors, tasks have similar properties as those defined for functions.

4.4.3 Selection Statements

SystemVerilog provides the following selection statements:

- If-else statements
- Case statements
- randcase statements

These constructs are described in the following subsections.

4.4.3.1 If-Else Statements

An *if-else statement* consists of a set of condition predicates and a conditional statement associated with each condition predicate. if-else statements allow program flow to be directed to the statement for the condition that evaluates to true. SystemVerilog allows keywords **priority** and **unique** to be specified for an if-else statement. An if-else statement has the following forms:

- Normal form (no keyword): if-else statements behave the same as if-else statements in Verilog. Conditional predicates, in programming order, are evaluated and program flow continues into the conditional statement of the first condition predicate that evaluates to true.
- Priority: The first if statement if prepended with keyword **priority**. The if-else statement behaves mostly similar to its normal form, with the exception that at least one of the condition predicates in the if-else statement must evaluate to true, or the if-else statement must have a final *else* clause. An error message is reported if this condition is not satisfied.
- Unique: The first if statement if prepended with keyword **unique**. In this form, exactly one condition predicate in the if-else statement must evaluate to true. This is in contrast with other forms where any number of condition predicates may evaluate to true. An error message is generated if this condition is not satisfied.

Priority and unique forms of if-else statements are closely related to their hardware implementation. The implementation of a priority if-else statement contains special priority decoding hardware, while the hardware implementation of a unique if-else statement does not require such special hardware, since at most one of the condition predicates are true. Examples of these forms of if-else statements are shown below:

```
Program 4.13: if-else statements
                    :
                    :
 1  :    int a, b, c;
 2  :
 3  :    if (a == 1) begin
 4  :            $display("a is one");
 5  :            $display("and b is", b);
 6  :    end
 7  :    else if (a == 2) $display("a is two");
 8  :    else $display("a is neither 1 nor 2");
 9  :
10  :    priority if (a == 1) $display("a is 1");
11  :    else $display("a is not 1");
12  :
13  :    unique if (a == 1) $display("a is 1");
14  :    else $display("a is not 1");
                    :
                    :
```

4.4.3.2 Case Statements

Case statements are similar to if-else statements in that they provide a mechanism for selectively controlling program flow. Case statements are, however, more limited in functionality since all case item expressions are compared to the same case expression. Limiting this usage, however, allows a more structured approach for writing such selection statements.

Similar to if-else statements, case statements can be marked with *unique* and *priority* keywords. The effect of these keywords are the same as those for if-else statements. The following program shows an example of a case statement:

```
Program 4.14: case statements
                    :
                    :
 1  :    int a, b, c, d;
 2  :    case (a**2)  // can be written as "priority case" or "unique case"
 3  .            c,(b+33): $display("a**2 is the same as either c or b+33");
 4  :            d+5: $display("a**2 is the same as d+5");
 5  :            9: $display("a**2 is 9");
 6  :            default: $display("a is none of the above");
 7  :    endcase
                    :
                    :
```

Case expression for the above example is expression (**a**2**). Case item expressions are (**c,(b+33)**), (**d+5**), and (**9**). Keyword ***default*** is used to specify a statement for conditions where none of the case item expressions match against the case expression.

Each case item expression is matched bitwise against the case expression. This means that a case item expression does not match if any of its bit values fail 4-valued (i.e., $0, 1, x, z$)

comparison with the corresponding bit in the case expression. SystemVerilog also provides special case statements *casex* and *casez* to relax the matching requirements. In a *casez* statement, value z is assumed to be a don't care and is matched against any bit value. In a *casex* statement, both x and z are assumed to be don't cares and match against any bit value.

4.4.3.3 Random Case Statements

A *random case statement* allows program flow to be randomly guided in different directions, according to a probability distribution. The SystemVerilog *randcase* construct is used to specify a random case statement. A *randcase* statement does not have a case expression or any case item expressions. Instead, each item is labeled with an expression that produces an unsigned integer value. During each execution of the *randcase* statement, the labels for all items are computed. The probability of each item is then computed as the value of the label for that item divided by the sum of all labels. The following program shows an example of a *randcase* statement:

```
Program 4.15: randcase statement
        ⋮
1  :        int a, b, c, d;                                 // assume a=4, b=2 in current pass
2  :        randcase                                        //----------------------------------------
3  :            a+b: $display("now in a+b branch");         // label = 6        prob=6/18
4  :            a-b: $display("now in a-b branch");         // label = 2        prob=2/18
5  :            a*b: $display("now in a*b branch");         // label = 8        prob=8/18
6  :            a/b: $display("now in a/b branch");         // label = 2        prob=2/18
7  :        endcase                                         //----------------------------------------
8  :                                                        // Sum = 18
        ⋮
```

Note that for each pass through the case statement, the probability for each case item may be different depending on the current values for the variables used for evaluating case labels. As such, constants should be used as labels if a static probability distribution is needed.

4.4.4 Loop and Jump Statements

SystemVerilog provides the following looping and jumping statements:

- *forever* statement
- *repeat* statement
- *while* statement
- *for* statement
- *do-while* statement
- *jump* statement
- *disable* statement

Jump statements include *return*, *break*, and *continue* keywords, which are familiar language constructs for returning from a function or task, and breaking or continuing from a loop structure. A *disable* statement is used to finish the execution of a block of code and move to the statement immediately after the block. If the block is not currently executing, then this statement has no effect. If the block is a loop body, the **disable** statement acts the same as a **continue** statement.

Examples of loop constructs are shown in the following example:

```
Program 4.16: SystemVerilog loop constructs
1   :    module top;
2   :        initial begin
3   :            fork
4   :                forever begin #1 $display ("in forever loop"); end
5   :                repeat (10) begin #1 $display("in repeat loop"); end
6   :                while (1==1) begin #1 $display("in while loop"); end
7   :                for (int i = 0; i <= 10; i++) begin #1 $display ("in for loop"); end
8   :                do begin #1 $display("in do-while loop"); end while (1==1);
9   :            join
10  :        end
11  :    endmodule
```

Note that a delay value is included before each display statement, so that all threads started by the fork statement become idle until their next execution time, so that other threads have the opportunity to execute.

4.4.5 Event Control Statements

Event control is provided by the following types of statements:

- Event trigger statements
- Wait statements

Trigger statements are used to activate an event while wait statements specified using the SystemVerilog **wait** keyword, are used to wait on an event. The use of these statements are described in detail in section 5.4.1.

4.5 Module Hierarchy

The expressive power of SystemVerilog in modeling an architecture is a major leap over what could be achieved with Verilog. The bulk of this improvement is due to one reason: SystemVerilog removes the fundamental restriction in Verilog that module ports be modeled as nets (i.e., wires and buses). In doing so, SystemVerilog allows module ports to be a *variable* data type as well as a net data type. This means that modules in SystemVerilog can correspond to blocks at any level of abstraction, and not just blocks that communicate through wires and buses. With this enhancement, SystemVerilog can be used not only to create RTL descriptions of a design but also the architectural description of the product with blocks whose ports communicate at higher levels of abstraction than wires and buses.

SystemVerilog maintains Verilog's module hierarchy modeling approach but improves expressiveness and efficiency in describing a model by:

- Allowing a module port to be a variable data type as well as a net data type
- Allowing one module declaration to be nested inside another module

- Providing shorthand notations for specifying port connectivities
- Allowing module ports to be bundled as an abstract interface object

As mentioned, allowing variable data types as module ports is the main reason for the improvement in SystemVerilog's modeling capabilities. This flexibility is provided in SystemVerilog by allowing variable data types to be driven not only by other variables, but also through a single continuous assignment (section 4.3.2). Keeping this property of variables in mind will be very helpful in understanding port connectivity rules described later in this section.

SystemVerilog allows module declarations to reside inside other modules. The motivation for this enhancement is to help better reflect the environment hierarchy when implementing the module hierarchy. In Verilog, all modules are declared at the top level and instantiated in their parent modules when necessary. In this approach, visual inspection of declared modules does not provide any hints as to the actual module hierarchy. In SystemVerilog, if a module is instantiated only once in its parent module, then it can be declared inside its parent module.

Shorthand notations when specifying port connectivities allow top level descriptions of modules with many thousands of ports to take a less daunting appearance. The use of more expressive constructs reduces the size of design descriptions, in turn leading to a lowered chance of mistakes in making such connections. Given the large number of design ports and also the fact that in most cases, the same group of ports connect multiple modules (e.g., ports corresponding to bus signals), a natural next step in optimizing port definitions is to bundle them into a larger abstract object. SystemVerilog provides the *interface* construct to support this enhancement (see section 4.5.2).

Modules are the basic building blocks in the SystemVerilog language and the module hierarchy of a SystemVerilog program defines the structural hierarchy of blocks and interconnections between these blocks. The following general properties hold for the module hierarchy in a SystemVerilog program:

- Top level programs can contain either packages or modules.
- Packages contain declarations for data, data types, classes, tasks, and functions, and can be imported to any program to make these declarations available to that program.
- All data, functions, and tasks are declared, instantiated, and used inside modules, except system task and functions, which are global.
- Modules can contain instances of other modules.
- Instance hierarchy is the expansion of the module hierarchy where each module instance is replaced by its own module hierarchy (note that if every module is used only once, then module and instance hierarchies would be the same).
- Any uninstantiated module (except when in a library or another module) is assumed to be at the top level of the module hierarchy. As such, the module hierarchy can have multiple top levels.
- Hierarchical names can be used to specify any named object from anywhere in the instance hierarchy (section 4.5.4).

4.5.1 Modules and Module Ports

A module may contain the following blocks:

- Instances of other modules
- Data Objects
- Task and function declarations
- *always*, *initial*, and *final* blocks containing procedural statements

In addition, a module can be assigned one of *automatic* or *static* properties. All objects declared inside an *automatic* module are by default assumed to have automatic semantics. Similarly, all objects inside a *static* module are assumed by default to have static semantics.

Module ports can be one of:

- Net
- Interface
- Event
- Variable of any type including arrays
- A structure or union

In addition, module ports can have one of the following directions:

- *input*
- *output*
- *inout*
- *ref*

The following program shows an example of using modules in SystemVerilog:

```
Program 4.17: Module declaration and instantiation
1  :    typedef struct packed {int ii; int jj;} twoval_t;
2  :
3  :    module leaf (input twoval_t tv, input wire w, output logic l, inout logic cc);
4  :            assign l = w;
5  :            assign cc = cc + 1;
6  :    endmodule;
7  :
8  :    module top;
9  :            twoval_t tv;        // a composite data variable
10 :            wire w;             // a net
11 :            logic l;            // a variable
12 :            wire l_cc;          // a variable
13 :
14 :            leaf leaf_1 (.*,.cc(l_cc));
15 :            //variations on instantiating module leaf
16 :            //leaf leaf_2 (.tv(tv),.w(w),.l(l),.cc(l_cc));
17 :            //leaf leaf_3 (tv, w, l, l_cc);
18 :
19 :    endmodule
```

The above example shows a module declaration having ports of type *input*, *output*, and *inout* (line 3). This module uses a composite data structure **tv** as an input port (line 3).

4.5.1.1 Port Connection Syntax

Ports can be connected using one of the following approaches:

- *Positional port connection*
- *Named port connection*
- *Implicitly connected ports*

Program 4.17 in the previous section shows an example of each of these notations. Implicit port connection is indicated by *(.*)* shorthand notation. This notation connects all local variables that have the same name as module's formal port names. Any local name that is not the same can be specified at the end of port map list (line 14). Lines 15 and 16 show examples of named and positional port connections respectively.

4.5.1.2 Port Connection Rules

Port connection rules define and limit how a module port can be connected to variable and net data objects. Port connection rules are defined separately for nets and variables. Connection rules specify how a instance port can be connected to the outside environment and how a port is used or assigned inside the module.

Port connection rules are derived from the following properties of variable and net assignments and the implicit continuous assignments that occur when ports are connected:

- A variable data type can be assigned only by one continuous assignment or multiple procedural assignments.
- Net data types can be driven by multiple continuous assignments but not by procedural statements.
- An outside connection to an input port is assumed to be driving the input port through a continuous assignment.
- An outside connection to an output port is assumed to be driven by the output port through a continuous assignment.
- The inside and outside connections for an inout port drive each other through continuous assignments.

Connection rules for ports having a variable data type are as follows:

- An *input* port can be driven on the outside by any expression of compatible type where the expression can be composed of variables or nets. An input port cannot be assigned inside the module. If an input port is left unconnected, then its value is the default value of its data type.
- An *output* port can be driven from inside the module by one continuous assignment or multiple procedural assignments. An output port can be connected on the outside to either a variable or a net data of compatible type. If the output port is connected to a variable data type, then no other procedural or continuous assignments are allowed for that external variable. If it is connected to a net, then other continuous assignments are allowed to drive that net but procedural assignments are not allowed.
- An *inout* port of an instance can only be connected to net data types on the inside and outside of the module. The reason for this requirement is that an inout port drives its connections using a continuous assignment. Therefore, if it is connected to a variable, then that variable cannot be assigned by any other means.

- A *ref* port can only be connected to an equivalent variable data type both inside the module and when the module is instantiated. A *ref* port cannot be left open. Access to a *ref* port is equivalent to a hierarchical reference.

Connection rules for ports having a net data type are as follows:

- A input port can be driven on the outside by any expression of compatible type where the expression can be composed of variables or nets. An input port can also be assigned inside the module. If an input port is left unconnected, then its value is set to *z* (tristated).
- An output port can be driven from inside the module by multiple continuous assignments. An output port can be connected on the outside to either a variable or a net data of compatible type. If the output port is connected on the outside to a variable data type, then no other procedural or continuous assignments are allowed for that variable. If it is connected to a net, then other continuous assignments are allowed for that net, but procedural assignments are not allowed.
- An inout port can only be driven from inside the module by a net data type. An inout port of an instance can only be connected to an actual net data type.

4.5.2 Interface Blocks

A major task in creating a design is defining and describing inter-block connections. In spite of the required effort in describing such communication mechanisms, design description languages have provided little more than single structural ports for specifying this inter-block connectivity. SystemVerilog addresses this shortcoming by introducing the *interface* construct. This construct is primarily used for the following purposes:

- Modeling communication between blocks at an abstract level as well as at a structural level (i.e., wires and buses).
- Allowing for ease of structural connectivity between blocks by providing a means to bundle signals.
- Allowing smooth migration from system level designs down to RTL descriptions.
- Facilitating design reuse by hiding communication details inside the interface.

Figure 4.3 shows the communication between a simplified CPU and a memory core.

The following program sample shows one possible implementation of these blocks and their interface:

```
Program 4.18: Module connection without an interface block
1  :    module mem_core (
2  :        input logic wen, input logic ren,
3  :        output logic mrdy=1, input logic [7:0] addr,
4  :        input logic [7:0] mem_din, output logic [7:0] mem_dout,
5  :        output logic status, input logic clk);
6  :
7  :        logic [7:0] mem [7:0];
8  :
9  :        task reply_read(input logic [7:0] data, integer delay);
10 :            #delay;
11 :            @(negedge clk);
12 :            mrdy = 1'b0;
13 :            mem_dout = data;
```

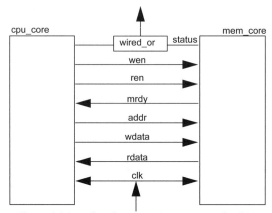

Figure 4.3 Interface between a Memory and a CPU

```
14  :              @ (negedge clk);
15  :              mrdy = 1'b1;
16  :          endtask
17  :
18  :          always @(negedge ren) reply_read(mem[addr],10);
19  :  endmodule
20  :
21  :  module cpu_core (
22  :          output logic wen=1, output logic ren=1,
23  :          input logic mrdy, output logic [7:0] addr=0,
24  :          input logic [7:0] cpu_din, output logic [7:0] cpu_dout,
25  :          output logic status=0, input logic clk);
26  :
27  :          task read_memory(input logic [7:0] raddr, output logic [7:0] data);
28  :          @(posedge clk);
29  :              ren = 1'b0;
30  :              addr = raddr;
31  :              @(negedge mrdy);
32  :              @(posedge clk);
33  :              data = cpu_din;
34  :              ren = 1'b1;
35  :          endtask
36  :
37  :          initial begin
38  :              logic [7:0] read_data;
39  :              read_memory (7'b00010000, read_data);
40  :              $display("Read Result", $time, read_data);
41  :          end
42  :  endmodule
43  :
44  :  module top;
45  :          logic mrdy; logic wen;
46  :          logic ren; logic [7:0] addr;
47  :          logic [7:0] d1; logic [7:0] d2;
48  :          wor status; logic clk = 0;
49  :
50  :          mem_core mem (.^,.mem_din(d1),.mem_dout(d2));
51  :          cpu_core cpu (.*,.cpu_din(d2),.cpu_dout(d1));
52  :
```

```
53  :          initial for (int i = 0; i <= 255; i++) #1 clk =!clk;
54  :  endmodule
```

The following observations can be made about this example:

- Most port signals connecting **cpu** and **mem** blocks are generated in one block and used in the other block, without being needed by other blocks outside of **cpu** and **mem**. These signals need not be visible anywhere but inside the **cpu** and **mem**.
- Some signals are generated outside the two blocks (i.e., **clk**) and used inside both **cpu** and **mem**.
- Some signals are generated inside one or all the blocks but used outside these blocks (e.g., **status**).
- Each block could be implemented either at the structural level or at the behavioral level. A behavioral implementation will use methods or procedure calls to drive or respond to its ports, a structural description will contain an actual RTL implementation. The example implementation above uses a procedural interface.
- Some signals have different meaning to different blocks. For example, a signal may be an output from one block and an input to another block (i.e., **mrdy** is generated by **mem** and used by **cpu**).

These observations suggest the following requirements for specifying an interface object:

- Ability to bundle signals into an interface
- Ability to specify the direction of interaction between signals in the interface and blocks attached by this interface as input, output, or inout. Such specification may be different for different blocks attached by the interface object.
- Ability to inject signals into the interface (i.e., **clk**) and extract signals from inside the interface (i.e., **status**)
- Ability to encapsulate behavioral descriptions inside the interface.

A graphical view of this interface is shown in figure 4.4.

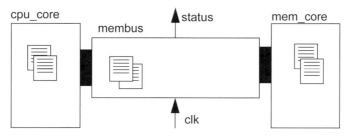

Figure 4.4 Interface between a Memory and a CPU

An interface block, or an interface for short, is implemented using the SystemVerilog *interface* construct. An interface block in SystemVerilog can include:

- Parameters
- Constants

- Variables
- Tasks and functions
- Processes (always, initial blocks)
- Continuous assignments

A port list can be defined for an interface block. An interface can be instantiated inside other interfaces (leading to hierarchical interfaces) and other modules. Modules cannot be instantiated inside interfaces.

Interfaces can contain tasks and functions thereby, allowing an interface to be modeled at an abstract level. This also allows for protocol checking routines to be included in the interface descriptions.

Both the declaration and instances of interfaces can be customized for different contexts. Parameters allow different instances of the same interface declaration to be customized when an instance is being created. The declaration of an interface can be customized by declaring only the function or task prototypes (the list of arguments) in an interface and defining the body in other modules. A module header can use a genetic interface when the interface contents is not yet defined, allowing module implementations to proceed without prior exact knowledge of the interface contents or composition of its signals.

The following SystemVerilog program shows the implementation of an interface block in SystemVerilog:

```
Program 4.19: Module connections with an interface block
1  :    interface membus (input logic clk, output wor status);
2  :        logic mrdy;
3  :        logic wen;
4  :        logic ren;
5  :        logic [7:0] addr;
6  :        logic [7:0] c2m_data;
7  :        logic [7:0] m2c_data;
8  :
9  :        task reply_read(input logic [7:0] data, integer delay);
10 :            #delay;
11 :            @(negedge clk)
12 :            mrdy = 1'b0;
13 :            m2c_data = data;
14 :            @(negedge clk);
15 :            mrdy = 1'b1;
16 :        endtask
17 :
18 :        task read_memory(input logic [7:0] raddr, output logic [7:0] data);
19 :            @(posedge clk);
20 :            ren = 1'b0;
21 :            addr = raddr;
22 :            @(negedge mrdy);
23 :            @(posedge clk);
24 :            data = m2c_data;
25 :            ren = 1'b1;
26 :        endtask
27 :
28 :        modport master (output wen, ren, addr, c2m_data, input mrdy, m2c_data);
29 :        modport slave (input wen, ren, addr, c2m_data, output mrdy, m2c_data);
30 :    endinterface: membus
31 :
32 :    module mem_core (membus.slave mb);
33 :        logic [7:0] mem [7:0];
```

```
34  :
35  :          assign mb.status = 0;
36  :
37  :          always @(negedge mb.ren) mb.reply_read(mem[mb.addr], 100);
38  :   endmodule
39  :
40  :   module cpu_core (membus.master mb);
41  :
42  :          assign mb.status = 0;
43  :
44  :          initial begin
45  :              logic [7:0] read_data;
46  :              mb.read_memory (7'b00010000, read_data);
47  :              $display("Read Result", $time, read_data);
48  :          end
49  :   endmodule
50  :
51  :   module top;
52  :       wor status;
53  :       logic clk = 0;
54  :       membus mb(clk, status);
55  :
56  :       mem_core mem (.mb(mb.slave));
57  :       cpu_core cpu (.mb(mb.slave));
58  :
59  :       initial for (int i = 0; i <= 255; i++) #1 clk =!clk;
60  :   endmodule
```

This example defines interface block **membus** which has two ports corresponding to signals **clk** and **status** (line 1). Interface block **membus** includes a list of data objects that corresponds to signals passing through the interface and connecting different modules (lines 2–7). This interface also includes procedural descriptions, allowing each module attached to it to drive the interface signals through procedure calls (lines 9–26). In addition, **membus** includes *modport* declarations specifying the port directions for different types of modules that can be connected by this interface (lines 28, 29). These *modport* types are then used when declaring the port list of modules that will be connected by this interface (lines 32, 40) and also when connecting instances of modules and interfaces (lines 56, 57). Note that modules connecting to this interface can use the tasks provided inside the interface to interact with the interface as shown in this example (lines 37, 46). These modules can also directly drive the signals inside the interface (lines 35, 42). This feature of the interface allows it to be driven both with structural and procedural modules.

4.5.3 Parameters

Often, it is necessary to customize different instances of the same object in a program's object hierarchy (i.e., memory size inside a memory module). SystemVerilog provides the following keywords for this purpose:

- *parameter*
- *localparam*
- *specparam*

Parameters are used to perform customizations for the following SystemVerilog blocks and constructs:

- Module
- Interface
- Program
- Class

Parameters have the following properties:

- Each parameter must be assigned a default value when declared.
- Parameters can be defined to have any data type. Parameters defined with no data type default to type *logic* of arbitrary size.
- Parameters are set during elaboration (creating the instance hierarchy) and remain the same throughout the program execution.
- Data types can also be defined as parameters so for example data objects in different instances of the same module declaration can have different data types.
- A parameter of integer data type can be assigned a value of "*$*".

4.5.4 Hierarchical Names

Hierarchical names allow objects to be referenced for reading or writing. Hierarchical names are also referred to as *nested identifiers*.

A hierarchical name consists of object names separated by periods. Object names follow these guidelines:

- The top of the program hierarchy is referred to as *$root*.
- A module object's name is the instance name used for instantiating that module.
- SystemVerilog syntax allows procedural blocks (e.g., *initial*, *always* blocks) to be labeled. This label is used as the name for that procedural block.
- The name of a task or function is used to refer to that task or function.
- Data object names are used in accessing data objects. Arrays member names are formed by using the array name and an index.

A hierarchical name provides an absolute path for accessing any object from any place in the hierarchy. It is, however, best to limit the use of such hierarchical names as it bypasses the modular programming style that should be followed while programming in SystemVerilog.

4.6 Processes and Execution Threads

SystemVerilog execution threads fall into two categories:

- Static processes
- Dynamic processes

Start and end time of static processes are determined at program start time. Creation of dynamic processes and their termination conditions can be decided during program runtime. Static and dynamic processes are described in the following subsections.

4.6.1 Static Processes

In SystemVerilog, *static processes* are created for each of the following constructs:

- *initial* block
- *final* block
- *always* block and its variations (e.g., *always_comb*)
- Continuous assignments
- *fork-join* statements

An *initial* block is always started at the beginning of the program execution. A *final* block is always started before program termination and after all execution threads have terminated. An *always* block and its variation *always_comb* block are started every time their sensitivity conditions are satisfied and if the previous start of the thread has already terminated (e.g., execution of an *always* block may be suspended midstream because of a wait on an event). Continuous assignments are similar to *always* blocks where any change in the signals on the right-hand side of the assignment causes a new evaluation and assignment to the left-hand side to take place. A new thread is started for each block in a *fork-join* statement once the *fork-join* statement is reached. The *fork-join* statement completes only after all threads started by the fork statement have been terminated.

4.6.2 Dynamic Processes

In SystemVerilog, dynamic processes are created using the following constructs:

- *fork-join_any*
- *fork-join_none*

These fork statements are similar to the static *fork-join* statement. However, in a *fork-join_any* statement, the parent process that contained the fork statement continues execution after *any* one of the processes spawned by the fork statement completes. In a *fork-join_none* statement, the parent process continues execution without waiting for any of the processes spawned by the fork statement to complete. In case of a *fork-join_none* statement, the spawned processes do not start executing until the parent is suspended or completes.

fork-join_any and *fork-join_none* are considered dynamic processes since they lead to new processes to be created in addition to the parent process that contained the fork statement.

4.7 Object-Oriented Programming and Classes

Object-oriented programming provides a programmer with the following benefits:

- Grouping data objects into more complex data structures
- Defining and grouping the operations that can be performed on these data objects
- Ability to hide the contents of an object from outside (other programmers) observa-

tion or modification, thereby providing predictable ways for the way data inside an object can be modified

- Ability to handle objects of different types (i.e., different data structures) uniformly (see section 4.7.4 on polymorphism).
- Ability to better deal with complex systems by modeling system components as separate objects.

SystemVerilog provides the ***class*** construct for building objects based on the object-oriented programming paradigm. The main flow in object-oriented programming is as follows:

1. Create a class containing properties (i.e., data objects) and methods (functions and tasks).
2. Optionally, create an extension of a previously defined class. This step will either define new properties and methods, or redefine the previous definition of the class that it extends.
3. Declare pointers that hold the address for instances of classes defined in the previous step.
4. Create instances whose address are stored in pointers declared in step 3.

Figure 4.5 shows a graphical view of this process. In this example, first a base class is defined. Classes c_1, c_2, and c_3 are defined by extending class c_0, and class c_4 is defined by extending class c_3. Variables i_1-i_{10} are pointers to classes of types c_1-c_4, where each pointer points at a memory location containing an object instance of that type. Note that a pointer can have value ***null***.

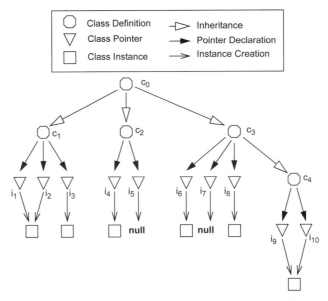

Figure 4.5 Class Inheritance and Instantiation Hierarchy

The following SystemVerilog program shows an example of how classes, derived classes, object pointers, and instances are created:

```
Program 4.20: Examples of class declaration and creation
1   :   module top;
2   :       class packet;
3   :           integer data1;
4   :           bit  flag;
5   :
6   :           task my_print();
7   :               $display("Packet: ",data1);
8   :           endtask
9   :       endclass: packet
10  :
11  :       class bigger_packet extends packet;
12  :           integer data2;
13  :           byte flag;
14  :
15  :           task my_print();
16  :               $display("Bigger Packet: ",data1, data2);
17  :           endtask
18  :       endclass: bigger_packet
19  :
20  :       packet p1, p2;
21  :       bigger_packet b1, b2, b3;
22  :
23  :       initial begin
24  :           p1 = new;
25  :           p1.data1 = 10;
26  :           p2 = p1;
27  :           p1.my_print();
28  :
29  :           b1 = new;
30  :           b1.data1 = 10;
31  :           b1.data2 = 20;
32  :           b2 = b1;
33  :           b3 = new b1;
34  :           b1.my_print();
35  :           b1 = null;
36  :           b2 = null;
37  :           b3 = null;
38  :       end
39  :
40  :   endmodule
```

In this example, class **packet** is created by declaring a class and its contents (lines 2–9). Class **packet** is then extended to declare a new class **bigger_packet** which includes a new data item (**data2**) and to redefine the definition for data item **flag** and method **my_print()** (lines 11–18). In this example **packet** is the *base class* or *super-class* and **bigger_packet** is the subclass or derived class.

Pointers p_1 and p_2 to class **packet** are declared on line 20. Pointers b_1, b_2, and b_3 to class **bigger_packet** are declared on line 21.

The SystemVerilog *new* construct is used to create an instance of a class and to assign it to a pointer. A new instance of class **packet** is assigned to p_1 on line 24. Pointer p_2 is pointed to the same object that p_1 is pointing to on line 26. Note that a new instance is not created, but rather both p_1 and p_2 point at the same instance.

Line 29 creates a new instance of **bigger_packet** class and sets b_1 to point to that instance. Pointer b_3 is set to point at the same instance as the one pointed to by b_1. A new instance of **bigger_packet** class is created on line 33 and contents of b_1 are copied into this new instance. Note that this is a shallow copy where the class objects pointed to by members of instance b_1 are not duplicated and only their pointer is copied.

The memory used for an instance of a class object is freed when no pointers point at that object. This memory reclamation is handled automatically through *garbage collection* mechanisms built into the program execution engine and as such, memory leak issues are not a concern when programming in SystemVerilog. In this example, the object created on line 29 is freed after executing line 36 since both pointers pointing to it have been set to a different value. Similarly, the memory associated with the object created on line 33 is freed after executing line 33 where the only pointer pointing to it is set to a different value.

4.7.1 Static Properties and Methods

Every instance of a class object creates dedicated memory for holding its data members and any values that must be maintained for its methods (i.e., static variables inside a method). Now consider a class description where one of its data members never changes and retains its value throughout the program execution, or a method that operates only on values that never change. It would be a waste of programming resources to create this never-changing data member or method for every instance. It is, therefore, helpful to specially tag such data members and methods so that they are created as part of elaborating the class declaration and not for every class instance. An additional advantage of this enhancement is that these properties and methods become accessible before any instances of the class are created, because their definition is bound to the class declaration, which is available at the beginning of the program when the program source is loaded into the execution engine.

SystemVerilog provides the keyword *static* to mark such data members and methods. Note that this keyword appears in the beginning of the declaration for such properties and methods and as such, is different from the static property assigned to a method indicating that all variables inside a method by default have a static lifetime.

The following program code shows an example of this concept:

```
Program 4.21: Class static data members and methods
1    :    module top;
2    :        class packet;
3    :            static integer data1 = 10;
4    :            bit   flag;
5    :
6    :            static task static my_print(time t);
7    :                time prev_t;
8    :                $display("Packet: ",t, prev_t, data1);
9    :                prev_t = t;
10   :            endtask
11   :        endclass: packet
12   :
13   :        packet p;
14   :
15   :        initial begin
16   :            $display(p.data1);          // p=null at this time
17   :            #1 p.my_print($time);       //prints   1    x    10
```

```
18  :              #4 p.my_print($time);     //prints    5    1    10
19  :              #8 p.my_print($time);     //prints   13    5    10
20  :         end
21  :    endmodule
```

In this example, property **data₁** of class **packet** is defined to be static. This means that this property can be accessed even without creating an instance and through a null pointer (line 16). In addition, method **my_print()** of class **packet** is declared to be a static method (first *static* keyword on line 6). Static methods can access only static properties of a class, as is the case for **my_print()** method accessing **data₁** property of class **packet**. Note that variables inside method **my_print()** are also declared to have static lifetime by default, as indicated by the second use of keyword *static* on line 6.

4.7.2 Class Hierarchy, Inheritance, and Abstract Classes

The ability to model a number of similar behaviors as derived classes of a base class provides a powerful mechanism for efficiently modeling complex behaviors. In using this modeling paradigm, however, a number of recurring requirements can be identified. These requirements include:

- In some cases, there is a need to not only extend a base class with a new property or method, but also to redefine a property or method from the base class in the derived class. Consider an example where most variations of a packet have the same CRC size except one variation. In this case, it is best to define the CRC size in the base class and then redefine the size in the subclass corresponding to packet format with a different CRC. In SystemVerilog, both data member and method definitions can be completely redefined in a derived class. Special keywords can be used to control the flexibility provided in allowing this type of redefinition.
- In cases where a data member or a method in a parent class is redefined, it may be necessary to access that data member or method as defined in the parent class. SystemVerilog provides the *super* keyword to support this requirement.
- Sometimes the base class for a group of objects is not a complete definition and as such it is not meant to be instantiated. SystemVerilog allows such classes to be marked as *abstract classes* by marking them with the keyword *virtual*.
- When defining a base class, the body of methods contained in that class may not be known until further development. In other cases, it may be helpful to place class declarations, including their method prototypes[5] and body definitions in separate files. SystemVerilog provides allows keyword *extern* to be used to mark such methods.
- Base class methods and their prototypes can be completely redefined in a derived class. This means that a method in a derived class can have a completely different return type and list of arguments than the one declared in the base class. At times, it may be needed to enforce the same method prototype for all new definitions of a base class method in derived classes. In such cases, only the body of methods can be redefined in derived classes. SystemVerilog allows such methods to be marked as *virtual methods*.

[5.] A method prototype refers to its return type, name, list of arguments and each argument type.

These special features for managing the definition of a class hierarchy are described in the following subsections.

4.7.2.1 Parent Class Scope: Super

SystemVerilog provides the ***super*** keyword to access parent class data members and methods that have been redefined in a derived class. This keyword can be applied to *only* the immediate parent class of a derived class. Use of this keyword is shown in the following example:

```
Program 4.22: Derived classes and super keyword
1   :   module top;
2   :       class delay_class;
3   :           integer delay = 5;
4   :           function integer get_delay();
5   :               get_delay = delay * delay;
6   :           endfunction
7   :       endclass: delay_class
8   :
9   :       class delay2_class extends delay_class;
10  :           integer delay= 10;
11  :           function integer get_delay();
12  :               get_delay = delay*delay + super.delay;
13  :           endfunction
14  :       endclass: delay2_class
15  :
16  :       delay2_class d;
17  :
18  :       initial begin
19  :           d = new;
20  :           $display(d.get_delay());
21  :       end
22  :   endmodule
```

In this example, both data member **delay** and method **get_delay()** of parent class **delay_class** have been redefined in derived class **delay2_class**. Keyword ***super*** is used in method **get_delay()** of **delay2_class** to access delay data member of class **delay_class** (line 12).

4.7.2.2 Abstract Classes

SystemVerilog provides the keyword ***virtual*** to mark classes that can be used only as a base class for derived classes and cannot be instantiated directly. Classes marked as virtual are known as *abstract classes*. An example of an abstract class is shown in the following program:

```
Program 4.23: Virtual Classes
1   :   module top;
2   :       virtual class base_packet;
3   :           integer data1;
4   :           function void size(); // body block is empty
5   :           endfunction
6   :       endclass: base_packet
7   :
8   :       class packet extends base_packet;
9   :           byte crc;
10  :           function integer size(int bits_in_word);
11  :               size = ($bits(data1) + $bits(crc))/bits_in_word;
```

```
12  :            endfunction
13  :        endclass: packet
14  :
15  :        packet pp;
16  :        initial begin
17  :            pp = new;
18  :            $display(pp.size(4));
19  :        end
20  :    endmodule
```

In this example, base class **base_packet** is defined as a virtual class. It includes data member **data1** and method **size()**. Class **packet** is derived from class **base_packet** and adds a new data member **crc** and completely redefines the definition for methods **size()**. A pointer to class **packet** is declared on line 15 and an instance is created on line 17. An attempt to use **base_packet** instead of **packet** on line 15 would lead to a compilation error.

4.7.2.3 Virtual Methods

As shown previously, both the body and the prototype of a base class method can be completely redefined in a derived class. Often, however, it is necessary to enforce the same method prototype[6] across all derived classes of a class declaration. SystemVerilog provides the keyword *virtual* to mark such methods. Virtual methods and abstract classes are not related. Virtual methods can be defined in both abstract and non-abstract classes.

The redefinition of a virtual method in a derived class must use the same prototype as the one in its parent class if and only if that method is marked as virtual in any of its direct or indirect parent classes. This means that using the same method prototype can be enforced starting from anywhere in the class hierarchy and not necessarily from the root of that class hierarchy. The following program shows an example of a virtual method declarations:

Program 4.24: extern methods
```
1   :    module top;
2   :        class base_packet;
3   :            function void send(); $display("no send() function defined"); endfunction
4   :        endclass: base_packet
5   :
6   :        class derived_packet extends base_packet;
7   :            virtual function integer send(byte data); $display(data+1); endfunction
8   :        endclass: derived_packet
9   :
10  :        class derived_packet1 extends derived_packet;
11  :            function integer send(byte data); $display(data+2); endfunction
12  :        endclass: derived_packet1
13  :
14  :        class derived_packet2 extends derived_packet1;
15  :            virtual function integer send(byte data); $display(data+3); endfunction
16  :        endclass: derived_packet2
17  :    endmodule
```

In this example, class **base_packet** contains a generic declaration of function **send()**. This function is not marked as virtual and, therefore, the redefinitions of this function in any

---

[6.] *Method prototype* or *method signature* is given by the method name, return type if any, and argument name(s), direction(s), and type(s).

derived class may have a different function prototype. Function **send()** is redefined in derived class **derived_packet** with a different function prototype and as a virtual function. The redefinition of function **send()** in any class derived either directly or indirectly from class **derived_class** must have the same function prototype as the one in class **derived_class**. This is shown in the redefinitions of this function in derived classes **derived_packet1** and **derived_packet2**. Using keyword *virtual* for function redefinition in class **derived_packet2** (line 15) is redundant since all function redefinitions in all derived classes of **derived_packet** must use its prototype definition of function **send()**.

4.7.2.4 Out of Block Declarations

At times, it is useful to declare the prototype for a class method and define its body outside class body definition. This features allows the body of a method to be defined in a separate file from where the class declaration is placed.

SystemVerilog provides the *extern* keyword for marking methods whose body is defined outside the class block declaration. The method prototype for method declaration inside the class and where method body is declared must be exactly the same.

```
Program 4.25: extern methods
1   :    module top;
2   :         class packet;
3   :              integer data1;
4   :              byte crc;
5   :              extern function integer size(int bits_in_word);
6   :         endclass: packet
7   :
8   :         function integer packet::size(int bits_in_word);
9   :              // body not shown
10  :         endfunction
11  :    endmodule
```

In this example, function **size()** is marked as an extern function in class packet (line 5). The body of this function is defined later outside the class block (lines 8–10). *Class scope resolution operator* "*::*" is used to identify the class containing the original method prototype declaration.

4.7.3 Parameterized Classes

Parameterized classes use a set of parameters to create a customized declaration of a generically defined class declaration. The use of parameters in defining classes is similar to using parameters in defining a module block to customize the generic description of a module to the actual requirements of its instances. A customization of a parameterized class with actual values for its parameters is referred to as a *class specialization*.

The following example show the use of parameterized classes to define class objects containing different types and sizes of fields using the same class declaration:

```
Program 4.26: Parameterized class declaration and instantiation
1   :    module test;
2   :         typedef bit [11:0] bits12;
3   :
```

```
 4  :        class pkt #(type T=byte, int S=10);
 5  :               T payload[S];
 6  :        endclass
 7  :
 8  :        class double_pkt #(type T1=byte, type T2=bit, int S=17) extends pkt #(T1, S);
 9  :               pkt #(T2, S+12) pkt2;
10  :        endclass
11  :
12  :        pkt #(bit, 12) pkt1;
13  :        pkt #(int) pkt2;
14  :        double_pkt #(real, bits12) dpkt;
15  :        double_pkt #(integer, integer) dpkt1;
16  :  endmodule
```

In this example, class **pkt** shows a simple example of using parameters to define a packet whose fields can be customized to be of different type and size. This class defines parameters **T** and **S**, each with a default value. Specialization "**pkt #(bit,12)**" (line 12) defines a class that contains an bit array of size **12**. Specialization "**pkt #(int)**", using the default value for parameter **S**, defines a class that contains an int array of size **10**.

Parameterized classes can be extended. This feature is shown in the definition of class **double_pkt** (lines 8–10). This class defines parameters T_1, T_2, and **S**. It uses parameters T_1 and **S** to specialize the base packet it is extending, and it uses parameters T_2 and **S** to define field pkt_2 whose type is class **pkt** specialized with parameters T_2 and **S**.

4.7.4 Polymorphism: Uniform Access to Diverse Objects

In software programming, _polymorphism_ refers to the ability of one variable to hold data objects of different types. A direct consequence of this flexibility is that objects of different types can be passed to the same argument of a method (i.e., task or function), in turn allowing a method to be generically used for a variety of data objects of different types. In this approach, the exact handling of each object type by that method is defined when a decision is made to support a new data type. Polymorphism provides great flexibility in both creating a program when details are not yet known, and to also extend a program at a later time to support new data types.

In SystemVerilog, polymorphism is defined within the scope of a class hierarchy. Consider a virtual base class **B** with a virtual method **M()**, a pointer **P** defined to have class type **B**, and a derived class **D** with data member **V** and a redefinition of method **M()**. In SystemVerilog, it is possible for pointer **P** to point to an instance of class **D**. In this case, pointer **P** behaves as a pointer to class **D**, where **P.M()** refers to method **M()** defined in class **D**, and **P.V** refers to data member **V** declared in class **D**. Generally, this feature allows pointer **P** to point to any class derived directly or indirectly from class **B**, thereby providing polymorphism within the scope of the class hierarchy rooted at class **B**. This concept is shown in the following example program:

```
   Program 4.27: Polymorphism and class object pointers
1  :  module top;
2  :        virtual class B;
3  :               virtual task M(); endtask
4  :        endclass: B
5  :
6  :        class D1 extends B;
```

```
7   :                task M(); $display("in class D1"); endtask
8   :            endclass: D1
9   :
10  :            class D2 extends B;
11  :                task M(); $display("in class D2"); endtask
12  :            endclass: D2
13  :
14  :            B B_ptr [1:0];
15  :            D1 D1_ptr;
16  :            D2 D2_ptr;
17  :
18  :            initial begin
19  :                D1_ptr = new;
20  :                D2_ptr = new;
21  :                B_ptr[0] = D2_ptr;
22  :                B_ptr[1] = D1_ptr;
23  :                for (int i = 0; i < 2; i++)      // this loop produces: in class D2
24  :                    B_ptr[i].M();                //                     in class D1
25  :            end
26  :    endmodule
```

In this program, pointer **B_ptr** is a two element unpacked array of pointers to class objects of type **B**. Because of polymorphism, however, **B_ptr** can be used to point to class objects of type D_1 and D_2 since these classes are derived from **B** (lines 21, 22). When accessing these objects, **B_Ptr[0]** will behave as if it was a pointer to D_2, and **B_ptr [1]** will behave as if it was a pointer to D_1. As shown in this example, this type of polymorphism allows an array of pointers to hold objects of diverse types.

4.7.5 Data Hiding

Hiding data members inside a class and allowing their value to be changed or viewed only through well defined methods also defined in that object leads to fewer programming errors compared to where object data members can be changed in an ad hoc manner. SystemVerilog provides the keywords *local* and *protected* to hide object data members. Properties marked as *local* can be read and modified only by methods defined in the same class. Properties marked as *protected* can be read and modified by methods defined in that and all classes derived directly or indirectly from the class containing that property. The following program segment shows this concept:

```
     Program 4.28: Local and protected class data members
1   :    module top;
2   :        class base_packet;
3   :            local byte partial_crc;
4   :            protected byte crc;
5   :
6   :            function void compute_partial_crc();
7   :                partial_crc = 10; // replace this with actual crc calculation
8   :            endfunction
9   :
10  :            function byte get_partial_crc();
11  :                get_partial_crc = partial_crc;
12  :            endfunction
13  :        endclass: base_packet
14  :
15  :        class packet extends base_packet;
16  :            function void compute_crc();
17  :                crc = 4; // replace this with actual crc calculation
```

```
18  :          endfunction
19  :
20  :          function byte get_crc();
21  :              compute_partial_crc();
22  :              compute_crc();
23  :              get_crc = crc + get_partial_crc();
24  :          endfunction
25  :      endclass: packet
26  :
27  :      packet p;
28  :
29  :      initial begin
30  :          p = new;
31  :          $display(p.get_crc());
32  :      end
33  :  endmodule
```

In this example, property **partial_crc** is only visible and editable inside the base class **base_packet**. As such, methods **compute_partial_crc()** and **get_partial_crc()** are provided for updating and accessing this data value. **crc** is visible inside the derived class **packet** but not outside this class. As such, methods **compute_crc()** and **get_crc()** are provided in class **packet** for accessing the combined **crc** value. Neither **partial_crc** nor **crc** can be accessed outside these class definitions.

CHAPTER 5

SystemVerilog as a Verification Language

SystemVerilog provides major enhancements over Verilog. These enhancements can be divided into two categories: 1) features that improve the programming paradigm of the language (e.g., complex data types, object-oriented programming, etc.), and 2) features that improve verification quality. The programming paradigm of SystemVerilog is described in chapter 4. This chapter focuses on verification related constructs and considerations of SystemVerilog.

Verification related enhancements in SystemVerilog include:

- Enhancing the scheduling semantics of the language beyond Verilog
- Facilitating cycle-based verification semantics through clocking blocks
- Promoting separation of testbench and design by introducing the program block
- Enhancing inter-process synchronization and communication mechanisms
- Constrained random generation features
- Native property specification constructs and assertion evaluation
- Coverage collection utilities

The scheduling semantics of SystemVerilog are extended in order to allow for scheduling of new language constructs (e.g., property evaluations) while maintaining backward compatibility with Verilog. Cycle-based verification approaches are facilitated through the introduction of clocking blocks that allow for automation of sampling and driving of design signals with respect to sampling clocks. Separation between testbench and design is facilitated by the introduction of program blocks. Inter-process synchronization is enhanced through the introduction of mailboxes and semaphores, thereby simplifying the interaction between independently running processes. SystemVerilog also provides new constructs for constrained random generation, property and assertion specification, and coverage collection.

Constrained random generation features of SystemVerilog are described in detail in chapter 10. Property specification and evaluation is described in chapter 15. Coverage collection syntax and semantics are described in chapter 17. This chapter describes the enhanced scheduling semantics in SystemVerilog (section 5.1), the clocking block (section 5.2), the program block (section 5.3), and inter-process communication and synchronization constructs (section 5.4).

5.1 Scheduling Semantics

The scheduling semantics in SystemVerilog is fully backward compatible with the scheduling semantics of Verilog. However, these semantics have been extended to provide support for the new constructs in SystemVerilog (e.g., program block, sequence evaluation). A good understanding of the scheduling semantics of SystemVerilog facilitates better understanding of the detailed operation of these new language constructs, and will help in avoiding potential programming pitfalls.

The semantics of SystemVerilog have been defined for event-driven simulation. A program consists of threads of execution (e.g., process blocks, concurrent statements, forked processes) that assign new values to data objects. A thread of execution is first started either statically at simulation start time or dynamically by using fork-join statements (section 4.6). A thread of execution is suspended either when its execution reaches the end of a block or by an explicit wait for an event or delay period (e.g., "**@rcv_pkt;**" waits until event **rcv_pkt** is triggered, "**#3ns;**" waits for **3** ns). The evaluation of a sleeping thread of execution is restarted either when an explicit sleep time in its sequential flow has passed or when the conditions for a wait statement are satisfied. A new evaluation thread is started either statically (e.g., *initial* block), upon changes in any of the signals in a sensitivity list (e.g., *always* block), or through *fork-join* statements. In this flow, time is advanced when restart times of all threads that are scheduled to be restarted are at a time in the future. The next simulation time, is consequently the next immediate time at which an execution thread restart is scheduled.

Each thread of execution evaluates its expressions by accessing values of data objects used in expressions and updating data objects that appear on the left-hand side of these expressions. Data values can be updated either with blocking assignments or non-blocking assignments. A *blocking assignments* takes effect (i.e., the result of evaluating the expression on the right-hand side of the assignment is moved into the data object on the left-hand side of assignment) immediately during the running of its thread of execution, and as that assignment is being carried out, whereas a *non-blocking assignment* takes effect only in the NBA scheduling region (figure 5.1). In other words, the result of evaluating the expression on the right-hand side of a non-blocking assignment is not moved into the left-hand side data object until its thread of execution is suspended. As such, the value of a variable assigned using a blocking assignment is immediately visible within the thread of execution after the assignment is made, but the value of a variable assigned using a non-blocking assignment becomes visible only after its execution thread is suspended.

A *time-slot* at a given simulation time T_s is the abstract unit of time within which all thread restarts and data object updates for time T_s take place. In SystemVerilog, thread restarts are given different priorities depending on the language construct that created the thread (e.g., *always* block, assertion action block, etc.). In addition, data object updates are grouped according to their update mechanisms (i.e., blocking vs. non-blocking). The *scheduling semantics of SystemVerilog* uses the concept of *scheduling regions* to describe the mechanism and ordering of thread restarts and data object updates within a given time-slot. Figure 5.1 shows the SystemVerilog simulation reference model and its predefined scheduling regions.

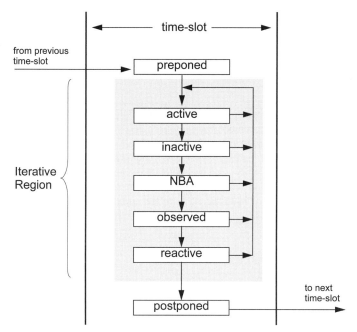

Figure 5.1 SystemVerilog Time-Slot and Scheduling Regions

Scheduling regions in this flow consist of preponed, active, inactive, NBA (non-blocking assignment), observed, reactive, and postponed. Except for observed and reactive regions, this flow essentially duplicates the standard simulation reference model in Verilog. The preponed region is specifically used as a PLI callback control point that allows PLI routines to access data at the current time-slot before any net or variable values are changed.

5.1.1 Active Region

At the start of the current time-slot, the active region holds thread evaluation restarts scheduled for the current time-slot in any of the previous time-slots. Upon reaching the active region, thread evaluations listed in this region are started. During each thread evaluation, any non-blocking assignment is scheduled to be carried out in the NBA region of the current time-slot. In addition, any "*#0*" delay causes the running thread to be suspended and scheduled for restart in the inactive region of the current time-slot.

5.1.2 Inactive Region

The inactive region holds all threads that are restarted in the active region of the current time-slot and executed a "*#0*" delay statement after being restarted. The reason for placing all such threads in the inactive region is that for all threads that are restarted in the current time-slot, all statements before any "*#0*" delay statement must be executed before any of these thread evaluations progress beyond the "*#0*" statement. Once all threads that are restarted in the active region are suspended, all threads scheduled for restart in the inactive region are moved to the active region, and iteration repeats by restarting the flow in the active region.

5.1.3 NBA Region

The NBA region is reached when no threads are scheduled for execution in the active or inactive regions. The NBA region holds data objects that were assigned using non-blocking assignments in threads executed so far in the active and inactive regions of the current time-slot. Upon reaching this region, all such assignments are carried out and threads sensitized to changes in these data objects are scheduled to be restarted. If any thread is scheduled to be restarted in the same time-slot, then that thread is scheduled for restart in the active region of the current time-slot. The scheduling of threads for restart in the current time-slot causes another iteration of the current time-slot to restart from the active region.

5.1.4 Observed Region

The observed region is reached when none of the assignments made in the NBA region result in scheduling a thread restart in the active region of the current time-slot. The observed region is introduced specifically for handling clocked assertions. Evaluating a clocked assertion requires that the clocking expression be evaluated, followed by its property expression evaluation if a clock trigger is detected (section 15.4). The values used for computing the property expression in a clocked assertion are sampled in the preponed region of the current time-slot. This means that any changes of property expression variables in the current time-slot are not visible to its evaluation in the current time-slot. The clocking expression of a clocked assertion is, however, evaluated using the current values of variables in its expression. The required behavior is that a clocking condition for an assertion should only be evaluated using stable values of signals in the current time-slot, after all signal activity in the current time-slot is completed and every data object has been assigned its final value. The reason for this requirement is that using non-stable variable values for evaluating a clocking expression may lead to false detection of a clock trigger. The observed region is introduced specifically to allow for this behavior where a clocking expression is evaluated only after all variable assignments for the current time-slot have been finalized.

5.1.5 Reactive Region

The reactive region is used for evaluating the pass/fail code attached to assertions. Assignments made to nets and variables in the reactive region can potentially lead to new thread evaluations to be scheduled in the active region of the current time-slot. This means that another iteration of the current time-slot starting at the active region may again be needed. Note that even if data objects used for evaluating the property expression of a clocked assertion are changed in this next pass through the current time-slot, these changes will not be visible to property evaluation, since values sampled in the preponed region are used for evaluating property expressions. The property will, however, be reevaluated if its clocking event is triggered. As such, it is important to take special care that assignments made in the pass/fail segment of a clocked assertion do not lead to triggering its clocking expression in the current time-slot.

5.1.6 Postponed Region

The postponed region is specifically for a PLI callback control point that allows user code to get suspended until all active, inactive, and NBA assignments have been completed. Signal values in the postponed region of a time-slot are exactly the same as those in the preponed region of the next time-slot. The *1step* time delay provided by SystemVerilog is a conceptual mechanism for sampling signal values during the postponed region of the previous time-slot. This sampling effectively means that stable values of the signal are sampled before the current time-slot is entered. Sampling in the postponed region of the previous time-slot is effectively the same as sampling in the preponed region of the current time-slot.

5.2 Clocking Blocks

Interaction with a DUV for verification purposes often follows cycle-based semantics where DUV signals are sampled and driven based on a clocking event. For verification purposes, it is usually a good practice to take advantage of the setup and hold time specifications of a design interface by driving DUV inputs slightly before a sampling event, and sampling outputs slightly after a clocking event in order to bypass any simulation-induced, spurious signal transitions at the exact time of the sampling event. An additional benefit of following this approach is that using the actual setup and hold time requirements of a design in sampling outputs and driving inputs leads to verifying the required setup and hold time behavior of a DUV.

As an example, consider a DUV whose outputs should be read at **2ns** before the positive edge of system clock and inputs should be driven **1ns** after the positive edge of the same clock (figure 5.2).

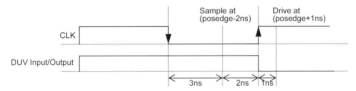

Figure 5.2 DUV Input/Output Sample and Driving Timing

The following program segment shows one approach for implementing this behavior:

```
Program 5.1: Signal sampling and setup/hold delays without a clocking block
1  :    module top;
2  :        bit clk=1;
3  :        reg [7:0] duv_in, duv_out, duv_io;
4  :        initial for (int i = 0; i <= 10; i++) #5ns clk = !clk; // Generate clk
```

```
5   :
6   :              always @(negedge clk) begin
7   :                  #3ns;
8   :                  $display (duv_io, duv_out); // read signal values at posedge - 2ns
9   :                  @(posedge clk);
10  :                  #1ns;
11  :                  duv_in = 10; // write signals at posedge + 1ns
12  :                  duv_io = 20;
13  :              end
14  :      endmodule
```

In this example, an always block is used to wait for **3ns** after the negative edge of clock (line 7) so that design outputs can be read **2ns** before the positive edge of clock, which occurs at time **10ns** (line 8). Design input signals are then driven **1ns** after the positive edge of the clock (lines 11, 12).

SystemVerilog provides the _clocking block_ construct to facilitate easy and straightforward implementation of this type of interaction with a DUV. A clocking block can only be instantiated in a module, program block, or interface.

A clocking block is identified by the following aspects:

- Name: Name of the clocking block
- Clocking event: Event used as the reference for setup/hold time calculations
- Unclocked signals: Hierarchical name for environment signals that are to be sampled or driven by the clocking block
- Clocked signals: A direction and an optional name for each unclocked signal managed by the clocking block
- Default input/output skews: Default delay values, with respect to clocking events, specifying timing for driving outputs and sampling inputs
- Skew overrides: An optional input and/or output skew override for each clocked signal

Figure 5.3 shows the relationship between the input skew, the output skew, and the clocking event defined for a clocking block. The event used for sampling the inputs is derived by assuming the input skew to be a negative value. The output driving event is derived by waiting for output skew time after the clocking event.

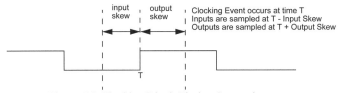

Figure 5.3 Clocking Block Timing Semantics

Figure 5.4 shows a pictorial view of the function of a clocking block. Any DUV or testbench signal can be managed by a clocking block both for sampling and driving. A clocking block implicitly defines _output driving clock_ and _input sampling clock_. Output driving clock is triggered output-skew-delay time after the clocking event, and input sampling clock is triggered input-skew-delay time before the clocking event. A clocking block allows separate output and input skews to be assigned to any clocked signal. As such, any clocked signal has its own dedicated and implicit output driving and input sampling clocks.

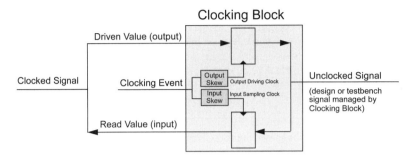

Figure 5.4 Clocking Block Behavior

Any value written to a clocked signal of a clocking block is assigned to its associated unclocked signal when its output driving clock occurs. This means that multiple writes to a clocking signal are filtered and only the last assignment to the clocked signal before the arrival of the output driving clock is driven to its associated unclocked signal. Reading from a clocked signal of a clocking block supplies the last value of its associated unclocked signal before its last input sampling event occurred. As such, all transitions in an unclocked signal between two occurrences of input sampling clocks are filtered out by the clocking block and only the last value of the unclocked signal before the last input sampling clock is available at the clocked signal.

The separation between clocked and their associated unclocked signals leads to some unexpected results. For example, writing from a clocking block *inout* element and reading the same value will not produce the value that was just written because the returned value is a value sampled when the input sampling clock had occurred (figure 5.4).

A clocking block supports *input*, *output*, and *inout* clocked signals. Configuration shown in figure 5.4 applies to inout elements. Input elements only have the input direction, output elements only have the output direction behavior.

Program segment 5.2 below shows an example of a clocking block:

Program 5.2:   Sample clocking block implementation

```
1  :        clocking cb @(posedge clk);
2  :            default input #2ns output #1ns;        //default i/o skews
3  :            input cb_out = duv_out;
4  :            output duv_in;
5  :            inout cb_io = top.module.duv_io;
6  :            input #1ns cb_out;
7  :            output #1ns duv_in;
8  :            input #1ns output #3ns cb_io;
9  :        endclocking
```

Line 1 shows the clocking block name and clocking event. Line 2 shows the default input and output skews. Lines 3–5 show examples of *input*, *output*, and *inout* element specifications. Each specification consists of the signal direction, clocked signal name (e.g., **cb_out** on line 3), and the unclocked signal (DUV or testbench signal) associated with this clocked signal (e.g., **duv_out** on line 3). Note that the unclocked signal can be specified using a hierarchical name (e.g., **top.module.duv_io** on line 5). Also, if the unclocked signal name is omitted, it is assumed to be a signal with the same name as the clocked signal and in the same scope as the clocking block (e.g., **duv_in** on line 4). If the input and output skews are different for an element, these skews can be specified explicitly. Input skew override is specified for input **cb_out** on line 6. Output skew override is specified for output **duv_in** on line 7, and input and output skew overrides are specified for *inout* **cb_io** on line 8.

The following program shows the use of clocking blocks to improve the implementation of the sampling and driving example shown in program 5.1:

```
Program 5.3: Signal sampling and setup/hold delays with a clocking block
1   :   module top;
2   :       bit clk=1;
3   :       reg [7:0] duv_in, duv_out, duv_io;
4   :
5   :       initial for (int i = 0; i <= 10; i++) #5ns clk = !clk;
6   :
7   :       clocking cb @(posedge clk);
8   :           default input #2ns output #1ns;
9   :           input cb_out = duv_out;
10  :           output cb_in = duv_in;
11  :           inout cb_io = duv_io;
12  :           input #1ns cb_out;
13  :           output #1ns cb_in;
14  :           input #1ns output #3ns cb_io;
15  :       endclocking
16  :
17  :       always @(posedge clk) begin
18  :           $display (cb.cb_io, cb.cb_out); // read signal values at posedge - 2
19  :           cb.cb_in <= 10; // write signals at posedge + 1
20  :           cb.cb_io <= 20;
21  :       end
22  :   endmodule
```

As shown in this example, the *always* block on line 17 is sensitive to the positive edge of the clock **clk**. Upon entering the *always* block, the values of **cb.cb_io** and **cb.cb_out** are read. The values read at this time, however, are those read **1ns** before the positive edge of the clock. Also, the values written to **cb.cb_in** and **cb.cb_io** on lines 19 and 20 will be applied to **duv_in** and **duv_io** at **1ns** and **3ns** respectively after the positive edge of the clock.

5.2.1 Input and Output Skews

SystemVerilog provides a rich set of options in specifying the input and output skews for clocking blocks. Some examples are shown below:

```
Example 1: input #1step var_name;
Example 2: input #10ns var_name;
Example 3: input negedge var_name;
Example 4: input negedge #1ns var_name;
Example 5: input #0 var_name;
```

Example 1 shows the use of keyword *#1step*, which is a special SystemVerilog construct for specifying that the input should be sampled in the postponed region of the previous time-slot of the clocking block sampling event. This is essentially the same as sampling the input in the preponed region of the time-slot for the sampling event of the clocking block (section 5.1). Example 2 shows an absolute value input skew. Example 3 shows that the sense of the clock can be changed from that of the sampling event for the clocking block. For example, if the sampling event for the clocking block is (**posedge clk**), then the input skew can be set to negative edge. Example 4 shows that the input skew can be set to an absolute delay offset from a changed sense of the sampling event. Example 5 shows the use of **#0** in specifying the skew. Inputs with explicit **#0** skew are sampled in the observed region of the time-slot for the clocking block sampling event. Outputs with explicit **#0** are driven in the NBA region of the time-slot for the clocking block sampling event. The default input skew is **#1step**. The default output skew is **#0**.

5.2.2 Default Clocking

The sampling event for a clocking block can be declared as the default clock for the block (e.g., module) that it is declared in. Given a default clock, the *cycle delay operator* "##" can be used within that block to specify delays as a count of default clock cycles. The following program uses the cycle delay operator.

```
Program 5.4: Use of cycle delay operator
1   :    module top;
2   :        bit clk=1;
3   :        int cnt=1;
4   :
5   :        initial for (int i = 0; i <= 10; i++) #5ns clk = !clk;
6   :
7   :        default clocking cb @(posedge clk); endclocking
8   :
9   :        initial begin
10  :            $display ($time); //prints 0
11  :            ##2;
12  :            $display ($time); //prints 20 (2 cycles of the 10ns period clk)
13  :            ##(cnt+2);
14  :            $display ($time); //prints 50 (cnt+2=3 cycles of the 10ns clk passed time 20)
15  :        end
16  :    endmodule
```

5.3 Program Block

SystemVerilog uses the same simulation semantics as that of Verilog. This means that SystemVerilog inherits not only the expressive power of event-driven simulation, but also the problem of race conditions that are an inherent part of event-driven simulation, as popularized by Verilog. Designers have developed an extensive set of design guidelines to avoid race conditions in their designs. These guidelines are focused mainly on following a modular and synchronous design style where, for example, the notion of combinational and sequential logic are modeled using blocking and non-blocking assignments. The same design guidelines migrate directly to designs created in SystemVerilog and as such, dealing with race conditions is not a main concern when creating designs in SystemVerilog.

For multiple reasons, however, the situation is different for verification engineers:

- Verification engineers follow a more software-oriented programming style where the notion of combinational versus sequential does not directly apply. This means that selective use of blocking versus non-blocking assignments is not a natural fit for avoiding races in testbenches.
- Detailed evaluation order of design signals is not an immediate concern for verification engineers. Verification engineers are more focused on verifying correct cycle-based operation of the design, and as such prefer to avoid having to deal with race conditions due to scheduling semantics of the simulator.
- Introduction of new verification related features such as assertions and properties, whose evaluation semantics are a new addition to SystemVerilog, require special considerations for how testbench evaluation is scheduled along with the design.

Consider the following design and its associated testbench:

```
Program 5.5: Design/testbench having a race condition
1  :    module duv (input clk);
2  :        bit siga,sigb;
3  :        always @(posedge clk)
4  :            sigb <= !siga;
5  :    endmodule
6  :
7  :    module test;
8  :        bit clk;
9  :
10 :        initial for (int i = 0; i <= 16; i++) #1 clk = !clk;
11 :
12 :        duv di(clk);
13 :
14 :        always @(posedge clk)
15 :            di.siga <= di.sigb;
16 :
17 :        always @(negedge clk) $display ($time, di.siga, di.sigb);
18 :    endmodule
```

The design to be verified is **duv** (lines 1–5). The testbench is implemented in module **test**. The design assigns to **sigb** the complement of **siga** on every positive edge of **clk**. The intention of this testbench is to take signal **sigb**, produced at the output of the design and assign it back to its input **siga** as the next test vector. This is accomplished on line 15 by moving the output value to the input at every positive edge of the clock.

The example, as shown above, has a race condition which leads to incorrect simulation results. The race condition is due to the non-blocking assignment on line 15 using the previous value of **sigb** before it is updated in the current cycle. As such, the value moved to the input of the design is not the value produced in this cycle but its previous value. It may seem that by changing the non-blocking assignment on line 15 to a blocking assignment, the problem would be solved, but this is not guaranteed. This is because the always blocks on lines 3 and 15 may be executed in any order at the positive edge of **clk**. A better fix would be to change the sense of clock on line 14 to **negedge** which would then lead to correct simulation results.

As shown, the problem with this testbench can be solved after some analysis, but the real issue is that first of all, these types of problems are very difficult to analyze for anything but the most non-trivial designs. Second, it would be best to avoid getting into these types of problems in the first place. SystemVerilog introduces the program block so that such problems can be prevented with ease.

The fundamental goal in introducing the program block is to provide verification engineers with a well defined ordering for the evaluation of design versus testbench. In order to achieve this goal, the following properties have been defined for a program block:

- A program block can contain only type and variable declarations and one or more initial blocks.
- A program block cannot contain always blocks, UDPs, modules, interfaces, or other program blocks.
- Variables inside a program block can only be assigned from inside the same or other program blocks (e.g., assignment to a program block variables from a module is illegal).
- Variables inside a program block can only be assigned using blocking assignments.
- From inside a program block, variables on the outside that are not in any program block, can only be assigned using non-blocking assignments.
- Statements from within a program block that are sensitized to design variables (e.g., **@posedge of design.clk**) are scheduled for evaluation in the reactive region.
- Initial blocks inside a program block are scheduled for evaluation in the reactive region. This is in contrast with initial blocks inside other blocks that are scheduled for evaluation in the active region.

The benefits gained because of these properties are described in the following bullets. In this description, design signals refer to any variable declared outside of program blocks.

- Suspended program block processes (e.g., an initial block suspended due to a wait on delay or event) are scheduled to be restarted in the reactive region. An immediate consequence of this property is that in any time-slot, the execution of code inside the program block is started only after all design signal transitions, due to any source other than the program block (e.g., scheduled from previous time-slots, 0-delay propagations in the current time-slot, etc.) are finalized.
- All program block variables are assigned using blocking assignments and all design signals driven from inside the program block are assigned using non-blocking assignments. An immediate consequence of this property is that once suspended processes inside program blocks are restarted, all signal evaluations inside a program block are finalized before any of the changes they cause in design signals cause design processes to be restarted. The reason is that blocking assignments made inside the program block take effect in the active region, and non-blocking assignments used for design signals take effect in the NBA region.
- These interactions produce the following order of evaluation for program blocks:
  - After entering the current time-slot, all design signal changes due to sources other than the program block are finalized.
  - Next, program block code is executed using the latest values of design signals in the current time-slot.
  - Next, all changes in program block variables are finalized, where all new values

to be applied to design using non-blocking assignments become available.
- New values for design variables are then applied to the design and their effect on design is computed.
- Another iteration of this sequence occurs if changes in design signals due to values applied from the program block lead to further restart of suspended program block processes in the next pass through the reactive region of the same time-slot.
- A very important consequence of scheduling program block evaluations in the reactive region is that results of property and assertion evaluations for the current time-slot are visible inside a program block. This is because properties are evaluated in the observed region, which occurs before the reactive region (figure 5.1). These results are not available for the current time-slot outside the program block.

In the following example, a program block is used to fix the problem with the race conditions in program 5.5.

```
Program 5.6: Using a program block to avoid race conditions
1   :   module dut (input clk);
2   :       bit siga,sigb;
3   :       always @(posedge clk)
4   :           sigb <= !siga;
5   :   endmodule
6   :
7   :   program bench(input clk);
8   :       initial
9   :           forever begin
10  :               @(posedge clk);
11  :                   test.di.siga <= test.di.sigb;
12  :           end
13  :   endprogram
14  :
15  :   module test;
16  :       bit clk;
17  :       initial for (int i = 0; i <= 16; i++) #10 clk = !clk;
18  :
19  :       dut di(clk);
20  :       bench bi(clk);
21  :
22  :       always @(negedge clk) $strobe ($time, di.siga, di.sigb);
23  :   endmodule
```

In this program, because of the semantics of the program block described in this section, assignment on line 11 is guaranteed to take place after assignment on line 4 is completed, even though they are both sensitized to the positive edge of the clock.

Design task and functions called from inside a program block are evaluated in the reactive region. This is in contrast to design task and function calls from inside a design which are evaluated in the active region. This means that in a given time-slot, the effect of non-blocking assignments are visible to design tasks and functions called from a program block but not visible to design and task functions called from outside the program block.

Additionally, a design task that suspends one or more times before returning (e.g., due to a wait for delay or on event) and that is called from inside a program block follows the scheduling semantics of the program block until it is suspended for the first time. However, from that point on, it follows the scheduling semantics of its containing block. This behavior, if not used carefully, can lead to unexpected results.

Given the scheduling complexity of design tasks and non-blocking assignments in design tasks and functions called from a program block, it is recommended that only design functions that use blocking assignments be called from a program block.

5.4 Inter-Process Communication and Synchronization

It is often necessary to synchronize or communicate between two independently running processes. SystemVerilog provides the following constructs to facilitate this requirement:

- Events
- Semaphores
- Mailboxes

Events and *semaphores* are used for thread synchronization, semaphores are also used for mutual exclusion, and *mailboxes* are used for inter-process communication. These constructs are described in the following subsections.

5.4.1 Events

Events are objects that can be triggered, and waited on to be triggered. SystemVerilog enhances the definition of Verilog events by defining an event to be a pointer to a synchronization object. As such, multiple event names can point to the same synchronization object, event pointers can be assigned to one another, and event pointers can be passed to functions and tasks. SystemVerilog events have the following properties:

- Can be triggered in the active region using the *blocking trigger operator* "->"
- Can be triggered in the NBA region using the *non-blocking trigger operator* "->>"
- Can be waited on using the @ operator
- Can provide a persistent state in addition to its event trigger, lasting throughout the time-slot in which it was triggered, that can be waited on using a wait statement
- Event variables can be assigned to one another
- Event variables can be passed to tasks and function and returned by functions
- Event variables can be compared using equality and inequality operators

The following program shows an example of using event triggering and waiting to synchronize between two process blocks, and also using event pointers as task arguments.

Program 5.7: Using events to synchronize between blocks

```
1 :    module top;
2 :        event e1, e2;
3 :        task trigger_event(event e); ->e; endtask
4 :
5 :        initial begin
6 :            #1; ->e1;
```

```
7    :              #1000 $finish;
8    :          end
9    :
10   :          always @(e1) begin
11   :                  #10 trigger_event(e2);
12   :                  $display ("e1", $time);
13   :          end
14   :
15   :          always @(e2) begin
16   :                  #10 trigger_event(e1);
17   :                  $display ("e2", $time);
18   :          end
19   :  endmodule
```

This example shows the implementation of task **trigger_event()** that triggers the event object that its argument identifies. Task **trigger_event()** is then used to trigger different events (lines 11, 16). Note that in this example, initial triggering of event e_1 (line 6) is delayed by 1 time unit in order to remove the race condition between triggering and checking of event e_1. If on line 6, e_1 is triggered at time **0**, then this triggering may occur after the always block on line 10 is activated, in which case, the trigger will not be seen by the always block and event e_2 never gets triggered.

The following program shows the use of persistent state of an event to eliminate this type of race condition.

```
Program 5.8: Events persistent states
1    :  module top;
2    :          event e1, e2;
3    :
4    :          initial begin
5    :                  wait(e1.triggered);
6    :                  $display ("e1 triggered in A");
7    :                  -> e2;
8    :                  @e1;
9    :                  if (e1 == e2) $display ("e1 and e2 the same in A");
10   :                  e1 = null;
11   :                  -> e2;
12   :          end
13   :
14   :          initial begin
15   :                  ->e1;
16   :                  @e2;
17   :                  $display ("e2 triggered in B");
18   :                  e2 = e1;
19   :                  ->e2;
20   :                  @e2;
21   :                  $display ("e2 triggered in B");
22   :                  if (e1 == null) $display ("e1 is null in B");
23   :          end
24   :  endmodule
```

The output produced by this example is:

```
e1 triggered in A
e2 triggered in B
e1 and e2 the same in A
e2 triggered in B
e1 is null in B
```

On line 5, the first thread waits on persistent triggered state of event e_1. The persistent triggered state of an event remains active throughout the duration of the time-slot in which it occurs. As such, this trigger will be visible by any thread waiting to be executed in the same time-slot (in this case thread 2 at line 15) regardless of which one is started first. Using the @ operator on line 5 may lead to a race condition where if thread 2 is started first, then the triggering of e_1 on line 15 will be missed by thread 1. This program also shows examples of how event pointers can be assigned to one another and compared against each other or the *null* value. Note that in this example, the synchronization object pointed to by variable e_2 on line 11 is the synchronization object that was initially pointed to by variable e_1.

5.4.2 Semaphores

Semaphores are used for the following purposes:

- Mutual exclusion
- Thread rendezvous

SystemVerilog provides a built-in semaphore construct. SystemVerilog provides the following methods for this construct:

```
function new (int keyCount = 0);
task put(int keyCount=1);
task get(int keyCount=1);
function try_get(int keyCount=1);
```

Function *new()* is used to allocate a new semaphore. Tasks *get()* and *put()* are used to procure and return keys to the semaphore. Function *try_get()* is used to check whether or not the requested number of keys are available in the semaphore.

Use of semaphore in implementing process synchronization is discussed in the following subsections.

5.4.2.1 Semaphore for Mutual Exclusion

Semaphores are ideal for providing *mutual exclusion* to a common resource. The program region that accesses a common resource is referred to as the active section. As an example, a driver interacting with a physical bus can potentially be called by multiple threads running in parallel. It is clear that access to the driver should be limited to one thread at a time.

The following program shows an example of using semaphores to limit access to an active section to one process at a time:

```
Program 5.9: Using semaphores for mutual exclusion
1  :    module top;
2  :        semaphore sem;
3  :        initial sem = new(1);
4  :
5  :        task automatic driver (input string nn, input time delay1, input time delay2);
6  :            #delay1;
7  :            sem.get(1);
8  :            $display($time, nn, "entering active section");
9  :            #delay2;
10 :            $display($time, nn, "leaving active section");
11 :            sem.put(1);
```

```
12  :          endtask
13  :
14  :          initial
15  :              fork
16  :                  driver("AgentA", 10, 30);
17  :                  driver("AgentB", 20, 40);
18  :              join
19  :  endmodule
```

First, note that task **driver()** on line 5 is specified to have automatic variables by default. Otherwise, given that the default mode for task variables is static, multiple simultaneous calls to this task would lead to problems. As shown in the example, the ***get()*** method of semaphore is called before entering the active section and the ***put()*** method of the semaphore is called after leaving the active section. This example produces the following output:

```
10 AgentA entering active section
40 AgentA leaving active section
40 AgentB entering active section
80 AgentB leaving active section
```

At time **0**, the fork statement on line 15 starts two processes, each calling task **driver()** with different delay parameters. Given that process **AgentA** has a shorter initial delay time of **10** (line 6), it acquires the semaphore first (line 7). Process **AgentB** finishes its initial delay at time **20**, and attempts to acquire a key from the semaphore, but suspends since the key is already held by process **AgentA**, which is still in its active section. At time **40**, process **AgentA** leaves the active section and returns its key to the semaphore (line 11). At this time, the key becomes available to process **AgentB**, which then enters the active section at time **40**, leaving it at time **80**, and returning the key to the semaphore.

Note that any number of processes can be started by calling **driver()** and this implementation would guarantee mutual exclusion across all processes for the active section in this task.

5.4.2.2 Thread Rendezvous

Thread synchronization can be modeled as a producer-consumer type relationship. In this model, producer threads can only proceed if their product is consumed by a consumer, and a consumer thread can only proceed when a product is available for it. This concept can be generalized to multiple producers and consumers where a producer can proceed when its product is consumed by any of the consumers, and a consumer can proceed when a product is available from any of the producers. Figure 5.5 shows a pictorial view of this relationship.

Figure 5.5 Producer-Consumer Model of Process Rendezvous

The following program shows how a rendezvous between multiple threads is implemented using two semaphores:

```
Program 5.10: Using semaphores for rendezvous between multiple threads
1   :   module top;
2   :       semaphore sem1 = new(0);
3   :       semaphore sem2 = new(0);
4   :
5   :       task automatic producer (input string name, input time delay1, input time delay2);
6   :           while (1) begin
7   :               #delay1;
8   :               // make product and place in mailbox
9   :               sem1.put(1);
10  :               sem2.get(1);
11  :               $display ($time, name, ": Product consumed, now making a new one");
12  :               #delay2;
13  :           end
14  :       endtask
15  :
16  :       task automatic consumer (input string name, input time delay1, input time delay2);
17  :           while (1) begin
18  :               #delay1;
19  :               sem1.get(1);
20  :               sem2.put(1);
21  :               $display ($time, name, ": Got product, now consuming");
22  :               // take product from mailbox and consume
23  :               #delay2;
24  :           end
25  :       endtask
26  :
27  :       initial begin
28  :           fork
29  :               producer("Producer1", 10, 30);
30  :               consumer("Consumer1", 20, 60);
31  :               consumer("Consumer2", 20, 60);
32  :               #150 $finish;
33  :           join_any
34  :       end
35  :   endmodule
```

Note that both semaphores are initialized with zero keys (lines 2, 3). In implementing a rendezvous, producers issue a *put()* on **sem1** and a *get()* on **sem2** before assuming their product is consumed, and consumers issue a *get()* on **sem1** followed by a *put()* on **sem2** before assuming a product is available. This program produces the following output:

```
20 Consumer1: Got product, now consuming
20 Producer1: Product consumed, now making a new one
60 Consumer2: Got product, now consuming
60 Producer1: Product consumed, now making a new one
100 Consumer1: Got product, now consuming
100 Producer1: Product consumed, now making a new one
140 Consumer2: Got product, now consuming
140 Producer1: Product consumed, now making a new one
```

Note that two slow consumers (turnaround time of **80**) are started for a relatively faster producer (turnaround time of **40**). Also note that any number of producers and consumers can be started in the fork statement (line 28) and the rendezvous mechanism would still guarantee that one consumer proceeds for any one produced item.

A simple case for using the above approach is where a thread can continue beyond point **A** in its program flow only when another thread has reached point **B** in its program flow and vice versa. In this case, the first thread can be assumed to produce when reaching point **A**, and the second thread is assumed to consume when reaching point **B**.

5.4.3 Mailboxes

Mailboxes are used for passing messages between independently running processes. Mailboxes provide the following features:

- Ability to pass messages from one process to another
- Behave like a FIFO, where messages placed first are retrieved first
- Can have bounded or unbounded size
- Message sender can suspend if a bounded mailbox is full
- Message receiver can suspend until a message becomes available

SystemVerilog provides a built-in mailbox construct. This construct provides the following methods:

```
function new (int bound = 0);
function int num();
task put(singular message);
function int try_put(singular message);
task get(ref singular message);
function try_get(ref singular message);
task peek(ref singular message);
function int try_peek(ref singular message);
```

Function *new()* is used to allocate a new mailbox. Function *num()* returns the number of messages in the mailbox. Tasks *put()*, *get()*, and *peek()* are used to place a message in a mailbox, retrieve a message from a mailbox, and retrieve a copy of a message from a mailbox without removing it. These tasks suspend execution if the mailbox is full (for *put()*) or if the mailbox is empty (for *get()* and *peek()*). Tasks *get()* and *peek()* produce a runtime error message if the mailbox content message type does not match their argument type. Functions *try_put()*, *try_get()*, *try_peek()* return 1 upon success, and 0 when the operation fails. Functions *try_get()* and *try_peek()* return -1 when a type mismatch is detected between mailbox content and the argument passed to these functions.

SystemVerilog mailboxes can be parameterized where the message type of the mailbox is specified when the mailbox is declared. This allows for message type checking to occur during compilation and prevents runtime errors because of message type mismatches.

The following program shows an example of using a mailbox to pass messages between a producer and a consumer.

Program 5.11: Using a mailbox to pass messages between processes

```
1  :   module top;
2  :       class envelope;
3  :           int letter;
4  :           function new(int ltr); letter=ltr; endfunction
5  :       endclass
6  :
7  :       task sender(input string name, input time delay1);
8  :           envelope envlp;
9  :           int count;
10 :           while (1) begin
11 :               #delay1;
12 :               envlp = new(count);
13 :               mbox.put(envlp);
14 :               $display ($time, name, ": sent msg: ", count);
15 :               count ++;
16 :           end
```

```
17  :        endtask
18  :
19  :        task receiver (input string name, input time delay1);
20  :            envelope envlp;
21  :            while (1) begin
22  :                #delay1;
23  :                mbox.get(envlp);
24  :                $display ($time, name, ": received msg: ", envlp.letter);
25  :            end
26  :        endtask
27  :
28  :        mailbox mbox;
29  :
30  :        initial begin
31  :            mbox = new(0);
32  :            fork
33  :                sender("Producer1", 10);
34  :                receiver("Consumer1", 35);
35  :                #50;
36  :            join_any
37  :            $display("Letters in mailbox before exit: ", mbox.num());
38  :            $finish;
39  :        end
40  :    endmodule
```

This example shows mailbox **mbox** declared (line 28) to transfer messages of type class **envelope** (lines 2–5). Tasks **sender()** and **receiver()** are defined to place objects of type **envelope** inside mbox (line 13) and collect objects of type **envelope** from mbox (line 23), respectively. Task **sender()** operates faster than task **receiver()** so that objects of type **envelope** accumulate inside **mbox**. Tasks **sender()** and **receiver()** are started in independent processes (lines 33, 34) and terminated at time **50ns**. Before ending the simulation, function **num()** is used to print the number of objects inside **mbox**.

5.5 Constrained Random Generation

Constrained Random Generation is presented in chapter 10.

5.6 Property Specification and Evaluation

Property specification and evaluation is presented in chapter 15.

5.7 Coverage Collection

Coverage collection is presented in chapter 17.

PART 3

Open Verification Methodology

CHAPTER 6

OVM Infrastructure

SystemVerilog provides a powerful programming environment for building an advanced verification environment. The rich set of constructs available in SystemVerilog provide a great deal of flexibility in building a verification environment. In spite of this flexibility, and because of the existence of a language independent verification methodology, the same set of approaches and practices for building verification environments appear repeatedly across diverse projects. Documenting these practices and capturing their implementation as reusable classes provides benefits by both reducing duplicated effort across projects, and also providing a framework for new engineers to leverage existing expertise in the field.

The Open Verification Methodology (OVM)[1] is an open-source, SystemVerilog-based class library developed based on extensive experience in building state-of-the-art verification environments. The primary purpose of OVM is to enable a greater number of verification engineers with varied degrees of programming experiences to quickly build well-constructed, object-oriented verification environments. In addition, the availability of predefined classes for building verification environments and writing tests allows verification engineers to meet their verification goals sooner and with higher confidence.

The OVM class library objects and classes are specially defined for implementing a multi-layer verification environment (chapter 3), and follows the coverage-driven verification methodology (chapter 1). As such, a good understanding of these topics is needed to fully realize the benefits of this class library.

The features of the OVM class library are divided into the following categories:

- Creating and managing class objects in the environment.
- Building and configuring the verification environment hierarchy, and managing the simulation runtime phases.
- Using TLM (transaction) interfaces for connecting verification environment blocks.
- Generating transaction sequences for modeling verification scenarios.

---

[1] OVM is an open source verification methodology and class library developed jointly by Cadence Design Systems and Mentor Graphics Corporation. Visit http://www.ovmworld.org to download the OVM package and to join the OVM community of users and contributors.

This chapter describes an overview of the OVM class library[2], and provides details of the core utilities provided in the library. The use of the OVM class library for building the verification environment hierarchy is described in chapter 7. Implementing transaction interfaces with the OVM class library is described in chapter 9. Transaction sequence generation using the OVM class library is described in chapter 8.

6.1 Verification Class Library Goals

The implementation of a verification environment using class objects requires that the following implementation issues be addressed by its predefined objects and classes:

- Class object utilities (e.g., creation, access, modification, configuration)
- Component hierarchy creation and configuration
- Transactions
- Transaction ports and interfaces (communication)
- Sequences of transactions (stimulus generation)
- Simulation phases
- Reporting and messaging

A class library should have the infrastructure to support the creation, modification, and management of class objects created throughout the lifetime of a verification environment. A verification class library should, therefore, provide the necessary infrastructure to support these core operations.

Creating a block hierarchy is the first step in creating a verification environment. In building a class-based block hierarchy, each block is modeled as a class object, with the object instantiation hierarchy (figure 4.5) representing the block hierarchy. In this implementation approach, many low-level details are shared between all blocks in the hierarchy (e.g., utilities to identify sub-blocks, parent blocks, blocks names, etc.). A verification class library should provide the base classes that provide these core features.

Verification components modeled using class objects should be implemented as independent objects where each component interacts with the outside environment only through its interfaces. The implementation of this behavior using class objects requires the use of transaction level model (TLM) interfaces. *TLM interfaces* (also known as *transaction interfaces*) allow each component to communicate with other components without any specific knowledge about the internal implementation of these other components. A verification class library should define the base classes that are needed for implementing transaction interfaces.

Interaction between verification environment blocks should take place through transactions. Transactions may carry data, status, or instructions from one block to another. It is in fact these transactions that are passed through transaction interfaces that connect verification

---

[2.] The presentation of the OVM class library in this book is based on OVM 1.0 release.

environment blocks. A verification class library should define the classes that provide these transaction level models.

Complex scenarios require the creation and synchronization of complex sequences of transactions, advancing in lock-step at multiple interfaces of the DUV. The modeling and creation of these complex scenarios is not a trivial task and requires its own techniques and utilities. A verification class library must provide the base classes and the necessary infrastructure for supporting the creation of such complex scenarios.

In SystemVerilog, simulation time is advanced without any consideration of abstract phases that may exist in the verification flow. Progression of time in a verification environment is, however, managed in phases where different sets of activities must take place in each phase (e.g., initialization phase, running phase, checking phase). A verification class library should define the infrastructure necessary for managing this high level view of simulation phases and the implicit synchronization requirement it imposes on concurrently running threads in different blocks of the environment.

Producing informative messages about the state of verification is an essential part of carrying out verification activities. Messages may be produced in different blocks and at different levels of severity. A verification class library should define the base utilities for specifying such severity levels and enabling or disabling the generation of such messages.

Features of the OVM class library are defined to address these requirements of a verification related class library. These features are summarized in the next section.

6.2 OVM Class Library Features

Features of the OVM class library are divided into the following broad categories:

- A: Object and component factory
- B: Core utilities
- C: Reporting utilities
- D: Hierarchy creation and management
- E: Thread synchronization
- F: Verification environment components
- G: Transaction objects
- H: Transaction interfaces
- I: Transaction channels
- J: Transaction items and sequences
- K: Sequence interfaces

The *factory* provides the ability to create objects during the simulation runtime while providing special features for overriding its default behavior. *Core utilities* provide a common set of utilities (e.g., comparing, printing) for use across objects in the environment. *Reporting utilities* allow global management and handling of reports generated by individual objects in the environment. *Hierarchy creation and management* features introduce the concept of "containment" where one block is contained in another block, thereby providing the

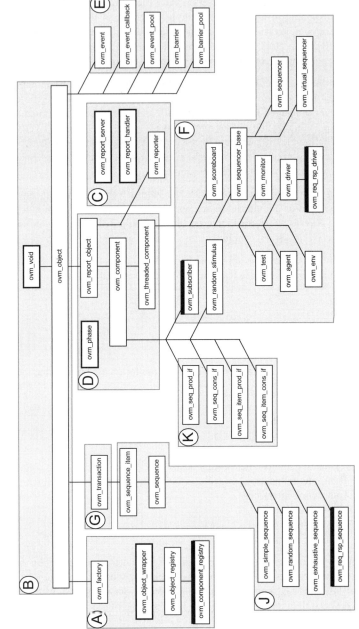

Figure 6.1 OVM Class Hierarchy

ability to create a hierarchical environment. In addition, this feature introduces the ability for each block to have its own thread of execution, and also introduces the concept of phasing by dividing the life cycle of each thread into multiple phases (e.g., run, extract, report, etc.), and synchronizing the start of each phase across multiple threads. In contrast with the phasing where the life of a thread is divided into multiple stages, *thread synchronization* features allow for synchronization between any two or more threads (e.g., using a semaphore to guarantee mutual exclusion between two or more threads). *Verification environment components* provide containers that model typical components in a verification environment (e.g., agents, monitors, scoreboards, etc.) and provide the control mechanisms for configuring, building, and controlling the simulation flow.

The OVM verification methodology promotes the use of transaction-based communication for modeling traffic flowing between components. To support this methodology, the OVM class library provides transaction objects for modeling traffic between components, transaction interfaces and transaction channels for modeling connectivity between components, and sequence interfaces to facilitate the generation of verification scenarios.

Figures 6.1 and 6.2 show an overview of the class inheritance hierarchy for the OVM class library. The classes shown in these figures are placed into groups that correspond to groups defined in the beginning of this section. Appendix A provides a full listing of all class declarations in the OVM class library, indicating the parent class, parameters for each class, and whether a class is a virtual class.

The core utilities of the OVM class library are described in this chapter.

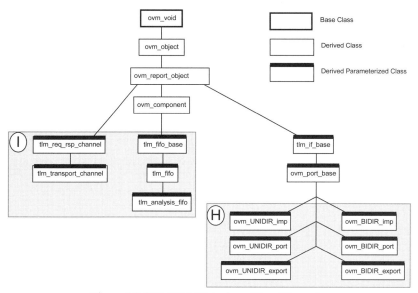

Figure 6.2 OVM TLM Interfaces Class Hierarchy

6.3 Object and Component Factories

A class-based verification environment is composed of hierarchical and non-hierarchical objects. Component objects modeling verification environment blocks represent structural hierarchy. Data objects represent transactions and environment properties and are considered as non-hierarchical objects. A common operation in building a verification environment and running scenarios is the creation of these components and data objects. The localization of all such object creation operations in a central factory provides not only a uniform approach for creating different kinds of objects, but also provides the ability to make global and instance-specific changes in how objects are created by the factory (e.g., type and instance overrides in section 6.3.1).

In its simplest form, a *factory* is a class-based object that provides specialized functionality, through its method interface, for creating objects of specialized types during simulation runtime. The following example illustrates the implementation of a simple factory:

```
Program 6.1: Simple implementation of an object factory
1    :    module top;
2    :        virtual class base_pkt;
3    :            string name;
4    :            rand byte payload;
5    :            function new(string pname=""); name=pname; endfunction
6    :            virtual task print(); endtask
7    :        endclass
8    :
9    :        class eth_pkt extends base_pkt;
10   :            constraint c1 {payload == 10;}
11   :            task print(); $display("Ethernet packet Payload: ", payload); endtask
12   :            function new(string pname=""); super.new(pname); endfunction
13   :        endclass
14   :
15   :        class usb_pkt extends base_pkt;
16   :            constraint c2 {payload == 20;}
17   :            task print(); $display("USB packet Payload: ", payload); endtask
18   :            function new(string pname=""); super.new(pname); endfunction
19   :        endclass
20   :
21   :        class simple_factory;
22   :            static function base_pkt create_pkt(string pkt_type_name, string pkt_name);
23   :                case (pkt_type_name)
24   :                    "eth_pkt":begin eth_pkt pkt; pkt=new(pkt_name); return pkt; end
25   :                    "usb_pkt":begin usb_pkt pkt; pkt=new(pkt_name); return pkt; end
26   :                endcase
27   :            endfunction
28   :        endclass
29   :
30   :        initial begin
31   :            base_pkt pkt;
32   :            pkt = simple_factory::create_pkt("eth_pkt", "packet1");
33   :            assert(pkt.randomize());
34   :            pkt.print();                // prints "Ethernet packet Payload: 10"
35   :
36   :            pkt = simple_factory::create_pkt("usb_pkt", "packet2");
37   :            assert(pkt.randomize());
38   :            pkt.print();                // prints "USB packet Payload: 20"
39   :        end
40   :    endmodule
```

This example defines **base_pkt**, a base packet data structure containing fields **name** (line 3) and **payload** (line 4), function **new()** (line 5), and virtual function **print()** (line 6). Derived classes **eth_pkt** and **usb_pkt** each provide a different implementation of virtual task **print()** (lines 11, 17). Each derived class also provides a different constraint for field **payload** of base class **base_pkt** (lines 10, 16). This example also shows the implementation of **simple_factory**, a simple packet factory that provides function **create_pkt()** (lines 22–27). This function returns a newly created packet data object whose type and name are provided by arguments **pkt_type_name** and **pkt_name** respectively. Note that this function is implemented to return an object of type **base_pkt** but because of polymorphism (section 4.7.4), this function can also return an object whose class type is derived from **base_pkt** (i.e., a specialized type). This means that in this example, function **create_pkt()** can return objects having types **eth_pkt** (line 24) and **usb_pkt** (line 25) since these classes are derived from class **base_pkt**.

Function **create_pkt()** (line 22) is defined as a static function, therefore this function can be called by using the class identifier (i.e., **simple_factory**) and the class scope resolution operator "*::*". This approach allows function **create_pkt()** to be called without creating an instance of this object factory.

This factory is used on line 32 to create a packet of type **eth_pkt** with name **packet₁,**. Randomizing this packet uses the constraint block specified for class **eth_pkt** (line 10). Therefore, randomizing this object sets the value of field **payload** to value **10**. The use of this factory for creating an object of type **usb_pkt** is shown on line 36.

Note that function **print()** is defined as a virtual function in the base class **base_pkt** (line 6). As such, calling this function through a pointer to an object of type **base_pkt** (lines 34, 38) has the same effect of calling the actual definition of this function for the true type of the object being pointed to by the pointer. This means that calling function **pkt.print()** (lines 34 and 38) results in calling function **print()** of the derived class that **pkt** is pointing at.

6.3.1 Type and Instance Overrides

The implementation of a factory in program 6.1 points to the following two benefits of using an object factory, namely the ability to define:

- Type overrides
- Instance overrides

A *type override* from type T_1 to T_2 configures a factory to return an object of type T_2 anytime an object of type T_1 is requested. An *instance override* for instance **INST** from type T_1 to T_2 configures a factory to create an object of type T_2 anytime an object of type T_1 is requested for instance **INST**. For non-hierarchical objects (i.e., objects that do not represent environment hierarchy), an instance is identified by instance name and the name of its hierarchical anchor component. For hierarchical objects (i.e., component objects), an instance is identified by full hierarchical name of that component. The implementation of the object factory shown in program 6.1 can easily be extended to include type and instance overrides by providing a task to define such overrides and then checking arguments **pkt_type_name** and **pkt_name** in function **create_pkt()** (line 21) for any such override before the actual objects are created.

The OVM library includes a built-in factory that provides the features presented in this section for both registering classes with the factory and also for defining instance and type overrides for registered classes. This factory can be used for the creation of objects and hierarchical components. These features are described in the following sections.

6.3.2 OVM Object Factory

In OVM, class **ovm_object** is used to model non-hierarchical objects, and provides the core utilities of the classes in the library (figure 6.1). All hierarchical and non-hierarchical classes in the OVM class library are derived from class **ovm_object**, thereby making these core utilities available to all the predefined classes of the library. The examples provided in this section derive from class **ovm_object** since the focus here is to highlight the utilities provided by this class. When building a verification environment according to OVM guidelines, verification environment elements should be derived from the predefined classes of OVM that are best suited for the intended implementation (e.g., a packet should be derived from the predefined class **ovm_sequence_item**). Chapters 13 and 14 show the appropriate base classes for verification environment element through an example implementation of a verification environment and its stimulus generator.

Any class derived from **ovm_object** can be registered with the OVM factory by using macro **ovm_object_utils()** in its declaration. This usage is shown in the following example:

```
Program 6.2: Registering a new class with the object factory
1  :    class packet extends ovm_object;
2  :        rand int unsigned size;
3  :        `ovm_object_utils(packet)
4  :        constraint c1 {size < 1000;}
5  :    endclass
```

The above program first defines class **packet** derived from base class **ovm_object** (line 1). This definition uses macro **ovm_object_utils()** to register class **packet** with the OVM factory (line 3).

The begin/end variation of macro **ovm_object_utils()** can be used to apply field automation 6.4) to fields in this class. This usage is shown below:

```
Program 6.3: Field automation for class fields
1  :    class packet extends ovm_object;
2  :        rand int unsigned size;
3  :        `ovm_object_utils_begin(packet)
4  :            `ovm_field_int(size, OVM_ALL_ON)
5  :        ovm_object_utils_end
6  :        constraint c1 {size < 1000;}
7  :    endclass
```

The implementation of macro **ovm_object_utils()** is based on class **ovm_object_wrapper**, where registering a new class is done by extending from class **ovm_object_wrapper** and defining functions **create_object()**, **create_component()**, and other helper functions. The use of this macro is, however, preferred since it simplifies the process of registering a new class with the factory.

Once a class is registered with the OVM factory, the following predefined methods of the OVM factory are used for creating objects and specifying object type and instance overrides:

```
Methods of class ovm_factory:
    static function ovm_object create_object(
                        string obj_type, string inst_path="", string inst_name="")
    static function void set_inst_override(string inst_id, string from_type, string to_type)
    static function void set_type_override(string from_type, string to_type, bit replace=1)
    static function void print_all_overrrides(bit all_types=0)
```

Function **create_object()** of the factory is used to create an instance of type **obj_type** whose name is assigned to argument **inst_name**. Optionally, argument **inst_path** of this function can be used to provide the hierarchical name of the block that contains the newly created object. This name can then be used to selectively apply type and instance override to objects based on their location in the hierarchy. Functions **set_inst_override()** and **set_type_override()** are used to specify instance and type overrides. These functions must be called before objects are created. Calling task **print_all_overrides()** with no arguments prints all overrides defined for the factory, while setting **all_types** to **1** results in the name of all classes currently registered with the factory to be printed. These methods are defined as static methods of class **ovm_factory** and can therefore be called directly through the class identifier **ovm_factory** and operator "::".

The following example shows the declaration of example packets derived from class **packet** (defined in program 6.2), and the use of macro **ovm_object_utils()** to register these newly defined classes with the OVM factory:

```
Program 6.4: Packet declarations to be created by the factory
1  :    class short_packet extends packet;
2  :        `ovm_object_utils(short_packet)
3  :        constraint c1 {size == 10;}
4  :    endclass
5  :
6  :    class long_packet extends packet;
7  :        `ovm_object_utils(long_packet)
8  :        constraint c1 {size == 100;}
9  :    endclass
```

Derived classes **short_packet** and **long_packet** each provide a different specialization of class **packet** by constraining the packet size to different values. Each of these classes are also registered with the OVM factory by using macro **ovm_object_utils()** (lines 2 and 7).

The use of OVM factory to create objects of this kind is shown in the following program:

```
Program 6.5: OVM Object Factory Example
1  :    module top;
2  :        `include "ovm.svh"
3  :        `include "program_6.2"      // packet class
4  :        `include "program_6.4"      // derived packet classes
5  :
6  :        packet pkt[5];
7  :        task create_packets();
8  :            ovm_object obj;
9  :            obj = ovm_factory::create_object("packet", "top", "pp1");
10 :            $cast(pkt[0], obj);
```

```
11  :
12  :                    $cast(pkt[1], ovm_factory::create_object("packet", "top", "pp2"));
13  :                    $cast(pkt[2], ovm_factory::create_object("packet", "top", "qq3"));
14  :                    $cast(pkt[3], ovm_factory::create_object("short_packet", "top", "pp4"));
15  :                    $cast(pkt[4], ovm_factory::create_object("long_packet", "top", "pp5"));
16  :        endtask
17  :
18  :        initial begin
19  :                    ovm_factory::set_inst_override("top.pp*", "packet", "short_packet");
20  :                    ovm_factory::set_type_override("packet", "short_packet");
21  :                    ovm_factory::set_type_override("packet", "long_packet");
22  :                    ovm_factory::set_type_override("short_packet", "packet");
23  :                    ovm_factory::set_type_override("short_packet", "long_packet", 0);
24  :                    ovm_factory::set_type_override("long_packet", "short_packet");
25  :                    ovm_factory::print_all_overrides(1);
26  :                    create_packets();
27  :        end
28  :  endmodule
```

Task **create_packets()** (lines 7–16) shows the use of function **create_object()** of OVM factory for creating new objects. This task creates five new objects. The creation of the first object shows the details of object creation and pointer casting (lines 8–10). First, a pointer to an object of type **ovm_object** is declared (line 8), then a new object is created as having type **packet**, residing in block **top** with name **pp1** (line 9), and then cast to **pkt[0]** which is a pointer of type **packet** (line 10). The next four objects are created (lines 12–15) using a short hand notation of directly casting the created objects to their corresponding pointers.

Task **create_packets()** is called on line 26 after specifying a number of overrides (lines 19–24). Task **print_all_overrides()** of the factory is called on line 25 to print a summary of all overrides specified for the factory. Override examples shown here illustrate the following features of override specification:

- Wild-card characters "*" and "?" can be used when specifying an instance name, where "*" matches any string of characters and "?" matches a single character. This means that instance name "**top.pp***" (line 19) matches all object names except "**top.qq3**".
- Both object type and instance name arguments of function **set_inst_override()** must match for an instance override to take effect. As such, instance override on line 19 applies only to instances "**top.pp1**" and "**top.pp2**".
- By default, a new type override overwrites the previous override for the same type. This means that the type override specified on line 21 overwrites the type override specified on line 20.
- Instance overrides take precedence over type overrides. This means that even though the type override specified on line 20 applies to instances "**top.pp1**", "**top.pp2**", and "**top.qq3**", this type override applies only to "**top.qq3**" since the first two instances are a match for the instance override specified on line 19.
- The default behavior can be changed so that a new type override does not take effect if a type override has been defined previously. By passing a value of **0** as the last argument of function **set_type_override()**, the type override on line 23 does not take effect, since a type override is specified for type **short_packet** on line 22.
- Type overrides do not chain. This means that specifying a type override from **packet₁** to **packet₂** and a type override from **packet₂** to **packet₃** does *not* result in a type override from **packet₁** to **packet₃**. In this case, any request for objects of type **packet₁** pro-

duces an object of type **packet₂**, and any request for an object of type **packet₂** produces an object of type **packet₃**. The same rule applies to instance overrides.

Object types generated by the above example without overrides (excluding lines 19–24) and with overrides is summarized below:

	Name	No Override	With Overrides
pkt[0]	pp1	packet	short_packet (line 19)
pkt[1]	pp2	packet	short_packet (line 19)
pkt[2]	qq3	packet	long_packet (line 21)
pkt[3]	pp4	short_packet	packet (line 22)
pkt[4]	pp5	long_packet	short_packet (line 24)

6.3.3 OVM Component Factory

In OVM, hierarchical components are derived from base classes **ovm_component** and **ovm_threaded_component**. Macro **ovm_component_utils()** is used to register a class derived from these classes with the OVM factory. Once a component is registered with the OVM factory, the same factory methods used for creating objects (section 6.3.2) can be used for creating components. However, OVM defines the following methods for the **ovm_component** base class in order to simplify the creation of components:

```
Methods for class ovm_component:
    function ovm_component create_component (string comp_type, string inst_name);
    function ovm_object create_object (string obj_type, string inst_name="");
    function void set_inst_override (string inst_path, string from_type, string to_type);
    static function void set_type_override (string from_type, string to_type, bit replace=1);
```

These methods call method **create_object()** of the OVM factory with the appropriate value for its **inst_path** argument derived from a component's hierarchical position. Components are class objects that represent hierarchical blocks and as such, include an explicit pointer to their containing block (i.e., parent component). Function **create_component()** creates a new component of type **comp_type** and name **inst_name** assumed to be structurally contained in the component from which this function is called (i.e., while this function calls function **create_component()** of **ovm_factory**, the **inst_path** of the new component is given as the full hierarchical path of the calling component). Function **create_object()** creates a new object of type **obj_type** and name **inst_name**, assumed to be structurally contained in the component from which this function is called. Functions **set_inst_override()** and **set_type_override()** behave the same as functions in **ovm_factory** except that parameter **inst_path** passed to **set_inst_override()** of **ovm_component** is given relative to the hierarchical path of the component from which this method is called (i.e., parent component).

In OVM, the root of a component hierarchy represents a testcase that contains the verification environment, as well as any customization of this environment for that specific test. The top level component representing this test is created by calling global function **run_test()** (section 7.4). The name of the class representing the top level component is either passed directly to this function as an argument, or specified as a plus-argument (section 7.4.1). This function uses global function **create_component()** defined by OVM. This function can also be used directly to create a top level component when no other component yet exists:

```
Methods for class ovm_factory:
    static function ovm_component create_component (
        string comp_type, string inst_path="", string inst_name, ovm_component parent);
```

The following example shows the use of OVM factory to register and create verification environment blocks derived from class **ovm_component**, and examples of overrides that can be specified when using this factory. It should be noted that this example is provided to show the use of OVM factory features, and the creation of a verification environment hierarchy according to OVM guidelines is shown in section 13.6.

```
Program 6.6: OVM Component Factory Example
1    :    module top;
2    :        `include "ovm.svh"
3    :        `include "program_6.2"      // packet class
4    :        `include "program_6.4"      // derived packet classes
5    :
6    :        class child_comp extends ovm_component;
7    :            packet pkt[3];
8    :            `ovm_component_utils(child_comp)
9    :
10   :            function new (string name, ovm_component parent);
11   :                super.new(name, parent);
12   :                $cast(pkt[0], create_object("short_packet", "p1"));
13   :                $cast(pkt[1], create_object("long_packet", "p2"));
14   :                $cast(pkt[2], create_object("short_packet", "p3"));
15   :            endfunction
16   :        endclass
17   :
18   :        class root_comp extends ovm_component;
19   :            child_comp ccomp;
20   :            `ovm_component_utils(root_comp)
21   :
22   :            function new (string name, ovm_component parent);
23   :                super.new(name, parent);
24   :                set_inst_override("s1.p1", "short_packet", "long_packet");
25   :                set_type_override("long_packet", "short_packet");
26   :                $cast(ccomp, create_component("child_comp", "cc1"));
27   :            endfunction
28   :        endclass
29   :
30   :        root_comp rcomp;
31   :        initial
32   :            $cast(rcomp, ovm_factory::create_component("root_comp", "top", "rcomp", null));
33   :    endmodule
```

The above example defines class **child_comp** derived from class **ovm_component**. This class is registered with the OVM factory by using macro **ovm_component_utils()** (line 8). The predefined function **create_object()** of class **ovm_component** is used to create three instances of types **short_packet, long_packet,** and **short_packet** respectively (lines 12–14). Also note that the argument list for function **create_object()** of **ovm_component** is different from the one defined for the OVM factory (as shown in section 6.3.2) where it does not require the name of the containing component. The reason is that function **create_object()** of **ovm_component**, automatically uses the name of the calling component (i.e., parent component) as the name of the component containing the newly created object.

Class **root_comp** is also derived from **ovm_component** and contains an instance of the class **child_comp**. This class is registered with the OVM factory by using macro **ovm_component_utils()** (line 20). Functions **set_inst_override()** and **set_type_override()** of **ovm_component** are called in the constructor for class **root_comp** (lines 24, 25) before an instance of class **child_comp** is created by calling function **create_component()** of

ovm_component (line 26). Note that instance name for the instance override (line 24) is given relative to the calling component.

The top level component is created by calling function **create_component()** of the OVM factory (line 32). The name of the top level module is used as the instance path of this new component (i.e., **"top"**). Also, this is a top level component so the parent component is set to *null*.

It should be noted that the OVM class library provides a specialized mechanism for creating the component hierarchy corresponding to a verification environment, and the implementation shown in the above example is provided only to illustrate features of the OVM factory and the facilities it provides. Section 7.2 describes the steps for creating a component hierarchy following the OVM guidelines. Section 7.4 describes the mechanism used for instantiating the verification environment hierarchy which is done as part of running a test.

6.4 Field Automation

The implementation of core utilities of the OVM class library (e.g., copy, clone, etc.) is based on the concept of field automation. *Field automation* is a powerful feature that provides a declarative approach for specifying class fields that participate in operations such as copying, comparing, etc.

The following program shows an example of using field automation to decide which fields of a data packet should be printed when the predefined **print()** method of a packet derived from class **ovm_sequence_item** is called:

```
Program 6.7: Example of field automation printing fields
 1   :   module top;
 2   :         `include "ovm.svh"
 3   :         typedef enum {SHORT, LONG} packet_type;
 4   :         class simple_packet extends ovm_sequence_item;
 5   :              rand bit error;
 6   :              rand byte size;
 7   :              rand packet_type ptype;
 8   :              rand byte addr;
 9   :              rand int unsigned data[];
10   :              constraint payload_size {data.size() == size;}
11   :
12   :              `ovm_object_utils_begin(simple_packet)
13   :                   `ovm_field_int(size, OVM_NOPRINT)
14   :                   `ovm_field_enum(packet_type, ptype, OVM_PRINT)
15   :                   `ovm_field_int(addr, OVM_PRINT)
16   :                   `ovm_field_array_int(data, OVM_PRINT)
17   :              `ovm_object_utils_end
18   :         endclass
19   :
20   :         simple_packet pkt = new;
21   :         initial begin
22   :              void'(pkt.randomize() with {size == 4;});
23   :              pkt.print();
24   :         end
25   :   endmodule
```

This example shows the declaration of class **simple_packet** derived from base class **ovm_seqence_item**, containing fields **error, size, ptype, addr,** and **data** (lines 5–9). Field automation macros **ovm_field_int(), ovm_field_enum(),** and **ovm_field_array_int()** are used (lines 13–16) to specify that field **size** should not be printed but fields **ptype, addr,** and **data** should be printed when method **print()** (predefined for class **ovm_object**) is called (line 23). No macro is specified for field **error**, and therefore, this field does *not* participate in field automation at all. For all classes derived from **ovm_object**, field automation macros should be placed inside predefined macro pair **ovm_object_utils_begin()** and **ovm_object_utils_end** (lines 12 and 17).

The OVM class library provides field automation macros for different types of fields. Table 6.1 shows a summary of field automation macros and the type of fields that are supported.

Field Kind		Field Automation Macro Prototype	Element Type
Scalar		`ovm_field_int (FIELD, FLAG)	any integral type (no enum)
		`ovm_field_enum (TYPE, FIELD, FLAG)	enum type
		`ovm_field_object (FIELD, FLAG)	derived from ovm_object
		`ovm_field_string (FIELD, FLAG)	string
Static Array		`ovm_field_sarray_int (FIELD, FLAG)	any integral type (no enum)
		`ovm_field_sarray_object (FIELD, FLAG)	derived from ovm_object
		`ovm_field_sarray_string (FIELD, FLAG)	string
Dynamic Array		`ovm_field_array_int (FIELD, FLAG)	any integral type (no enum)
		`ovm_field_array_object (FIELD, FLAG)	derived from ovm_object
		`ovm_field_array_string (FIELD, FLAG)	string
Queue		`ovm_field_queue_int (FIELD, FLAG)	any integral type
		`ovm_field_queue_object (FIELD, FLAG)	derived from ovm_object
		`ovm_field_queue_string (FIELD, FLAG)	string
Associative Array	key: integral	`ovm_field_aa_string_int (FIELD, FLAG)	string
		`ovm_field_aa_object_int (FIELD, FLAG)	derived from ovm_object
	key: string	`ovm_field_aa_int_string (FIELD, FLAG)	any integral type
		`ovm_field_aa_object_string (FIELD, FLAG)	derived from ovm_object
		`ovm_field_aa_string_string (FIELD, FLAG)	string
	key: Note 1	`ovm_field_aa_int_<key_type> (FIELD, FLAG)	any integral type
Note1: <key_type> can be one of: int, integer, int_unsigned, integer_unsigned, byte, byte_unsigned, shortint, shortint_unsigned, longint, longint_unsigned. Note2: Fields handled by ovm_field_int() must be packed integral fields of at most 4096 bits			

Table 6.1: Field Automation Macros

Field automation attributes (argument **FLAG** in table 6.1) are used to include or exclude fields from the set of predefined operations. These attributes are shown in table 6.2. Multiple attributes can be specified by combining attributes using the bitwise-OR operator (e.g., "**OVM_ALL_ON | OVM_DEC**"). Alternatively, attributes can be added arithmetically, but adding the same attribute multiple times will result in unexpected behavior (e.g., "**OVM_ALL_ON + OVM_DEC + OVM_READONLY**").

Feature	Attribute	Description
Copy	OVM_COPY	Copy this field (default)
	OVM_NOCOPY	Do not copy this field
Compare	OVM_COMPARE	Compare this field (default)
	OVM_NOCOMPARE	Do not compare this field
Print	OVM_PRINT	Print this field (default)
	OVM_NOPRINT	Do not print this field
	OVM_NODEFPRINT	Do not print the field if it is the same as its default value
	OVM_BIN, OVM_DEC, OVM_UNSIGNED, OVM_OCT, OVM_HEX, OVM_STRING, OVM_TIME, OVM_NORADIX	Radix settings for integral types (default: OVM_HEX)
Pack/Unpack	OVM_PACK	Pack and unpack this field (default)
	OVM_NOPACK	Do not pack/unpack this field
	OVM_PHYSICAL	Treat as a physical field
	OVM_ABSTRACT	Treat as an abstract field
Misc	OVM_READONLY	Do not apply configuration settings (section 7.2)
	OVM_ALL_ON	Set all operations on (default)
	OVM_DEFAULT	Use the default flag settings

Table 6.2: Field Automation Attributes

The OVM class library defines composite attributes in order to simplify the setting of common combinations of field automation attributes. These composite attributes are shown in table 6.3.

Predefined Flags	OVM_COPY	OVM_NOCOPY	OVM_COMPARE	OVM_NOCOMPARE	OVM_PRINT	OVM_NOPRINT	OVM_RECORD	OVM_NORECORD	OVM_PACK	OVM_NOPACK	OVM_DEEP	OVM_SHALLOW	OVM_REFERENCE	OVM_PHYSICAL	OVM_ABSTRACT
OVM_DEFAULT	☑		☑		☑		☑		☑		☑			☑	☑
OVM_ALL_ON	☑		☑		☑		☑							☑	☑
OVM_FLAGS_ON	☑		☑		☑		☑		☑						
OVM_FLAGS_OFF															

Table 6.3: Field Automation Composite Attributes

6.5 Core Utilities

The OVM class library provides the following core utilities for class **ovm_object**:

- Copy
- Clone
- Compare

- Print
- Pack/Unpack

Object cloning is implemented by creating a new object and using the copy utility to set the contents of the newly created object to the contents of the source object. Copy, compare, print, and pack/unpack utilities are described in the following subsections.

6.5.1 Copy

OVM defines the following predefined methods to support the copy operation for classes derived from **ovm_object**:

```
Methods defined for class ovm_object:
    function void copy (ovm_object rhs)
    virtual function void do_copy (ovm_object rhs)
```

Function **copy()** is used to copy all automated fields of **rhs** that are configured to participate in the copy operation. The recursion behavior of this function is controlled by the recursion policy for object fields (e.g., **OVM_SHALLOW, OVM_REFERENCE**). Function **do_copy()** provides a callback mechanism for handling fields of **rhs** that require special handling, or are not configured by field automation macros to be included in the copy operation.

The following program shows an example of using these predefined functions:

```
Program 6.8: Using copy() and do_copy()
1  :   module top;
2  :       `include "ovm.svh"
3  :
4  :       class payload extends ovm_sequence_item;
5  :           rand byte capacity;
6  :           rand byte size;
7  :
8  :           `ovm_object_utils_begin(payload)
9  :               `ovm_field_int(capacity, OVM_ALL_ON|OVM_NOCOPY)
10 :               `ovm_field_int(size, OVM_ALL_ON)
11 :           `ovm_object_utils_end
12 :
13 :           function void do_copy (ovm_object rhs);
14 :               payload pl; $cast(pl,rhs); // rhs is guaranteed to be non-null
15 :               if (pl.capacity < 10) capacity = pl.capacity;
16 :               size = 100; // size will be over-written by automated field copy
17 :           endfunction
18 :       endclass
19 :
20 :       class hier_packet extends ovm_sequence_item;
21 :           time collection_time;
22 :           rand byte addr;
23 :           rand payload pload = new;
24 :
25 :           `ovm_object_utils_begin(hier_packet)
26 :               `ovm_field_int(addr, OVM_ALL_ON)
27 :               `ovm_field_object(pload, OVM_ALL_ON)
28 :           `ovm_object_utils_end
29 :       endclass
30 :
31 :       hier_packet pkt1 = new;
32 :       hier_packet pkt2 = new;
33 :       initial begin
34 :           void'(pkt1.randomize());
```

```
35  :            pkt2.copy(pkt1);
36  :       end
37  :    endmodule
```

This example shows the implementation of hierarchical object **hier_packet** having fields **collection_time**, **addr**, and **pload**. Field **collection_time** is not automated, but fields **addr** and **pload** are both automated for all operations by using attribute **OVM_ALL_ON** (lines 26, 27). Field **pload** is an instance of class **payload** having fields **capacity** and **size**. Both fields **capacity** and **size** are automated for printing (lines 9, 10), but **capacity** is excluded from the automated copy operation (line 9) since it should be copied only if its value is less than **10**. Function **do_copy()** of class **payload** is defined to perform this conditional copy operation for field **capacity**. Note that function argument **rhs** should be casted to the derived type **payload** (line 14) so that access to the fields of the derived type are possible. Function **do_copy()** is called before automated copy operations take place, therefore writing to fields that are automated for copy operation (line 16) will not be visible outside this function.

6.5.2 Compare

OVM defines the following predefined methods to support the compare operation for classes derived from **ovm_object**:

```
Compare Methods defined for class ovm_object:
    function bit compare (ovm_object rhs, ovm_comparer comparer=null);
    function bit do_compare (ovm_object rhs, ovm_comparer comparer);
```

Function **compare()** is used to compare all automated fields of **rhs** that are configured to be included in the compare operation. The recursion behavior of this function is controlled by the recursion policy for object fields (e.g., **OVM_SHALLOW**, **OVM_REFERENCE**). Function **do_compare()** provides a callback mechanism for handling fields of **rhs** that require special handling or are not configured by field automation macros to be included in the compare operation.

The following program shows an example of using these functions:

```
Program 6.9: Field automation for compare, and using do_compare()
1   :    class simple_packet extends ovm_sequence_item;
2   :         rand byte addr;
3   :         rand byte data;
4   :
5   :         `ovm_object_utils_begin(simple_packet)
6   :             `ovm_field_int(addr, OVM_ALL_ON|OVM_NOCOMPARE)
7   :             `ovm_field_int(data, OVM_ALL_ON)
8   :         `ovm_object_utils_end
9   :
10  :         function bit do_compare(ovm_object rhs, ovm_comparer comparer);
11  :             simple_packet pkt;
12  :             $cast(pkt, rhs); // rhs is guaranteed to be non-null
13  :             do_compare = (data == 1) ? 1 : (addr != pkt.addr);
14  :         endfunction
15  :    endclass
```

This example shows the implementation of class **simple_packet** having fields **addr** and **data**. Both fields are automated (lines 6, 7) but field **addr** is not included in the automated compare operation (line 6). The implementation of **do_compare()** for this class compares the values for **addr** only if **data** has a value of 1 (lines 10–14).

The use of compare operation is shown in the following program:

```
Program 6.10: Comparing two objects using the built-in function compare()
1   :   module top;
2   :       `include "ovm.svh"
3   :       `include "program_6.9"      // simple_packet class
4   :
5   :       simple_packet pkt1 = new;
6   :       simple_packet pkt2 = new;
7   :       initial begin
8   :           `message(OVM_LOW, (pkt2.compare(pkt1)))
9   :       end
10  :   endmodule
```

The compare operation is carried out by calling the compare function of one of the objects with the other object as its argument (line 8). Generally, the compare operation is symmetric. This means that function **compare()** of either of the two objects being compared can be called with the other object as an argument. In this example, however, the compare operation is not symmetric because of the special implementation of function **do_compare()** where the value of field **data** of the calling object is used to guide the compare operation.

The compare operation makes use of compare policy object **ovm_comparer**. This object contains settings for guiding the compare operation, as well as predefined methods for comparing objects or fields (one method for each type). It is possible to define a new policy object that redefines the settings of the default comparer and hence achieve a modified compare behavior. The following program shows an example of using a modified **ovm_comparer** object:

```
Program 6.11: Using a modified ovm_comparer
1   :   module top;
2   :       `include "ovm.svh"
3   :       `include "program_6.9"      // simple_packet class
4   :
5   :       class custom_comparer extends ovm_comparer;
6   :           int unsigned show_max = 1;           // Maximum miscompares to print
7   :           int unsigned verbosity = 500;        // Verbosity setting for miscompare
8   :           ovm_severity sev = OVM_INFO;         // Severity setting for miscompare
9   :           string miscompares = "";             // Last set of miscompares
10  :           bit physical = 1;                    // compare physical fields
11  :           bit abstract = 1;                    // compare abstract fields
12  :           bit check_type = 1;                  // verify that object types match
13  :           ovm_recursion_policy_enum policy = OVM_DEFAULT_POLICY;
14  :       endclass
15  :
16  :       custom_comparer cc = new;
17  :       simple_packet pkt1 = new;
18  :       simple_packet pkt2 = new;
19  :       initial begin
20  :           cc.show_max = 0;
21  :           `message(OVM_LOW, (pkt2.compare(pkt1, cc)))
22  :       end
23  :   endmodule
```

In this example, class **custom_comparer** is derived from **ovm_comparer**. For illustration purposes, the definition of this derived class lists properties that are available in class **ovm_comparer** and their default settings. The setting for these properties can be changed either during class definition (lines 5–14) or before the policy object is passed to the compare operation (line 21). In this example, field **show_max** of the compare policy object is set to zero so that no compare results are printed, and only the result of calling function **compare()** (line 21) is shown.

6.5.3 Print

OVM defines the following predefined methods to support the print operation for classes derived from **ovm_object**:

```
Print Methods defined for class ovm_object:
    function void print (ovm_printer printer=null)
    function string sprint (ovm_printer printer=null)
    virtual function void do_print (ovm_printer printer)
```

Function **print()** is used to print all automated fields of the calling object that are configured to be included in the print operation. Function **print()** recursively calls the **print()** function of all automated fields that are objects derived from base class **ovm_object**. Function **sprint()** is the same as **print()** except that it returns a string instead of printing the result to the screen. Function **do_print()** provides a callback mechanism for handling fields of the calling object that require special handling or are not configured by field automation macros to be included in the print operation. The use of **print()** and **do_print()** functions is similar to the use model for the copy operation.

The print operation makes use of print policy object **ovm_printer**. This policy object contains settings for controlling the print operation, as well as predefined methods that customize the way object data is printed. It is possible to define a new print policy object that redefines the settings of the default printer and hence achieves a modified print behavior. The following print policy objects are automatically created by loading the OVM class library:

- Global object **ovm_default_printer** (initialized to **ovm_default_table_printer**)
- Global object **ovm_default_line_printer** of type **ovm_line_printer**
- Global object **ovm_default_tree_printer** of type **ovm_tree_printer**
- Global object **ovm_default_table_printer** of type **ovm_table_printer**

If no printer policy object is passed to print functions (i.e., **print()** and **sprint()**), then the global printer **ovm_default_printer** is used by default. Each printer policy object contains field **knobs** that can be used for customizing the printer output. Table 6.4 shows a summary of knob properties that can be configured.

The implementation of the print utility allows the output of print functions to either follow the global setting of the printer policy object or to be customized depending on the local requirements. Local customizations are done by instantiating a local copy of a printer policy object and then modifying its properties before passing it explicitly to the print function. The printer policy object that is passed to callback function **do_print()** is the same printer policy object that is provided as argument to the print functions.

Type	Field Name	Default Value	Description
Class ovm_printer_knobs:			
int	column	0	Current column the printer is writing to.
int	max_width	999	Do not print anything beyond this column number.
string	truncation	"+"	Append this string to end of truncated fields.
bit	header	1	Print a header if set to 1.
bit	footer	1	Print a footer if set to 1.
int	global_indent	0	Indent size at the beginning of each new line.
bit	full_name	1	xx
bit	identifier	1	Print field identifiers if set to 1.
int	depth	-1	How many levels of objects to print (-1 means all).
bit	reference	1	Print object pointer value if set to 1.
bit	type_name	1	Print field type name if set to 1.
bit	size	1	Print field sizes if set to 1.
int	begin_elements	5	Print this many elements from the beginning of array.
int	end_elements	5	Print this many elements from the end of array.
bit	show_radix	1	Show radix in printed values if set to 1.
int	mcd	OVM_STDOUT	File pointer where the print result is sent.
radix_enum	default_radix	OVM_HEX	Formatting text when using OVM_NORADIX radix
string	bin_radix	"'b"	Formatting text when using OVM_BIN radix
string	oct_radix	"'o"	Formatting text when using OVM_OCT radix
string	dec_radix	"'d"	Formatting text when using OVM_DEC radix
string	unsigned_radix	"'d"	Formatting text when using OVM_UNSIGNED radix
string	hex_radix	"'h"	Formatting text when using OVM_BIN radix
Class ovm_hier_printer_knobs derived from ovm_printer_knobs:			
string	indent_str	" " (2 spaces)	String to use for each indentation level.
bit	show_root	0	Print the root object where printing is started.
Class ovm_table_printer_knobs derived from ovm_hier_printer_knobs:			
int	name_width	25	Name column width (not printed if set to 0).
int	type_width	20	Type column width (not printed if set to 0).
int	size_width	5	Size column width (not printed if set to 0).
int	value_width	20	Value column width (not printed if set to 0).
Class ovm_tree_printer_knobs derived from ovm_hier_printer_knobs:			
string	separator	"{}"	Place each tree level string inside these two characters.

Table 6.4: Printer Knob Configuration Fields

The following program shows examples of changing the default printer object, as well as creating local printer objects:

Program 6.12: Using printer policy objects with print() method

```
1  :    module top;
2  :        `include "ovm.svh"
3  :        class simple_packet extends ovm_sequence_item;
4  :            rand byte addr;
5  :            rand byte data;
6  :
7  :            `ovm_object_utils_begin(simple_packet)
8  :                `ovm_field_int(addr, OVM_ALL_ON)
9  :                `ovm_field_int(data, OVM_ALL_ON|OVM_NOPRINT)
10 :            `ovm_object_utils_end
```

```
11  :          endclass
12  :
13  :          ovm_line_printer local_line_printer = new;
14  :          ovm_tree_printer local_tree_printer = new;
15  :          ovm_table_printer local_table_printer = new;
16  :
17  :          simple_packet pkt = new;
18  :          initial begin
19  :               //ovm_default_printer = ovm_default_table_printer; //default, so not needed.
20  :               pkt.print();
21  :               ovm_default_printer = ovm_default_line_printer;
22  :               pkt.print();
23  :               ovm_default_printer = ovm_default_tree_printer;
24  :               pkt.print();
25  :               local_table_printer.knobs.type_width = 20;
26  :               local_table_printer.knobs.value_width = 20;
27  :               pkt.print(local_table_printer);
28  :          end
29  :   endmodule
```

This example shows the definition of class **simple_packet** with fields **data** and **addr**, where automation macros are used to include **addr** in (line 8) and exclude **data** from (line 9) the print output. This example shows the creation of local printer objects **local_line_printer**, **local_tree_printer**, and **local_table_printer** (lines 13–15). These objects can be modified locally to change the default print behavior. By default, **ovm_default_printer**, is assigned to **ovm_default_table_printer** (line 19). Calling **print()** without any arguments results in using **ovm_default_printer** (line 20). The global default printer is assigned to the global default line printer **ovm_default_line_printer** (line 21). Therefore, calling function **print()** on line 22 results in **ovm_default_line_printer** being used as the default printer. The customization of printer knobs (table 6.4) for the local printer object **local_table_printer** is shown on lines 25 and 26. When calling **print()** with this local printer object (line 27), this customized local printer object is used instead of the global default printer object.

6.5.4 Packing and Unpacking

The OVM class library provides the following functions, defined for class **ovm_object**, for packing and unpacking of a class object:

```
Methods defined for class ovm_object:
     function int pack (ref bit bitstream[], input ovm_packer packer=null);
     function int unpack (ref bit bitstream[], input ovm_packer packer=null);
Callback methods defined for class ovm_object:
     virtual function void do_pack (ovm_packer   packer);
     virtual function void do_unpack (ovm_packer   packer);
```

Calling function **pack()** of a class object appends the packed contents of this object to bit array **bitstream**. The contents of the class object are packed according to the settings of, and by using the helper functions provided in, **packer**. Function **pack()** first processes all automated fields of a class object, followed by executing virtual callback function **do_pack()** to perform any special handling required by the model being implemented.

Calling function **unpack()** of a class object unpacks the contents of bit array bitstream into the class object. The unpacking is performed according to the settings of, and by using the helper functions provided in, **packer**. As with function **pack()**, function **unpack()** first processes automated fields of the class object, followed by executing virtual callback function **do_unpack()** to perform any special handling required by the model being implemented.

The packing and unpacking utility of the OVM class library is implemented using the helper functions provided by the class **ovm_packer**. This class provides the following methods for packing and unpacking data types:

```
Methods defined for class ovm_packer:
        virtual function void pack_field_int (logic[63:0] value, int size);
        virtual function void pack_field (bitstream_t value, int size);
        virtual function void pack_string (string value);
        virtual function void pack_time (time value);
        virtual function void pack_real (real value);
        virtual function void pack_object (ovm_void value);
        virtual function logic[63:0] unpack_field_int (int size);
        virtual function bitstream_t unpack_field (int size);
        virtual function string unpack_string ();
        virtual function time unpack_time ();
        virtual function real unpack_real ();
        virtual function void unpack_object (ovm_void value);
        virtual function int get_packed_size();
        virtual function bit is_null ();
```

In the remainder of this section, an example is shown where these helper functions are used in the definition of callback functions **do_pack()** and **do_unpack()** to pack and unpack a class object. The example shown in this section does not show any automated fields, but any field that is automated for packing and unpacking is processed using the same helper functions shown explicitly in this example. Class fields are included in and excluded from packing and unpacking by using automation attributes **OVM_PACK** and **OVM_NOPACK**, respectively (table 6.2). It should be noted that all automated fields are processed before a callback function is executed.

The following program shows the definition of two class objects that will be used to describe the packing and unpacking mechanism of the OVM class library:

```
     Program 6.13: Example classes to be packed and unpacked
 1  :   class scalars extends ovm_object;
 2  :       string addr;
 3  :       time days;
 4  :       real prob;
 5  :       byte bits_0008;
 6  :       bit [1023:0] bits_1024;
 7  :
 8  :       extern function void do_pack (ovm_packer packer);
 9  :       extern function void do_unpack (ovm_packer packer);
10  :   endclass
11  :
12  :   class composites extends ovm_object;
13  :       string string_array[];
14  :       scalars one_obj = new;
15  :       scalars obj_array[];
16  :
17  :       extern function void do_unpack (ovm_packer packer);
18  :       extern function void do_pack (ovm_packer packer);
19  :   endclass
```

This program shows the implementation of classes **scalars** and **composites**, each containing the different types of class fields that may need to be packed or unpacked. Callback functions **do_pack()** and **do_unpack()** are defined as *extern* functions that must be defined as part of this implementation (lines 8–9, 17–18).

The implementation of function **do_pack()** for classes **scalars** and **composites** is shown in the following program:

```
Program 6.14: Implementation of do_pack()
1   :    function void scalars::do_pack (ovm_packer packer);
2   :        packer.pack_string(addr);
3   :        packer.pack_time(days);
4   :        packer.pack_real(prob);
5   :        packer.pack_field_int(bits_0008, $bits(bits_0008));
6   :        packer.pack_field(bits_1024, $bits(bits_1024));
7   :    endfunction
8   :
9   :    function void composites::do_pack (ovm_packer packer);
10  :        int unsigned arr_size;
11  :
12  :        arr_size = string_array.size();
13  :        packer.pack_field_int(arr_size, $bits(arr_size));
14  :        for (int i=0; i<arr_size; i++)
15  :            packer.pack_string(string_array[i]);
16  :
17  :        packer.pack_object(one_obj);
18  :
19  :        arr_size = obj_array.size();
20  :        packer.pack_field_int(arr_size, $bits(arr_size));
21  :        for (int i=0; i<arr_size; i++)
22  :            packer.pack_object(obj_array[i]);
23  :    endfunction
```

Class **scalars** contains only non-composite fields, and the packing of each of its fields into the packer object **packer** passed into this function is shown above (lines 2–6). In packing integral fields, function **pack_field()** is used to pack an integral field of any size up to **4096** bits, and function **pack_field_int()** is used to pack fields of at most **64** bits. In this implementation, SystemVerilog system function *$bits()* is used to get the number of bits in variables **bits_0008** and **bits_1024** (lines 5, 6).

Packing composite fields is shown for class **composites** (lines 9–23). The convention in packing an array is to first pack the size of this array as an integer and then pack each member of this array. This process is shown for array **string_array** (lines 12–15). First the size of array is packed using function **pack_field_int()** (line 13) and then each member of the array is packed using function **pack_string()** (line 15). The packed size value will be used during the unpacking process.

A single object is packed using function **pack_object()**. Calling function **pack_object()** on field **one_obj** results in calling function **do_pack()** of that object (lines 1–7). The packing of an object array (lines 19–22) follows the same flow as that of **string_array**.

The implementation of function **do_unpack()** of classes **scalars** and **composites** is shown in the following program:

```
Program 6.15: Implementation of do_unpack()
1   :    function void scalars::do_unpack (ovm_packer packer);
2   :        addr = packer.unpack_string();
3   :        days = packer.unpack_time();
4   :        prob = packer.unpack_real();
```

```
5  :          bits_0008 = packer.unpack_field_int($bits(bits_0008));
6  :          bits_1024 = packer.unpack_field($bits(bits_1024));
7  :     endfunction
8  :
9  :     function void composites::do_unpack (ovm_packer packer);
10 :          int unsigned arr_size;
11 :
12 :          arr_size = packer.unpack_field_int($bits(arr_size));
13 :          for (int i=0; i<arr_size; i++)
14 :              string_array[i] = packer.unpack_string();
15 :
16 :          if (one_obj != null)
17 :              packer.unpack_object(one_obj);
18 :
19 :          arr_size = packer.unpack_field_int($bits(arr_size));
20 :          for (int i=0; i<arr_size; i++)
21 :              obj_array[i] = new();
22 :              packer.unpack_object(obj_array[i]);
23 :          end
24 :     endfunction
```

The implementation of **do_unpack()** for class **scalars** shows the unpacking of values from packer object **packer** in the same order that these objects were packed (lines 1–7). Also, the implementation of the unpacking process for composite objects in class **composties** follows the same order that these objects were packed (lines 9–24). Array **string_array** is unpacked by first unpacking the size of this array (line 12) and then using a loop to unpack each member of this array. Calling function **unpack_object()** on field **one_obj** results in calling function **do_unpack()** of class **scalars** (lines 1–7). The unpacking of an object array (lines 19–22) follows the same flow of unpacking arrays.

The use of packing and unpacking functions is shown in the following program:

```
     Program 6.16: Calling pack() and unpack() functions
1  :     module top;
2  :          `include "ovm.svh"
3  :          `include "program_6.13"    // declarations of scalars and composites
4  :          `include "program_6.14"    // do_pack() functions
5  :          `include "program_6.15"    // do_unpack() functions
6  :
7  :          composites cmpst1 = new;
8  :          composites cmpst2 = new;
9  :          bit stream[];
10 :          initial begin
11 :              // populate fields of cmpst1 with arrays and values.
12 :              void'(cmpst1.pack(stream));
13 :              `message(OVM_LOW, (stream.size()))
14 :              void'(cmpst2.unpack(stream));
15 :          end
16 :     endmodule
```

This program shows that object **cmpst₁** is packed by calling its predefined function **pack()** (line 12). The resulting stream is then unpacked into **cmpst₂** by calling its predefined function **unpack()** (line 14). Calling functions **pack()** and **unpack()** in turn calls the hook methods **do_pack()** and **do_unpack()** respectively.

In most applications, a data object is packed so that the packed bit stream can be applied to a DUV interface. Similarly, unpacking is needed where a class object must be populated by the bit stream collected from a DUV interface. In such cases, it is important that the unpacking flow mirrors the steps taken for collecting data from the environment, and that the packing process satisfies the format needed for applying the packed stream into the DUV interface.

6.5.4.1 Packing and Unpacking of Automated Fields

Automating class fields allows these fields to automatically be included in the packing and unpacking processes. The internal implementation of field automation for packing and unpacking mirrors the flow described in this section. During the packing process, first, automated fields of a class object are packed and then its callback function **do_pack()** is called. During the unpacking process, first automated fields of a class object are unpacked and then its callback function **do_unpack()** is called.

6.5.4.2 Packing and Unpacking Metadata

An important assumption about the default behavior of packing and unpacking of automated object fields is that an object is packed if it is not null, and a bit stream is unpacked into an object if that object is not null. This means that before unpacking into a class object, all its fields that are also class object must be initialized to non-null values.

The OVM packer class **ovm_packer** defines field **use_metadata** which is set to false by default. When this field is set to true, it causes metadata to be added to a packed stream when automated dynamic fields are packed. Metadata is collected for the following dynamic elements:

- Strings
- Class objects
- Arrays

When packing strings with an active **use_metadata** flag, a null byte is added after a string is packed. This behavior is intended to duplicate the string handling behavior of the C language where each string is terminated with a null byte.

When packing a class object with an active **use_metadata** flag, four bits are packed before an object is packed, indicating whether the object has a null value. During unpacking, function **is_null()** can be used to check the value of these bits and to decide if an object should be allocated and unpacked into. In contrast with default behavior of the unpack operation (i.e., when **use_metadata** is set to false. and where all objects that are unpacked into must be allocated before unpacking is started), this feature allows object allocation to be decided during the unpacking process.

When packing arrays with an active **use_metadata** flag, a 32 bits value indicating the size of the array is packed before array contents are packed. The same field is used during the unpacking process of automated fields to resize the array before is members are unpacked into.

It is important that the same setting for field **use_metadata** be used for packing and unpacking of the same object.

CHAPTER 7   *OVM Component Hierarchy*

In a class-based verification environment, it is possible to build the environment hierarchy during simulation runtime since class objects representing components can be created after simulation has been started. This ability is in contrast with an RTL design or a module-based verification environment where the hierarchy is modeled with module blocks leading to a fixed structure before simulation runtime is started.

The ability to create the verification environment hierarchy during simulation runtime leads to great flexibility in how the verification environment can be created. Taking advantage of this flexibility, however, requires that a consistent approach be followed during hierarchy creation, and that a powerful infrastructure for effective implementation of this consistent approach is available.

This chapter describes the features provided by the OVM class library for building the verification environment hierarchy and managing simulation phases of components in this hierarchy. Section 7.1 provides an abstract view of hierarchical components and objects, and principles that must be followed when building the environment hierarchy. Section 7.2 describes the constructs provided by the OVM class library for building the environment hierarchy and shows a detailed example of hierarchy construction for an environment containing the types of cases that can be handled by these constructs. Section 7.3 describes the predefined class types provided by the OVM class library for building different components in a verification environment. Section 7.4 introduces the predefined simulation phases of the OVM class library and describes the constructs provided for activating and controlling the execution of these phases.

7.1 Abstract View of the Component Hierarchy

Guidelines for creating the environment component hierarchy is in part related to the principles of object-oriented programming. These guidelines are:

- Self-containment
- Recursive construction

.   • Configurability

Self-containment guideline refers to the need that a component behavior or implementation be independent of any value not contained within its sub-hierarchy. This guideline is a necessary requirement for achieving component reuse. The need for port-based connectivity is a direct result of enforcing the self-containment guideline (see section 9.7 on transaction interfaces). A clear example of where this guideline must be strictly enforced is in the implementation of a verification component.

Recursive construction refers to how the hierarchy is created. In this approach, each parent component builds only its immediate children components, and the children components in turn, build their own immediate children components. The recursive nature of this approach leads to the creation of the full hierarchy where each parent component is created before its child components are created. During this recursive construction process, the build method of each component follows these steps:

• Local fields that can locally be decided are initialized (e.g., default values).
• Local hierarchy configuration fields (usually set to default values and initialized by parent components as needed) are used to decide which children components must be created.
• Each child component is created and then the child component's build mechanism is activated to build its sub-hierarchy.
• Local fields that must be decided by the contents of children components and their sub-hierarchies are initialized.
• Transaction interfaces that must link children components are connected.

Configurability refers to the ability for a component to configure the structure and behavior of its component sub-hierarchy. The need for this ability is a direct consequence of enforcing the self-containment guideline, since self-containment implies that a child component is not aware of its parent component, and as such, configuration information should be passed from the higher layers of the hierarchy to the lower layers of the hierarchy. When using the recursive construction approach, the configurability challenge is that when a component is starting to build its children components, the sub-hierarchy rooted at these children components has not yet been created and, therefore, configuration fields within this sub-hierarchy do not yet exist. This means that a dedicated mechanism is required for controlling configuration fields deep within the sub-hierarchy when the sub-hierarchy is recursively constructed. Support for this feature is provided in the OVM class library.

Figure 7.1 shows a graphical view of verification environment elements from the perspective of hierarchy construction. A hierarchical component may contain any of the following elements:

• Fields
    • Regular
    • Hierarchy configuration
    • Behavior configuration
• Children components
    • Fixed components
    • Conditional components
    • Reference components

- Children objects
  - Source objects
  - Cloned objects
  - Reference objects

A *regular field* is used for the internal operation of a component. A *hierarchy configuration field* is used to decide the hierarchical structure of a component (e.g., passive/active flag in an interface verification component indicating whether or not an agent should contain a driver and sequencer). A *behavior configuration field* is used to control the behavior of the component (e.g., how many packets to generate in a sequencer). Hierarchy and behavior configuration fields are set to default values and then initialized by parent components during hierarchy construction.

A *fixed child component* is always present in the component hierarchy (e.g., the monitor in an interface verification component). A *conditional child component* is present if indicated by a hierarchy configuration field (e.g., sequencer and driver components are present only in an active interface verification component). A *reference child component* is in fact a pointer to a component that is physically located at a different level of the hierarchy (e.g., components at the lower level of the hierarchy need to access components that sit at higher layers of the hierarchy).

A *source child object* is a container of a collection of data items (e.g., configuration settings). A source child object is referred to as "source" since it is neither cloned nor a reference and hence contains the source of its content. A *cloned child object* is created by cloning another object that is physically located at a higher level of the hierarchy (e.g., copying the global configuration object to the local scope for local use and modification). A *reference child object* is in fact a pointer to an object that is physically located at a different level of the hierarchy (e.g., a reference to the global configuration object may be made available in the lower layers of the hierarchy).

Figure 7.1 shows examples of these fields, objects, and component types. For example, **TOP_COMP** is a fixed component that is physically located in the top level of the hierarchy, and **RefTOP_COMP** components in **SystemComp** and **ModuleComp** components are both reference components that point at fixed component **TOP_COMP**. Also, source object **GlobConf** is a configuration object that is physically located in the top level of the hierarchy, and **RefGlobConf** objects in **SystemComp** and **ModuleComp** are both reference objects that point to source object **GlobConf** in the top level of the hierarchy. Also, field **HierFlag** is a hierarchical configuration field in component **ModuleComp** whose value should come form field **GlobFlag** in the top level of the hierarchy.

The arrows that point from each layer of the hierarchy to the lower layers indicate the required order of construction. For example, at the top level of the hierarchy, object **GlobConf**, component **TOP_COMP**, and field **GlobFlag** control the content and structure of the hierarchy rooted at component **SystemComp**, and must therefore be created before component **SystemComp** is created. The relationships shown by arrows in figure 7.1 are specified using the configuration construct of the OVM class library. The next section introduces the constructs provided by the OVM class library for creating and configuring a component hierarchy.

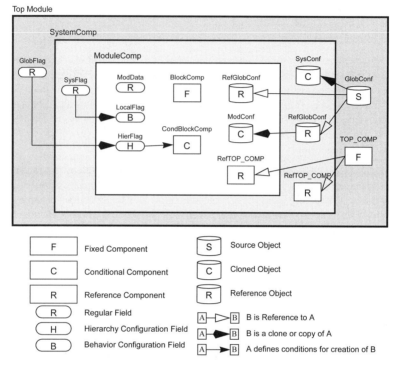

Figure 7.1 Hierarchical Components, Objects, and Fields

7.2 Hierarchy and Configuration Constructs

In the OVM class library, class **ovm_component** provides the necessary facilities for building a component hierarchy. Class **ovm_threaded_component** derived from **ovm_component**, in turn, provides the necessary facilities for controlling the runtime behavior of these hierarchical components (section 7.4). The predefined verification environment components of the OVM class library (e.g., **ovm_monitor**, section 7.3) are derived from **ovm_threaded_component**. This means that the features of classes **ovm_component** and **ovm_threaded_component** are available to all predefined verification environment components of the OVM class library.

The OVM provides specific guidelines for using its predefined verification environment components to build a verification environment hierarchy. A complete example showing this flow is provided in section 13.6. This section, however, uses class **ovm_component** to illustrate the general steps for building and configuring a component hierarchy. The techniques described in this section are then used with all classes derived from class **ovm_component**.

Hierarchical building and configuration of components is supported through the following methods:

```
Methods Defined for class ovm_component:
    function void build();
    function void set_config_int(string inst_name, string field_name, ovm_bitstream_t value);
    function void set_config_object(string inst_name, string field_name, ovm_object value,bit clone=1);
    function void set_config_string(string inst_name, string field_name, string value);

Global Methods:
    function void set_config_int(string inst_name, string field_name, ovm_bitstream_t value);
    function void set_config_object(string inst_name, string field_name, ovm_object value, bit clone=1);
    function void set_config_string(string inst_name, string field_name, string value);
```

The steps for building the contents of a component are implemented in function **build()** of that component. Configuration functions **set_config_*()** provide a name-based approach for setting fields within sub-components that are not yet created. An instance name **inst_name** and a field name **field_name** are specified with each configuration function. As the hierarchy is created, configuration settings are applied if the instance name and a field name in the newly created component match one of the configuration settings specified before the component was created. Configuration setting functions allow fields of integral type, string type, and **ovm_object** type to be configured. Function **set_config_object()** additionally provides argument **clone** that indicates whether a field should be set to either a reference or a copy of the argument specified with argument **value** of function **set_config_object()**. Global functions corresponding to configuration functions of class **ovm_component** are provided in order to allow configurations to be set at the top-most level of hierarchy where no component of type **ovm_component** is yet created. The following comments apply to component configuration usage:

- Configuration functions can manage only automated fields (section 6.4).
- Instance name and field name arguments (i.e., **inst_name**, **field_name**) may optionally include wild-card characters "*****" and "**?**" allowing the same configuration setting to be applied to different fields within the same component and/or to different components across the sub-hierarchy.
- Base class **ovm_component** is defined in a way that configuration settings for a component instance are applied as part of calling function **build()** of that instance. As such, using function **build()** is mandatory for having the configuration settings for an instance to take effect. A consequence of this implementation is that all configuration settings for a component instance have been applied by the time its function **build()** is called, and therefore these settings can be used during the building of the sub-hierarchy rooted at that instance.
- The argument **inst_name** specified with each configuration function is assumed to be relative to the hierarchical path of the component from which it is called.
- Configuration settings in a higher scope take precedence to the ones in a lower scope by default. The reason for this ordering is to allow configuration settings at the higher layers of the hierarchy to override those specified at the lower layers.
- Within the same scope, the last configuration setting matching a field takes precedence over previous settings for the same field.

The use of configuration functions is illustrated by showing the construction of the component hierarchy shown in figure 7.1. Even though the component hierarchy is built recursively from top to bottom, the implementation of the program that creates this hierarchy is started from the lowest level of the hierarchy. These steps are shown in the remainder of this section.

The first step is to create the object and components at the lowest level of the hierarchy. The content of components at the lowest level of hierarchy do not affect the build process and as such are not shown in this implementation:

```
Program 7.1: Leaf component and object class declarations
1   :   class ex_config extends ovm_object;
2   :       `ovm_object_utils(ex_config)
3   :   endclass
4   :
5   :   class ex_block extends ovm_component;
6   :       function new(string name, ovm_component parent);
7   :           super.new(name, parent);
8   :       endfunction
9   :       `ovm_component_utils(ex_block)
10  :   endclass
11  :
12  :   class ex_top_comp extends ovm_component;
13  :       function new(string name, ovm_component parent);
14  :           super.new(name, parent);
15  :       endfunction
16  :       `ovm_component_utils(ex_top_comp)
17  :   endclass
```

This program shows the implementation of object **ex_config**, and components **ex_block** and **ex_top_comp**. It is assumed that contents of **ex_top_comp** may need to be accessed by components at lower layers of the hierarchy. In addition, note that as required, these class declarations include the appropriate automation macros (lines 2, 9, and 16) to allow these classes to be handled by the OVM factory (section 6.3). Also, function **new()** must be defined for all classes derived from **ovm_component** (lines 6, 13).

The next step is to define the class for module component **ModuleComp**:

```
Program 7.2: ex_module class declaration, showing function build()
1   :   class ex_module extends ovm_component;
2   :       int ModData, LocalFlag;
3   :       string HierFlag;
4   :       ex_block BlockComp, CondBlockComp;
5   :       ex_config RefGlobConf, ModConf;
6   :       ex_top_comp RefTOP_COMP;
7   :
8   :       function new(string name, ovm_component parent);
9   :           super.new(name, parent);
10  :       endfunction
11  :
12  :       function void build();
13  :           super.build();
14  :           $cast(BlockComp, create_component("ex_block", "BlockComp"));
15  :           BlockComp.build();
16  :           if (HierFlag == "must have CondBlockComp") begin
17  :               $cast(CondBlockComp, create_component("ex_block", "CondBlockComp"));
18  :               CondBlockComp.build();
19  :           end
20  :       endfunction
21  :
22  :       `ovm_component_utils_begin(ex_module)
23  :           `ovm_field_int(ModData, OVM_DEFAULT)
```

```
24  :               `ovm_field_int(LocalFlag, OVM_DEFAULT)
25  :               `ovm_field_string(HierFlag, OVM_DEFAULT)
26  :           `ovm_component_utils_end
27  :   endclass
```

The implementation of class **ex_module** is shown in the above program. Note that no configuration is passed from this module to lower level components (no arrows from this module to lower level components in figure 7.1). Therefore, the implementation of function **build()** for this class requires only that the appropriate components be constructed, and no configuration settings are needed. It is assumed that any configurations applied to this component by higher layer components have already taken effect before entering function **build()**. The first step in function **build()** is to call the **build()** method of the super class (line 13). Component **BlockComp** is then created and built (lines 14, 15). Conditional component **CondBlock-Comp** is then created only if hierarchical configuration field **HierFlag** is appropriately set (lines 16–19). Note that **RefGlobConf**, **ModConf**, and **RefTOP_COMP** are all set to their appropriate values (set through configuration from higher layer components) by the time function **build()** is called. This configuration mechanism is shown in the implementation of **ex_system**, shown in the following program:

```
    Program 7.3: ex_module class declaration, showing function build()
1   :   class ex_system extends ovm_component;
2   :           int SysFlag;
3   :           ex_module ModuleComp;
4   :           ex_config RefGlobConf, SysConf;
5   :           ex_top_comp RefTOP_COMP;
6   :
7   :           function new(string name, ovm_component parent);
8   :                   super.new(name, parent);
9   :                   SysFlag = 15;
10  :           endfunction
11  :
12  :           function void build();
13  :                   super.build();
14  :                   set_config_int("ModuleComp", "LocalFlag", SysFlag);
15  :                   set_config_object("ModuleComp", "ModConf", RefGlobConf, 1);
16  :                   $cast(ModuleComp, create_component("ex_module", "ModuleComp"));
17  :                   ModuleComp.build();
18  :           endfunction
19  :
20  :           `ovm_component_utils_begin(ex_system)
21  :                   `ovm_field_int(SysFlag, OVM_DEFAULT)
22  :                   `ovm_field_object(ModuleComp, OVM_DEFAULT)
23  :                   `ovm_field_object(RefGlobConf, OVM_DEFAULT)
24  :                   `ovm_field_object(SysConf, OVM_DEFAULT)
25  :                   `ovm_field_object(RefTOP_COMP, OVM_DEFAULT)
26  :           `ovm_component_utils_end
27  :   endclass
```

Component **SystemComp** is an instance of class **ex_system** shown above. This component contains field **SysFlag** and component **RefGlobConf** whose values should be passed to component **ModuleConf** when building that component. Field **SysFlag** is initialized in the constructor for class **ex_system** (line 9) and component **RefGlobConf** is initialized through configuration from the higher layer and therefore, has a valid value when function **build()** is entered. Configuration functions **set_config_int()** and **set_config_object()** are used to specify that fields **LocalFlag** and **ModConf** of instance **ModuleComp** should be set to **SysFlag** and **RefGlobConf** respectively (lines 14, 15). In addition, argument **clone** of **set_config_object()** is set to **1** in order to indicate that a cloned copy of **RefGlobConf** should be assigned to **ModConf** of instance **ModuleComp**.

The implementation of the environment top level is shown in the following program:

```
Program 7.4: Top level program for creating the component hierarchy
1  :   module top;
2  :       `include "ovm.svh"
3  :       `include "program-7.1"
4  :       `include "program-7.2"
5  :       `include "program-7.3"
6  :
7  :       string GlobFlag;
8  :       ex_system SystemComp;
9  :       ex_top_comp TOP_COMP;
10 :       ex_config GlobConf;
11 :
12 :       initial begin
13 :           GlobFlag = "must have CondBlockComp";
14 :           $cast(GlobConf, ovm_factory::create_object("ex_config", "", "GlobConf"));
15 :           $cast(TOP_COMP,
16 :               ovm_factory::create_component("ex_top_comp", "", "TOP_COMP", null));
17 :           TOP_COMP.build();
18 :
19 :           set_config_string("SystemComp.ModuleComp", "HierFlag", GlobFlag);
20 :           set_config_object("SystemComp", "SysConf", GlobConf, 1);
21 :           set_config_object("*", "RefGlobConf", GlobConf, 0);
22 :           set_config_object("*", "RefTOP_COMP", TOP_COMP, 0);
23 :
24 :           $cast(SystemComp,
25 :               ovm_factory::create_component("ex_system", "", "SystemComp", null));
26 :           SystemComp.build();
27 :           ovm_print_topology();
28 :       end
29 :   endmodule
```

Field **GlobFlag**, component **TOP_COMP**, and object **GlobConf** are assigned and created first (lines 13–17) since they affect the sub-hierarchy rooted at component **SystemComp**. Note that this program is in the scope of a module block, and as such, the globally defined **ovm_factory** is used to create the appropriate components and objects (lines 14, 16). For the same reason, global configuration functions are used to specify configuration settings for the sub-hierarchy rooted at component **SystemComp** (lines 19–22). Function **set_config_string()** is first used to indicate that the value of field **HierFlag** in instance **SystemComp.ModuleComp** should be set to the value of field **GlobFlag** (line 19). Next, global function **set_config_object()** with clone argument set to **1**, is used to indicate that component **SysConf** of **SystemComp** should be set to a cloned copy of object **GlobConf** (line 20). Global function **set_config_object()** with clone argument set to **0**, is then used to indicate that object **RefGlob-Conf** and component **RefTOP_COMP** in any instance (as indicated by "*") should point to object **GlobConf** and component **TOP_COMP** in the top level of hierarchy respectively (lines 21, 22). With these configuration settings in place, instance **SystemComp** is then created and built by using the factory and calling function **build()** (lines 24–26).

7.3 Verification Environment Component Types

A verification environment is composed of a set of hierarchical components that communicate to produce the desired behavior. Given this general view, the implementation of a verification environment can be described in terms of the following:

- Creating a component hierarchy
- Specifying the interconnection between environment components
- Implementing the specific requirements of each component for their intended use (e.g., a monitor has different implementation requirements than a driver)

Implementation of a component hierarchy is described in section 7.2. Transaction-based connectivity between components is described in chapter 9. This section provides a generalized view of the verification environment in terms of the different kinds of components that are present in the verification environment (subsection 7.3.1) and the constructs provided in the OVM class library for implementing these specialized components (subsection 7.3.2).

7.3.1 Verification Environment Components

Figure 7.2 shows the architectural view of a verification environment described in chapter 3. The main focus in this view is on how different components in the verification environment are grouped to form the hierarchy of the verification environment. The following hierarchical components can be identified in this view:

- Verification environment top level
- Software verification components
- Interface verification components
- Module verification components
- System verification components

Verification environment top level is the main container for all components in the verification environment. An interface verification component interacts directly with the DUV. Each module verification environment interacts with multiple interface verification environment to implement module level verification environments. Software verification components provide the abstraction necessary for interacting with a DUV's software stack during the simulation runtime. A system level verification component interacts with multiple module, software, and interface verification components to carry out the system level verification scenarios.

Figure 7.2 shows only interface, module, and system verification components. The specific view of the verification environment for a project, however, depends on its integration schedule where a layer of module/cluster/system level verification components will be in place for each integration of smaller components into larger components (e.g., blocks to modules to clusters to chips to systems). Features of these components are described in chapter 3.

The implementation of a verification environment should proceed in a hierarchical fashion. In the first step, interface verification components are implemented. In the next step,

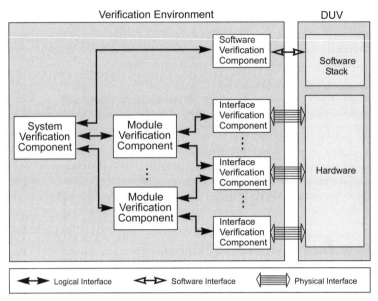

Figure 7.2 Complete Architecture of a Verification Environment

module verification components are implemented and used in verifying modules. In the next step, system verification components are implemented to verify system level behavior.

The implementation view of an interface verification component is shown in figure 7.3. This component contains the following:

- Driver
- Monitor
- Sequencer

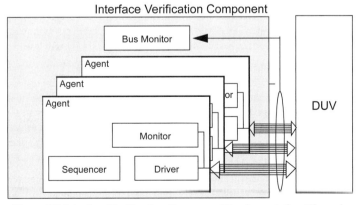

Figure 7.3 Interface Verification Component Implementation Hierarchy

- Verification component agent
- Verification component

An interface verification environment encapsulates the abstraction necessary for interacting with a device port that follows a well defined protocol (e.g., USB, PCI-Express). Given that a design may have multiple ports that communicate using the same protocol (e.g., a network switch with multiple Ethernet ports), one instance of an interface verification component should be able to interact with multiple device ports of the same type. An agent provides the abstraction for the interaction with a single device port, and can be used to model the varying types of devices supported by a single protocol. An interface verification environment may contain multiple agent instances, each communicating with a different device port. This configuration allows a single interface verification component to be used for all device ports that follow the same protocol. Each agent contains a driver, a monitor/coverage collector, and a sequencer.

A module verification component interacts with multiple interface verification components to verify a module. Module verification components interact with the DUV through interface verification components and therefore do not require a driver. They do, however, contain a sequencer, and a monitor for properties relevant at the module level. A system verification component interacts with multiple module and interface verification components to verify the functionality at the system level.

Figure 7.4 shows a graphical view of different types of components that are present in a verification environment. This view also identifies two types of component connectivity: physical interfaces and transaction interfaces. Physical interfaces are implemented using SystemVerilog port and interface constructs (see section 12.7 for an example implementation). The implementation of transaction interfaces using the OVM class library is described in chapter 9. The following component types, categorized based on their interface types, can be identified in this figure:

- Environment
- Sequencer (layered and non-layered)
- Driver (master and slave)
- Monitor (DUV and transaction)
- Scoreboard

Based on this view, an interface verification component consists of sequencer, driver, and monitor components placed in an environment component. Module and system verification components consist of sequencer, monitor, and scoreboard components placed in an environment component. All verification components are also placed in an environment component modeling the top level of the verification environment hierarchy. It should be noted that in a class-based implementation, the physical interface of a component is provided as a virtual interface that is a field of the class modeling that component (section 13.3).

The implementation model of these components using the OVM class library is described in the next section.

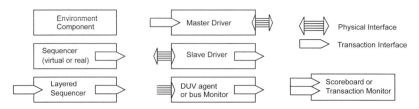

Figure 7.4 Component Interface Connectivity

7.3.2 OVM Models of Verification Environment Components

The hierarchical structure of an OVM-based verification environment is shown in figure 7.5. This structure is composed of the following OVM classes derived from class **ovm_threaded_component**:

- **ovm_test**
- **ovm_env**
- **ovm_agent**
- **ovm_monitor**
- **ovm_driver**
- **ovm_sequencer, ovm_virtual_sequencer**
- **ovm_scoreboard**

Environment components are modeled using class **ovm_env**. An environment component is the container for either an interface or a module/system verification component, as well as the container for the top level of the verification environment hierarchy. An environment modeling a verification component may contain multiple instances of an agent component modeled using class **ovm_agent**, with each agent component corresponding to an instance of the core functionality of a verification component. A verification component may optionally include a bus monitor (section 3.2). An agent may be passive or active. An active agent contains a monitor modeled using class **ovm_monitor**, a sequencer modeled using class **ovm_sequencer** and a monitor modeled using class **ovm_monitor**. A passive agent contains a monitor. A module VC contains the definition of a virtual sequencer modeled using class **ovm_virtual_sequencer** and a set of virtual sequences placed in the sequence library of this virtual sequencer. The actual instance of the virtual sequencer can, however, be placed in the top level component of the verification environment.

A driver is modeled using class **ovm_driver** and contains all functionality that is necessary for an agent to interact with the DUV such that either information is driven into the DUV port or the necessary handshaking for collecting DUV outputs is applied at the DUV ports. A monitor is modeled using class **ovm_monitor** and contains all functionality that is necessary to passively observe DUV port activity or the monitors in other verification environment components. A monitor component contains the necessary checking and coverage collection functionality. A sequencer is modeled using class **ovm_sequencer** and contains the functionality to create scenarios relevant to the next downstream component it interacts with. The next downstream component may be the DUV port, or a verification component. A

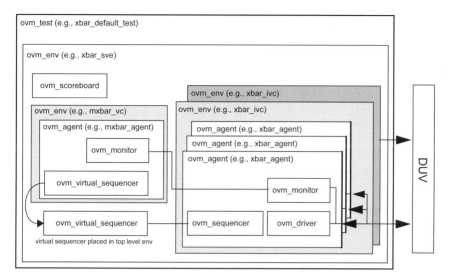

Figure 7.5 Verification Environment Component Types Provided by OVM

sequencer component may act autonomously or be controlled by the sequencer component in another verification component.

The system level container of all verification components is also modeled using an object of type **ovm_env**. All interface and module/system verification components are instantiated inside this top level environment component. This component is the top-most structural block in the verification environment, in that it represents the structural make-up of the verification environment. An implementation of a verification environment represented by an **ovm_env** component may be driven using different initial conditions, generation constraints, and test-specific configurations. All such test-specific settings are captured in a *test component* modeled with class **ovm_test**, which also acts as the container of the top-most environment component. Given this configuration, creating a new test requires the creation of a new test component that includes an instance of the top-most environment component along with its related test-specific settings. A unit testcase requiring a customized verification environment can be created by instantiating a customized top level environment component. This organization of the verification environment hierarchy allows all testcases to be uniformly maintained as top level test components where customizations of the verification environment for each testcase are managed through instantiation of the appropriate top level environment component in that testcase.

Component-specific classes provided by the OVM class library are mainly used to clearly mark the intent in implementing each environment component. Providing a dedicated class name for each component type allows implementation intent to be clarified by using the appropriate class type. In the current release of the OVM class library, class **ovm_sequencer** provides special methods for generating and managing sequences (section 8.2.2). In addition, classes **ovm_env** and **ovm_test** provide special features for starting and stopping the simulation and for handling simulation phases (section 7.4). The future release of the OVM class library may add additional features to each component definition as the need for such features are identified.

7.4 Simulation Phase Control

Simulation of a verification environment can naturally be divided into multiple phases. These phases correspond to steps for building the environment, simulating the environment, and collecting and reporting results.

In the OVM class library, the concept of simulation phases is implemented as part of the following classes:

- **ovm_component**
- **ovm_threaded_component**
- **ovm_env**
- **ovm_test**

An **ovm_component** implements the notion of hierarchy and is used for building a hierarchical environment. Additionally, this class implements simulation phases that do not consume simulation time (i.e., occur in zero time). An **ovm_threaded_component** is derived from an **ovm_component** and adds a time consuming phase to the set of predefined phases. An **ovm_env** is derived from **ovm_threaded_component**, and adds special utilities for controlling the execution of individual simulation phases. All components in a verification environment should be derived from **ovm_env**.

An **ovm_test** is derived from **ovm_env**, and models the top level component in the hierarchy. This top level component contains an instance of the verification environment hierarchy customized to the requirements of the specific test to be run by this top level test component. Using this approach, different tests running on the same verification environment hierarchy are created as follows:

- Class **test$_1$** is derived from **ovm_test**, and contains an instance of the verification environment hierarchy (an object of type **ovm_env**) initialized to the requirements of the specific test to be carried out by **test$_1$**.
- Class **test$_2$** is derived from **ovm_test**, and contains an instance of the verification environment hierarchy (an object of type **ovm_env**) initialized to the requirements of the specific test to be carried out by **test$_2$**.
- Verification is started by calling global function **run_test()** with the name of the test class that should be executed in the current simulation run (e.g., **run_test("test1")**). A test name specified using plus-argument **OVM_TESTNAME** overrides any name passed to function **run_test()** (section 7.4.1).

Table 7.1 shows the predefined phases defined by the OVM class library. It is important to note that functions **build()** and **resolve_all_bindings()** are called implicitly as part of executing this flow.

Phase	Callback Type	Defined in Class	Description
post_new	function	ovm_component	-First phase called. -Function build() of component is called before entering this function.
elaborate	function	ovm_component	-Binding of transaction ports is automatically performed at the end of this phase by calling function resolve_all_bindings() of each component
pre_run	function	ovm_threaded_component	-It is assumed that by the time this phase is started, the hierarchy is fully created and all component fields are initialized.
run	task	ovm_threaded_component	-The only time-consuming phase. -May be suspended, stopped, or resumed through methods defined in ovm_env.
extract	function	ovm_component	-Used for extracting information from the simulation run.
check	function	ovm_component	-Used for checking results extracted from the simulation run.
report	function	ovm_component	-Used for reporting the result of checking simulation run results.

Table 7.1: Predefined Simulation Phases

Table 7.2 lists the predefined callback methods used for customizing the execution of these phases to specific requirements of a verification environment components. Table 7.3 lists function and methods calls used for controlling the execution and termination of these simulation phases.

Phase	Type	Returns	Name	Defined in Class	Called After
post_new	virtual function	void	post_new()	ovm_component	run_test()
elaborate	virtual function	void	end_of_elaboration()	ovm_component	run_test()
pre_run	virtual function	void	pre_run()	ovm_threaded_component	run_test()
run	virtual task		run()	ovm_threaded_component	run_test()
run	virtual task		stop(string ph_name)	ovm_component	global_stop_request()
extract	virtual function	void	extract()	ovm_component	global_stop_request()
check	virtual function	void	check()	ovm_component	global_stop_request()
report	virtual function	void	report()	ovm_component	global_stop_request()

Table 7.2: Phase Callback Methods

7.4.1 Starting the Simulation Phases

The OVM class library provides global function **run_test()** for starting the execution of phases listed in table 7.2. The execution of phases for the verification environment is organized in terms of *top level components*.

A top level component is the top-most component for a verification environment hierarchy. A top level component is assumed to be of type **ovm_test** (figure 7.5). It is possible for a simulation runtime to contain more than one top level component, as described below. The top level components that participate in a simulation run are decided as follows:

- The name of a class derived from **ovm_test** can optionally be passed to function

Type	Returns	Name	Defined in class
function	string	get_current_global_phase()	ovm_component
task		global_stop_request()	ovm_component
function	void	set_global_timeout(time t)	ovm_component
function	void	set_global_stop_timeout(time t)	ovm_component
task		stop_request(stop_enum s=OVM_STOP_ALL) (one of OVM_STOP_CHILDREN, OVM_STOP_SELF, OVM_STOP_ALL)	ovm_component
virtual function	void	kill()	ovm_threaded_component
task		run_test(string test_name)	ovm_env
task		run_test(string test_name)	Global Function

Table 7.3: Phase Start and Control Methods

run_test(). In this case, an instance of this class is created and this instance is used as the top level component.

- If no argument is passed to function **run_test()**, and plus-argument **OVM_TESTNAME** is not given, then each object of type **ovm_test** that is instantiated in the SystemVerilog code is assumed to be a top level component.
- Simulation plus-argument **+OVM_TESTNAME=<test_name>** can be used to specify the name of the test that is to be started for a given simulation run. Test name **test_name** specifies a class type derived from class **ovm_test**. This form of specifying a test name has precedence over a test name that is passed as argument to function **run_test()**. This behavior allows tests to be selected without having to recompile the SystemVerilog code.

All top level components are processed concurrently. Given a top level component, methods for each phase are executed using a depth-first *postorder* traversal, where the phase method of a component is called after the phase method for its child components (e.g., function **pre_run()** of a component is called after function **pre_run()** of its child component). The exception to this behavior is that for the run phase, task **run()** of each component is started using a depth-first *preorder* traversal where task **run()** of a component is started before the task **run()** of its child components.

7.4.2 Stopping the Simulation Run Phase

Except for the run phase, all simulation phases are modeled using functions, and therefore, occur in zero simulation time. The run phase is the only phase that consumes simulation time. At the start of the run phase, task **run()** of all components in the hierarchy are started using a depth-first preorder traversal.

The end of run phase is decided by one of the following mechanisms:

- By default, the run phase of the hierarchy rooted at a top level component ends when task **run()** of all components in this hierarchy have completed.
- Function **set_global_timeout()** of class **ovm_component** can be used to specify a time value at which the run phase of a component should end. The default value for this timeout is **0** which indicates that no such timeout exists.
- Task **stop-request()** of class **ovm_component** can be used to selectively end the run

phase of a single component, the hierarchy rooted below a component, or both (see argument options in table 7.3). The default behavior is that task **run()** of all components affected by calling this task are terminated immediately.

- Field **enable_stop_interrupt** and virtual task **stop()** of class **ovm_component** allow the default stop behavior to be modified. This modification mechanism, described later in this section using an example, allows any component to raise an objection to, and therefore prevent, the ending of the run phase for this component, and therefore, the hierarchy in which it exists.

- Function **set_global_stop_timeout()** of class **ovm_component** can be used to specify a timeout value for the maximum length of time a component may hold an objection to ending the run phase. The default value for this field is **10,000** time units.

- Task **global_stop_request()** of class **ovm_component** can be used to call **stop_request()** for all active top level components.

- The global run phase completes when the run phase of all top level components have completed.

The mechanisms described in this section can be applied to any component types derived from **ovm_component** (e.g., **ovm_monitor**, **ovm_env**, **ovm_test**, etc.)

The following program shows an example of redefining simulation phase callback methods to control the completion of the run phase:

```
Program 7.5: Redefining simulation phase callback methods
1  :    class top_sve extends ovm_env;
2  :         `ovm_component_utils(top_sve)
3  :
4  :         function new (string name="", ovm_component parent=null);
5  :              super.new(name, parent);
6  :         endfunction: new
7  :
8  :         function void raise_objection(); enable_stop_interrupt ++; endfunction
9  :         function void lower_objection(); enable_stop_interrupt --; endfunction
10 :
11 :         function void pre_run();
12 :              raise_objection();
13 :         endfunction
14 :
15 :         task stop(string ph_name="run");
16 :              while (enable_stop_interrupt) @(enable_stop_interrupt);
17 :         endtask
18 :
19 :         function void extract();
20 :              `message(OVM_INFO, ("Now in phase:", get_current_global_phase()))
21 :              `message(OVM_INFO, ("phase extract entered at time",$time))
22 :         endfunction
23 :
24 :         task run();
25 :              `message(OVM_INFO, ("Now in phase:", get_current_global_phase()))
26 :              #1000; // represents simulation time consumed by this component run phase
27 :              lower_objection();
28 :         endtask
29 :    endclass
```

This program shows the implementation of class **top_sve**, the top level component containing the verification environment hierarchy. The hierarchy rooted at this component does not relate to the focus of this example and is not shown. The implementation of this class shows the use of predefined field **enable_stop_interrupt** of class **ovm_component** for preventing the run phase of this class from being stopped by a parent component. This approach is based on the behavior that if field **enable_stop_interrupt** is larger than zero, then a call to task **stop()** of this class must be completed before the run phase of this class can be terminated. In this implementation user defined functions **raise_objection()** and **lower_objection()** are defined to raise and lower the value of field **enable_stop_interrupt** (lines 8, 9). Before the run phase is started, function **raise_objection()** is called in function **pre_run()** (line 12). This means that as long as this objection remains raised and the stop timeout value, if provided, has not expired, then the run phase of this component will not end. Function **stop()** is also defined so that this function completes only when the value of field **enable_stop_interrupt** is set to **0** (line 16). Function **extract()** of this class is also defined to print the time at which this phase starts, thereby giving the simulation time at which the run phase completes (lines 19–22). Finally, task **run()** is defined to call function **lower_objection()** after some simulation time has passed.

The use of this class in a test is shown in the following example:

```
Program 7.6: Defining and running a new testcase
1  :   module top;
2  :       `include "ovm.svh"
3  :       `include "program-7.5"        // class top_sve
4  :
5  :       class my_test extends ovm_test;
6  :           `ovm_component_utils(my_test)
7  :           top_sve sve;
8  :
9  :           function new (string name="", ovm_component parent=null);
10 :               super.new(name, parent);
11 :           endfunction: new
12 :
13 :           virtual function void build();
14 :               super.build();
15 :               $cast(sve, create_component("top_sve", "sve_15"));
16 :               sve.build();
17 :           endfunction
18 :
19 :           task run();
20 :               global_stop_request();
21 :               // Alternatively call function below to just stop hierarchy rooted here
22 :               //stop_request(OVM_STOP_ALL);
23 :           endtask
24 :       endclass
25 :
26 :       initial run_test("my_test");
27 :   endmodule
```

The above example shows the implementation of testcase **my_test** which is derived from class **ovm_test** (line 5). This class instantiates class **top_sve** (line 7) which is configured and built in function **build()** (line 13–17). Task **run()** of this class is defined to stop all running components anywhere in the environment by immediately calling **global_stop_request()** (line 20). The use of this function is in contrast with function **stop_request()** which only controls the termination of the run phase for components in the hierarchy of its calling component (line 22). The use of **global_stop_request()** is recommended over **stop_request()** unless there is specific requirement for stopping the run phase for only a portion of the verification environment hierarchy. Global function **run_test()** is used to run testcase **my_test** (line 26).

In this implementation, even though task **global_stop_request()** is called at simulation time **0** immediately after entering task **run()** of **my_test** (line 20), the run phase continues until time **1,000** when task **run()** of **top_sve** completes and lowers its objection to ending the run phase, thereby allowing task **stop()** to complete.

The mechanism for raising objections to ending the simulation run phase is useful in providing distributed control for when the run phase can end. This approach is also useful for preventing the run phase from terminating during activities that must be completed once started. For example, a transaction that has already been generated by a sequencer must be processed before the run phase can end. In this case, an objection can be raised by the sequencer before a new transaction is generated and then lowered after the processing of this transaction is completed.

CHAPTER 8

OVM Transaction Sequences

Effective creation of verification scenarios is perhaps the most important part of carrying out a verification project. After all, everything in a verification environment is put in place to support the ultimate goal of creating and monitoring all of the scenarios that must be verified.

In modern verification environments, verification scenarios are modeled as a sequence of items where both the sequence items and the sequence itself can be randomly or deterministically defined and created at simulation runtime. This approach brings the power of randomization to scenario generation, and allows for fine-grain runtime control of how sequences are built. The ability to define a sequence item at any level of abstraction (i.e., from low-level driving of signals to high level issuing a command to a verification component) allows this approach to be applicable at any level of abstraction. This approach also facilitates the creation of hierarchies of sequences where complex sequences are created by combining lower level sequences.

Effective construction of verification scenarios as sequences of items requires a mix of language constructs and an infrastructure for sequence generation and driving. A sequence generation infrastructure should provide the ability to define:

- Flat sequences (series of sequence items driven by one driver)
- Hierarchical sequences (sequence of sequences driven by one driver)
- Virtual sequences (sequence of sequences driven by multiple drivers)
- Layered sequences (sequences driving other sequences)
- Reactive sequences (ability for a sequence to react to its environment)

This chapter provides a detailed description of sequence generation capabilities provided by the OVM class library. This chapter also provides small implementation examples to better illustrate the concepts discussed in this chapter. A comprehensive and detailed example of sequence generation is provided in chapter 14.

8.1 Verification Scenarios and Sequences

Verification scenarios can be modeled as a sequence of transactions, where each transaction models an atomic interaction with a module in the verification environment. For example, in verifying a memory model, a verification scenario may consist of writing to a memory location and then reading back the value at that memory location in order to make sure that the read value is in fact the same as the value that was initially written to that memory location.

Verification scenarios can be categorized as single-sided or multi-sided. A *single-sided scenario* interacts with only a single DUV interface (e.g., writing to a memory location and then reading back that memory location). A *multi-sided scenario*, however, requires interaction with multiple DUV interfaces (e.g., injecting a packet at DUV interface **1** and then injecting a packet at DUV interface **2** to verify that DUV transmits these packets on interface **3** with the correct priority).

In its simplest form, a sequence-based model of a verification scenario consists of a single stream of transactions that is to be consumed by a single driver. This simple configuration consists of the following elements:

- Sequence item
- Sequencer
- Sequence item interface
- Driver

Figure 8.1 shows a general view of this architecture. A *sequence item* refers to a transaction describing an atomic interaction with the environment. In the memory verification example, writing to memory can be considered an atomic step and hence defined as a sequence item. Sequence items may describe complex activities such as initializing a system, or an activity as simple as applying a value to a signal. In describing a memory write operation as an atomic operation, all details related to how the memory is written and the fact that this operation may take multiple cycles are considered to be a part of the sequence item description, which is to be handled by the driver. This abstraction allows the sequence generation mechanism to focus on generating the sequence without considering the low-level details of how each item is handled by the environment. In most cases, sequence items contain randomly generated properties. For example, in a memory write operation, data and the address values may be randomly generated. A *sequence item declaration* defines a new sequence item type and refers to the description of a sequence item. A *sequence item instance* refers to the actual item created while applying the relevant random generation constraints.

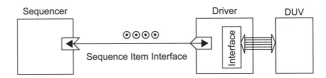

Figure 8.1 Single-Sided Sequence Generation Architecture

A *sequencer* produces a single stream of sequence items where all of the sequence items have the same type. The ability of a sequencer to produce only a single stream of items limits this configuration to single-sided scenarios. As will be shown later in this chapter, a virtual sequencer is used to remove this limitation and allow multi-sided scenarios to be handled by the sequence generation facilities of the OVM class library.

A *driver* is the consumer of sequence items produced by a sequencer. A driver may drive the sequence items directly into a DUV interface (figure 8.1). A driver may also represent the sequencer in a lower layer of the verification scenario generation hierarchy. For example, a TCP/IP layer sequencer, producing items representing TCP/IP layer traffic, may pass its items to an Ethernet sequence that uses a single TCP/IP layer item to generate a sequence of Ethernet layer items.

A *sequence item interface* is used to connect a sequencer to a driver. A sequence item interface is a transaction interface (chapter 9) that is customized to the requirements of sequence generation architecture (i.e., it supports a customized set of methods instead of the standard transaction interface methods listed in section 9.3).

The interaction between a sequencer and a driver can be one of:

- Push mode
- Pull mode

In *push mode*, a sequencer drives a produced item into a driver when that item is generated, and waits until the driver consumes this item. In *pull mode*, a driver requests the sequencer to provide it with a sequence item. The pull mode of interaction is superior to push mode. The reason is that first, in pull mode, a sequence item is consumed immediately after it leaves the sequencer. This means that the sequencer can customize the contents of the sequence item to the timing of sequence item consumption. Second, the single stream of sequence items leaving a sequencer may represent multiple concurrently running scenarios, and pull mode allows the sequencer to arbitrate between items generated by these concurrently running scenarios based on the item that is best suited for consumption at the time the driver requests the next item (see **is_relevant()** in section 8.8.2). In addition, a pull mode implementation can easily be turned into a push mode implementation by adding an active transaction channel between the sequencer and the driver, containing a thread of execution that reads the next available sequence item from the sequencer, passes it to the driver, and blocks until this sequence item is consumed by the driver. The OVM class library fully supports the pull mode of operation, with support of push mode planned for future versions.

The configuration in figure 8.1 shows a pull mode interaction between the sequencer and the driver. In this mode, the driver is the initiator component and the transaction consumer, and the sequencer is the target component and the transaction producer. The sequence item interface defined in OVM supports a bidirectional transaction transfer across this interface where the driver requests the next sequence item from the sequencer and then returns the result of executing that item through the interface.

The remainder of this chapter describes the sequence generation utilities of the OVM class library.

8.2 Sequencers

The architecture of a sequencer component is shown in figure 8.2. This architecture is identified by:

- A default sequence item type
- A library of predefined and user defined sequences
- A set of running sequences
- An arbiter
- A sequence item interface

A sequencer produces a single stream of sequence items whose base type is given by the sequencer's default sequence item type. A sequencer contains a *sequence library* which is a container of predefined and user defined sequences that can either be started as running sequences each having an independent thread of execution, or used as subsequences in hierarchical sequences. Each running sequence generates a stream of sequence items, feeding these items into an arbiter that uses a first-in-first-out (FIFO) policy to select among relevant items from the incoming streams. The OVM class library provides a mechanism for allowing each sequence to define whether or not the items it generates are relevant to the current verification context (see **is_relevant()** in section 8.8.2). The driver connects with the sequencer through a sequence item interface that forwards driver requests for a new item to the arbiter.

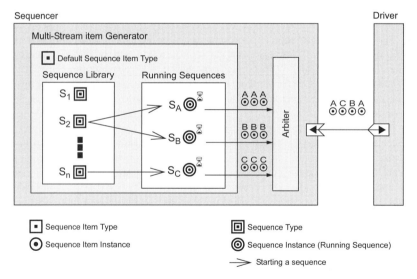

Figure 8.2 Sequencer Architecture

The implementation of a sequencer using the OVM class library is described through the following steps:

- Sequence item definition
- Sequencer and the default sequence item declaration

- Defining flat and hierarchical sequences
- Sequence library and the predefined sequences it contains by default
- Sequence activation
- Arbitration mechanisms
- Sequence item interface

These topics are discussed in the following subsections.

8.2.1 Sequence Items

A sequence item is the atomic object that is produced by a sequencer. The lifetime of a sequence item consists of the following major stages:

- Creation
- Randomization
- Transfer to driver
- Execution

All sequence items are generated by sequences, which then pass these sequence items to the sequencer for transfer to a driver. A sequence item is created in a sequence. The timing for the transfer of a sequence item to a driver is decided by the interaction between the sequence, sequencer, and the driver. This means that a sequence item may be passed to a driver some time after it is created. A sequence item can be randomized immediately after it is created (i.e., *early randomization*) or right before it is transferred to the driver (i.e., *late randomization*). The mechanism provided in the OVM class library for controlling this randomization behavior is described in section 8.6.2.

The implementation of a sequence item using the OVM class library is shown in the following example (see section 12.2 for XBar design specification):

```
Program 8.1: Sequence item Implementation
1  :    class xbar_xmt_packet extends ovm_sequence_item;
2  :        rand byte payload;
3  :        `ovm_object_utils_begin(xbar_xmt_packet)
4  :            `ovm_field_int(payload, OVM_ALL_ON)
5  :        `ovm_object_utils_end
6  :        function new (string name = "xbar_xmt_packet",
7  :                ovm_sequencer_base sequencer = null, ovm_sequence parent_seq = null);
8  :            super.new(name, sequencer, parent_seq);
9  :        endfunction: new
10 :    endclass: xbar_xmt_packet
```

The above example highlights the following general guidelines that must be followed when implementing these elements of a sequence generation facility:

- Sequence item classes must be derived from class **ovm_sequence_item** (line 1).
- The declaration of a new sequence item must include the declaration of its constructor (lines 6–9).
- Macro **ovm_object_utils()** must be used in order to allow a newly defined sequence item to be managed by the OVM·factory. Field automation macros can also be specified by using the begin/end variation of this macro (lines 3–5).

8.2.2 Sequencer Declaration

Sequencer implementation using the OVM class library is shown in the following example:

```
Program 8.2: Sequencer implementation
1  :   class xbar_xmt_sequencer extends ovm_sequencer;
2  :        int unsigned port_num;
3  :        `ovm_sequencer_utils_begin(xbar_xmt_sequencer)
4  :            `ovm_field_int(port_num, OVM_ALL_ON)
5  :        `ovm_sequencer_utils_end
6  :
7  :        function new (string name="", ovm_component parent=null);
8  :            super.new(name, parent);
9  :            `ovm_update_sequence_lib_and_item(xbar_xmt_packet)
10 :        endfunction: new
11 :   endclass: xbar_xmt_sequencer
```

The example shown the implementation of sequencer **xbar_xmt_sequencer** derived from class **ovm_sequencer**. Macro **ovm_update_sequence_lib_and_item()** is used in the constructor to mark class **xbar_xmt_packet** (defined in program 8.1) as the default sequence item (line 9). This means that sequencer **xbar_xmt_sequencer** will be passing transactions of type **xbar_xmt_packet** through its sequence item interface.

The above example highlights the following general guidelines that must be followed when implementing a sequencer:

- A sequencer class must be derived from **ovm_sequencer** (line 1).
- Macro **ovm_sequencer_utils()** or its begin/end variation must be used with a new sequencer declaration (lines 3–5) to initialize its sequencer utilities. The begin/end variation of this macro is used when the newly defined class contains fields that must be automated. The argument to this macro is the name of the newly declared class in which the macro is used.
- The declaration of a new sequencer must include the declaration of its constructor (lines 7–10). Additionally, macro **ovm_update_sequence_lib_and_item()** must be used in this constructor to define the default sequence item handled by this sequencer (line 9). The argument to this macro is the name of the default sequence item to be handled by this newly declared sequencer. This default sequence item also gives the sequence item type generated by sequence **ovm_simple_sequence** (section 8.5.1).

The above example creates a minimal sequencer that produces a stream of sequence items of type **xbar_xmt_packet**, and contains a sequence library with a set of predefined sequences. The addition of user defined sequences to this sequence library is shown in the next section. A predefined sequence of this sequencer is started by default, producing a stream of randomized items of base type **xbar_xmt_packet** (section 8.5.1). This means that this sequencer, as implemented, can be used for initial verification steps. Creating more interesting scenarios, however, requires that new sequences be added to the sequence library and started. This step is described in the next section.

8.3 Sequences

A *sequence* contains a recipe for generating an ordered list of sequence item instances. A *sequence declaration* describes these instructions and may contain randomizable fields and fields that get customized to the specific conditions when the sequence is created. A sequence declaration defines a new *sequence type*. A *sequence instance* refers to a specific instance of sequence type that generates a sequence of item instances during the simulation runtime. Multiple sequence instances may be created from a single sequence type, each behaving differently because of their randomizable fields and other fields initialized to the specific conditions when that sequence instance was created.

A *flat sequence* is defined only in terms of sequence items. A flat sequence contains the following types of information:

- Sequence item(s) to generate
- Dynamic constraints[1] that should be applied to each item during generation
- Randomization control (e.g., use of functions **constraint_mode()** and **rand_mode()** to modify sequence item static constraints)
- Flow control information (e.g., timing)
- How environment conditions affect item generation (reactive sequences)
- Relationship between consecutively generated items

A sequence declaration is identified by:

- Sequence items and/or subsequences
- Action block

Sequence *action block* describes how and in what order items and subsequences are generated. A graphical view of this process is shown in figure 8.3. In this example, sequence S_1 contains three sequence items **A**, **B**, and **C**. The action block for this sequence indicates that item **A** should be generated, followed by item **B**, followed by item **A**, and followed by item **C**. The generation of sequence S_1 produces a sequence of items **A**, **B**, **A**, and **C** which are passed to the sequencer in the order of their generation.

The implementation of a flat sequence using the OVM class library is shown in the following example:

```
 Program 8.3: Flat sequence implementation
1  :    class xbar_xmt_seq_flat extends ovm_sequence;
2  :        rand byte default_payload;
3  :        rand byte count;
4  :        constraint c {default_payload < 10;}
5  :
6  :        `ovm_sequence_utils_begin(xbar_xmt_seq_flat, xbar_xmt_sequencer)
7  :            `ovm_field_int(default_payload, OVM_ALL_ON)
8  :        `ovm_sequence_utils_end
9  :
10 :        function new(string name="", ovm_component parent=null);
11 :            super.new(name);
12 :        endfunction
```

---

[1] Static constraints are constraints that are specified as part of an item declaration while dynamic constraints are in-line constraints provided when an item instance is being randomized.

Sequence Declaration: Defining sequence S_1

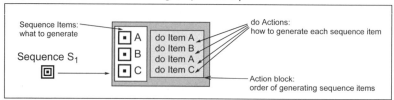

Sequence Instance: Creating sequence S_1

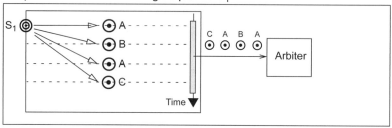

Figure 8.3 Flat Sequence Declaration and Generation

```
13  :
14  :        virtual task body();
15  :            xbar_xmt_packet this_seq_item;
16  :            `ovm_do_with(this_seq_item, {payload==default_payload;})
17  :            repeat (count)
18  :                `ovm_do(this_seq_item)
19  :        endtask
20  :  endclass: xbar_xmt_seq_flat
```

Flat sequence **xbar_xmt_seq_flat** is declared in the above example. This class is derived from the predefined base class **ovm_sequence** (line 1). Macro **ovm_sequence_utils()** is used to register this class with the factory and to add it to the sequence library for sequencer **xbar_xmt_sequencer** implemented in program 8.2 (line 6). This sequencer is defined to contain a random field **default_payload**, and a random field **count** for controlling the number of generated items (lines 2, 3). A constraint defining the desired range for this payload is also included in this description (line 4). As will be shown in program 8.4, fields **default_payload** and **count** can be used to customize this sequence when it is used as a subsequence in a hierarchical sequence.

The action block for sequence **xbar_xmt_seq_flat** is specified by defining virtual task **body()** and using execution macros **ovm_do_with()** and **ovm_do()** to execute sequence item **this_seq_item** (lines 14–19). Macro **ovm_do_with()** is used to execute sequence item **this_seq_item** with dynamic constraints, constraining field **payload** to field **default_payload** of the sequence (line 16). Macro **ovm_do()** is used to execute sequence item **this_seq_item** with its static randomization constraints (line 18). Every execution of this sequence will produce **count+1** sequence items. The OVM class library defines a set of execution macros that are used for executing sequences and sequence items (section 8.6.2).

It should be noted that depending on the execution macro, a new instance of sequence item **this_seq_item** may be created and randomized for each execution of this sequence item (lines 16, 18). Table 8.1 provides a summary of actions performed by each execution macro. As such, the definition of a sequence should not depend on the content of a sequence item that is created or randomized by an execution macro. Given that both execution macros **ovm_do()** and **ovm_do_with()** create and randomize the sequence item, the implementation shown above follows this guideline by defining a new field holding the default payload value and constraining sequence item **this_seq_item** when it is passed to an execution macro.

The above example highlights the following general guidelines that must be followed when implementing a flat sequence:

- A new sequence must be derived from **ovm_sequence** (line 1).
- The declaration of a new sequence must include the declaration of its constructor (lines 10–12).
- Macro **ovm_sequence_utils()**, or its begin/end variations must be used to register a new sequence type with the sequencer whose sequence library should contain this newly declared sequence (lines 6–8). This macro also registers this new sequence type with the OVM factory so that override operations can be supported. The begin/end variation of this macro is used when the newly defined class contains fields that must be automated. The arguments to this macro are the name of the class in which this macro is used, and the sequencer class whose sequence library should contain this newly declared sequence.
- A sequence action block is specified by defining the contents of virtual task **body()** (lines 14–19).
- In some cases, a new sequence is only defined to be used later as a base class for other sequences, and hence, should not be placed in the sequence library of its sequencer. For such sequences, macro **ovm_object_utils()** or its begin/end variations can be used instead of macro **ovm_sequence_utils()**. In this case, the new sequence is registered with the OVM factory without being placed into a sequence library.

The flat sequence created in the above example is automatically added to the sequence library for sequencer **xbar_xmt_sequencer** and can be used in hierarchical sequences belonging to that sequencer, or started as the root sequence of a new running sequence, or set as the default sequence for this sequencer. The use of this sequence in a hierarchical sequence is shown in the next section. Starting this sequence as a root sequence is shown in section 8.6.

8.4 Hierarchical Sequences

A *hierarchical sequence* is defined in terms of both subsequences and sequence items. Hierarchical sequences allow previously defined sequences to be reused, and also provide a means of organizing a long sequence into smaller interelated sequences. Consider a verification sequence generating 20–30 **SIZED** Ethernet packets followed by a **PAUSE** packet, followed by 40–50 **QTAGGED** packets. It may be helpful to model this sequence as a hierarchical sequence where the generation of **SIZED** and **QTAGGED** packets are defined as flat sequences that are then used in the final hierarchical sequence.

Figure 8.4 shows an example of a hierarchical sequence. In this example sequence S_2 makes use of sequence S_1 defined in figure 8.3, and sequence S_3 makes use of sequence S_2. It is important to note that the internal organization of a sequence (i.e., hierarchical versus flat) is not visible to the sequencer, and the sequencer is unaware of the fact that the sequence of items generated by sequence S_3 are generated using a hierarchical sequence.

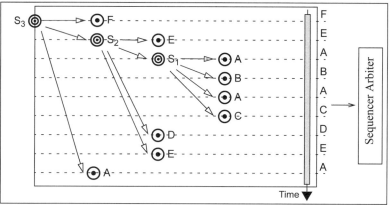

Figure 8.4 Hierarchical Sequence Declaration and Generation

Two types of sequences can be identified during the execution of a hierarchical sequence:

- Root sequences
- Subsequences

A *root sequence* is the start point of the execution of a new independent sequence tree. The difference between a root sequence and a subsequence is that a *subsequence* has a parent sequence but a root sequence does not have a parent sequence. Having a parent sequence impacts the way a running sequence is treated by the sequencer. For example, a grabbed sequencer accepts items from a subsequence if the sequence that is currently grabbing the sequencer is an immediate or distant parent of that subsequence (section 8.8.1). The default sequence of a sequencer is started as a root sequence (section 8.5.1).

A root sequence is started in its own thread of execution and a subsequence executes in the execution thread of its parent sequence. This behavior is not, however, mandatory. For example a sequence S_1 can execute a sequence S_2 in its execution thread as a root sequence thereby denying S_2 any privileges granted to S_1 (e.g., interaction with a sequencer currently grabbed by S_1), and wait for S_2 to complete before continuing. Alternatively, a sequence S_1 can execute sequences S_2 and S_3 as parallel subsequences (i.e., by using a fork statement), so that these subsequences inherit the privileges currently granted to sequence S_1.

Section 8.6 describes how root sequences and subsequences are started. The remainder of this section shows the implementation of hierarchical sequences using the predefined execution macros of the OVM class library.

The implementation of a hierarchical sequence using the OVM class library is shown in the following example:

```
Program 8.4: Hierarchical sequence implementation
1   :   class xbar_xmt_seq_hier extends ovm_sequence;
2   :           `ovm_sequence_utils(xbar_xmt_seq_hier, xbar_xmt_sequencer)
3   :
4   :           function new(string name="", ovm_component parent=null);
5   :                   super.new(name);
6   :           endfunction
7   :
8   :           virtual task body();
9   :                   xbar_xmt_seq_flat this_flat_seq;
10  :                   xbar_xmt_packet this_seq_item;
11  :
12  :                   `ovm_do(this_seq_item)
13  :                   `ovm_do(this_flat_seq)
14  :                   `ovm_do_with(this_flat_seq, {default_payload == 4 && count == 4;})
15  :           endtask
16  :   endclass: xbar_xmt_seq_hier
```

This example shows how flat sequence **xbar_xmt_seq_flat** (defined in program 8.3) is used in the declaration of hierarchical sequence **xbar_xmt_seq_hier**. This new sequence is derived from the predefined base class **ovm_sequence** (line 1), and is added to the sequence library for sequencer **xbar_xmt_sequencer** by using macro **ovm_sequence_utils()** (line 2). The action block for this sequence is specified by defining virtual task **body()** and using macros **ovm_do()** and **ovm_do_with()** to start the execution of sequence item **this_seq_item** (line 12) followed by execution of subsequence **this_flat_seq** once without any constraints (line 13) and once with constraints applied to randomized fields of sequence **this_flat_seq** (line 14). The use of macro **ovm_do_with()** with a sequence argument (line 14) shows how each execution of a subsequence in a hierarchical sequence can be customized to its execution context.

The guidelines for creating a hierarchical sequence are similar to those for a flat sequence, except that a hierarchical sequence contains instances of previously defined sequences (line 9) and can optionally execute sequence items. A hierarchical sequence may contain instances of both flat and other hierarchical sequences. It should be noted that all sequence instances used in a hierarchical sequence must belong to the same sequence library, and hence the same sequencer.

8.5 Sequence Library

Every sequence that is to be executed by a sequencer should be placed in the sequence library of its sequencer by using macro **ovm_sequence_util()** or its being/end variations. Sequence declarations that provide a base class for deriving other sequences, and hence are never executed, need not be placed in any sequence library. Every sequence in a sequence library is identified by its type name and kind.

The OVM class library provides the following fields and methods for locating and creating a sequence from the sequence library.

```
Methods and fields for class ovm_sequencer_base:
    string sequences[$];
    function int unsigned get_seq_kind(string seq_type_name);
    function ovm_sequence get_sequence(int unsigned seq_kind);
Methods and fields for class ovm_sequence:
    function int unsigned get_seq_kind(string seq_type_name);
    function ovm_sequence get_sequence(int unsigned seq_kind);
```

Array **sequences** in class **ovm_sequencer** holds all sequences in the sequence library of this sequencer. The total number of sequences in the sequence library of a sequencer is given by the size of this field. Function **get_seq_kind()** returns the kind for sequence type name **seq_type_name**. Function **get_sequence()** creates a new instance of a sequence of kind **seq_kind**. The resulting sequence instance is not randomized. These functions are defined for both a sequencer and a sequence. Calling these functions from inside a sequence has the effect of calling the same function in the sequencer that contains that sequence.

The fields and methods described above allow access to any sequence from inside a sequencer or a sequence. The following sections show how a sequence created through this interface can be started.

8.5.1 Predefined and User Defined Sequences

The OVM class library provides the following predefined sequences for every sequence library:

- Sequence **ovm_random_sequence**
- Sequence **ovm_exhaustive_sequence**
- Sequence **ovm_simple_sequence**

In addition, the following fields defined for a sequencer class are used to control the execution of these predefined sequences:

```
Fields defined fro class ovm_sequencer_base:
    protected string default_sequence = "ovm_random_sequence";
    int count = OVM_UNDEF;
    int unsigned max_random_count = 10;
```

Sequence **ovm_simple_sequence** executes the default sequence item of its containing sequencer once. This means that running this sequence once produces a single sequence item sent to the sequencer.

Sequence **ovm_exhaustive_sequence** executes every user defined sequence and sequence **ovm_simple_sequence** once and in a random order.

The behavior of sequence **ovm_random_sequence** depends on fields **count** and **max_random_count**. If **count** is not negative, then this sequence executes **count** number of sequences selected randomly from **ovm_simple_sequence** and user defined sequences registered with the sequence library. If count is less than zero, then the sequencer generates a random value between **1** and **max__random_count**, and executes that many number of sequences selected randomly from **ovm_simple_sequence** and user defined sequences registered with the sequence library.

Field **default_sequence** of a sequencer determines which sequence from its sequence library is automatically started when the run phase of simulation is entered. This field can be changed in order to allow a user defined sequence to be started instead of sequence **ovm_random_sequence**.

The fields shown above can be changed through field configuration constructs (section 7.2) to customize a sequencer to behave according to the requirements of its environment.

8.6 Executing Sequences and Sequence Items

Sequences can be executed using either methods calls or through predefined macros. Sequence items are executed by calling predefined macros. Executing root sequences and subsequences using methods is described in section 8.6.1. Executing subsequences and sequence items using the predefined macros of the OVM class library is described in section 8.6.2.

8.6.1 Executing Root Sequences and Subsequences using Methods

The OVM class library provides the following methods for executing sequences:

```
Method for class ovm_sequencer_base:
      task start_sequence(ovm_sequence this_seq, ovm_sequencer_base this_sqnsr=null);
Methods for class ovm_sequence:
      task start(ovm_sequencer_base parent_sqnsr, ovm_sequence parent_seq = null);
      task do_sequence_kind(int unsigned seq_kind);
```

Task **start_sequence()** of class **ovm_sequencer_base** is used to start a new root sequence in sequencer **this_sqnsr**. If argument **this_sqnsr** is not provided, then the sequence is started on the calling sequencer. Argument **this_seq** passed to this task must be a sequence that is already created, and if necessary, randomized.

Task **start()** of class **ovm_sequence** is used to start a new sequence on sequencer **parent_sqnsr**. If argument **parent_seq** is set to *null*, then this new sequence is started as a root sequence. If argument **parent_seq** is provided, then the new sequence is executed as a subsequence of sequence **parent_seq**.

Task **do_sequence_kind()** of class **ovm_sequence** is used to start a new subsequence of kind **seq_kind** as a subsequence of the calling sequence. This task always results in a subsequence. Task **do_sequence_kind()** is useful for executing sequences through distribution or exclusion constraints, where each sequence kind is selected randomly and then executed using this task. Other than this special use model, the use of execution macros (section 8.6.2) is recommended over this task.

The following example program highlights two aspects of sequencer implementation: Overriding the default behavior of a sequencer, and starting root sequences and subsequences. This implementation uses sequence library methods (section 8.5) and sequence start methods shown above.

```
Program 8.5: Overriding sequencer behavior and starting a root sequence
 1  :   module test;
 2  :       `include "ovm.svh"
 3  :       `include "program-8.2"
 4  :       `include "program-8.3"
 5  :       `include "program-8.4"
 6  :
 7  :       class xbar_xmt_main extends ovm_sequence;
 8  :           `ovm_sequence_utils(xbar_xmt_main, xbar_xmt_sequencer)
 9  :
10  :           function new(string name="", ovm_component parent=null);
11  :               super.new(name);
12  :           endfunction
13  :
14  :           virtual task body();
15  :               int unsigned key;
16  :               xbar_xmt_seq_flat fseq;
17  :               xbar_xmt_seq_hier hseq;
18  :
19  :               fork
20  :                   begin
21  :                       key = get_seq_kind("xbar_xmt_seq_flat");
22  :                       $cast(fseq, get_sequence(key));
23  :                       assert(fseq.randomize() with {count == 5;});
24  :                       p_sequencer.start_sequence(fseq);
25  :                   end
26  :                   begin
27  :                       key = get_seq_kind("xbar_xmt_seq_hier");
28  :                       $cast(hseq, get_sequence(key));
29  :                       hseq.start(p_sequencer, null); //start as a root sequence
30  :                   end
31  :               join_none
32  :
33  :               do_sequence_kind(get_seq_kind("xbar_xmt_seq_hier"));
34  :           endtask
35  :       endclass: xbar_xmt_main
36  :
37  :       initial begin
38  :           xbar_xmt_sequencer sqnsr;
39  :           set_config_string("my_sqnsr", "default_sequence", "xbar_xmt_main");
40  :           $cast(sqnsr, ovm_factory::create_component(
41  :                               "xbar_xmt_sequencer", "", "my_sqnsr", null));
42  :           sqnsr.build();
43  :       end
44  :   endmodule
```

The first step in modifying the default behavior of a sequencer is to define a new sequence that will replace the default sequence started by the sequencer and registering it with the sequencer. Sequence **xbar_xmt_main** is defined in the above example (lines 7–35). Configuration method **set_config_string()** is used to change the value of the field **default_sequence** in sequencer **sqnsr** to the name of this newly defined sequence (line 39). The OVM factory is then used to create an instance of the sequencer (line 40), and the **build()**

method of this new instance is used to create its content (line 42). Sequencer **sqnsr** will now start sequence **xbar_xmt_main** when it enters the run phase of simulation.

The action block for sequencer **xbar_xmt_main** (lines 14–34) shows the start of two new root sequences (lines 19–31) and executing of a subsequence (line 33). An instance of sequence **xbar_xmt_seq_flat** is started as a root sequence by first getting the key index for the sequence type (line 21), creating a new instance of this key (line 22), randomizing the contents of this sequence according to the local requirements (line 23), and then starting this sequence instance by calling function **start_sequence()** of its parent sequencer accessed through predefined field **p_sequencer** (line 26). The alternative approach of using task **start()** of the sequence is used to start an instance of sequence **xbar_xmt_seq_hier** (lines 27–29) without the randomization step, since this sequence does not contain any field requiring randomization. Task **do_sequence_kind()** of class **ovm_sequence** is then used to start a subsequence (line 33).

The use of macros to execute subsequences and sequence items is described in the next section.

8.6.2 Executing Subsequences and Sequence Items using Macros

The execution of a sequence item or a subsequence in the action block of a sequence results in the execution of a number of steps. These execution steps are described in this section.

The execution flow of a sequence item (e.g., **this_seq_item** on lines 12 in program 8.4) consists of the following steps:

- Create and initialize the sequence item and let the sequencer know that it is available
- Sync: wait for sequencer to indicate that it is ready to accept an item
- Execute **pre_do()** method of the calling sequence
- Randomize the sequence item
- Call **mid_do()** method of the calling sequence
- Post-Sync: let sequencer know that randomization is complete and item can be sent, and wait until sequencer indicates that the item has been consumed
- Call method **post_do()** of the calling sequence

In the first step, the sequence item is created and initialized with pointers to its sequencer and parent sequence. Next, the execution waits for the sequencer to announce that it is ready to accept a new item. The sequencer selects this sequence only if it is relevant to the current verification context (see sequence selection in section 8.8.2). The sequence informs the sequencer that it has an item available and then task **pre_do()** of the calling sequence is called. In the next step, the contents of the sequence item are randomized according to the static (embedded) and dynamic (in-line) randomization constraints of the sequence item. Additional constraints that may have been provided during the activation of this sequence item (e.g., by using macro **ovm_do_with()**) are also used as dynamic constraints during this randomization. In the next step, task **mid_do()** of the calling sequence is called, allowing user to modify or observe the randomized contents of the sequence item. In the next step, the sequence informs the sequencer that the item is randomized, and ready to be sent, and waits for the sequencer to indicate that the item was consumed. In the last step, task **post_do()** is called.

The execution flow of a subsequence (e.g., **this_flat_seq** on lines 13 in program 8.4) consists of the following steps:

- Create and initialize the subsequence
- Execute **pre_do()** method of the calling sequence
- Randomize the subsequence
- Call **mid_do()** method of the calling sequence
- Call method **body()** of the subsequence
- Call method **post_do()** of the calling sequence

Execution steps for a subsequence are similar to those for a sequence item. The main difference is that executing a subsequence does not involve any synchronization with the driver. Also a subsequence has an action block defined by the contents of task **body()** which is called after calling task **mid_do()**.

	Macros	create	sync	pre_do()	randomize()	constrained randomization	mid_do()	post-sync	Action Block (body())	post_do()
Sequence Items	ovm_do(item)	☑	☑	☑	☑		☑	☑	not related	☑
	ovm_do_with(item, {constraints})	☑	☑	☑		☑	☑	☑		☑
	ovm_create(item)	☑								
	ovm_send(item)		☑	☑			☑	☑		☑
	ovm_rand_send(item)		☑	☑	☑		☑	☑		☑
	ovm_rand_send_with(item, {constraints})		☑	☑		☑	☑	☑		☑
Subsequence	ovm_do(subseq)	☑	not related	☑	☑		☑	not related	☑	☑
	ovm_do_with(subseq, {constraints})	☑		☑		☑	☑		☑	☑
	ovm_create(subseq)	☑								
	ovm_send(subseq)			☑			☑		☑	☑
	ovm_rand_send(subseq)			☑	☑		☑		☑	☑
	ovm_rand_send_with(subseq, {constraints})			☑		☑	☑		☑	☑

Table 8.1: Item and Subsequence Execution Macros

Table 8.1 lists the predefined macros provided by the OVM class library for executing sequence items and subsequences. Each of the macros listed in table 8.1 cover different steps of execution, therefore allowing these macros to be combined to achieve a number of different randomization behaviors. Some possible scenarios include:

- Execute an item with late randomization (section 8.2.1) and with item's default constraints:
  - Use macro **ovm_do()** to execute the item
- Execute an item with early randomization (section 8.2.1) and with item's default con-

straints:
  - Use macro **ovm_create()** to create the item. Then explicitly randomize the item. Then use **ovm_send()** to send the item. This macro does not do any further randomization and, therefore, the item is sent with the early randomization that is explicitly performed.
- Execute an item with late randomization and with constraints in addition to the item's default constraints:
  - Use macro **ovm_do_with()** to execute the item
- Execute an item with late randomization and with modification of its default randomization constraints:
  - Use **ovm_create()** to create the item. Explicitly turn off *rand* statements or constraint blocks in the item using randomization methods. Use **ovm_rand_send()** or **ovm_rand_send_with()** to send the item.

The OVM class library defines a set of callback methods for a sequence object. These methods can be used to customize the behavior of sequence generation steps. For example, task **mid_do()** can be redefined to over-write the result of randomization for some fields of a subsequence before the action block for that subsequence is executed. Table 8.2 summarizes the list of callback methods for a sequence object.

Method Type	Return	Name	Arguments	Notes
task		pre_body	()	Called only for root sequences
task		body	()	Called for both root sequences and subsequences
task		post_body	()	Called only for root sequences
task		pre_do	(bit is_item)	Called when executing both items and subsequences
function	void	mid_do	(ovm_sequence_item this_item)	Called when executing both items and subsequences
function	void	post_do	(ovm_sequence_item this_item)	Called when executing both items and subsequences

Table 8.2: Sequence Callback Methods

It is important to note that if a sequence executes multiple sequence items and subsequences, then the same hook methods are called when executing any of these items or sequences (e.g., the same **mid_do()** method is called for every execution of sequence item and/or subsequence). As such, use of hook methods in sequences that execute multiple subsequences and/or sequence items requires special facilities for making clear which sequence item or subsequence is being executed when that hook method is called.

Figure 8.5 shows an example of the order in which these callback methods are called during the execution of a root sequence, subsequences, and sequence items. Note that the flow in this figure shows only the order of calling these callback methods and does not show the full details of the steps that are carried out during the execution of sequence items and sequences. Method names shown in this example directly correspond to steps shown in table 8.1.

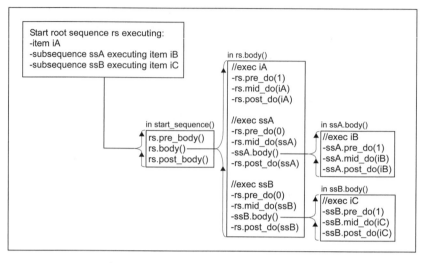

Figure 8.5 Callback Method Calling Sequence

8.7 Sequence Item Interfaces

The OVM class library provides a sequence item interface for connecting a sequencer with a driver. A sequence item interface is a specialized transaction interface that supports methods customized to the requirements of sequence item exchange (figure 8.6).

Figure 8.6 Sequence Item Interface Architecture

In using a sequence item interface, it is assumed that the driver is an initiator component that is a transaction consumer, and the sequencer is a target component that is a transaction producer. The sequence item interface consists of two connector object kinds:

- Imp object kind **ovm_seq_item_cons_if**
- Port object kind **ovm_seq_item_prod_if**

Connector object kind **ovm_seq_item_cons_if** is instantiated inside the producer compo-
nent (i.e., **ovm_sequencer**) and connector object kind **ovm_seq_item_prod_if** is instantiated inside the consumer component (i.e., **ovm_driver**). Connector object **ovm_seq_item_cons_if**

provides the implementation for the predefined methods supported by this interface. Once these connector objects are connected, these supported methods can be called from inside the driver to exchange sequence items with the sequencer. Table 8.3 lists the methods supported by a sequence item interface.

Type	Returns	Name	Arguments	Description
task		get_next_item	(output ovm_sequence_item item)	Returns the next available sequence item from the sequencer. Blocks if no item is immediately available.
task		try_next_item	(output ovm_sequence_item item)	Returns immediately the next available sequence item from the sequencer. Returns null if no item is available.
function	void	item_done	(ovm_sequence_item item = null)	Is called by the driver when a received sequence item is processed. Can optionally return a sequence item in reply to the sequence item that was received from the sequencer.
function	bit	has_do_available	()	Returns 1 if a sequence item is available immediately from the sequencer.
function	void	connect_if	(ovm_seq_item_cons_if sqnsr_if)	Connects this connector object with a connector object of kind ovm_seq_item_cons_if.

Table 8.3: Methods Supported by Connector Object **ovm_seq_item_prod_if**

The implementation of a sequencer, as provided by the OVM class library, contains a connector object of kind **ovm_seq_item_cons_if**. Therefore, connecting a driver to a sequencer requires that a connector object of type **ovm_seq_item_prod_if** be instantiated inside a driver and then connected with the connector object inside the sequencer when the environment hierarchy is being constructed. The implementation of the Xbar verification environment shows a complete example of instantiating and connecting a sequence item interface (section 13.6.1.4).

8.8 Sequencer Arbitration Mechanism

The arbiter component inside a sequencer interacts with multiple streams of sequence items and selects one sequence item at a time to be passed to the driver (figure 8.2). This arbiter then provides the next available sequence item to the driver through the sequence item interface described in section 8.7.

The operation of the arbiter is described in terms of:

- Interaction with a single sequence producing a stream of sequence items
- Interaction with multiple sequences, deciding which sequence should provide the next sequence item

These topics are described in the following subsections.

8.8.1 Sequence Interaction

The interaction between a sequencer arbiter and a single sequence is shown in figure 8.7. A sequence producing a stream of sequence items, and a sequencer arbiter each have their own execution threads. Initially, the arbiter loop waits for the driver to request a new sequence item by calling task **get_next_item()** of the sequence item interface. At this point, the arbiter waits for a new sequence item to become available in its queue. It then emits event **do_gen** of the sequence that placed the sequence item on its queue. Upon detecting event **do_gen**, the sequence thread randomizes that sequence item and calls task **mid_do()** and emits event **gen_done**. Upon detecting event **gen_done**, the arbiter passes the sequence item to the driver and waits for the driver to emit event **item_done** which is triggered when the driver calls method **item_done()**. Upon detecting event **item_done**, the sequence thread continues with the remainder of its execution steps, and the arbiter thread returns to the beginning of its loop.

The description above assumes that when the driver requests a new sequence item, no item is available in the sequencer queue. This assumption, however, is not necessary since it is possible for a sequence to place a sequence item in the sequencer queue before the driver makes a request for a sequence item. In this case, when the driver request the next sequence item, the arbiter realizes that a sequence item is already present in the queue and immediately proceeds by emitting event **do_gen** and the steps that follow.

It should be noted that figure 8.7 shows only a logical view of the interaction between a sequencer and a sequence thread, and does not reflect the actual implementation of this interaction. The actual interaction may also vary from this description. For example, depending on the execution macro that is being used, no randomization may take place before calling task **mid_do()**.

Figure 8.7 shows the sequencer interaction with a single sequence thread. This interaction can, however, support multiple sequence threads feeding items to the sequencer arbiter. The reason is that each sequence item passed to the arbiter has a pointer to the sequence that produced it, and as such, the arbiter can target this interaction to the sequence that produced the sequence item being handled at the time of this interaction.

8.8.2 Sequence Selection

The sequencer arbiter uses a first-in-first-out (FIFO) mechanism for deciding which sequence that is relevant to the current verification context should provide the next sequence item. By default, all sequences are assumed to be relevant to the current verification context.

Two mechanisms are provided by the OVM class library for allowing better control over arbiter sequence selection:

- Grabbing
- Relevance

Grabbing refers to the ability of a sequence to grab a sequencer, thereby gaining exclusive access to the arbitration mechanism. A grabbed sequencer selects sequence items from only the sequence that has currently grabbed the sequencer or any of its subsequences. Since the sequencer does not select sequence items from any other sequence, all other sequences

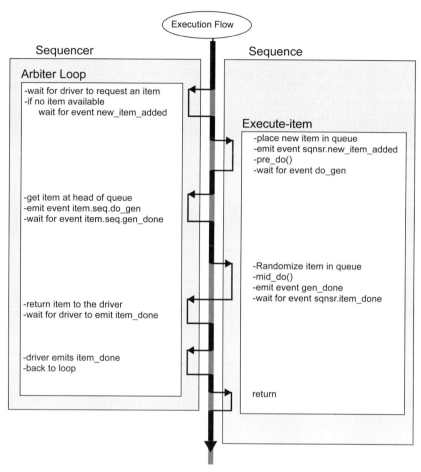

Figure 8.7 Sequence and Sequencer Interaction

appear to block until the sequencer is ungrabbed. The OVM class library provides the following methods for allowing sequences to grab the sequencer:

```
Methods defined fro class ovm_sequencer:
    task grab(ovm_sequence_seq seq);
    function void ungrab(ovm_sequence_seq seq);
    function ovm_sequence current_grabber();
    function bit is_grabbed();
Methods defined fro class ovm_sequence:
    function bit is_blocked();
```

Task **grab()** is used to grab a sequencer. If the sequencer is already grabbed, then this task blocks until the sequence that has already grabbed this sequencer calls function **ungrab()**. Function **current_grabber()** returns a pointer to the sequence that is currently grabbing the sequencer. Function **is_grabbed()** returns **1** if the sequencer is currently grabbed. A call to **grab()** in a subsequence of a sequence that has already grabbed the sequencer does not block (i.e., succeeds immediately). Method **is_blocked()** of a sequence returns **1** if that sequence is currently blocked on a call to **grab()**.

Relevance calculation allows the sequencer arbiter to decide if items produced by a sequence are relevant to the current verification context. For example, a sequence that should only generate items during the reset phase, is not relevant to verification when the reset phase is completed. The OVM class library provides the following methods for allowing sequences to identify their relevance to the sequencer:

```
Methods defined fro class ovm_sequence:
      virtual function bit is_relevant();
      virtual task wait_for_relevant();
```

Method **is_relevant()** is a virtual method of a sequence that returns a value of **1** by default. The user can modify the definition of this task to return a **1** only if a sequence item generated by this sequence is relevant to the current environment conditions. The relevance of a sequence to the current conditions may change at any time during the simulation run-time. As such, a special mechanism is needed to notify the arbiter, which may be idle due to no additional items being generated after its last cycle, that items produced by this sequence should now be processed. Task **wait_for_relevant()** is a virtual task that should block and complete only when sequence items produced by this sequence become relevant to the current environment conditions. The completion of task **wait_for_relevant()** forces the sequencer arbiter to reprocess its sequence item queue. Task **wait_for_relevant()** should be redefined if task **is_relevant()** is redefined.

Examples of grabbing sequences and relevance calculation are given in section 14.10.

8.9 Virtual Sequencers

The OVM class library provides the *virtual sequencer* construct for creating multi-sided verification scenarios. Figure 8.8 shows a graphical view of a virtual sequencer and its interaction with downstream sequencers. A virtual sequencer uses *sequence interfaces* to interact with downstream sequencers. A sequence interface allows a virtual sequence to execute subsequences belonging to the sequence library of downstream sequencers. A sequence interface also allows a virtual sequence to interact with (e.g., grab) downstream sequencers. Virtual sequences can only execute subsequences. As such, a virtual sequencer does not have a default sequence item type. A subsequence executed by a virtual sequence may belong to the sequence library of the local virtual sequencer or any downstream sequencer connected to the local sequencer through a sequence interface.

The implementation of a virtual sequencer is shown in the following program:

```
Program 8.6: Virtual sequencer implementation
1   :    class xbar_xmt_virtual_sequencer extends ovm_virtual_sequencer;
2   :        int unsigned port_num;
3   :        `ovm_sequencer_utils_begin(xbar_xmt_sequencer)
4   ;            `ovm field int(port num, OVM ALL ON)
5   :        `ovm_sequencer_utils_end
6   :
7   :        function new (string name="", ovm_component parent=null);
```

```
8   :              super.new(name, parent);
9   :                 `ovm_update_sequence_lib
10  :          endfunction: new
11  :     endclass: xbar_xmt_virtual_sequencer
```

The core implementation of a virtual sequencer is similar to that of a regular sequencer except that a virtual sequencer is derived from base class **ovm_virtual_sequencer** (line 1), and also, predefined macro **ovm_update_sequence_lib** should be used to initialize the sequence library of a virtual sequencer (line 9).

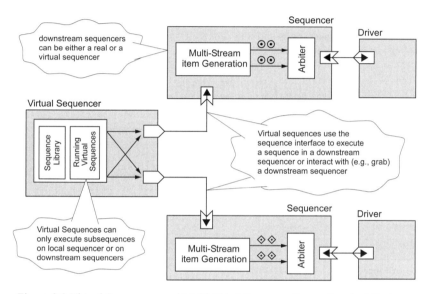

Figure 8.8 Virtual Sequencers and Multi-Sided Sequence Generation Architecture

The use of virtual sequencers for generating multi-sided scenarios is shown using an example in section 14.7.

8.10 Sequence Interfaces

The OVM class library provides a sequence interface construct for connecting a virtual sequencer with a downstream sequencer. A *sequence interface* is a specialized interface that supports methods customized to the requirements of sequence exchange (figure 8.9).

In using a sequence interface, it is assumed that the virtual sequencer is the initiator component, and the downstream sequencer is a target component. The interface consists of two connector object kinds:

- Port object kind **ovm_seq_cons_if**
- Imp object kind **ovm_seq_prod_if**

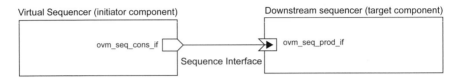

Figure 8.9 Sequence Item Interface Architecture

Port connector object kind **ovm_seq_cons_if** is instantiated inside the producer component (i.e., **ovm_virtual_sequencer**) and imp connector object kind **ovm_seq_prod_if** is instantiated inside the consumer component (i.e., downstream **ovm_sequencer** or **ovm_virtual_sequencer**). Once these connector objects are connected, these supported methods can be called from inside the virtual sequencer to execute it on the downstream sequencer. Table 8.3 lists the methods supported by a sequence interface.

Type	Returns	Name	Arguments	Description
task		start_sequence	(ovm_sequence this_seq)	pass to downstream sqnsr
task		grab	(ovm_sequence this_seq)	pass to downstream sqnsr
function	void	ungrab	(ovm_sequence this_seq)	pass to downstream sqnsr
function	ovm_sequence	current_grabber	()	pass to downstream sqnsr
function	bit	is_grabbed	()	pass to downstream sqnsr
function	bit	is_connected	()	returns 1 if connected
function	bit	is_virtual_sequencer	()	returns 1 if downstream sequencer is virtual
function	string	get_sequencer_type_name	()	name of downstream sequencer type
function	void	connect_if	(ovm_seq_prod_if sqnsr_if)	connect this connector object with the one in the downstream sequencer

Table 8.4: Methods Supported by Connector Object **ovm_seq_cons_if**

The implementation of a virtual sequencer, as provided by the OVM class library, contains an associative array of connector objects of kind **ovm_seq_cons_if**. The following field and method are provided for class **ovm_virtual_sequencer**:

```
Method and field defined fro class ovm_virtual_sequencer:
    ovm_seq_cons_if seq_cons_if[string];
    virtual function void add_seq_cons_if(string if_name);
```

Method **add_seq_cons_if()** is used to add a new connector object to a virtual sequencer. Once a connector object is added to the virtual sequencer, its name can be used in virtual sequence execution macros to execute a given sequence on the downstream sequencer to which this named connector object is connected. This newly added connector object can directly be accessed through field **seq_cons_if** which is an associative array. A complete implementation of this approach is shown in section 14.7.

The execution macros available for use in the action block of a sequence defined in a virtual sequencer are shown in table 8.5.

Macros	create	pre_do()	randomize()	constrained randomization	mid_do()	Action Block (body())	post_do()
				Execution Steps			
ovm_do_seq(subseq, seq_cons_if)	☑	☑	☑		☑	☑	☑
ovm_do_seq_with(subseq, seq_cons_if)	☑	☑		☑	☑	☑	☑
ovm_create_seq(subseq, seq_cons_if)	☑						
ovm_send(subseq)		☑			☑	☑	☑
ovm_rand_send(subseq)		☑	☑		☑	☑	☑
ovm_rand_send_with(subseq, {constraints})		☑		☑	☑	☑	☑

Table 8.5: Subsequence Execution Macros for Virtual Sequencers

Macros **ovm_do_seq()** and **ovm_do_seq_with()** can be used to directly execute a subsequence on the downstream sequencer that **seq_cons_if** connector object is connected with. Alternatively, macro **ovm_create_seq()** can be used to create a new subsequence object, and then macros **ovm_send()**, **ovm_rand_send()**, and **ovm_rand_send_with()** can be used without referring to the actual connector object to execute this subsequence on the downstream sequencer connected with **seq_cons_if** object used when creating this subsequence instance.

A new root sequence can be created on a downstream sequencer by calling task **start_sequence()** of a sequence interface.

Full examples of creating, connecting, and driving sequences through virtual sequencers are given in section 14.7.

CHAPTER 9

OVM Transaction Interfaces

In a modular verification environment, communication between verification environment components are carried out through exchange of transactions. Transactions are containers of information that one component must send to another. This information may carry data, status, or commands. In essence, a transaction can model any content once the participating components agree on how that content will be handled. Transactions operate at an abstraction level which can vary from physical wires all the way to abstractions that exist at the product level description of the design. This means that transaction interfaces can be used at any level of abstraction.

Transaction-based communication involves two components that interact over a transaction interface. A *transaction interface* is created by binding two transaction connector objects in each of the two components. A *transaction connector object* serves the same purpose as port objects in connecting SystemVerilog module blocks. During a transaction-based interaction, transactions are moved from a transaction producer to a transaction consumer. A *transaction producer* creates a transaction while a *transaction consumer* uses that transaction to perform an activity. Transactions can optionally move in both directions on a transaction interface. This bidirectional transfer of transactions is useful in cases where one component sends a request transaction to another component and expects to receive a response transaction in return. In this case, both components act as a producer and a consumer of transactions, where the master, the initiator of the transfer, produces a transaction request and consumes the reply transaction, and the slave consumes the request transaction and produces a reply transaction. Figure 9.1. shows the architectural view of transaction-based connectivity and the movement of transactions from producers to consumers.

A transaction-based communication model has a data flow and a control flow property. *Transaction data flow* is always from the producer of a transaction to the consumer of that transaction. A *transaction transfer request* marks the beginning of an exchange between a producer and a consumer. A transaction transfer request is made by the *transaction initiator*. Either the producer or the consumer can be the transaction initiator (i.e., a transaction initiator sends a transaction if it is a producer, and requests a transaction if it is a consumer). A *transaction target* is the recipient of, and responds to, a transaction transfer request (a transaction target accepts a transaction if it is a consumer, and returns a transaction if it is a producer). *Transaction control flow* is always from the transaction initiator to the transaction

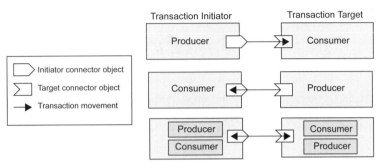

Figure 9.1 Transaction-Based Communication Model

target. Transaction control and data flows do not have to be in the same direction. The transaction-based communication model shown in figure 9.1 allows either the producer or the consumer to be the transaction initiator. In this case, if the producer is the initiator, then the consumer is the target, and the producer puts a transaction into the consumer. If the consumer is the initiator, then the producer is the target, and the consumer requests that the producer give it a new transaction.

Concepts of push mode and pull mode (section 8.1) are related to data and control flow directions. In a push mode interaction, the transaction initiator is also the transaction producer. In a pull mode interaction, the transaction initiator is the transaction consumer.

Transaction data flow can be bidirectional. In this type of connection, the transaction initiator can be both the producer and consumer of transactions. For example, a transaction initiator may produce a transaction, pass this transaction to the target for consumption, and then expect the target to reply back with a reply transaction. In a *unidirectional transaction interface*, transactions move in only one direction. In a *bidirectional transaction interface*, transactions move in both directions over the same transaction interface.

Transaction movement in a class-based environment is achieved through *transaction connector objects* and method calls. In this approach, the initiator component contains a connector object that provides it with a set of predefined methods. While developing the initiator component, these methods are used as needed, with the understanding that the actual implementation of these methods will be provided by the target component that the initiator will eventually get connected to. At the same time, a target component contains a connector object that must provide the implementation of methods that are assumed to be available by any initiator component connecting to this target component. *Transaction connector object kind* refers to the different kinds of connector objects that are used in the initiator and target components, and for routing transaction interfaces through layers of component hierarchy (section 9.1). *Transaction connector object type* is defined by the set of methods that is supported by a connector object.

Transaction connector objects are linked when the component hierarchy is created. Once this link is in place, calling a predefined method of the connector object in the initiator component has the effect of calling the implementation of that method in the target component. A major advantage of a communication infrastructure implemented using this approach is that both the initiator and target components can be implemented independently, and without requiring any special knowledge about the internal implementation of the other component.

A common use of a transaction-based connection is where multiple consumer components initiate requests to a common producer component asking for a transaction. This means that transaction interfaces must support connections between multiple transaction consumers that are also the initiator with a single transaction producer which is also the transaction target. Another common use of a transaction-based connection is where a transaction producer broadcasts its next transaction to multiple target components that each receive a copy of the broadcasted transaction. A classic example of this use model is where multiple verification components (e.g., scoreboard, coverage collector, etc.) receive packets from a monitor component. An *analysis interface* defines a special type of transaction interface where an initiator component that is the producer of transactions can broadcast its transactions to multiple subscribing target components. Transaction-based connectivity does not support the case where a single initiator component that is a transaction consumer is connected to multiple target components that are transaction producers. The reason is that transaction-based connectivity does not support any arbitration mechanism for determining which producer should supply the transaction requested by the consumer.

The OVM class library provides the following transaction interface types:

- Unidirectional transaction interfaces
- Bidirectional transaction interfaces
- Analysis interfaces
- Transaction channels

The implementation of unidirectional and bidirectional interfaces are described in sections 9.3 and 9.4, respectively. Analysis interfaces provide a specialized transaction-based mechanism for allowing multiple target components that are transaction consumers to subscribe to a single initiator component that is a transaction producer. Analysis interfaces are described in section 9.5. Transaction channels provide specialized class objects that contain the implementation of the predefined methods required by transaction connector objects, thereby simplifying both the modeling and the implementation of transaction interfaces. Transaction channels are described in section 9.7.

9.1 Transaction Connector Objects

Figure 9.2 shows an example of a hierarchical verification environment. In this example, components $comp_0$, $comp_1$, $comp_2$, and $comp_4$ are transaction initiators, while components $comp_3$ and $comp_5$ are transaction targets. While building the environment hierarchy, connector objects are needed for the following purposes:

- To instantiate in transaction initiators (e.g., p_0, p_1, p_2, p_5)
- To instantiate in transaction targets (e.g., i_0, i_1)
- To route connections to higher layers of the hierarchy (e.g., p_3, p_4)
- To route connections to other layers of the hierarchy (e.g., e_0)

The OVM class library defines three connector object kinds: imp objects, port objects, and export objects. *Imp objects* are used inside target components to provide the implementation of the predefined methods that are supported by a transaction interface (e.g., i_0, i_1 in figure 9.2). *Port objects* are used inside initiator components to provide access to the predefined methods of the transaction interface (e.g., p_0, p_1, p_2, p_5 in figure 9.2). Port objects are also used to route transaction interfaces to the higher layers of the hierarchy (e.g., p_3, p_4 in figure 9.2). *Export objects* are used to route transaction interfaces to the other layers of the hierarchy (e.g., e_0 in figure 9.2).

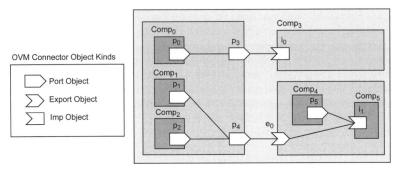

Figure 9.2 OVM Transaction Connector Objects and Hierarchical Connections

The OVM class library defines the following unidirectional connector objects:

```
ovm_UNIDIR_TYPE_imp #(trans_type, imp_parent_type)
ovm_UNIDIR_TYPE_port #(trans_type)
ovm_UNIDIR_TYPE_export #(trans_type)
```

In the above description, **UNIDIR_TYPE** refers to one of the unidirectional interface types supported by the library (section 9.3). Parameter **trans_type** identifies the class type of the transaction moving across the interface, and **imp_parent_type** identifies the class type of the target component in which the imp connector object is instantiated. Examples of using these connector object kinds are given in section 9.3.

The OVM class library defines the following bidirectional connector objects:

```
ovm_BIDIR_TYPE_imp #(req_trans_type, rsp_trans_type, parent_class_type)
ovm_BIDIR_TYPE_port #(req_trans_type, rsp_trans_type)
ovm_BIDIR_TYPE_export #(req_trans_type, rsp_trans_type)
```

In the above description, **BIDIR_TYPE** refers to one of the bidirectional interface types supported by the library (section 9.4). Parameter **req_trans_type** identifies the class type of the transaction object moving from the initiator component to the target component. Parameter **rsp_trans_type** identifies the class type of the transaction object moving from the target component to the initiator component. Examples of using these connector object kinds is given in section 9.4.

9.2 Binding Connector Objects

Every connector object class includes a predefined method used to connect it to the next connector object. The syntax for this method is:

```
function void connect(this_type next_connector_object)
```

Each connector object is linked with the next connector object by calling its **connect()** function with argument **next_connector_object**. In this context, next connector object is defined based on a directional path starting from an initiator component to a target component. For example, given the connection path from component **comp$_2$** to **comp$_5$** in figure 9.2, next connector object for **p$_2$** is **p$_4$**, next connector object for **p$_4$** is **e$_0$**, and next connector object for **e$_0$** is **i$_1$**.

Connector objects in two subcomponents should be connected by the common parent component of these subcomponents. This approach is part of recursive construction guideline (section 7.1) for building a hierarchical environment.

Assuming connector object **from_co** is being connected to connector object **to_co** through statement "**from_co.connect(to_co)**", the following rules should be followed:

- A connector object can be connected only to a single next connector object. In other words, function **connect()** of **from_co** cannot be called with any other connector object once it is called with argument **to_co**. A connector object can, however, receive connections from multiple connector objects. For example, connector object **p$_4$** in figure 9.2 is receiving two connections but is connected only to one object **e$_0$** (see analysis interfaces in section 9.5 for an exception to this rule).
- If **from_co** is a port connector object, then **to_co** can be a port connector object, an export connector object, or an imp connector object.
- If **from_co** is an export connector object, then **to_co** can be an export connector object or an imp connector object.
- An imp connector object cannot be connected to any other connector objects since it is always the last connector on a connection path.

Function **connect()** is used only to specify which connector objects must be connected. It does not connect these objects. Function **resolve_all_bindings()** of the top level component in the hierarchy is used after all connections between connector objects are specified by using function **connect()** to actually establish the necessary connections. Note that by default, function **resolve_all_bindings()** is called as part of the elaboration phase of simulation (table 7.1). As such, calling this function explicitly is only required for specialized implementations where the predefined simulation phases of OVM are not being used.

The following program shows an example of creating a unidirectional and a bidirectional transaction interface across two components. Note that in this example, the focus is on the mechanics of implementing the methods supported by a transaction interface and on binding the connector objects that form this transaction interface. Details of unidirectional and bidirectional interfaces are described in sections 9.3 and 9.4. In addition, the use of transaction interfaces in building a verification environment according to the guidelines of OVM is shown in chapter 13.

```
          Program 9.1: Binding transaction interfaces
 1   :    module top;
 2   :        `include "ovm.svh"
 3   :
 4   :        class request extends ovm_transaction; byte packet; endclass
 5   :        class response extends ovm_transaction; byte packet; endclass
 6   :
 7   :        class initiator extends ovm_component;
 8   :            ovm_blocking_put_port #(request) bp_port;
 9   :            ovm_nonblocking_transport_port #(request, response) nbtr_port;
10   :
11   :            function new(string name, ovm_component parent);
12   :                super.new(name, parent);
13   :                bp_port = new("bp_port", this);
14   :                nbtr_port = new("nbtr_port", this);
15   :            endfunction
16   :        endclass
17   :
18   :        class target extends ovm_component;
19   :            ovm_blocking_put_imp #(request, target) bp_imp;
20   :            ovm_nonblocking_transport_imp #(request, response, target) nbtr_imp;
21   :
22   :            function new(string name, ovm_component parent);
23   :                super.new(name, parent);
24   :                bp_imp = new("bp_imp", this);
25   :                nbtr_imp = new("nbtr_imp", this);
26   :            endfunction
27   :
28   :            task put(input request req); `message(OVM_INFO, (req.packet)) endtask
29   :            function bit nb_transport(input request req, output response rsp); return 1;
30   :            endfunction
31   :        endclass
32   :
33   :        class top_comp extends ovm_component;
34   :            initiator i0;
35   :            target t0;
36   :
37   :            function new(string name, ovm_component parent);
38   :                super.new(name, parent);
39   :                i0 = new("i0", this);
40   :                t0 = new("t0", this);
41   :                i0.bp_port.connect(t0.bp_imp);
42   :                i0.nbtr_port.connect(t0.nbtr_imp);
43   :            endfunction
44   :        endclass
45   :
46   :        top_comp tc;
47   :
48   :        initial begin
49   :            tc = new("tc", null);
50   :            tc.resolve_all_bindings();
51   :        end
52   :    endmodule
```

This example provides a unidirectional interface of type **blocking_put** and a bidirectional interface of type **nonblocking_transport** between an initiator and a target component. Classes **request** and **response** define transaction types, and are defined first (lines 4–5). Class **initiator** (lines 7–16) is defined to include two port connector objects **bp_port** and **nbtr_port** (lines 8, 9). These objects are then initialized in the constructor for this class (lines 13, 14). Class **target** (lines 18–31) is defined to include two imp connector objects **bp_imp** and **nbtr_imp** (lines 19–20). These objects are initialized in the constructor for this class (lines 24, 25). The inclusion of these imp connector objects in class **target** requires that the implementation for the predefined methods of these connector objects also be defined in class **target** (section 9.3). The implementation for these predefined methods is given in class **target** (lines 28–30). The top level component for this example, **top_comp** contains i_0 and t_0, instances of classes **initiator** and **target** respectively (lines 34, 35). These instances are initialized in the constructor for this class (lines 39, 40), and the port and imp connector objects inside each instance are then connected using function **connect()**, and according to the ordering rule required for making such connections (lines 41, 42). The top level component is then instantiated in the top level module (line 46), initialized (line 49), and all of its connections finalized by calling its predefined function **resolve_all_bindings()** (line 50).

9.3 Unidirectional Interfaces

The semantics of transaction flow across a transaction interface is defined by the methods that an imp connector object supports. Table 9.1 lists all of the predefined methods that may be supported by a unidirectional transaction interface.

Category	Type	Return	Name	Arguments
Blocking Put	task	void	put	(input TR t)
Non-blocking Put	function	bit	try_put	(input TR t)
	function	bit	can_put	();
Blocking Get	task	void	get	(output TR t)
Non-blocking Get	function	bit	try_get	(output TR t);
	function	bit	can_get	();
Blocking Peek	task	void	peek	(output TR t);
Non-blocking Peek	function	bit	try_peek	(output TR t);
	function	bit	can_peek	();

Table 9.1: Transaction-Based Communication Methods

The behaviors implemented by these methods are as follows:

- **put()**: Sends a transaction of type **TR** from the initiator to the target. A target implementing the interface will block the calling thread if it cannot immediately accept delivery of the transaction. Because of the potential for waiting, only tasks may call this method.
- **try_put()**: If possible, sends a transaction of type **TR** from the initiator to the target. If the target is ready to accept the transaction argument, it does so and returns **1**. Otherwise it returns **0**.
- **can_put()**: Returns **1** if target is ready to accept a transaction from the initiator, else it returns **0**.
- **get()**: Returns a new transaction of type **TR** from the target to the initiator. The calling thread is blocked if target cannot immediately provide the requested transaction. The new transaction is returned in the provided output argument. The implementation of **get()** must regard the transaction as consumed. Subsequent calls to **get()** must return a

different transaction instance. Because of the potential for waiting, only tasks may call this method.

- **try_get()**: Returns a new transaction of type **TR** from the target to the initiator. If a transaction is immediately available, it is returned in the provided output argument and function returns **1**. Otherwise, the output argument is not modified and **0** is returned.
- **can_get()**: Returns **1** if target is ready to return a transaction immediately upon calling **get()** or **try_get()**. Otherwise it returns **0**.
- **peek()**: Returns a new transaction from target without consuming it. If a transaction is available, then it is written to the provided output argument. If a transaction is not available, the calling thread is blocked until one becomes available. The returned transaction is not consumed. A subsequent call to **peek()** or **get()** will return the same transaction. Because of the potential for waiting, only tasks may call this method.
- **try_peek()**: Returns a new transaction without consuming it. If available, a transaction is written to the output argument and **1** is returned. A subsequent call to **peek()** or **get()** will return the same transaction. If a transaction is not available, the argument remains unmodified and **0** is returned.
- **can_peek()**: Returns **1** if a new transaction is available, **0** otherwise.

The OVM class library defines the following unidirectional interface types (*xxx* indicates connector object kind, and can be one of "**port**", "**export**", or "**imp**"):

- **ovm_blocking_put_*xxx***
- **ovm_nonblocking_put_*xxx***
- **ovm_put_*xxx***
- **ovm_blocking_get_*xxx***
- **ovm_nonblocking_get_*xxx***
- **ovm_get_*xxx***
- **ovm_blocking_peek_*xxx***
- **ovm_nonblocking_peek_*xxx***
- **ovm_peek_*xxx***
- **ovm_blocking_get_peek_*xxx***
- **ovm_nonblocking_get_peek_*xxx***
- **ovm_get_peek_*xxx***

The different interface connector object kinds (i.e., port, export, imp) are used to make a physical connection between components where imp connector objects are instantiated inside target components and port connector objects are instantiated inside initiator components. On the other hand, the different connector object types listed above, define the direction and semantics of data exchange between the initiator and the target components.

Unidirectional interface types differ in the methods they support. Table 9.2 summarizes the methods supported by each of these unidirectional interface types. For example, connector object kinds **ovm_put_port**, **ovm_put_imp**, and **ovm_put_export** support only methods **put()**, **try_put()**, and **can_put()**.

The set of methods supported by each interface type also define the data flow direction of the interface. For example, **peek()** is supported by only an imp connector object that is inside a producer component. Similarly, **put()** is supported by only an imp connector object that is inside a consumer component. This means that an **ovm_peek_xxx** interface is used when the initiator component is the transaction consumer, while an **ovm_put_xxx** interface is used when the initiator component is the transaction producer.

Used when target is	TLM Methods	Unidirectional Connector Object Types (xxx gives connector kind: port, export, imp)											
		ovm_blocking_put_xxx	ovm_nonblocking_put_xxx	ovm_put_xxx	ovm_blocking_get_xxx	ovm_nonblocking_get_xxx	ovm_get_xxx	ovm_blocking_peek_xxx	ovm_nonblocking_peek_xxx	ovm_peek_xxx	ovm_blocking_get_peek_xxx	ovm_nonblocking_get_peek_xxx	ovm_get_peek_xxx
Consumer	put()	☑		☑									
	try_put()		☑	☑									
	can_put()		☑	☑									
Producer	get()				☑		☑				☑		☑
	try_get()					☑	☑					☑	☑
	can_get()					☑	☑					☑	☑
	peek()							☑		☑	☑		☑
	try_peek()								☑	☑		☑	☑
	can_peek()								☑	☑		☑	☑

Table 9.2: Methods Supported by Unidirectional Transaction Interfaces

Figure 9.3 shows an example of the interaction between a producer and a consumer component. In this example, both the producer and the consumer can be the transaction initiator. If a transaction is initiated by the producer, then it places a transaction into the consumer component through its **put_port**. If a transaction is initiated by the consumer component, then it can either peek into, or get a transaction, from the producer through its **get_peek_port**. A level of hierarchy is added to show how connector objects should be used to route transaction interfaces through hierarchy layers. Because of the inclusion of a **put_port** and a **get_peek_port**, the implementation of this example highlights the use of all predefined methods listed in table 9.2. The implementation of this example is shown in the remainder of this section.

Top Level Block

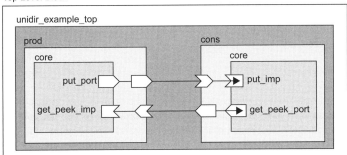

Figure 9.3 Unidirectional Transaction Interface Example

The first step in defining this environment is to define the base transaction type. This definition is shown in the following program:

```
Program 9.2: Defining the transaction object
1  :    class transaction extends ovm_transaction;
2  :         byte packet;
3  :    endclass
```

The implementation of producer core component highlights the use of connector objects **ovm_put_port, ovm_get_peek_imp** and implementation of methods that must be supported by imp connector object **get_peek_imp**. This implementation is shown below:

```
Program 9.3: Producer core implementation
1  :    class producer_core extends ovm_component;
2  :         ovm_put_port #(transaction) put_port;
3  :         ovm_get_peek_imp #(transaction, producer_core) get_peek_imp;
4  :
5  :         function new(string name, ovm_component parent);
6  :              super.new(name, parent);
7  :              put_port = new("put_port", this);
8  :              get_peek_imp = new("get_peek_imp", this);
9  :         endfunction
10 :
11 :         transaction to_consumer[$];
12 :
13 :         function bit can_get(); return (to_consumer.size() > 0); endfunction
14 :
15 :         task get(output transaction tr);
16 :              if (can_get() == 0) @(can_get());
17 :              tr = to_consumer.pop_front();
18 :         endtask
19 :
20 :         function bit try_get(output transaction tr);
21 :              if (can_get() == 0) return 0;
22 :              tr = to_consumer.pop_front();
23 :              return 1;
24 :         endfunction
25 :
26 :         function bit can_peek(); return (to_consumer.size() > 0); endfunction
27 :
28 :         task peek(output transaction tr);
29 :              if (can_get() == 0) @(can_get());
30 :              tr = to_consumer[0];
31 :         endtask
32 :
33 :         function bit try_peek(output transaction tr);
34 :              if (can_peek() == 0) return 0;
35 :              tr = to_consumer[0];
36 :              return 1;
37 :         endfunction
38 :    endclass
```

In this implementation, class **producer_core** is defined to have port connector object **put_port** of type **ovm_put_port** (line 2) and imp connector object **get_peek_imp** of type **ovm_get_peek_imp** (line 3). These connector objects are initialized in the constructor for this class (lines 7, 8). The implementation of methods that must be supported by **get_peek_imp** (lines 13–37) is based on the assumption that produced transactions are placed on queue **to_consumer** (line 11). The part of implementation that interacts with **put_port** is not shown, but is assumed that a call to any of the predefined methods of **put_port** results in calling the implementation of that method in the consumer core component. Any call to predefined methods of a port object connector of type **ovm_get_peek_port** in another component that is connected to **get_peek_imp** of this class, results in the implementation of that method in this class to be called.

The implementation of consumer core component highlights the use of **ovm_put_imp**, **ovm_get_peek_port** and implementation of methods that must be supported by imp connector object **get_put_imp**. This implementation is shown below:

```
Program 9.4: Consumer core implementation
1    :    class consumer_core extends ovm_component;
2    :        ovm_put_imp #(transaction, consumer_core) put_imp;
3    :        ovm_get_peek_port #(transaction) get_peek_port;
4    :
5    :        function new(string name, ovm_component parent);
6    :            super.new(name, parent);
7    :            put_imp = new("put_imp", this);
8    :            get_peek_port = new("get_peek_port", this);
9    :        endfunction
10   :
11   :        transaction from_producer[$:5];
12   :
13   :        function bit can_put();
14   :            return (from_producer.size() < 5);
15   :        endfunction
16   :
17   :        task put(input transaction tr);
18   :            if (can_put() == 0) @(can_put());
19   :            from_producer.push_back(tr);
20   :        endtask
21   :
22   :        function bit try_put(input transaction tr);
23   :            if (can_put() == 0) return 0;
24   :            from_producer.push_back(tr);
25   :            return 1;
26   :        endfunction
27   :    endclass
```

In this implementation, class **consumer_core** is defined to have imp connector object **put_imp** of type **ovm_put_imp** (line 2) and port connector object **get_peek_port** of type **ovm_get_peek_port** (line 3). These connector objects are initialized in the constructor for this class (lines 7, 8). The implementation of methods that must be supported by **put_imp** (lines 13–26) is based on the assumption that transactions to be consumed are placed on queue **from_producer** (line 11). The part of implementation that interacts with **get_peek_port** is not shown, but it is assumed that a call to any of the predefined methods of **get_peek_port** results in calling the implementation of that method in the producer core component. Any call to predefined methods of a port object connector of type **ovm_put_port** (e.g., **put()**) in another component that is connected to **put_imp** of this class, results in the implementation of that method in this class to be called.

The implementations of producer and consumer components highlight the inclusion of connector objects for the purpose of crossing hierarchy layers. These implementations are shown in the following program:

```
Program 9.5: Producer and consumer component implementation
1   :   class producer extends ovm_component;
2   :       ovm_put_port #(transaction) put_port;
3   :       ovm_get_peek_export #(transaction) get_peek_export;
4   :       producer_core core;
5   :
6   :       function new(string name, ovm_component parent);
7   :           super.new(name, parent);
8   :           put_port = new("put_port", this);
9   :           get_peek_export = new("get_peek_export", this);
10  :           core = new("producer_core", this);
11  :           core.put_port.connect(put_port);
12  :           get_peek_export.connect(core.get_peek_imp);
13  :       endfunction
14  :   endclass
15  :
16  :   class consumer extends ovm_component;
17  :       ovm_put_export #(transaction) put_export;
18  :       ovm_get_peek_port #(transaction) get_peek_port;
19  :       consumer_core core;
20  :
21  :       function new(string name, ovm_component parent);
22  :           super.new(name, parent);
23  :           put_export = new("put_export", this);
24  :           get_peek_port = new("get_peek_port", this);
25  :
26  :           core = new("consumer_core", this);
27  :           put_export.connect(core.put_imp);
28  :           core.get_peek_port.connect(get_peek_port);
29  :       endfunction
30  :   endclass
```

The implementation of class **producer** (lines 1–14) contains object **core** which is an instance of **producer_core**, port connector object **put_port** used to connect **core.put_port** to the higher layer, and export connector object **get_peek_export** used to connect the higher layer to **core.get_peek_imp**. These objects are initialized in the class constructor (lines 8–10) and then appropriate connections are made between connector objects in the local scope and connector objects in object **core** (lines 11, 12). The implementation of class **consumer** (lines 16–30) follows the same flow.

The implementation of component **unidir_example_top** highlights the linking of connector objects of components that exist in the same level of the hierarchy. In this implementation, shown below, connector objects inside instances of producer and consumer components are connected in the class constructor for class **unidir_example_top**:

```
Program 9.6: Example top component implementation
1   :   class unidir_example_top extends ovm_component;
2   :       producer prod;
3   :       consumer cons;
4   :
5   :       function new(string name, ovm_component parent);
6   :           super.new(name, parent);
7   :           prod = new("prod", this);
8   :           cons = new("cons", this);
9   :
10  :           prod.put_port.connect(cons.put_export);
11  .           cons.get_peek_port.connect(prod.get_peek_export);
```

```
12  :          endfunction
13  :      endclass
```

The implementation of environment top level, shown below, highlights the step for resolving all bindings made in the hierarchy rooted at a component, and illustrates the use of a transaction port by calling its predefined method:

```
Program 9.7: Top level component instantiation and binding resolution
1   :    module top;
2   :        `include "ovm.svh"
3   :        `include "program_9.2"      // transaction class
4   :        `include "program_9.3"      // producer_core class
5   :        `include "program_9.4"      // consumer_core class
6   :        `include "program_9.5"      // producer and consumer class
7   :        `include "program_9.6"      // unidir_example_top class
8   :
9   :        transaction tr;
10  :        unidir_example_top extop;
11  :
12  :        initial begin
13  :            extop = new("unidir_example_top", null);
14  :            extop.resolve_all_bindings();
15  :            tr = new();
16  :            extop.prod.core.put_port.put(tr);
17  :        end
18  :    endmodule
```

In this implementation, an instance of component **unidir_example_top** is first created (line 13). The connections between all components in the hierarchy rooted at **extop** are then resolved by explicitly calling predefined function **resolve_all_bindings()** of **extop** derived from base class **ovm_component**. A new transaction is then created (line 15) and passed to method **put()** of port object **put_port** of component **extop.prod.core**. This call results in calling method **put()** of instance **extop.cons.core** with argument **tr**.

To keep the implementation concise, the example shown in this section uses the class constructor to create and link connector objects. In a full-scale verification environment, the steps for creating and linking connector objects are performed as part of verification hierarchy construction flow (section 7.2). In addition, function **resolve_all_bindings()** is called by default in the elaboration phase of a verification flow (section 7.4), therefore removing the need for explicitly calling this function in a verification environment managed through the predefined simulation phases of the OVM class library.

9.4 Bidirectional Interfaces

Unidirectional interfaces allow transactions to move in only one direction. In contrast, bidirectional interfaces allow transactions to move in both directions across the interface. A bidirectional interface is identified by two transaction types, one for each transfer direction. Bidirectional interfaces use the methods defined for unidirectional interfaces (table 9.1) to move data in both directions. In addition, bidirectional interfaces may support methods listed in table 9.3.

Category	Type	Return	Name	Arguments
Transport	task		transport	(input REQ req, output RSP rsp)
Non-blocking Transport	function	bit	nb_transport	(input REQ req, output RSP rsp)

Table 9.3: Transaction-Based Communication Bidirectional Methods

The behavior implemented by methods listed in table 9.3 is as follows:

- **transport()**: Sends a transaction request to the target component for execution. Upon return, a response is provided by the target in the output argument **rsp**. Blocking might occur during execution, so only tasks may call this method.
- **nb_transport()**: Sends a transaction request to the target component for immediate execution. Execution must occur without blocking. The response is provided by the target in the output argument. If for any reason the request could not be executed immediately, a **0** must be returned, otherwise **1** is returned.

The OVM class library defines the following bidirectional interface types (**xxx** indicates connector object kind, and can be one of "**port**", "**export**", or "**imp**"):

- **ovm_blocking_master_xxx**
- **ovm_nonblocking_master_xxx**
- **ovm_master_xxx**
- **ovm_blocking_slave_xxx**
- **ovm_nonblocking_slave_xxx**
- **ovm_slave_xxx**
- **ovm_blocking_transport_xxx**
- **ovm_nonblocking_transport_xxx**
- **ovm_transport_xxx**

Bidirectional interface types have the ability to use a single interface to send one type of transaction from the transaction initiator to the transaction target, and receive a different kind of transaction from the transaction target. The types of these transactions are given by the parameters specified when instantiating bidirectional interface objects (see section 9.1 for the required parameter list for bidirectional connector objects). Master or slave connector objects use methods defined for unidirectional interfaces to move transactions between the initiator and the target on a single interface. Transport connector objects use methods especially introduced for bidirectional transfer of transactions. Table 9.4 summarizes the methods supported by each of these bidirectional interface types.

A transaction initiator that is a producer contains a *master connector object* (e.g., **ovm_blocking_master_port**), uses **put()** methods to move a transaction of type **req** to the target component, and uses **get()** or **peek()** methods to ask the target component for a transaction of type **rsp**. In contrast, a transaction initiator that is a consumer contains a *slave connector object* (e.g., **ovm_blocking_slave_port**), uses **get()** or **peek()** methods to receive a transaction of type **req** from the target component, and uses **put()** methods to return to the target component a transaction of type **rsp**.

A *transport connector object* uses a single method call to send a transaction of type **req** and receive a transaction of type **rsp**. This type of interface can be only used by transaction initiators that are producers. Master interface types allow the sending and receiving of transactions to be performed using separate method calls. Transport interface types require that this exchange be performed using a single method call.

TLM Methods	Bidirectional Connector Object Types (xxx gives connector kind: port, export, imp)								
	ovm_blocking_master_xxx	ovm_nonblocking_master_xxx	ovm_master_xxx	ovm_blocking_slave_xxx	ovm_nonblocking_slave_xxx	ovm_slave_xxx	ovm_blocking_transport_xxx	ovm_nonblocking_transport_xxx	ovm_transport_xxx
put()	req		req	rsp		rsp			
try_put()		req	req		rsp	rsp			
can_put()		req	req		rsp	rsp			
get()	rsp		rsp	req		req			
try_get()		rsp	rsp		req	req			
can_get()		rsp	rsp		req	req			
peek()	rsp		rsp	req		req			
try_peek()		rsp	rsp		req	req			
can_peek()		rsp	rsp		req	req			
transport()							req,rsp		req,rsp
nb_transport()								req,rsp	req,rsp

req and rsp are first and second parameters of bidirectional connector objects (section 9.1)
Each table entry indicates the transaction type handled by the corresponding method

Table 9.4: Methods Supported by Bidirectional Transaction Interfaces

Figure 9.4 shows an example of interaction between a producer and a consumer component. In this example, the producer is the transaction initiator. The producer component contains two bidirectional ports of types **ovm_transport_port** and **ovm_blocking_master_port**. In both these connections, the producer component is the transaction initiator. The difference between these two interfaces is that in the **ovm_transport** interface, the sending of the request transaction and the receiving of a response transaction occurs with one method call, where in the **ovm_blocking_master** interface, this exchange occurs using separate method calls. The implementation of this example is shown in the remainder of this section.

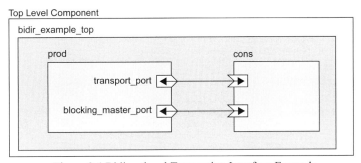

Figure 9.4 Bidirectional Transaction Interface Example

The first step in implementing this environment is to define the base request and response transaction types. This definition is shown in the following program:

```
Program 9.8: Defining the request and response transaction objects
1   :   class request_tr extends ovm_transaction;
2   :        byte request;
3   :   endclass
4   :   class response_tr extends ovm_transaction;
5   :        byte response;
6   :   endclass
```

The implementation of a producer component highlights the use of **ovm_transport_port**, and **ovm_blocking_master_port** connector object types. This implementation is shown below:

```
Program 9.9: Producer implementation
1   :   class producer extends ovm_component;
2   :        ovm_transport_port #(request_tr, response_tr) transport_port;
3   :        ovm_blocking_master_port #(request_tr, response_tr) b_master_port;
4   :
5   :        function new(string name, ovm_component parent);
6   :             super.new(name, parent);
7   :             transport_port = new("transport_port", this);
8   :             b_master_port = new("b_master_port", this);
9   :        endfunction
10  :   endclass
```

In this implementation, class **producer** is defined to have port connector objects **transport_port** of type **ovm_transport_port** (line 2), and **b_master_port** of type **ovm_blocking_master_port** (line 3). These connector objects are initialized in the constructor for this class (lines 7, 8). The part of implementation that interacts with **transport_port** and **b_master_port** is not shown, but it is assumed that a call to any of the predefined methods of these connector objects results in calling the implementation of that method in the consumer component.

The implementation of a consumer component highlights the use of imp connector object types **ovm_transport_imp**, and **ovm_blocking_master_imp**, and the implementation of methods that must be supported by these objects. This implementation is shown below:

```
Program 9.10: Consumer implementation
1   :   class consumer extends ovm_component;
2   :        ovm_transport_imp #(request_tr, response_tr, consumer) transport_imp;
3   :        ovm_blocking_master_imp #(request_tr, response_tr, consumer) b_master_imp;
4   :
5   :        function new(string name, ovm_component parent);
6   :             super.new(name, parent);
7   :             transport_imp = new("transport_imp", this);
8   :             b_master_imp = new("b_master_imp", this);
9   :        endfunction
10  :
11  :        function bit must_wait_for_response(request_tr req_tr); endfunction
12  :        function void handle_request(request_tr req_tr); endfunction
13  :        function response_tr get_response(); endfunction
14  :        function response_tr peek_at_response(); endfunction
15  :        task wait_until_next_request_can_be_accepted(); endtask
16  :        task wait_until_response_is_ready(); endtask
17  :
18  :        task transport(input request_tr req_tr, output response_tr rsp_tr);
```

```
19  :                    wait_until_next_request_can_be_accepted();
20  :                    handle_request(req_tr);
21  :                    wait_until_response_is_ready();
22  :                    rsp_tr = get_response();
23  :              endtask
24  :
25  :              function bit nb_transport(input request_tr req_tr, output response_tr rsp_tr);
26  :                    if (must_wait_for_response(req_tr)) return 0;
27  :                    handle_request(req_tr);
28  :                    rsp_tr = get_response();
29  :                    return 1;
30  :              endfunction
31  :
32  :              task put(input request_tr req_tr);
33  :                    wait_until_next_request_can_be_accepted();
34  :                    handle_request(req_tr);
35  :              endtask
36  :
37  :              task get(output response_tr rsp_tr);
38  :                    wait_until_response_is_ready();
39  :                    rsp_tr = get_response();
40  :              endtask
41  :
42  :              task peek(output response_tr rsp_tr);
43  :                    wait_until_response_is_ready();
44  :                    rsp_tr = peek_at_response();
45  :              endtask
46  :     endclass
```

In this implementation, class **consumer**, derived from base class **ovm_component**, is defined to have imp connector objects **transport_imp** of type **ovm_transport_imp** (line 2), and **b_master_imp** of type **ovm_blocking_master_imp** (line 3). These connector objects are initialized in the constructor for this class (lines 7, 8). This class includes a number of methods used for handling request and response transactions (lines 11–16). The implementation of these methods is not shown, but should be clear from usage and method names. The implementation of methods that must be supported by imp connector object **transport_imp** is shown on lines 18–30. The implementation of methods that must be supported by imp connector object **b_master_imp** is shown on lines 32–45. It should be noted that the argument type for task **put()** (line 32) is **request_tr** which is the first parameter used in declaring **b_master_imp** (line 3), and the argument type for tasks **get()** and **peek()** is **response_tr** which is the second parameter used in declaring **b_master_imp** (line 3).

The implementation of component **bidir_example_top** highlights the linking of connector objects at the same level of the hierarchy. In this implementation, shown below, connector objects inside instances of producer and consumer components are connected in the constructor for class **bidir_example_top**:

```
      Program 9.11: Example top component implementation
1   :     class bidir_example_top extends ovm_component;
2   :              producer prod;
3   :              consumer cons;
4   :
5   :              function new(string name, ovm_component parent);
6   :                    super.new(name, parent);
7   :                    prod = new("prod", this);
8   :                    cons = new("cons", this);
9   :
10  :                    prod.transport_port.connect(cons.transport_imp);
```

```
11  :                    prod.b_master_port.connect(cons.b_master_imp);
12  :            endfunction
13  :        endclass
```

The implementation of environment top level, shown below, highlights the step for resolving all bindings made in the hierarchy rooted at a component, and illustrates the use of a transaction port:

```
Program 9.12: Top level component instantiation and binding resolution
1   :   module top;
2   :            `include "ovm.svh"
3   :            `include "program_9.8"      // request/response classes
4   :            `include "program_9.9"      // producer class
5   :            `include "program_9.10"     // consumer class
6   :            `include "program_9.11"     // bidir_example_top class
7   :
8   :            request_tr req_tr;
9   :            response_tr rsp_tr;
10  :            bidir_example_top extop;
11  :
12  :            initial begin
13  :                extop = new("bidir_example_top", null);
14  :                extop.resolve_all_bindings();
15  :                req_tr = new();
16  :                extop.prod.transport_port.transport(req_tr, rsp_tr);
17  :                `message(OVM_INFO, (rep_tr.response))
18  :            end
19  :   endmodule
```

In this implementation, an instance of component **bidir_example_top** is first created (line 13). The connections between all components in the hierarchy rooted at **extop** is then resolved by explicitly calling the predefined function **resolve_all_bindings()** of **extop** (line 14). A new request transaction is then created (line 15) and passed to method **transport()** of port object **transport_port** of component **extop.prod**. This call results in calling method **transport()** of instance **extop.cons** with argument **req_tr and rsp_tr**. The value of **rsp_tr** is updated by the time statement on line 17 is reached.

9.5 Analysis Interface

The implementation of transaction interfaces, as presented so far, does not allow a single initiator component to be connected to multiple target components. The reason for this limitation is that in this type of connection, and when the initiator component is the transaction consumer, it is not clear which target component should respond when task **get()** is called by the initiator component. Connecting a single initiator component to multiple target components is, however, very useful if the initiator component is the transaction producer. This type of connection provides these important benefits:

- A transaction producer can broadcast its transactions to multiple target components.
- The transaction producer does not need any knowledge of how many consumer components are receiving the transaction that is being broadcasted.
- Transaction consumers can subscribe to the broadcast as needed.

One common use model for this type of connection is when a monitor component collects packets from a DUV port, and then broadcasts these collected packets. The broadcasted packet can then be received and processed by multiple components requiring access to this packet (e.g., scoreboard).

The OVM class library provides the *analysis interface* for implementing this type of broadcast connectivity. The analysis interface supports the following connector object kinds:

```
ovm_analysis_port #(tr_type)
ovm_analysis_export #(tr_type)
ovm_analysis_imp #(tr_type, imp_parent_type)
```

In this syntax, **tr_type** gives the type of broadcasted transaction, and **imp_parent_type** gives the class type for the component in which the imp connector object is placed.

An analysis interface supports only a single method given by the following function prototype:

```
function void write(input tr_type tr);
```

The implementation of this function should be supplied in a target component, which by definition of an analysis interface, is also the transaction consumer. Calling this function in the initiator component results in calling the implementation of this function in all of the target components that are attached to this initiator component. Note that each target component may consume the broadcasted transaction in a different way, and as such, the implementation of this function in each target component may be customized to the local scope of that target component.

Figure 9.4 shows an example of interaction between a broadcaster that produces transactions and multiple subscriber components. In this example, the initiator component contains an analysis port of type **ovm_analysis_port**. The target components each contain an analysis imp connector object **analysis_imp** of type **ovm_analysis_imp**. The implementation of this example is shown in the remainder of this section.

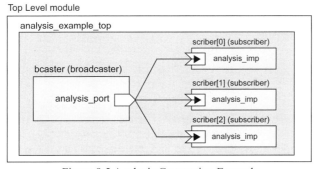

Figure 9.5 Analysis Connection Example

The first step in defining this environment is to define the base request and response transaction types. This definition is shown in the following program:

```
Program 9.13: Defining the transaction object
1  :    class transaction extends ovm_transaction;
2  :        byte packet; endclass
3  :    endclass
```

The implementation of component **broadcaster** highlights the use of port connector object **ovm_analysis_port**. This implementation is shown below:

```
Program 9.14: Broadcaster implementation
1  :    class broadcaster extends ovm_component;
2  :        ovm_analysis_port #(transaction) analysis_port;
3  :
4  :        function new(string name, ovm_component parent);
5  :            super.new(name, parent);
6  :            analysis_port = new("analysis_port", this);
7  :        endfunction
8  :    endclass
```

In this implementation, class **broadcaster** is defined to contain analysis port connector object **analysis_port** of type **ovm_analysis_port** (line 2). This connector object is initialized in the constructor for this class (lines 6). The part of implementation that interacts with this **analysis_port** is not shown, but it is assumed that calling the predefined function **write()** of **analysis_port** results in calling the implementation of that method in *all* of the target components attached to this port object.

The implementation of component **subscriber** highlights the use of analysis imp connector object **ovm_analysis_imp**, and the implementation of its predefined function **write()**. This implementation is shown below:

```
Program 9.15: Subscriber implementation
1  :    class subscriber extends ovm_component;
2  :        ovm_analysis_imp #(transaction, subscriber) analysis_imp;
3  :
4  :        function new(string name, ovm_component parent);
5  :            super.new(name, parent);
6  :            analysis_imp = new("analysis_imp", this);
7  :        endfunction
8  :
9  :        function void write(transaction tr);
10 :            `message(OVM_INFO, ("received tr in subscriber ", get_name()))
11 :        endfunction
12 :    endclass
```

In this implementation, class **subscriber** is defined to contain analysis imp connector object **analysis_imp** of type **ovm_analysis_imp** (line 2). This connector object is initialized in the constructor for this class (lines 6). The implementation of function **write()** that must be provided by **analysis_imp** is shown on lines 9–11. This is a generic implementation that simply displays the received transaction, but can be changed to any required processing of the incoming transaction.

The implementation of component **analysis_example_top** highlights the linking of one analysis port connector object to multiple analysis imp connector objects:

Program 9.16: Analysis example top component implementation

```
1   :   class analysis_example_top extends ovm_component;
2   :           broadcaster bcaster;
3   :           subscriber scribers[3];
4   :
5   :           function new(string name, ovm_component parent);
6   :                   super.new(name, parent);
7   :                   mon = new("mon", this);
8   :                   for (int i = 0; i <= 3; i++) begin
9   :                           string inst_name; $sformat(inst_name, "ms[%0d]", i);
10  :                           scribers[i] = new(inst_name,this);
11  :                           bcaster.analysis_port.connect(scribers[i].analysis_imp);
12  :                   end
13  :           endfunction
14  :   endclass
```

In this implementation, class **analysis_example_top** is defined to include **bcaster**, an instance of **broadcaster** (line 2), and **scribers**, an array of objects of type **subscriber** (line 3). Instance **bcaster** is initialized in the constructor (line 7), and then in a loop, each subscriber is created (line 10) and connected to the broadcaster through its connector object (line 11).

The implementation of environment top level, shown below, highlights the steps for resolving all bindings made in the hierarchy rooted at a component, and illustrates the use of the analysis interface:

Program 9.17: Top level component instantiation and binding resolution

```
1   :   module top;
2   :           `include "ovm.svh"
3   :           `include "program_9.13"    // transaction class
4   :           `include "program_9.14"    // broadcaster class
5   :           `include "program_9.15"    // subscriber class
6   :           `include "program_9.16"    // analysis_example_top class
7   :
8   :           transaction tr;
9   :           analysis_example_top extop;
10  :
11  :           initial begin
12  :                   extop = new("analysis_example_top", null);
13  :                   extop.resolve_all_bindings();
14  :                   tr = new();
15  :                   extop.bcaster.analysis_port.write(tr);
16  :           end
17  :   endmodule
```

In this implementation, an instance of component **analysis_example_top** is first created (line 12). The connections between all components in the hierarchy rooted at **extop** is then resolved by explicitly calling predefined function **resolve_all_bindings()** of **extop** (line 13). A new request transaction is then created (line 14) and passed to method **write()** of port object **analysis_port** of component **extop.bcaster**. This call results in calling method **write()** of every instance of **subscribers** that is connected with **analysis_port**.

9.6 Multiple Connector Objects in One Component

Instantiating an imp connector object in a component leads to predefined method(s) being added to the definition of that component (tables 9.2 and 9.4, and section 9.5). The behavior supported by a transaction interface is implemented by defining the body of these methods. One complication of this approach is that two imp connector objects that require the same method cannot be added to the same component. For example, two or more **ovm_blocking_put_imp** connector objects cannot be placed inside the same component since each of these objects requires a dedicated function **put()**, and the class that models a component can contain only one definition of function **put()**.

The OVM class library resolves this issue by providing special macros for declaring new imp connector object types whose predefined method names are different from the default method names assumed by the standard imp object types of the class library. Column 1 in table 9.5 summarizes the macros that are available for declaring new imp connector objects for different types of transaction interfaces. Column 2 shows the new type that is created by each macro.

Macro for Declaring New Imp Type	Imp Connector Type Name
`ovm_blocking_put_imp_decl(SFX)	ovm_blocking_put_imp_SFX
`ovm_nonblocking_put_imp_decl(SFX)	ovm_nonblocking_put_imp_SFX
`ovm_put_imp_decl(SFX)	ovm_put_imp_SFX
`ovm_blocking_get_imp_decl(SFX)	ovm_blocking_get_imp_SFX
`ovm_nonblocking_get_imp_decl(SFX)	ovm_nonblocking_get_imp_SFX
`ovm_get_imp_decl(SFX)	ovm_get_imp_SFX
`ovm_blocking_peek_imp_decl(SFX)	ovm_blocking_peek_imp_SFX
`ovm_nonblocking_peek_imp_decl(SFX)	ovm_nonblocking_peek_imp_SFX
`ovm_peek_imp_decl(SFX)	ovm_peek_imp_SFX
`ovm_blocking_get_peek_imp_decl(SFX)	ovm_blocking_get_peek_imp_SFX
`ovm_nonblocking_get_peek_imp_decl(SFX)	ovm_nonblocking_get_peek_imp_SFX
`ovm_get_peek_imp_decl(SFX)	ovm_get_peek_imp_SFX
`ovm_blocking_master_imp_decl(SFX)	ovm_blocking_master_imp_SFX
`ovm_nonblocking_master_imp_decl(SFX)	ovm_nonblocking_master_imp_SFX
`ovm_master_imp_decl(SFX)	ovm_master_imp_SFX
`ovm_blocking_slave_imp_decl(SFX)	ovm_blocking_slave_imp_SFX
`ovm_nonblocking_slave_imp_decl(SFX)	ovm_nonblocking_slave_imp_SFX
`ovm_slave_imp_decl(SFX)	ovm_slave_imp_SFX
`ovm_blocking_transport_imp_decl(SFX)	ovm_blocking_transport_imp_SFX
`ovm_non_blocking_transport_imp_decl(SFX)	ovm_non_blocking_transport_imp_SFX
`ovm_transport_imp_decl(SFX)	ovm_transport_imp_SFX
`ovm_analysis_imp_decl(SFX)	ovm_analysis_imp_SFX

Table 9.5: Macros for Defining New Imp Connector Object Types

The use of this approach to include multiple imp connector objects in one component is shown in the following program fragment:

```
┌──────────────────────────────────────────────┐
│ Program 9.18:  Declaring new imp object types  │
└                                                
                      ⋮

 1   :    'ovm_blocking_put_imp_decl(_rcv)
 2   :    'ovm_blocking_put_imp_decl(_xmt)
 3   :
 4   :    class rcv_xmt_component #(type T=int) extends ovm_component;
 5   :          ovm_blocking_put_imp_rcv #(T) rcv_imp;
 6   :          ovm_blocking_put_imp_xmt #(T) xmt_imp;
 7   :
 8   :          function void put_rcv(input T t);
 9   :                .
10   :                .
11   :          endfunction
12   :
13   :          function void put_xmt(input T t);
14   :                .
15   :                .
16   :          endfunction
17   :    endclass
                      ⋮
└──────────────────────────────────────────────
```

In this implementation, macro **ovm_blocking_put_imp_decl()** is used to declare two new imp connector objects types (line 1, 2) that support the blocking put behavior. Note that these macros define new class types, and as such, are placed at the same syntactical level as a class declaration.

The use of macro **ovm_blocking_put_imp_decl()** (lines 1, 2) defines new imp connector object types **ovm_blocking_put_imp_rcv** and **ovm_blocking_put_imp_xmt**. These new imp connector types are then used to instantiate imp connector objects **rcv_imp** and **xmt_imp** in class **rcv_xmt_component** (lines 5,6), adding functions **put_rcv()** and **put_xmt()** respectively. Calling function **put()** of a port connector object linked with imp connector object **rcv_imp** results in calling function **put_rcv()**, while calling function **put()** of a port connector object linked with imp connector object **xmt_imp** results in calling function **put_xmt()**.

A full implementation, using this approach to add two analysis imp connector objects to a scoreboard, is shown in section 13.10.

9.7 Transaction Channels

Transaction interfaces described so far in this chapter, are passive in nature. This means that the interface simply acts as a conduit of transactions, and one side of the interface must act as the transaction initiator and the other side must act as the target providing the implementation of methods that are called by the transaction initiator.

Introducing a communication channel that connects a producer and consumer allows components on both sides of the interface to both be either the transaction initiator or the target. In this configuration, the communication channel would hold the infrastructure that is necessary for managing the transfer of transactions from the producer to the consumer. Table 9.6 shows a summary of the roles a transaction producer and consumer can take in exchanging transactions.

Producer	Consumer	Channel Type	Control Flow	Notes
Initiator	Target	Not Needed	Producer to Consumer	Producer decides when a transaction should be created and passed to the consumer.
Target	Initiator	Not Needed	Consumer to Producer	The consumer decides when it needs a new transaction and requests the producer to create a new transaction.
Initiator	Initiator	Passive	From both Initiators to the Channel	Producer decides when it needs to send a new transaction, the consumer decides when it needs a new transaction. The channel stores each request and acts as the intermediary between the initiators. The channel has to have the ability to store transactions.
Target	Target	Active	From Channel to both targets	The channel actively requests the next transaction from the producer and pushes that transaction into the consumer. The timing of all transactions is decided by the channel. The channel can be pass-through or have memory to store transactions.

Table 9.6: Transaction Producer and Consumer Roles

Rows 1 and 2 summarize the case where one of the two communicating components is the initiator and the other side is the target. These two cases are implemented using transaction interfaces described in chapter 9.

Row 3 summarizes the case where both the producer and the consumer are initiators. In this case, a producer decides when to pass its transaction to the channel, and a consumer decides when to take that transaction from the channel. In this configuration, the channel is passive (i.e., does not decide when transfers occur), and must have the ability to store transactions received from the producer.

Row 4 summarizes the case where both the producer and consumer are targets. In this case, the channel is active (i.e., decides transaction transfer timing), and can either be a pass-through or store the transactions received from the producer.

Figure 9.6 shows the architectural view of a passive transaction channel. As shown, the producer and consumer contain port connector objects, and the channel contains the imp connector objects. An important benefit derived from this configuration is that the implementation of all methods required by the imp connector objects must be provided as part of the channel. This means that once a passive channel is implemented for a given transaction type, there is no longer a need to provide method implementations inside either the producer or the consumer, effectively eliminating a major part of the effort required for building a transaction-based connection. So, given a passive channel for a given transaction type, implementing the connection between a producer and consumer is as simple of instantiating port connector objects inside each component and connecting them to the channel.

Passive channels are more useful than active channels. The reason is that passive channels eliminate the need for providing method implementations in the producer and consumer components, but at the same time, leave the timing of transaction transfer to the producer and consumer components. Active channels, however, require that method implementations be

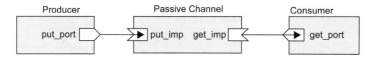

Figure 9.6 Architectural View of Passive Channel Connections

provided by the producer and the consumer, while taking control of the timing for transaction movement. Clearly, a passive channel is a more useful structure for connecting components.

The following passive channel types are supported by the OVM class library:

- TLM FIFO
- Analysis FIFO
- Request/response channel

These channel types are described in the following subsections.

9.7.1 TLM FIFO Channel

The OVM class library provides class **tlm_fifo** for modeling a TLM FIFO channel. The architecture of this component is shown in Figure 9.7. This component provides an instance of all unidirectional connector object types along with the implementation of the methods that must be supported. The name and type of each connector object is given in this figure. A producer component can connect to any of the **put()** type connector objects, and a consumer component can connect with any of the **get()** or **peek()** type connector objects. This implementation also provides an analysis interface for put operations and an analysis interface for get operations. These analysis interfaces can be connected to components that need to be informed anytime a transaction is passed to the FIFO channel and anytime a transaction is received from the FIFO channel.

Given a TLM FIFO channel, the connection of a transaction producer and consumer is implemented as follows:

- A producer component containing a port connector object supporting its required methods is instantiated.
- A consumer component containing a port connector object supporting its required methods is instantiated.
- A TLM FIFO channel, with its transaction type defined using parameter **tr_type**, is instantiated.
- Port connector objects in the producer and consumer components are connected with the appropriate imp connector objects in the channel.

With this implementation, the producer decides when to pass a transaction to the channel, and the consumer decides when to receive a transaction from the channel. Meanwhile, analysis ports **put_ap** and **get_ap** can also be used to listen to the transaction that was put into or received from the channel.

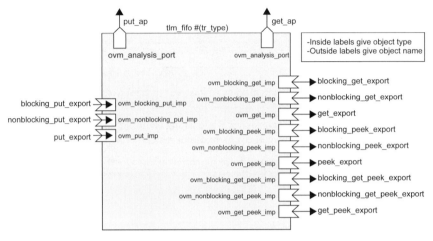

Figure 9.7 Implementation View of tlm_fifo

9.7.2 Analysis FIFO Channel

An analysis interface is a powerful construct for broadcasting transactions to multiple sub-scriber components. One limitation of a straight connection between an analysis port object and an analysis imp connector object is that problems can arise if the transaction producer creates multiple transactions in the same simulation time when an analysis interface sub-scriber cannot handle multiple transactions in one simulation time. An analysis FIFO chan-nel provides a buffer between the transaction producer and any of its subscribers that may not be able to handle multiple incoming transactions. The use of an analysis fifo channel is shown in figure 9.8 where slow subscribers use an analysis channel so that they can take the next transaction broadcasted by the producer at their own pace.

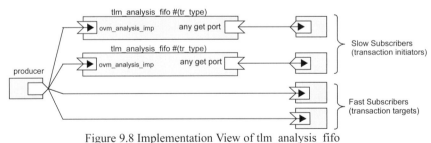

Figure 9.8 Implementation View of tlm_analysis_fifo

The OVM class library provides class **tlm_analysis_fifo** for modeling an analysis FIFO. This class is implemented by adding analysis imp connector object **analysis_export** of type **ovm_analysis_imp** to an unbounded TLM FIFO channel. The implementation of function

write() for this component writes the incoming transaction into the TLM FIFO. A producer is then connected to **analysis_export**, and subscribers are connected to **put_ap**.

9.7.3 Request/Response Channel

The OVM class library provides class **tlm_req_rsp_channel** for modeling a two-way transaction channel. This channel contains two TLM FIFO channels, one channel identified by transaction type **req_type** is used for moving request transactions from the producer to the consumer, and one channel identified by transaction type **rsp_type** is used for returning a response transaction from the consumer to the producer (figure 9.9).

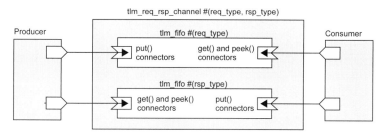

Figure 9.9 Implementation View of tlm_req_rsp_channel

PART 4

Randomization Engine and Data Modeling

CHAPTER 10

Constrained Random Generation

Constrained random generation is a key technology and a fundamental requirement for implementing a coverage-driven verification environment. SystemVerilog provides the full range of constructs and features necessary for generating random data objects subject to a set of constraints, where these constraints can be selectively activated, deactivated, or further extended.

Effective use of SystemVerilog randomization features requires a good understanding of how random values are assigned to variables and how constraints affect the value and probability distribution of the generated values. This knowledge will prove especially useful as program size grows and constraint complexity and interdependencies lead to seemingly unexpected problems in both failed generations and unexpected probability distributions of the generated values.

This chapter provides a detailed look at the constrained random generation feature of SystemVerilog. Section 10.1 describes the abstract operation of a constraint solver. Section 10.2 provides an overview of random generation in SystemVerilog and the use of constraint blocks for controlling randomization. Sections 10.3 and 10.4 describe constraint operators and constraint guards respectively. Section 10.5 describes how constraint operators and constraints guards are used to control randomization. Section 10.6 defines random stability and describes how it is achieved in SystemVerilog. Section 10.7 summarizes SystemVerilog randomization system functions.

10.1 Random Generators and Constraint Solvers

Random generation engines and constraint solvers are only as good as their implementation. Two constrained random generators that provide the same interface and look very similar on the surface can in practice behave very differently. Implementation quality of a constrained random generation engine is measured in terms of:

- Its ability to find solutions to a set of constraints, if one exists
- Uniformity of the random values it generates within its _reachable set_[1]

- How quickly it converges on a solution

A poorly implemented constraint solver may not be able to identify all corner cases that are reachable based on the given set of constraints. This problem may occur when the randomized variables are assigned one at a time instead of considering all the randomized variables at the same time. Once the randomization engine identifies a reachable space defined by the constraints, it should produce random variables that are uniformly distributed within that reachable set. Correct implementation of these goals requires the constraint solver and the randomization engine to solve more complex problems and, therefore, take longer to complete a given task. As such, speed becomes a major consideration when rating randomization engines. As described later in this section, the SystemVerilog constrained random generation engine is implemented to produce results that meet these targets, with the computation speed subject to different vendor offerings.

Constrained random generation is a simple concept to understand. However, its effective application to a real problem requires a good understanding of the following issues:

- How constraints are solved
- How random numbers are assigned
- The impact of constraints on the generated values (reachable set)
- The impact of constraints on the probability distribution of generated values
- The impact of explicit and implicit variable orderings, imposed because of constraints, on the probability distribution of generated values
- How randomness can be controlled in a predictable manner (i.e., random stability)

SystemVerilog random generation constructs can be explained in two phases. The first step is to understand how constraint solving and random generation work for a set of random variables and constraints. The second step is to understand the utilities and constructs that SystemVerilog provides for deciding what variables are randomized and how constraints are specified and controlled.

10.1.1 Constrained Randomization and Variable Ordering Effects

A *constrained randomization problem* is stated as follows: Given a set of integral variables (e.g., taking discrete values) and a set of constraints describing a relationship between these variables, assign random values to these variables that meet the specified constraints.

Consider the following simple randomization problem:

Example 10.1: Assign random values to bits v_1 and v_2 subject to constraint:

   $v_2 >= v_1$

First, the reachable set for this problem is computed subject to the specified constraint. This reachable set is $RS(v_1.v_2)=\{(0,0),(0,1),(1,1)\}$. Note that combination $v_1.v_2=(1,0)$ is not reachable since $v_1=1$ is greater than $v_2=0$.

The next step is to assign values to random variables v_1 and v_2. The SystemVerilog random generation engine considers all variables at the same time. This means that it does not assign val-

---

[1.] The reachable set $RS(v_1.v_2...v_n)$ for random variables v_1, v_2, ...v_n, is defined as the set of all valid simultaneous value assignments to these variables that satisfy a set of randomization constraints.

ues to v_1 and v_2 one at a time, but instead picks a value from the reachable set. In this case, the random generation engine picks a value from the set **{(0,0),(0,1),(1,1)}** with equal probability of **1/3** for each possible value.

It is instructive to compute the probability of variables v_1 and v_2 taking different values. It can be seen from **RS(v_1.v_2)** that v_1=1 for one out of three choices in the reachable set giving **prob(v_1==1)=1/3**, and v_2=1 for two out of three choices in the reachable set giving **prob(v_2==1)=2/3**. In summary:

prob(v_1==1)=1/3	**prob(v_1.v_2==00)=1/3**	**prob(v_1.v_2==10)=0**
prob(v_2==1)=2/3	**prob(v_1.v_2==01)=1/3**	**prob(v_1.v_2==11)=1/3**

The above example is simple. In practice, constraints are more complex and may in fact lead to cases where a variable has to be decided before the reachable set for another variable can be computed. Consider the following randomization problem:

Example 10.2: Assign random values to bits v_1 and v_2 subject to constraint:

$v_2 >=$ **myfunc(v_1)**

In this example, the relationship between v_1 and v_2 cannot be immediately understood by simply looking at the given constraint, since function **myfunc()** may implement any function of variable v_1. In such cases, the value for variable v_1 must be known before the constraint for variable v_2 can be considered. This requirement imposes an ordering for the assignment of random values to variables v_1 and v_2, where v_1 must be assigned a random value before v_2 is assigned a random value.

For simplicity, assume **myfunc()** returns the value of its argument. Therefore, this constraint is in reality the same as v_2>=v_1. As mentioned, v_1 must be assigned a value before the constraint for v_2 can be solved, therefore the focus is to first do random assignment for v_1.

First, the reachable set for variable v_1 is computed. No constraints apply exclusively to v_1, therefore **RS(v_1)**, the reachable set for v_1 is the set of all possible values for v_1 which is the set **{0,1}**. The random generation engine then randomly picks a value for v_1 with equal probability from **RS(v_1)**.

Next, depending on the value assigned to v_1, the reachable set for variable v_2 is computed. If v_1 is assigned a **0**, then **RS(v_2)={0,1}**. If v_1 is assigned a **1**, then **RS(v_2)={1}**.

It is instructive to compute the probability of a variable or a set of variables being assigned each of their possible single or combined values. Variable v_1 is assigned first where a value is selected with equal probability from the set **{0,1}**, therefore **prob(v_1==1)=1/2**. If v_1 is set to **0**, then v_2 may be assigned either a value of **0** or **1** with equal probability of **1/2** each, making **prob(v_1.v_2==00)=1/4**, and **prob(v_1.v_2==01)=1/4**. If v_1 is set to **1**, then v_2 must be assigned to **1**, making **prob(v_1.v_2==11)=1/2**. Considering the probability for each combination, gives **prob(v_2==1)=3/4**. In summary:

prob(v_1==1)=1/2	**prob(v_1.v_2==00)=1/4**	**prob(v_1.v_2==10)=0**
prob(v_2==1)=3/4	**prob(v_1.v_2==01)=1/4**	**prob(v_1.v_2==11)=1/2**

As can be seen from this example, ordering of variables led to completely different variable probabilities than those in example 10.1 because of the use of a function in describing a constraint. Having a good sense for the probability distributions of a set of randomly generated variables, therefore, requires good understanding of the orderings that may be imposed during the generation process.

Variable ordering that is imposed because of constraints can cause the random generation engine to fail when there is in fact a viable random assignment of variables that meets the specified constraints. Consider the following example:

Example 10.3: Assign random values to bits v_1 and v_2 subject to constraint:

$v_2 > \text{myfunc}(v_1)$

In this example, the use of a function call in specifying the constraint imposes an ordering in solving the constraint. For simplicity, assume **myfunc()** returns the value of v_1.

In this example, $RS(v_1.v_2)=\{(0,1)\}$ since $v_1=0$ and $v_2=1$ is the only assignment where v_2 is strictly larger than v_1. But the randomization engine may fail to find this possible valid assignment. The constraint solver first assigns a random value to v_1 because of the ordering imposed by the use of **myfunc()** function call. Given that no other constraints on variable v_1 exists, the random generation engine may assign a value of **1** to variable v_1. In this case, random generation fails because no value for v_2 will satisfy the constraint when v_1 is set to **1**.

As shown in this example, variable ordering can cause the random generation engine to fail when there does in fact exist a viable solution to the randomization problem. As such, constraints that impose a variable ordering should be avoided as much as possible. Constraints are labeled as _unidirectional constraint_ if they impose a variable ordering, and _bidirectional constraint_ if no such ordering is imposed.

Variable ordering has two effects on the random generation process:

- It may lead to false fails of the generation engine.
- It changes the probability distribution of the values assigned to random variables.

The first problem should be avoided as much as possible. The second side effect, however, can be useful at times. Consider the following example:

Example 10.4: Assign random values to bit v_1 and 32-bit unsigned integer v_2 subject to the following implication constraint:

$(v_1==0 \text{ implies that } v_2==0)$

In this example, $RS(v_1.v_2)=\{(0,0),(1,0),...(1,2^{32}-1)\}$. Note that this set contains $2^{32}+1$ elements where $v_1=0$ for only the first element. The random generation engine picks a value with equal probability from this set. This means that $\text{prob}(v_1==0)$ is $1/(2^{32}+1)$ which is almost zero. Therefore, the solution provided by this generator will almost never assign v_1 to a value of **0**.

Recall that random value generation consists of two phases: 1) computing the reachable set for all random variables involved, and 2) selecting an entry from this reachable set which simultaneously assigns a value to all variables involved (e.g., in the above example, selecting **(1,0)** from $RS(v_1.v_2)$ assigns $v_1=1$ and $v_2=0$). In some cases, it is possible to better control the probability distribution of random variables by specifying a variable ordering for the second phase of random value generation. This type of variable assignment ordering does not suffer from the drawback of constraint imposed orderings where the randomization engine may fail even when a viable assignment exists.

In the above example, assume v_1 is to be assigned a value before v_2 but after $RS(v_1.v_2)$ is computed. This is in contrast with selecting a value from $RS(v_1.v_2)$ which assigns values to both variables v_1 and v_2 at the same time. In this case, first $RS(v_1)$ is computed by including all values for v_1 that appear in $RS(v_1.v_2)$. In the above example, $RS(v_1)=\{0,1\}$ and a value from this set is randomly selected for variable v_1. Second, $RS(v_2)$ is computed by including all values for v_2 that appear in $RS(v_1.v_2)$ whose value assignment for v_1 is the currently selected value for v_1. A value for v_2 is then selected randomly from $RS(v_2)$. By allowing variable v_1 to be assigned before variable v_2, it is now possible to assign v_1 to both **0** and **1** with equal probability. Note that the process described in this example can easily be extended to multiple variables (e.g., assign v_1 and v_2 before v_3 and v_4).

Examples provided in this section identify three *modes of operation* for a constrained random generator:

- *Non-ordered*: No variable ordering
- *Assignment-based ordered*: Variable ordering only during random value assignment
- *Constraint-based ordered*: Variable ordering during constraint solving (and hence during value assignment)

A constrained random generation engine should optimally be operating in non-ordered mode, with selective use of assignment-ordered mode to control random value probabilities. Constraint-ordered mode will be imposed by some constraints and at times cannot be avoided. The following sections describe the random generation utilities of SystemVerilog with these properties and behaviors in mind.

10.1.2 Random Generation Engine

Operation of a random generation engine is affected by assignment-based and constraint-based ordering requirements. Details of how these orderings are implicitly or explicitly imposed will be described as part of introducing SystemVerilog randomization constructs. In this section, the operation of the random generation engine is described assuming these orderings have already been indicated.

Given a set of random variables and a set of constraints describing the relationships between these variables, the random generation engine operation can be outlined as shown in the following pseudo-code. Note that this pseudo-code is a logical view of how the engine operates, and the actual implementation will vary from this description.

```
Program 10.1: Random Generation Engine Pseudo-Code:
1   :   -Rule out circular dependencies in constraint-based and assignment-based orderings.
2   :   -Group random variables based on constraint-based ordering of variables.
3   :   -For each group G in the ordered set of groups,
4   :       -Identify constraints to consider for variables in G.
5   :       -Solve the constraint and compute the reachable set for variables in group G.
6   :       -Identify the reachable set for variables in group G marked with randc.
7   :       -Assign values for variables in group G marked with randc.
8   :       -Group unassigned vars in G into G1 and G2 based on assignment-based ordering.
9   :       -Identify reachable set RS1 for the variables in G1 given randc assignments.
10  :       -Select a member with uniform probability from RS1 and assign to variables in G1.
11  :       -Identify reachable set RS2 for variables in G2 given G1 and randc assignments.
12  :       -Select a member with uniform probability from RS2 and assign to variables in G2.
13  :       -Continue with the next group G, if any.
```

The first step in solving the randomization problem is to rule out any circular dependencies in any constraint orderings. Consider the following example:

Example 10.5: Assign random values to bits v_1 and v_2 subject to constraints:

$v_1 > myfunc(v_2)$

solve v_1 **before** v_2

The set of constraints for this example leads to a circular dependency. The first constraint leads to a constraint-based ordering of variables where the reachable set for v_2 must be computed first and v_2 assigned a value before v_1 can be assigned a value. The second constraint leads to an assignment-based ordering requiring that v_1 is assigned a value before v_2. An error message will be generated when such circular dependencies are detected.

The next step is to partition the random variables into ordered groups of variables where the variables in each group must be assigned values before variables in the following group can be processed. Constraint-based ordering is used to identify these partitions. Consider the following example:

Example 10.6: Assign random values to 2-bit v_1, v_2, v_3, v_4, v_5 subject to:

> 1: $v_3 >$ **myfunc**(v_2)
> 2: $v_3 >$ **myfunc**(v_4)
> 3: $v_5 >$ **myfunc**(v_4)
> 4: $v_1 < v_3$
> 5: $v_2 < v_4$
> 6: **solve** v_3 **before** v_1

A general guideline for this grouping is to postpone assigning a variable to as late a time as possible. The goal here is to increase the flexibility in assigning values to variables in the later groups. Based on this guideline, and the constraint-based required ordering of assigning v_2 before v_3, assigning v_4 before v_3, and assigning v_4 before v_5, the ordered groups obtained for this example are: $\{v_2, v_4\}$ followed by $\{v_1, v_3, v_5\}$. Note that v_1 is not involved in any required ordering so it is placed in the last group.

Given a group **G** (e.g., group $\{v_2, v_4\}$ in example 10.6), the next step is to identify the set of constraints that must be considered for the variables in this group. Any constraint that includes at least one reference to variables in this group, and depends on constants and *state variables*[2] is included. Constraints that include variables that have not yet been processed are excluded from this set. In the previous example, only constraint 5 is considered for group $\{v_2, v_4\}$. Other constraints depend on variables that are not yet processed. Note that when processing group $\{v_1, v_3, v_5\}$, the set of constraints will include constraints 1, 2, 3, and 4. Also note that when this second group is being processed, values for v_2 and v_4 have already been assigned and as such, v_2 and v_4 are considered as state variables when group $\{v_1, v_3, v_5\}$ is being processed.

The next step is to compute the reachable set for the set of variables in each group **G** of all groups identified for a randomization problem. Continuing with the results in example 10.6, the following two examples show this calculation for group $\{v_2, v_4\}$ solved along with its relevant constraint 5, and group $\{v_1, v_3, v_5\}$ solved along with its relevant constraints 1, 2, 3, and 4.

Example 10.7: Assign random values to 2-bit integers v_2, v_4 subject to constraint:

> 5: $v_2 < v_4$

In this case $RS(v_2.v_4)=\{(0,1),(0,2),(0,3),(1,2),(1,3),(2,3)\}$.

Assume we select member **(0,1)**, thereby setting $v_2=0$ and $v_4=1$. Note that a peek into the requirements for the next group shows that viable assignments to variables v_1, v_3, and v_5 are only possible for $v_2.v_4=\{(0,1),(0,2),(1,2)\}$. As such, during the processing of this group, selecting any

---

[2] State variables in the context of randomization constraints refers to variables that have been assigned a value when the current random assignment iteration starts and as such whose value can be considered a constant.

member of set $v_2.v_4$={(0,3),(1,3),(2,3)} will lead to generation failure when processing the next group of random variables.

Example 10.8: Assign random values to 2-bit integers v_1, v_3, v_5 subject to constraints:

1: $v_3 > 0$

2: $v_3 > 1$

3: $v_5 > 1$

4: $v_1 < v_3$

This randomization problem is for the second group of variables assuming that v_2=0 and v_4=1, and that function **myfunc()** returns the value of its argument.

In this case, $RS(v_1.v_3.v_5)$={(0,2,2), (0,2,3), (0,3,2), (0,3,3), (1,2,2), (1,2,3), (1,3,2), (1,3,3), (2,3,2), (2,3,3)}.

The next step is to order the variables in each group according to assignment-based ordering requirements. Group $\{v_2,v_4\}$ does not have any assignment-based ordering requirements. Group $\{v_1,v_3,v_5\}$ does, however, require that v_3 is assigned a value before v_5. This operation is shown in the following example:

Example 10.9: Assign random values to 2-bit integers v_1, v_3, v_5 with the reachable set computed in example 10.8, and constraint:

solve v_3 before v_1

The variable assignment groups are identified as $\{v_3\}$ and then $\{v_1,v_5\}$ where v_5 is placed in the last group in order to leave maximum flexibility in assigning values to later variables.Given that variable v_3 is to be assigned first and $RS(v_1.v_3.v_5)$, then $RS(v_3)$={2,3}. Variable v_3 is assigned to a randomly selected member of $RS(v_3)$ before considering assignment for group $\{v_1,v_5\}$.

If v_3=2, then $RS(v_1.v_5)$={(0,2),(0,3),(1,2),(1,3)}.

If v_3=3, then $RS(v_1.v_5)$={(0,2),(0,3),(1,2),(1,3),(2,2),(2,3)}.

Once a value is assigned to v_3 and $RS(v_1.v_5)$ is computed, a member is selected randomly from $RS(v_1.v_5)$ to simultaneously assign values to variable v_1 and v_5.

Without a constraint-based or assignment-based ordering requirement for the example solved in this section, the reachable set for all variables would be computed at the same time, and an entry selected from this set to simultaneously assign values to all random variables.

The examples in this section also highlight the fact that constraint-based ordering requirements can lead to the possibility of assigning values to v_2 and v_4 that could have resulted in generation failure. In addition, constraint-based and assignment-based orderings led to different random probability distributions for each variable in this example.

10.2 Randomization in SystemVerilog

Using random generation in SystemVerilog requires knowledge of the following topics:

- Random variables: How variables are marked as random
- Constraint blocks: How constraints are specified
- Randomization methods: How to assign random values to variables

These topics are described in the following subsections.

10.2.1 Random Variables

This section describes how variables are marked as random in SystemVerilog and how unconstrained random variables are randomized. Constraint specification is described in the next section.

In SystemVerilog, only _integral_[3] variable types can be randomized. This randomization considers only 2-state values. This means that 4-state values (_x_, _z_) and 4-state operators (e.g., ===, !==) are illegal and their use in randomization constructs results in an error. In general, any integral variable declared in modules, tasks, functions can be randomized (i.e., scope variable randomization). The main focus in SystemVerilog, however, is on modeling randomization using objects defined as classes. The reason is that random variables and their associated constraints can be packaged as a reusable class object which can be later extended, inherited, constrained, overridden, enabled, disabled, and merged with or separated from other objects.

The following program segment shows examples of how random variables can be specified in a SystemVerilog program:

```
Program 10.2: Specifying random variables
1  :   module top;
2  :       typedef enum {short, med, long} packet_type;
3  :       class rand_class;
4  :           rand int unsigned int_var;
5  :           rand bit bit_var;
6  :           rand bit [10:0] dynamic_array_var[];
7  :           rand byte static_array_var[10];
8  :           rand rand_class class_ptr_var;
9  :           rand packet_type enum_var;
10 :           randc packet_type enum_cyclic_var;
11 :       endclass
12 :
13 :       logic [10:0] module_var [];
14 :
15 :       initial begin
16 :           int scope_int_var;
17 :           rand_class rc;
18 :           rc = new();
19 :           rc.class_ptr_var = new();
20 :           assert(randomize(scope_int_var,module_var)); // 1 for success, 0 for failure
21 :           assert(rc.randomize());   //returns 1 for success, 0 for failure
22 :       end
23 :   endmodule
```

In general, any integral variable in the scope of a module, program, or interface can be randomized by calling the system function **_randomize()_**. In the example above, variable **scope_int_var** and **module_var** are randomized by passing them as arguments to the system function **_randomize()_**. This function returns a **1** upon success and a **0** upon failure.

As mentioned earlier, randomization is best leveraged when random variables are packaged in a class object. Class **rand_class** (lines 3–11) contains variables that are marked as **_rand_** or **_randc_**. As shown in the class definition, variables of integral type can be random-

---

[3.] The term _integral_ refers to data types that can represent a single basic integer data type, packed array, packed struct, packed union, enum, or time.

ized. Variable **int_var** (line 4) is an integer, variable **bit_var** (line 5) is a bit, **dynamic_array_var** (line 6) is a dynamic array of 11-bit words, **static_array_var** (line 7) is a static array of ten bytes, **class_ptr_var** (line 8) is a pointer to a class object, **enum_var** (line 9) is an enumerated type variable (defined on line 2), and **enum_cyclic_var** (line 10) is a cyclic random variable of the same enum type.

A class object is randomized by calling the ***randomize()*** predefined function of its class (line 21). When calling the ***randomize()*** function of a class object, all class members that are marked with ***rand*** or ***randc*** are randomized.

In the absence of any constraint, each scalar variable is set to a random variable within its valid range. For example, after executing line 21, **bit_var** in object **rc** is set to a value in the range {0:1}, **int_var** is set to a value in the range $\{0:2^{32}\text{-}1\}$. Static arrays have a fixed size, therefore the contents of static arrays are randomized within the range of their type. Each of the ten members of **static_array_var** (line 7) are set to a random value in the range {0:255}. The size for dynamic arrays is not fixed, so first the size of a dynamic array is randomly assigned, and once the size is set, each member is set to a random value within the range of its type. Object pointers are ignored if the pointer is null. Otherwise, the content of the object is randomized recursively, according to the same condition.

Each call to ***randomize()*** assigns a random non-repeating value to a variable marked with ***randc***. Once all possible values for that variable have been generated randomly, a new iteration is started where the order of the new set of generated values is different from the previous pass through all possible values. Consider the following example:

```
Program 10.3: rand versus randc class fields
1  :    class rand_container;            // Consecutive calls to randomize() for this object:
2  :        rand bit [1:0] rand_var;     // 0 1 2 1   3 2 0 0   1 3 3 2...
3  :        randc bit [1:0] randc_var;   // 0 3 1 2   2 1 3 0   3 0 1 2...
4  :    endclass
```

One possible set of values generated for this object for consecutive calls to ***randomize()*** is shown in the comment section of the above example. As shown, values generated for **randc_var** (line 3) are random but every possible value for this variable is generated before a new iteration of values is started. Values generated for **rand_var** may be any of the values in the range of {0:3}, for example, value 1 is generated two times before value 3 is generated (line 2). The permutation sequence for a ***randc*** variable is recomputed when constraints on that variable change, or none of the remaining values satisfies the constraints on that variable. The behavior of a ***randc*** variable is similar to that of dealing every card in a shuffled deck of cards before it is shuffled again. The behavior of a ***rand*** variable is similar to that of throwing a dice where at every roll, all possible values may appear. It should be noted that using a ***randc*** variable that has a large set of possible values makes the constraint problem more difficult to solve.

Variables marked with ***randc*** have a strict requirement to go through all possible values before a generated value can be repeated. Because of this requirement, such variables are always generated before variables marked with ***rand***. Also, for dynamic arrays, the size of the array must be generated before array elements can be randomized. As such, the implicit variable that defines the size of a dynamic array is generated before the elements of that array. This requirement imposes an implicit constraint-based ordering between the size of a dynamic array and the elements of that dynamic array.

The following properties apply to random variables:

- Any integral variable in the scope of a module, program, or interface can be randomized by calling system function *randomize()*.
- Random variables are best packaged in a class, since they can be grouped along with their constraints and reused.
- Class members marked with *randc* are assigned values that cycle through all of the values in a random permutation of their declared range. Such variables can be of type *bit* (or packed bit array) or an enumerated type.
- Class members marked with *rand* are assigned a value (possibly repeating) from their valid range, where this value has a uniform distribution over its valid range subject to randomization constraints that must be met.
- An object pointer in a class can be marked with *rand* in which case all of this object pointer's variables and constraints are solved and randomized concurrently with the variables and constraints of the object that contains the pointer.
- A *null* object pointer in a class marked with *rand* is ignored by the randomization engine.
- When randomizing a class object, an object pointer in that class not marked with *rand* will not be randomized, even if it has members that are marked as *rand* or *randc*.
- Variables marked as *randc* are assigned before variables marked as *rand*.

Random dynamic arrays introduce special constraint-based ordering and also require special considerations when pointing to class objects. Random dynamic arrays and constraint-based random generation are discussed in the following sections.

10.2.2 Random Dynamic Arrays

Random dynamic arrays are used extensively in building dynamically sized data objects. These constructs do, however, require special handling for randomization purposes. These considerations are described in this section.

The size of a randomized array must be decided and the array resized before any of its members can be randomized. Therefore, randomization constraints specified for the size of a dynamic array must be solved before any of the constraints specified for array members. This requirement imposes an implicit constraint-based ordering between the size of a dynamic array and members of that dynamic array. Given that the size of the array is already decided by the time array members are being randomized, the size of a dynamic array is considered as a state variable when constraints for array members are being solved.

Array randomization consists of three steps:

- Array size randomization
- Array Resizing
- Array member randomization

Array size randomization is performed by considering the size of a dynamic array as a random variable, solving any constraints specified for this random variable to identify its reachable set, and then randomly selecting a value from this reachable set. All constraints involving array members are excluded from the set of constraints that are solved to compute the reachable set for the size of a random array. This exclusion leads to the implicit constraint-based ordering that exists between the size of an array and its elements.

Array resizing is the process of changing the number of elements in an array to the newly generated size. In this step, the main focus is on how array member values are maintained across the resizing process. This special handling allows an array of objects to be resized without loosing the object pointers at indices that remain in the array after resizing. Given $size_{new}$ (the new randomly decided size of a dynamic array) and $size_{old}$ (its size before randomization started), the following guidelines are used for maintaining array member values during the resizing of the array:

- If $size_{new}$ is the same as $size_{old}$ then array size or members are not modified and after resizing the value of each array member remains the same as before randomization started.
- If $size_{new}$ is larger than $size_{old}$ then array size is increased to the new size. After resizing, the value for the first ($size_{old}$) members of the array remain the same as before randomization started. This means that if array members are object pointers, then these pointers are not lost and remain as before randomization started. The remaining ($size_{new}$ - $size_{old}$) members are set to the default value of the array member data type (e.g., *null* for array of objects, 0 for *integer*, etc.).
- If $size_{new}$ is smaller than $size_{old}$ then array size is reduced to the new size. After resizing, the value for the first ($size_{new}$) members of the array remain the same as before randomization started.

Array member randomization is performed after the array is resized. During this step, constraints involving array members are solved while considering array size as a state variable. Each member of the array is then randomized by randomly selecting a value from its reachable set computed by solving its constraints.

The randomization engine never allocates a new object. This means that for an array of objects, each array member is randomized if its value is not *null*.

10.2.3 Constraint Blocks

Constraints can be specified as constraint blocks in classes, or in-line when the *randomize()* function is called. A *constraint block* contains a list of expressions that specify a limit for a single variable or relationships between multiple variables. Constraints are inherited along with other class properties. This feature allows a hierarchy of constraints to be built along with class inheritance hierarchy. SystemVerilog also provides mechanisms for disabling existing constraint blocks as needed by a specific generation scenario.

The following program segment shows examples of constraint blocks:

Program 10.4: Specifying constraint blocks

```
1  :    module top;
2  :        typedef enum {short, average, tall} box_type;
```

```
3   :        class box;
4   :            rand box_type bt;
5   :            rand int unsigned width;
6   :            rand int unsigned height;
7   :            constraint valid_range;
8   :            constraint short_box {bt == short -> height < 10;}
9   :            constraint average_box { bt == average -> height inside {[30:70]};}
10  :            constraint tall_box {bt == tall -> height > 90;}
11  :        endclass
12  :        constraint box::valid_range {width < 100 && height < 100;}
13  :
14  :        class short_box extends box;
15  :            constraint sb { bt == short;}
16  :        endclass
17  :
18  :        class short_and_wide_box extends short_box;
19  :            constraint swb { width > 90 ;}
20  :            constraint short_box {bt == short -> height < 20;}
21  :        endclass
22  :
23  :        initial begin
24  :            short_and_wide_box swb;
25  :            short_box sb;
26  :            swb = new();
27  :            sb = new();
28  :            assert(sb.randomize());
29  :            assert(sb.randomize() with {width == 95;});
30  :            assert(swb.randomize());
31  :        end
32  :    endmodule
```

The above example shows a hierarchy of constraints used to implement an object with properties in different range of values. Class **box** (lines 3–11) contains the generic description of a box and constraint blocks describing the valid ranges of its width and height properties. It also contains implication constraints constraining the height property, depending on the box type (lines 8–10). A constraint box can be declared outside a class declaration. Constraint name **valid_range** is first declared as part of class declaration (line 7) and its description is then specified outside the class declaration (line 12).

Class **short_box** is a class inherited from **box** and contains only an additional constraint that the generated box type property should be constrained to **short**. Class **short_and_wide_box** further extends this definition to include a constraint for its **width** property. It also overrides the **short_box** constraint defined in its parent class in order to redefine the range for a short box.

Random values generated for variable **sb** (line 28) will meet all constraint blocks on lines 8, 9, 10, 12, and 15. The **randomize()** function can be called with in-lined constraints (line 29). In this example, the random values generated for variable **sb** (line 29) will meet the additional constraint defined using *with* keyword. Random values generated for variable **swb** (line 30) will meet all constraint blocks on lines 9, 10, 12, 15, 19 and 20.

Constraint-specific operators are discussed in the next section.

10.3 Constraint-Specific Operators

A constraint can be any SystemVerilog expression with integral variables and constants, or one of the constraint-specific operators. Constraint-specific operators are described in the following subsections.

10.3.1 Set Membership Constraints

The *inside* operator is used to specify that a random variable should be assigned a value from a set specified with this operator. Absent any other constraints, a value is selected from the given set with uniform probability. The negation of this operator indicates that the random value should not be in the indicated set.

The *inside* operator is a bidirectional constraint operator. This means that variables used in specifying the set, and the random variables being assigned are solved concurrently. In fact, the inside operator can also be written as a disjunction of equality constraints:

constraint {a inside {b,c,d}} is equivalent to {a == b || a ==c || a==d}

If variables are used to specify members of the set, it is possible that the ranges specified for the set overlap. The probability of each set member is still uniformly distributed even if a set member is repeated multiple times in describing the set. Consider the following example:

```
Program 10.5: Repeated set member in specifying "inside" constraint
1  :    class randobj;
2  :        integer b=2;
3  :        rand integer a;
4  :        constraint c1 {a inside {[1:3],[b:b+2]};}
5  :    endclass
```

In the above example, values **2** and **3** are specified two times in the set description. Each value in the set (i.e., **1**, **2**, **3**, **4**), however, is assigned with equal probability.

Examples of this operator are shown below:

```
Program 10.6: examples of "inside" constraint operator
1  :    class randobj;
2  :        rand integer a, b, c;
3  :        integer d;
4  :        constraint c1 {a inside {1,3,5,[6:9], [b:2*b],[c:c+14]};}
5  :        constraint c2 {!(a inside {b,c};}
6  :        constraint c3 {d inside {a,b,c};}
7  :    endclass
```

Non-random variables used in specifying the arguments to the *inside* operator are considered as state variables whose value at the time of randomization is used to solve the constraint.

10.3.2 Distribution Constraints

The *distribution operator* allows the value assigned to a random value to be selected with a weighted probability distribution from a set of values. Distribution constraints act both as a relational test for set membership and also to specify a statistical distribution for set members.

The distribution operator evaluates to true if the value of the random variable is in the specified set. In the absence of any other constraints which may prevent the assignment of a set member to the random variable, the probability of selecting each member in the set follows its given weight.

The distribution set is a comma-separated list of integral expressions and ranges. A weight can be assigned to each expression or range. For ranges, it is possible to assign a range for each member of that range (using the ":=" operator) or assign a weight that will be divided equally between members of that range (using the ":/" operator). The total weight specified for all set members need not add to **100**, and each weight assignment acts as only a relative weight to other set members. In the absence of a weight operator, a default setting of ":=1" is assumed.

The distribution operator cannot be used with variables marked with **randc**. Also, a distribution expression must contain at least one variable marked with **rand**.

The distribution operator is a bidirectional constraint and does not impose any ordering on the random generation process.

An example of distribution operator are shown below:

```
Program 10.7: Constraint distribution operator
1   :    class randobj;
2   :        rand integer a,b;
3   :        constraint c1 {a dist {1:=1, 2:=3, [4:5]:=5, [b:b+2]:/3};}
4   :    endclass
```

In the above example, value **1** has a weight of **1**, value **2** has a weight of **3**, values **4** and **5** each have a weight of **5**, and values in the range **b** to **b+2** each have a weight equal to the number of values in this range divided by **3**.

10.3.3 Implication Constraints

The implication operator "->" is used to declare a conditional (predicated) relation between logical conditions.

An implication operator has the following general form:

boolean_condition1 -> boolean_condition2

This form is equivalent to the following Boolean constraint:

! boolean_condition1 || boolean_condition2

As such, the implication operator is a bidirectional operator that does not impose any ordering on the random generation process.

An example of the implication operator is shown below.

```
Program 10.8: Implication constraint operator
1  :   module top;
2  :        typedef enum {short, legal, long} packet_type;
3  :        class packet;
4  :             rand packet_type pt;
5  :             rand integer packet_length;
6  :             rand bit payload[];
7  :             constraint payload_size { payload.size() == packet_length;}
8  :             constraint short_pack { pt == short -> packet_length < 64;}
9  :             constraint legal_pack { pt == legal -> packet_length inside {[64:1024]};}
10 :             constraint long_pack { pt == long -> packet_length > 1024;}
11 :        endclass
12 :
13 :        initial begin
14 :             packet p;
15 :             p = new();
16 :             assert(p.randomize() with {pt == legal;});
17 :        end
18 :   endmodule
```

In the above example, the class declaration of a packet contains implication constraints deciding the packet size depending on the packet enumerated type of **short, legal,** or **long.** The payload size is also constrained to be set by variable **packet_length.** This implementation allows packet type to be decided when the packet content is being randomized (line 16).

10.3.4 If-Else Constraints

SystemVerilog *if-else* constraints can be considered as a compound implication constraint. This constraint operator has the following general form:

```
if (boolean_expression) constraint_set₁ [else constraint_set₂]
```

This operator can be written as an equivalent implication operator:

```
boolean_expression -> constraint_set₁;
!boolean_expression -> constraint_set₂;
```

As such, *if-else* operator is also a bidirectional operator that does not impose any ordering on the generation order.

The *if-else* operator provides a more structured look for writing long constraint sets and also provides a more efficient way by relating constraint sets to the value of a single boolean expression.

The following example, shows the packet declaration in the previous example rewritten using an if-else constraint.

```
Program 10.9: if-else constraint operator
1  :   class packet;
2  :        rand packet_type pt;
3  :        rand integer packet_length;
4  :        rand bit payload[];
5  :        constraint payload_size {payload.size() == packet_length;}
6  :        constraint packet_size {
7  :             if (pt == short)
8  :                  packet_length < 64;
```

```
 9  :              else if (pt == legal)
10  :                     packet_length inside {[64:1024]};
11  :              else if (pt == long)
12  :                     packet_length > 1024;
13  :         }
14  :   endclass
```

The drawback with the above approach, however, is that individual constraints for **short**, **legal**, and **long** packets cannot be disabled as can be done when separate constraint blocks are given for each constraint.

10.3.5 Iterative Constraints

Iterative constraints allow array members to be constrained using indexing expressions and loop variables. This construct acts as a shorthand notation for specifying constraints for each member of an array and relationships between array members and other random and state variables. Iterative constraints provide a compact syntax for describing constraints for members of static arrays whose size is known. Iterative constraints are, however, a necessary construct for dynamic arrays since the number of elements is not known beforehand and constraints must, therefore, be described in terms of indexing expressions.

An example of an iterative constraint is shown below:

```
Program 10.10: Iterative constraint operators
1  :   module top;
2  :       class randobj;
3  :           //        2   3   4          1   2    dimension numbers
4  :           //        k   l   m          i   j    iterative var name
5  :           rand bit [5:0] [4:0] [3:1] bit_var [10:1] [9:1];
6  :           constraint c1 {foreach (bit_var [i,j,k,l,m]) bit_var[i][j][k][l][m] == 0;}
7  :       endclass
8  :   endmodule
```

The above example shows the relationship between index variables (i.e., **i,j,k,l,m**) and the dimension of the array variable.

The following properties apply to iterative constraints:

- The number of loop variables must not exceed the number of array dimensions.
- The scope of each loop variable is the context of the *foreach* construct (line 6).
- The type of each loop variable is implicitly declared to be consistent with the type of array index.
- A loop variable can be skipped by leaving its place in the order of loop variables blank (hence two commas appearing back to back), in which case, that dimension is not iterated over.

Size of an array can be used in iterative constraints. This usage is shown in the following example:

```
Program 10.11: Array size and iterative constraint operators
1  :   module top;
2  :       class randobj;
3  :           rand bit dba[];
4  :           constraint c1 { dba.size() == 100;}
```

```
5   :              constraint c2 {foreach (dba[i]) (i < dba.size()-1) -> (dba[i+1] == dba[i]);}
6   :  endmodule
```

Recall that the use of a constraint on the size of dynamic array causes an implicit constraint-based variable ordering where the size of array is decided before any of the constraints on its members are solved. As such, when solving constraint **c2** (line 5), the size of array is used as a state variable and is assumed to be a fixed value.

Iterative constraints provide a shorthand notation for describing relationships between array members and other random variables. As such, they do not impose any ordering on the random generation order unless the constraint specified in the foreach constraint block imposes such an ordering (i.e., using a function call in specifying the constraint) or using the array size predicate as described in the previous paragraph.

10.3.6 Global Constraints

Global constraints refer to constraints that specify relationships between members of two different class objects.

Consider the following example:

```
Program 10.12: Global constraints across two separate class objects
1   :  module top;
2   :      class payload;
3   :          rand bit data [];
4   :          rand int unsigned length;
5   :          constraint c1 { length < 1024;}
6   :          constraint c2 {data.size() == length;}
7   :      endclass
8   :
9   :      class packet;
10  :          rand payload pl1;
11  :          rand payload pl2;
12  :          constraint c1 { pl1.length > pl2.length;}
13  :          function new();
14  :              pl1 = new();
15  :              pl2 = new();
16  :          endfunction
17  :      endclass
18  :
19  :      initial begin
20  :          packet p;
21  :          p = new();
22  :          assert(p.randomize());
23  :      end
24  :  endmodule
```

In this example, constraint block c_1 (line 12) describes a relationship between the length parameter of two objects contained inside its class. As such, this constraint is a global constraint.

The call to ***randomize()*** (line 22) solves the constraints for all variables in all involved objects concurrently. The set of variables to randomize and applicable constraints are derived as follows:

- First all objects that are to be randomized are found. The set of objects starts with the object whose *randomize()* method is called and any object with a *rand* pointer declared inside that object (lines 10, 11). This definition is recursive in that any *rand* pointers inside the newly identified object are also added to the set.

- All variables marked with *rand* or *randc* inside the identified objects are added to the list of variables to be randomized. Any variable that is disabled using *rand_mode()* function (section 10.5.2) are removed from the set of variables to be randomized.
- All constraints in the identified objects that relate to the identified variables to be randomized are included in the set of constraints to be solved. Any constraints specified along with the *randomize()* function is added to this list. And any constraints disabled using *constraint_mode()* function (section 10.5.1) is removed from this list.

Once the set of all random variables and relevant constraints are identified, all constraints are solved concurrently, subject to any implicit/explicit constraint-based or assignment-based orderings.

10.3.7 Variable Ordering Constraints

Variable ordering constraints allow some variables to be assigned before other variables are assigned values. Note that variable ordering constraints do no impose an order on how the constraints are solved but only how variables are assigned random values (see description for example 10.4 in section 10.1.1).

An example of an ordering constraint is shown in the following program:

```
Program 10.13: Ordering constraint operator
1  :    class payload;
2  :        rand bit v₁;
3  :        rand int unsigned v₂;
4  :        constraint c1 {v₁ == 1'b0 -> v₂ == 0;}
5  :        constraint c2 {solve v₁ before v₂;}
6  :    endclass
```

In the above example, the reachable set for variables v_1 and v_2 is given by set {(0,0), (1,0),...(1,2^{32}-1)}. If both v_1 and v_2 are assigned a member from this set with equal probability, then the probability of setting v_1 to 0 is $1/(2^{32}+1)$ which will almost never occur. By adding constraint c_2 (line 5), variable v_1 is assigned a value first from the possible values in the reachable set of $v_1.v_2$. This means that both values 0 and 1 will be assigned to v_1 with equal probability. After v_1 is assigned, then v_2 is assigned a value from the newly computed reachable set for v_2. This means that if v_1 is set to 0, then the reachable set for v_2 is {0}, and if v_1 is assigned a 1, then the reachable set for v_2 is {0,1,...2^{32}-1}. In either case, a value is selected from the reachable set for v_2 with equal probability.

The following properties apply to ordering constraints:

- Only variables marked with *rand* can be used in an ordering constraint.
- Variables marked with *randc* are not allowed in ordering constraints. As mentioned earlier, these variables are always assigned before any variable marked with *rand*.
- Explicit ordering constraints, along with other implicit ordering constraints should not lead to circular dependencies (e.g., solve a before b, solve b before c, solve c before a is not allowed).

10.3.8 Function-Call Constraints

Constraint expressions containing a function call impose an explicit constraint-based ordering requirement. This means that the constraints for any random variables passed as arguments to such a function are solved first and assigned random values before the constraint containing the function call is solved. Consequently, all variables passed to a function call in a constraint are treated as state variables whose values are assumed to be fixed.

The following guidelines apply when using function calls in constraint expressions:

- Arguments passed to functions used in a constraint expression cannot be an output of type *ref* (*const ref* is allowed).
- Functions used in constraint expressions should not contain any state information (i.e., should include only automatic variables).
- Functions used in constraint expressions cannot modify the randomization process (e.g., by calling *rand_mode()* or *constraint_mode()*).
- Functions used in constraint expressions may be called multiple times. This is one reason that such functions should not have state information, as all calls to this function must behave exactly the same.

10.4 Constraint Guards

When evaluating a constraint expression, it is possible that variables used in this expression may not have valid settings. For example, in writing a global constraint which uses object pointers to specify a relationship between multiple objects, it is possible that an object pointer is set to *null* and as such accessing a member of that object may lead to a runtime errors. As another example, consider an iterative constraint that specifies that each array member should be larger than the next array member. Obviously, for the last member of this array, no next member exists and as such, accessing that variable will lead to a runtime error.

In such cases, it is, therefore, necessary to predicate the constraint expression with an expression that provides conditions which must be satisfied before that constraint expression is included in the randomization process.

Constraint Guards are expressions included in a constraint block that protect constraints from such runtime errors. Constraint guards are sub-expressions written as part of the expression in a constraint block and are only differentiated from other sub expressions in that they include only the following items:

- Constants
- State variables
- Object pointer comparisons
- Loop variables in iterative constraints
- Array size in iterative constraints

Consider the following example:

Program 10.14: Constraint guards

```
1  :   module top;
2  :       class payload;
3  :           rand bit data [];
4  :           rand int unsigned length;
5  :           rand int unsigned tlength;
6  :           constraint c1 { length < 10;}
7  :           constraint c2 {data.size() == length;}
8  :       endclass
9  :
10 :       class packet;
11 :           rand payload pl [];
12 :           int unsigned length;
13 :           rand int unsigned tlength;
14 :           constraint c1 {foreach (pl[i]) (i == 0)-> (pl[i].tlength == pl[i].length);}
15 :           constraint c2 {foreach (pl[i]) (i>0)-> (pl[i].tlength == pl[i-1].tlength + pl[i].length);}
16 :           constraint c3 {foreach (pl[i]) (i == length)-> (tlength == pl[i].tlength);}
17 :           constraint c4 {foreach (pl[i]) (i > length)-> (pl[i].length == 0);}
18 :
19 :           function new();
20 :               pl = new[6];
21 :               for (int i = 0; i < 6; i++) pl[i] = new();
22 :           endfunction
23 :       endclass
24 :
25 :       initial begin
26 :           packet p;
27 :           p = new();
28 :           p.length = 3;
29 :           assert(p.randomize());
30 :       end
31 :   endmodule
```

This example shows the implementation of class **packet** composed of an array of **payload** objects. Field **length** of **payload** specifies the size of its data payload, and field **tlength** of **payload** gives the total length of all payloads in its containing **packet** before and including this **payload**. Field **length** of **packet** specifies the number of payloads that are contained in **packet** (active payloads), and the field **tlength** of **packet** gives the total **length** of all active payloads. Note that field **length** of class **packet** is not a random variable.

Constraint blocks in **packet** class declaration (lines 14–17) provide the relationships that must be maintained between class object fields during randomization. Constraint c_1 specifies that for the first payload in dynamic array **pl**, the field **tlength** should be equal to field **length**. Constraint block c_2 specifies that for payloads after the first payload, the **tlength** field is computed by adding the **length** field for that payload, and the **tlength** field for the previous payload. Constraint c_3 specifies that the **tlength** field of **packet** should be set to the **tlength** field of the last active payload. Constraint c_4 specifies that the payload size for all inactive payloads should be set to **0**.

Each of these constraints contain a guard expression. For constraint c_1, c_2, c_3, and c_4, the guard expressions are **(i==0)**, **(i>0)**, **(i==length)**, and **(i>length)** respectively. Note that these guard expressions are composed of either loop variables, constants, or state variables (i.e., **length**).

10.5 Controlling Constrained Randomization

The generic model of a random object, as described in its class declaration, is not applicable to all randomization uses of that object. The randomization utility should provide constructs that allow for modification of the default randomization assumptions as defined in a class declaration. These constructs should handle the following requirements:

- It may be needed to disable or enable a constraint block for a specific use of a randomized object.
- It may be needed to prevent the randomization of a variable already marked with *rand* or *randc*.
- Building a hierarchical random object requires that the object hierarchy be prepared for randomization before randomization starts, and final steps carried out after randomization takes place. Hook methods should be provided for programming these steps as part of randomization.

These topics are discussed in the following subsections.

10.5.1 Controlling Constraints

Constraint blocks can be activated or deactivated during program runtime. Turning on or off a constraint block marked as static affects that constraint block for all instances of that object. Turning on or off a constraint block not marked as static affects only the given instance of the object for which that constraint block was disabled.

SystemVerilog provides a task and a function for controlling constraints. The syntax is as follows:

```
task object[.constraint_identifier]::constraint_mode(bit on_off);
function int object.constraint_identifier::constraint_mode();
```

The task is used to change the active state of a constraint block. The function is used to query the current status of a constraint block. The use of these methods is shown in the following example:

Program 10.15: Constraint block activation and deactivation

```
1  :   module top;
2  :       typedef enum {short, average, tall} box_type;
3  :       typedef enum {valid, incorrect_area} error_type;
4  :       class box;
5  :           rand box_type bt;
6  :           rand error_type et;
7  :           rand int unsigned width;
8  :           rand int unsigned height;
9  :           rand int unsigned area;
10 :           static constraint valid_area { (et == valid) == (area == width * height);}
11 :           constraint short_box   { bt == short  -> height < 10;}
12 :       endclass
13 :
14 :       initial begin
15 :           int result; box b1, b2;
16 :           b1 = new(); b2 = new();
17 :           result = b1.valid_area.constraint_mode();     // result = 1;
18 :           result = b2.valid_area.constraint_mode();     // result = 1;
19 :           b1.valid_area.constraint_mode(0);             // turns off valid_area in b1
```

```
20  :              result = b1.valid_area.constraint_mode();      // result = 0;
21  :              result = b2.valid_area.constraint_mode();      // result = 0;
22  :              b1.short_box.constraint_mode(0);               // turn off short_box in b1
23  :              result = b1.short_box.constraint_mode();       // result = 0;
24  :              result = b2.short_box.constraint_mode();       // result = 1;
25  :              b1.constraint_mode(1);                         // turn on all constraints in b1
26  :              result = b1.short_box.constraint_mode();       // result = 1;
27  :              result = b1.valid_area.constraint_mode();      // result = 1;
28  :              result = b2.valid_area.constraint_mode();      // result = 1;
29  :          end
30  :   endmodule
```

The initial active state of constraint block **valid_area** for both fields b_1 and b_2 of **box** object is printed on lines 17 and 18, respectively. Note that **valid_area** is marked as a static constraint. The active state of this constraint block is set to off for field b_1 on line 19. This change will affect not only instance b_1, but also instance b_2, as shown on lines 20 and 21. On line 22, constraint block **short_box** of b_1 is set to off. This change, however, does not affect instance b_2 since this constraint block is not marked as static. All constraint blocks of instance b_1 are set to active state on line 25. Note that this change also affects constraint block **valid_state** which is a static constraint. Therefore the statement on line 25 also affects instance b_2. This is shown on lines 26–28.

10.5.2 Disabling Random Variables

All variables marked with *rand* or *randc* are initially active. This means that if the object containing these variables is randomized, these variables are also randomized by default. These random variables can be activated or deactivated during program runtime. A disabled random variable is treated as a state variable during the randomization process.

SystemVerilog provides a task and a function for controlling this feature. The syntax is as follows:

```
task object[.random_variable]::rand_mode(bit on_off);
function int object.random_variable::rand_mode();
```

Task *rand_mode()* is used to change the active state of a random variable. Function *rand_mode()* is used to query the current status of a random variable. The following properties apply to this usage:

- For unpacked array variables, a single array element or the entire array can be used with these methods. Using an index limits the method to a single element of the array. Omitting the index applies the method to all elements of the array.
- For unpacked structure variables, individual members of the structure can be used with these methods. Specifying a member limits the method to that member. Omitting any member name applies the method to all elements of the structure.
- A compiler error will be generated if the specified variable is not marked with either *rand* or *randc*.
- The function form of *rand_mode()* does not accept arrays. As such, if the random variable is an unpacked array, then a member of that array should be specified when using this function.

Consider the following initial block in combination with the object declaration in program example 10.15:

```
       Program 10.16: Random variable activation and deactivation
1    :   module top;
2    :       initial begin
3    :           int result;
4    :           box b1;
5    :           b1 = new();
6    :           result = b1.bt.rand_mode();        // result = 1;
7    :           result = b1.et.rand_mode();        // result = 1;
8    :           b1.rand_mode(0);                    // turns off all random_variables in b1
9    :           result = b1.bt.rand_mode();        // result = 0;
10   :           result = b1.et.rand_mode();        // result = 0;
11   :           b1.bt.rand_mode(1);                // turns off valid_area constraint in b1
12   :           result = b1.bt.rand_mode();        // result = 1;
13   :           result = b1.et.rand_mode();        // result = 0;
14   :       end
15   :   endmodule
```

The initial active state for random variables **bt** and **et** are printed on lines 6 and 7. The statement on line 8 deactivates all random variables in instance **b₁**. Lines 9 and 10 show that the active states for **bt** and **et** are changed to off. The statement on line 11 activates random variable **bt**. The result of this activation is shown on lines 12 and 13 to only affect random variable **bt**.

10.5.3 Randomization Flow Methods

Randomizing an object often requires pre-processing and post-processing operations to be performed on the randomized object. These operations can be performed as part of the program that calls the *randomize()* function to randomize an object. This approach, however, has two drawbacks. First, the steps that must be performed are usually the same regardless of where the object is randomized, so repeating these steps every time such randomization is needed leads to reduced productivity. Second, performing these steps requires detailed knowledge of the internal structure of a randomized object. This intimate knowledge may not be available if the randomized object is a part of a package developed separate from the program using that randomized object. As such, it is best to have a mechanism to include such pre- and post-processing steps as part of the object.

SystemVerilog defines predefined functions *pre_randomize()* and *post_randomize()* to facilitate this objective when dealing with class objects. Each class object has the following default declarations for these functions:

```
       Program 10.17: default declaration of pre_randomize() and post_randomize()
1    :   function void pre_randomize();
2    :       if( super) super.pre_randomize();
3    :   endfunction
4    :
5    :   function void post_randomize();
6    :       if( super) super.post_randomize();
7    :   endfunction
```

The following pseudo-codes describe two functions that are called before the randomization is started, and after randomization is completed:

```
┌─────────────────────────────────────────────────────────────────────────────────┐
 Program 10.18: hierarchical call order to pre_randomize() and post_randomize()
 1   :   pre_randomize_prepare(obj_ptr) {
 2   :        foreach member mem_obj of obj_ptr that is an object ptr and an active rand variable {
 3   :             pre_randomize_prepare(mem_obj);
 4   :        }
 5   :        obj_ptr.pre_randomize();
 6   :   }
 7   :   post_randomize_wrapup(obj_ptr) {
 8   :        foreach member mem_obj of obj_ptr that is an object ptr and an active rand variable {
 9   :             post_randomize_wrapup(mem_obj);
 10  :        }
 11  :        obj_ptr.post_randomize();
 12  :   }
└─────────────────────────────────────────────────────────────────────────────────┘
```

Note that these functions are only meant to provide an overview of the order of execution for hierarchical objects and actual implementation will be different from what is shown above. As shown in the pseudo-codes, the ***pre_randomzie()*** and ***post_randomize()*** functions are called in a depth-first order where the function for each object is called before its parent function is called.

A typical use of ***pre_randomize()*** is in preparing an object containing a dynamic array of class objects for randomization. In this case, randomizing each array member requires that the array position already points at an object (section 10.2.2). The randomization problem with this setup is that each member of a such a dynamic array should be allocated explicitly before it can be randomized. This creates a conflict, since the size of the array is not known before randomization and, therefore, it is not clear how to allocate the dynamic array before randomization starts. The strategy is to assume a maximum size for the dynamic array, initialize the dynamic array size to this maximum size in function ***pre_randomize()*** and then constrain the size of dynamic array to the randomly generated size that is less than the maximum size, so that after the array is resized during randomization, all its members point to allocated objects that will be randomized.

A typical use of ***post_randomize()*** function is in computing packet properties based on the randomly generated values. Checksum fields are one such field that must be computed after randomization is completed.

The following example shows the implementation of these behaviors using the randomization methods.

```
┌─────────────────────────────────────────────────────────────────────────────────┐
 Program 10.19: Example of using pre_randomize() and post_randomize()
 1   :   class payload; bit pl; endclass
 2   :   class packet;
 3   :        rand payload packet_payload [];
 4   :        rand byte size;
 5   :        int max_size = 100;
 6   :        byte crc;
 7   :        constraint c0 {size > 0 && size <= max_size;}
 8   :        constraint c1 {packet_payload.size() == size;}
 9   :
 10  :        function void pre_randomize();
 11  :             packet_payload = new[max_size];
 12  :             for (int i = 0; i < max_size; i++) packet_payload[i] = new;
 13  :        endfunction
 14  :
 15  :        function void post_randomize();
 16  :             crc = 0;
```

```
17  :                    for (int i = 0; i < packet_payload.size(); i++) crc += packet_payload[i].pl;
18  :           endfunction
19  :    endclass
```

In this example, dynamic array packet_payload is initially sized to **max_size** in **pre_randomize()** (line 1) and a new object allocated for each array position (line 12). The array size is constrained to be less than **max_size** (lines 7, 8). During randomization, **packet_payload** is resized to its new randomly decided size and since each position of this array already points to an allocated object, the content of each object is also randomized. After randomization is completed, function **post_randomize()** is used to update the **crc** field of the packet.

10.6 Random Stability

One of the most important requirements for a randomized program is that it should predictably generate the same sequence of random values across multiple runs of the same program and using the same random seed value. If this property is not maintained, then such a program becomes impossible to debug, and impossible to quantify as a contributor to the overall verification progress. In addition to this requirement, it is also desirable that incremental changes in a program do not drastically modify its random behavior. _Random stability_ refers to this property of a randomized program and steps taken to minimize variations in program behavior because of localized changes to the program.

Execution of a SystemVerilog program consists of concurrently running threads of execution, operating on multiple instances of class objects. SystemVerilog takes advantage of this architecture for minimizing the effects of incremental program changes on random behavior of the program by localizing random generation to each thread of execution and each instance of class objects. In this approach, the sequence of generated random numbers in each thread or each object is controlled by only its initial seed value. This means that the creation of new threads or instantiating new objects has minimal effect on the random behavior of previously existing threads and instances. In SystemVerilog, _Random Stability_ refers to this property.

Each time a new thread or object is created, a new random number generator context is created and assigned to the newly created thread or object. The seed for this new randomization context is set from the next available random number from the thread that created that new thread or object. Given this approach, random stability in SystemVerilog is discussed in terms of the following properties:

- Thread stability
- Object stability

Thread stability is achieved by creating a new random generation context for each newly created thread. This behavior is shown in the following example:

Program 10.20: SystemVerilog thread random stability

```
1  :    module top;
2  :           //initial $display($urandom);
```

```
3   :        initial begin
4   :            int x, y, z;
5   :            //$display ($urandom);
6   :            fork
7   :                begin $display ($urandom,,$urandom); end
8   :                begin $display ($urandom,,$urandom); end
9   :                begin $display ($urandom,,$urandom); end
10  :                begin $display ($urandom,,$urandom); end
11  :                begin $display ($urandom,,$urandom); end
12  :            join
13  :        end
14  :    endmodule
```

In the above example, the initial block is assigned a new random generation context when it is created. Also, each branch of the fork statement is assigned a new random generation context when that thread is created, where the seed for each new thread is taken from the next available random number from its parent thread (i.e., the thread for the initial block). Note that the seed assigned to each sub-thread of the fork is independent of the order of execution of these sub-threads. This is because the order of execution is independent of the order of creating these threads; order of thread creation follows program order. Because of the properties described, the above program example generates the same random values for every execution of this program.

Random stability of above program segment can be affected in two ways. First, if the display statement on line 5 is un-commented, then the seed for each thread started by the fork statement becomes different and as such, the program will generate a completely different set of values for each of the display statements. Second, if the initial block on line 2 is un-commented, then the seed value assigned to the initial block on line 3 will become different, therefore causing the program to display completely different random values.

The solution to above problems is to self-seed each thread if the values to be generated by that thread are important to remain the same when the thread is moved or code leading to start of a new thread is modified. This modification is shown in the following program segment.

```
Program 10.21: Self-seeding threads to improve thread random stability
1   :    module top;
2   :        //initial $display($urandom);
3   :        initial begin
4   :            process::self.srandom(100);
5   :            //$display ($urandom);
6   :            fork
7   :                begin process::self.srandom(1); $display ($urandom,,$urandom); end
8   :                begin process::self.srandom(2); $display ($urandom,,$urandom); end
9   :                begin process::self.srandom(3); $display ($urandom,,$urandom); end
10  :                begin process::self.srandom(4); $display ($urandom,,$urandom); end
11  :                begin process::self.srandom(5); $display ($urandom,,$urandom); end
12  :            join
13  :        end
14  :    endmodule
```

In the above program segment, the initial block on line 3 is self-seeded on line 4, and each thread started by the fork statement is also self-seeded with the first statement of that thread. In this new program, un-commenting lines 2 and 5 will not change the values produced by the program. As such, this modified program using self-seeded threads exhibits full thread stability.

Object Stability is achieved by creating a new random generation context for each newly created object. This behavior is shown in the following example:

```
Program 10.22: SystemVerilog object random stability
1   :   module top;
2   :       class packet;
3   :           rand byte payload;
4   :       endclass
5   :
6   :       //initial $display($urandom);
7   :       initial begin
8   :           packet p;
9   :           //$display($urandom);
10  :           p = new();
11  :           assert(p.randomize());
12  :       end
13  :   endmodule
```

In the above program, the initial block on line 6 is assigned a seed value when it is created. In addition, object **p** is assigned a new random generation context and initialized with a seed. This seed is the next available random number in the context of the initial block. The random value assigned to **p.payload** is dependent on the seed assigned to the context of object **p**.

The above program will generate the same value for **p.payload** for consecutive runs of the same program. Object stability of this program will, however, be disturbed if either lines 6 or 9 are un-commented. Un-commenting line 6 will change the seed value set for the initial block, therefore changing the seed value for object **p**. Un-commenting line 9 will result in a different seed value for object **p**. In both cases, a different value will be generated for **p.pay-load**.

The solution to the above problem is to self-seed the object when it is created. The updated program is shown below.

```
Program 10.23: Self-seeding threads to improve object random stability
1   :   module top;
2   :       class packet;
3   :           rand byte payload;
4   :           function new(int seed);
5   :               this.srandom(seed);
6   :           endfunction
7   :       endclass
8   :
9   :       //initial $display($urandom);
10  :       initial begin
11  :           packet p;
12  :           //$display($urandom);
13  :           p = new(10);
14  :           assert(p.randomize());
15  :       end
16  :   endmodule
```

The above program will produce the same result for **p.payload** even if lines 9 or 12 are un-commented.

It is not always practical or desired to self-seed every thread or every object. A good policy to follow is to add new threads to the end of a program so that seeds assigned to the existing threads do not change. This practice can significantly contribute to random stability.

10.7 System Functions

SystemVerilog provides system functions and tasks for random number generation and control. These functions are described in the following subsections.

10.7.1 $urandom

The prototype for this function is:

    function int unsigned $urandom [(int seed)];

This function returns a new 32-bit unsigned random number every time it is called. The seed argument is optional and determines the sequence of generated random numbers. This function returns the same sequence of numbers when the same seed is used.

The *$urandom* function is different from the *$random* system function in that *$urandom* returns unsigned integers and it is automatically thread stable.

10.7.2 $urandom_range()

The prototype for this function is:

    function int unsigned $urandom_range(int unsigned maxval, int unsigned minval=0);

This function returns a new 32-bit unsigned random number within the specified range of **minval** and **maxval** every time it is called. The **minval** argument can be omitted and defaults to **0**. The **maxval** argument can be less than **minval** in which case, the program automatically reverses the two argument. *$urandom_range()* function is automatically thread stable.

10.7.3 srandom()

The prototype for this function is:

    function void srandom(int seed)

This function initializes an object or thread's random number generator with the provided seed value. The following example shows the use of this function for a thread and for an object.

```
Program 10.24. Use of srandom() function
1  :  module top;
2  :      class packet;
```

```
3   :              rand bit data [];
4   :               rand byte size;
5   :               constraint c1 { data.size() == size;}
6   :          endclass
7   :
8   :          initial begin
9   :               int local_rand;
10  :               packet p;
11  :               p = new();
12  :               process::self.srandom(10);
13  :               assert(randomize(local_rand));
14  :               p.srandom(100);
15  :               assert(p.randomize());
16  :          end
17  :     endmodule
```

In this example, the seed for random number generator of the initial thread is initialize on line 13. This seed affects random values that are generated in the context of this thread. The randomization of local scope variable **local_rand** (line 14) is affected by the seed set on line 13. The statement on line 15 initializes the seed for the random number generator in the packet object. The randomization of packet **p** (line 16) is affected by the seed set on line 15.

CHAPTER 11   *Data Modeling*

Modern verification environments deal with data at different layers of abstractions. At the lowest level, bits and bytes are assigned and read from physical wires in the environment. At the highest level, objects encapsulating bundled values are routinely generated, manipulated, and discarded throughout the environment. Dealing with data at transaction level leads to a more productive and modular program, and also allows for operations related to that data type to be packaged with its abstraction, thereby reducing the low-level complexity that has to be managed.

Data can be created, duplicated, and discarded during simulation runtime. And it can, as it usually does, travel from object to object. These common behaviors across data objects suggests that a structured approach for creating and managing complex data objects can lead to benefits in productivity and reducing the potential for mistakes in data manipulations.

Data in a verification environment can be put into two broad categories:

- Composite data objects
- Command and status (or actions and reactions)

Composite data objects represent a collection of interrelated data values that usually represent objects in a standard or proprietary protocol (i.e., an Ethernet packet). Commands are used to instruct a module to perform a certain activity (e.g., instructing a memory driver to read a memory location). Status is used to provide feedback to the object issuing a command. Note that as with data packets, commands and status are generated, used, discarded, and must travel (e.g., command traveling from a sequencer to a driver, or status moving from monitor where it is observed to the scoreboard). As such, it is natural to model commands and status similar to data that represents packets and signal values.

Ultimately, all abstract data types (i.e., command, status, or data objects) that must travel through a DUV at the register transfer level must be transformed to its physical form. For example, a data object representing an Ethernet packet should be translated into a bit stream to be sent into a DUV port or a bit stream collected from an Ethernet port must be translated into an abstract representation of an Ethernet packet. Packing and unpacking techniques are used to control translation between abstract and physical forms.

This chapter introduces a general view of data modeling and discusses issues related to generation, and its related manipulations.

11.1 Data Models in SystemVerilog

Data models are more than just a container of interrelated data values. In fact, the main goal in creating a data model is to provide an atomic object to the outside world where the data object can be manipulated at an abstract level without intimate knowledge of its internals. Some benefits for this approach are:

- Including data values and applicable operations in a data model inherently leads to a reusable object that can be used in any project operating on such data type.
- Any implementation bug related to that data model is confined to its definition which helps in debugging.
- Not all verification engineers dealing with this data type may have knowledge of its internals and may only need to use it and manipulate it as it travels through their verification jurisdiction.

Hiding the internal complexity of a data model requires that commonly defined operations associated with an abstract data type be packaged with the data model. As such, all composite data types should be modeled using the SystemVerilog *class* construct. The following properties of class construct motivate the need for this requirement:

- Only class-based objects can include constraint blocks.
- Only class-based objects can have a subset of its members defined as random.
- Classes can have properties and methods allowing for data behavior to be embedded in the data object by using class methods.
- Class-based objects can be created and discarded during the simulation runtime.
- Class-based objects are inherently accessed by pointers (i.e., passing objects in task and function calls), and as such, data movement is very efficient.

It maybe tempting to use the *struct* construct to model a composite data object. The following limitations of this construct, however, discourage such usage:

- Struct-based objects are copied by value and not by reference unless *ref* qualifier is specifically used when passing it as a task or function argument.
- Struct-based objects can only be randomized as a whole.
- Methods cannot be embedded in a struct-based object.

The following program shows an example of a simple data packet modeled as a class:

Program 11.1: Data packet modeled as a class object

```
1   :   module top();
2   :       class my_packet;
3   :           rand bit [3:0] field1;
4   :           rand bit [3:0] field2;
5   :           rand bit [3:0] field3;
6   :           constraint c1 {field1 == field2 * field3;}
7   :       endclass
8   :
```

```
9   :        initial begin
10  :            my_packet mp;
11  :            mp = new;
12  :            for(int i=0; i<10; i++)
13  :                assert(mp.randomize() with {field1==10;});
14  :        end
15  :    endmodule
```

In the above example, the constraint solver assigns values to **field₂** and **field₃** in order to satisfy the constraints specified on lines 6 and 13.

11.2 Data Model Fields and Constraints

The abstraction implemented in a data model is achieved through its set of fields (i.e., properties) and constraints describing relationships between these fields. These topics are described in the following subsections.

11.2.1 Data Model Fields

Data model abstractions consist of two types of fields:

- Physical fields
- Virtual fields

Physical fields contain values that represent the content of the abstract data object and are present in the physical form of the data object (i.e., source address in an Ethernet packet). *Virtual fields* contain either instructions for how the packet should be generated or status fields indicating conditions detected when extracting a packet from the physical environment (i.e., crc status in an Ethernet packet). Virtual fields may also be used to hold array sizes inside the data model.

Physical fields follow closely the description of an abstract data type. For example, the physical fields in an Ethernet packet model correspond directly to the fields defined in an Ethernet packet. A data model that represents only the content of a packet contains only physical fields. Virtual fields, however, are included based on the operations defined for a given data model. For example, an Ethernet packet must have a field indicating whether or not it holds a valid crc. In a generator, this field is used to control the random generation of an Ethernet packet so that an incorrect crc is generated only when this flag is set. In a monitor and during collection, this field indicates whether or not a crc error was detected when a packet was collected from a DUV port. Virtual fields are also used to carry instructions about how a packet should be handled as it travels through the verification environment. For example, an Ethernet packet may contain a virtual field indicating the number of idle clocks before the packet preamble is started. During transmission, this field is used by the driver to control when this packet is sent. During receive, this field is updated by the driver to indicate how many idle cycles were detected on the channel before this packet was received.

Figure 11.1 shows the structure of an Ethernet packet. In keeping with the general guidelines of hiding data model details, a model of an Ethernet packet should include the following features and utility methods:

- Physical fields for:
  - Source address
  - Destination address
  - Size
  - Payload
  - crc
- Virtual fields used during generation:
  - Generate short, valid size, or long packet
  - Generate valid or invalid crc
  - Payload size to be generated (derived from valid)
- Virtual fields set during packet collection from DUT, indicating:
  - If the collected packet was short, valid size, or long
  - If the collected packet had a valid or invalid crc when it was collected
  - Whether a collision was detected when receiving this packet
  - Payload size of the collected packet
- Utility methods to:
  - Unpack a bit array into the packet structure
  - Pack the physical fields and return a bit array
  - Methods to copy, print, compare, record, and clone packets
- Random Generation facilities to allow for randomly setting the packet fields

Note that a data object is either generated and transmitted or is received from the DUV, and as such, it is common practice to use the same virtual fields for both generation and collection (i.e., use **valid_crc** to indicate if a valid **crc** should be generated during generation, and to set the same field to true or false when the packet is received from the DUV).

	48	48	16	46 to 1536 bytes	32
SIZED	DEST	SRC	Size [46...1536]	DATA	CRC

Figure 11.1 The Base Ethernet Packet Format

The following program shows a typical implementation for the payload portion of an Ethernet data packet, showing only the fields.

```
Program 11.2: Payload implementation of an Ethernet packet
1  :   typedef enum bit {FALSE, TRUE} bool;
2  :   typedef enum {TOO_SHORT, SHORT, MEDIUM, LONG, TOO_LONG} eth_length_t;
3  :
4  :   class ethernet_frame_sized_payload;
5  :       rand bool legal_size;
6  :       rand eth_length_t ltype;
7  :       rand bit [15:0] tag_info;
8  :       rand int unsigned data_size;
9  :       rand byte data [];
10 :   endclass
```

The physical fields in this implementation are **tag_info** and **data**. The virtual fields are **legal_size**, **ltype**, and **data_size**. These three virtual fields are included in order to provide the ability to control the size of generated payload at different levels of granularity. Field **legal_size** is used to specify if the payload size should be legal or not, field **ltype** is used to specify payload size in general terms as indicated by *enum* on line 2, and field **data_size** is used to specify exact size of payload that should be generated.

The real challenge in implementing this data model is that all virtual and physical fields must be set to their appropriate values when any of the other virtual of physical fields are constrained using an in-line constraint when the object is being randomized. For example, if **data_size** is set to **20** as a constraint when this data model is generated, then **legal_size** should be set to **FALSE**, and **ltype** should be set to **TOO_SHORT** by the random generator. Alternatively, if **legal_size** is constrained to **FALSE** during generation, then **ltype** should be assigned one of **TOO_SHORT** or **TOO_LONG** by the random generator and **data_size** should match the range defined by the setting of **ltype**. This goal is achieved through appropriate inclusion of constraints in this data model. Data model constraints are described in the following section.

11.2.2 Data Model Constraints

Ideally, the abstraction in a data model should be implemented only through constraint blocks that describe the relationship between its fields. This means that procedural assignment statements should be avoided as much as possible when assigning values to the data object, and all such assignments should be left to the randomization engine. The approach that should be avoided is a flow where a series of alternating value assignments followed by randomization are used to assign values to the data object. This guideline provides two benefits:

- The random generation engine can provide more uniform random behavior when considering all data fields at the same time.
- A procedural programming approach imposes an order where some data fields must be set before other fields can be assigned. No such ordering requirement exists when randomization constraints are used to assign values to data fields, since the constraint solver considers all fields at the same time. This means that in a fully constraint-based implementation of a data model, any field can be constrained knowing that other fields will be assigned values in the expected range.

The real challenge in specifying the constraints included in the implementation of a data model is in making sure that all fields are assigned valid values for the initial set of constraints, no matter which fields are constrained using in-line constraints when an object is being randomized.

The following program shows program 11.2 completed to include constraint blocks that implement target features described for that example:

```
     Program 11.3: Using randomization constraints for computing data model fields
1  :    typedef enum bit {FALSE, TRUE} bool;
2  :    typedef enum {TOO_SHORT, SHORT, MEDIUM, LONG, TOO_LONG} eth_length_t;
3  :
4  :    class ethernet_frame_sized_payload;
5  :        rand bool legal_size;
```

```
 6  :        rand eth_length_t ltype;
 7  :        constraint c1 {(legal_size) == (ltype inside {SHORT, MEDIUM, LONG});}
 8  :
 9  :        rand bit [15:0] tag_info;
10  :        constraint c2 {tag_info <= 1536;}
11  :
12  :        rand int unsigned data_size;
13  :        constraint c3 {(legal_size) == (data_size == tag_info);}
14  :        constraint c4 {(ltype==TOO_SHORT) -> (data_size inside {[1:45]});}
15  :        constraint c5 {(ltype==SHORT) -> (data_size inside {[46:800]});}
16  :        constraint c6 {(ltype==MEDIUM) -> (data_size inside {[801:1200]});}
17  :        constraint c7 {(ltype==LONG) -> (data_size inside {[1201:1536]});}
18  :        constraint c8 {(ltype==TOO_LONG) -> (data_size inside {[1536:2000]});}
19  :
20  :        rand byte data [];
21  :        constraint c9 {data.size() == data_size;}
22  :    endclass
```

Constraint c_1 uses an *equivalence constraint* instead of an implication constraint. An equivalence constraint is used to represent mutual implication between two Boolean conditions. This relationship is shown in the following example:

```
constraint impl_constr {(A) -> (B) && !(A) -> !(B);};
constraint equiv_constr {(A) == (B);};
```

In this example, **A** and **B** are Boolean conditions and constraints **impl_constr** and **equiv_constr** represent the same constraint between **A** and **B**. As such, constraint block c_1 in the above example, requires that if virtual field **legal_size** is set to **TRUE**, then **ltype** should be assigned to either **SHORT**, **MEDIUM**, or **LONG**, and vice versa (this is a bidirectional constraint). It also requires that if virtual field **legal_size** is set to **FALSE**, then **ltype** is not set to **SHORT**, **MEDIUM**, or **LONG**, which means **ltype** should be set to either **TOO_SHORT** or **TOO_LONG**. Note that because of using an equivalence constraint, the value assigned to **legal_size** will always reflect the value assigned to **ltype** and vice versa. As such, if **ltype** is constrained during randomization using an in-line constraint, then **legal_size** is automatically set to a value reflecting the setting for the constrained value of **ltype**, and if **legal_size** is constrained during randomization, then **ltype** is automatically set to a value reflecting the setting for the constrained value of **legal_size**. Constraints c_4-c_8 specify valid ranges for each setting of **ltype**. Note that, again, if **data_size** is constrained using an in-line constraint during randomization, then these constraint blocks will result in **ltype** being assigned a value appropriate to the setting for **data_size**, which in combination with constraint block c_1 will set appropriate value for field **legal_size**.

In summary, the provided set of constraints will result in a behavior where any of the virtual fields or physical fields can be constrained using an in-line constraint during randomization and all other data fields will be assigned appropriately. This is shown in the following example:

Program 11.4: Data model randomization constraints based on any of its fields

```
1  :    module top();
2  :        'include "program_11.3"
3  :
4  :        ethernet_frame_sized_payload efsp;
5  :
6  :        initial begin
7  :            efsp = new();
8  :            assert(efsp.randomize() with {legal_size == FALSE;});
```

```
9  :                    assert(efsp.randomize() with {ltype == TOO_SHORT;});
10 :                    assert(efsp.randomize() with {data_size == 199;});
11 :                    assert(efsp.randomize() with {data_size == 2100;});
12 :        end
13 :    endmodule
```

In this example, randomization on line 8 results in **ltype** to be generated as either
TOO_SHORT or **TOO_LONG** with **data_size** set to a random value in the corresponding range.
Randomization on line 9 results in **legal_size** set to **FALSE** with **data_size** set to a random value
in the [1:45] range. Randomization on line 10 results in **legal_size** set to **TRUE** and **ltype** set to
SHORT. Randomization on line 11 will fail because of a contradiction.

11.3 Hierarchical Models

Some data models are naturally described as a hierarchy of smaller composite objects. It is,
therefore, a good strategy to define such models to mirror their description. As will be discussed in the next section, a hierarchical model is implemented as a hierarchy of class
objects where a class object has other class objects as its members.

The important consideration in creating a hierarchical model is that it will contain pointers to other class objects. Care should be taken that these lower level class objects are also
created when the top level object is created or before randomization is started.

The following program shows the hierarchical implementation of a **SIZED** Ethernet
packet. Even though using a hierarchy for just one subtype is not necessary, this example is
shown here so that the addition of other subtypes can be shown in the next section.

```
Program 11.5: Hierarchical model of an Ethernet packet
1  :    typedef enum {SIZED} eth_frame_t;
2  :
3  :    class ethernet_sized_frame;
4  :          rand eth_frame_t ptype;
5  :          rand eth_length_t ltype;
6  :
7  :          rand bool legal_size;
8  :          rand bool legal_crc;
9  :
10 :          rand bit [47:0] dest_addr;
11 :          rand bit [47:0] src_addr;
12 :
13 :          rand int unsigned data_size;
14 :
15 :          rand ethernet_frame_sized_payload sized_payload;
16 :          constraint c0 {(ptype == SIZED) ->
17 :                              sized_payload.legal_size == legal_size;
18 :                              sized_payload.data_size == data_size;
19 :                              sized_payload.ltype == ltype;}
20 :
21 :          bit [31:0] crc;
22 :          constraint c6 {(legal_crc) == (crc == compute_crc(legal_size));}
23 :
24 :          function bit [31:0] compute_crc(bool flag);
25 :          endfunction
26 :
```

```
27  :          function void pre_randomize();
28  :              if(sized_payload == null) sized_payload = new();
29  :          endfunction
30  :      endclass
```

This example shows a hierarchical implementation where the Ethernet frame contains the payload class defined in program 11.3. A *hierarchical constraint block* is used to specify the relationship between the payload object and the class being defined here. Note that all hierarchical constraints in this example are specified in the parent object. The reason for this guideline is that class **ethernet_frame_sized_payload** may potentially be used as a stand-alone object as shown in example 11.4, but class **ethernet_sized_frame** defined in this example cannot be used without the payload object contained in it. The approach of placing all hierarchical constraints in the parent object allows the implementation of the lower level object to remain independent of the parent object.

A constraint guard should be used when defining hierarchical constraints. In this example, a constraint guard is not used since special code is put in place (line 28) to make sure that **sized_payload** is never null when randomization is taking place.

In this example, **crc** is computed using a function call in a constraint block (line 22). The reason field **legal_size** is passed to this function is that **crc** should be calculated only when all other fields are assigned random values. Using a function call with **legal_size** as an argument guarantees that **crc** is assigned only after **legal_size** is assigned a value which requires that all other fields also be assigned values. An alternative approach would be to assign **crc** in the *post_randomize()* function of this class.

11.4 Data Model Subtypes

Any reasonably complex data model describes subtypes for which fields and field values may be different. It may seem intuitive to model such a data object and its subtypes using a base class containing common members and derived classes that contain specialized fields for each subtype. This approach, however, is not well suited for modeling subtypes of a data model. To better understand the reason for this shortcoming, consider the following properties of classes in SystemVerilog:

- SystemVerilog does not support multiple inheritance[1]. This means that a set of members and methods common to some but not all derived classes of a parent class must be explicitly implemented in all derived classes that contain these members and methods.
- Consider two derived classes **B** and **C** of a parent class **A**. In SystemVerilog, it is not possible to randomize an object of type **A** to produce objects of type **B** or **C**. In fact, the only way to create objects of either type **B** or **C** is to declare a pointer of that type and allocate an object for that pointer.

---

[1] A language supporting multiple inheritance allows a derived class to inherit properties and methods from more than one parent class.

- Class members defined using tagged unions cannot participate in constraint specifications.

The lack of support for multiple inheritance implies that if data subtypes are modeled as derived classes of a parent class, then properties and methods that are present in most but not all subtypes have to be explicitly and separately implemented for each subtype, including them. This is not a scalable approach, since a change in any of these properties or methods would mean that all relevant subtypes have to be modified to reflect the new change.

The inability to choose randomly between derived classes of a parent class implies that if data subtypes are modeled as derived classes of a parent class, then creating a data object requires advance knowledge of its subtype. Since randomization occurs after object creation, then data subtype is fixed when data randomization takes place. This behavior leads to multiple drawbacks in using derived classes for modeling data subtypes:

- If data object subtypes must be decided before object creation and randomization, then they cannot be decided based on randomly generated values for other fields of that data object.
- When creating data objects, its subtype must be explicitly decided even if data subtype is not a focus of verification.
- Subtype randomization cannot be packaged inside a class object. The reason is that the subtype for a data object is already decided by the time randomization is taking place, and therefore, any special requirements for generating different subtypes with different probabilities should be implemented outside the class describing the data model.

Given the limitations of using derived classes in modeling data subtypes, it is best to avoid using derived classes and use one class to represent all subtypes. In this case, subtypes can be modeled using either a flat or a hierarchical approach. In a flat approach, all fields for all subtypes are explicitly included in the class declaration of the base model. In a hierarchical approach, fields specific to each subtype are modeled with an independent class declaration, which is then instantiated inside the class declaration of the base model. A hierarchical approach leads to a modular and structured model but it has the disadvantage that constraint guards should be used to deal with potentially *null* object pointers. A flat modeling approach has the advantage of not needing constraint guards but tends to become difficult to manage for anything but the simplest models.

The following guidelines should be followed when modeling a sub-typed data model:

- Use one class definition to represent all subtypes of a data model.
- Include a virtual field having an enumerated type indicating the subtype.
- Define constraints that dictate which fields are affected by the subtype field.
- Implement subtype fields either as a flat or hierarchical model.
- Do not use tagged unions in data models.

Figure 11.2 shows two subtype definitions for an Ethernet packet. Class declaration for ethernet_frame_sized_payload is shown in program 11.3. The following program shows the implementation for ethernet_frame_qtagged_payload. The implementation of the QTAGGED Ethernet packet subtype payload follows the same guidelines as the one described for the SIZED Ethernet packet subtype.

SIZED Ethernet Packet

QTAGGED Ethernet Packet

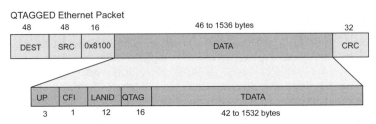

Figure 11.2 Ethernet Packet Subtypes

```
Program 11.6: Qtagged subtype implementation of an Ethernet payload
1  :    class ethernet_frame_qtagged_payload;
2  :        rand bool legal_size;
3  :        rand eth_length_t ltype;
4  :        constraint c1 {(legal_size) == (ltype inside {SHORT, MEDIUM, LONG});}
5  :
6  :        rand bit [15:0] tag_info;
7  :        constraint c2 {tag_info == 16'h8100;}
8  :
9  :        rand bit [3:0] user_priority;
10 :        rand bit     CFI;
11 :        rand bit [11:0] VLAN_id;
12 :
13 :        rand bit [15:0] tag_length;
14 :
15 :        rand int unsigned data_size;
16 :        constraint c4 {(data_size == tag_length);}
17 :        constraint c5 {(ltype==TOO_SHORT) -> (data_size inside {[1:41]});}
18 :        constraint c6 {(ltype==SHORT) -> (data_size inside {[42:800]});}
19 :        constraint c7 {(ltype==MEDIUM) -> (data_size inside {[801:1200]});}
20 :        constraint c8 {(ltype==LONG) -> (data_size inside {[1201:1532]});}
21 :        constraint c9 {(ltype==TOO_LONG) -> (data_size inside {[1533:2000]});}
22 :
23 :        rand byte data[];
24 :        constraint c10 {data.size() == data_size;}
25 :    endclass
```

Given class declarations for **SIZED** and **QTAGGED** Ethernet packet subtype payloads shown in programs 11.3 and 11.6, respectively, Hierarchical Implementation of an Ethernet packet is shown below.

```
Program 11.7: Hierarchical implementation of an Ethernet packet
1  :    typedef enum {SIZED, QTAGGED} eth_frame_t;
2  :
3  :    class ethernet_frame;
4  :        rand eth_frame_t ptype;
5  :        rand eth_length_t ltype;
6  :        rand bool legal_size;
7  :        rand bool legal_crc;
```

```
8   :      rand bit [47:0] dest_addr;
9   :      rand bit [47:0] src_addr;
10  :      rand int unsigned data_size;
11  :
12  :      rand ethernet_frame_sized_payload sized_payload;
13  :      constraint c0 {(ptype == SIZED) ->
14  :                    sized_payload.legal_size == legal_size;
15  :                    sized_payload.data_size == data_size;
16  :                    sized_payload.ltype == ltype;}
17  :
18  :      rand ethernet_frame_qtagged_payload qtagged_payload;
19  :      constraint c1 {(ptype == QTAGGED) ->
20  :                    qtagged_payload.legal_size == legal_size;
21  :                    qtagged_payload.data_size == data_size;
22  :                    qtagged_payload.ltype == ltype;}
23  :
24  :      bit [31:0] crc;
25  :      constraint c6 {(legal_crc) == (crc == compute_crc(legal_size));}
26  :
27  :      function bit [31:0] compute_crc(bool flag);
28  :              //compute crc here
29  :      endfunction
30  :
31  :      function void pre_randomize();
32  :              if(sized_payload == null) sized_payload = new();
33  :              if(qtagged_payload == null) qtagged_payload = new();
34  :      endfunction
35  :
36  :      function void post_randomize();
37  :              if (ptype==SIZED) qtagged_payload= null;
38  :              if (ptype==QTAGGED) sized_payload= null;
39  :      endfunction
40  :   endclass
```

In the above example, *pre_randomize()* method of class **ethernet_frame** is used to make sure that **sized_payload** and **qtagged_payload** pointers are not *null*. If memory consumption is a concern, the object pointer that is not relevant after random assignment can be freed after randomization is complete. This is done in *post_randomize()* where depending on the randomly generated data subtype, the non-relevant object pointer is set to *null* resulting in its allocated memory to be reclaimed by the garbage collection feature of SystemVerilog. Also note that in this implementation, constraint guards are not used with object pointers since the implementation guarantees that object pointers are never *null* during randomization.

11.5 Data Model Views

A data model should provide the following views:

- Method view
- Constraint view

The *method view* is used to access data object properties. A *constraint view* defines how the object can be constrained during randomization. These interfaces are discussed in the following sections.

11.5.1 Method View

Ideally, properties of a data model should only be accessed or modified through well defined methods. This can be achieved by using the *local* and *private* keywords when declaring a class. This approach, however, is not practical when additional constraints must be defined for randomizable fields in a data model.

Either functions or tasks can be used to provide a procedural interface to a data model. It is best to use only functions to provide such an interface. The reason is that a data model is used to hold contents of a composite data object and not store any information related to the state of simulation. Functions return in zero simulation time and as such are the preferred mode of interacting with a data object where no simulation time is expected to pass when interacting with the data object.

The following guidelines should be followed when hiding data model contents:

- All *rand* and *randc* data fields should be *public* (not *local* or *private*).
- Fields used for internal states or flags should be marked as *local* or *private*.
- Only functions should be used in data models. If tasks must be used, they must be non–time-consuming tasks.

11.5.2 Constraint View

To improve user interaction with a data model, generation constraints should also be included for the following purposes:

- Defining default values for valid data generation
- Identifying valid and invalid variations of the data model that are useful for verification, and providing constraint blocks to easily generate such variations

The following subsections discuss approaches for defining such constraint blocks.

11.5.2.1 Abstract Ranges

Data model properties are controlled through values assigned to their fields. Even though a given field can potentially be assigned many different values, it is usually ranges of values that are of interest for verification purposes. *Abstract ranges* refer to ranges of parameters defined for a data model that signify a more abstract concept such as validity, corner cases, or qualitative size measurements (e.g., large, small, etc.).

Abstract ranges provide an easy mechanism for constraining an object during randomization to within a range of interest. Abstract ranges are identified by an enum type variable. Defining abstract ranges also simplifies the specification of non-contiguous ranges during randomization.

In program 11.3, enumerated type eth_length_t is an abstract range where the exact value of packet size is abstracted to concepts of illegal values (TOO_SHORT, TOO_LONG) and sub-ranges within the valid range (SHORT, MEDIUM, LONG).

11.5.2.2 Coordinated Ranges

Coordinated ranges are used to define interesting relationships between different fields of a data model. Coordinated ranges are used as a quick means of providing constraints for commonly used combinations of parameters. The following example shows the definition of coordinated ranges for an Ethernet packet:

```
Program 11.8: Use of coordinated ranges in data modeling
1   :    typedef enum bit {FALSE, TRUE} bool;
2   :    typedef enum {TOO_SHORT, SHORT, MEDIUM, LONG, TOO_LONG} eth_length_t;
3   :    typedef enum {OTHER, SHORT_GOODCRC, LONG_BADCRC} eth_pkt_gen_t;
4   :    class ethernet_frame;
5   :        rand eth_length_t ltype;
6   :        rand bool legal_crc;
7   :        rand eth_pkt_gen_t pg_type;
8   :        constraint c1 {(pg_type==SHORT_GOODCRC) == (ltype==SHORT && legal_crc);}
9   :        constraint c2 {(pg_type==LONG_BADCRC) == (ltype==LONG && !legal_crc);}
10  :    endclass
```

Only the beginning part of the implementation is shown in this example. Enumerated type **eth_pkt_gen_t** is defined as interesting combinations of packet length and crc value. Constraint blocks c_1 and c_2 specify the relationship between coordinated range parameter **pg_type** and values for **ltype** and **legal_crc**. Note that if **pg_type** is not constrained using an in-line constraint during randomization, then its value will be assigned according to randomly generated values for **ltype** and **legal_crc**, and as such can be used as a field to quickly identify the specific coordinated range that was generated during randomization. Also note that if the combination of **ltype** and **legal_crc** does not correspond to those in constraint blocks c_1 and c_2, then **pg_type** will be assigned to **OTHER** since assigning it to any other value would violate constraint blocks c_1 and c_2, and **OTHER** is the only remaining possible value.

11.5.2.3 Default Ranges

A data model should by default be implemented to produce typical behavior. This means that *default ranges* should be provided as part of data model implementation to produce such basic behavior. It is, however, necessary to override such constraints when generating variations that contradict the typical behavior of the data object. SystemVerilog provides mechanisms to override previously defined constraint blocks to achieve this target. This use model is shown in the following example:

```
Program 11.9: Overriding default ranges for a data model
1   :    module top()
2   :        class ethernet_frame;
            ⋮
3   :            constraint default_setting {pg_type == SHORT_GOODCRC;}
            ⋮
4   :        endclass
5   :
6   :        ethernet_frame e;
7   :
8   :        initial begin
9   :            e = new;
```

```
10  :                 assert(e.randomize());
11  :                 e.default_setting.constraint_mode(0);    //turn off default_setting constraint
12  :                 assert(e.randomize() with {
13  :                     legal_crc == FALSE;
14  :                     ptype == SIZED;
15  :                 });
16  :         end
17  :   endmodule
```

This example shows the Ethernet frame model with an additional constraint block (line 3) which is used to indicate that in the absence of any constraints, short packets with good crc should be generated. However, this default behavior can be disabled using a *constraint_mode()* function call (line 11) and the default behavior changed (lines 12–15).

11.6 Transactions: Command and Status

Building randomized verification environments requires not only random data generation, but also random sequence of activities. Traditionally, such activities were modeled with tasks where a customized loop would generate the scenario of interest. However, modeling an activity and its resulting effect as objects that can be created, transferred, and destroyed, opens an entirely new range of possibilities for generating random sequences of actions in a verification environment.

Modeling commands as data objects has the following advantages:

- A command can be randomly generated during simulation.
- A command can be transferred from one verification module to another (i.e from sequencer to a driver).
- Data relevant to a command can be embedded in the command itself (i.e., command to transmit the enclosed packet).
- A command object can be scoreboarded.

Random generation of a command is the enabling idea behind detaching scenario generation from a fixed programming loop that cannot be changed during the simulation process. By modeling a command as an object that can be generated, a variety of factors can control the next action that will take place in the verification environment. A command object can also travel from one module to another, possibly in non-zero time where it is queued before reaching its destination, enabling the separation of command generation from command execution. Additionally, methods related to a command can be encapsulated inside the command object, and a command object can be scoreboarded by inserting it inside a scoreboard.

Modeling status conditions as objects has similar advantages to modeling commands as objects. Status objects are created when status is observed in the verification environment. For example, a collision detected on an Ethernet connection can be packaged in a status object indicating a collision, which can then be sent to a scoreboard that is expecting a collision condition to be detected.

The modeling of data and commands as objects is the fundamental requirement for transaction level modeling of activity in a verification environment (chapter 9).

PART 5

*Environment Implementation
and Scenario Generation*

CHAPTER 12

Module-Based VE Implementation

Two fundamentally different approaches can be used to implement a verification environment:

- Module-based approach
- Class-based approach

In a *module-based implementation*, each component in the verification environment is implemented using a SystemVerilog module construct, the component hierarchy is modeled using the module hierarchy, and connections between components modeled as ports or interface components. *Class-based implementation* is a completely different approach where each component in the verification environment is modeled as a class object, component states are modeled as object fields and properties, and component behavior is implemented using tasks and functions. In a class-based approach, the component hierarchy is implemented as a hierarchy of objects defined using class declarations, with communication between components modeled using transaction interfaces.

Either module-based or class-based implementation approaches can be used to implement a verification environment that follows the architectural guidelines of a modern verification environment (chapter 3). A module-based approach has the advantage of being familiar to engineers with experience in HDL-based programming. As such, a module-based implementation approach can be quickly adopted and used by all members of a design and verification team. A module-based approach, however, is not well suited to large-scale verification projects whose success depends on flexibility, scalability, and reusability of the underlying verification environment. The main reason for this shortcoming is that, first, a module-based implementation is a fixed implementation that cannot be changed after the simulation runtime is started. In addition, the randomization features of the SystemVerilog language are best used with class objects, and therefore, using modules to represent components reduces the flexibility of environment randomization.

Following a class-based implementation approach has the additional advantage of allowing developers to take full advantage of object-oriented programming techniques (e.g., polymorphism, property hiding, object encapsulation). Benefiting from this advantage, however, requires good knowledge of object-oriented programming paradigms.

This chapter illustrates a module-based implementation approach for building a verification environment. Section 12.1 provides a general understanding of a module-based implementation approach through an example of a small module-based implementation. Section 12.2 introduces the XBar design which will act as the DUV for the verification environment described in the remainder of this chapter. The class-based implementation approach is discussed in chapter 13.

12.1 Module-Based Implementation Overview

This section provides an overview of the module-based implementation approach by showing a module-based implementation for a small example. The focus in providing this example is not on following correct methodology but on providing a clear overview of elements involved in a module-based implementation. Class-based implementation of this example is shown in chapter 13.1 and can be used to contrast between these two implementation approaches.

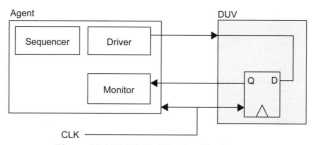

Figure 12.1 D-FF Verification Environment

Consider the D-FF and its verification environment shown in figure 12.1. The implementation of this DUV is shown in the following program.

```
Program 12.1: Implementation of a DFF and its interface wrappers
1   :   module dff(input byte unsigned D, input bit clk, output byte unsigned Q);
2   :       always @(posedge clk)
3   :           Q <= D;
4   :   endmodule
5   :
6   :   interface dff_if(input bit clk);
7   :       byte unsigned D;
8   :       byte unsigned Q;
9   :   endinterface
10  :
11  :   module dff_wrapper(dff_if phy_if, input bit clk);
12  :       dff dffi(phy_if.D, clk, phy_if.Q);
13  :   endmodule
```

The first step in building the verification environment for this component is to define an interface block and define a wrapper that allows other components to interact with this DUV by using the interface block. In the context of a verification environment, this interface block is considered the physical interface.

The verification environment architecture for this design (figure 12.1) consists of a sequencer, a driver, and a monitor that simply prints the values collected from the physical interface.

Module-based implementation of this verification environment is shown in the following program. It should be emphasized that this implementation does not strictly follow the guidelines for implementing a verification environment (e.g., using ports to communicate between drivers and sequencer components, etc.). The focus in this example is to highlight the structure of a module-based implementation of a verification environment.

```
Program 12.2: Module-based verification environment for a DFF
1   :   `include "program-12.1"      //dff implementation
2   :
3   :   module xmt_driver(dff_if phy_if);
4   :       task drive(byte unsigned value);
5   :           @(negedge phy_if.clk);
6   :           phy_if.D = value;
7   :       endtask
8   :   endmodule
9   :
10  :   module monitor(dff_if phy_if);
11  :       always @(negedge phy_if.clk)
12  :       $display("Data Collected ", phy_if.Q);
13  :   endmodule
14  :
15  :   module xmt_sequencer(dff_if phy_if);
16  :       class transaction;
17  :           rand byte unsigned A;
18  :       endclass
19  :
20  :       transaction tr;
21  :
22  :       task gen_and_drive(input int count);
23  :           tr = new;
24  :           for (int i=0; i<count; i++) begin
25  :               void'(tr.randomize());
26  :               $display("driving ", tr.A);
27  :               xmt_drvr.drive(tr.A);
28  :           end
29  :       endtask
30  :   endmodule
31  :
32  :   module agent(dff_if phy_if);
33  :       xmt_driver xmt_drvr(phy_if);
34  :       xmt_sequencer xmt_sqnsr(phy_if);
35  :       monitor moni(phy_if);
36  :   endmodule
37  :
38  :   module dff_module_based_test();
39  :       initial
40  :           dff_testbench.ve_agent.xmt_sqnsr.gen_and_drive(4);
41  :   endmodule
42  :
43  :   module dff_testbench();
44  :       bit clk;
45  :       dff_if dff_if(clk);
46  :
47  :       dff_wrapper dff_wrapper(dff_if, clk);
```

```
48  :           dff_module_based_test dff_test();
49  :           agent ve_agent(dff_if);
50  :
51  :           always #5 clk = ~clk;
52  :   endmodule
```

In module-based implementation of the environment, a SystemVerilog module is used to implement each component in the verification environment (lines 3, 10, 15, 32). The hierarchy is implemented by instantiating each of these components in their intended place in the hierarchy (e.g., instantiating the driver, sequencer, and monitor in the agent on lines 33–35). Functions and tasks are used to implement the procedural behavior of each component (e.g., task **gen_and_drive()** on lines 22–29), and *always* blocks and *initial* blocks are used to initiate the functions in each component (e.g., starting the sequencer on line 40). The testbench is implemented by instantiating the design wrapper, the module for the top level agent containing the verification environment components, and a module block that contains the activation of the sequencer in the agent.

The next section introduces the XBar design. The remainder of this chapter illustrates the implementation of the verification environment for this design using a module-based approach.

12.2 XBar Design Specification

Figure 12.2 shows the interface view of the XBar crossbar switch. This design consists of four receive and transmit ports.

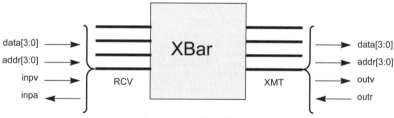

Figure 12.2 XBar Design

A receive port consists of the following signals:

- **data**: (4-bit input to design). Data received by design.
- **addr**: (4-bit input to design). Address of port to route data to.
- **inpv**: (1-bit input to design). Indicates input is valid.
- **inpa**: (1-bit output from design). Indicates that device is ready to accept data.

The transmit port consists of the following signals:

- **data**. (4-bit output from design). Data that was routed to this port.
- **addr**: (4-bit output from design). Receive port where this data came from.

- **outv**: (1-bit output from design). Indicates output data is valid.
- **outr**: (1-bit input to design). Indicates that outside agent has read current output.

The receive port protocol is as follows: the device samples inputs and updates the output on the negative edge of the clock. Inputs are applied to the device at the positive edge of clock. If **inpv** is not set (current input is not valid), then new input can be applied at any time (**inpv** should be set when data is applied). If **inpv** is set then data at the receive port can be changed only when **inpa** is set to **1** (meaning device has read the input signals **data** and **addr**).

The transmit port protocol is as follows: the device transfers data from a receive port to the transmit port indicated on the **addr** line of the receive port. It sets the transmit port signal **addr** to the number of the receive port where the data was received. Device updates transmit port outputs on the negative edge of the clock. If **outv** is not set, then device can write to the output at any time. If **outv** is set, then device can write to an output port if **outr** signal is set (meaning last data applied was read by the outside agent).

The implementation of XBar design is shown in the following program:

Program 12.3: XBar Design implementation

```
1  :   module xbar_duv(input wire  [15:0] rcv_data, input wire  [15:0] rcv_addr,
2  :                    output logic [3:0] rcv_inpa, input wire  [3:0] rcv_inpv,
3  :                    output logic [15:0] xmt_data, output logic [15:0] xmt_addr,
4  :                    input wire  [3:0] xmt_outr, output logic [3:0] xmt_outv,
5  :                    input wire reset, input wire clk);
6  :
7  :       int pending_active_inputs;
8  :
9  :       always @(negedge clk or posedge reset) begin
10 :           if (reset) begin
11 :               rcv_inpa = 4'b1111;
12 :               xmt_data = 12'bz;
13 :               xmt_addr = 12'bz;
14 :               xmt_outv = 4'b0000;
15 :               pending_active_inputs = 0;
16 :           end
17 :           else begin
18 :               pending_active_inputs = 0;
19 :               for (int i = 0; i < 4; i++) if (xmt_outr[i] === 1'b1) xmt_outv[i] = 1'b0;
20 :               for (int i = 0; i < 4; i++) begin
21 :                   bit [3:0] dest_addr;
22 :                   if (rcv_inpv[i] !== 1'b1) continue;
23 :                   dest_addr = rcv_addr[4*i +:4];
24 :                   if (xmt_outv[dest_addr] === 1'b1)begin
25 :                       rcv_inpa[i] = 1'b0;
26 :                       pending_active_inputs ++;
27 :                   end else begin
28 :                       rcv_inpa[i] = 1'b1;
29 :                       xmt_outv[dest_addr] = rcv_inpv[i];
30 :                       xmt_addr[4*dest_addr +:4] = i;
31 :                       xmt_data[4*dest_addr +:4] = rcv_data[4*i +:4];
32 :                   end
33 :               end
34 :           end
35 :       end
36 :   endmodule
```

In defining the XBar sample design, the goal has been to keep the low-level details (i.e., protocol complexity) to a minimum while including features that make the structural composition of its verification environment and sequence type requirements a super-set of what needs to be covered in a majority of designs. These features include:

- Interacting with multiple design ports that use the same protocol, therefore needing multiple agents per interface verification component.
- DUV receive port requiring active interaction with the verification environment for receiving an input (therefore, requiring a master transactor).
- DUV transmit port can be set to operate with no verification environment interaction (by setting **outr** signals to a constant **1**) and could also be driven by a slave transactor that manipulates signal **outr**.
- Ability to verify the XBar design through independently running random stimulus generators at each port, therefore allowing this design to be verified by using only interface verification components. An extension to this design, described in section 14.1, is used to show the implementation of hierarchical sequences that require an environment containing module and system verification components.

12.3 XBar VE Architecture

The architecture of the verification environment for the XBar design is shown in figure 12.3. The following components are identified in this architecture:

- Receive interface: Abstractions for XBar receive port signals.
- Transmit interface: Abstraction for XBar transmit port signals.
- **xbar_wrapper**: Provides an abstraction of XBar to the verification environment.
- XBar RCV agent: Contains sequencer, slave driver, and monitor/collector components to interact with transmit port of the XBar.
- XBar XMT agent: Contains sequencer, master driver, and monitor/collector components to interact with receive port of the XBar.
- **xbar_ivc_env**: Represents an interface verification component containing two agents that interact with a receive and transmit port of XBar.
- **xbar_sve**: Represents the verification environment top level containing the full hierarchy of the verification environment components.
- **xbar_test**: Represents the abstraction of a testcase in a verification environment where a testcase represents a specific configuration of **xbar_sve**.
- **xbar_testbench**: This component is the container of the entire environment.

Component **xbar_sve** represents the top level of the verification environment hierarchy. Component **xbar_test** implements the specific scenario that is carried out by the infrastructure provided by **xbar_sve**. Both **xbar_sve** and **xbar_test** are placed inside component **xbar_testbench**. The implementation of the verification environment architecture shown in figure 12.4 is described in the remainder of this chapter.

xbar_testbench

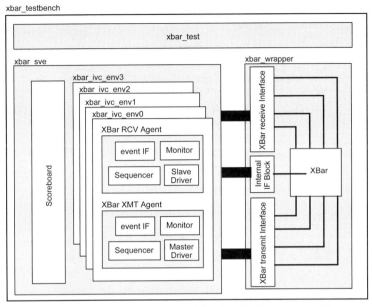

Figure 12.3 XBar Module-Based Verification Environment Architecture

12.4 DUV Wrapper

The implementation of receive, transmit, and internal interface components are shown in the following program. The internal interface component is used to selectively make internal DUV signals available to the verification environment. In the implementation below, internal DUV signal **pending_active_inputs** is an internal design signal that is included in the internal interface.

Program 12.4: XBar Design Interface Blocks

```
1  :   interface xbar_duv_internal_if(input wire reset, input wire clk);
2  :       int pending_active_inputs;
3  :   endinterface
4  :
5  :   interface xbar_duv_rcv_if(input wire reset, input wire clk);
6  :       logic [15:0] data;
7  :       logic [15:0] addr;
8  :       logic [3:0] inpv;   // input is valid (input to DUV)
9  :       logic [3:0] inpa;   // input allowed (output from DUV)
10 :
11 :       task get_data_addr(input int port, output logic [3:0] idata, output logic [3:0] iaddr);
12 :           idata = data[4*port +:4]; iaddr = addr[4*port +:4];
13 :       endtask
14 :
15 :       task set_data_addr(input int port, input logic [3:0] idata, input logic [3:0]iaddr);
```

```
16  :                    data[4*port +:4] <= idata;
17  :                    addr[4*port +:4] <= iaddr;
18  :            endtask
19  :    endinterface: xbar_duv_rcv_if
20  :
21  :    interface xbar_duv_xmt_if(input wire reset, input wire clk);
22  :            logic [15:0] data;
23  :            logic [15:0] addr;
24  :            logic [3:0] outv;   // output is valid (output from DUV)
25  :            logic [3:0] outr;   // output was read (input to DUV)
26  :
27  :            task get_data_addr(input int port, output logic [3:0] idata, output logic [3:0] iaddr);
28  :                    idata = data[4*port +:4]; iaddr = addr[4*port +:4];
29  :            endtask
30  :    endinterface: xbar_duv_xmt_if
```

The XBar design wrapper, implemented using the receive, transmit, and internal interface blocks, is shown in the following program:

Program 12.5: XBar design wrapper module

```
1   :    module xbar_duv_wrapper (xbar_duv_rcv_if xbar_duv_rcvi,
2   :                    xbar_duv_internal_if xbar_duv_inti, xbar_duv_xmt_if xbar_duv_xmti);
3   :
4   :            assign xbar_duv_inti.pending_active_inputs = duv.pending_active_inputs;
5   :
6   :            xbar_duv duv(
7   :                    .rcv_data(xbar_duv_rcvi.data),.rcv_addr(xbar_duv_rcvi.addr),
8   :                    .rcv_inpa(xbar_duv_rcvi.inpa),.rcv_inpv(xbar_duv_rcvi.inpv),
9   :                    .xmt_data(xbar_duv_xmti.data),.xmt_addr(xbar_duv_xmti.addr),
10  :                    .xmt_outv(xbar_duv_xmti.outv),.xmt_outr(xbar_duv_xmti.outr),
11  :                    .reset(xbar_duv_xmti.reset),.clk(xbar_duv_xmti.clk));
12  :    endmodule
```

Components in the verification environment interact with the DUV only through this
wrapper and interface blocks exposed by its ports. Each interface block contains a set of
helper functions to read and write values to the DUV port.

12.5 Library Package

A library package can be defined to hold type declarations, constants specific to a given
implementation, and global functions and tasks. The package file for the XBar example is
shown below:

Program 12.6: XBar Package Declaration

```
1   :    package xbar_pkg;
2   :            `include "ovm.svh"
3   :
4   :            typedef enum bit {FALSE, TRUE} bool;
5   :
6   :            class xbar_packet extends ovm_transaction;
7   :                    // logical fields
8   :                    rand int unsigned wait_cycle;
9   :                    rand int port;
10  :
11  :                    // physical fields
```

```
12  :              rand bit [3:0] src_addr;
13  :              rand bit [3:0] dest_addr;
14  :              rand bit [3:0] data;
15  :
16  :              constraint c0 {src_addr == port;}
17  :              constraint c1 {src_addr != dest_addr;}
18  :              constraint c2 {src_addr < 4;}
19  :              constraint c3 {dest_addr < 4;}
20  :              constraint c4 {wait_cycle < 20;}
21  :
22  :              `ovm_object_utils_begin(xbar_packet)
23  :                  `ovm_field_int(data, OVM_ALL_ON)
24  :                  `ovm_field_int(src_addr, OVM_ALL_ON)
25  :                  `ovm_field_int(dest_addr, OVM_ALL_ON)
26  :                  `ovm_field_int(wait_cycle, OVM_ALL_ON|OVM_NOCOMPARE)
27  :                  `ovm_field_int(port, OVM_ALL_ON|OVM_NOCOMPARE)
28  :              `ovm_object_utils_end
29  :
30  :              function new (int pn=0, string name="");
31  :                  super.new(name);
32  :                  port = pn;
33  :              endfunction
34  :          endclass
35  :
36  :          function void print_2_packets(xbar_packet pkt1, xbar_packet pkt2);
37  :              pkt1.print(""); pkt2.print("");
38  :          endfunction: print_2_packets
39  :      endpackage: xbar_pkg
```

This package first includes the header file for the OVM class library (line 2). Including this file allows all features of the OVM class library to be available when package **xbar_pkg** is loaded. This package includes the declaration of special data type **bool** (line 4) which can be used by importing this package. This package also contains the declaration of XBar packet data type. This packet is described in section 12.6.

The packet declaration also includes helper functions that can be used throughout the verification environment. Function **print_2_packets()** (lines 36–38) is one such function that prints two packets.

This package can be used by importing it into all modules making use of its contents. Alternatively, the name resolution operator can be used to directly access the contents of the package (e.g., **xbar_pkg::xbar_packet**). Importing the package into each module instead of into the global space is a better approach since modules in the same file may use different packages. This usage is shown in the example below:

```
Program 12.7: Importing a package into a module
1  :  module xbar_ivc_env(interface xbar_ve_rcvi, interface xbar_ve_xmti);
2  :      import xbar_pkg::*;
3  :  endmodule
```

12.6 XBar Data Packet

Class objects must be used to model anything but the most simple stimulus. The use of a class object allows data to be generated during program runtime, randomized, and moved around using pointers. The use of a class object also allows methods operating on a data type (e.g., clone, compare, etc.) to be packaged along with the data description.

The implementation of the XBar data packet **xbar_packet** is shown in program 12.6 (lines 6–34). Class **xbar_packet** is used for both transmitted and received packets. This model contains logical fields **wait_cycle** and **port**, representing the number of cycles to wait before applying a packet to the DUV port and the port number to which a packet belongs. This model also includes physical fields **data**, **src_addr**, and **dest_addr**. A set of named constraints are used to define legal behavior for this model (lines 16–20). The name of each constraint can be used to disable that constraint during simulation runtime.

Class **xbar_packet** is derived from base class **ovm_transaction** (line 4) which provides all infrastructure utilities of class **ovm_transaction** (e.g., **copy()**, **clone()**, **print()**, **compare()**) to class **xbar_packet**. Field automation macros are used to indicate which fields are included in the operation of each of these utilities (lines 22–28). For example, field **wait_cycle** is included in all utility functions (e.g., **wait_cycle** is printed when function **print()** of xbar_packet is called) except compare operation (line 26). Field automation feature of the OVM class library is described in detail in section 6.4.

12.7 Transaction Interfaces

Communication between components in a verification environment falls into two categories:

- Physical connections
- Procedural interfaces

Physical connections are used for communicating with the device physical ports. Procedural interfaces are used for transaction based communication between two verification environment components where communication is handled through procedure calls. The use of a procedural interface allows each module interacting through this procedural interface to be developed without the other module being available. The reason for this flexibility is that each module interacts with only the procedural interface and is not aware of the other module being attached to this interface. Figure 12.4 shows a pictorial view of physical and procedural connections between modules using interface blocks.

The implementation of the interface block used for connecting to the XBar design is shown in section 12.2. It is important that all interactions with the DUV take place through such physical interface blocks. This approach provides a clean boundary between the design and the verification environment.

A procedural interface is used for communication between two verification environment components. Transaction based communication model (e.g., blocking, non-blocking calls, etc.) should be used when implementing procedural interaction between two compo-

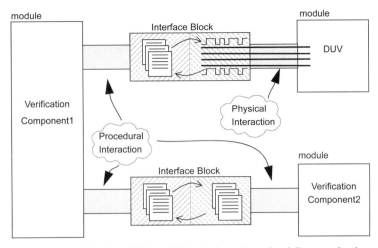

Figure 12.4 Module-Based View of Physical vs. Procedural Communication

nents. In the module-based implementation approach, the facilities that provide transaction based communication should be implemented in an interface block.

The following program shows the procedural interface block used for communication between the sequencer and driver in the verification environment. This implementation is used for both receive and transmit agents and is used to pass an XBar data packet from the sequencer to the driver. As will be shown, on the transmit side of the verification environment (i.e., receive port of DUV), a packet is used to indicate the transfer content. On the receive side of the verification environment (i.e., DUV transmit port), a packet sent to the driver indicates the number of wait cycles before a packet should be collected from the DUV transmit port.

```
     Program 12.8: Transaction interface block
1  :    interface xbar_driver_if;
2  :        import xbar_pkg::*;
3  :
4  :        xbar_packet put_pkt;       // placed by put()
5  :        bit put_pkt_ready = 0;
6  :
7  :        xbar_packet done_pkt;      // last transfer done();
8  :        event done_pkt_ready;
9  :
10 :        semaphore driver_sem = new(1);
11 :
12 :        task automatic put(inout xbar_packet pkt);
13 :            driver_sem.get();
14 :            $cast(put_pkt, pkt.clone());
15 :            put_pkt_ready = 1;
16 :            @done_pkt_ready; // Wait transaction to be taken by get();
17 :            pkt = done_pkt; // return the packet returned by consumer
18 :            driver_sem.put();
19 :        endtask
20 :
21 :        task automatic get(output xbar_packet pkt);
22 :            while (put_pkt_ready == 0) @(put_pkt_ready);
```

```
23  :              put_pkt_ready = 0;
24  :              pkt = put_pkt;
25  :          endtask
26  :
27  :          function automatic void done(input xbar_packet pkt);
28  :              $cast(done_pkt, pkt.clone());
29  :              -> done_pkt_ready;
30  :          endfunction
31  :  endinterface: xbar_driver_if
```

The above program shows the implementation of the passive transaction channel interface **xbar_driver_if** shown in figure 9.6 using an interface block. The methods supported by this interface allow the transaction producer to perform a blocking put into the channel and the transaction consumer (i.e., driver) to perform a blocking get from the channel. In addition, this implementation allows the transaction producer to synchronize with the consumer by waiting until the last transaction placed into the channel is consumed (line 16). The interaction carried through this interface block consists of the following steps:

- Producer places a packet into the interface by calling function **put()**. The interaction implemented here guarantees that the last packet is consumed by the time this function is called again, and therefore the packet can be placed in the interface immediately.
- A consumer calls function **get()**. This function blocks until a packet becomes available (line 22). Meanwhile, the producer is blocked, waiting for the processing of this packet to be completed by the consumer (line 16).
- Upon processing the packet, the consumer calls function **done()**, triggering event **done_pkt_ready** (line 29).
- Triggering event **done_pkt_ready** allows function **put()** to continue beyond line 16. Before returning, the packet returned by the consumer is copied into inout argument **pkt** of function **put()**. This mechanism allows the producer to receive a reply packet from the consumer in return to the packet it had placed inside the interface.

Note that method **put()** is a time consuming task, and therefore, uses a semaphore to create mutual exclusion among possibly multiple callers to this task. This means that no new packet is placed into the transaction interface until the packet that is already placed in the interface is consumed.

12.8 Event Interfaces

Event interfaces are used as a means of event based communication between verification environment components. For example, event interfaces are used by a monitor to broadcast information about conditions that are being monitored. Other components in the environment can track events defined in an event interface to perform tasks related to conditions flagged by these events. An event interface is not as powerful as a transaction interface, but is simple to implement and easy to understand. Module-based implementation of XBar agents makes use of the following event interfaces implemented using interface blocks:

```
Program 12.9: Event interface implementation
1  :    interface xbar_xmt_agent_event_if();
2  :        import xbar_pkg::*;
3  :
4  :        event start_all;
5  :        event stop_all;
6  :        event input_to_duv_collected;
7  :        xbar_packet xbar_xmt_pkt;
8  :    endinterface
9  :
10 :    interface xbar_rcv_agent_event_if();
11 :        import xbar_pkg::*;
12 :
13 :        event start_all;
14 :        event stop_all;
15 :        event duv_valid_output_observed;
16 :        event output_from_duv_collected;
17 :        xbar_packet xbar_rcv_pkt;
18 :    endinterface
```

The transmit agent event interface (lines 1–8) contains event **input_to_duv_collected** which is emitted by the transmit agent monitor indicating that an input to DUV was collected (defined as when a packet applied to the input is accepted by the DUV). In this case, the monitor sets **xbar_xmt_pkt** to the packet collected from the DUV receive port.

Receive agent event interface (lines 10–18) contains event **duv_valid_output_observed** emitted by the receive agent monitor indicating that the DUV has produced a valid output, and event **output_from_duv_collected** emitted by the receive agent monitor indicating that a packet was collected from the DUV output (defined as when the receive driver accepts the packet). In both cases, **xbar_rcv_pkt** is set to the observed packet.

The internal engines of both receive and transmit agents (e.g., sequencer) start their operation when event **start_all** is detected and stop when event **stop_all** is detected. These events are used as a means of controlling verification start and stop time.

As will be shown in the following sections, these event interfaces will be used by both the sequencer and the scoreboarding processes.

12.9 Building the Hierarchy

Now that XBar package and all interfaces have been defined, the hierarchy of the verification environment can be built. In this section, the focus is on how verification environment components are declared, instantiated, and connected. The core function of each component is described in the following sections.

The implementation of the hierarchy for the receive agent (figure 12.3) is shown in the following program:

```
Program 12.10: Receive Agent Hierarchy
1  :    module xbar_rcv_driver(interface phy_if, interface driver_if, interface event_if);
2  :        import xbar_pkg::*;
3  :        parameter int PORT_NUM = 0;
```

```
4   :    endmodule: xbar_rcv_driver
5   :
6   :    module xbar_rcv_monitor(interface phy_if, interface event_if);
7   :        import xbar_pkg::*;
8   :        parameter int PORT_NUM = 0;
9   :    endmodule: xbar_rcv_monitor
10  :
11  :    module xbar_rcv_sequencer(interface driver_if, interface event_if);
12  :        import xbar_pkg::*;
13  :        parameter int DEF_COUNT = OVM_UNDEF;
14  :        parameter int PORT_NUM = 0;
15  :        parameter int MAX_RANDOM_SEQS = 10;
16  :    endmodule: xbar_rcv_sequencer
17  :
18  :    module xbar_rcv_agent(interface phy_if);
19  :        import xbar_pkg::*;
20  :        parameter ovm_active_passive_enum AP_TYPE = OVM_ACTIVE;
21  :        parameter int PORT_NUM = 0;
22  :        parameter int DEF_COUNT = 0;
23  :
24  :        xbar_rcv_agent_event_if event_if();
25  :        xbar_rcv_monitor #(.PORT_NUM(PORT_NUM)) rcv_monitor(phy_if, event_if);
26  :
27  :        // instantiate driver, driver_if, and sequence driver if active
28  :        generate
29  :            if (AP_TYPE == OVM_ACTIVE) begin: active
30  :                xbar_driver_if driver_if();
31  :                xbar_rcv_driver #(.PORT_NUM(PORT_NUM))
32  :                        driver(phy_if, driver_if, event_if);
33  :                xbar_rcv_sequencer #(.PORT_NUM(PORT_NUM),
34  :                        .DEF_COUNT(DEF_COUNT)) sequencer(driver_if, event_if);
35  :            end
36  :        endgenerate
37  :    endmodule: xbar_rcv_agent
```

The following observations apply to this implementation:

- XBar package is imported into all modules (lines 2, 7, 12, 19).
- Physical interface passed to the receive agent (line 18) is the interface block attaching directly to the transmit port of the DUV (program 12.4 line 21).
- An event interface event_if is instantiated at the top level of receive agent (line 24) and passed as a port to all of its sub-modules (i.e., driver, monitor, sequencer).
- Parameter AP_TYPE of receive agent (line 20), in combination with a *generate* statement, is used to decide (line 28) if the driver and the sequencer should be instantiated in the receive agent.
- Physical transaction interface driver_if of type xbar_driver_if (program 12.8) is instantiated inside an active receive agent (line 30) and used in conjunction with event_if to connect the driver and the sequencer.
- Each DUV port is attached to a receive agent. This port number is identified by parameter PORT_NUM (line 21) and is used to set the port number for the monitor, driver and the sequencer (lines 25, 31, and 33).
- Parameter DEF_COUNT (line 22) is used to control the default behavior of the sequencer module by using it to set parameter DEF_COUNT of the sequencer. Use of this parameter is shown in section 12.12.

The implementation hierarchy of XBar transmit agent **xbar_xmt_agent** (figure 12.3) is the same as the one for the receive agent. As such, this implementation is not shown in this text.

An interface verification component for the XBar design (**xbar_ivc_env** in figure 12.3) contains one receive and one transmit agent. The implementation of this component is shown in the following program:

```
Program 12.11: XBar interface verification component implementation
1   :   module xbar_ivc_env(interface xbar_ve_rcvi, interface xbar_ve_xmti);
2   :       import xbar_pkg::*;
3   :       parameter ovm_active_passive_enum AP_TYPE = OVM_ACTIVE;
4   :       parameter int PORT_NUM = 0;
5   :       parameter int RCV_DEF_COUNT = OVM_UNDEF;
6   :       parameter int XMT_DEF_COUNT = OVM_UNDEF;
7   :
8   :       xbar_xmt_agent #(.AP_TYPE(AP_TYPE),.PORT_NUM(PORT_NUM),
9   :               .DEF_COUNT(XMT_DEF_COUNT)) xmt_agent (.phy_if(xbar_ve_xmti));
10  :       xbar_rcv_agent #(.AP_TYPE(AP_TYPE),.PORT_NUM(PORT_NUM),
11  :               .DEF_COUNT(RCV_DEF_COUNT)) rcv_agent (.phy_if(xbar_ve_rcvi));
12  :   endmodule: xbar_ivc_env
```

Component **xbar_ivc_env** contains ports **xbar_ve_rcvi** and **xbar_ve_xmti** connecting to the receive and transmit ports of the DUV. This component contains an instance of receive agent and an instance of the transmit agent (lines 8, 10). Parameters defined for component **xbar_ivc_env** (lines 3–6) are used to configure these two instances. This allows the receive and transmit agents to be configured by specifying the parameters for component **xbar_ivc_env**. Each agent instance is also connected to the appropriate DUV port through port objects **xbar_ve_rcvi** and **xbar_ve_xmti**.

The structure of the verification environment takes shape in **xbar_sve** component (figure 12.3) implemented in the following program. This component contains four **xbar_ivc_env** components.

```
Program 12.12: Component xbar_sve implementation
1   :   module xbar_sve(interface xbar_ve_rcvi, interface xbar_ve_inti, interface xbar_ve_xmti);
2   :       import xbar_pkg::*;
3   :       parameter ovm_active_passive_enum AP_TYPE = OVM_ACTIVE;
4   :
5   :       xbar_scoreboard #(.NUM_PORTS(4)) sb();
6   :       `include "program-12.21"      //connecting the scoreboard to monitors
7   :
8   :       xbar_ivc_env #(.AP_TYPE(AP_TYPE),.PORT_NUM(0),
9   :               .RCV_DEF_COUNT(1000000),.XMT_DEF_COUNT(OVM_UNDEF)
10  :       ) xbar_ivc_env0 (.xbar_ve_rcvi(xbar_ve_rcvi),.xbar_ve_xmti(xbar_ve_xmti));
11  :
12  :       xbar_ivc_env #(.AP_TYPE(AP_TYPE),.PORT_NUM(1),
13  :               .RCV_DEF_COUNT(1000000),.XMT_DEF_COUNT(OVM_UNDEF)
14  :       ) xbar_ivc_env1 (.xbar_ve_rcvi(xbar_ve_rcvi),.xbar_ve_xmti(xbar_ve_xmti));
15  :
16  :       xbar_ivc_env #(.AP_TYPE(AP_TYPE),.PORT_NUM(2),
17  :               .RCV_DEF_COUNT(1000000),.XMT_DEF_COUNT(OVM_UNDEF)
18  :       ) xbar_ivc_env2 (.xbar_ve_rcvi(xbar_ve_rcvi),.xbar_ve_xmti(xbar_ve_xmti));
19  :
20  :       xbar_ivc_env #(.AP_TYPE(AP_TYPE),.PORT_NUM(3),
21  :               .RCV_DEF_COUNT(1000000),.XMT_DEF_COUNT(OVM_UNDEF)
```

```
22  :          ) xbar_ivc_env3 (.xbar_ve_rcvi(xbar_ve_rcvi),.xbar_ve_xmti(xbar_ve_xmti));
23  :    endmodule: xbar_sve
```

This component contains four instances of **xbar_ivc_env** module (lines 8–22) and an instance of a scoreboard defined to have four ports (line 5). For each instance of **xbar_ivc_env**, the port number, the active status, and the default count for receive and transmit sequencers are specified as parameters. Note that the default receive is set to a very large number since by default we would expect the environment to receive any number of packets transmitted by DUV. The default transmit count is set to **OVM_UNDEF**, which as will be shown, indicates that a random number of packets should be transmitted on that port.

Component **xbar_sve** implemented above is the top level of the verification environment hierarchy. The use of this module to create the complete testbench is shown below:

```
Program 12.13: Testbench top level implementation
1   :    module xbar_testbench();
2   :         import xbar_pkg::*;
3   :
4   :         bit reset = 0;
5   :         bit clk = 0;
6   :
7   :         xbar_duv_xmt_if xbar_duv_xmti(reset, clk);
8   :         xbar_duv_rcv_if xbar_duv_rcvi(reset, clk);
9   :         xbar_duv_internal_if xbar_duv_inti(reset, clk);
10  :
11  :         xbar_duv_wrapper xbar_duvw(.*);
12  :         xbar_sve xbar_sve(.xbar_ve_rcvi(xbar_duv_xmti),
13  :              .xbar_ve_inti(xbar_duv_inti),.xbar_ve_xmti(xbar_duv_rcvi));
14  :         xbar_test xbar_test(.*);
15  :
16  :         always #5 clk = ~clk;
17  :
18  :         initial begin
19  :              #0 reset = 1'b1;
20  :              #51 reset = 1'b0;
21  :         end
22  :    endmodule: xbar_testbench
```

Three interfaces are instantiated in **xbar_testbench**, the top level corresponding to receive, transmit, and internal interface with the DUV. The top level contains an instance of the DUV (line 11), **xbar_sve** an instance of the verification environment hierarchy (line 12), and an instance of **xbar_test** which is used for carrying out a target scenario using the infrastructure available in **xbar_sve**. This test component acts as the central controller of the verification activation control. The implementation of this component is shown in section 12.14.

12.10 Monitor

Receive and transmit monitors of the verification environment track signal activity on the transmit and receive ports of the DUV respectively. These monitors serve the following purposes:

- Marking DUV port status through events

- Extracting data from DUV ports
- Verifying correct DUV port traffic
- Collecting coverage on monitored traffic

The monitor components depend on only DUV port values, and are independent of other components in the agent. This independence allows monitors to be used in passive agents that do not contain a driver or a sequencer.

The implementation of receive agent monitor is shown in the following program:

```
Program 12.14: XBar receive monitor implementation
1  :    module xbar_rcv_monitor(interface phy_if, interface event_if);
2  :        import xbar_pkg::*;
3  :        parameter int PORT_NUM = 0;
4  :
5  :        int port_num = PORT_NUM;
6  :        xbar_packet rcv_pkt = new(PORT_NUM);
7  :        event cov_pkt_collected;
8  :        cov_packet cov = new;
9  :
10 :        task rcv_monitor_main_loop(input int port);
11 :            forever begin
12 :                @(posedge phy_if.clk iff phy_if.outv[port] === 1);
13 :                phy_if.get_data_addr(port, rcv_pkt.data, rcv_pkt.src_addr);
14 :                rcv_pkt.dest_addr = port;
15 :
16 :                $cast(rcv_pkt, rcv_pkt.clone());
17 :                event_if.xbar_rcv_pkt = rcv_pkt;
18 :                -> event_if.duv_valid_output_observed;
19 :
20 :                @(negedge phy_if.clk iff phy_if.outr[port] === 1);
21 :                -> event_if.output_from_duv_collected;
22 :                -> cov_pkt_collected;
23 :            end
24 :        endtask: rcv_monitor_main_loop
25 :
26 :        covergroup cov_packet @cov_pkt_collected;
27 :            packet_src_addr: coverpoint rcv_pkt.src_addr;
28 :            packet_dest_addr: coverpoint rcv_pkt.dest_addr;
29 :            packet_data: coverpoint rcv_pkt.data;
30 :        endgroup
31 :
32 :        always @(negedge phy_if.clk) begin
33 :            assertAddrUnknown:assert property (disable iff(phy_if.reset)
34 :                ((phy_if.outv[port_num]) |-> !$isunknown(phy_if.addr[4*port_num +:4]))
35 :            ) else $error("Address X or Z when outv=1 on duv transmit port");
36 :        end
37 :
38 :        initial rcv_monitor_main_loop(port_num);
39 :    endmodule: xbar_rcv_monitor
```

This program highlights the implementation of port monitoring, coverage collection (lines 26–30), and assertion specification (lines 32–36).

Task **rcv_monitor_main_loop()** (lines 10–24) is the start point of the main loop for passive monitoring of the DUV port connected through port **phy_if**. The main loop of the monitor performs a number of operations:

- It identifies when valid data is placed on the DUV output. Upon detecting this condition, it sets **xbar_rcv_pkt** in the event interface **event_if** to information collected from the physical interface (data and address fields) and emits **duv_valid_output_observed** in **event_if** (lines 16, 17). This information is used by the receive sequencer to set field **wait_cycle** in the next generated packet, according to the source address of the incoming packet.

- It identifies when DUV output is read, as signified by assertion of **outpr** signal (line 19). Upon detecting this condition, it sets **xbar_rcv_pkt** in **event_if** and emits event **output_from_duv_collected** in **event_if** (lines 21, 22).
- It emits event **cov_pkt_collected** which is used by the covergroup (lines 26–30) to collect coverage on the collected packet.

The implementation of this monitor is self contained and depends on only its module ports. As will be shown, events emitted in **event_if** are used by the receive sequencer to synchronize the generation of next packet (used only for passing value of field **wait_cycle**) to be passed to the receive driver.

The implementation of the transmit agent monitor is similar in structure and style to receive agent monitor and is not shown in this text.

12.11 Driver

Transmit and receive drivers interact with transmit and receive sequencers, respectively, to transmit and receive packets. The implementation of receive driver is shown in the program below:

```
Program 12.15: XBar receive slave driver implementation
1    :     module xbar_rcv_driver(interface phy_if, interface driver_if, interface event_if);
2    :         import xbar_pkg::*;
3    :         parameter int PORT_NUM = 0;
4    :         int port = PORT_NUM;
5    :
6    :         task get_packet_and_collect();
7    :             xbar_packet driver_packet;
8    :             driver_if.get(driver_packet); //number of cycles to wait before collecting
9    :             collect_packet(port, driver_packet);
10   :             driver_if.done(driver_packet);
11   :         endtask
12   :
13   :         task collect_packet(int port, xbar_packet pkt);
14   :             @(posedge phy_if.clk iff phy_if.outv[port] === 1'b1);
15   :             repeat (pkt.wait_cycle) @(posedge phy_if.clk);
16   :             phy_if.outr[port] <= 1'b1;
17   :             pkt.dest_addr = port;
18   :             phy_if.get_data_addr(port, pkt.data, pkt.src_addr);
19   :             @(negedge phy_if.clk);
20   :             phy_if.outr[port] <= 1'b0;
21   :         endtask: collect_packet
22   :
23   :         always @(negedge phy_if.reset)
24   :             phy_if.outr = 1'b0; // reset the interface
25   :
26   :         initial begin
27   :             @(event_if.start_all);
28   :             $display("RCV collector started on port ", PORT_NUM);
```

```
29  :                forever get_packet_and_collect();
30  :            end
31  :    endmodule: xbar_rcv_driver
```

As shown in the above implementation, the receive driver interacts with **phy_if** (physical port), **driver_if** (transaction interface), and **event_if** (event interface). It uses **driver_if** to receive transactions from the sequencer connected to the other end of this port (line 8) by doing a blocking get, and indicate that transfer is completed (line 10). The value of field **wait_cycle** in the packet received from the sequencer is used to determine the number of cycles to wait before a packet read is acknowledged on the DUV interface (line 15). Receive driver uses **phy_if** to collect the packet from the DUV transmit port. The event interface **event_if** is passed to the driver as a general guideline and is not used in this implementation. The important observation about this implementation is that because of the use of different types of interfaces, the implementation of this driver is completely self contained. The implementation of the transmit agent driver is similar in structure and style to receive agent driver and is not shown in this text.

12.12 Sequencer

Receive and transmit sequencers are used to generate and pass packets to receive and transmit drivers, respectively. Sequencers form the core of scenario generation utilities, and as such, should provide a rich set of features that allow for all scenarios to be generated.

The implementation of a sequencer is divided into four aspects:

- Structure and initialization
- Sequencer main loop
- Item generation
- Sequencer activation

The following program shows the implementation of the XBar receive sequencer using a module block. This implementation highlights the initialization of the sequencer using module parameters.

```
Program 12.16: XBar receive sequencer module
1   :    module xbar_rcv_sequencer(interface driver_if, interface event_if);
2   :        import xbar_pkg::*;
3   :        parameter int DEF_COUNT = OVM_UNDEF;
4   :        parameter int PORT_NUM = 0;
5   :        parameter int MAX_RANDOM_SEQS = 10;
6   :
7   :        int count = DEF_COUNT;
8   :        int port_num = PORT_NUM;
9   :
10  :        `include "program-12.17"    //main loop functions
11  :        `include "program-12.18"    //item generation fields and functions
12  :        `include "program-12.19"    //start of generation
13  :    endmodule: xbar_rcv_sequencer
```

XBar receive sequencer has ports **driver_if** connected to the receive driver and **event_if** connected to all subcomponents of the receive agent. Module parameters (lines 3–5) are used to initialize this sequencer.

The following program shows the implementation of the main generation methods of this sequencer:

```
Program 12.17: XBar receive sequencer main sequence generation loop
1  :    function void set_count(input int new_cnt);
2  :        if (count != OVM_UNDEF && new_cnt != count)
3  :            $display("Setting main's count to a new value, %0d ", new_cnt);
4  :        count = new_cnt;
5  :    endfunction: set_count
6  :
7  :    task main();
8  :        if (count == OVM_UNDEF) assert (randomize(count) with
9  :                {count inside {[1:MAX_RANDOM_SEQS]};}) else $fatal;
10 :
11 :        for (int i = 0; i < count; i++) begin
12 :            randcase
13 :                1: simple();
14 :                1: reactive_receive();
15 :            endcase
16 :        end
17 :    endtask: main
```

Task **main()** (lines 7–16) is the start point of generation activity and is called when this sequencer is activated (program 12.19). Variable **count** is used to decide how many packets should be generated. The value of **count** is set to a random value if it is initially set to **OVM_UNDEF**. Function **set_count()** is also provided so that the value of **count** can be set by a top level testcase component before the sequencer is activated. Task **main()** uses a *randcase* statement to randomly choose between functions **simple()** and **reactive_receive()**. These functions, shown in the next program, generate packets and pass the generated packet to the driver through interface **driver_if**.

The implementation of packet generation methods are shown in the following program:

```
Program 12.18: XBar receive sequencer packet generation functions
1  :    xbar_packet template_pkt;
2  :
3  :    function void override_template_item(xbar_packet tpkt);
4  :        $cast(template_pkt, tpkt.clone());
5  :    endfunction
6  :
7  :    task automatic simple();
8  :        xbar_packet rpkt;
9  :        $cast(rpkt, template_pkt.clone());
10 :        assert (rpkt.randomize() with {
11 :                            rpkt.src_addr == port_num;
12 :                            rpkt.port == port_num;}) else $fatal;
13 :        driver_if.put(rpkt);
14 :    endtask: simple
15 :
16 :    task automatic reactive_receive();
17 :        xbar_packet rpkt;
18 :        xbar_packet mpkt;
19 :        $cast(rpkt, template_pkt.clone());
20 :        assert (rpkt.randomize() with {
21 :                            rpkt.src_addr==port_num;
```

```
22  :                                 rpkt.port==port_num;}) else $fatal;
23  :
24  :             @(event_if.duv_valid_output_observed);
25  :             mpkt=event_if.xbar_rcv_pkt;
26  :             rpkt.wait_cycle=mpkt.data;
27  :             driver_if.put(rpkt);
28  :     endtask: reactive_receive
```

The above implementation is included in the module block that implements the receive sequencer (program 12.16 line 11). This means that the above declarations exist in the body of the sequencer module block.

This implementation includes field **template_pkt** which is an instance of the default item type **xbar_packet** that is to be generated by this sequencer (line 1). This default item will be initialized before the sequencer starts and only if it has not already been initialized by the testcase that starts this sequencer (program 12.19 line 4). Overriding the default behavior of this sequencer is achieved by assigning **template_item** to a class object derived from the default type **xbar_packet**. For example, class **xbar_packet_new** can be derived from **xbar_packet** containing a new constraint block. Because of polymorphism, assigning **template_item** to an object of type **xbar_packet_new** and randomizing **template_item** produces results matching the additional constraint block specified for class **xbar_packet_new**. Note that in this implementation approach, the default sequence item type for this sequencer is indicated through the object type that is stored in **template_item**, and losing this object means losing information of what sequence type should be generated. This consideration plays a role in the how sequence generation methods are implemented.

Function **override_template_item()** (lines 3–5) is provided as a means of overriding the default item type through class polymorphism (section 4.7.4). The use of this function is described in section 12.15.

Function **simple()** (lines 7–14) operates by first creating a clone of template item **template_pkt** (line 9). Working on a cloned copy of **template_pkt** is mandatory since a sequencer may have multiple concurrently running threads that use **template_pkt** as a template item and as such, **template_pkt** should not be used to carry out operations specific to any one thread. Function **clone()** used in this step is a predefined function of class **ovm_transaction** which is the parent class of **xbar_packet**. The use of this function guarantees that the cloned object created on line 9 and assigned to **rpkt**, has the true type of object stored in **template_pkt** even when this type is one derived from **xbar_packet**. Note that because of polymorphism, randomizing **rpkt** produces a result that satisfies any constraint specified for the true type of **template_pkt** object. Function **put()** overwrites the value of its argument, therefore after returning from call to **put()**, the object pointed to by **rpkt** is the object returned by the consumer.

Function **reactive_receive()** (lines 16–28) interacts with the receive monitor to decide the value of **wait_cycle** depending on the source address of the packet that is currently arriving at the DUV transmit port connected to this receive agent. The implementation of this function is similar to function **simple()**, except that after randomizing **rpkt**, the sequencer waits for event **duv_valid_output_observed** in event interface **event_if** to be emitted by the monitor, and then sets the value of **wait_cycle** to the data field of the packet currently being received on the DUV port (line 26). It then passes **rpkt** to the consumer by calling function **put()** of **driver_if** (line 28).

The following program shows the activation mechanism for this sequencer:

```
Program 12.19: XBar receive sequencer activation
1  :   always @(event_if.start_all) begin
2  :       $display("RCV sequencer started on port ", PORT_NUM);
3  :       if(template_pkt == null)
4  :           $cast(template_pkt, ovm_factory::create_object("xbar_packet"));
5  :       fork
6  :           begin
7  :               main();
8  :               $display("RCV sequencer completed on port ", PORT_NUM);
9  :           end
10 :           begin
11 :               @(event_if.stop_all);
12 :               $display("RCV sequencer stopped on port ", PORT_NUM);
13 :           end
14 :       join_any
15 :       template_pkt = null;
16 :   end
```

Start and stop of this sequencer is controlled by events **start_all** and **stop_all** defined in its event interface **event_if**. The always loop is entered when event **start_all** is emitted (line 1). This component first creates an object for template item **template_pkt** if it is not already assigned explicitly by calling function **override_template_item()** (program 12.19 line 3). Note that the OVM factory is used to create this object, and therefore, type override mechanisms (section 6.3.1) can be used to modify the default behavior of this sequencer by changing the object type that is created in this step. This component then executes task **main()**, the sequencer main loop (lines 6–9) in parallel with a thread waiting the occurrence of event **stop_all** (lines 10–13) by using a *fork-join_any* statement. If event **stop_all** is emitted before task **main()** is completed, then the thread of task **main()** is killed. Before completing this always block, field **template_pkt** is se to *null* so that factory override can take effect for the next activation of this sequencer. The always block is restarted at the next occurrence of event **start_all**.

Sequence generation in a module-based implementation has limited flexibility. Adding new behaviors requires that new functions be added to this module, and the weight of *rand-case* statement in task **reactive_receive()** to be changed. Generating multi-sided scenarios (section 8.1) is also challenging when using modules to implement sequencers. Chapter 14 presents the use of the OVM class library for implementing sequencers using class objects while addressing these sequence generation challenges.

12.13 Scoreboarding

Scoreboards check for correct data transfer between DUV ports. The following program shows the scoreboard interface methods for the XBar verification environment:

```
Program 12.20: XBar scoreboard implementation
1  :   module xbar_scoreboard(),
2  :       import xbar_pkg::*;
3  :       parameter int NUM_PORTS = 1;
4  :
```

```
5   :          function void insert(xbar_packet pkt);
6   :                  //implementation not shown
7   :          endfunction
8   :
9   :          function void match(xbar_packet pkt);
10  :                  //implementation not shown
11  :          endfunction
12  :   endmodule
```

The internal implementation of the scoreboard is not shown. The scoreboard, however, creates an array of scoreboards, one for each port. Inserting a packet into the scoreboard places the packet in the scoreboard for its destination address. Matching a packet to the scoreboard, matches that packet against its destination address as well.

The scoreboard for XBar design is instantiated in **xbar_sve** (program 12.12 line 5). This is the scope that contains agent instances for all four ports of the design and as such, monitor components for all four agents can be accessed. The following program shows the content of file included in program 12.12 at line 6 for connecting the scoreboard to the receive and transmit monitors inside each agent:

Program 12.21: Connecting XBar scoreboard to receive and transmit monitors

```
1   :          always @(xbar_ivc_env0.rcv_agent.event_if.output_from_duv_collected)
2   :                  sb.match(xbar_ivc_env0.rcv_agent.event_if.xbar_rcv_pkt);
3   :          always @(xbar_ivc_env1.rcv_agent.event_if.output_from_duv_collected)
4   :                  sb.match(xbar_ivc_env1.rcv_agent.event_if.xbar_rcv_pkt);
5   :          always @(xbar_ivc_env2.rcv_agent.event_if.output_from_duv_collected)
6   :                  sb.match(xbar_ivc_env2.rcv_agent.event_if.xbar_rcv_pkt);
7   :          always @(xbar_ivc_env3.rcv_agent.event_if.output_from_duv_collected)
8   :                  sb.match(xbar_ivc_env3.rcv_agent.event_if.xbar_rcv_pkt);
9   :
10  :          always @(xbar_ivc_env0.xmt_agent.event_if.input_to_duv_collected)
11  :                  sb.insert(xbar_ivc_env0.xmt_agent.event_if.xbar_xmt_pkt);
12  :          always @(xbar_ivc_env1.xmt_agent.event_if.input_to_duv_collected)
13  :                  sb.insert(xbar_ivc_env1.xmt_agent.event_if.xbar_xmt_pkt);
14  :          always @(xbar_ivc_env2.xmt_agent.event_if.input_to_duv_collected)
15  :                  sb.insert(xbar_ivc_env2.xmt_agent.event_if.xbar_xmt_pkt);
16  :          always @(xbar_ivc_env3.xmt_agent.event_if.input_to_duv_collected)
17  :                  sb.insert(xbar_ivc_env3.xmt_agent.event_if.xbar_xmt_pkt);
```

As shown in this program, events in event interfaces of receive and transmit agents are tracked and their collected packet is either inserted into the scoreboard (for transmit agents) or matched against the scoreboard (for receive agents).

The implementation of scoreboarding in this design is such that the same scoreboarding implementation continues to check for correct packet transfer when the agent components are changed from active to passive and the packets are generated by other components in the DUV and not by the verification environment. The reason is that this scoreboarding depends on only the monitor and event interface implementations which are present in passive agents.

12.14 Test Component

A test component is used to carry out specific verification scenarios. The following example shows a simple test component making use of the default behavior of the XBar verification environment:

```
Program 12.22: XBar test component using default behavior
1  :   module xbar_test();
2  :       import xbar_pkg::*;
3  :
4  :       initial begin
5  :           @(xbar_testbench.reset == 1'b0);
6  :           xbar_testbench.xbar_sve.start();
7  :           #10000;
8  :           $finish;
9  :       end
10 :   endmodule
```

Module **xbar_test** shown above is instantiated in the top level testbench. Upon entering the initial block, the test component waits for the global reset signal to get deactivated (line 5). It then calls function **start()** of the **xbar_sve** component which in turn emits event **start_all** in the event interface blocks of all agents. All sequencers are activated after this function is called. Transmit sequencers generate a random number of packets since their count variable is initialized to **OVM_UNDEF**, and receive sequencers receive up to **1,000,000** packets. The test component shown above waits for **10,000** time units after starting the environment and then ends the simulation by calling function *$finish* (line 8).

A test component can also be used to create a directed test. A directed-test is shown in the following example:

```
Program 12.23: XBar test component for a directed test
1  :   module xbar_test();
2  :       import xbar_pkg::*;
3  :
4  :       initial begin
5  :           xbar_testbench.xbar_sve.disable_all_xmt_agent_sequencers();
6  :           @(xbar_testbench.reset == 1'b0);
7  :           xbar_testbench.xbar_sve.start();
8  :
9  :           xbar_testbench.xbar_sve.xmt_directed_packet(0,1,2);
10 :           repeat (2) wait_for_packet_collected_on_port(1);
11 :           xbar_testbench.xbar_sve.xmt_directed_packet(3,1,5);
12 :           repeat (5) wait_for_packet_collected_on_port(1);
13 :           #1000;
14 :           $finish;
15 :       end
16 :   endmodule
```

In the first step, the above directed test disables the sequencers in all transmit agents (line 5) by calling function **disable_all_xmt_agent_sequencers()** of **xbar_sve**. This function sets variable **count** of all transmit sequencers to **0** by calling the **set_count()** function of all transmit sequencers (program 12.17). The test then waits for the global reset to be deactivated (line 6) and then starts the verification environment (line 7). Next, this test sends two packets from XBar port **0** to XBar port **1** by calling function **xmt_directed_packet()** of **xbar_sve** component.

This function in turn calls a function in the transmit sequencer for port **0** to send **2** packets to destination port **1**.

Function **wait_for_packet_collected_on_port()** waits for event **output_from_duv_collected** in the event interface block of **xbar_agent** on port **1** to be emitted (line 10). The same process is then repeated for sending five packets from XBar port **3** to XBar port **1** (line 12) and then waiting for these packets to be received at XBar port **1**.

12.15 Modifying Sequencer Default Behavior

The default behavior of a sequencer can be changed through one of these mechanisms:

- Adding new functions for generating specific sequences of items.
- Calling function **override_template_item()** of the sequencer to explicitly override its default sequence item type before sequencer is started.
- Using type override for the OVM factory to implicitly modify the object type created by the OVM factory for **template_pkt** when the sequencer is being started.

Functions **simple()** and **reactive_receive()** (section 12.12) show examples of how new packet generation capabilities can be added to this sequencer. The same approach can be used for adding new functions that add new generation behaviors to the sequencer.

Both explicit and implicit modification of the sequencer default item require that a new class type be derived from the default sequence item of a sequencer. In the explicit approach, the default sequence item of a sequencer is replaced with an instance of the new class type by calling function **override_template_item()**. In the implicit approach, a type override from the default sequence item to the newly defined class type is specified for the OVM factory before the sequencer is activated.

The following program shows the implementation of a testcase that explicitly and implicitly modifies the sequencers in the XBar verification environment:

```
Program 12.24: XBar test component for a directed test
1   :   module xbar_test();
2   :       import xbar_pkg::*;
3   :
4   :       class xbar_packet_wait_5 extends xbar_packet;
5   :           constraint nowait {wait_cycle == 5;}
6   :           `ovm_object_utils(xbar_packet_wait_5)
7   :       endclass
8   :
9   :       class xbar_packet_wait_8 extends xbar_packet;
10  :           constraint nowait {wait_cycle == 8;}
11  :           `ovm_object_utils(xbar_packet_wait_8)
12  :       endclass
13  :
14  :       initial begin
15  :           xbar_packet_wait_8 pkt8;
16  :           pkt8 = new;
17  :
18  :           @(xbar_testbench.reset == 1'b0);
19  :           xbar_testbench.xbar_sve.ivc_override_rcv_template_item(2, pkt8);
20  :           xbar_testbench.xbar_sve.ivc_override_rcv_template_item(3, pkt8);
```

```
21  :                    ovm_factory::set_type_override("xbar_packet", "xbar_packet_wait_5");
22  :                    xbar_testbench.xbar_sve.start();
23  :                       #10000;
24  :                       $finish;
25  :             end
26  :       endmodule
```

The above implementation shows the definition of class **xbar_packet_wait_5** (lines 4–7) and class **xbar_packet_wait_8** (lines 9–12) which are derived from class **xbar_packet**. Note that macro **ovm_object_utils()** is specified for both these classes so that they are handled correctly by the OVM factory and the predefined functions provided by the OVM class library (e.g., **clone()**). The test is then implemented by first creating class object **pkt$_8$** of type **xbar_packet_wait_8** (line 16), and then using function **ivc_override_rcv_template_item()** to explicitly set the default sequence item for receive sequencers at ports **2** and **3** to **pkt$_8$**. Function **ivc_override_rcv_template_item()** is implemented as part of module **xbar_sve** and in turn calls function **override_template_item()** of the sequencer at the port identified by its first argument. A type override is specified for the OVM factory to generate an object of type **xbar_packet_wait_5** anytime an object of type **xbar_packet** is requested (line 21). This override causes the default sequence item for all sequencers whose default sequence types are not explicitly initialized to be set to an object of type **xbar_packet_wait_5** (see program 12.19 lines 3–4 for the implementation that achieves this behavior). With this configuration, receive sequencers at ports **2** and **3** use type **xbar_packet_wait_8** as their default sequence item type, and receive sequencers at ports **0** and **1** and all transmit sequencers use class type **xbar_packet_wait_5** as their default sequence item type. All sequencers are then started by calling function **xbar_sve.start()** of **xbar_sve** which in turn starts the sequencers in all receive and transmit agents.

CHAPTER 13

Class-Based VE Implementation

Class-based implementation of a verification environment uses classes to model verification environments and their hierarchies. Using classes to model the verification environment and hierarchy leads to great flexibility in how the verification environment can be created and manipulated.

The following tasks must be handled in creating a verification environment:

- Creating the components
- Creating the environment hierarchy
- Interconnecting
- Generating sequences of transactions

Verification environments and their hierarchy can naturally be modeled using classes. In this approach, a class object represents an environment component and class object containment represents the environment hierarchy. Creation of transaction interfaces and transaction sequences is not a concept native to classes and, therefore, requires extensive infrastructure supporting the implementation of these concepts using class objects. The OVM class library provides the full set of classes and utilities required to create a class-based implementation of a verification environment. Features of OVM for implementing these aspects of a verification environment are presented in detail in chapters 6 through 8.

This chapter illustrates the use of a class-based implementation approach for building a complete verification environment. First, an example of a small class-based implementation is provided in section 13.1 to provide a general feel for this implementation approach. The remainder of this chapter provides an in-depth view of a class-based implementation of the XBar design (introduced in section 12.2). Generation of transaction sequences is presented in chapter 14.

13.1 Class-Based Implementation Overview

This section provides an overview of the class-based implementation approach by showing a class-based implementation for the DFF design first introduced in section 12.1. The focus in providing this example is not on following correct methodology but on providing a clear overview of elements involved in a class-based implementation. The class-based implementation shown in this example should be contrasted with the module-based implementation of the same example (section 12.1). The implementation of a verification environment following OVM guidelines is described in section 13.6.

The following program shows class-based implementation of the verification environment shown in figure 12.1:

Program 13.1: Class-based verification environment for a DFF

```
1  :    module dff_class_based_test(dff_if phy_if, input bit clk);
2  :         typedef class xmt_agent;
3  :         class transaction;
4  :             rand byte unsigned A;
5  :         endclass
6  :         class xmt_driver;
7  :             xmt_agent parent;
8  :             task drive(transaction tr);
9  :                 @(negedge parent.pif.clk);
10 :                 parent.pif.D = tr.A;
11 :             endtask
12 :             function new(xmt_agent p=null); parent =p; endfunction
13 :         endclass
14 :         class xmt_monitor;
15 :             xmt_agent parent;
16 :             task collect();
17 :                 forever @(negedge parent.pif.clk) $display(parent.pif.Q);
18 :             endtask
19 :             function new(xmt_agent p=null); parent =p; endfunction
20 :         endclass
21 :         class xmt_sequencer;
22 :             xmt_agent parent;
23 :             transaction tr;
24 :             task gen_and_drive(input int count);
25 :                 tr = new;
26 :                 for (int i=0; i<count; i++) begin
27 :                     assert(tr.randomize());
28 :                     parent.xmt_drvr.drive(tr);
29 :                 end
30 :             endtask
31 :             function new(xmt_agent p=null); parent =p; endfunction
32 :         endclass
33 :         class xmt_agent;
34 :             virtual dff_if pif;
35 :             xmt_driver xmt_drvr;
36 :             xmt_sequencer xmt_sqnsr;
37 :             xmt_monitor xmt_mntr;
38 :             function new();
39 :                 xmt_drvr = new(this); xmt_sqnsr = new(this); xmt_mntr = new(this);
40 :             endfunction
41 :         endclass
42 :
43 :         xmt_agent ve_xmt_agent;
44 :         initial begin
45 :             ve_xmt_agent = new;
46 :             ve_xmt_agent.pif = phy_if;
47 :             fork
48 :                 ve_xmt_agent.xmt_sqnsr.gen_and_drive(10);
49 :                 ve_xmt_agent.xmt_mntr.collect();
50 :             join_any
51 :             $finish;
```

```
52  :          end
53  :     endmodule
```

In a class-based implementation of the verification environment, all components are modeled as class objects instantiated inside a top level module block. The class object representing the agent (lines 33–41) is composed of other class objects representing the driver (lines 6–13), monitor (lines 14–20), and the sequencer (lines 21–32). The agent is then instantiated in a module block (line 43) and activated in an ***initial*** block (lines 48, 49) to drive traffic to and collect traffic from the design.

An important step in this implementation is the creation of a pointer to the physical interface in class **xmt_agent** (line 34) and initializing it with the actual interface to the design (line 46). After initializing the physical interface, methods in the class hierarchy can access the design through this field in the class hierarchy.

The top level testbench for class-based implementation is shown below.

```
     Program 13.2: DFF top level testbench
1   :    module dff_testbench();
2   :        bit clk;
3   :
4   :        dff_if dff_if(clk);
5   :
6   :        dff_wrapper dff_wrapper(dff_if, clk);
7   :        dff_class_based_test   dff_test(dff_if, clk);
8   :
9   :        always #5 clk = ~clk;
10  :    endmodule
```

The major difference between this top level environment and the one for module-based implementation is that in class-based implementation, the verification environment hierarchy is modeled as a class hierarchy, where in a module-based implementation, the verification environment hierarchy is modeled as a module hierarchy.

It should be noted that the class-based implementation shown above is only meant to highlight the general structure of a class-based implementation, and this implementation does not follow the recommended guidelines for implementing a verification environment. For example, this implementation does not follow the component self-containment guideline since in this example, each component makes method calls into other components in the environment (e.g., the sequencer directly calling the **drive()** method of the driver).

The remainder of this chapter focuses on showing the implementation of the verification environment for the XBar design using the OVM class library, and by following the class-based implementation approach.

13.2 XBar Data Packet

The first step in building the verification environment for the XBar design is to define the data object that will be used in the environment. The class declaration for this data model is shown below:

```
Program 13.3: XBar Packet model
1  :   class xbar_packet extends ovm_sequence_item;
2  :       rand bit [3:0] data;
3  :       rand bit [3:0] src_addr;
4  :       rand bit [3:0] dest_addr;
5  :       rand int unsigned wait_cycle;
6  :
7  :       `ovm_object_utils_begin(xbar_packet)
8  :           `ovm_field_int(data, OVM_ALL_ON)
9  :           `ovm_field_int(src_addr, OVM_ALL_ON)
10 :           `ovm_field_int(dest_addr, OVM_ALL_ON)
11 :           `ovm_field_int(wait_cycle, OVM_ALL_ON|OVM_NOCOMPARE)
12 :       `ovm_object_utils_end
13 :
14 :       constraint c10 {src_addr < 4; dest_addr < 4; dest_addr != src_addr;}
15 :       constraint c12 {wait_cycle < 300;}
16 :
17 :       function new(string name="xbar_packet_inst");
18 :           super.new(name);
19 :       endfunction: new
20 :   endclass: xbar_packet
```

It is expected that data objects are generated by sequences. As such, classes representing a data model should be inherited from **ovm_sequence_item** (line 1). The implementation
above shows the use of begin/end variation of macro **ovm_object_utils()** to register class
xbar_packet with the OVM factory (line 7). In addition, field automation macros (section 6.4)
are specified to allow members of this data model to be managed by the OVM facilities
(lines 8–11). The constructor for this model allows for specifying a logical name for an
instance, if necessary.

13.3 Physical Interfaces

Class-based implementation of a verification environment uses the SystemVerilog interface
construct to communicate between the verification environment and the DUV. In class-based
implementations a virtual interface is used as a means of allowing classes to access a SystemVerilog interface. This means that classes representing components in the verification
environment have a pointer to the physical interface to the DUV. This pointer is initialized to
point to the DUV interface when the verification environment hierarchy is built. The following small program shows the use of a virtual interface as a field of a class object. This physical interface can then be accessed through this pointer:

```
Program 13.4: Virtual interface use model
1  :   interface duv_if();
2  :       bit clk;
3  :   endinterface
4  :
5  :   module duv(duv_if dif);
6  :       initial forever #1 dif.clk = ~dif.clk;
7  :   endmodule
8  :
9  :   module test(duv_if dif);
10 :       class my_class;
11 :           virtual duv_if virtual_dif;
```

```
12  :              task run();
13  :                    repeat (10) @(virtual_dif.clk) $display($time, virtual_dif.clk);
14  :                    $finish;
15  :              endtask
16  :         endclass
17  :
18  :         my_class sve;
19  :       · initial begin
20  :              sve = new();
21  :              sve.virtual_dif = dif;
22  :              sve.run();
23  :         end
24  :    endmodule
25  :
26  :    module testbench();
27  :         duv_if mdif();
28  :         duv duvi(mdif);
29  :         test test(mdif);
30  :    endmodule
```

The above example shows the declaration of class **my_class** containing virtual interface **virtual_dif** (line 11). Once this virtual interface is initialized (line 21) to point to an instance of an interface (line 27), it can be used in a class object for accessing the physical signals inside that physical interface (line 13).

13.4 Transaction Ports and Interfaces

The connection between two components depends on the communication requirements of the components being connected. The OVM class library provides the following types of transaction-based connections:

- Transaction interfaces (introduced in chapter 9.3 and 9.4)
- Transaction channels (introduced in section 9.7)
- Analysis ports and Channels (introduced in sections 9.5 and 9.7.2)
- Sequence item Interfaces (introduced in section 8.7)
- Sequence interfaces (introduced in section 8.8.1)

In the XBar verification environment, transaction interfaces are used for connecting sequencers and monitors (section 13.6). Analysis ports are used with monitors to broadcast collected packets (section 13.6.1.1), and then used by scoreboards (section 13.10) to check correct flow of packets between design ports. Sequence item interfaces are used for connecting sequencers with drivers in both the receive and transmit agents (section 13.6.1.4). Sequence interfaces are used for connecting virtual sequencers to downstream sequencers (section 14.7).

13.5 Event-Based Synchronization

Event objects are used as a means of event-based synchronization between verification environment components. OVM provides class **ovm_event** which can be used to exchange data objects derived from **ovm_object**. The provider of the data object triggers the event while providing the data to be exchanged, and the consumer of the data object waits for the event to be triggered and then collects the data object by calling a predefined method of the event object. Event-based synchronization is similar to a non-blocking put and a blocking get operation by the producer and consumer, respectively. As such, event-based synchronization provides a very simple form of transaction-based synchronization. OVM also provides the predefined class **ovm_event_callback** that can be used to initiate methods calls when an event is triggered instead of passing data objects.

The use of event-based synchronization is shown in the following example program. Note that this example does not strictly follow the OVM guidelines for creating an environment hierarchy (section 7.2) since the focus here is on how an event object are used for synchronization purposes. The implementation of a verification environment following OVM guidelines is described in section 13.6.

Program 13.5: Use model for class ovm_event

```
1   :   module top;
2   :       `include "ovm.svh"
3   :
4   :       class packet extends ovm_object;
5   :           `ovm_object_utils(packet)
6   :           int data;
7   :       endclass
8   :
9   :       class monitor extends ovm_monitor;
10  :           `ovm_component_utils(monitor)
11  :           ovm_event packet_ready;
12  :
13  :           function new (string name, ovm_component parent=null);
14  :               super.new(name,parent);
15  :               packet_ready = new("packet_ready");
16  :           endfunction
17  :
18  :           virtual task run ();
19  :               packet collected_packet;
20  :               collected_packet=new();
21  :               collected_packet.data = 123;
22  :               packet_ready.trigger(collected_packet);
23  :           endtask
24  :       endclass
25  :
26  :       class target extends ovm_env;
27  :           `ovm_component_utils(target)
28  :           ovm_event monitor_got_pkt;
29  :
30  :           function new (string name, ovm_component parent=null);
31  :               super.new(name,parent);
32  :               monitor_got_pkt = new("monitor_got_pkt");
33  :           endfunction
34  :
35  :           virtual task run ();
36  :               packet collected_packet;
37  :               monitor_got_pkt.wait_ptrigger();
38  :               $cast(collected_packet, monitor_got_pkt.get_trigger_data());
```

```
39  :                          $display("got packet with data=%0d",collected_packet.data);
40  :                  endtask
41  :          endclass
42  :
43  :          monitor mntr = new("mntr");
44  :          target tgt = new("tgt");
45  :
46  :          initial begin
47  :                  tgt.monitor_got_pkt = mntr.packet_ready;
48  :                  run_test();
49  :          end
50  :  endmodule
```

The above example defines classes **monitor** and **target**. Class **monitor** contains event **packet_ready** of type **ovm_event** (line 11). The monitor triggers this event by passing **collected_packet**, the packet currently collected in the monitor and derived from **ovm_object**, to function **trigger()** of event object **packet_ready** (line 22). Event **packet_ready** is allocated in the constructor for class **monitor** (line 15). Class **target** contains event **monitor_got_pkt** of type **ovm_event**. This event is used by first waiting for it to be triggered (line 37) and then collecting the data from this event object (lines 38–39). Note that event **monitor_got_pkt** is allocated inside the constructor for class **target** (line 32) even though it will be set to point to the event object in the monitor during hierarchy construction.

The top level of this example instantiates monitor **mntr** (line 43) and target **tgt** (line 44). It then overrides event pointer **monitor_got_pkt** in **tgt** by setting it to event **packet_ready** in **mntr** (line 47) before running the test (line 48).

The implementation of **target** and **monitor** classes shown in this example are specially defined to allow each component to operate even if the other component is not yet available, hence achieving self-containment. This is accomplished by creating the event object in each component in its constructor even though it is understood that the event pointer in the target will be changed to point to the event object in the monitor when the hierarchy is being built.

Events provide an easy-to-implement approach for synchronizing the activities of multiple components. The use of events can however lead to problems when a verification environment is moved from a simulation-based platform to a hybrid platform (e.g., simulation and emulation). For example, in moving a verification environment to an emulation platform, the monitor may be evaluated by the emulation platform while the sequencer may be evaluated in the simulator. For such cases, it is best to use transaction interfaces (chapter 9) in order to avoid issues that may arise when accessing event objects across verification platforms. As such, the implementation of the verification environment for the XBar design uses transaction interfaces to synchronize between interacting components (section 13.6).

13.6 Building the Hierarchy

Building a class-based verification environment using the OVM class library consists of the following steps:

- For each environment component, create a custom class derived from an OVM predefined class appropriate for that component (section 7.3).

- Customize the new class by adding fields specific to that component.
- Use appropriate macros to register each class and its fields with the OVM factory.
- Instantiate interface connector objects as needed by the communication requirements of environment components.
- Define the constructor for each component (function **new()**).
- Define the builder for each component (task **build()**).

The architecture of a class-based implementation of the XBar verification environment according to the guidelines of the OVM is described in this section starting from the components in the lowest layers of the verification environment ending with the top level component. This section is focused on creating the hierarchy and the connectivity between components. The implementation of each component is then described in the following sections.

13.6.1 XBar Receive Agent

Figure 13.1 shows the architecture of the XBar receive agent. This agent consists of a monitor, a driver, and a sequencer. The implementation of components in this hierarchy are shown in the following subsections.

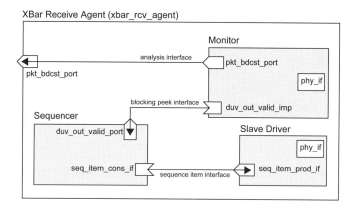

Figure 13.1 XBar Receive Agent Architecture

13.6.1.1 Receive Monitor

The monitor component (figure 13.1) contains analysis port **pkt_bdcst_port** used for broadcasting the latest packet collected by the monitor, and an event object **duv_output_is_valid** which is emitted when the monitor detects the start of a valid packet on the DUV interface. The monitor also contains virtual interface **phy_if** which is initialized to point to the top level interface block that connects with the transmit port of the DUV.

The implementation of this monitor is shown in the following program:

```
     Program 13.6: Receive Monitor class declaration
 1   :   class xbar_rcv_monitor extends ovm_monitor;
 2   :        virtual xbar_duv_xmt_if phy_if;
 3   :        int unsigned port_num;
 4   :        xbar_packet rcv_pkt;
 5   :
 6   :        event duv_out_is_valid_event;
 7   :        event cov_pkt_collected;
 8   :
 9   :        ovm_analysis_port #(xbar_packet) pkt_bdcst_port;
10   :        ovm_blocking_peek_imp#(xbar_packet,xbar_rcv_monitor) duv_out_valid_imp;
11   :
12   :        `ovm_component_utils_begin(xbar_rcv_monitor)
13   :            `ovm_field_int(port_num, OVM_ALL_ON)
14   :            `ovm_field_object(rcv_pkt, OVM_ALL_ON)
15   :        `ovm_component_utils_end
16   :
17   :        covergroup cov_packet @cov_pkt_collected;
18   :            packet_src_addr: coverpoint rcv_pkt.src_addr;
19   :            packet_dest_addr: coverpoint rcv_pkt.dest_addr;
20   :            packet_data: coverpoint rcv_pkt.data;
21   :        endgroup
22   :
23   :        function new (string name="", ovm_component parent=null);
24   :            super.new(name, parent);
25   :            cov_packet = new();
26   :            pkt_bdcst_port = new("pkt_bdcst_port", this);
27   :            duv_out_valid_imp = new("duv_out_valid_imp", this);
28   :        endfunction
29   :
30   :        task peek(output xbar_packet pkt);
31   :            @duv_out_is_valid_event;
32   :            $cast(pkt, rcv_pkt.clone());
33   :        endtask
34   :
35   :        `include "program-13.17"    // implementation of method run() shown in section 13.7
36   :   endclass: xbar_rcv_monitor
```

This program defines class **xbar_rcv_monitor** derived from class **ovm_monitor** (line 1). Field **phy_if** (line 2) will be initialized to point to the top level interface block that connects with the transmit port of the DUV. Field **port_num** (line 3) identifies DUV port to which this monitor is attached. Field **rcv_pkt** (line 4) holds the latest packet collected from the DUV transmit interface. Analysis port connector object **pkt_bdcst_port** (declared on line 9 and initialized on line 26) is used to broadcast packets collected from the DUV interface. Event **cov_pkt_collected** (line 7) activates coverage group **cov_packet** (declared on lines 17–21 and initialized on line 25).

Blocking peek interface **duv_out_valid_imp** (declared on line 10 and initialized on line 27) is provided to allow other components to synchronize with the beginning time of when a new packet is placed by the DUV on its transmit port. Function **peek()** is defined to block until event **duv_out_is_valid_event** is emitted, and then to return a copy of **rcv_pkt**. Event **duv_out_is_valid_event** is emitted in task **run()** after the packet placed by the DUV on its transmit port is collected and stored in **rcv_pkt** (section 13.7). This interface is implemented as a blocking interface so that outside components can synchronize by waiting for task **peek()** to complete. Also, because of using a peek interface, multiple outside components can use this interface to synchronize with this monitor.

Macros are added to this class declaration (lines 12–15) in order to register this class and its field with the OVM factory, include predefined methods of OVM classes (line 12) and to also allow fields in this class to participate in OVM field automation. No hierarchy exists below this monitor component. As such, task **build()** of this class is not required to be defined.

Class **ovm_monitor** does not implement protocol-specific behavior, and therefore, the run phase behavior of this monitor should be implemented in the predefined task **run()** of class **ovm_monitor**. The statement on line 35 includes that implementation (program 13.17) in this class.

13.6.1.2 Receive Sequencer

The sequencer component (figure 13.1) contains the blocking peek port connector object **duv_out_valid_port** connected to imp connector object **duv_out_valid_imp** in the monitor component. This transaction interface is used by sequences running in the sequencer to synchronize to the arrival of a new packet on a DUV output, as detected by the monitor. The sequencer also contains sequence item interface **seq_item_cons_if** that is used by the driver to receive the packets generated by the sequencer.

The implementation of receive sequencer is shown in the following:

```
Program 13.7: Receive sequencer
1   :    class xbar_rcv_sequencer extends ovm_sequencer;
2   :        int unsigned port_num;
3   :        virtual xbar_duv_xmt_if phy_if;
4   :
5   :        ovm_blocking_peek_port#(xbar_packet) duv_out_valid_port;
6   :
7   :        `ovm_sequencer_utils_begin(xbar_rcv_sequencer)
8   :            `ovm_field_int(port_num, OVM_ALL_ON)
9   :        `ovm_sequencer_utils_end
10  :
11  :        function new (string name="", ovm_component parent=null);
12  :            super.new(name, parent);
13  :            `ovm_update_sequence_lib_and_item(xbar_rcv_packet)
14  :            duv_out_valid_port = new("duv_out_valid_port", this);
15  :        endfunction: new
16  :    endclass: xbar_rcv_sequencer
```

This program defines class **xbar_rcv_sequencer** derived from class **ovm_sequencer** (line 1). Field **port_num** (line 2) identifies the DUV port to which this sequencer is attached. Virtual interface **phy_if** is included to allow sequences running in this sequencer to access the DUV physical interface (line 3). Blocking peek interface **duv_out_valid_port** (declared on line 5 and initialized on line 14) will be connected to the blocking peek interface of the receive monitor (program 13.6 line 10) when building the agent containing this sequencer (program 13.10). This interface is used with reactive sequences (section 14.6) to synchronize to the time when a new packet appears on the DUV transmit port. No hierarchy exists below this sequencer, therefore, task **build()** of this class is not defined in this program.

The begin/end variation of OVM macro **ovm_sequencer_utils()** (section 8.2.2) is used to register class **xbar_rcv_sequencer** with the OVM factory, and to also create the sequence library container for this sequencer (line 7–9). Any sequence added to this sequencer by using macro **ovm_sequence_utils()** (e.g., program 13.19 line 2) is placed in the sequence library created in this step.

OVM macro **ovm_update_sequence_lib_and_item()** is used (line 13) to specify the default sequence item for this sequencer and to also initialize the sequencer with the needed sequencing infrastructure. The use of this macro is mandatory.

Note that the implementation of class **xbar_rcv_sequencer** does not include the sequence item interface port **seq_item_cons_if** since this object is included by default in class **ovm_sequencer.**

The transaction type generated by the sequencer has a type of **xbar_packet**. In the receive direction, this packet contains parameter **wait_cycle** which instructs the slave driver on how many cycles to wait before accepting a packet from the DUV. In the transmit direction, the packet produced by the sequencer is transmitted by the driver into a DUV receive port.

The default behavior of the receive and transmit sequencers is to execute sequence **ovm_simple_sequence** a number of times defined by field **count**, where each execution of this sequence generates one sequence item whose type is given by the default sequence type of the sequencer. This means that class **xbar_packet** cannot be used directly as the default sequence item type for either the receive or the transmit sequencers if the default behavior of the sequencers is to be used. The reason is that the default implementation of **xbar_packet** (program 13.3) does not include information on which port it is being generated on. It is, however, required that the source address of a packet generated by the transmit sequencer be set to the local port number, and the destination address of a packet generated by the receive sequencer to be set to the local port number. Because of this requirement, the default sequence item type for the receive sequencer is set to class **xbar_rcv_packet** shown below:

```
     Program 13.8: Receive sequencer transaction type
1  :    class xbar_rcv_packet extends xbar_packet;
2  :            rand int port_num;
3  :
4  :            `ovm_object_utils(xbar_rcv_packet)
5  :
6  :            constraint valid_dest_addr {dest_addr == port_num;}
7  :
8  :            function new(string name="xbar_rcv_packet");
9  :                    super.new(name);
10 :            endfunction: new
11 :
12 :            function void pre_randomize();
13 :                    xbar_rcv_sequencer sqnsr;
14 :                    $cast(sqnsr, get_sequencer());
15 :                    port_num = sqnsr.port_num;
16 :            endfunction
17 :    endclass: xbar_rcv_packet
```

Class **xbar_rcv_packet** is derived from **xbar_packet** and includes field **port_num**. The goal is to have the value of **port_num** set to the local port number before randomization of this packet is started so that this field can be used to constrain the destination address of this packet to the current port during randomization (line 6). Function **pre_randomize()** (section 10.5.3) is used to set the value of field **port_num** before randomization is started. Function **get_sequencer()** of class **ovm_sequence_item** (the parent class of **xbar_packet**) is used in

pre_randomize() (line 14) to set field **port_num** to the port number of the sequencer that is generating this packet type.

In the transmit direction, the default sequence item type is set to **xbar_xmt_packet** which is implemented similar to **xbar_rcv_packet** except that constraint on line 6 is replaced with a constraint setting the value of **src_addr** to field **port_num**.

13.6.1.3 XBar Driver

The default implementation of class **ovm_driver** contains sequence item interface **seq_item_prod_if** which should be connected to the sequencer so that the driver can receive sequence items from the sequencer. The driver component (figure 13.1) also contains virtual interface **phy_if** which during hierarchy construction is initialized to point to the top level interface block that connects with the transmit port of the DUV.

The implementation of receive driver is shown below:

```
Program 13.9: Receive driver
1   :    class xbar_rcv_driver extends ovm_driver;
2   :            int unsigned port_num;
3   :
4   :            virtual xbar_duv_xmt_if phy_if;
5   :
6   :            `ovm_component_utils_begin(xbar_rcv_driver)
7   :                    `ovm_field_int(port_num, OVM_ALL_ON)
8   :            `ovm_component_utils_end
9   :
10  :            function new (string name="", ovm_component parent=null);
11  :                    super.new(name, parent);
12  :            endfunction: new
13  :
14  :            `include "program-13.18"    // implementation of method run() shown in section 13.8
15  :    endclass: xbar_rcv_driver
```

This program defines class **xbar_rcv_driver** derived from class **ovm_driver** (line 1). Field **port_num** (line 2) identifies the DUV port to which this driver is attached. Field **phy_if** (line 4) will be set to point to the top level interface block that connects with the transmit port of the DUV. Sequence item producer interface **seq_item_prod_if** which is a default field of class **ovm_driver** is used to receive sequence items from the sequencer.

Macros are added to this class declaration (lines 6–8) to include predefined methods of the OVM classes (line 6) and to also allow fields in this class to participate in OVM field automation (line 7). No hierarchy exists below this monitor component. As such, task **build()** of this class is not redefined.

The run phase behavior of this monitor is implemented in the predefined task **run()** of class **ovm_driver**. The statement on line 35 includes that implementation (program 13.18) in this class.

13.6.1.4 XBar Agent Top Level Component

The agent component (figure 13.1) is the container for the driver, sequencer, and the monitor, and also has an analysis port **pkt_bdcst_port** that is used to expose the monitor analysis port **pkt_bdcst_port** to the higher layer components.

The implementation of receive agent is shown below:

```
Program 13.10: XBar receive agent
1  :   class xbar_rcv_agent extends ovm_agent;
2  :        protected ovm_active_passive_enum is_active = OVM_ACTIVE;
3  :        protected int port_num = 0;
4  :
5  :        xbar_rcv_monitor monitor;
6  :        xbar_rcv_driver driver;
7  :        xbar_rcv_sequencer sequencer;
8  :
9  :        `ovm_component_utils_begin(xbar_rcv_agent)
10 :             `ovm_field_enum(ovm_active_passive_enum, is_active, OVM_ALL_ON)
11 :             `ovm_field_int(port_num, OVM_ALL_ON)
12 :        `ovm_component_utils_end
13 :
14 :        function new (string name="", ovm_component parent=null);
15 :             super.new(name, parent);
16 :        endfunction: new
17 :
18 :        virtual function void build();
19 :             super.build();
20 :
21 :             set_config_int("monitor", "port_num", port_num);
22 :             $cast(monitor, create_component("xbar_rcv_monitor", "monitor"));
23 :             monitor.build();
24 :
25 :             if(is_active == OVM_ACTIVE) begin
26 :                  set_config_int("sequencer", "port_num", port_num);
27 :                  $cast(sequencer, create_component("xbar_rcv_sequencer", "sequencer"));
28 :                  sequencer.build();
29 :
30 :                  // connect peek port between sequencer and monitor
31 :                  sequencer.duv_out_valid_port.connect(monitor.duv_out_valid_imp);
32 :
33 :                  set_config_int("driver", "port_num", port_num);
34 :                  $cast(driver, create_component("xbar_rcv_driver", "driver"));
35 :                  driver.build();
36 :
37 :                  driver.seq_item_prod_if.connect_if(sequencer.seq_item_cons_if);
38 :             end
39 :        endfunction: build
40 :
41 :        function void assign_vi(virtual interface xbar_duv_xmt_if phy_if);
42 :             monitor.phy_if = phy_if;
43 :             if (is_active == OVM_ACTIVE) begin
44 :                  driver.phy_if = phy_if;
45 :                  sequencer.phy_if = phy_if;
46 :             end
47 :        endfunction: assign_vi
48 :   endclass: xbar_rcv_agent
```

This program defines class **xbar_rcv_agent** derived from class **ovm_agent** (line 1). Field **is_active** (line 2) indicates whether this is an active or passive agent. Field **port_num** (line 3) identifies DUV port to which this monitor is attached.

The purpose of this class is to instantiate the monitor, driver, and the sequencer, and to make the necessary connections between these components. Task **build()** is redefined in this implementation (lines 18–39) to build the hierarchy rooted at this component.

The creation of each component follows a three step process:

- Specifying configuration settings for the component
- Creating an instance of the component
- Calling task **build()** of component to build its sub-hierarchy

The monitor is created first. Before creating an instance of the monitor (line 22), configuration function **set_config_int()** is used to set field **port_num** of the monitor to field **port_num** of the agent. Task **build()** of the monitor is called after the monitor is created (line 23). Note that this task is called even though there is no hierarchy below the monitor component. This is recommended, since later changes may require adding sub-components to the monitor.

A passive agent does not contain the driver and the sequencer. As such, these components are created only if the agent is active (line 25). The sequencer is created (lines 26–28) with the same flow as that of the monitor. Blocking peek interface used for synchronization between the sequencer and monitor is initialized by connecting blocking peek port object **duv_out_valid_port** of the sequencer to the blocking peek imp object **duv_out_valid_imp** of the monitor (line 31).

Driver is created (lines 33–35) with the same steps as that of the monitor. The sequence item interface connector objects in the driver and sequencer are connected after both are created (line 37).

This class also defines function **assign_vi()** which is used by higher layer components to initialize the virtual interfaces in this agent (lines 41–47). As such, field **phy_if** of driver and monitor are not set when building the agent, since these fields will be initialized procedurally after the environment hierarchy is built.

13.6.2 XBar Transmit Agent

The implementation of XBar transmit agent **xbar_xmt_agent**, is similar to the implementation for XBar receive agent discussed in the previous section, and is not shown in this text.

13.6.3 XBar Interface VC

Figure 13.2 shows the architecture of an XBar interface verification component. This component contains an instance of XBar receive agent and an instance of XBar transmit agent.

The implementation of XBar interface verification component is shown below:

```
     Program 13.11: XBar interface verification component
1  :    class xbar_ivc extends ovm_env;
2  :        protected int unsigned port_num = 0;
3  :        protected ovm_active_passive_enum is_active = OVM_ACTIVE;
4  :
5  :        xbar_xmt_agent xmt_agent;
6  :        xbar_rcv_agent rcv_agent;
7  :
```

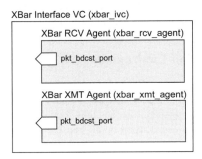

Figure 13.2 XBar Interface VC Architecture

```
8   :        `ovm_component_utils_begin(xbar_ivc)
9   :              `ovm_field_int(port_num, OVM_ALL_ON)
10  :              `ovm_field_enum(ovm_active_passive_enum, is_active, OVM_ALL_ON)
11  :        `ovm_component_utils_end
12  :
13  :        function new(string name="", ovm_component parent = null);
14  :              super.new(name, parent);
15  :        endfunction: new
16  :
17  :        function void build();
18  :              super.build();
19  :
20  :              set_config_int("xbar_xmt_agent0", "port_num", port_num);
21  :              set_config_int("xbar_xmt_agent0", "is_active", is_active);
22  :              $cast(xmt_agent, create_component("xbar_xmt_agent", "xbar_xmt_agent0"));
23  :              xmt_agent.build();
24  :
25  :              set_config_int("xbar_rcv_agent0", "port_num", port_num);
26  :              set_config_int("xbar_rcv_agent0", "is_active", is_active);
27  :              $cast(rcv_agent, create_component("xbar_rcv_agent", "xbar_rcv_agent0"));
28  :              rcv_agent.build();
29  :        endfunction: build
30  :
31  :        function void assign_vi(virtual interface xbar_duv_xmt_if xmt_phy_if
32  :                                             virtual interface xbar_duv_rcv_if rcv_phy_if);
33  :              xmt_agent.assign_vi(rcv_phy_if);
34  :              rcv_agent.assign_vi(xmt_phy_if);
35  :        endfunction: assign_vi
36  :  endclass: xbar_ivc
```

This program defines class **xbar_ivc** derived from class **ovm_env** (line 1). Field **is_active** (line 2) indicates whether this is an active or passive verification component. Field **port_num** (line 3) identifies the DUV port to which this component is attached.

The creation of each component follows the same three-step process outlined for creating the components in the receive agent (section 13.6.1.4). Component **xmt_agent** is created (line 22) after its relevant configuration settings are made (lines 20, 21), followed by calling task **build()** of this component. The receive agent is created using the same process (lines 25–28).

This class also defines function **assign_vi()** which is used by higher layer components to initialize the virtual interfaces in this verification component (lines 31–35). This function is implemented by calling function **assign_vi()** of receive and transmit agents.

13.6.4 XBar Verification Environment

Figure 13.3 shows the architecture of the top level component of the XBar verification environment. This component contains four **xbar_ivc** components, each interacting with one port of the XBar design. This component also contains four **xbar_scoreboard** components. Each scoreboard listens to packets broadcasted by all transmit monitors and places packets destined to its port address on its queue. Each scoreboard listens to packets broadcasted by the receive monitor attached to its local port and matches incoming packets against packets in its queue (section 13.10).

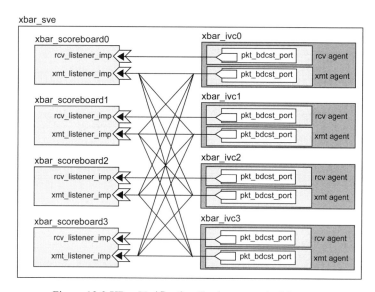

Figure 13.3 XBar Verification Environment Architecture

The implementation of the XBar verification environment top level is shown below:

```
     Program 13.12: XBar verification environment top level
1  :     class xbar_sve extends ovm_env;
2  :         `ovm_component_utils(xbar_sve)
3  :         int unsigned num_ports=4;
4  :
5  :         xbar_ivc ivcs[];
6  :         xbar_scoreboard1 sbs [];
7  :
8  :         function new (string name="", ovm_component parent=null);
9  :             super.new(name, parent);
```

```
10  :          endfunction
11  :
12  :          virtual function void build();
13  :              string inst_name;
14  :              super.build();
15  :
16  :              ivcs = new[num_ports];
17  :              sbs = new[num_ports];
18  :              for (int i=0; i< num_ports; i++) begin
19  :                  $sformat(inst_name, "xbar_ivc[%0d]", i);
20  :                  set_config_int(inst_name, "port_num", i);
21  :                  $cast(ivcs[i], create_component("xbar_ivc", inst_name));
22  :                  ivcs[i].build();
23  :
24  :                  ivcs[i].assign_vi(xbar_testbench.xbar_duv_xmti,
25  :                                              xbar_testbench.xbar_duv_rcvi);
26  :
27  :                  $sformat(inst_name, "xbar_sb[%0d]", i);
28  :                  set_config_int(inst_name, "port_num", i);
29  :                  $cast(sbs[i], create_component("xbar_scoreboard1", inst_name));
30  :                  sbs[i].build();
31  :              end
32  :              for (int i=0; i< num_ports; i++) begin
33  :                  ivcs[i].rcv_agent.monitor.pkt_bdcst_port.connect(sbs[i].rcv_listener_imp);
34  :                  for (int j=0; j< 4; j++)
35  :                      ivcs[i].xmt_agent.monitor.pkt_bdcst_port.connect(sbs[j].xmt_listener_imp);
36  :              end
37  :          endfunction: build
38  :      endclass: xbar_sve
```

This program defines class **xbar_sve** derived from class **ovm_env** (line 1). This component contains field **num_ports** (line 3) which controls the number of ports supported by this
environment. Dynamic arrays **ivcs** and **sbs** (lines 5, 6) hold objects corresponding to
instances of **xbar_ivc** and **xbar_scoreboard** components; one for each port.

The virtual interface in the receive and transmit agents of each **ivcs** are initialized by
calling function **assign_vi()** of the interface verification component with the appropriate interface block as argument (line 24).

Each scoreboard contains two listener ports that should be connected to the broadcast
analysis ports of each **ivcs** component according to the diagram in figure 13.3. These connections are made by calling function **connect()** of the analysis port objects (lines 32–36). The
implementation of the scoreboard components is shown in section 13.10.

13.6.5 XBar Tests

A testcase represents a specific customization of a verification environment for a desired
behavior. In the OVM class library, class **ovm_test** is intended to represent a testcase. Different testcases are modeled as classes derived from **ovm_test**. A library of testcases can be created by defining multiple classes, each containing an instance of the verification
environment with specific configurations required for carrying out the desired verification
scenario.

The following program shows the implementation of a testcase for the XBar design:

```
     ┌ Program 13.13: XBar default testcase
 1   :    class xbar_test_default extends ovm_test;
 2   :         `ovm_component_utils(xbar_test_default)
 3   :
 4   :         xbar_sve xbar_sve;
 5   :
 6   :         function new(string name = "xbar_base_test", ovm_component parent=null);
 7   :              super.new(name, parent);
 8   :         endfunction: new
 9   :
10   :         virtual function void build();
11   :              super.build();
12   :              $cast(xbar_sve, create_component("xbar_sve", "xbar_sve0"));
13   :              xbar_sve.build();
14   :         endfunction: build
15   :
16   :         task run();
17   :              #200000;
18   :              global_stop_request();
19   :         endtask: run
20   :    endclass: xbar_test_default
     └
```

This example shows the implementation of testcase **xbar_test_default** that only creates an instance of **xbar_sve**, the top level component of the verification environment, without modifying any of its default settings. Task **run()** of this test provides a simple stop mechanism where the test is terminated after a fixed length of time (line 16–19). Section 7.4.2 describes the infrastructure provided by the OVM class library for supporting more elaborate requirements for ending the run phase of the simulation.

The following example shows the implementation of a new testcase derived from class **xbar_test_default** that creates an environment with passive transmit agents and active receive agents:

```
     ┌ Program 13.14: XBar testcase with passive transmit agents
 1   :    class xbar_test_passive_xmt extends xbar_test_default;
 2   :         `ovm_component_utils(xbar_test_passive_xmt)
 3   :
 4   :         function new(string name = "xbar_base_test", ovm_component parent=null);
 5   :              super.new(name, parent);
 6   :         endfunction: new
 7   :
 8   :         virtual function void build();
 9   :              set_config_int  ("*.xbar_xmt_agent0","is_active", OVM_PASSIVE);
10   :              super.build();
11   :         endfunction: build
12   :    endclass: xbar_test_passive_xmt
     └
```

Testcase **xbar_test_passive_xmt** is derived from class **xbar_test_default** (line 1). This derived class does no redefine task **run()** of **xbar_test_default**, and therefore, the run behavior for this test is the same as class **xbar_test_default**. Task **build()** of this class is, however, redefined to re-configure all transmit agents in the sub-hierarchy rooted at this component before calling task **build()** of its parent class (i.e., task **build()** of class **xbar_test_default**). The configuration setting is done by calling function **set_config_int()** to set to **OVM_PASSIVE** field **agent is active** of all components in the sub hierarchy rooted at this component whose names end with string "**.xbar_xmt_agent0**". The priority scheme for applying configuration settings (section 7.2) guarantees that the configuration setting specified at this level overrides any settings made in the lower layers of the hierarchy.

The use of global function **run_test()** to start a previously defined testcase is shown in the next section.

13.6.6 XBar Testbench

Figure 13.4 shows the architecture of the XBar testbench. This architecture consists of top level module block **xbar_testbench**. This top level component contains the following objects:

- An instance of **xbar_wrapper**
- An instance of **xbar_test_launcher**
- Clock or reset generation facilities

Module block **xbar_wrapper** contains the XBar design and its interfaces (section 12.4). A module block is used for implementing **xbar_test_launcher**, which is used to create an instance of a testcase and start the execution of simulation phases. An example is shown below:

```
Program 13.15: XBar test launcher block
1  :    module xbar_test_launcher();
2  :        // first include all class defined so far
3  :        `include "top.svh"
4  :
5  :        // use function run_test() to allocate and start a previously defined testcase
6  :        initial begin
7  :            run_test("xbar_test_passive_xmt");
8  :        end
9  :    endmodule
```

In the above example, the implementation of all classes is first included (line 3). An initial block is then used to call global function **run_test()** with the name of a previously defined testcase. Section 7.4.1 describes the infrastructure provided by the OVM class library for selecting a test and starting the run phase of the simulation.

The implementation of **xbar_testbench** is shown below:

```
Program 13.16: XBar testbench
1  :    module xbar_testbench();
2  :        reg clk, reset;
3  :
4  :        xbar_duv_xmt_if xbar_duv_xmti(reset, clk);
5  :        xbar_duv_rcv_if xbar_duv_rcvi(reset, clk);
6  :        xbar_duv_internal_if xbar_duv_inti(reset, clk);
7  :
8  :        xbar_duv_wrapper duvw(.*);
9  :        xbar_test_launcher mt();
10 :
11 :        always #5 clk = ~clk;
12 :
13 :        initial begin
14 :            reset = 1'b0; #0 reset = 1'b1; clk = 1'b1; #51 reset = 1'b0;
15 :        end
16 :    endmodule
```

xbar_testbench (module block)

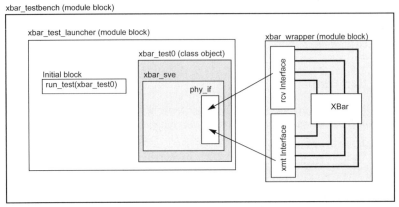

Figure 13.4 XBar Testbench

The implementation of **xbar_testbench** contains instances of **xbar_duv_wrapper**, interfaces to be connected to this instance (lines 4–6), and an instance of **xbar_test_launcher**. This block also includes the necessary code for clock generation (line 11) and reset signal generation (line 14).

13.7 Monitor Run Phase

The implementation of the monitor run phase in class-based implementation is shown in the following program:

```
Program 13.17: XBar receive monitor Run Phase (included in program 13.6)
1   :   task run();
2   :       forever begin
3   :           // wait for duv to indicate output is valid
4   :           @(posedge phy_if.clk iff phy_if.outv[port_num] === 1);
5   :           rcv_pkt = new();
6   :           phy_if.get_data_addr(port_num, rcv_pkt.data, rcv_pkt.src_addr);
7   :           rcv_pkt.dest_addr = port_num;
8   :
9   :           //allow function peek() (program 13.6) to complete when valid packet appears
10  :           -> duv_out_is_valid_event;
11  :
12  :           // wait for outside agent to indicate packet was read
13  :           if (phy_if.outr[port_num] !== 1'b1)
14  :               @(posedge phy_if.outr[port_num]);
15  :           @(negedge phy_if.clk);
16  :
17  :           //activate coverage group cov_packet
18  :           -> cov_pkt_collected;
19  :
20  :           // broadcast packet after DUV receives acknowledgement that it was accepted
21  :           pkt_bdcst_port.write(rcv_pkt);
```

```
22  :          end
23  :    endtask: run
```

This implementation emits event **duv_out_is_valid_event** when the DUV places a new packet on its transmit port. Emitting this event allows task **peek()** of the monitor (program 13.6) to complete, therefore allowing all components blocked on this task to synchronize to this condition detected by the monitor. Note that the monitor is unaware components, if any, that are blocked and waiting for this condition to be detected.

Event **cov_pkt_collected** is emitted (line 18) after the monitor detects that the DUV has received acknowledgement that the packet placed by the DUV on its transmit interface was accepted by the outside agent (i.e., the driver in the receive agent in active mode, and a design component in passive mode), thereby activating coverage group **cov_packet**. After emitting this event, the monitor uses analysis port **pkt_bdcst_port** to broadcast the packet it collected from the DUV transmit port (line 21). The monitor is unaware of components, if any, that use the packets it broadcasts.

The implementation for the transmit agent monitor is similar to the one for receive agent monitor.

13.8 Driver Run Phase

The core function of receive and transmit agent drivers are defined using tasks. The prototypes for these tasks in the agent receive driver were shown in the class declaration of the driver (program 13.9). Task **run()** of class **xbar_rcv_driver** is automatically called as part of executing the OVM predefined simulation phases (section 7.4) and as such, provides an entry for the driver function to get started. The implementation for the receive agent driver is shown below:

```
Program 13.18: XBar Driver Run Phase (included in program 13.9)
1   :   task run();
2   :       fork
3   :            get_packet_from_sequencer_and_drive(port_num);
4   :            reset_signals();
5   :       join
6   :   endtask: run
7   :
8   :   task get_packet_from_sequencer(output xbar_packet pkt);
9   :       ovm_sequence_item item;
10  :       seq_item_prod_if.get_next_item(item);
11  :       $cast(pkt, item);
12  :   endtask: get_packet_from_sequencer
13  :
14  :   task get_packet_from_sequencer_and_drive(int port);
15  :       @(negedge phy_if.reset)
16  :       forever begin
17  :           xbar_packet rcv_pkt;
18  :           get_packet_from_sequencer(rcv_pkt);
19  :           collect_packet(port, rcv_pkt);
20  :           seq_item_prod_if.item_done(rcv_pkt);
21  :       end
22  :   endtask: get_packet_from_sequencer_and_drive
```

```
23  :
24  :   task collect_packet(int port, xbar_packet pkt);
25  :        assert(phy_if.outr[port] == 1'b0);
26  :        @(posedge phy_if.clk iff phy_if.outv[port] === 1'b1);
27  :        repeat (pkt.wait_cycle) @(posedge phy_if.clk);
28  :        phy_if.outr[port] <= 1'b1;
29  :        pkt.dest_addr = port;
30  :        phy_if.get_data_addr(port, pkt.data, pkt.src_addr);
31  :        @(negedge phy_if.clk);
32  :        phy_if.outr[port] <= 1'b0;
33  :   endtask: collect_packet
34  :
35  :   task xbar_rcv_driver::reset_signals();
36  :        forever @(negedge phy_if.reset) phy_if.outr = 1'b0;
37  :   endtask: reset_signals
```

An important aspect of the above implementation is the mechanism for this driver to receive packets from the receive sequencer. The driver uses field **wait_cycle** of the packet it receives from the sequencer to decide how many cycles to wait before collecting the next packet from the DUV transmit port (line 27). The interaction between the driver and the sequencer is shown in function **get_packet_from_sequencer** (lines 8–12). The driver first calls task **get_next_item()** of its sequence item interface connector **seq_item_prod_if** (line 10). Once the driver has completed driving the next packet from the DUV transmit port, it informs the sequencer that it has completed processing the previous item by calling function **item_done()** of **seq_item_prod_if** (line 20). Sequence item interface connector **seq_item_prod_if** is linked with the sequencer when building the receive agent component (program 13.10 line 42).

13.9 Sequencer

The implementation of sequencers, their interaction with the driver, and their associated features are described in detail in chapter 14. However, a simple example is shown in this section on how to override the default behavior of sequencer for the receive agent sequencer. This implementation is shown below:

```
Program 13.19: Overriding default behavior for receive sequencer
1   :   class xbar_rcv_seq_idle extends ovm_sequence;
2   :        `ovm_sequence_utils(xbar_rcv_seq_idle, xbar_rcv_sequencer)
3   :
4   :        function new(string name="", ovm_object parent=null);
5   :             super.new(name);
6   :        endfunction
7   :
8   :        virtual task body();
9   :             `message(OVM_INFO, ("idle rcv sequence"))
10  :        endtask
11  :   endclass: xbar_rcv_seq_idle
12  :
13  :   class xbar_test_idle_rcv extends xbar_test_default;
14  :        `ovm_component_utils(xbar_test_idle_rcv)
15  :
16  :        function new(string name = "xbar_base_test", ovm_component parent=null);
17  :             super.new(name, parent);
18  :        endfunction: new
19  :
```

```
20  :              virtual function void build();
21  :                  set_config_string("*.xbar_rcv_agent0.rcv_sqnsr",
22  :                                    "default_sequence", "xbar_rcv_seq_idle");
23  :                  super.build();
24  :              endfunction: build
25  :  endclass: xbar_test_passive_xmt
```

In this example, a new sequence **xbar_rcv_seq_idle** is first defined where the body of the sequence (lines 8–10) is defined so that no sequence item is generated. A new testcase **xbar_test_idle_rcv** is created by deriving from **xbar_test_default** (line 13). The default sequence started by sequencers in receive agents is then changed using function **set_config_string()** to set field **default_sequence** of any sequencer whose instance name matches string **"*.xbar_rcv_agent0.rcv_sqnsr"** to **xbar_rcv_seq_main** (lines 21–22). The **build()** method of parent class is then called (line 23) which creates the verification environment as described in **xbar_test_default** (program 13.13). Testcase **xbar_test_idle_rcv** can then be run using global function **run_test(xbar_test_idle_rcv)** (program 13.15 line 7).

13.10 Scoreboarding

The xbar scoreboard, as described in figure 13.3, is defined to have two analysis imp connector objects for listening to packets broadcasted by transmit and receive monitors. The complication with requiring two analysis imp connector objects in the same class object is that a single class declaration cannot contain two standard analysis imp objects since a class declaration can contain only one function **write()**, and each standard analysis imp connector object requires a dedicated function **write()** (section 9.5).

Approaches for implementing this behavior include:

- Defining new analysis imp types thereby allowing two analysis imp objects to coexist in the same component
- Using a subscriber component as a subcomponent of the scoreboard, that listens on each of the incoming analysis interfaces of the scoreboard

These approaches are described in the following sections.

13.10.1 Implementation with User Defined Analysis Imp Types

The OVM class library provides the **ovm_IF_decl()** macros (table 9.5 on page 228) for defining new imp connector object types that use a modified method name, thereby allowing multiple imp connector objects to be instantiated in the same component (section 9.6). The implementation of **xbar_scoreboard**, shown below, makes use of this approach for including two imp connector objects in the scoreboard that listen to packets broadcasted by receive and transmit agents in the interface verification components.

```
Program 13.20: XBar scoreboard
1  :  `ovm_analysis_imp_decl(_xmt)
2  :  `ovm_analysis_imp_decl(_rcv)
3  :
```

```
4    :   class xbar_scoreboard extends ovm_scoreboard;
5    :       int unsigned port_num;
6    :       xbar_packet pkt_queue[$];
7    :
8    :       ovm_analysis_imp_xmt #(xbar_packet, xbar_scoreboard) xmt_listener_imp;
9    :       ovm_analysis_imp_rcv #(xbar_packet, xbar_scoreboard) rcv_listener_imp;
10   :
11   :       `ovm_component_utils_begin(xbar_scoreboard)
12   :           `ovm_field_int(port_num, OVM_ALL_ON)
13   :           `ovm_field_queue_object(pkt_queue, OVM_ALL_ON)
14   :       `ovm_component_utils_end
15   :
16   :       function new (string name, ovm_component parent);
17   :           super.new(name, parent);
18   :           xmt_listener_imp = new("xmt_listener_imp", this);
19   :           rcv_listener_imp = new("rcv_listener_imp", this);
20   :       endfunction
21   :
22   :       virtual function void write_xmt(input xbar_packet t);
23   :           if (t.dest_addr == port_num) insert(t);
24   :       endfunction
25   :
26   :       virtual function void write_rcv(input xbar_packet t);
27   :           if (t.dest_addr == port_num)
28   :               match(t);
29   :           else
30   :               `message(OVM_INFO, ("rcv packet dest_addr does not match port_num"))
31   :       endfunction
32   :
33   :       function void insert(xbar_packet pkt);
34   :           // Implementation not shown
35   :       endfunction
36   :
37   :       function void match(xbar_packet pkt);
38   :           // Implementation not shown
39   :       endfunction
40   :   endclass
```

In this implementation, macro **ovm_analysis_imp_decl()** is used to declare analysis imp connector object types **ovm_analysis_imp_xmt** and **ovm_analysis_imp_rcv** (lines 1, 2). These new types are then used to create imp connector objects **xmt_listener_imp** and **rcv_listener_imp** (lines 8, 9). Functions **write_xmt()** (lines 22–24) and **write_rcv()** (lines 26–31) are then defined for imp connector objects **xmt_listener_imp** and **rcv_listener_imp** respectively.

With this implementation, a call to function **write()** of an analysis port connection object connected to **xmt_listener_imp** results in calling function **write_xmt()**, and a call to function **write()** of an analysis port connection object connected to **rcv_listener_imp** results in calling function **write_rcv()**. With this behavior, and given the connectivity shown in figure 13.3, packets broadcasted by the receive agent are passed to function **write_rcv()** and packets broadcasted by the transmit agent are passed to function **write_xmt()**. The implementation of these functions then uses functions **insert()** (lines 33–35) and **match()** (lines 37–39) of the scoreboard to carry out the necessary scoreboarding activities.

13.10.2 Implementation with Listener Subcomponents

The predefined class **ovm_subscriber** to create subcomponents inside the scoreboard that listen on the incoming analysis interfaces. Class **ovm_subscriber** is derived from class

ovm_component, and contains a predefined analysis imp object. In this approach, two components of type **ovm_subscriber** are placed inside class **ovm_scoreboard**. Each **ovm_subscriber** object contains a reference to its parent scoreboard, and function **write()** in each **ovm_subscriber** object can be redefined to perform the required operation on the scoreboard in the parent component. Since a single class object can contain multiple export connector objects, the analysis imp connector in each **ovm_subscriber** object can then be routed to components outside **xbar_scoreboard** through analysis export connectors placed inside the **xbar_scoreboard** object.

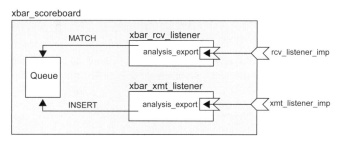

Figure 13.5 XBar Scoreboard Architecture

Figure 13.5 shows the internal architecture of the XBar scoreboard component. The implementation of this scoreboard contains two analysis export connectors **rcv_listener_imp** and **xmt_listener_imp** of type **ovm_analysis_export** (note that these objects are export objects but are named as imp objects since they appear as imp objects to outside components). These connector objects are connected to the analysis imp objects inside **ovm_subscriber** components. Function **write()** of **xbar_xmt_listener** block derived from **ovm_subscriber** is defined to place the incoming packet in the scoreboard queue if the packet destination address matches the port number for this scoreboard. Function **write()** of **xbar_rcv_listener** component derived from **ovm_subscriber** is defined to match the incoming packet against the contents of the scoreboard queue. Connector objects **rcv_listener_imp** and **xmt_listener_imp** of **xbar_scoreboard** are named as imp objects even though these are in fact export connector objects. The reason is that these connector objects appear as analysis imp connectors to components outside the scoreboard component.

The implementation of **xbar_xmt_listener** component is shown in the following:

```
     Program 13.21: XBar xmt listener component
1  :     class xbar_xmt_listener extends ovm_subscriber #(xbar_packet);
2  :         xbar_scoreboard sb;
3  :
4  :         `ovm_component_utils_begin(xbar_xmt_listener)
5  :             `ovm_field_object(sb, OVM_ALL_ON)
6  :         `ovm_component_utils_end
7  :
8  :         function new(string name, ovm_component parent);
9  :             super.new(name,parent);
10 :         endfunction
11 :
12 :         virtual function void write(input xbar_packet t);
```

```
13  :                  if (t.dest_addr == sb.port_num) sb.insert(t);
14  :             endfunction
15  :    endclass
```

Class **xbar_xmt_listener** is derived from **ovm_subscriber** and is specified to be listening to transactions of type **xbar_packet** (line 1). Field **sb** is a reference to the scoreboard that contains this component and is initialized by the scoreboard when the scoreboard hierarchy is being built. Function **write()** is defined to call function **insert()** of the scoreboard if the destination address of the incoming packet matches the port number for this scoreboard (line 13). This function places the incoming transaction in the ordered list of transactions that are expected to be received at this port. Note that it is not required to create an instance of an analysis imp connector since class **ovm_subscriber** by default contains connector **analysis_export** of type **ovm_analysis_imp**.

The implementation of the **xbar_rcv_listener** is similar to the implementation of **xbar_xmt_listener** except that its function **write()** is defined to call function **match()** of the scoreboard with the incoming packet.

The implementation of **xbar_scoreboard** is shown in the following:

```
    Program 13.22: XBar scoreboard
1   :    class xbar_scoreboard extends ovm_scoreboard;
2   :        int unsigned port_num;
3   :        xbar_packet pkt_queue[$];
4   :
5   :        `ovm_component_utils_begin(xbar_scoreboard)
6   :            `ovm_field_int(port_num, OVM_ALL_ON)
7   :            `ovm_field_queue_object(pkt_queue, OVM_ALL_ON)
8   :        `ovm_component_utils_end
9   :
10  :        ovm_analysis_export #(xbar_packet) xmt_listener_imp;
11  :        ovm_analysis_export #(xbar_packet) rcv_listener_imp;
12  :
13  :        xbar_xmt_listener xmt_listener;
14  :        xbar_rcv_listener rcv_listener;
15  :
16  :        function new (string name, ovm_component parent);
17  :            super.new(name, parent);
18  :        endfunction
19  :
20  :        virtual function void build();
21  :            super.build();
22  :
23  :            xmt_listener_imp = new("xmt_listener_imp", this);
24  :            rcv_listener_imp = new("rcv_listener_imp", this);
25  :
26  :            set_config_object("xmt_listener", "sb", this, 0);
27  :            $cast(xmt_listener, create_component("xbar_xmt_listener", "xmt_listener"));
28  :            xmt_listener.build();
29  :
30  :            set_config_object("rcv_listener", "sb", this, 0);
31  :            $cast(rcv_listener, create_component("xbar_rcv_listener", "rcv_listener"));
32  :            rcv_listener.build();
33  :
34  :            xmt_listener_imp.connect(xmt_listener.analysis_export);
35  :            rcv_listener_imp.connect(rcv_listener.analysis_export);
36  :        endfunction: build
37  :
38  :        extern function void insert(xbar_packet pkt);
```

```
39  :          extern function void match(xbar_packet pkt);
40  :   endclass
```

This implementation contains components **xmt_listener** and **rcv_listener** (lines 10, 11). Task **build()** of **xbar_scoreboard** is defined to first create connector objects **xmt_listener_imp** and **rcv_listener_imp** (lines 23, 24). It then creates object **xmt_listener** (line 27) after using function **set_config_object()** to set field **sb** of **xmt_listener** to point to this scoreboard object (line 26). Object **rcv_listener** is created using the same process (lines 30–32). In the last step, connector objects for **xbar_scoreboard** are each connected to their corresponding listener component (lines 34, 35). With this implementation, any packet arriving at **xmt_listener_imp** is routed to the analysis imp connector of **xmt_listener**, causing function **write()** of **xmt_listener** to be called with the incoming packet, which in turn inserts the packet into the scoreboard. Similarly, any packet arriving at **rcv_listener_imp** is routed to the analysis imp connector of **rcv_listener**, which in turns matches the incoming packet against the scoreboard.

CHAPTER 14

Verification Scenario Generation

The OVM class library provides powerful constructs and concepts for modeling verification scenarios as a sequence of transactions. The concepts and constructs for implementing this model of a verification scenario is described in detail in chapter 8.

Chapter 13 introduces the XBar crossbar switch as a sample design and showed the implementation of its verification environment containing only interface verification components. This chapter introduces the XBar communication protocol and describes in detail the implementation of a complete verification environment that uses transaction sequences generated across multiple layers of interface, module, and system verification components to verify the features of this communication protocol. Techniques and features of generating sequences using the OVM class library are described through the presentation of this sample environment.

14.1 XBar Communication Protocol

The XBar communication protocol is based on the single-cycle packet routed through the XBar crossbar switch (section 12.2).

The following data encapsulations are used in constructing the XBar communication protocol:

- The *XBar Packet* is the fundamental item of communication, consisting of:
  - Source address (**src_addr**)
  - Destination address (**dest_addr**)
  - Payload (**data**)
- The *XBar Frame* defines an abstraction over the XBar packet where values of field **data** are mapped into the following object kinds: **SOF, BEACON_REQ, BEACON_REPLY, DATA_REQ_A, DATA_REQ_B, DATA_REPLY_A**, and **DATA_REPLY_B**.
- The *XBar Transfer* is composed of XBar frames and supports the following types of transfers across XBar ports:
  - Beacon request

- Beacon reply, which is sent in response to receiving a beacon request
- Data request in either protocol A or B
- Data reply which is sent in response to receiving a data request

The composition of XBar transfers, as well as the data encoding for each XBar frame kind, are shown in table 14.1. The protocol semantics are as follows:

- Beacon request and beacon reply transfers consist of a single XBar frame.
- Data request and data reply transfers consist of two XBar frames.
- Sending a data request or data reply transfer at a given port must be completed before another data transfer is started by that port's agent.
- Sending of a beacon request or beacon reply transfer at a port may interleave the two frames composing a data request or data reply transfer.

Transaction	Frame Kinds	Packet Data Field	Notes
Beacon Request	1: BEACON_REQ	4'b0000	
Beacon Reply	1: BEACON_REPLY	4'b0001	
Data Request/Protocol A	1: SOF	4'b0010	
	2: DATA_REQ_A	4'b100-	bit 0 holds the payload
Data Request/Protocol B	1: SOF	4'b0010	
	2: DATA_REQ_B	4'b101-	bit 0 holds the payload
Data Reply/Protocol A	1: SOF	4'b0010	
	2: DATA_REPLY_A	4'b110-	bit 0 holds the payload
Data Reply/Protocol B	1: SOF	4'b0010	
	2: DATA_REPLY_B	4'b111-	bit 0 holds the payload

Table 14.1: XBar Communication Protocol

The XBar communication protocol is defined to facilitate the illustration of the variety of protocol handling requirements that may exist in real designs, while including as few low-level details as possible (e.g., the reader may note that the XBar protocol supports only the transfer of a single bit in each data transfer). The changes required to turn this protocol into a real-life protocol, however, do not affect the techniques described for verification related handling of this protocol. For example, in a real protocol, the data field size may be increased arbitrarily to support larger payloads or the packet definition may be redefined to occur over multiple cycles, allowing for more complex data exchange scenarios. This added protocol complexity can be handled by the driver component that drives the packet at the XBar physical interface.

The XBar communication protocol highlights the following features of a generalized communication protocol:

- XBar packet routing through source and destination addressing
- XBar frame assigning protocol-related meanings to packet data values
- Composite transfers consisting of multiple frames
- Support for multiple protocols A and B, through the same device port
- The need for a multi-layer stack for handling (i.e., generating and collecting) the protocol. The implementation of the environment supporting the XBar communication protocol requires a physical layer for driving packets into the DUV ports, a link layer

for managing beacon request and replies and for abstracting packets into transfers, and an application layer handling the generation of data request transfers and responding to data request transfers with data reply transfers.

XBar frames generated by the verification environment and arriving at a DUV receive port must follow the ordering requirements described for the XBar protocol (e.g., two frames belonging to a transfer must appear before a frame belonging to a new transfer appears). On the other hand, XBar frames arriving at a DUV transmit port and collected by the verification environment may come from any of the other DUV ports. As such, XBar frames arriving at a DUV transmit port may appear in any order (two **SOF** frames, coming from two separate DUV ports, appearing back to back). This behavior affects the monitoring requirements at the transmit and receive ports of the XBar design.

14.2 XBar Transfer and Frame Models

The implementation of class **xbar_frame** is shown in the following program. An XBar frame is used to provide protocol related meaning to fields of an XBar packet. This class, therefore, is derived from class **xbar_packet**:

```
Program 14.1: XBar Frame
1  :   typedef enum {INVALID, SOF, BEACON_REQ, BEACON_REPLY, DATA_REQ_A,
2  :                 DATA_REQ_B, DATA_REPLY_A, DATA_REPLY_B} xbar_packet_kind;
3  :
4  :   class xbar_frame extends xbar_packet;
5  :       // logical fields
6  :       rand xbar_packet_kind kind;
7  :       rand bit payload;
8  :
9  :       `ovm_object_utils_begin(xbar_frame)
10 :           `ovm_field_enum(xbar_packet_kind,kind,OVM_ALL_ON)
11 :           `ovm_field_int(payload, OVM_ALL_ON)
12 :       `ovm_object_utils_end
13 :
14 :       constraint c1 {(data[3:1]==3'b000) == (kind==SOF);}
15 :       constraint c2 {(data[3:1]==3'b001) == (kind==BEACON_REQ);}
16 :       constraint c3 {(data[3:1]==3'b010) == (kind==INVALID);}
17 :       constraint c4 {(data[3:1]==3'b011) == (kind==BEACON_REPLY);}
18 :       constraint c5 {(data[3:1]==3'b100) == (kind==DATA_REQ_A);}
19 :       constraint c6 {(data[3:1]==3'b101) == (kind==DATA_REQ_B);}
20 :       constraint c7 {(data[3:1]==3'b110) == (kind==DATA_REPLY_A);}
21 :       constraint c8 {(data[3:1]==3'b111) == (kind==DATA_REPLY_B);}
22 :       constraint c9 {(data[0:0]==payload);}
23 :
24 :       //optionally allow this object to be initialized from the content of an xbar_packet
25 :       function new(string name="xbar_frame_inst", xbar_packet pkt=null);
26 :           super.new(name);
27 :           if(pkt== null) return;
28 :           src_addr = pkt.src_addr; dest_addr = pkt.dest_addr;
29 :           data = pkt.data; wait_cycle=pkt.wait_cycle;
30 :           void'(randomize(kind, payload));
31 :       endfunction: new
32 :   endclass: xbar_frame
```

Class **xbar_frame** includes logical fields **kind** and **payload** that provide a view of this object as an XBar frame. This class also includes fields **data, src_addr, dest_addr,** and **wait_cycle** since it is derived from class **xbar_packet**. This class should contain the set of constraints necessary for generating random values that are consistent across the set of logical and physical fields, regardless of which field is constrained. For example, if **kind** is constrained to **DATA_REQ_B** and **payload** is constrained to **1**, then randomization should set field **data** to **4'b1011**. Alternatively, if field **data** is constrained to value **4'b1011**, then randomization should set **kind** and **payload** to **DATA_REQ_B** and **1**, respectively (section 11.2.2). Constraints defined for this class (lines 14–22) implement this behavior. These constraints are used for initializing this class to the contents of an **xbar_packet** object. In the constructor for **xbar_frame** (lines 24–31), fields **src_addr, dest_addr, data,** and **wait_cycle** are initialized from argument **pkt**, and then fields **kind** and **payload** are assigned by randomizing their value.

Given the simple description of the XBar protocol, no special class is defined for an XBar transfer. In this implementation, class **xbar_frame** and its field **kind** is used to indicate the type of transfer that is to be sent.

14.3 XBar Sequence Generation Architecture

The XBar communication protocol, as outlined in section 14.1, reflects functionality beyond that described for the XBar crossbar switch introduced in section 12.2. The XBar switch has the simple function of routing single-cycle packets through XBar ports, subject to handshaking at both the source and destination ports. The XBar communication protocol, however, reflects the existence of additional hardware layers that depend or act on beacon and data transfers.

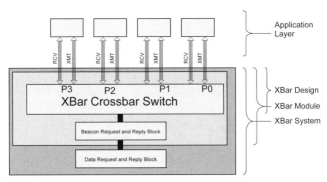

Figure 14.1 XBar Block to XBar System Evolution

Figure 14.1 shows a possible evolution of the XBar design from a block to a system that supports the XBar communication protocol. XBar block contains only the XBar crossbar switch. *XBar module* is created by adding a component that requires traffic passing through the XBar switch to follow transfer ordering requirements, and beacon request and reply transfers to be appropriately sent by all ports. *XBar system* is created by adding a component that requires data reply transfers to be sent back from ports that receive data request transfers. It should be noted that the integration flow for moving from an XBar block to an XBar system, as described here, is decided specifically to motivate the need for different sequence generation techniques described in this chapter.

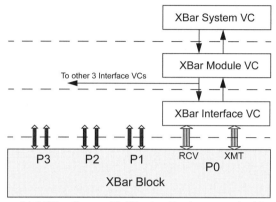

Figure 14.2 XBar System Verification Environment Architecture

The verification environment architecture for the XBar system level design is shown in figure 14.2. This architecture reflects the multi-layer implementation of the XBar system. In full deployment of this environment during system level verification, each verification component performs the following activities:

- XBar Interface VC:
    - Implements the abstraction of **xbar_packet** for interacting with the XBar design through XBar packets.
    - During block level verification, randomly generates XBar packets to be transmitted and generates random packets indicating the latency with which packets should be collected from DUV ports.
    - During module and system level verification, acts as the driver of traffic generated by the module and system VC components.
    - Has the necessary scoreboarding structure in place to check for correct transmission of packets across the XBar switch.
    - Can remain in place in passive mode as the real application layer is attached to the system and continues to scoreboard for packets traveling across the XBar design.
- XBar Module VC
    - Is not present during block level verification.
    - Implements the abstraction of XBar transfers composed of XBar frames, and interacts with interface VC components using the abstraction of XBar frames.
    - During module level verification, generates random beacon request transfers, replies to incoming beacon request transfers, and generates random data request and reply transfers to any of the interface VC components. Data request and response frame traffic generated at this level does not comply with the request/reply requirements for data transfers.
    - During system level verification, continues to generate beacon request and beacon reply transfers, making beacon transfer handling invisible to system VC

components. Also provides to system VC component the facilities for sending data transfers through any of the downstream interface VC components.

- Monitors that incoming and outgoing XBar frames follow the ordering requirements of the XBar communication protocol.
- Can remain in place in passive mode when the real application layer is attached to monitor to check for correct ordering of XBar frames injected into the DUV port by the application layer and XBar frames received by the application layer from the DUV ports.
- XBar System VC:
  - Is not present during block and module level verification.
  - During system level verification, generates data reply transfers in response to incoming data request transfers, and generates data request transfers.
  - Can remain in place in passive mode when the real application layer is connected to monitor that data reply transfers are received in reply to data request transfers generated by the application layer.

An advantage of this verification environment architecture is that it provides a clear migration path from block to module to system level verification. During block level verification, only the interface VCs are present and are attached to all ports. In this configuration, each interface VC randomly generates all types of packets and in any order since at this level the focus is only on verifying the XBar crossbar switch. During module level verification, interface and module verification components are present. In this configuration, interface VCs take on a supporting role where they provide the infrastructure necessary for higher level VCs to transmit their generated data. During system level verification, both interface and module VCs take on a supporting role where interface VCs provide the infrastructure needed by module VCs and in turn, module VCs provide the infrastructure needed by system VCs.

There is great flexibility in deciding the detailed architecture of a verification environment. This means that the final form of an architecture will ultimately be decided by the specific requirements of a project. One requirement for deciding the architecture presented in this section is to help illustrate different sequence generation techniques. These techniques include:

- Reactive sequences responding to environment conditions.
- Interaction between a flat sequence and a sequencer.
- Interaction between a hierarchical sequence and a sequencer.
- Interaction between multiple sequences and a single sequencer, and techniques for:
  - Allowing the sequencer to choose the sequence that has the item relevant to current environment conditions.
  - Allowing one of the sequences to grab the sequencer, thereby preventing that sequencer from interacting with any of the other sequences until it is released.
- Using virtual sequencers for interaction between one sequence and multiple sequencers, thereby allowing a sequence to interact with multiple DUV interfaces.
- Use of transaction ports to communicate between VCs at different layers of the verification environment (e.g., between system VC and module VC), and conditions that make this use model preferred over other means.
- Reuse of infrastructure developed during block level verification in the module level verification environment, and from module to system level verification environment.

These techniques will be illustrated in the following sections where the implementation for each layer of the verification environment is described.

14.4 Flat Sequences

The interaction between a flat sequence and a sequencer is described in section 8.8.1. Flat sequences produce only sequence items which are then passed to a driver through synchronized interaction with a sequencer. Figure 14.3 shows the structural relationship between these components. As shown, a sequencer may contain one or more sequences that interact with the sequencer to pass their generated items to the driver. Sequences may require status information from the environment in order to generate their next item (see reactive sequences in section 14.5). The architecture is defined so that all such information is provided by only the monitor. A sequencer can interact with multiple sequences, in which case, the next available item by a relevant sequence is selected by the sequencer. In addition, sequences are defined to allow the sequencer to choose from the next relevant verification item available (see conditional sequences in section 14.10).

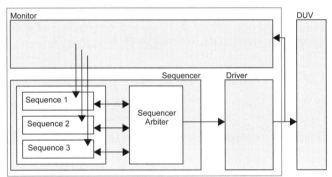

Figure 14.3 Sequencer and Driver Interaction

The simplest form of a sequence consists of a non-reactive flat sequence being passed to the driver through the pull-mode interaction. A non-reactive sequence does not need environment status information to generate the next item. The generation of this simple form of sequence is described in this section. The discussion in this section is used to introduce more advanced sequence types in the following sections.

The first step in creating a sequencer is to define a default sequence item. This sequence item is used in generating the default behavior for a sequencer as described later in this section. The following program shows the declaration for a class object that will be used as the default sequence item for the transmit direction of the sequencer for XBar interface verification environment:

Program 14.2: default sequence item xbar_xmt_packet

```
1  :    class xbar_xmt_packet extends xbar_packet;
2  :          `ovm_object_utils(xbar_xmt_packet)
3  :
```

```
4  :          int port_num;
5  :          constraint valid_src_addr {src_addr == port_num;}
6  :          constraint valid_dest_addr {dest_addr != src_addr;}
7  :
8  :          function new(string name="xbar_xmt_packet");
9  :              super.new(name);
10 :          endfunction: new
11 :
12 :          function void pre_randomize();
13 :              xbar_xmt_sequencer sqnsr;
14 :              $cast(sqnsr, get_sequencer());
15 :              if (sqnsr != null) port_num = sqnsr.port_num;
16 :          endfunction
17 :      endclass: xbar_xmt_packet
```

Class **xbar_packet** used as base class for **xbar_xmt_packet** is derived from **ovm_sequence_item** (see program 13.3). Even though it is possible to use class **xbar_packet** as the default sequence item for **xbar_xmt_sequencer**, it is recommended that a dedicated class type be defined for each sequencer type so that it can be customized for the specific requirements of its sequencer. In this example, declaration of class **xbar_xmt_packet** includes the necessary code to initialize its **port_num** field to that of the port that is generating this sequence item. Additionally, this class includes a constraint for setting the source address of this packet to the correct port number before it is passed to the driver.

The default sequence item defined in the previous program is used in declaration of a sequencer. This setting is shown in the following program segment:

```
   Program 14.3: Setting default sequence item for XBar transmit sequencer
1  :    class xbar_xmt_sequencer extends ovm_sequencer;
            .
            .
            .
2  :        function new (string name="", ovm_component parent=null);
3  :            super.new(name, parent);
4  :            `ovm_update_sequence_lib_and_item(xbar_xmt_packet)
5  :        endfunction: new
6  :    endclass: xbar_xmt_driver
```

In this example, class **xbar_xmt_packet** is defined as the default sequence item for driver **xbar_xmt_sequencer** (line 4). The full implementation of this sequencer is similar to that of **xbar_rcv_sequencer** shown in program 13.7.

In an interface verification component, sequence items are generated by the sequencer and passed to the driver. The following program shows the implementation of a task in a driver that interacts with the sequencer to get the next generated sequence item:

```
   Program 14.4: XBar transmit driver interaction with sequencer
1  :    task xbar_xmt_driver::get_packet_drive_and_respond(int port);
2  :        xbar_packet xmt_pkt;
3  :        ovm_sequence_item item;
4  :
5  :        seq_item_prod_if.get_next_item(item);
6  :        cast(xmt_pkt, item);
7  :        drive_packet(port, xmt_pkt);
8  :        seq_item_prod_if.item_done(xmt_pkt);
9  :    endtask: get_packet_drive_and_respond
```

This interaction consists of two main steps: 1) driver requesting and receiving the sequence item from the sequencer (line 5), and 2) driver informing the sequencer that the item has been processed so that the sequencer can complete the generation steps for this sequence item (line 8). This example shows a pull-mode implementation where the driver requests the next item from the sequencer when it is ready to process that item, and blocks if necessary, until the sequencer can produce an item. Instantiation and connection of sequence item producer interface **seq_item_prod_if** is similar to that for the receive driver (programs 13.9 and 13.10).

In the implementation of the XBar verification environment, reactive sequences receive their required information through the monitor and the sequencer. In some cases, however, the information required by a sequence may be available from only the driver (e.g., driver's internal status on the result of executing an item). In such cases, the driver can return an item to the sequencer when calling function **item_done()** (line 8). This returned item can then be accessed by the sequence that provided the item currently being executed.

The OVM class library provides the predefined sequence type **ovm_req_rsp_sequence** to automate the handling of separate request and response item types.

14.4.1 Sequencer Default Behavior

In the absence of any user defined sequences, the default behavior of a sequencer is defined by the following aspects (section 8.5.1):

- Field **default_sequence** of sequencer (default is **ovm_random_sequence**)
- Fields **count** and **max_random_count** of sequencer (default is **OVM_UNDEF** and **10**)
- Predefined sequence **ovm_random_sequence**
- Predefined sequence **ovm_exhaustive_sequence**
- Predefined sequence **ovm_simple_sequence**

The first step, before sequence execution starts, is to decide the value of field **count**. In this step, if the value of **count** is the default value of **OVM_UNDEF**, then it is assigned a positive random value less than **max_random_count**. If the user has changed the value of **count** by using function **set_config_int()** to a value equal to or larger than **0** (e.g., line 9 in program 14.6), then its value is not changed.

Next, the value of field **default_sequence** is used to decide which sequences to execute. If **default_sequence** is set to its default setting of **ovm_random_sequence**, then the sequencer executes **count** sequences selected randomly among user defined sequences and the pre-defined sequence **ovm_simple_sequence**. Sequence **ovm_simple_sequence** is defined to execute the default sequence item of the sequencer (i.e., **xbar_xmt_packet**) once.

If no user defined sequences are defined, and given that the default values of fields **default_sequence** and **count** are **ovm_random_sequence** and **OVM_UNDEF** respectively, the sequencer by default generates a random number of sequence items (less than value given by field **max_random_count**) of type **xbar_xmt_sequence** when started.

The implementation of the default sequence item **xbar_xmt_sequence** shows how its source address is set to the port number of its parent sequencer. Any other constraints needed for this default behavior of the sequencer can also be added to the implementation of **xbar_xmt_packet** in a similar fashion.

14.4.2 Adding Sequences to the Sequence Library

The sequence generation architecture allows for user defined sequences to be defined and added to the sequence library of a sequencer. Since the default behavior of the sequencer is to randomly select among sequence **ovm_simple_sequence** and user defined sequences, simply defining a new sequence brings this new sequence into the mix of sequences that are executed.

The following example shows the declaration of a sequence **xbar_xmt_seq_send_beacon** for sequencer **xbar_xmt_sequencer**:

```
Program 14.5: User defined sequence for xbar_xmt_sequencer
1   :   class xbar_xmt_seq_send_3_packets extends ovm_sequence;
2   :           `ovm_sequence_utils(xbar_xmt_seq_send_3_packets, xbar_xmt_sequencer)
3   :
4   :       function new(string name="", ovm_object parent=null);
5   :           super.new(name);
6   :       endfunction
7   :
8   :       virtual task body();
9   :           xbar_xmt_packet this_transfer;
10  :           for (int i=0; i< 4; i++)
11  :               if (i!=p_sequencer.port_num)
12  :                   `ovm_do_with(this_transfer, {dest_addr == i;})
13  :       endtask
14  :   endclass: xbar_xmt_seq_send_3_packets
```

Sequence **xbar_xmt_seq_send_3_packets** is derived from class **ovm_sequence** (line 1) and is specifically defined to belong to sequencer **xbar_xmt_sequencer** (line 2). This sequence is a flat sequence and sends one XBar packet to each of the other ports of the XBar design. A *for-loop* (line 10) is used to loop over all destination addresses. An *if-statement* (line 11) is used to skip a destination address if it is the same as the port number for the generating sequencer, since a constraint involving this destination address would conflict with the constraint set in the declaration of **xbar_xmt_packet** requiring the destination address to be different than the current port number. OVM macro **ovm_do_with()** is used to execute the sequence item and to define the constraint for setting the destination address (line 12).

It is especially important to note that any field values in sequence item **this_transfer** are lost before the item is executed (line 12). The reason is that item execution with macro **ovm_do_with()** allocates a new object for this item at the beginning. This means that values of fields of **this_transfer** before calling **ovm_do_with()** cannot be used for any purposes, and any customization should be performed through constraints specified with the macro executing this item.

Adding sequence **xbar_xmt_seq_send_3_packets** to the sequence library of sequence **xbar_xmt_sequencer** has the effect of including this sequence in the list of randomly selected sequences when executing the predefined sequence **ovm_random_sequence**.

14.4.3 Modifying the Default Behavior

Sequencer default behavior can be modified in a number of ways:

- Changing the value of field **count** in the sequencer
- Adding new sequences to the sequence library
- Changing the value of field **default_sequence** in the sequencer
- Changing task **run()** of the sequencer

The addition, and effect, of adding a new sequence to the sequence library is shown in the previous section. The following example shows how the value of fields **count** and **default_sequence** can be customized as part of building the verification environment:

```
Program 14.6: XBar testcase with passive transmit agents
1  :   class xbar_test_modifed_behavior extends xbar_test_default;
2  :       `ovm_component_utils(xbar_test_modifed_behavior)
3  :
4  :       function new(string name = "xbar_base_test", ovm_component parent=null);
5  :           super.new(name, parent);
6  :       endfunction: new
7  :
8  :       virtual function void build();
9  :           set_config_int("*.xbar_xmt_agent0.xmt_sqnsr","count", 0);
10 :           set_config_int ("*.xbar_ivc[0].xbar_xmt_agent0.xmt_sqnsr","count", 1);
11 :           set_config_string ("*.xbar_ivc[0].xbar_xmt_agent0.xmt_sqnsr",
12 :                               "default_sequence", "xbar_xmt_seq_send_3_packets");
13 :           super.build();
14 :       endfunction: build
15 :   endclass: xbar_test_modifed_behavior
```

The above program defines new test **xbar_test_modifed_behavior** that can be executed by passing its name to the global function **run_test()** (section 13.6.6), and follows the procedure described for defining new testcases for the XBar verification environment (section 13.6.5). In this implementation, configuration function **set_config_int()** is first used to set field **count** of all transmit sequencers to value **0** (line 9). Functions **set_conf_int()** and **set_config_string()** are then used to redefine the values for fields **count** and **default_count** of the sequencer at port **0** (lines 10–12), thereby overriding the setting for port **0** made on line 9. These settings will take effect while the environment hierarchy is being built by calling function **build()** (line 11). With these configuration settings, the running of this testcase results in one execution of sequence **xbar_xmt_seq_send_3_packets** by the sequencer at port **0**, and no sequences in the sequencer of any of the other ports.

Most behaviors can be implemented by adding a new sequence to the sequence library, redefining the default sequence, and changing field **count** of the sequencer. For behaviors that cannot be implemented through these steps, the default behavior of a sequencer can be modified by redefining its predefined task **run()**. The following example shows this approach:

```
Program 14.7: Modifying default definition of task run() of a sequencer
1  :   task xbar_xmt_sequencer::run ();
2  :       fork
3  :           super.run();
4  :           start_sequence(get_sequence(get_seq_kind("xbar_xmt_seq_send_3_packets")));
5  :       join
6  :   endtask
```

In this example, an instance of sequence **xbar_xmt_seq_send_3_packets** is started as a root sequence (section 8.6) by using functions **get_seq_kind()** and **get_sequence()** of the sequencer (line 4). Note that the predefined task **run()** of the sequencer must be started in a parallel thread in order for the sequencer operation to begin (line 3).

14.5 Hierarchical Sequences

Hierarchical sequences allow a sequence to be defined in terms of other previously defined sequences. As such, hierarchical sequences allow complex sequences to be described more efficiently and more clearly. A hierarchical sequence generates a single stream of sequence items and as such appears to the sequencer as a single sequence.

A sequence that can be called as a subsequence is described in terms of its:

- Action block
- Configuration fields

The *action block* for a sequence describes the steps performed in the sequence for generating the target scenario. The action block may execute sequence items or subsequences. *Configuration fields* of a sequence allow it to be customized when executed by a parent sequence. An example of a hierarchical sequence executing a configurable subsequence is shown in this section.

A subsequence that is executed by another sequence is created and randomized similar to how sequence items are executed. This means that configurable fields of a subsequence can be modeled using randomizable fields of a sequence class. The following program shows the implementation of a sequence that contains fields that can be configured by a calling sequence:

```
Program 14.8: Sequence definition containing configurable fields
1  :   class xbar_xmt_seq_send_special extends ovm_sequence;
2  :       `ovm_sequence_utils(xbar_xmt_seq_send_special, xbar_xmt_sequencer)
3  :
4  :       rand xbar_packet pkt;
5  :       rand int seq_param1;
6  :       rand int seq_param2;
7  :
8  :       constraint valid_dest_addr {pkt.dest_addr != p_sequencer.port_num;}
9  :       constraint valid_src_addr {pkt.src_addr == p_sequencer.port_num;}
10 :       constraint param1 {seq_param1 < 1000;}
11 :       constraint param2 {seq_param2 < 2000;}
12 :
13 :       function new(string name="", ovm_object parent=null);
14 :           super.new(name);
15 :           $cast(pkt, ovm_factory::create_object("xbar_packet", "", "pkt"));
16 :       endfunction
17 :
18 :       virtual task body();
19 :           xbar_xmt_packet this_transfer;
20 :           `message(OVM_INFO, ("Sequence Parameter 1 randomized to:", seq_param1))
21 :           `message(OVM_INFO, ("Sequence Parameter 2 randomized to:", seq_param2))
22 :           `ovm_do_with(this_transfer, {dest_addr == pkt.dest_addr;
23 :                   data == pkt.data; wait_cycle == pkt.wait_cycle;})
```

```
24  :          endtask
25  :     endclass: xbar_xmt_seq_send_special
```

This example shows sequence **xbar_xmt_seq_send_special** (line 1) belonging to sequencer **xbar_xmt_sequencer** (line 2). Randomizable fields **pkt**, **seq_param$_1$**, and **seq_param$_2$** are also defined in this class (lines 4–6). Note that these fields are marked as *rand* so they can be assigned by the randomization engine when a subsequence is randomized as part of its execution flow. If this sequence is executed as a subsequence, then any constraints specified in the calling macro (e.g., **ovm_do_with()**) is considered along with the constraints in the local scope (lines 8–11). If this sequence is executed as a root sequence, then only constraints in the local scope are considered. SystemVerilog randomizes only non-null objects. Therefore, random fields that are object classes must be allocated in the constructor for this sequence (line 15) so that they have non-null value during randomization.

It can be assumed that by the time the action block of a subsequence is executed, its random fields have already been assigned a value meeting any randomization constraints specified in its local and the calling scopes. These values can then be used to customize the flow of the action block (lines 20, 21) or provide further constraints for sequence items or subsequences being executed in the local scope (lines 22, 23).

The following program shows the implementation of a hierarchical sequence:

```
     Program 14.9: Hierarchical sequence
1   :    class xbar_xmt_seq_send_multiple_packets extends ovm_sequence;
2   :         `ovm_sequence_utils(xbar_xmt_seq_send_multiple_packets, xbar_xmt_sequencer)
3   :
4   :        function new(string name="", ovm_object parent=null);
5   :             super.new(name);
6   :        endfunction
7   :
8   :        rand bit [3:0] seq_dest_addr;
9   :        constraint valid_addr {seq_dest_addr < 4;seq_dest_addr != p_sequencer.port_num;}
10  :
11  :        virtual task body();
12  :             xbar_xmt_seq_send_special send_special_seq;
13  :             xbar_xmt_packet xmt_item;
14  :             `ovm_do_with(send_special_seq, {
15  :                      sequence_param1 == 20;
16  :                      sequence_param2 == 20;
17  :                      pkt.wait_cycle == 20;
18  :                      pkt.data == 4'b1111;
19  :                      pkt.dest_addr == seq_dest_addr;})
20  :             `ovm_do_with(send_special_seq, {
21  :                      pkt.data == 4'b0101;
22  :                      pkt.dest_addr == seq_dest_addr;})
23  :            repeat (10)
24  :                 `ovm_do(xmt_item)
25  :        endtask
26  :    endclass: xbar_xmt_seq_send_multiple_packets
```

This example shows sequence **xbar_xmt_seq_send_multiple_packets** (line 1) belonging to sequencer **xbar_xmt_sequencer** (line 2). Configuration field **seq_dest_addr** and its related constraints (lines 8, 9) contains the destination address of all packets generated by this sequence. This sequence executes subsequence **send_special_seq** two times (lines 14–22) while providing constraints for its configurable fields. Note that fields within configuration field **pkt** of this subsequence can be constrained directly when using the execution macros (e.g., lines 18,

19). It then executes sequence item **xmt_item** a total of ten times without providing any constraints.

14.6 Reactive Sequences

Only in rare conditions is a sequence completely independent of its outside environment. Most sequences are *reactive sequences* that either follow the current configuration settings of the verification environment or produce stimulus in reply to current state values in the verification environment and the DUV. It is, therefore, necessary to have a clear strategy for modeling the interaction between verification environment components that provide a sequence with the information it needs to generate reactive scenarios.

A reactive sequence receives two types of information from the environment:

- Configuration settings related to its location in the environment hierarchy (e.g., the port number for the agent containing the sequencer).
- Live data being generated by a monitor (e.g., generating a read-reply transfer in response to a read-request transfer arriving at the DUV port).

The sequencer is the focal point of all sequence generation activity since it mediates the generation of items before they are sent into the environment. As such, a sequencer is the obvious choice for localizing information needed by a sequence or a sequence item. When building the environment, special care should be taken to include in the sequencer, all configuration fields that sequences and sequence items may need to access. An example of this approach is adding parameter **port_num** to the implementations of **xbar_xmt_sequencer** and **xbar_rcv_sequencer** (program 13.7) which was initialized when building the environment hierarchy (program 13.10). This parameter was consequently used for specifying a constraint for the source address of **xbar_xmt_packet**, the default sequence item for **xbar_xmt_sequencer** (line 5 in program 14.2).

Reacting to live data during sequence generation is somewhat more challenging since the changing nature of data values requires careful timing and ordering of sequence generation activity with value changes in the environment. XBar packets generated in the transmit path of the XBar verification environment do not depend on live data generated by the environment, since both the content of the packet as well as the wait cycle for the packet are decided in the sequence. The receive channel of the XBar verification environment may, however, need to generate a wait cycle value that depends on the source port of the packet being received on the XBar transmit port. This wait cycle value is used by the receive path slave driver to decide how many cycles to wait before accepting the incoming packet from the DUV. This requirement is a clear example of a strict reactive sequence where both the timing and the value of the generated sequence item depends on observations made at the design transmit port. In this example, timing is important since the sequence in the receive sequencer should produce a wait cycle value as soon as a new packet has been produced by the DUV. The remainder of this section shows the implementation of a sequencer that implements this requirement. The implementation approach shown here can easily be applied to cases requiring similar types of interactions between a sequencer and a DUV interface. Examples include generating a read-reply transfer in response to receiving a read-request transfer, producing an error condition at a DUV port upon a specific value observed at the DUV port, etc. A sequence that requires information from multiple design ports should be placed in module or system VCs where conditions at all DUV interfaces can be tracked through the monitors in interface VCs.

In deciding the best implementation for a reactive sequence, the following issues must be considered:

- A sequence is not aware of the driver and the driver is not aware of the sequence. They interact only through the sequencer. As such, a sequence cannot read from a driver and a driver cannot write to a sequence.

- A monitor is not aware of any of the other components in the environment. A monitor provides status about the current state of the environment. Other components in the environment subscribe to this status information as needed. This behavior is necessary to allow a monitor to be used in passive mode where the driver and the sequencer are removed.

Given this independence requirement between verification environment components, the following approach is used for implementing a reactive sequence:

- Identify all environment status information needed by a reactive sequence to take the next step in its flow.

- Implement the monitor to provide this information to the sequencer, either through broadcasting on an analysis port or through transaction ports.

- Add to the sequencer the necessary fields that allow access to this status information in the monitor. By using this approach for reading status information produced by the monitor, it is possible to remove the sequencer in passive mode without needing to change the monitor implementation.

- In a reactive sequence, use transaction interfaces made available in its sequencer to detect and react to relevant environment conditions.

The approach outlined above allows the component independence requirement to be satisfied while providing a reactive sequence with the information it requires. The following example shows the implementation of a reactive sequence that generates wait-cycle values based on the source address of the incoming packet on the receive channel.

```
Program 14.10: Reactive Sequence/receiving packets from XBar transmit port
1  :   class xbar_rcv_seq_rand_wait_cycle extends ovm_sequence;
2  :       `ovm_sequence_utils(xbar_rcv_seq_rand_wait_cycle, xbar_rcv_sequencer)
3  :
4  :       function new(string name="", ovm_object parent=null);
5  :           super.new(name);
6  :       endfunction
7  :
8  :       xbar_rcv_packet this_transfer;
9  :       rand int unsigned seq_wait_cycle;
10 :       constraint reasonable_wait {seq_wait_cycle < 200;}
11 :
12 :       virtual task body();
13 :           xbar_packet partial_rcved_pkt;
14 :           p_sequencer.duv_out_valid_port.peek(partial_rcved_pkt);
15 :
16 :           case (partial_rcved_pkt.src_addr)
17 :               0: `ovm_do_with(this_transfer, {wait_cycle == 10;})
18 :               1: `ovm_do_with(this_transfer, {wait_cycle == 20;})
```

```
19  :                        2: `ovm_do_with(this_transfer, {wait_cycle == seq_wait_cycle;})
20  :                        3: `ovm_do_with(this_transfer, {wait_cycle == seq_wait_cycle;})
21  :                    endcase
22  :            endtask
23  :    endclass: xbar_rcv_seq_rand_wait_cycle
```

The definition for **xbar_rcv_packet** is not shown, but is similar to the one for **xbar_xmt_packet** (program 14.2). The declaration of blocking peek port connector object **duv_out_valid_port** in sequencer **xbar_rcv_sequencer**, and connecting it to the blocking peek imp connector object in **xbar_rcv_monitor** is shown in section 13.6. The implementation of sequence **xbar_rcv_seq_rand_wait_cycle** contains configuration field **seq_wait_cycle** (line 9, 10). Execution of this sequence starts by calling function **peek()** of transaction interface **duv_out_valid_port** (line 14). This function call returns when the monitor detects that the DUV has placed a new packet on its transmit port. The sequence then generates an item with a wait cycle value that depends on the source address of the incoming packet (lines 16–21). Note that in this implementation, no direct interaction with the receive slave driver takes place. In this flow, the receive slave driver waits to receive the first item from its sequencer providing information on how many cycles to wait before collecting an incoming packet from the port, while the monitor is independently looking for the arrival of the first packet. Once this packet arrives, the monitor allows function **peek()** to complete allowing the sequence to proceed, thereby generating the next item. This item is then passed to the receive slave driver, which will in turn use this item to decide how long to wait before collecting the incoming packet.

The mechanism shown in the above example can be used multiple times in a row to generate a complex sequence of handshaking with a DUV port. The sequence shown in the above example must replace the default behavior for the **xbar_rcv_sequencer**. The mechanisms described in section 14.4.3 can be used to carry out this task.

14.7 Virtual Sequences

Figure 14.4 shows the block diagram corresponding to interface and module VCs for the XBar design. The XBar verification environment as shown in figure 13.3, is limited to single-sided verification scenarios since interface VCs can interact with only one DUV interface. Additionally, interface VCs are not aware of the XBar communication protocol and work only with **xbar_packet** items. However, module VCs in the XBar verification environment:

- Are aware of the Xbar frame abstraction defined in table 14.1
- Can interact with multiple interface VCs to generate multi-sided scenarios
- Automatically generate beacon request transfers
- Automatically generate beacon reply transfers in response to incoming beacon request transfers
- Provide the abstraction of multi-frame data request and reply transfers, and can generate random data request and reply transfers
- Do not differentiate between data request and reply transfers, and leave it to the system VC to generate data request transfers and reply to data reply transfers

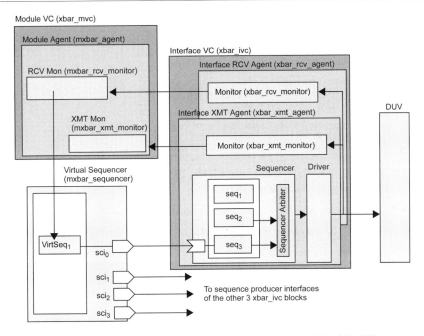

Figure 14.4 Virtual Sequences Connecting Interface and Module VCs

A *virtual sequencer* allows a single sequence to interact with multiple sequencers and hence interact with multiple drivers. A virtual sequence can only execute subsequences, either in the local virtual sequencer or in a downstream sequencer. This means that a virtual sequence can execute a subsequence on any sequencer in the verification environment as long as that subsequence is in the sequence library of the target sequencer. The sequencer belonging to the XBar module VC is implemented using a virtual sequencer so that each instance of the module level sequencer can interact with transmit sequencers in all of the interface VCs. Note that the virtual sequencer for the module VC is placed in the top level environment so that its implementation can be changed if needed without needing to modify the implementation of the module VC.

The virtual sequencer of the module VC is implemented through the following steps:

- Implementing the virtual sequencer (**mxbar_sequencer** in figure 14.4)
- For each virtual sequencer, adding one sequence consumer interface (section 8.9) for each downstream sequencer, and connecting it with the sequence producer interface in the downstream sequencer (**sci** connectors in figure 14.4)
- Implement sequences in the sequence library of downstream sequencers that will be executed by local virtual sequences (sequence **seq$_3$** in figure 14.4)
- Implement virtual sequences that execute local sequences and sequences on down-stream sequencers through appropriately connected sequence consumer interfaces (sequence **VirtSeq$_1$** in figure 14.4)

These steps are described in the following sections:

14.7.1 Virtual Sequencer

The implementation of XBar module VC sequencer is shown in the following program:

```
Program 14.11: XBar module VC sequencer
1    :    class mxbar_sequencer extends ovm_virtual_sequencer;
2    :         int unsigned port_num = 0;
3    :         int unsigned num_duv_ports = 4;
4    :
5    :         ovm_blocking_peek_port#(xbar_frame) beacon_requested_port;
6    :         ovm_seq_item_prod_if sve_pkt_prod_if;
7    :
8    :         `ovm_sequencer_utils_begin(mxbar_sequencer)
9    :              `ovm_field_int(port_num, OVM_ALL_ON)
10   :              `ovm_field_int(num_duv_ports, OVM_ALL_ON)
11   :         `ovm_sequencer_utils_end
12   :
13   :         function new (string name="", ovm_component parent=null);
14   :              super.new(name, parent);
15   :              `ovm_update_sequence_lib
16   :              beacon_requested_port = new("beacon_requested_port", this);
17   :              $cast(sve_pkt_prod_if,
18   :                   create_component("ovm_seq_item_prod_if","sve_pkt_prod_if"));
19   :         endfunction: new
20   :
21   :         function ovm_seq_cons_if get_seq_cons_if(int index);
22   :              string seq_if_name;
23   :              $sformat(seq_if_name, "mxbar_seq_if[%0d]", index);
24   :              if(seq_cons_if.exists(seq_if_name)==0)
25   :                   add_seq_cons_if(seq_if_name);
26   :              return seq_cons_if[seq_if_name];
27   :         endfunction: get_seq_cons_if
28   :    endclass: mxbar_sequencer
```

Sequencer **mxbar_sequencer** is derived from class **ovm_virtual_sequencer**, and contains blocking peek port object **beacon_requested_port** (line 5), and sequence item producer interface **sve_pkt_prod_if** (line 6) used for receiving sequence items from the higher layer sequencer (see layered sequences in section 14.9).

A virtual sequencer can only execute subsequences, and cannot generate sequence item. This means that it is not necessary to define a default sequence item for a virtual sequencer. Therefore, instead of using macro **ovm_update_sequence_lib_and_item()** which is used with real sequencers to specify a default sequence item, macro **ovm_update_sequece_lib** is used in the constructor (line 15) to initialize sequence generation facilities of this virtual sequencer without specifying a default sequence item.

A virtual sequencer by default contains associative array **seq_cons_if** used for storing interface objects connecting to downstream sequencers. Function **get_seq_cons_if()** is defined (line 21–27) to return a connector for an index value. This function adds a new connector in array **seq_cons_if** if one for that index does not already exist. This function provides an simple-to-use mechanism for both the creation and access to these interface objects through an index value.

Building the hierarchy for the XBar module VC is similar to that defined for the XBar Interface VC and is not shown in this text. The next section shows how each virtual sequencer in a module VC is connected to each of the downstream sequencers in the interface VCs.

14.7.2 Sequence Interface Connectivity

The following program shows the implementation of XBar verification environment top level that includes both the interface and module VCs. Note that the implementation of this verification environment is derived from that of the implementation for the verification environment containing only the interface VCs (program 13.12).

```
Program 14.12: Module level XBar verification environment
1    :    class mxbar_sve extends xbar_sve;
2    :        `ovm_component_utils(mxbar_sve)
3    :
4    :        xbar_mvc mvcs[];
5    :
6    :        function new (string name="", ovm_component parent=null);
7    :            super.new(name, parent);
8    :        endfunction
9    :
10   :        virtual function void build();
11   :            string inst_name;
12   :            super.build();
13   :
14   :            mvcs = new[num_ports];
15   :            for (int i=0; i< num_ports; i++) begin
16   :                $sformat(inst_name, "xbar_mvc[%0d]", i);
17   :                set_config_int(inst_name, "port_num", i);
18   :                set_config_int(inst_name, "num_duv_ports", num_ports);
19   :                $cast(mvcs[i], create_component("xbar_mvc", inst_name));
20   :                mvcs[i].build();
21   :            end
22   :
23   :            for (int i=0; i< num_ports; i++) begin
24   :                ivcs[i].rcv_pkt_bdcst_port.connect(mvcs[i].agent.rcv_monitor.lstn_imp);
25   :                ivcs[i].xmt_pkt_bdcst_port.connect(mvcs[i].agent.xmt_monitor.lstn_imp);
26   :                for (int j=0; j< num_ports; j++) begin
27   :                    ovm_seq_cons_if sci;
28   :                    sci = mvcs[i].agent.sqnsr.get_seq_cons_if(j);
29   :                    sci.connect_if(ivcs[j].xmt_agent.xmt_sqnsr.seq_prod_if);
30   :                end
31   :            end
32   :        endfunction: build
33   :    endclass: mxbar_sve
```

The top level environment **mxbar_sve** is derived from class **xbar_sve** (line 1). This environment instantiates a dynamic array of type **xbar_mvc** type objects (line 4). Task **build()** of this class is implemented to first call task **build()** of its parent class (line 12), thereby building the environment shown in figure 13.3. It then creates objects in array **mvcs** (line 14) and builds the module VC at each index (lines 15–21).

In the next part, connections are made between each module VC and downstream interface VCs. For the module VC at port **i**, packet listeners in receive and transmit monitors (implemented as analysis imp objects) are connected with the corresponding packet broadcasters (implemented as analysis port objects) of the interface VC at port **i** (lines 24, 25). Next, a loop is used to create four sequence consumer interface objects for the virtual sequencer at port i (line 28), and then connecting each with the sequence producer interface in its corresponding downstream sequencer (line 29). Note that each new sequence consumer interface is created by calling function **get_seq_cons_if()** (line 28), since this function creates an object if one doesn't exist.

Note that each sequence consumer interface is connected to four different sequence producer interfaces in the downstream sequencers. And each sequence producer interface in the downstream sequencers receives connections from four different virtual sequencers. This structure shows an example of virtual sequencers executing sequences on different downstream sequencers, and downstream sequencers allowing multiple virtual sequencers to execute sequences on them.

14.7.3 Downstream Sequences

Virtual sequencers can only execute sequences and not sequence items. As such, a special sequence must be defined in a downstream sequencer in order to provide a mechanism for virtual sequencers to execute its sequence item type. The following program shows the implementation of this downstream sequence:

```
Program 14.13: Defining a sequence on a downstream sequencer
1  :   class xbar_xmt_seq_send_packet extends ovm_sequence;
2  :       `ovm_sequence_utils(xbar_xmt_seq_send_packet, xbar_xmt_sequencer)
3  :
4  :       rand xbar_packet pkt;
5  :       constraint valid_dest_addr {pkt.dest_addr != p_sequencer.port_num;}
6  :       constraint valid_src_addr {pkt.src_addr == p_sequencer.port_num;}
7  :
8  :       function new(string name="", ovm_object parent=null);
9  :           super.new(name);
10 :           pkt = new();
11 :       endfunction
12 :
13 :       virtual task body();
14 :       xbar_xmt_packet this_transfer;
15 :           `ovm_do_with(this_transfer, {dest_addr == pkt.dest_addr;
16 :               data == pkt.data; wait_cycle == pkt.wait_cycle;})
17 :       endtask
18 :   endclass: xbar_xmt_seq_send_packet
```

This program shows the implementation of sequence **xbar_xmt_seq_send_packet** derived from **ovm_sequence** and placed in the sequence library for **xbar_xmt_sequencer**. This sequence includes configurable field **pkt** that allows sequences executing this sequence as a subsequence to execute items on **xbar_xmt_sequencer**.

14.7.4 Virtual Sequence Library

Virtual sequences are placed in the sequence library of a virtual sequencer, and can execute either local sequences, sequences in downstream sequencers, or virtual sequences in downstream virtual sequencers. Downstream sequencers may optionally be virtual sequencers that drive a downstream sequencer.

The following program shows the implementation of a configurable virtual sequence that allows each module VC to send a packet through any of the downstream sequencers:

```
Program 14.14: Virtual Sequence using macro ovm_so_seq_with()
1  :    class mxbar_seq_send_frame extends ovm_sequence;
2  :          `ovm_sequence_utils(mxbar_seq_send_frame, mxbar_sequencer)
3  :
4  :          rand xbar_frame xfr;
5  :          constraint waitcycles {xfr.wait_cycle < 10;}
6  :
7  :          function new(string name="", ovm_object parent=null);
8  :                super.new(name);
9  :                $cast(xfr, ovm_factory::create_object("xbar_frame", "", "xfr"));
10 :          endfunction
11 :
12 :          virtual task body();
13 :                xbar_xmt_seq_send_packet seq_send_pkt;
14 :                ovm_seq_cons_if sci;
15 :
16 :                sci = p_sequencer.get_seq_cons_if(xfr.src_addr);
17 :                `ovm_do_seq_with(seq_send_pkt, sci, {
18 :                                    pkt.dest_addr==xfr.dest_addr;
19 :                                    pkt.data == xfr.data;
20 :                                    pkt.wait_cycle == xfr.wait_cycle;})
21 :          endtask
22 :    endclass: mxbar_seq_send_frame
```

This implementation defines class **mxbar_seq_send_frame** derived from **ovm_sequence** (line 1) and belonging to virtual sequencer **mxbar_sequencer** (line 2). This sequence contains configurable field **xfr** which provides the XBar frame abstraction implemented in class **xbar_frame** (section 14.2), allowing it to be constrained based on frame kind. The source and destination of **xfr** may be set to any port number. Therefore, the action block for this virtual sequence first uses **xfr.src_addr** to identify **sci**, the sequence consumer interface on which its subsequence should be executed (line 16), and then uses macro **ovm_do_seq_with()**, along with **sci** to execute sequence **seq_send_pkt** (section 14.7.3) on the sequencer connected to sequence consumer interface **sci** (lines 17–20).

Note that by the time the action block for this sequence is called, field **xfr** is randomized, and therefore, if any constraint is set for **xfr.kind**, then the value of **xfr.data** is set to a value consistent with this constraint. This data value is then used to constrain the configuration field of subsequence **seq_send_pkt** which executes on the downstream sequencers (line 19).

Once virtual sequence **mxbar_seq_send_frame** is defined, a virtual sequence in any of the module VCs can use this sequence to execute XBar frames on any of the downstream sequencers. This is shown in the following example:

```
Program 14.15: Hierarchical virtual sequence sending a beacon request frame
1  :    class mxbar_seq_send_beacon_request extends ovm_sequence;
2  :          `ovm_sequence_utils(mxbar_seq_send_beacon_request, mxbar_sequencer)
3  :
4  :          function new(string name="", ovm_object parent=null);
5  :                super.new(name);
6  :          endfunction
7  :
8  :          rand int pkt_dest;
9  :          constraint valid_dest_addr {pkt_dest < 3; pkt_dest != p_sequencer.port_num;}
10 :
```

```
11  :          virtual task body();
12  :              mxbar_seq_send_frame seq_send_frame;
13  :
14  :              `ovm_do_with(seq_send_frame, {
15  :                             xfr.kind==BEACON_REQ;
16  :                             xfr.dest_addr==pkt_dest;
17  :                             xfr.src_addr==p_sequencer.port_num;})
18  :              #1000; // wait some time. Can be a configurable field
19  :          endtask
20  :      endclass: mxbar_seq_send_beacon_request
```

This example shows virtual sequence **mxbar_seq_send_beacon_request** which is used to send a beacon request transfer to any of the downstream sequencers. This sequence has configuration field **pkt_dest**. It uses macro **ovm_do_with()** (line 14) to execute the local virtual sequence **mxbar_seq_send_frame** to send a frame with kind **BEACON_REQ** (line 15) through the downstream sequencer at local port (line 17) to destination port **pkt_dest** (line 16). This virtual sequence can in turn be used as a subsequence in any other local sequence by simply constraining its field **pkt_dest** to send a beacon request transfer to any destination port. The same approach can be used to send a data request transfer by sending two frames in the action block of a sequence. This implementation is described in the next section when grabber sequences are introduced.

14.8 Grabber Sequences

The main difficulty when multiple sequences are supplying packets to a single sequencer is that the order in which packets are processed by the sequencer is dynamically decided depending on the current state of the environment. As such, the sequence of items produced by one sequence can be interleaved by items produced by another sequence passing items to the same sequencer. Consider the structure shown in figure 14.5. In this configuration, the module VC for each port may generate data request frames and pass them to the interface verification components at any of the ports. The XBar communication protocol states that the two frames corresponding to a transfer generated at a port can be interleaved only by a beacon request or beacon reply frame. Consider a case when the module VCs at ports **0** and **3** are both sending a transfer to the driver at port 1. Given that the order of interaction between each sequence and the sequencer in interface VC at port **1** is dynamically decided, it is possible that the sequencer may send the **SOF** frame for each transfer first before sending the second frame in each transfer. This behavior violates the protocol requirement that frames corresponding to a transfer be interrupted only by a beacon request or reply frame.

The solution to this problem is to provide a mechanism for a sequence to grab the sequencer that it is interacting with, thereby giving that sequence exclusive access to that sequencer. The grabbing mechanism provided by the OVM class library is described in section 8.8.2. This section provides an example of how the grabbing constructs are used to resolve the issue raised in figure 14.5.

The following program shows the implementation of the default sequence that is started for each module VC:

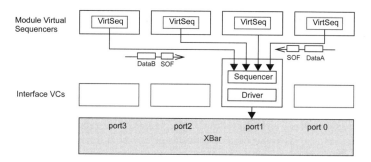

Figure 14.5 Multiple Sequences per Sequencer Needing Exclusive Access

```
Program 14.16: Default sequence for XBar module VC
1    :    class mxbar_seq_main extends ovm_sequence;
2    :         `ovm_sequence_utils(mxbar_seq_main, mxbar_sequencer)
3    :
4    :         function new(string name="", ovm_object parent=null);
5    :              super.new(name);
6    :         endfunction
7    :
8    :         virtual task body();
9    :              mxbar_seq_send_beacon_request send_beacon_req_seq;
10   :              mxbar_seq_send_beacon_reply send_beacon_reply_seq;
11   :              mxbar_seq_send_data_transfer send_data_seq;
12   :
13   :              fork
14   :                   forever
15   :                        `ovm_do(send_beacon_req_seq)
16   :                   forever
17   :                        `ovm_do(send_beacon_reply_seq)
18   :                   repeat(p_sequencer.count)
19   :                        `ovm_do(send_data_seq)
20   :              join
21   :         endtask
22   :    endclass: mxbar_seq_main
```

This program shows the implementation of virtual sequence **mxbar_seq_main** (line 1) belonging to virtual sequencer **mxbar_sequencer** (line 2). Field **default_sequence** of virtual sequencer **mxbar_sequencer** is configured during hierarchy construction to run this sequence by default. The action block of this sequence starts three threads using a *fork-join* statement (lines 13–20). The first thread (line 14) uses a *forever* loop to continuously execute sequence **send_beacon_req_seq** of type **mxbar_seq_send_beacon_request** (defined in program 14.15). Each execution of this sequence sends a beacon request transfer, and can optionally include a randomized or user defined wait time after the request is sent. The second thread (line 16) continuously executes sequence **send_beacon_reply_seq** of type **mxbar_seq_send_beacon_reply** which waits for the receive monitor to indicate that a beacon request transfer has been received, and then sends a beacon reply transfer from the local port to the source port of the incoming beacon request transfer (implementation not shown in this text). The third thread (line 18), executes sequence **send_data_seq** of type **mxbar_seq_send_data_transfer** a number of times given by the field **count** of this sequence's parent sequencer. Note that the default sequence of a sequencer is not started at all if field **count** of the sequencer is set to zero. As such, if field **count** is used as a controlling field in a newly defined sequence (line 18), care should be taken so that it is never set to zero. Sequences started in all these threads are treated as subsequences and have this sequence as their parent sequence. This distinction is important because of how it affects the behavior of grabbing sequence. The implementation of grabbing sequence **mxbar_seq_send_data_transfer** is described next.

A data transfer requires two frames to be transmitted. The XBar communication proto-col indicates that these two frames can be interrupted only by beacon request or reply frames. The implementation of the sequence implementing this behavior is shown next:

```
Program 14.17: Virtual sequence sending an XBar transfer
1   :    class mxbar_seq_send_data_transfer extends ovm_sequence;
2   :         `ovm_sequence_utils(mxbar_seq_send_data_transfer, mxbar_sequencer)
3   :
4   :         rand xbar_data_frame dxfr;
5   :
6   :         function new(string name="", ovm_object parent=null);
7   :             super.new(name);
8   :             $cast(dxfr, ovm_factory::create_object("xbar_data_frame", "", "dxfr"));
9   :         endfunction
10  :
11  :         virtual task body();
12  :             mxbar_seq_send_frame seq_send_frame;
13  :             ovm_seq_cons_if sci;
14  :
15  :             sci = p_sequencer.get_seq_cons_if(dxfr.src_addr);
16  :
17  :             sci.grab(get_parent_seq());
18  :             `ovm_do_with(seq_send_frame, {xfr.kind==SOF;
19  :                     xfr.dest_addr==dxfr.dest_addr; xfr.src_addr==dxfr.src_addr;})
20  :             `ovm_do_with(seq_send_frame, {xfr.kind==dxfr.kind;
21  :                     xfr.dest_addr==dxfr.dest_addr; xfr.src_addr==dxfr.src_addr;})
22  :             sci.ungrab(get_parent_seq());
23  :             #1000; // wait for some time, optionally randomize by using a field instead
24  :         endtask
25  :    endclass: mxbar_seq_send_data_transfer
```

The implementation of sequence **mxbar_seq_send_data_transfer** is similar to the imple-mentation of **mxbar_seq_send_frame** (program 14.14). The main difference is that this sequence first generates an **SOF** frame (line 18), and then sends a frame whose kind is con-strained to the value given by its configuration field **dxfr** (line 20). Field **kind** of **dxfr** is guar-anteed to be a data transfer kind since **dxfr** has type **xbar_data_frame** (line 4). Therefore, this sequence can generate only one of the four data transfer types. Also note that the use of vir-tual sequence **mxbar_seq_send_frame** allows this data transfer to be sent through any of the DUV ports, and not just the local port. The source port of this transfer is identified by field **src_addr** of **dxfr** which is used to get the sequence consumer interface connected to that port (line 15).

Functions **grab()** and **ungrab()** of the sequence consumer interface are used to grab and ungrab the downstream sequencer before sequence execution starts and after it ends (lines 17 and 22).

An important aspect of this example is that the grabbing is performed on the parent sequence of this sequence (i.e., **mxbar_seq_main** in program 14.16). The parent sequence is obtained by calling the predefined function **get_parent_seq()** of **ovm_sequence** (line 17, 22). The reason is that by grabbing the parent sequence, any subsequence started by the parent sequence can still access the downstream sequencer that is being grabbed by this sequence, therefore allowing beacon request and reply frames started by the root sequence to interleave the two frames generated by this sequence. Note that this interleaving is allowed if both the data transfer and beacon request/reply transfers need to use same downstream sequencer to execute. In other words, a local beacon request transfer cannot interleave the frames being sent to the local downstream sequencer by the virtual sequencer in another module VC.

14.9 Layered Sequences

A _layered sequence_ consists of multiple layers of sequencers where a sequence in one layer receives sequence items from the higher layer sequencers. This architecture is ideally suited for implementing layered protocols. Figure 14.6 shows a view of this relationship between the system and module VCs in the XBar verification environment. In this implementation, the sequence in module VC gets the next sequence item from the sequencer in the system VC and then uses this item to decide what action to take next. The connection between the sequence in the module VC and the sequencer in the system VC is implemented using sequence item producer and consumer interfaces (section 8.7). Note that in this architecture, the implementation of the sequencer in the system VC would be the same, regardless of whether its sequences are being received by a downstream sequence or a driver.

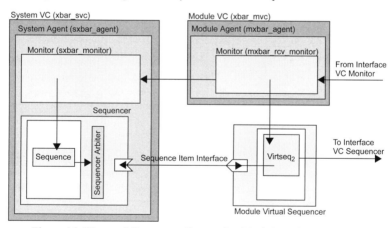

Figure 14.6 Layered Sequences Connecting Module and System VCs

Implementation of the architecture shown in figure 14.6 follows these steps:

- Defining a default sequence item produced by the sequencer in system VC
- Implementing the system VC including its sequencer
- Building the verification environment top level to include the system VC component, and connecting the module virtual sequencer with system sequencer

- Implementing the module virtual sequence that receives sequence items from the sequencer in the system VC
- Modifying the default behavior of the system VC sequencer by implementing new sequences in its sequence library

These implementation steps are described in the remainder of this section.

The first step is to define a default sequence item type for the system VC sequencer. In this implementation, class **xbar_frame** (program 14.1) can be used to model the type of transfers that the system VC sequencer may need to generate. Given, however, that system VC is aware only of data transfers, a new class must be defined so that the default behavior of the system VC sequencer produces only data transfer items. This implementation is shown in the following program:

```
Program 14.18: Class xbar_data_frame, default sequence item for system VC
1   :   class xbar_data_frame extends xbar_frame;
2   :       `ovm_object_utils(xbar_data_frame)
3   :       constraint data_kind {kind
4   :           inside {DATA_REQ_A,DATA_REQ_B,DATA_REPLY_A,DATA_REPLY_B};}
5   :
6   :       function new(string name="xbar_frame_inst", xbar_packet pkt=null);
7   :           super.new(name);
8   :       endfunction: new
9   :   endclass: xbar_data_frame
```

Class **xbar_data_frame** is derived from class **xbar_frame** and only adds a constraint that limits the kind of transfers that can be represented by this object. Note that the definition of this new class is necessary for the default behavior of the system VC sequencer to be useful. Another option is to use class **xbar_frame** as the default sequence item for the system VC sequencer, but in that case, the default sequence of this sequencer must be modified to run a sequence that executes an item whose kind is limited to data transfers.

The implementation of the system VC sequencer is the same as the one for interface VC sequencer (program 13.7), with the difference that sequence item **xbar_data_frame** is used as the default sequence item type for the system VC sequencer. With this implementation, the system VC sequencer will start generating random data transfer frames at the start of the run phase of the verification.

The implementation of module VC sequencer was shown to include sequence item producer interface **sve_pkt_prod_if** (program 14.11, line 6). The implementation **sxbar_sve**, XBar environment top level that includes system VC components **xbar_svc**, is similar to the implementation of **mxbar_sve** (program 14.12). In this implementation, class **sxbar_sve** is derived from class **mxbar_sve** and adds the system VC components to the environment while making the necessary connections between system VC and module VC components. The connection between the sequence item producer interface **sve_pkt_prod_if** of the module VC sequencer and system VC sequencer is carried out in this step and follows the same syntax shown for connecting XBar receive driver **xbar_rcv_driver** to XBar transmit sequencer **xbar_rcv_sequencer** (program 13.10 line 44).

The default implementation of system VC sequencer starts by generating a series of data transfer frames which are passed to the sequence item producer interface in the module VC sequencer. The next step is to write a sequence belonging to the sequence library of the module VC sequencer that uses this interface to receive the next data frame it sends to downstream sequencers. The implementation of this sequence is shown in the following program:

```
Program 14.19: Sequence in Module VC receiving items from System VC
1   :   class mxbar_layered_seq_send_data_transfer extends ovm_sequence;
2   :       `ovm_sequence_utils(mxbar_layered_seq_send_data_transfer, mxbar_sequencer)
3   :
4   :       function new(string name="", ovm_object parent=null);
5   :           super.new(name);
6   :       endfunction
7   :
8   :       task get_req(output xbar_data_frame dfr);
9   :           ovm_sequence_item item;
10  :           p_sequencer.sve_pkt_prod_if.get_next_item(item);
11  :           $cast(dfr, item);
12  :       endtask
13  :
14  :       task put_rsp(input xbar_data_frame dfr);
15  :           p_sequencer.sve_pkt_prod_if.item_done(dfr);
16  :       endtask
17  :
18  :       virtual task body();
19  :           mxbar_seq_send_frame seq_send_frame;
20  :           ovm_seq_cons_if sci;
21  :           xbar_data_frame dxfr;
22  :
23  :           get_req(dxfr);
24  :           sci = p_sequencer.get_seq_cons_if(dxfr.src_addr);
25  :           sci.grab(get_parent_seq());
26  :
27  :           `ovm_do_with(seq_send_frame, {xfr.kind==SOF;
28  :               xfr.dest_addr==dxfr.dest_addr; xfr.src_addr==dxfr.src_addr;})
29  :           `ovm_do_with(seq_send_frame, {xfr.kind==dxfr.kind;
30  :               xfr.dest_addr==dxfr.dest_addr; xfr.src_addr==dxfr.src_addr;})
31  :
32  :           sci.ungrab(get_parent_seq());
33  :           put_rsp(dxfr);
34  :           #1000; // wait for some time, optionally randomize by using a field instead
35  :       endtask
36  :   endclass: mxbar_layered_seq_send_data_transfer
```

The implementation of sequence **mxbar_layered_seq_send_data_transfer** (line 1), belonging to the sequence library of virtual sequencer **mxbar_sequencer** (line 2) is shown in the above example. This sequence defines tasks **get_req()** (lines 8–12) and **put_rsp()** (lines 14–16) used for interacting with the sequence item producer interface in its parent sequencer. Task **get_req()** blocks until it receives the next sequence item (line 10) from the sequencer connected to **sve_pkt_prod_if** (i.e., system VC sequencer), and task **put_rsp()** indicates the completion of sequence item execution to the sequencer connected to **sve_pkt_prod_if** (line 15). The sequence action block (lines 18–35) starts by getting the next sequence item from the upstream sequencer (line 23), identifying the downstream sequencer through which this packet should be sent (line 24), grabbing that sequencer while identifying itself as the parent sequence that started this sequence (line 25), and then using subsequence **seq_send_frame** of sequence type **mxbar_seq_send_frame** (program 14.14) to send the two frames that compose the requested data transfer (lines 27–30). After sending the frames, the sequence ungrabs the downstream sequencer (line 32), and indicates to the upstream sequencer that it is finished executing its sequence item (line 33). Note that grabbing the downstream sequencer as the parent of this sequence (line 25) allows other subsequences started by the parent sequence (i.e., sequences to send beacon request and reply frames) to have access to this downstream sequencer. This approach allows the transfer of beacon request and reply to interleave a data transfer, but prevents other data transfers to interleave another data transfer.

One possible configuration for making use of this layered sequence is as follows:

- Implement a sequence in module sequencer that starts three parallel subsequences for sending beacon request transfers, sending beacon reply transfers, and executing sequence **mxbar_layered_seq_send_data_transfer** a given number of times controlled by field **count** of the module VC sequencer.
- Configure the system VC sequencer to continuously generate sequence items. The actual number of data transfers injected into the DUV is controlled by the number of sequence items that the module virtual sequencer is configured to receive from the sequencer in system VC. The system VC sequencer blocks if the module VC sequencer stops accepting the items it is producing.

Generation of data transfer sequences, as described in this section, does not differentiate between data request and reply transfers. The extension of this environment to comply with data transfer requirements of the XBar communication protocol is described in the next section.

14.10 Conditional Sequences

Multiple sequences can pass their generated items to their sequencer. A sequencer picks the next sequence item in a first-in-first-out (FIFO) order from those sequence items that are relevant to the current verification context. The default implementation is to assume all sequence items produced by all sequences are relevant. This default behavior, however, must be changed in order to support sequence generation schemes where not all sequence items are relevant at all times.

Consider a requirement that the XBar system VC sequencer should reply immediately to an incoming data request transfer even if an outgoing data request transfer is pending. One approach to support this requirement is to create two concurrently running sequences in the XBar system VC sequencer: one for replying to incoming data request transfers, and one for generating outgoing data request transfers. The required behavior for the sequencer is then to pick the next sequence item from the sequence generating data reply transfers if an incoming data request transfer is detected.

Conditional sequences provide a mechanism for specifying when a sequence is relevant to the current verification context. In turn, a sequencer selects its next sequence item from those sequences that are marked as relevant at the time the next item is being selected.

Conditional sequences are used in the XBar verification environment to allow the sequencer in XBar system VC to reply to data request transfers first, even if an outgoing data request transfer is also available for transmission. This implementation follows these steps:

- XBar system VC monitor detects all incoming data request transfers by listening to the analysis port of the module VC receive monitor.

- The sequencer in system VC continuously listens to the event port in the monitor and adds any incoming data request frames to queue **data_req_pkt_queue**. Having the sequencer extract this information from the monitor is necessary since the monitor is unaware of all other blocks, so the sequencer has to extract the needed information from the monitor.
- Each sequence has a predefined function **is_relevant()** whose return value is checked by the sequencer to select sequences relevant to the current verification context:
  - The sequence that generates data reply transfers returns true for this method when queue **data_req_pkt_queue** is not empty.
  - The sequence that generates data request transfers returns true for this method when queue **data_req_pkt_queue** is empty.
- Each sequence has a predefined task **wait_for_relevant()** that completes only when the sequence containing this task becomes relevant to the current verification context. The completion of this task is used as a means of triggering the sequencer arbiter to process sequence items as they become relevant. This task must be defined is function is_relevant() is redefined.

The following program shows the implementation of system VC sequencer:

```
Program 14.20: system VC driver for computing relevant sequences
1     class sxbar_sequencer extends ovm_sequencer;
2         int unsigned port_num;
3
4         ovm_blocking_peek_port#(xbar_data_frame) data_req_collected_port;
5         xbar_frame data_req_pkt_queue[$];
6
7         `ovm_sequencer_utils_begin(sxbar_sequencer)
8             `ovm_field_int(port_num, OVM_ALL_ON)
9         `ovm_sequencer_utils_end
10
11        function new (string name="", ovm_component parent=null);
12            super.new(name, parent);
13            `ovm_update_sequence_lib_and_item(xbar_data_frame)
14            data_req_collected_port = new("data_req_collected_port", this);
15        endfunction: new
16
17        task update_data_req_queue();
18            xbar_data_frame rcv_data_frame;
19            forever begin
20                data_req_collected_port.peek(rcv_data_frame);
21                rcv_data_frame = new rcv_data_frame;
22                data_req_pkt_queue.push_back(rcv_data_frame);
23            end
24        endtask
25
26        task run();
27            fork
28                super.run();
29                update_data_req_queue();
30            join
31        endtask
32    endclass: sxbar_sequencer
```

Queue **data_req_pkt_queue** (line 5) is defined to hold incoming data request frames detected by the monitor. Task **update_data_req_queue()** (lines 17–24) is defined to receive the next data request transfer received by the system VC monitor by calling task **peek()** of blocking peek transaction port **data_req_collected_port**, and add the received data request to the queue. The definition for the **run()** method of the sequencer is also modified to start this method in parallel with the default behavior of the driver (lines 26–31). Given the above implementation, queue **data_req_pkt_queue** will contain all unprocessed data request transfers in the order of their arrival.

The following program shows the implementation of function **is_relevant()** and task **wait_for_relevant()** for sequences that generate and reply to a data request transfers:

```
Program 14.21: Function is_relevant() of data req and reply sequences
1   :   class sxbar_send_data_reply extends ovm_sequence;
2   :       `ovm_sequence_utils(sxbar_send_data_reply, sxbar_sequencer)
            .
            .
            .
3   :       function bit is_relevant();
4   :           return (p_sequencer.data_req_pkt_queue.size() > 0);
5   :       endfunction
6   :
7   :       task wait_for_relevant();
8   :           if (!is_relevant()) @(if_relevant());
9   :       endtask
10  :   endclass: sxbar_send_data_reply
11  :
12  :   class sxbar_send_data_request extends ovm_sequence;
13  :       `ovm_sequence_utils(sxbar_send_data_request, sxbar_sequencer)
            .
            .
            .
14  :       function bit is_relevant();
15  :           return (p_sequencer.data_req_pkt_queue.size() == 0);
16  :       endfunction
17  :
18  :       task wait_for_relevant();
19  :           while (!is_relevant()) @(p_sequencer.data_req_pkt_queue.size() == 0);
20  :       endtask
21  :   endclass: sxbar_send_data_request
```

Sequence **sxbar_send_data_reply** (lines 1–10) responds to data request transfers being received at this port. Function **is_relevant()** of this sequence is defined to return true if array **data_req_pkt_queue** contained in its parent sequencer **p_sequencer** has any entries (line 4). Task **wait_for_relevant()** of this sequence is defined to return when function **is_relevant()** succeeds. The *if-statement* allows this task to return immediately if function **is_relevant()** succeeds at the current time.

Sequence **sxbar_send_data_request** (lines 12–21) generates data request transfers. Function **is_relevant()** of this sequence returns false anytime there is a pending data request transfer that has not yet been replied to (line 11). The definition of task **wait_for_relevant()** for this sequence is the same as that for sequence **sxbar_send_data_reply**.

Note that function **is_relevant()** returns true by default. As such, if a conditional sequence scheme is implemented for a sequencer, then function **is_relevant()** of all new sequences must be redefined to take into account the relevance scheme.

The above example provides a simple definition for when a sequence is relevant to the verification context. The same approach can, however, be used to define any relevant criteria as needed by the verification context.

14.11 Sequence Synchronization with End of Run

Some verification scenarios may require that a chain of sequence items produced by a sequence be fully processed by the driver before the simulation run phase is ended. In other cases, verification scenarios may require that a reply to an outgoing sequence item be received before the run phase is completed. The OVM class library provides a mechanism for a component to raise an objection to ending the run phase of the hierarchy in which is exists (section 7.4.2). This mechanism can be used to synchronize the end of run phase with the operating state of sequences.

One example of this requirement is in the XBar module VC where a data transfer consisting of two frames is generated. The goal is to prevent the run phase to end if a data transfer is started but both frames have not yet been processed.

The following implementation shows the additional functions that are added to the implementation of the module VC sequencer (program 14.11) to support this requirement:

```
Program 14.22: Implementing sequencer support for objection to end of run phase
1   :    class mxbar_sequencer extends ovm_virtual_sequencer;
                  ⋮
                  ⋮
2   :            function void raise_objection();
3   :                enable_stop_interrupt ++;
4   :            endfunction
5   :            function void drop_objection();
6   :                enable_stop_interrupt --;
7   :            endfunction
8   :
9   :            task stop(string ph_name="run");
10  :                while (enable_stop_interrupt) @(enable_stop_interrupt);
11  :            endtask
12  :    endclass: mxbar_sequencer
```

Functions **raise_objection()** and **drop_objection()** increase and decrease the value of field **enable_stop_interrupt** (a predefined member of class **ovm_component**, a parent class of **ovm_virtual_sequencer**) respectively. The addition of these functions are necessary since field **enable_stop_interrupt** is a protected field and as such, cannot directly be modified by sequences in the sequence library of this sequencer. Function **stop()** is defined so that it completes when the value of **enable_stop_interrupt** is, or has reached, **0**.

The implementation sequence **mxbar_seq_send_data_transfer** (program 14.17) is modified as follows to prevent the run phase from ending after the generation of the first frame is started and before the second frame is processed by the driver:

```
Program 14.23: Sequence action block raising objection to end of run
1   :    class mxbar_seq_send_data_transfer extends ovm_sequence;
                  ⋮
                  ⋮
2   :            virtual task body();
3   :                mxbar_seq_send_frame seq_send_frame;
4   :                ovm_seq_cons_if sci;
5   :
6   :                sci = p_sequencer.get_seq_cons_if(dxfr.src_addr);
7   :                sci.grab(get_parent_seq());
```

```
 8  :              p_sequencer.raise_objection();
 9  :
10  :              `ovm_do_with(seq_send_frame, {xfr.kind==SOF;
11  :                        xfr.dest_addr==dxfr.dest_addr; xfr.src_addr==dxfr.src_addr;})
12  :              `ovm_do_with(seq_send_frame, {xfr.kind==dxfr.kind;
13  :                        xfr.dest_addr==dxfr.dest_addr; xfr.src_addr==dxfr.src_addr;})
14  :              sci.ungrab(get_parent_seq());
15  :
16  :              p_sequencer.drop_objection();
17  :              #1000; // wait for some time, optionally randomize by using a field instead
18  :          endtask
19  :  endclass: mxbar_seq_send_data_transfer
```

This behavior is achieved in the action block of this sequencer by calling function **raise_objection()** of its sequencer before executing the first sequence item (line 8), and calling function **drop_objection()** of its sequencer after executing the second sequence item (line 16).

Depending on the synchronization requirements of a sequence with the end of run phase, the functions to raise or drop objections can be placed in the predefined callback methods of a sequence. For example, if the run phase should not end while the action block of a root sequence is executing, then functions to raise and drop objections can be placed in tasks **pre_body()** and **post_body()** of that sequence. Figure 8.5 provides a view of the order in which callback methods are called for root sequences, subsequences, and sequence items, and can be used as a guide to deciding the best place for a sequence to raise and lower objections to ending the run phase.

PART 6

Assertion-Based Verification

CHAPTER 15

Property Specification and Evaluation Engine

A major factor affecting verification productivity is how concisely verification intent can be described. A concise description makes verification intent easier to specify and also easier to understand. The need to describe a property, either in the design or the verification environment, is an inherent part of any verification activity. As such, the ability to write concise, yet clear descriptions of design properties not only increases verification productivity, but also improves verification environment reusability by allowing other engineers to better understand the intent behind property descriptions.

The quality of a proprety specification language is measured in its expressiveness, a measure that is meant to maximize the following competing priorities:

- The ability to model as complex a description as possible
- The ability to write as concise a description as possible
- The ability to write as readable a description as possible

As in any other natural or computer language, one's ability to reach a good balance between these competing priorities is developed over time and through practice and experience.

To address the need for a powerful property specification mechanism, property specification languages have been defined, either as independent standards (e.g., Property Specification Language [PSL]) or as part of hardware verification languages (e.g., temporal expressions in the e language). SystemVerilog provides an extensive set of constructs for writing property specifications.

Assertion-based verification (ABV) is a verification approach that makes extensive use of property specifications. ABV methodology provides best practices for improving verification quality by using assertions. A good understanding of how properties are specified is essential for taking maximum advantage of the benefits provided by ABV. This chapter describes in detail how properties are described in SystemVerilog. Assertion-based verification, where property specification is needed, is described in chapter 16.

15.1 Property Specification Hierarchy

A property, in its most abstract form, is a relationship between Boolean conditions across multiple time steps. The simplest property is a single Boolean condition defined at one point in time, and the most complex property is a relationship between multiple Boolean conditions within one and across multiple time-steps. As such, a property specification language should provide language constructs for defining Boolean conditions based on design and verification environment signals, and for specifying relationships between these Boolean conditions across multiple time-steps.

In addition to these constructs, a powerful property specification language should also provide facilities for managing the following aspects of property specification:

- Ability to define a property based on Boolean conditions sampled (i.e., evaluated) at multiple asynchronous (i.e., unrelated) clocks in order to facilitate properties defined across multiple clock domains.
- Ability to define properties in a hierarchical fashion so that a complex property can be constructed from simpler properties.
- Ability to write a property based on formal arguments so that a given specification can be used in multiple places in the environment using different sets of actual signals replacing the formal arguments.
- Efficient ways to define when a property should hold (i.e., defining property sampling event).
- Efficient ways to define when a property need not hold (i.e., disabling property).

SystemVerilog provides three abstraction layers for defining a property:

- Boolean Expressions
- Sequences
- Properties

Boolean expressions define conditions that are evaluated in zero time. In general, SystemVerilog allows any expression that produces a Boolean result to be used as a Boolean expression (section 15.2). In addition, SystemVerilog provides system functions (e.g., *$rose()*) to extract relevant Boolean conditions from signals in the environment (section 15.2.5). *Sequences* are composed of Boolean expressions and sequence operators, and are used to define a relationship between Boolean expressions across multiple time-steps. *Properties* are composed of sequences and property operators, and provide a true or false result indicating whether the given property was maintained throughout the simulation runtime.

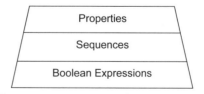

Figure 15.1 Property Specification Hierarchy

Sequences and properties have very different semantic meanings. The relationship between sequences and properties is the same as the relationship between behaviors and rules. Behaviors describe a manner of behaving or acting, while rules outline legal behaviors. For example, a behavior for a reset signal may state that "the cpu reset signal stays active for five clock cycles" while a rule about that reset signal may state that "the cpu reset signal *must* stay active for at least five clock cycles." Rules often use some behaviors as qualifying conditions for legal behaviors. For example, a rule may state that "if system reset becomes active, then the cpu reset signal must stay active for at least five clock cycles." In this case, the behavior "system reset becomes active" is used as the qualifying condition for the second behavior.

Properties provide a mechanism for specifying rules about design behaviors described with sequences. SystemVerilog sequences and sequence operators provide a powerful mechanism for specifying complex design behaviors, while SystemVerilog properties and property operators allow legal relations to be specified between behaviors described by sequences. In the cpu reset example, sequences are used to describe behaviors "system reset becomes active" and "cpu reset stays active for five clock cycles," and properties are used to specify the allowed relationship between these two behaviors.

In addition to this conceptual difference, SystemVerilog sequences and properties   have different evaluation models. For a given simulation trace, a sequence may match multiple times in one or more evaluation cycles and fails only if it never matches. All the match conditions computed for a sub-sequence are tracked as part of the evaluation and used to guide the evaluation of the sequence containing that sub-sequence (section 15.3.2). Evaluation of a property, however, produces only a true or false statement indicating whether the given property was satisfied in any possible way. Consider a design having two reset signals. Assume sequence S states that "either $reset_1$ or $reset_2$ stays active for two to five cycles" and property P states that "either $reset_1$ or $reset_2$ *must* stay active for two to five cycles." Property P is satisfied if either $reset_1$ or $reset_2$ stay active for two to five cycles. This means that if one of these conditions is observed, then the property can be considered as satisfied, and there is no need to find out if the other condition is satisfied. However, if sequence S is used to describe a more complex sequence, then all possible ways it can succeed must be found and considered.

The requirement to keep track of all possible matches for a sequence is illustrated in the following example:

```
S₁: (V₁==10) ##1 [1:2] (V₁==20)
P₁: S₁
P₂: S₁ ##1 (V₁==30)
Trace Tr: (10,20,20,30)
```

Sequence S_1 describes a behavior where variable V_1 is equal to **10** in the first evaluation cycle, and equal to **20** in the following one or two evaluation cycles. As such, sequence S_1 matches traces **(10,20)** and **(10,20,20)**, thereby producing two matches for trace **Tr** at evaluation cycles **2** and **3**. Property P_1 is described as sequence S_1 and succeeds for either trace **(10,20)** or **(10,20,20)**. Property P_2 is described as sequence S_1 followed in the next evaluation cycle with variable V_1 being equal to **30**, and therefore, succeeds for traces **(10,20,30)** or **(10,20,20,30)**. When evaluating property P_1, only the first match of sequence S_1 is sufficient for deciding that the property succeeds. However, in evaluating property P_2, both matches of sequence S_1 must be considered, since considering only the first match (i.e., **(10,20)**) would result in missing the actual success of this property for trace **Tr**. Clearly, if sequence **s₁** fails for any trace (e.g., **(10,50,20,30)**), then neither property **P₁** nor **P₂** will match for that trace.

Boolean expressions, sequences and properties are described in the following sections of this chapter.

15.2 Boolean Expressions

Boolean expressions are the building blocks of sequences and property specifications. In general, any expression that produces a Boolean result without any side effects[1] can be used as a Boolean expression in a sequence or property specification. Such an expression is treated in the same way as the expression in the *if-clause* of an *if-statement*, where a value of **1** is assumed to be true and values of **0**, *x*, and *z* are assumed to be false.

Examples of valid Boolean expressions with different operand types are shown below:

```
( A && !B)          // A and B are bits
( cnt == 53)        // cnt is an integer
( arrayA == arrayB) // arrayA and arrayB are 2-dimensional arrays
( A.X == B.Y)       // X and Y are integer members of structs A and B respectively
```

Boolean expressions, in the context of sequence and property specifications, are defined by the following aspects:

- Allowed operand types
- Operators
- Sampling events
- Operand value sampling
- Sampled value functions

Sampled value functions are system provided functions that allow for writing conditions based on changes in signal values. These topics are discussed in the following subsections.

15.2.1 Operand Types

Boolean expression operands can be one of literals (i.e., constants), variables, or function calls. Literals with the following types are not allowed in Boolean expressions:

- Non-integer types (*shortreal, real, realtime*)
- *string*
- *event*
- *chandle*
- *class*
- Associative arrays
- Dynamic arrays

[1.] A side effect, in this context, refers to a change in the value of any data object in the environment.

Variables that return a valid operand type (i.e., variable types not in the previous list) can be used in a Boolean expression. These variables, however, must be a static design variable declared in programs, interfaces, clocking blocks, or tasks.

Function calls that return one of the valid types (i.e., types excluding those listed above) can be used in a Boolean expression. However, the following semantic restrictions are imposed on function calls used in a Boolean expression:

- Function arguments cannot be of type *ref* (*const ref* is allowed)
- Functions should not contain any static variables
- Functions should not have any side effects (e.g., changing values in other scopes).

These restrictions are required in order to prevent side effects when a property is being evaluated. Preventing side effects is needed since a property may get evaluated multiple times in a single time-slot because of race conditions in its sampling event. And any side effect in evaluation of a Boolean expression used in a property can, therefore, lead to unpredictable behavior.

15.2.2 Operators

All operators that are valid for the operands types described in the previous section can be used in Boolean expressions. However, operators that produce side effects when used in expressions are not allowed. Disallowed operands are:

- Assignment operator (=)
- Increment operator (++)
- Decrement operator (--)

15.2.3 Sampling Events

The sampling event for a Boolean expression is the condition that causes the Boolean expression in a sequence or property specification to be evaluated. The sampling event for a Boolean expression can either be explicitly specified or derived from the context in which it is used. The discussion of the sampling event for a Boolean expression is the same as discussion for sampling event for sequences (section 15.6).

15.2.4 Operand Value Sampling: Sampled Value vs. Current Value

Every simulation time-slot in the execution engine of a SystemVerilog simulator starts with the preponed region, goes through at least one, and potentially multiple, passes from active through to reactive regions, and ends by passing through the postponed region (section 5.1). This flow implies that a signal value may change multiple times during a single time-slot.

In order to avoid race conditions in evaluating a property, and also to avoid evaluating a property multiple times at the same simulation time, Boolean expressions in a sequence or property are evaluated in the postponed region using the variable values sampled in the preponed region This means that there is only one evaluation of a Boolean expression occurring at a given simulation time-slot, and the values used are the stable values right before entering that simulation time-slot. It is, however, important to note that the current value of the sampling event are used to decide when a Boolean expression is evaluated. This means that if the sampling event of a property (and hence, Boolean expressions used in that property) makes multiple transitions in a single simulation time-slot, it is possible to evaluate that Boolean expression multiple times in a single time-slot.

Figure 15.2 shows how this approach provides a consistent behavior even when signals used for evaluating a property change at the same time as the sampling event of a property. In this figure, Boolean expression (**@(posedge clk) clk**) never evaluates to true. The reason is that the current value of signal **clk**, which is set in the main scheduling loop of the current time-slot, is used to detect the sampling event while the value of **clk**, sampled in the preponed region before clock changed to **1**, is used to evaluate the Boolean expression. Boolean expression (**@(posedge clk) !clk**) evaluates to true for all sampling events because of the same reason. The values of expression (**@(posedge clk) A**) at times **2, 3, 6, 7** and **8** show examples of using variable values immediately before the sampling event to evaluate a property. This example also shows the usefulness of the sampled values of variables used in a Boolean expressions, where this approach leads to predictable evaluations even when signals change at the same time as the sampling event. Also, this approach is consistent with cycle-based verification semantics where signal values are sampled before a clock edge (section 5.2).

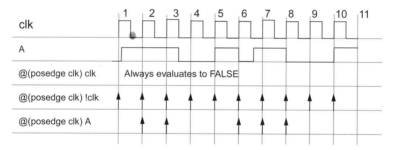

Figure 15.2 Sampled Values in Property and Sequence Evaluation

It is important that the sampling event for all sequences and properties are glitch free and change only once at each simulation time-slot. Using the current value for evaluating sampling events means that a sampling event with race conditions (e.g., signal **clk** changing multiple times in the same simulation time-slot) leads to multiple evaluations of a sequence or property in the same time-slot. In this case, the sequence evaluation engine assumes the next sampling event at a next simulation time to have arrived, when, in fact, simulation time has not yet advanced. Given that properties are usually described in terms of consecutive occurrences of sampling events, any such misunderstanding of the actual arrival of the sampling event can lead to errors in correct evaluation of a property.

15.2.5 Sampled Value Functions

SystemVerilog provides special functions to help detect a change in sampled value, the current sampled value, or the past sampled value of variables. The use of these functions is not limited to sequence and property specifications, and can be used anywhere a function return-ing a Boolean value can be used. These system functions and their syntax are:

```
$sampled(expr)
$rose(expr)
$fell(expr)
$stable(expr)
$past(expr [, number_of_sampling_events] [, gating_expr])
```

Function **$sampled(expression)** returns the sampled value of expression in the current simulation time-slot. The value returned by this function is the value used for **expr** in evaluat-ing a property in which **expr** is used.

Functions **$rose()**, **$fell()**, and **$stable()** compare the sampled value of **expr** in the current simulation time-slot to the sampled value of **expr** in the previous simulation time-slot when the sampling event for the function occurred. Function **$rose()** returns true if the least signifi-cant bit changed from zero to one. Function **$fell()** returns true if the least significant bit changed from one to zero, and function **$stable()** returns true if the sampled value did not change.

Function **$past()** returns the sampled value of **expr** at the time-slot for a previous sam-pling event. Function **$past()** can be used to retrieve the sampled value of **expr** for any number of sampling events in the past by specifying arguments **number_of_sampling_events** and **gating_expr**. The number of sampling events in the past is counted only for sampling events at which **gating_expr** evaluates to true. Both these arguments are optional, with **number_of_sampling_events** having a default value of **1**.

Figure 15.3 shows examples of values returned for these sampled value functions. Sig-nal **clk** is used as the sampling event, and row 2 shows when this sampling event occurs. The value for signal **A** (row 3) goes through all transitions (**0→0, 0→1, 1→0, 1→1**) both at the ris-ing edge of **clk** and at the falling edge of **clk**, thereby providing examples for all possible cor-ner cases. Row 5 shows the value returned by function **$sample()**. Note that the value returned for the first sampling event is x since initially, all variables are initialized to x. Rows 6, 7, and 8 show transition values computed for signal **A**. Rows 9, 10, and 12 show values returned by function **$past()**. Row 9 shows values returned for sampled value of signal **A** that is delayed by one sampling-event. Row 10 shows values returned for sampled values of signal **A** that is delayed by two sampling events. Row 12 shows the effect of using a gating expression to decide which past sampled value of signal **A** to return. Note that the Boolean expression shown in row 12 is still evaluated for every occurrence of the sampling event shown in row 2, but the number of sampling events counted into the past is taken from row 11.

Boolean expressions are the building blocks of sequences and properties. The use of Boolean expressions in writing sequences and properties are described in the following sec-tions.

15.3 Sequences

Sequences specify behaviors that span zero or more simulation time. Sequences are con-structed by using the *sequence delay operator* (##) to specify what Boolean expressions must

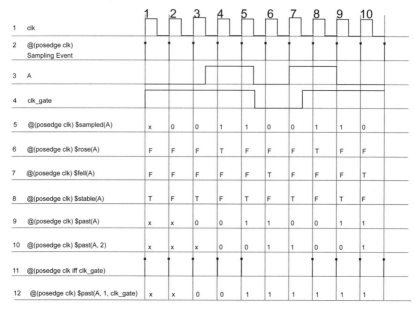

Figure 15.3 Sampled Value System Functions

evaluate to true across consecutive sampling cycles. Evaluation cycles for a sequence are defined by the sequence sampling event. For example, sequence (**A ##1 B**) indicates a condition where **A** is true in a given cycle and **B** is true in the following cycle.

A *linear sequence* is the simplest form of a sequence and specifies Boolean conditions that must evaluate to true in consecutive cycles (e.g., **A ##1 B ##1 C**). A linear sequence is said to match when all Boolean expressions, as ordered by the unit delay operator, are true in their corresponding cycles. Note that a sequence of type (**A ##3 B**) is also a linear sequence, since this form indirectly states that in the three cycles from **A** to **B**, no Boolean condition is necessary to be true in order for this sequence to match. In other words:

A ##3 B   is equivalent to: A ##1 (1) ##1 (1) ##1 B where (1) matches any condition

All other sequence operators are essentially provided as efficient means of specifying long linear sequences or composite sequences where a single expression represents a group of linear sequences. For example, the delay repeat operator (e.g., **A ##60 B**) helps in defining a very long linear sequence without explicitly writing the condition for each cycle. An "or" sequence operator helps in writing one sequence expression that represents multiple sequences. A *composite sequence* may represent zero, finitely many, or infinitely many linear sequences. Table 15.1 shows examples of composite sequences each representing one or more linear sequences.

The sequence operator that is used to create a composite sequence defines how the results of individual sequences are combined in order to compute the match or fail condition

Composite Sequence	Linear Sequences Represented	Number of Linear Sequences Represented
A [*0]	This is an empty sequence. Doesn't match any trace.	0
A ##1 B	A ##1 B	1
A ##[1:3] B	A ##1 B A ##1 (1) ##1 B A ##1 (1) ##1 ('true) ##1 B	3
A ##[1:$] B	A ##1 B A ##1 (1) ##1 B . A ##1 (1) ##1...##1 (1) ##1 B .	Infinite

Table 15.1: Composite Sequences Representing a Group of Linear Sequences

for the composite sequence. The evaluation model of sequences is described in section 15.3.2.

15.3.1 Sequence Declarations and Formal Arguments

Sequences can be written in-line as part of a property or assertion declaration. Sequences can also be declared as a *named sequence*, which can then be instantiated in other sequences and properties. Named sequences provide the following benefits:

- A declared sequence can be defined in terms of formal arguments, allowing declared sequences to be reused for different sets of signals and repeat counts.
- A declared sequence can contain local variables, allowing a declared sequence's matching conditions to be defined in terms of state information stored in a local variable.
- A declared sequence can be used to better organize the description of a complex scenario, leading to more readable implementation of a sequence.

Sequences can be declared in the following blocks:

- Module block
- Interface block
- Program block
- Clocking block
- Package

Sequence instantiation refers to using the name of a declared sequence in writing other sequences or properties. Such usage is equivalent to replacing the actual declaration of a named sequence with the instance of that sequence, while replacing that sequence's formal arguments with the actual argument provided in its instantiation.

The following program shows examples of sequence declarations and instantiations:

Program 15.1: Named sequence declaration and instantiation

```
1  :   module top;
2  :       bit a, b, c, clk;
3  :       int data_in, data_out;
4  :
```

```
 5   :        initial begin for (int i = 0; i <= 10; i++) #1 clk = !clk ; end
 6   :
 7   :        sequence S1(AA);
 8   :            AA [*2:4];
 9   :        endsequence
10   :
11   :        sequence S2;
12   :            bit [7:0] local_var;
13   :            @(negedge clk) (S1(b), local_var = data_in) ##5 (data_out == local_var);
14   :        endsequence
15   :
16   :        sequence S3 (S_CLK, AA, BB, CC, min1, max1, max2);
17   :            @(posedge S_CLK) AA ##[min1:max1] BB ##[1:max2] CC;
18   :        endsequence
19   :
20   :        sequence S4;
21   :            S3(clk, a, S1(a), (a==b), 1, 10, "$");
22   :        endsequence
23   :    endmodule
```

The following observations apply to the above examples. These topics are covered in more detail in the following subsections.

- Sequences are specified by using sequence operators to combine Boolean expressions and previously declared sequences (lines 8, 13, 17, 21).
- Sequence sampling events can either be specified explicitly or derived from the context of where the sequence is used. In the above example, no sampling event is specified for sequence S_1. As such, S_1 derives its sampling event from its instantiation context. The sampling event for sequence S_1 is the negative edge of **clk** when S_1 is used in sequence S_2 (line 13), positive edge of **clk** when S_1 is used in sequence S_3 (line 17), and positive edge of **clk** when S_1 is passed to S_3 as an actual argument to its instance in sequence S_4 (line 21).
- *Sequence evaluation state* can be one of "started", "matched", or "failed".
- Formal arguments can be defined for a sequence declaration in order to customize an instance of a sequence to its instantiation context. Formal arguments of a declared sequence can replace the following elements of a sequence declaration:
    - Identifier: Identifier **a** as actual for formal argument **AA** of S_3
    - Sequence: Sequence S_1(a) as actual for formal argument **BB** of S_3
    - Expression: (a==b) as actual for formal argument **CC** of S_3
    - Event control expression: **clk** as actual for formal argument **S_CLK** of S_3
    - Repeat range: Passing **1**, **10**, and "$" for formal arguments of S_3
- Sequence declarations can include procedural code (including function calls) that will be invoked when a given part of sequence matches (e.g., invoking (**local_var = data_in**) when sub-sequence (S_1(b) on line 13 matches)).
- Local variables which persist throughout evaluation of a sequence can be used in a sequence specification. These local variables simplify the transfer of information from one part of a sequence to another (storing the value of **data_in** to be later used in a Boolean expression on line 13).
- Any identifier used in a sequence declaration that is not a local variable or a formal argument is resolved according to the scoping rules of the block in which the sequence declaration is placed. For example, variables **data_in** and **data_out** are not local variables of sequence S_2. As such, the variables used are the ones in the scope

where sequence S_2 is declared (line 3). This means that even if this sequence is used in a property in a different module (using its hierarchical name), variables **data_in** and **data_out** from this module (line 3) are used.

- Formal arguments are type independent. As such, a sequence instance actual argument can have any type as long as the resulting sequence definition is legal.

Details of sequences are described in the following subsections.

15.3.2 Sequence Evaluation Model

Figure 15.4 shows the abstract evaluation model for a linear sequence. In this model, an evaluation thread is started in the first cycle to check for the Boolean condition for the first sampling period. Boolean expressions for each cycle are checked in consecutive cycles until either one of the Boolean expressions is detected as false, in which case the sequence fails and evaluation thread is terminated, or until all Boolean expressions in their corresponding cycles are detected to be true and sequence matches. A linear sequence will match or fail only one time.

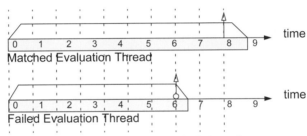

Figure 15.4 Abstract Evaluation Model of Linear Sequence

Evaluating a composite sequence is more involved. Figure 15.5 shows the abstract evaluation model of a composite sequence. The sampling event cycles are shown on top, along with their corresponding cycles. The overall result of sequence evaluation is shown on top, where evaluation is started at cycle **0** (first cycle this evaluation is started) and in this example ends at time **10**. The evaluation result of a composite sequence is computed from the results of evaluation threads for its sub-sequences. The operator used to create the composite sequence from its subsequences defines how the overall evaluation of the sequence is derived from the results produced by its evaluation sub-threads. For example, composite sequence ($S = S_1$ or S_2) has two evaluation sub-threads corresponding to sequences S_1 and S_2. Sequence **S** is then said to match any time one of its sub-sequences matches.

In figure 15.5, the match or fail status of the overall sequence (shown on top) does not depend directly on the match or fail condition of its sub-threads, since the actual results will depend on the operator used to combine the sub-threads. The presentation of sequence operators in the following section will describe each operator based on how it combines the results of its evaluation sub-threads.

The following aspects define the abstract evaluation model of a composite sequence:

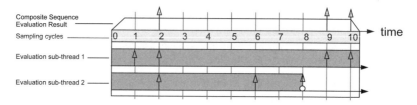

Figure 15.5 Abstract Evaluation Model of a Composite Sequence

- *Sequence match condition*: How match or fail results of evaluation sub-threads are combined to produce match/fail results for the sequence
- *Sequence termination condition*: when evaluation thread is terminated

Sequence operators (section 15.3.3) will be defined, based on this view of the sequence evaluation model.

15.3.2.1 Evaluation Sub-Threads and Multiple Matches

Depending on the operator used, evaluation of a composite sequence may match multiple times. These multiple matches may occur at different cycles or even in the same cycle. For example, sequence (**S** = **S₁** or **S₂**) may match twice in the same cycle if both **S₁** and **S₂** match in the same cycle. Note that the evaluation sub-threads shown in figure 15.5 represent evaluation threads of their corresponding sub-sequences, and each may contain multiple sub-threads producing their evaluation results. As such, each sub-thread may match multiple times and the effect of such multiple matches in sub-threads to the overall sequence result is defined by the sequence operator used to combine the evaluation sub-threads.

The number of times a sequence matches is important only when a sequence is used in building a larger sequence. Consider the following two examples:

P_1:	s_1 or s_2	(s_1, s_2, s_3 are multiple cycle sequences)
P_2:	(s_1 or s_2) ##1 s_3	P_2 is equivalent to: (s_1 ##1 s_3) or (s_2 ##1 s_3)

Only one match is sufficient for a property to succeed. As such, P_1 is satisfied if either s_1 or s_2 produce a match, and it is not necessary to search for a second match. Therefore, only the first match of sequence (s_1 or s_2) is relevant when considering P_1. On the other hand, both matches for sequences s_1 and s_2 are important in evaluating P_2. The reason is that either one of (s_1 ##1 s_3) or (s_2 ##1 s_3) may match, and ignoring one of the matches of the (s_1 or s_2) may lead to missed matched results.

Figure 15.6 shows a view of the evaluation flow for sequence (s: s_1 ##1 s_2) started at time **22**, where sequences s_1 and s_2 are composite sequences. In this example, evaluation of sequence s_1 is started at time **22**, producing matches at times **24, 28**, and **29**. Note that these matches are produced because of the description of sequence s_1 which is not shown in this example. For every match of sequence s_1, a new evaluation thread is started for sequence s_2 in the cycle after the match for s_1 occurred (using ##0 would start the evaluation for s_2 in the same cycle that the match for s_1 occurred). An evaluation sub-thread is terminated if it fails, but such failure is not reported. The evaluation of sequence s started at time **22** fails if all

evaluation sub-threads for evaluating s_2 fail. In this example, if (s_1 ##1 s_2) is a property definition, then the property succeeds on the first match produced by evaluation thread for S_2 (at
time **27**). If, however, this sequence is used in building a larger sequence (e.g., (s_1 ##1 s_2) ##1
s_3) then all matches produced by sub-threads started for evaluation of s_2 (times **27, 31, 32, 33,
35**) will lead to the start of an evaluation sub-thread for sequence **s3**.

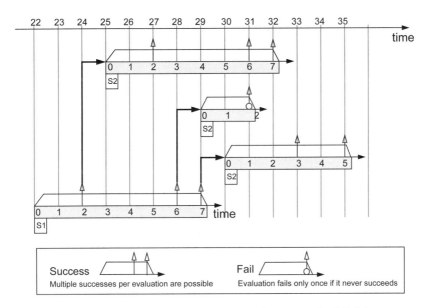

Figure 15.6 Abstract Evaluation Model of Sequence (S_1 ##1 S_2)

15.3.3 Sequence Operators

SystemVerilog sequence operators are listed in table 15.2, with highest precedence listed
first. Sequence operators can be either a *base sequence operator* or a *composite sequence
operator*. A composite sequence operator can be expressed in terms of base sequence operators. In the following subsections, the equivalent description of each composite operator in
terms of base operators is provided.

Some operators accept sequences as operands while others accept only Boolean expressions. In the description of these operators, an **s** is used to represent a sequence operand
while a **B** is used to represent a Boolean expression operand. An operator accepting a
sequence operand can also accept Boolean expressions as operands. Sequence operators are
described in the following subsections.

15.3.3.1 Sequence Delay Repeat Operators

Sequence *delay repeat operator* is used to specify a number of repetitions for the delay operator. The delay repeat operator can have one of the following forms:

Type	Operator	Associativity	Base/Composite
Delay Repetition	##n	----	
Sequence Repetition	[*] [=] [->]	----	
Delay	##	Left	base
Range	throughout	right	composite
	within	left	composite
	intersect	left	base
Boolean	and	left	base
	or	left	base

Table 15.2: Sequence Operators

##n:	n is an integer constant
##identifier	identifier is an object that evaluates to an integer at compile time
##(expression)	expression evaluates to an integer at compile time
##[start:end]	start and end are identifiers or expressions that evaluate to an integer at compile time. "end" can be set to "$" meaning any number of cycles.

Note that the specified delay value should be a constant that results in an integer equal to or larger than zero at compile time. The first three forms of the delay operator, as shown above, represent the same form of a *simple delay repeat operator* with different means of specifying a delay value. The last form shows a *range delay repeat operator*, which is a shorthand notation for multiple linear sequences. Range delay repeat operators can be specified in terms of the simple form of delay, and the "*or*" sequence operator as follows:

$$S_1 \text{ \#\#[start:end] } S_2 \qquad (S_1 \text{ \#\#start } S_2) \text{ or } (S_1 \text{ \#\#(start+1) } S_2) \text{ or } ...$$
$$\text{or } (S_1 \text{ \#\#(end-1) } S_2) + (S_1 \text{ \#\#(end) } S_2)$$

Examples of simple and range repeat operators and their equivalent sequences are shown below:

S_1 ##3 S_2 S_1 ##1 (1) ##1 (1) ##1 S_2
                where (1) is a Boolean expressions always evaluating to TRUE
S_1 ##[1:2] S_2 $(S_1$ ##1 B) or $(S_1$ ##1 (1) ##1 $S_2)$
                where match in either sequence will match the main sequence

A simple delay repeat operator results in a linear sequence and as such, the evaluation model discussed in section 15.3.2 applies to sequences defined using the simple delay repeat operator. A range repeat operator can be restated as the grouping of multiple linear sequences using the "*or*" sequence operator. As such, the evaluation model of sequence repeat operators follows that of the sequence "*or*" operator.

15.3.3.2 Sequence Repeat Operators

Sequence repeat operators are used to specify a repeat parameter for a Boolean expression or a sequence, the same way a delay repeat operator specified a repeat parameter for the delay operator. The following types of sequence repeat operators are provided in SystemVerilog:

(S) [*n]   Consecutive Repeat Operator applied to a sequence
(B) [=n]   Non-Consecutive Repeat Operator applied to a Boolean Expression
(B) [->n]   Goto Operator applied to a Boolean Expression

Sequence *consecutive repeat operator* specifies a sequence that matches a trace in which **s** occurs **n** times in consecutive cycles. This operator can be applied to both Boolean expressions and sequences. The match occurs at the cycle where the last required match of **s** occurs. Applying the consecutive repeat operator is equivalent to concatenating sequence **S** a total of **n** times using the unit delay operators (##*1*). In specifying a repeat operator, a range can be used instead of a single value. In this case, the range will result in the sequence matching any trace containing a match in the given range. The following shows examples of this operator:

(S$_1$ ##1 S$_2$) [*3]	(S$_1$ ##1 S$_2$) ##1 (S$_1$ ##1 S$_2$) ##1 (S$_1$ ##1 S$_2$)
(S$_1$ ##1 S$_2$) [*2:3]	(S$_1$ ##1 S$_2$) ##1 (S$_1$ ##1 S$_2$) or
	(S$_1$ ##1 S$_2$) ##1 ((S$_1$ ##1 S$_2$) ##1 (S$_1$ ##1 S$_2$)
(S) [*1:$]	S or (S ##1 S) or (S ##1 S ##1 S) or …
	Match 1 or more occurrence of S
(S) [*0]	no match. Never matches.

Sequence *non-consecutive repeat operator* specifies a sequence that matches a trace in which **B** occurs, possibly not consecutively, a total of **n** times. The resulting sequence matches not only at the cycle where the *nth* occurrence of **B** matches, but also at every cycle after that for which **B** does not match. This operator can be applied only to Boolean expressions. The following shows examples of this operator:

(B$_1$) [=3]	matches at end of any of following example traces:
	(B$_1$, B$_1$, B$_1$)
	(B$_1$, B$_1$, B$_2$, B$_1$)
	matches at cycle where 3rd. B$_1$ occurs and at any cycle after that:
	(B$_1$, B$_2$, B$_1$, B$_2$, B$_1$, B$_2$, B$_2$, B$_2$)
(B) [=1:2]	is equivalent to sequence (B [=1]) or (B [=2]))

Sequence *goto repeat operator* specifies a sequence that matches a trace in which **B** occurs, possibly not consecutively, a total of **n** times. This sequence matches only at the cycle where the *nth* occurrence of **B** matches. This operator can be applied only to Boolean expressions. The following shows examples of this operator:

(B$_1$) [->3]	matches at the end of following traces:
	(B$_1$, B$_1$, B$_1$)
	(B$_1$, B$_2$, B$_1$, B$_1$)
	(B$_1$, B$_2$, B$_1$, B$_2$, B$_1$)
(B) [->1:2]	is equivalent to sequence (B [->1]) or (B [->2]))

It is important to note that the non-consecutive and goto repeat operators produce different result only when used as part of other sequences or properties. Consider the following properties:

```
       Program 15.2: Sequence repeat operators
                        ⋮

1   :          property p1;
2   :                 @(posedge clk) a [=3];
3   :          endproperty
4   :
5   :          property p2;
6   :                 @(posedge clk) a [->3];
7   :          endproperty
8   :
9   :          property p3;
10  :                 @(posedge clk) a [=3] ##1 b;
11  :          endproperty
12  :
13  :          property p4;
```

```
14  :                    @(posedge clk) a [->3] ##1 b;
15  :            endproperty
                         .
    |_____     .
                         .
```

Consider trace (**a, c, a, a, c, c, b**) occurring during time interval (**1, 2, 3, 4, 5, 6, 7**). Properties p_1 and p_2 both succeed at time **4**, even though property p_1 uses the non-consecutive repeat operator and property p_2 uses the goto repeat operator. The reason is that the sequence expression for both these properties match time **4**, and a property evaluation is terminated after its first match. Property p_3 succeeds at time **7** when **b** is true, but property p_4 fails since it requires **b** to occur immediately after the last cycle where **a** occurred.

Conceptually, sequences created by sequence repeat operators can be represented as a group of linear sequences combined with the "**or**" sequence operator. As such, the evaluation model of sequence repeat operators follows that of the sequence "*or*" operator.

15.3.3.3 Sequence AND Operator

The sequence "*and*" operator has the following syntax:

S = S$_1$ and S$_2$

Match condition: An evaluation of sequence **s** produces a match in any cycle where the following conditions are satisfied:

- Sequences s_1 and s_2 both match at least once
- Sequence s_1 matches at least once while sequence s_2 has already matched at least once in any of the previous cycles
- Sequence s_2 matches at least once while sequence s_1 has already matched at least once in any of the previous cycles

An evaluation of sequence **s** produces only one match in any cycle, regardless of how many times its operands match in that cycle. An evaluation of sequence **s** may, however, match multiple times across its lifetime. If sequence s_1 matches n_1 times and sequences s_2 matches n_2 times, then an evaluation of sequence **s** produces less than (n_1+n_2) matches, and at least $min(n_1, n_2)$ matches. The exact number of matches depends on the ordering between matches from sequence s_1 and matches from sequence s_2.

Termination condition: Evaluation of sequence **s** terminates immediately if any of the evaluation sub-threads fail. Otherwise, evaluation is terminated when both evaluation sub-threads have completed.

Figure 15.7 shows the evaluation model of the sequence "*and*" operator. The evaluation threads for each sub-sequence is shown inside the main evaluation box for sequence **s**. As shown in the figure, sequence s_1 matches at times **3** and **10**, and sequence s_2 matches at times **2** and **8**. Sequence **s** matches once at time **3** (for s_1 match at time **3** and s_2 match at previous time **2**), once at time **8** (for s_2 match at time **8** and s_1 match at previous time **3**) and once at time **10** (for s_1 match at time **10** and s_2 previous match at either time **2** or **8**). The example shows that evaluation of sequence **s** continues even after evaluation sub-thread for s_2 is terminated, since no fail was produced by that evaluation sub-thread.

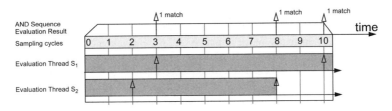

Figure 15.7 Evaluation Model of AND Sequence Operator

15.3.3.4 Sequence OR Operator

The sequence "*or*" operator has the following syntax:

$$S = S_1 \text{ or } S_2$$

Match condition: Sequence **S** matches when either evaluation sub-threads of S_1 or S_2 match. Sequence **S** may match multiple times in one cycle or at difference cycles, depending on sequences S_1 and S_2. If sequence S_1 matches n_1 times and sequences S_2 matches n_2 times, then sequence **S** produces (n_1+n_2) matches, one for every match produced by S_1 and one for every match produced by S_2.

Termination condition: Evaluation of sequence **S** terminates when both evaluation sub-threads have completed.

Figure 15.8 shows the evaluation model of the sequence "*or*" operator. The evaluation threads for each sub-sequence is shown inside the main evaluation box for sequence **S**. As shown in the figure, sequence S_1 matches at times **3**, **8**, and **10**, and sequence S_2 matches at times **2** and **8**. Sequence **S** matches once at times **2**, **3**, **8** (two times), and **10**. The example shows that evaluation of sequence **S** continues even after evaluation sub-thread for S_2 is terminated in order to wait for evaluation of S_2 to complete.

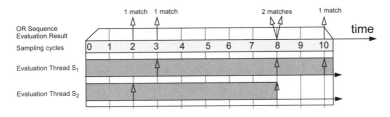

Figure 15.8 Evaluation Model of OR Sequence Operator

15.3.3.5 Sequence INTERSECT Operator

The sequence "*intersect*" operator has the following syntax:

S = S$_1$ intersect S$_2$

Match condition: Sequence **s** matches when both evaluations of **s$_1$** and **s$_2$** match in the *same* cycle. An evaluation of sequence **s** produces only one match in any cycle, regardless of how many times its operands match in that cycle. An evaluation of sequence **s** may, however, match multiple times across its lifetime. If sequence **s$_1$** matches **n$_1$** times and sequences **s$_2$** matches **n$_2$** times, then an evaluation of sequence **s** produces at most **min(n$_1$, n$_2$)** matches, and possibly no matches if matches from **s$_1$** and **s$_2$** do not overlap. The exact number of matches depends on the ordering between matches from sequence **s$_1$** and matches from sequence **s$_2$**.

Termination condition: Evaluation of sequence **s** terminates immediately if any of the evaluation sub-threads completes with either a fail or match condition. The reason is that it is no longer possible to produce a match if one of the sub-threads terminates.

Figure 15.9 shows the evaluation model of the sequence "*intersect*" operator. The evaluation threads for each sub-sequence is shown inside the main evaluation box for sequence **s**. As shown in the figure, sequence **s$_1$** matches at time **3**. Sequence **s$_2$** matches at times **2** and **8**. Sequence **s** fails when evaluation sub-thread for sequence **s$_2$** terminates. In doing so, evaluation of sequence **s$_1$** is also terminated even though it is not completed yet.

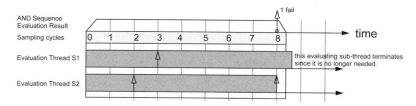

Figure 15.9 Evaluation Model of INTERSECT Sequence Operator

15.3.3.6 Sequence THROUGHOUT Operator

The sequence "*throughout*" operator has the following syntax:

S = B throughout S$_1$

This operator is used to specify that a Boolean condition must be true throughout the evaluation of sequence **s$_1$**. This operator is a composite operator and can be specified equivalently as:

S = (B) [*0:$] intersect (S$_1$)

The first part of this expression matches for zero or more occurrences of Boolean expression **B**. Sequence **s** matches if sequence **s$_1$** matches while Boolean expression **B** has been continuously valid since the evaluation started. Sequence **s** either fails or matches the same number of times that sequence **s$_1$** matches.

15.3.3.7 Sequence WITHIN Operator

The sequence "*within*" operator has the following syntax:

$S = S_1$ within S_2

This operator is used to specify that sequence S_1 must match within the period that sequence S_2 matched. As such, assuming both sequence S_1 and S_2 match, the start of evaluation for S_1 can be no sooner than the start of evaluation for S_2, and the end of evaluation for S_1 can be no later than the end of evaluation for S_2.

This operator is a composite operator and can be specified equivalently as:

$S = (1 [*0:$] ##1 (S_1) ##1 (1[*0:$]))$ intersect (S_2)

15.3.3.8 Sequence "first_match" Operator

The sequence "*first_match*" operator has the following syntax:

$S = first\_match(S_1)$

The sequence *first_match* operator is used to terminate the evaluation of sequence S_1 after its first match is detected. Sequence S can match multiple times if sequence S_1 has multiple matches in the first cycle in which its first match occurs.

This operator is used to limit the number of threads that are started in evaluating a composite sequence. Consider sequence (**first_match(S_1) ##1 S_2**) shown in figure 15.10. In this example, evaluation of sequence S_1 is terminated after its first match is identified at time **2**. Because of this termination, evaluations of S_2 at times **7** and **8** are never started. Note that if S_1 had matched twice at time **2**, then two evaluations of S_2 would have been started at that time.

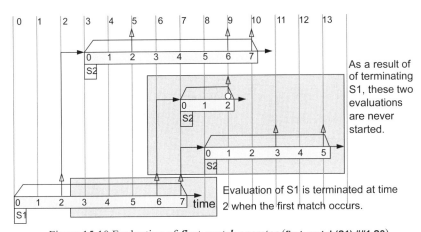

Figure 15.10 Evaluation of *first_match* operator (**first_match(S1) ##1 S2**)

15.4 SystemVerilog Properties

In SystemVerilog, design rules are described using the property construct. Properties are created by using property operators to combine sequences and properties. Both sequences and properties used to create a larger property can be either in-lined (i.e., written explicitly) or instantiated (instance of a named sequence or property). The result of a property evaluation is a true or false statement indicating whether or not the given property succeeded starting at a given point in time.

SystemVerilog property declarations are used for:

- Checking whether or not a sequence produces any match.
- Combining the results of smaller properties using property Boolean operators
- Specifying conditions for when a property should be evaluated

A SystemVerilog *base property* is one that is expressed with a single sequence (note that this sequence may in fact represent a very complex behavior)[2]. Property declarations are then used to combine the result of base properties using Boolean operators and to specify conditions for when a given property should be evaluated.

15.4.1 Property Declarations and Formal Arguments

Properties can be written in-line as part of an assertion declaration. Properties can also be declared as a *named property*, which can then be instantiated in other properties. Named property declarations are very similar to named sequence declarations in that both can include local variables and formal arguments. Named properties are, however, different from named sequences in that they cannot be used where properties are not allowed.

Consider the following example:

```
     Program 15.3: Named property declaration and instantiation
1  :   module top;
2  :       bit a, b, c, clk;
3  :       initial begin for (int i = 0; i <= 10; i++) #1 clk = !clk ; end
4  :       property P1(AA); AA [*2:4]; endproperty
5  :       sequence S1(AA); AA [*2:4]; endsequence
6  :
7  :       property valid_prop;
8  :           @(negedge clk) disable iff (reset==1'b0)  (S1(a)) |=> (P1(b));
9  :       endproperty
10 :
11 :       property invalid_prop1;
12 :           @(negedge clk) (P1(a)) |=> (P1(b)); // invalid property
13 :       endproperty
14 :
15 :       property invalid_prop2;
16 :           @(negedge clk) P1(a) ##1 S1(a); // invalid property
17 :       endproperty
18 :   endmodule
```

[2.] A base property declaration is one that does not contain any property specific operators (i.e., *not*, implication) and does not specify multiple clocks for clauses of Boolean operators (i.e., *and*, *or*).

Sequence S_1 and property P_1 have the exact same definition (lines 4, 5). However, even though property valid_prop (line 7) is a valid property, properties invalid_prop$_1$ (line 11) and invalid_prop$_2$ (line 15) are not valid. The reason is that the implication operator (line 12) accepts only sequences as an antecedent clause (section 15.4.3). Also, properties cannot be combined using sequence operators, therefore sequence operator ##1 cannot be used to combine property P_1 with sequence S_1 (line 16).

Named properties may include a *disable clause*, which contains a reset expression. If the reset expression evaluates to true between the time a property evaluation is started and when its evaluation is completed, then the property is assumed to be true. The reset expression is evaluated for every independent evaluation of a property (section 15.4.2). In the above example, property valid_prop includes a disable clause with reset expression "reset==1'b0". Disable clauses cannot be nested. In other words, a property, after collapsing all its named properties, cannot contain more than one disable clause.

Properties can be declared in the following blocks:

- Module block
- Interface block
- Clocking block
- Package
- Compilation unit scope

Named property instantiation refers to using the name of a declared property in writing other properties. Such usage is equivalent to replacing the actual declaration of a named property with the instance of that property while replacing that property's formal arguments with the actual argument provided in its instantiation.

Details of SystemVerilog properties are described in the following subsections.

15.4.2 Property Evaluation Model

Property evaluation produces either a true or false result. Evaluation of a property is said to succeed if it evaluates to true, and to fail if it evaluates to false.

Property operators fall into three categories:

- Sequence evaluation
- Implication operators
- Boolean operators

Sequence evaluation is used to check whether or not a sequence matches at least one time. A base property, used to evaluate a sequence, is declared by writing that sequence in-line or using an instance of a named sequence in the property expression. Consider a property (P_1= S_1). The evaluation of property P_1 consists of evaluating first_match(S_1) where property evaluation succeeds if sequence S_1 matches at least one time, and fails if sequence S_1 produces no match. The evaluation of a base property started at a given cycle continues until its sequence fails or matches once.

Figure 15.11 shows the abstract evaluation model of a base property (evaluating a single sequence). In this figure, evaluation of sequence S_1 is shown to match twice at times **5** and **9**.

Evaluation of property P_1 (defined as sequence S_1), however, starts at time **0** and ends at time **5** when the first match of sequence S_1 is observed. When evaluating property P_1, the evaluation of sequence S_1 is terminated after its first match is observed, since the property has already succeeded. Property P_1 would fail if sequence S_1 does not match at all. A property evaluation succeeds or fails only once. This is in contrast with sequence evaluation, where a sequence may match multiple times. As such, a property evaluation thread is identified by its start time, its end time, and its final success or fail result.

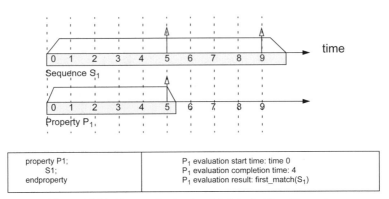

property P1; S1; endproperty	P_1 evaluation start time: time 0 P_1 evaluation completion time: 4 P_1 evaluation result: first_match(S_1)

Figure 15.11 Abstract Evaluation Model of a Base Property

A *composite property* is created by combining base properties using property operators. Figure 15.12 shows the abstract evaluation model of a composite property created by using the "*or*" property operator. As can be seen, each evaluation sub-thread is identified with a start time (which is the same as the evaluation start time for property **P**), an evaluation completion time, and a final result. In this figure, evaluation of property P_1 starts at time **0**, ends at time **10**, and succeeds. Also, evaluation of property P_2 starts at time **0**, ends at time **8**, and fails. The evaluation of the composite property ends at time **10** and succeeds. If the property operator used in this example was (P_1 **and** P_2), then the evaluation of the composite property would complete at time **8** and produce a fail result. Note that the evaluation thread of the composite property is the same as the one for a base property, in that it is identified by a start time, a completion time, and a single success or fail result. This means that the evaluation model shown in this figure can be recursively applied to base and composite properties.

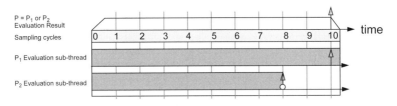

Figure 15.12 Abstract Evaluation Model of a Composite Property

As described in this section, property evaluation can be described in terms of the following aspects:

- Property evaluation start time
- Property evaluation completion time
- How property results are combined to derive the result for a composite property

Implication and Boolean property operators (section 15.4.3) will be described in terms of these aspects of property evaluation.

15.4.2.1 Evaluation Threads: Properties and Sequences

It is important to have a clear understanding of all the threads used to evaluate a composite property. A composite property evaluation consist of the following thread types

- Property evaluation thread
- Property evaluation sub-thread
- Sequence evaluation thread
- Sequence evaluation sub-thread

Consider a composite property (**P = P₁ or P₂**) created by using property operator "*or*" to combine base properties **P₁** and **P₂**. A property evaluation thread is started at every cycle of the sampling event for property **P**. Each property evaluation thread will then launch multiple property evaluation sub-threads, one for each base property **P₁** and **P₂**. Each property evaluation sub-thread will then launch a sequence evaluation thread (figure 15.12). If necessary, each sequence evaluation thread will then launch multiple sequence evaluation sub-threads for evaluating that sequence (figure 15.5). Note that the flow described for thread creation is a logical view of the evaluation process and the actual implementation may in fact be different.

15.4.2.2 Property Evaluation Start Points

At every sampling event of a property, a new evaluation of that property is started. This means that at any time—and depending on the time it takes for a property evaluation to complete—multiple evaluations of the same property started at different times may be active. This is an important concept that should be carefully understood, since the success or failure of a property reported in a cycle depends on the collective result of all evaluations running in parallel.

Figure 15.13 shows an example of how multiple evaluation threads of a property started at different cycles can lead to matches or fails at different times during the simulation runtime. Rows 5 through 11 show evaluation threads started at times **1** through **7** for each new sampling event of the property. As can be seen in this figure, at each sampling event, some evaluations may fail, some may match, and some may be in the "evaluation started" phase. For example, at time **5**, the evaluation started at time **1** succeeds, and evaluation started at time **5** fails. At time **11**, both evaluations started at times **7** and **11** fail.

Success or failure of a property at a sampling event is the result of a combination of all evaluations that complete in that sampling event. This means that in each cycle, only one

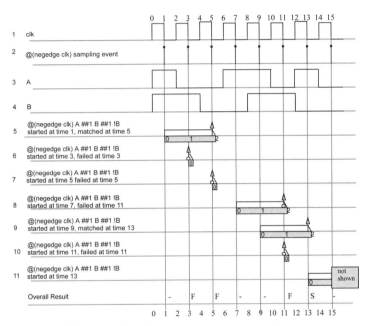

Figure 15.13 Multiple Property Evaluation Threads

result is reported for all property evaluation threads, even if multiple threads of evaluation fail or succeed in that cycle. The following rules apply to this evaluation:

- A property succeeds in a cycle, if and only if no property evaluation thread fails in that cycle and one or more property evaluation threads succeed in that cycle (time **13** in figure 15.13).
- A property fails in a cycle if and only if one or more of its evaluation threads fail in that cycle (time **5** in figure 15.13).
- In a given cycle, a property is in the "evaluation started" state if none of its evaluation threads produce a result in that cycle (time **7** in figure 15.13).

The example in figure 15.13 is based on a linear sequence, producing a single success or fail result for each evaluation thread. It is important to point out that any property, regardless of its complexity, produces only a single success or fail result, and as such, the model above can be used to compute the overall result for that property evaluation.

The following program segment based on values shown in figure 15.13, produces a match at time **13**, and fails at times **3**, **5**, and **11**.

Program 15.4: Multiple evaluation threads during property evaluation

```
            .
            .
            .
1  :        sequence s_abb;
2  :            a ##1 b ##1 !b;   // a linear sequence
3  :        endsequence
4  :
5  :        property p_abb ;
```

```
6  :              @(negedge clk) s_abb; // a base property (made up of a single sequence)
7  :         endproperty
8  :
9  :         env_prop: assert property (p_abb)
10 :              $display("PASS",,$time);
11 :         else
12 :              $display("FAIL",,$time);
                    ⋮
```

15.4.2.3 Properties and Degenerate Sequences

SystemVerilog sequences can be classified based on the number of matches they can produce. These categories are:

- Sequences that never match
- Sequences that produce only an empty match
- Sequences that produce a non-empty match

A sequence that never matches is a sequence that fails for every possible simulation trace. Some examples of sequences that never match are shown below:

S_1: (a == !a);   // never matches since the Boolean expression can never be true
S_2: (a intersect (b ##1 c)); // never matches since **intersect** operands must have the same duration

An empty match refers to a match for an empty trace[3]. An empty match is usually used to specify cases where a sub-sequence can appear zero or more times in a larger sequence. As such, the ability to define an empty match is introduced in order to allow for more concise sequence descriptions. Consider the following example:

S_1: (a) or (a ##1 b)
S_2: (a ##1 b [*0]) or (a ##1 b)
S_3: a ##1 b[*0:1]

Sequence S_1 is defined as Boolean expression (a), or Boolean expression (a) followed by Boolean expression (b) in the following cycle. Sequence S_2 makes use of the empty match sequence ([*0]b) to rewrite the description of sequence S_1 into a form that can be further simplified into sequence S_3 which is a more concise description of sequence S_1.

Sequence degeneracy is defined in terms of what number of matches a sequence admits. Table 15.3 shows the definition for degenerate and non-degenerate sequences.

Sequence Type	Admits Empty Match	Admits Non-Empty Match	Example
Strictly Degenerate	no	no	A intersect B [*2]
Degenerate	yes	no	A [*0]
Non-Degenerate	yes	yes	A [*0:2]
Strictly Non-Degenerate	no	yes	A [*1:2]

Table 15.3: Degenerate and Non-Degenerate Sequences

[3.] A simulation trace is a set of signal values in consecutive cycles (e.g., $\{a,b,c,\overline{a},\overline{b}\}$). An empty trace refers to the absence of any cycles. For example, if T_1, T_2, and T_3 are three simulation traces and trace T_2 is an empty trace, then trace $\{T_1,T_2,T_3\}$ (concatenation of these three traces) is the same as trace $\{T_1,T_3\}$.

SystemVerilog enforces the following restrictions for using sequences in writing properties:

- A sequence used to define a base property should be strictly non-degenerate.
- A sequence used as the antecedent of an overlapping implication (|->) should be non-degenerate or strictly non-degenerate. In other words, it has to admit a non-empty match.
- A sequence used as the antecedent of a non-overlapping implication (|=>) should not be strictly degenerate. In other words, it has to admit at least one match even if it is an empty match.

Overlapping and non-overlapping implication operators are further discussed in section 15.4.3.

15.4.3 Property Operators

SystemVerilog property operators are listed in table 15.4. Property operators fall into two major categories:

- Boolean operators
- Implication operators

Boolean operators are used to combine the results of their operands. Implication operators are used to control when a given property should be evaluated.

Operator Type	Operator	Associativity
Boolean	not	----
	and	left
	or	left
Implication	if-else	right
	|->	right
	|=>	right

Table 15.4: Property Operators

These operators are described in the following sections. The description of these operators is based on the property abstract evaluation model presented in section 15.4.2. Given a composite property **P** created by using a property operator to combine operand properties (e.g., in (**P** = **P₁** and **P₂**) property operator "*and*" is used to combine operand properties **P₁** and **P₂** to create property **P**), and assuming that a property evaluation thread is started at the current cycle for property **P**, each operator is described in terms of:

- Start time of property evaluation sub-threads for operands properties P_1, P_2.
- End time of evaluation thread for property **P**
- Evaluation result for property **P** as a function of evaluation results for its operands

15.4.3.1 Boolean Operators

SystemVerilog property evaluation results can be combined using the full set of Boolean operators. These include:

- "*not*" property operator
- "*and*" property operator
- "*or*" property operator

The "*not*" Boolean operator (**P: not (P₁)**) is defined as follows:

- Sub-thread start time: Evaluation sub-thread for property **P₁** is started when evaluation of property **P** is started.
- End time: Evaluation of property **P** is completed when evaluation of property **P₁** is completed.
- Result: The evaluation result for property **P** is the Boolean complement of evaluation result for property **P₁**.

The "*or*" Boolean operator (**P: P₁ or P₂**) is defined as follows:

- Sub-thread start time: Evaluation sub-threads for properties **P₁** and **P₂** are started when evaluation of property **P** is started.
- End time: Evaluation of property **P** is completed either when evaluation for both properties **P₁** and **P₂** complete (when both **P₁** and **P₂** fail) or when evaluation of either properties **P₁** or **P₂** complete (when either **P₁** or **P₂** succeed).
- Result: Property **P** succeeds if either of properties **P1** or **P2** succeed. It fails otherwise.

The "*and*" Boolean operator (**P: P₁ and P₂**) is defined as follows:

- Sub-thread start time: Evaluations of sub-threads for properties **P₁** and **P₂** are started when evaluation of property **P** is started.
- End time: Evaluation of property **P** is completed either when evaluation for both properties **P₁** and **P₂** are completed (when both **P₁** and **P₂** succeed) or when evaluation of either properties **P₁** or **P₂** complete (when either **P₁** or **P₂** fail).
- Result: Property **P** succeeds if both properties **P₁** and **P₂** succeed. It fails otherwise.

15.4.3.2 Implication Operators

The evaluation result of a property is used as a condition for other verification activity. For example, the evaluation result of a property used in an *assert* statement is used to decide whether the pass or fail statement of its action block should be executed. Under some circumstances, however, the evaluation result of a property may not be relevant to correct operation of the design and must be ignored. These conditions fall into two categories:

- Success of a property evaluation is obviated by other concurrent events in the simulation environment (e.g., a reset condition).
- Success of a property evaluation is required only when a qualifying condition has occurred.

The first category of conditions includes situations where a property evaluation has already started but concurrent circumstances make the result of that property evaluation irrelevant. For example, a property evaluation for a system bus may have already been started when a reset condition is detected. Similarly, a property evaluation for a cache coherency protocol may have already been started when the cache is flushed. In both cases, the result of the already started evaluation is no longer relevant. SystemVerilog provides the **disable** clause (section 15.4.1) to handle such situations. The evaluation of a property is terminated when the qualifying condition for the disable clause is satisfied any time after the evaluation of that property is started.

A more commonly occurring situation, however, is when the success or failure of a property is meaningful only when a qualifying condition has already occurred. Such circumstances can be identified anywhere from properties defined for individual wires of a design all the way to properties defined for system level behaviors. For example, at the bit level, the address lines of a bus must hold valid binary values only when the bus is in a read or write mode. At the system level, the burst size of a memory bus should be of a given size only when the device was initially configured to operate with that burst size. SystemVerilog provides the implication operators for specifying such conditional design behaviors.

Implication operators introduce the notion of _vacuous success_ of a property. A property that succeeds vacuously is a property whose qualifying condition is not met and, therefore, the evaluation result of the property attached to the qualifying condition is found to be irrelevant to the correct operation of the design. A vacuous success of a top level property (e.g., a property at the top level of an assert or cover statement) is treated as though that property was never evaluated. For example, if a property used in an assert statement succeeds vacuously, then neither the pass nor fail statements of that assert statement are executed. Vacuous success of properties that are used as operands to form a larger property are treated as real successes. For example, a vacuous fail of property P_1 in property P defined as (P: **not** (P_1)) results in fail of property P.

SystemVerilog provides the following implication operators:

- Overlapping implication: |->
- Non-overlapping implication: |=>
- if-else operator

Property _overlapping implication operator_ has the following form:

$P: S_1$ |-> P_1

The left-hand side operand of the overlapping implication operator is called the _antecedent_. Only sequences can be used as the antecedent expression. The right-hand side of the implication operator is called the _consequent_. Antecedent is the qualifying condition, while the consequent is the property to be evaluated. The operation of overlapping implication operator is defined as follows:

- Sub-thread start time: Evaluation sub-thread for sequence S_1 is started when evaluation thread for P is started. An evaluation thread for property P_1 is started _for every match_ of sequence S_1 and in the _same cycle_ that the match was produced.
- End time: Evaluation of property P is completed when either sequence S_1 fails, or when evaluation of sequence S_1 completes and every evaluation sub-thread that was started for property P_1 completes.
- Result: Evaluation of property P succeeds vacuously if sequence S_1 fails. Otherwise, evaluation of property P_{oi} fails if any of the evaluation threads started for property P_1 fail. Otherwise, evaluation of property P_{oi} succeeds.

Property *non-overlapping implication operator* has the following form:

P: S₁ |=> P₁

As with the overlapping implication operator, only sequences can be used as the antecedent expression. The operation of a non-overlapping implication operator is defined as follows:

- Sub-thread start time: Evaluation sub-thread for sequence **s₁** is started when evaluation thread for **P** is started. An evaluation thread for property **P₁** is started *for every match* of sequence **s₁** and in the *next cycle* that the match was produced.
- End time: Same as that for overlapping implication
- Result: Same as that for overlapping implication

The *if-else operator* has the following form:

P: if (B) P₁ [else P₂]   // else P2 is optional

Only a Boolean expression is allowed as the if-clause. The operation of an if-else operator is defined as follows:

- Sub-thread start time: Evaluation sub-thread for property **P₁** is started when evaluation thread for **P** is started and only if Boolean expression **B** evaluates to true. Evaluation sub-thread for property **P₂** is started when evaluation thread for **P** is started and only if Boolean expression **B** evaluates to false.
- End time: Evaluation of property **P** is completed when evaluation of either property **P₁** or property **P₂**, whichever was started, is completed.
- Result: Evaluation of property **P** succeeds if **B** is true and property **P₁** succeeds or **B** is false and property **P₂** succeeds. Otherwise, evaluation of property **P** fails.

Implication operators are different from other property operators in that they include an implicit requirement that the subsequent property should succeed for *every* match of the antecedent sequence. This is in contrast with base property evaluations where only the first match of a sequence leads to the property succeeding. This behavior of the implication operator can be leveraged to gain information about all matches produced by a sequence. Consider the following program segment:

```
     Program 15.5: Implication operator showing every match of consequent clause
1   :    module top;
2   :        bit a, b, c, clk;
3   :
4   :        sequence ss;
5   :            (a ##[1:$] b);
6   :        endsequence
7   :
8   :        property all_matches(tt, seq);
9   :            ($time ==tt) |-> seq |-> (1, $display(t,,$time));
10  :        endproperty
11  :
12  :        env_prop: assert property (@(negedge clk) all_matches(4, ss));
13  :    endmodule
```

In this example, property **all_matches** is defined to print the time for all matches of sequence **seq** for evaluations started at time **tt** (lines 8–10). The declaration of this property takes advantage of the overlapping implication operator. The first antecedent is used to produce a vacuous success for any time other than time **tt**. This means that property evaluation continues only for a start time of **tt**. If the current simulation time is the same as **tt**, then the evaluation of sequence **seq** is started in the same cycle (because of the use of an overlapping implication operator). Sequence **seq** is the antecedent of the next nested implication operator. As such, for every match of sequence **seq**, the consequent property is evaluated. In this case, the consequent property always succeeds, since it is simply a constant value **1**, and upon success, displays the current simulation time. Note that since an overlapping implication operator is used, the success time of property is the same as the cycle where the corresponding match for sequence **seq** was produced. Property **all_matches** is used on line **12** to print the time at which a match occurred for all matches of sequence **ss** started at time **4**.

15.5 Base Operators vs. Derived Operators

SystemVerilog provides a rich set of sequence and property operators. These operators are meant to provide an intuitive set of constructs for specifying complex behaviors. This means that some operators can be expressed in terms of other operators. This is similar to Boolean expressions where an XOR operation can be defined in terms of AND, OR, and NOT operations, but is provided as an operator since an intuitive behavior can be attached to an XOR operation.

Base sequence and property operators are shown in table 15.5. All other sequence and property operators can be defined in terms of the operators shown in this table.

Type	Name	Syntax
Sequence	Concatenation	S_1 ##1 S_2
	Fusion	S_1 ##0 S_2
	Disjunction	S_1 or S_2
	Intersect	S_1 intersect S_2
	First Match	first_match(S)
	Null Repetition	S [*0]
	Unbounded Repetition	S [1:$]
Property	Negation	not P
	Disjunction	P_1 or P_2
	Conjunction	P_1 and P_2
	Overlapping Implication	S |-> P

Table 15.5: Sequence and Property Base Operators

Tables 15.6 and 15.7 show derived sequence and property operators and their implementation in terms of base operators.

When learning SystemVerilog sequences and properties, the focus should be on learning how to use each property in an intuitive way. However, as behavior complexity grows, understanding the operation of base operators allows for better insight into how each derived operator is expected to behave.

Name	Syntax	Base Implementation
Consecutive Repeat	S [*m]	S ##1 S ... S ##1 S // repeats m times
Consecutive Repeat Range	S [*n:m]	S[*n] or S[*n+1] or...or S [*m-1] or S[*m] //m-n+1 clauses
Goto Repeat	B [->n:m]	(!B [*0:$] ##1 B) [*n:m]
Non-consecutive Repeat	B [=n:m]	(!B [*0:$] ##1 B) [*n:m] ##1 !B [*0:$]
Delay Range	S_1 ##[*n:m] S_2	S_1 ##1 1[*(n-1):(m-1)] ##1 S_2
Conjunction	S_1 and S_2	((S_1 ##1 1[*0:$]) intersect S_2) or (S_1 intersect (S_2 ##1 1[*0:$]))
Within	S_1 within S_2	(1[*0:$] ##1 S_1 ##1 1[*0:$]) intersect S_2
Throughout	B throughout S	(B [*0:$]) intersect S

Table 15.6: Sequence Derived Operators

Name	Syntax	Base Implementation
Non-overlapping Implication	S |=> P	(S ##1 1) |-> P
if	if (B) P	(B |-> P)
if-else	if (B) (P_1) else (P_2)	(B |-> P_1) and (!B |-> P_2)

Table 15.7: Property Derived Operators

15.6 Multi-Clock Sequences and Properties

In SystemVerilog, a clocked sequence or property can be created by pre-pending that sequence or property with a clocking event. In turn, these clocked sequences and properties can be combined using sequence and property operators to create multi-clocked sequences and properties. Some examples of multi-clocked sequences and properties are shown below:

```
Sc1: @(posedge clk) S1        //S1 does not include any clocking specification
Sc2: @(negedge clk) S2        //S2 does not include any clocking specification
Sc12: Sc1 ##1 Sc2
Pc12: @(posedge clk) S1 or @(negedge clk) S2
```

S_{c1} and S_{c2} are singly clocked sequences, S_{c12} is a multi-clocked sequence, and P_{c12} is a multi-clocked property (using different edges of signal **clk**).

The last clocking event in a cascaded set of clocking events overrides all previous clocking events. Sequence S_{c1} in the following example is in fact a singly clocked sequence whose behavior is equivalent to sequence S_{c2}.

```
Sc1 : @(posedge clk3) @(posedge clk2) @(posedge clk1) S1
Sc2 : @(posedge clk1) S1
```

SystemVerilog imposes restrictions on how clocked and multi-clocked sequences and properties can be created and combined using operators. All such restrictions are specified in order to enforce a set of semantic requirements on multi-clock sequences and properties.

The following section describes the semantic requirements of multi-clock sequences and properties, and the resulting restrictions on how sequence and property operators can be used.

15.6.1 Semantic Requirements

SystemVerilog imposes a set of semantic requirements on multi-clock sequences and properties. Understanding these semantic requirements clarifies the reason for restrictions on how sequence and property operators can be used to create multi-clock properties and also creates a more intuitive understanding of the types of multi-clocked sequences and properties that can be created in SystemVerilog.

SystemVerilog *multi-clock semantic requirements* are:

- *Merge rule*: All sequence evaluation sub-threads whose results are combined to compute the result of a composite sequence must be singly clocked sequences that have the same clocking event.
- *Concatenation rule*: In transitioning from one clocking event to another while evaluating a multi-clock sequence, the first cycle of a new clocking event should be strictly after the last cycle of the previous clocking event (they cannot overlap).
- *Repeat rule*: The clocking event used for the next evaluation cycle of a sequence should be strictly known. In other words, no ambiguities should exist in what the next clocking event will be.

The first requirement affects merging of concurrently running evaluation threads. For example, in evaluating sequence S_c defined as (S_{c1} **intersect** S_{c2}), both sequences S_{c1} and S_{c2} must be singly clocked sequences that are clocked using the same clocking event. The reason is that the evaluation results of S_{c1} and S_{c2} are combined to decide whether or not sequence S_c matches or fails.

The second requirement affects how sequences and properties can be concatenated. Consider the following examples where S_1 and S_2 are un-clocked sequences:

S_{c1}: @(clk$_1$) S_1
S_{c2}: @(clk$_2$) S_2
SS_{c1}: S_{c1} ##1 S_{c2} //legal
SS_{c2}: S_{c1} ##0 S_{c2} //illegal
PP_{c1}: S_{c1} |-> S_{c2} //illegal
PP_{c2}: S_{c1} |=> S_{c2} //legal
PP_{c3}: @(clk1) S_1 |-> (@(clk1) S_3 ##1 @(clk2) S_2) //legal

In the above examples, SS_{c2} is not a valid multi-clocked sequence. The reason is that in using the fusion operator (##0), the first evaluation cycle of S_{c2} overlaps the last evaluation cycle of S_{c1}, requiring that the clocking event for the last cycle of S_{c1} to be the same as the clocking event for the first cycle of S_{c2}. And this requirement is violated since S_{c1} and S_{c2} use different clocking events. Similarly, property PP_{c1} is an invalid multi-clocked property. The reason is that in using the overlapping implication operator (|->), the first evaluation of sequence S_{c2} starts in the last evaluation cycle of sequence S_{c1} and this violates the concatenation requirement since S_{c1} and S_{c2} use different clocking events. Property PP_{c3} is, however, a legal multi-clocked property since the consequent clause is a valid multi-clocked sequence, and also the sampling event of the first cycle of consequent (i.e., clk$_1$) is the same as the clocking event of the last cycle of the antecedent (clk$_1$).

The third requirement affects how repeat operators can be used in concatenating sequences. For example, assuming sequences S_{c1} and S_{c2} are singly clocked sequences with different clocking events, sequence S_c defined as (S_{c1} ##1 S_{c2}) is an invalid sequence if sequence S_{c2} permits empty matches (e.g., S_{c2} = A[*0:1]). In this case, upon an empty match of sequence S_{c2}, it is not clear whether the last cycle of S_c ends on the clocking event for sequence S_{c1} or the clocking event for sequence S_{c2}.

The semantic requirements discussed above impose restrictions on the clocking properties of the operands to sequence and property operators. These restrictions are summarized in table 15.8.

Type	Name	Syntax	
Sequence	Concatenation	S_{c1} ##1 S_{c2}	No Restrictions
	Fusion	S_{c1} ##0 S_{c2}	$LCLK(S_{c1}) = FCLK(S_{c2})$
	Disjunction	S_{c1} or S_{c2}	Both singly clocked. $CLK(S_{c1}) = CLK(S_{c2})$
	Conjunction	S_{c1} and S_{c2}	Both singly clocked. $CLK(S_{c1}) = CLK(S_{c2})$
	Intersect	S_{c1} intersect S_{c2}	Both singly clocked. $CLK(S_{c1}) = CLK(S_{c2})$
	Within	S_{c1} within S_{c2}	Both singly clocked. $CLK(S_{c1}) = CLK(S_{c2})$
	Throughout	B_c throughout S_c	S_c singly clocked. $CLK(B_c) = CLK(S_c)$
	First Match	first_match(S_c)	No Restrictions
	Null Repetition	S_c [*0]	Only allowed when clocking events for the previous and next sequences are the same as $CLK(S_c)$
	Unbounded Repetition	S_c [1:$]	No Restrictions
Property	Negation	not P_c	No Restrictions
	Disjunction	P_{c1} or P_{c2}	No Restrictions
	Conjunction	P_{c1} and P_{c2}	No Restrictions
	Overlapping Implication	S_c |-> P_c	$LCLK(S_c) = FCLK(P_c)$
	Non-overlapping Implication	S_c |=> P_c	No Restrictions
	if	if (B_c) P_c	$CLK(B_c) = FCLK(P_c)$
	if-else	if (B_c) (P_{c1}) else (P_c)	$CLK(B_c) = FCLK(P_{c1}) = FCLK(P_{c2})$

B_c is a clocked Boolean expression, S_c is a clocked sequence, Pc is a clocked property
$CLK(S_c)$: Clocking event for singly clocked sequence S_c
$FCLK(S_c)$: Clocking event for the first cycle of multiple-clocked sequence S_c
$LCLK(S_c)$: Clocking event for the last cycle of multiple-clocked sequence S_c

Table 15.8: Multi-Clock Rules for Sequence and Property Operators

The following observations summarize the restrictions listed in this table:

- The concatenation sequence operator can be used to combine any singly or multi-clocked sequences.
- The clocking event for the first cycle of the second term in the fusion sequence operator should be the same the clocking event for the last cycle of its first term.
- All operand sequences for sequence disjunction, conjunction, intersect, within, and throughout operators must be singly clocked sequences that have the same clocking event.
- Null sequence repetition can be used only in places where a null match does not result in ambiguity about the next clocking event. This means that the clocking event of the last cycle before a null match and the clocking event of the first cycle after a

possible null match should be the same clock.

- Property Boolean operators can be used to combine singly or multiple clocked properties with no restrictions. The reason is that property Boolean operators depend on only the true or false result of each operand, and exact timing of their evaluation is not relevant to the final result.
- For an overlapping implication property operator, the first cycle of the consequent overlaps with the last cycle of the antecedent. As such, the clocking event for the first cycle of the consequent must be the same as the last clocking cycle of the antecedent.

15.7 Sequence and Property Dictionary

Describing a design property consists of two steps:

- Using the sequence construct to specify design behaviors
- Using the property construct to specify the allowed relationship between behaviors described using sequences

These topics are covered in the following sections.

15.7.1 Sequence Dictionary

Design behaviors are described using sequences. Two types of elements are used in describing a sequence:

- Condition: A condition is described by a Boolean expression. It takes zero time to evaluate, and therefore has no beginning and no end time.
- Behavior: A behavior is described by a sequence. A behavior takes more than one evaluation cycle to complete and as such has a beginning cycle and an end cycle.

The use of one multi-cycle behavior in describing a more complex behavior should be clear as to the intended relationship between the timing between these behaviors. Consider a bus read operation that takes multiple cycles to complete and has a start time and an end time. For some behaviors, only the end time of this bus read cycle is relevant. For example, the starting cycle of the bus read operation or how many cycles it took is not relevant to the expected behavior that "a read-reply operation should take place only after a bus read cycle has occurred." For other behaviors, however, the start time and duration of the bus read operation must be known. For example, the starting cycle and duration of a bus read operation is relevant to the expected behavior that "signal **rd** should be active throughout a bus read cycle."

If only the end time of a sub-behavior is relevant in describing a more complex behavior, it is a good practice to separate the evaluation of this sub-behavior from the evaluation of the more complex behavior. This can be accomplished by using either SystemVerilog's predefined sequence methods (i.e., *ended()*, *matched()*, *triggered()*), or by using the action block of a property that evaluates the sub behavior to set an appropriate flag. In either case, the effect of this separation is that the success of failure of a sub-behavior can be treated as a condition that takes zero time to evaluate, thereby reducing the complexity that must be dealt with in writing sequences.

Examples of common design behaviors and their corresponding implementation using sequences are described in the following subsections.

15.7.1.1 Sequences Based on One Condition

The following behaviors depend on a single condition. Condition **B** in the following behaviors can be any valid sequence Boolean expression (section 15.2).

Condition **B** holds for one cycle

This behavior states that condition **B** is observed for one cycle. The use of this sequence in a property with a sampling clock implies that this condition must hold for every occurrence of the property sampling clock.

Sequence:
    (B)

Condition **B** holds for exactly **N** cycles

This behavior states that condition **B** holds for **N** evaluation cycles but not for more than **N** cycles.

Sequence:
    (B) [*N] ##1 !(B)

Condition **B** holds for at least **N** cycles

This behavior states that condition **B** holds for **N** evaluation cycles and the condition may or may not repeat in the following cycles.

Sequence:
    (B) [*N]

Condition **B** holds for at most **N** cycles

This behavior states that condition **B** holds for any number of cycles between **0** and **N** consecutive cycles but not after that.

Sequence:
    (B) [*0:N] ##1 !(B)

Condition **B** holds for [N₁:N₂] cycles

This behavior states that condition **B** holds for anywhere between N_1 to N_2 consecutive cycles but not more than N_2 cycles.

Sequence:
    (B)[*N1:N2] ##1 !(B)

Condition **B** occurs within **M** cycles from now

This behavior states that condition **B** holds once within the next **M** cycles.

Sequence:
    (1) ##[0:M] (B)

Condition B occurs within M cycles from now and then holds for at least N cycles

This behavior states that the first occurrence of condition **B** is within the next **M** cycles and it holds for **N** consecutive cycles after its first occurrence.

Sequence:
(1) ##[0:M] (B)[*N]

Condition B occurs [M$_1$:M$_2$] cycles from now and then holds for [N$_1$:N$_2$] cycles

This behavior states that even if condition **B** occurs in the first **M$_1$** cycles, it also occurs within **M$_1$** to **M$_2$** cycles and after this occurrence, it holds for **N$_1$** to **N$_2$** consecutive cycles.

Sequence:
(1) ##[M1:M2] (B)[*N1:N2]

Condition B occurs first within [M$_1$:M2] cycles and then holds for [N$_1$:N$_2$] cycles

This behavior states that condition **B** does not occur in the first **M$_1$** cycle and it does occur within **M$_1$** to **M$_2$** cycles, and after this occurrence, it holds for **N$_1$** to **N$_2$** consecutive cycles.

Sequence:
!(B) [*M1:M2] ##1 (B)[*N1:N2]

Condition B occurs exactly N times

This behavior states that condition **B** occurs exactly **N** times but not necessarily in consecutive evaluation cycles. This sequence makes use of the goto repeat operator.

Sequence:
(B)[->N] ##1 !(B)[0:$]

Condition B occurs exactly N times within the next M cycles

This behavior states that condition **B** occurs exactly N times in the next **M** cycles but not necessarily in consecutive evaluation cycles.

Sequence:
((1)[*M]) intersect ((B)[->N] ##1 !(B)[0:$])

15.7.1.2 Sequences Based on Two Conditions

The following behaviors depend on two conditions. Conditions **B$_1$** and **B$_2$** in the following behaviors can be any valid sequence Boolean expression (section 15.2).

Conditions B$_1$ and B$_2$ occur only in the same cycle

This behavior states that conditions **B$_1$** and **B$_2$** always evaluate to the same value. This condition is implemented using an equivalence operator.

Sequence:
(B1) == (B2)

At least one of conditions B$_1$ or B$_2$ occurs in the next M cycles

This behavior states that in the next **M** cycles, one of conditions **B$_1$** and **B$_2$** evaluate to true. The use of a Boolean OR operator to combine conditions **B$_1$** and **B$_2$** indicates that the implementation shown here can easily be extended to any number of conditions.

Sequence:
((B1) || (B2))[*M]

Condition B₁ occurs before condition B₂ occurs

This behavior states that conditions B_1 and B_2 both occur but condition B_2 does not occur before condition B_1. The implementation shown here provides an open-ended range where conditions B_1 and B_2 can occur within any number of evaluation cycles.

Sequence:
```
!(B2) [*0:$] ##0 (B1) ##[1:$] (B2)
```

Condition B₁ occurs within the next N₁ cycles, and within N₂ cycles before B₂ occurs

This behavior states that conditions B_1 and B_2 both occur but condition B_2 does not occur before condition B_1. The implementation shown here provides a closed range where conditions B_1 must occur within N_1 cycles and condition B_2 must occur within N_2 cycles after condition B_1 occurs.

Sequence:
```
!(B2) [*0:N1] ##0 (B1) ##[1:N2] (B2)
```

Condition B₂ does not occur before condition B₁ occurs

This behavior states only that condition B_2 does not occur before condition B_1 occurs. It does not require that condition B_2 occurs after condition B_1 has occurred.

Sequence:
```
!(B2) [*0:$] ##1 (B1)
```

Condition B₁ occurs before and holds until condition B₂ occurs

This behavior states that both conditions B_1 and B_2 occur, and that B_1 occurs before condition B_2, and that once B_1 occurs, it holds until condition B_2 occurs.

Sequence:
```
(B1) [*1:$] ##0 (B2)
```

Condition B₁ occurs before and holds until N cycles after condition B₂ occurs

This behavior states that both conditions B_1 and B_2 occur, and that B_1 occurs before condition B_2, and that once B_1 occurs, it holds until N cycles after condition B_2 occurs.

Sequence:
```
(B1) [*1:$] ##0 (B2) ##1 (B1) [*N]
```

Conditions B₁ and B₂ occur exactly N times each within the next M cycles

This behavior states that conditions B_1 and B_2 each occur N times within the next M cycles. It does not, however, require that the occurrence of each condition be in any specific order or that the occurrences of each condition be consecutive.

Sequence:
```
((1)[*M]) intersect (((B1)[->N] ##1 !(B1)[0:$]) and ((B2)[->N] ##1 !(B2)[0:$]))
```

15.7.1.3 Sequences Based on Multi-Cycle Behaviors

The following behaviors depend on a condition and a multi-cycle behavior. Condition B in the following behaviors can be any valid sequence Boolean expression (section 15.2). Behavior S can be any valid sequence.

Behavior S₁ starts and ends while behavior S₂ is taking place

This behavior states that sub-behaviors s_1 and s_2 both occur, but the start time of s_1 is at the same time or after the start time of s_2, and that the end time of s_1 is before or at the same time as the end time for s_2.

    Sequence:
        (S1) within (S2)

Condition B occurs exactly N times while behavior S is taking place

This behavior states that from the start of evaluation to the end of evaluation of sub-behavior s, condition B occurs exactly N times and not more than N times.

    Sequence:
        ((B)[->N] ##1 !(B)[0:$]) within (S)

Condition B holds during the last N cycles of behavior S taking place

This behavior states that condition B occurs in N consecutive evaluation cycles with the last cycle being the same as the end cycle for evaluation of sub-behavior s.

    Sequence:
        ((1) ##[0:$] (B)[*N]) intersect (S)

Condition B holds during the first N cycles of behavior S taking place

This behavior states that condition B occurs in N consecutive evaluation cycles with the first cycle being the same as the first cycle for evaluation of sub-behavior s.

    Sequence:
        ((B)[*N] ##1 (1) ##[0:$]) intersect (S)

Condition B holds while behavior S is taking place

This behavior states that condition B holds from the first cycle the evaluation of sub-behavior s is started until the cycle in which the evaluation of sub-behavior s ends.

    Sequence:
        (B) throughout (S)

15.7.2 Property Dictionary

The challenging part of writing a property is in turning the description of relevant behaviors into sequences. Once each intended behavior is described with a sequence, writing properties is as simple as deciding the qualifying behavior (to be used as the antecedent clause), the qualified behavior (to be used as the consequent clause), and the relative timing between these behaviors (to determine the implication operator type).

As an example, consider the property "If condition B_1 occurs before and holds until condition B_2, then conditions B_3 and B_4 occur exactly N times each within the following M cycles." The implementation of this property is given by:

    (B1) [*1:$] ##0 (B2) |->
        ((1)[*M]) intersect ((((B3)[->N] ##1 !(B3)[0:$]) and ((B4)[->N] ##1 !(B4)[0:$]))

This seemingly complex property is easily implemented by using the appropriate implementations for the qualifying and qualified behaviors, as shown in section 15.7.1, for antecedent and consequent clauses of the property implication operator.

Examples of common design properties and their corresponding implementation using the SystemVerilog property construct are shown in the following subsections. Given these implementations, many design properties can be expressed by the combination of sequences shown in section 15.7.1 and property implementation shown in this section.

15.7.2.1 Properties using a Condition as a Qualifying Condition

Condition B must always hold

```
property prop;
        @(posedge clk) disable iff (reset) B;
endproperty
```

If condition B_1 occurs, then condition B_2 must occur in the next cycle

```
property prop;
        @(posedge clk) disable iff (reset) B1 |=> B2;
endproperty
```

If condition B_1 occurs, then condition B_2 must occur in the same cycle

```
property prop;
        @(posedge clk) disable iff (reset) B1 |-> B2;
endproperty
```

If condition B has occurred, then evaluation of behavior S started in the next cycle after B occurred must succeed

```
property prop1;
        @(posedge clk) disable iff (reset) B |=> S;
endproperty
```

If condition B has occurred, then evaluation of behavior S started in the same cycle that B occurred must succeed

```
property prop1;
        @(posedge clk) disable iff (reset) B |-> S;
endproperty
```

15.7.2.2 Properties using a Multi-Cycle Behavior as a Qualifier

If behavior S succeeds, then condition B must occur in the next cycle after S succeeded

```
property prop;
        @(posedge clk) disable iff (reset) S |=> B;
endproperty
```

If behavior S succeeds, then condition B must occur in the same cycle that S succeeded

```
property prop1;
        @(posedge clk) disable iff (reset) S |-> B;
endproperty
```

If behavior S_1 succeeds, then evaluation of behavior S_2 started in the next cycle after S_1

succeeded must also succeed

```
property prop1;
    @(posedge clk) disable iff (reset) S1 |=> S2;
endproperty
```

If behavior S₁ succeeds, then evaluation of behavior S₂ started in the same cycle that S₁ succeeded must also succeed

```
property prop1;
    @(posedge clk) disable iff (reset) S1 |-> S2;
endproperty
```

15.7.2.3 Properties Used for Debugging Sequences

These properties are used to help in debugging named sequences.

Print evaluation end time of all matches for sequence S whose evaluation started in time range [T₁:T₂]

This property is used to print the evaluation end time of all matches for sequence S whose evaluation started between time T₁ and T₂ for a named sequence S.

```
property all_matches_starting_between(seq, t1, t2);
    time start_time;
    ($time <=t2 && $time>= t1, start_time = $time) |-> seq |-> (1, $display(start_time, $time));
endproperty
```

This property can be used as follows in an assertion statement for a previously defined named sequence **S**:

```
debug_assert: assert property (
    @(posedge clk)   all_matches_starting_between(ss, 2, 40)
);
```

The clocking event specified for the assert statement should be the same as the clocking event for the first cycle of sequence **ss**.

Print evaluation start time of all matches for sequence S that are matched in time range [T₁:T₂]

This property is used to print the evaluation start time of all matches produced between time T₁ and T₂ for a named sequence **S**.

```
property all_matches_produced_between(seq, t1, t2);
    time start_time;
    ($time <=t2, start_time = $time) |-> seq
                |-> ($time>=t1 && $time <=t2) |-> (1, $display(start_time, $time));
endproperty
```

This property is can be used as follows in an assertion statement for a previously defined named sequence **ss**:

```
debug_assert: assert property (
    @(posedge clk)   all_matches_produced_between(ss, 10, 16)
);
```

The clocking event specified for the assert statement should be the same as the clocking event for the first cycle of sequence **ss**.

CHAPTER 16

Assertion-Based Verification (ABV)

An important observation about functional verification is that design properties that must be verified remain the same as the design implementation progresses through different levels of abstraction, regardless of what verification tools and methodologies are used to carry out the verification tasks. Regardless of design flow (top-down or bottom-up), properties that must be verified accumulate. For example, in a top-down design style starting from the architectural specification, a property that must be held at the architectural level, must still be maintained when the detailed block level design is created. And in a bottom-up design style where individual blocks are created first, a micro-code design implementation property that had to be maintained during block level design must still hold when blocks are combined to create the complete system.

These observations lead to the straightforward conclusion that the use of a robust and practical mechanism for specifying, modeling, and collecting such properties throughout the design process leads to immediate gains in verification completeness (i.e, all scenarios are verified), correctness (i.e., each scenario is verified correctly), and productivity. Completeness is improved because of the accumulating nature of these properties throughout the design and verification process. Correctness is improved because these properties will be verified using multiple verification technologies during the full verification cycle (e.g., formal verification, simulation, acceleration and emulation) and at different levels of design abstraction. Productivity improves both directly, as result of using well-defined procedures for specifying and verifying properties, and indirectly as a result of improvements in verification completeness and correctness. *Assertion-based verification (ABV) methodology* describes the tools, techniques, and best-in-class practices that allow the benefits of this approach to be realized.

The enabling technology for assertion-based verification is a powerful mechanism for specifying design properties. SystemVerilog provides the sequence and property constructs to describe design properties in a concise and expressive manner. These constructs were described in chapter 15. This chapter describes the approach used for identifying and organizing assertions, and deploying assertion-based verification using SystemVerilog.

16.1 Assertion Definition Flow

Two questions must be answered when defining the set of assertions for a DUV:

- Who should identify the asserted properties?
- When should these asserted properties be identified?

DUV behavior is the collective effect of its properties at all levels of abstraction (e.g., transaction level, RTL) and in all levels of the design hierarchy (e.g., module, block). It is therefore clear that an effective assertion definition strategy must include all actors involved in the design, verification, and implementation, and must span the complete design life cycle. This section describes guidelines for the type of feedback that should be provided by each project participant and the type of information that should be collected during each phase of the design process.

16.1.1 Participants and Roles

Both designers and verification engineers must participate in defining the set of assertions. The general trend is that design engineers contribute fine-grain assertions that describe low level properties of design signals and blocks. And verification engineers contribute abstract assertions that relate more to the end-to-end operation of the design. The following discussion provides general guidelines that design and verification engineers must follow in defining assertions related to their respective activities.

A block designer continuously makes assumptions about the operating environment of blocks, using these assumptions to decide how to implement low level design features, and considering what it means for the implemented features to work as expected. When participating in assertion definition, a block designer's goal should be to capture this thought process as it takes place. The reason is that only the block designer has specific knowledge of these assumptions, low level design decisions, and relevant verification scenarios. And if the block designer does not capture this knowledge as it takes shape, then it either has to be reverse engineered by verification engineers or re-discovered by the designer at a later time. To capture this thought process, assertions defined by a block designer must reflect the following information (section 16.1.2.2):

- Assumptions made about the block operating environment
- Properties of the interaction between block ports and the outside environment
- Properties of the interaction between sub-blocks
- Properties that define predictable error conditions
- Coverage points for corner cases and tricky areas of the design
- Coverage points for state machine transitions that are less frequently traversed

System design engineers focus on transaction level behavior and end-to-end behavior of a design. As such, assertions defined by system design engineers must reflect the transaction level and end-to-end behavior of a DUV (section 16.1.2.1). Implementation engineers may modify the design to satisfy design constraints (e.g., introducing a multi-cycle path to meet timing constraints). Assertions defined by implementation engineers must describe properties that should be satisfied by these specialized design implementations.

A verification engineer's focus is more on features extracted from the design specification and less on how these features are implemented. Not all design properties are suitable for assertion-based verification. Data oriented scenarios are best verified using scoreboarding techniques whereas control oriented properties are better candidates for assertion-based verification. A verification engineer should decide on the design properties that are best verified using assertions. Block level verification engineers can identify assumptions and properties relevant to the local blocks they work on, and system level verification engineers can focus on end-to-end scenarios and system-wide properties. In addition to local and end-to-end verification scenarios that can be verified through assertions, verification engineers must also define assertions about the following types of information (section 16.1.2.3 and 16.1.2.4):

- Assumptions made about the verification environment
- Properties defining correct DUV configuration
- Properties defining valid combinations of configuration and control registers, status registers, and DUV pin values
- Properties for standard DUV interfaces

16.1.2 Assertions and Project Phases

Different types of properties should be considered during each phase of the design flow. These phases are:

- Architectural design
- Block design and verification
- Cluster/chip integration and verification
- System integration and verification

Considerations relevant to each phase are discussed in the following sections.

16.1.2.1 Architectural Design

There is usually very little detailed information available during architectural design. As such, properties derived from design specification at this stage are fairly abstract and consist mostly of end-to-end design behaviors. The execution model of the design at this stage, if available, consists of a transaction level model described at a high granularity level built in SystemC. Assertions at this level of abstraction are, therefore, described at the transaction level.

16.1.2.2 Block Design and Verification

Formal verification is used to verify assertions specified during the block design phase. The main reason for this usage is that there is usually no simulation environment available when blocks are being designed and in fact multiple blocks must be attached together before a simulation environment can be built.

Given the limitations inherent in formal verification, it may not be possible to evaluate all assertions specified during block level design. These assertions must be marked and considered for evaluation when the block under consideration is being verified as part of a larger module or chip using a simulation environment.

The natural order of execution for block related verification is as follows:

- Bring-up checks
  - Reset stuck
  - Clock not active
- Interface verification
- Operational mode verification
  - Control registers
  - Mode pins
- Internal functionality verification
  - Operational modes are considered assumptions during formal verification.
  - Assertions are specified for each operational mode.
- End-to-end functionality verification

Bring-up checks cover design conditions that must be satisfied before the block can operate correctly. Examples include reset lines and clock connections.

Interface verification is considered next. The block can operate only if it can communicate with its enclosing environment. Depending on the interface complexity, it may not be possible to specify all interface properties as assertions. And not all assertions specified at block level may be verifiable by the formal verification tool. All such interface properties must be marked for consideration in the simulation environment.

A block can usually operate in different modes through control register settings or mode pins. The formal verification tool's ability to verify assertions improves with an increasing number of assumptions and decreasing assertion complexity. Using block operation modes as assumptions to the formal verification tool allows more assertions to be covered by the formal verification tool. In this approach, assertions for block properties are specified separately for each operating mode.

Internal functionality is considered next. Internal functionality is specified for each set of operating and interface modes. End-to-end behavior of a block may not be a good candidate for assertion-based verification because such properties are usually data-path oriented behaviors. As such, such properties are best verified in the simulation environment. However, end-to-end properties that can be specified using assertions should be considered in this stage of verification.

16.1.2.3 Cluster/Chip Integration and Verification

In this phase, individual blocks designed in the previous phase are grouped together to form clusters and chip level designs. The focus of verification at this stage is mostly on verifying correct communication between blocks and that the operating environment of each block is as expected. Assertions added at this stage should check the following properties:

- Environmental assumptions for each block are satisfied
- Each block operating mode and configuration is valid
- Interactions between blocks follow assumptions made at the block level
- Properties that could not be checked during block level design

- Properties about the overall function of the cluster

Assertions specified for these properties are either inherited from the block level design or are added because of functionality provided by the increased level of integration. A simulation-based environment is used at this level to collect coverage and to make sure no assertions fail.

16.1.2.4 System Integration and Verification

The increasing complexity of a design at the system level requires the use of hardware acceleration and emulation systems. Assertions added at this level are similar in nature to the ones added during chip and cluster creation, where in this case, clusters are connected to form a complete system. An additional consideration in this phase is the ability to evaluate assertions using the acceleration and emulation systems. Generally, acceleration and emulation systems can handle the same assertions as formal verification and simulation tools, and tool vendors provide the ability to compile assertions to be evaluated on such systems.

16.2 Assertions vs. Assumptions

Both assumptions and assertions define properties that must be satisfied by signal values of a design block. *Assumptions* are, however, statements about the operating environment of a block, while assertions are statements about how a block should operate under the given assumptions.

Assumptions are an important consideration when using a formal verification tool. To better understand this need for assumptions, consider the example shown in figure 16.1. This example shows a block with three inputs **A**, **B**, and **C**, and two outputs **D** and **E**. It also gives property P_1 for the input signals, and property P_2 for the output signals. A formal verification tool operates by first computing the equation describing the relationship between the output signals and then proving that property P_2 is always satisfied by the equation describing this relationship between the output signals (see example in section 1.4.1.2). Property P_1 defines a relationship that must be maintained between the input signals and as such, can be used to identify input combinations that will never occur (i.e., input don't care conditions). If property P_1 is not considered during this proof construction, then property P_2 must hold for all possible combinations of input variables (i.e., area **Dom** in figure 16.1). However, in reality, property P_2 need to be satisfied only for valid combination of the input signals as described by property P_1 (i.e., area **Dom$_A$** in figure 16.1). This means that not including property P_1 as an assumption during formal verification of property P_2 can lead to false assertion failures for combinations of the input signals that never occur.

Assumptions can be *over-specified* or *under-specified*. An over-specified set of assumptions (area **Dom$_o$** in figure 16.2) does not include all input space combinations for which design properties must hold. This means that an over-specified set of assumptions may lead the formal verification engine to miss and not report a failed property. An under-specified set of assumptions (area **Dom$_u$** in figure 16.2) includes input space combinations that never occur. This means that an under-specified set of assumptions may lead to the formal verifica-

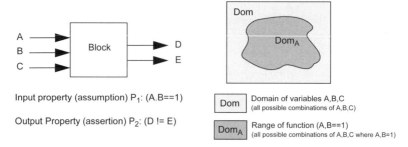

Input property (assumption) P$_1$: (A.B==1)

Output Property (assertion) P$_2$: (D != E)

Dom — Domain of variables A,B,C
(all possible combinations of A,B,C)

Dom$_A$ — Range of function (A,B=1)
(all possible combinations of A,B,C where A,B=1)

Figure 16.1 Assumptions and Formal Verification of Assertions

tion engine falsely reporting assertion failures for input space combinations that never occur. Not including assumptions during formal verification is an extreme case of having an under-specified set of assumptions. As an example, using property (**A.B.C==1**) instead of property (**A.B==1**) as an assumption for the example in figure 16.1 leads to having an over-specified assumption where the formal verification engine may not report a failed assertion when (**A.B.$\overline{\text{C}}$=1**). Alternatively, using property (**A==1**) as an assumption for the example in figure 16.1 leads to having an under-specified assumption where the formal verification engine may falsely report the failure of an assertion for the impossible case when (**A.$\overline{\text{B}}$=1**). During formal verification, it is, therefore, important that assumptions made about any property are carefully examined before being added to the verification environment.

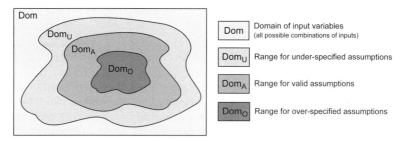

Dom — Domain of input variables
(all possible combinations of inputs)

Dom$_U$ — Range for under-specified assumptions

Dom$_A$ — Range for valid assumptions

Dom$_O$ — Range for over-specified assumptions

Figure 16.2 Over-Specified vs. Under-Specified Assumptions

Assumptions and assertions take alternating roles when verifying each one of a set of interacting blocks. Figure 16.3 shows two interacting blocks **B$_1$** and **B$_2$**. When verifying block **B$_1$**, properties defined for the output port of **B$_1$** are verified while considering properties defined on its input port as assumptions. The situation is reversed when verifying block **B$_2$** where properties on block **B$_2$**'s output are now verified with properties on its input considered as assumptions.

Differentiating between assumptions and assertions is not necessary when using a simulation tool. The reason is that a simulation tool verifies an assertion by computing the values of all signals used in that assertion, and these computed values already reflect any properties or assumptions that must be satisfied anywhere else in the design.

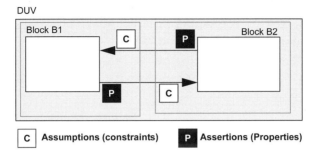

Figure 16.3 Interchanging Roles of Assumptions and Assertions

16.3 SystemVerilog Assertions

In SystemVerilog, assertions can be activated using different mechanisms. In addition, SystemVerilog provides system tasks that allow the programmer to assign different severity (i.e., warning, error, info) to assertions and to also control the behavior and logging of assertions. These topics are discussed in the following subsections.

16.3.1 Assertion Activation

SystemVerilog provides three methods for activating and evaluating assertions:

- Immediate assertions
- Concurrent assertions
- Procedural assertions

Immediate assertions are used for non-temporal properties (i.e., only Boolean expressions are allowed) within procedural code. Concurrent assertions are instantiated in a module, program, or interface (in parallel with procedural blocks) where a new evaluation of the asserted property is started at every new sampling event for that assertion. Procedural assertions follow the same semantics as concurrent assertions but can be embedded in procedural code under special considerations. These assertions types are described in the following subsections.

16.3.1.1 Immediate Assertions

Immediate assertions are used to check for non-temporal behaviors. This means that only Boolean expressions can be used to define a property checked by immediate assertions. Immediate assertions can be placed anywhere procedural code is allowed, using the following syntax:

```
[ label ] assert boolean_expression [action_block];
```

An immediate assertion is evaluated immediately when it is reached in the procedural code. If **action_block** is not defined, then *$error* system task is called when **boolean_expression** evaluates to false and no action is taken when **boolean_expression** evaluates to true. The default behavior for pass and fail of this assertion can be changed by defining the **action_block**.

An example of an immediate assertion is shown in the following code fragment.

```
Program 16.1:  Immediate Assertion Statement

           :
           :
1    :    always @(negedge clk) begin
2    :          assert(m_task === `read_memory || m_task === `write_memory)
3    :                if(done) $display("%t Finished command %b",$time,last_task);
4    :          else
5    :                $error("Unsupported memory task command %b",m_task);
6    :    end
           :
           :
```

Immediate assertions are also useful for checking issues that may arise during program execution. The following example shows how an immediate assertion is used to check that the *randomize()* function produces valid results:

```
Program 16.2:  Checking program behavior using immediate assertions

           :
           :
1    :    always @(negedge clk) begin
2    :          rand_value_randomize_ok: assert (randomize(rand_value))
3    :                else $fatal(1, "Randomization failed for variable rand_value");
4    :    end
           :
           :
```

16.3.1.2 Concurrent Assertions

Concurrent assertions allow for continuous checking of a property while simulation is in progress. A new evaluation of a concurrent assertion is started for every new sampling event of its property definition, leading to multiple concurrent evaluations of a multi-cycle property. As such, a concurrent assertion is used to continuously monitor a given design property. Concurrent assertions can be specified for Boolean expressions as well as properties spanning multiple cycles. Concurrent assertions are placed inside modules, program blocks, or interfaces in parallel with procedural blocks (e.g., always block).

Concurrent assertions have the following general syntax:

[label] directive property (property_expression) [action_block];

SystemVerilog provides the following directives for concurrent assertions:

- *assert*
- *assume*
- *cover*

The *assert* directive is used to specify a property as a checker to make sure that the property holds for the design. Both formal verification and simulation tools check that assertions defined with the **assert** directive are checked and any failed evaluations are reported. The syntax is:

[label] assert property (property_expression) [action_block];

The **assume** directive is used to specify an assumption about the operating environment of the design. Formal verification tools do not check properties defined using the **assume** directive. Rather, such properties are used for verifying the properties that must be solved by the formal verification engine. Simulation tools, however, treat assertions defined using the **assume** directive the same as those defined with the **assert** directive. Note that no **action_block** is allowed for this directive. Syntax for this directive is:

[label] assume property (property_expression);

The **cover** directive is used to include the results of assertion evaluation in coverage results. A pass statement can be specified for this directive, which will be evaluated when the property succeeds.

[label] cover property (property_expression) [pass_statement];

The following code fragment shows examples of these concurrent assertion types:

```
Program 16.3:  Concurrent assertion directives
                      ⋮

1   :        property assert_prop;
2   :             @(posedge (clk)) (a ##1 b);
3   :        endproperty
4   :        assert property (assert_prop) else -> error_detected;
5   :
6   :        property assume_prop;
7   :             @(posedge (d)) (a ##1 b);
8   :        endproperty
9   :        p3_label: assume property (assume_prop);
10  :
11  :        property cover_prop;
12  :             @(posedge clk) a |=> b ##2 c;
13  :        endproperty
14  :        cover property (cover_prop) $display("Covering C1");
                      ⋮
```

16.3.1.2.1 Procedural Assertions

Procedural assertions are similar to concurrent assertions but are placed inside procedural code and are evaluated when program control flow reaches the assertion.

Procedural assertions require that:

- If property has no explicit clocking event, then one is inferred from the procedural block. This inference requires that the first term in the event control of the procedural block be defined using a *posedge* or *negedge* specifier, and that the variables used in the expression for this specifier are not used in the body of the procedural block.
- If property has an explicit clocking event defined, then this clocking event must be the same as the inferred clocking event for the procedural block.
- No time consuming statements (i.e., tasks with delays, delays) can be present between the beginning of the block until assertion is reached.

• The procedural assertion cannot be placed inside a looping statement.

Evaluation semantics of procedural assertions are the same as concurrent assertions with the exception that the evaluation of the property is conditioned upon program execution reaching the assertion statement. Consider the following code segment:

```
Program 16.4:  Procedural assertions
                        :
                        :
1    :       property prop1;
2    :           q1 != d1;
3    :       endproperty
4    :       always @(posedge clk) begin
5    :           q1 <= d1;
6    :           prop1_proc_asrt: assert property (prop1);
7    :       end
8    :
9    :       property prop2;
10   :           @(posedge clk)(q2 != d2);
11   :       endproperty
12   :       always @(posedge clk) begin
13   :           if (a) begin
14   :               q2 <= d2;
15   :               prop2_proc_asrt: assert property (prop2);
16   :           end
17   :       end
                        :
                        :
```

In this example, assertions defined on lines 6 and 15 are procedural assertions. The assertion on line 6 infers its clocking event from the always block, and the assertion on line 15 has its own clocking event defined, which is the same as the inferred clock for the always block but is placed inside a conditional block. The following code fragment shows how these same assertions can be specified using concurrent assertions:

```
Program 16.5:  Rewriting procedural assertions as concurrent assertions
                        :
                        :
1    :       property prop1c;
2    :           @(posedge clk) q1 != d1;
3    :       endproperty
4    :       prop_concur_asrt: assert property (prop1c);
5    :
6    :       always @(posedge clk) begin
7    :           q1 <= d1;
8    :       end
9    :
10   :
11   :       property prop2c;
12   :           @(posedge clk) a |-> (q2 != d2);
13   :       endproperty
14   :       prop2_concur_asrt: assert property (prop2c);
15   :
16   :       always @(posedge clk) begin
17   :           if (a) begin
18   :               q2 <= d2;
19   :           end
20   :       end
                        :
                        :
```

The definition for property **prop1** is modified to include an explicit clocking event before it can be used in a concurrent assertion. The definition for **prop2** is modified so that the condition for reaching procedural assertion is used as the antecedent of an implication property whose consequent is the original property definition.

16.3.2 Severity System Tasks

SystemVerilog provides the following *assertion severity levels*:

- fatal
- error
- warning
- info

A system task is provided for each severity level, which when called produces the desired behavior on simulation flow. These system tasks have the following syntax:

```
$fatal ( level, message[ , args ]);
$error (message[ , args ])
$warning (message[ , args ])
$info (message[ , args ])
```

$fatal() is used to immediately terminate simulation. The first argument passed to *$fatal()* is the same argument passed to *$finish()* system task. The effect of *$error()* task depends on settings for the simulation tools and is customizable. *$warning()* and *$info()* system tasks produce logging message of the corresponding severity.

Severity tasks can be used anywhere procedural statements are allowed. *$error* system task is called by the simulator by default when an assertion fails. The action block for an assertion can be used to modify this behavior or call a system task with a different level of severity.

16.3.3 Assertion Control System Tasks

SystemVerilog provides the following system tasks for controlling assertion checking through the SystemVerilog program:

- *$asserton()*
- *$assertoff()*
- *$assertkill()*

Arguments to these tasks are interpreted in the same way as for *$dumpvars()* system task. The general syntax is:

```
$assert_control_task [(level[, list_of_modules_or_assertions])];
```

Each assertion control task can be called either with no arguments, with the **level** argument, or with **level** and **list_of_modules_or_assertions**. If no arguments are specified, then the task affects all assertions in the hierarchy. **level** specifies the number of hierarchy levels below each specified module instance that are affected. The number of levels is counted from the top of module instance and not from where the task is located. **level** cannot be set to zero when any assertions are specified as arguments. If **level** is set to **0**, then all assertions in the specified module instances will be affected.

list_of_modules_or_assertions provides the scope to which the command applies. The arguments in this list can be either modules or assertions within modules. Arguments in this list can be instance names, hierarchical instance names, or hierarchical references to properties. These arguments cannot be a reference to a sequence or out of module reference to individual assertions.

Task *$assertoff()* suspends checking of all specified assertions until *$asserton()* is encountered. Assertions that are already executing, including assertion action blocks, will continue executing. Task *$asserton*, resumes checking all specified assertions that were disabled by a previous call to *$assertoff()*. Task *$assertkill()* halts checking of all specified assertions that are currently executing, then suspends checking of all specified assertions until *$asserton()* is encountered.

16.4 Capturing Assertion Requirements

Assertions are added at different levels of design abstraction and during different stages of the design and verification flow. As such, it is necessary to follow a consistent view for analyzing a DUV and its verification environment, and expressing verification targets as assertions. Section 16.1 describes the types of assertions that must be contributed by each project participant and during each phase of the design process. This section describes a methodology that provides a consistent view of assertion extraction from a project planning perspective.

Use the following steps when capturing assertions for a design:

- Consider verification objectives.
- Partition the verification problem.
- Identify requirements for each partition.
- Map requirements to assertions.
- Define clocking and reset/interrupt conditions.
- Add assertions to the design.

These steps are described in the following subsection.

16.4.1 Step 1: Consider Verification Objectives

Complete functional verification of a DUV requires that the following behaviors be considered in verification objectives:

- DUV configuration
- DUV interaction with its environment (interface behavior)
- Core functionality of the DUV

Not all of these behaviors may be necessary for all verification projects. As such, it is necessary to define the scope of a verification project before considering what assertions must be specified.

16.4.2 Step 2: Partition the Problem

Complete DUV verification requires that:

- DUV function is verified
- DUV usage in its target environment is verified

Verifying that a DUV functions as expected requires that:

- DUV interface requirements are specified
  - How the design communicates with its environment (i.e., protocols)
  - DUV configuration is valid
  - Valid DUV pin values
- DUV core functionality is fully verified
  - Individual subcomponents work correctly
  - Overall DUV works correctly in all modes

Verifying that a DUV is used correctly in its target environment requires that:

- DUV is tied correctly to its environment
  - DUV is correctly integrated into the global clocking/reset/test/power lines
  - Communication protocols are implemented correctly
- DUV static configuration and dynamic re-configuration is valid
  - Valid combinations of configuration parameter values
  - Valid transitions between configurations or operating modes
- Environment correctly drives the DUV
  - Valid control inputs in any state
  - Data inputs within valid ranges
  - Inputs stable when required

These verification requirements are described in the following subsections in the context of DUV interface, core function, and outputs.

16.4.2.1 Interface

DUV interface refers not only to its boundary pins but also to any interaction between the DUV and its outside environment. Correct operation of this interface is the initial, and a required, step in verifying a DUV, since without an operational interface, the DUV cannot be verified. Interface requirements are also used as assumptions in formal verification tools.

DUV interface consists of the following:

- Configuration
- DUV input pins
- Protocol
- Register interface

Configuration refers to how a block is configured (e.g., through configuration parameters) to play a specific role in its target environment. DUV input pins refer to behavior at the DUV boundary pins. Protocol refers to complex multi-cycle interaction between the DUV and its containing environment. Register interface refers to how the outside environment manipulates the register space of the DUV. These aspects of interface verification are discussed in the following subsections.

16.4.2.1.1 Configuration

Design and verification IPs are commonly used to improve productivity through reuse. The widespread use of such IPs and IP developers' desire to make their product as commonly useful as possible means that each IP is usually designed to be adaptable to multiple use models. Different approaches for design configuration during different stages of the design process include:

- Source code generation: creating different files for different configurations
- Source code compilation: using conditional compilation (e.g., using ifdef in Verilog)
- Design elaboration: using generating parameters and "generate" statements
- Design operation: assigning values to configuration inputs and registers

The following assertions must be specified for checking design configuration:

- Combined setting of all configuration parameters represents a valid configuration mode
- If allowed, dynamic transitions from one configuration to another take place correctly
- DUV is configured as planned in its operating environment

The first two types of assertions are added by block designers. The third type is added when that block is integrated into a larger block.

16.4.2.1.2 DUV Input Pins

DUV inputs refer to pins connecting the DUV to other blocks. Assertions about inputs must be added by the designers of a block so that when that block is integrated in a larger module, valid values for its pins are checked without requiring extra work by other designers.

Assertions about the following DUV input properties should be specified:

- Control inputs are presented at the appropriate times and in the right combination and/or sequence
- Data input values are in the valid set or within the valid range of allowed values
- Input signals are stable when required

Assertions added for DUV input pins are used as assumptions for formal verification tools. Assumptions about input pins of a block turn into assertions about internal functionality of larger design blocks containing that block.

Design input pin assertions are added by block designers.

16.4.2.1.3 Protocol

Any design of reasonable complexity uses a predefined protocol to communicate with its environment. A protocol may be a bus type interface where the design can act either as bus master, a bus slave, or both, or a point-to-point connection where communication takes place using a predefined syntax over multiple clock cycles (e.g., UART, USB).

The signal activity at a block interface depends on the detailed description of its protocol and the activity originating from inside the block and from outside the environment. When defining assertions for a block interface protocol, decisions made by the outside environment are not known. This means that interface behaviors that depend on the outside activity cannot be verified by using assertions when the operating environment of that block is not available. For example, in a UART interface, it is straightforward to verify that all stop-bits appearing on the interface are valid, since the size of UART data word is available as a setting in the internal configuration of the block that uses the UART interface. Some UART behaviors, however, cannot be verified by simply looking at the interface signals. For example, if the environment driving the UART input to a block asserts the break condition (forcing the data value to a constant **0**), it is not possible to decide by just looking at the interface signals and block internal setting whether or not the constant zero value on the input line is due to an environment error or due to a UART break condition.

Figure 16.4 shows a pictorial view of this distinction between protocol internal and external properties. Assertions defined for interface protocols of a block should include at least all interface properties that can be checked by looking at the interface signals and internal state of the design (i.e., protocol internal properties). These assertions must be added by the block designer. Designers can potentially identify external conditions that are needed to decide all protocol properties and ask for such conditions to be elaborated when the design is integrated into the larger design. Alternatively, protocol checkers can assume a worst case scenario policy where any unexpected observation is assumed to be an error unless overridden when the design is integrated in the target design.

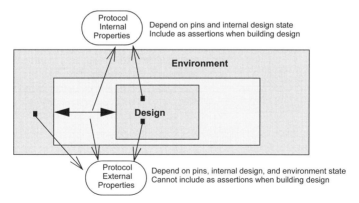

Figure 16.4 Protocol Internal and External Properties

16.4.2.1.4 Register Interface

A register bank is a common component of any design. It allows design interaction to take place through memory-mapped transactions, thereby minimizing the number of interface pins required for such configurations. Registers can be divided into two broad categories:

- Control registers: written to by the outside environment to control DUV behavior
- Status registers: updated by DUV and read by the outside environment

Any register that can be updated both by the DUV and from the outside environment should be included in both categories. Assertions about control registers should be included in the interface verification of the design. Properties that should be included for control registers include:

- Values assigned by the outside environment are valid
- Register values change only as allowed by specification or don't change at all after initial setting if required by the specification
- Combined setting of input registers represents a valid state

Assertions about status registers should be included when verifying design outputs (section 16.4.2.3).

16.4.2.2 Core Function

Assertions about the core functionality of a design should include the following:

- Implementation specific assumptions
- Core properties that are required for most fundamental operations to work

It is not possible to define all properties of a DUV as assertions. As such, the focus in defining design core assertions should be: 1) to check properties that overall indicate the design works correctly, and 2) properties that if failed, would be difficult to debug either because they include micro-code assumptions little known by anyone but the designer or because it would take them many cycles to become visible at the system boundary.

In general, assertions about the following core function properties should be included:

- FSM properties including state transitions and sequences
- Data transfer control logic including muxes, addressing, decoding, etc.
- Data transformation logic including ALUs, multipliers, and other complex blocks
- Parallel operation of multiple elements (e.g., pipeline behavior, interacting state machines)
- Correct configuration and operation of subcomponents
- Correct setting of status registers

16.4.2.3 Design Outputs

The setting of a value on a design output can be viewed from two different perspectives. First, it is clear that design outputs are assigned because of complex end-to-end behaviors. However, specifying assertions for such end-to-end behaviors is usually complicated and verifying this behavior is best done using scoreboarding techniques during the simulation process. A different view on setting of design output values is how these signals are assigned as a function of the blocks driving them. Such properties are usually more tractable and do not require end-to-end property descriptions. In addition, properties specified using such local assignment considerations are more manageable by formal verification tools. As such, it is recommended that design output assertions be specified using their local assignment instead of their end-to-end behaviors.

Assertions on design outputs can be considered as design core assertions and as such follow the same general guidelines discussed for design core assertions.

16.4.3 Step 3: Identify Requirements for Each Partition

Each partition described in the previous section consists of many properties that may be good candidates for including as assertions. In writing assertions it is best to start from most general properties applicable to typical design behavior and work towards more dedicated properties. A suggested flow for extracting such properties is as follows:

- Nominal functionality
- Boundary conditions
- Startup behavior
- Predictable errors

Nominal functionality refers to the typical behavior at the given partition. Examples include: default configuration settings, typical traces on design inputs, properties that are needed before the design core can work as expected, and design output properties.

Boundary conditions describe corner-case conditions and properties that must hold for such corner cases to work correctly. Examples include: combinations of configuration and inputs settings, and their effect on design behavior; and error conditions that must be detected by the design, either by reacting to such error conditions or setting status registers.

Startup behavior describes how the design is expected to be reset, initialized, and brought into a new mode of operation. Examples include: how the reset sequence should be executed, what effect the reset sequence will have on the core functionality, and how the output values change as a result of the reset process.

Predictable errors describe conditions that must never occur. These errors fall into two categories: 1) errors generated by the outside environment, and 2) errors generated because of design problems. Error conditions at the design input that the design is expected to detect and react to are considered part of the design functionality and are included in the design boundary condition properties. Error conditions that must be included here include errors on the design input that cannot be detected by the design and would, therefore, either go unnoticed by the design or cause a fatal problem. It is a good practice to add new assertions as bugs are detected so that same bug does not reappear in the design.

16.4.4 Step 4: Map Requirements to Assertion Forms

Assertions are statements about design behaviors that should be satisfied either unconditionally or when some qualifying behavior is satisfied. As such, mapping requirements to assertions requires the following steps:

- Identify the target behavior that must be satisfied
- Identify the qualifying behavior, if one is needed
- Decide the timing relationship between the qualifying and the target behavior

Section 15.7.1 provides a range of behaviors and their equivalent representation using the SystemVerilog sequence construct. Section 15.7.2 provides examples of how qualifying and target behaviors can be combined to form a property. Section 16.3.1 then describes assertion directives (e.g., *assert*, *assume*) that can be used to turn a property into an assertion statement.

16.4.5 Step 5: Define Clocking and Reset/Interrupt Conditions

DUV properties should be evaluated using the appropriate clocking event. For local properties, selection of such clocks is straightforward and obvious. As the property under consideration spans more of the design and turns into an end-to-end property, then clock selection may not be obvious and special steps must be taken in order to define a clock or combination of clocks for which that property must hold. SystemVerilog allows properties to be defined based on different clocking events (section 15.6). However, special care must be taken when defining such properties.

Additionally, not all properties should be maintained at all times. Obvious examples are properties that fail during reset condition. Other examples include cases where a specific property must hold only under a specific operating mode. SystemVerilog provides the "*disable iff*" construct for disabling assertions when they need not be evaluated. This is shown in the following example:

Program 16.6: Disabling an assertion using "disable iff"
```
1  :      property abc;
2  :          @(negedge clk) disable iff (reset) s1;
3  :      endproperty
```

16.4.6 Step 6: Add the Assertions to the Design

Assertions can be added to a design using three approaches:

- Embedded in the design
- Placed in a property file (module later bound to design)
- Placed in a verification component (module including assertions and coverage)

Table 16.1 summarizes the advantages and disadvantages of each approach.

Use the following guidelines in deciding placement for assertions:

- Designers should place assertions either in their design code or in a property file.
- Verification engineers should place assertions about the design in a property file and assertions about the design interface in the testbench.
- Assertions for common interface protocols should be placed in a verification component that can be reused across multiple projects.

Location	Advantages	Disadvantages
Embedded	• Always travels with the design • Can be placed near the logic with which it is associated • Assertions that document behavior are in the same location as code • One file contains all information for verification and synthesis	• Must guard that supporting HDL code does not get synthesized or affect code coverage results • Cannot disable without special provisions • Assertions can clutter an RTL file
Module bound to design	• No need to touch the design • Easy to categorize assertions for performance optimizations • Easy to separate auxiliary code so that it does not affect code coverage and synthesis tools	• Multiple files are required • The parser will not complain if the file is missing
Stand-alone verification component	• Portable • Easy to instantiate in design • Easy to control parsing by using ifdefs	• Multiple files are required • It is more work to instantiate the assertions in the design • An extra level of hierarchy adds a little complexity to any analysis

Table 16.1: Assertion Placement: Advantages and Disadvantages

16.5 Assertion-Based Verification IPs

Assertion-based verification IPs (ABVIPs) provide a set of built-in assertions and coverage collection mechanisms for common design properties, including design behaviors, design structures, and protocols. ABVIPs can be divided into two categories:

- Assertion libraries
- Assertion-based protocol checkers

The following subsections describe each category of verification IPs.

16.5.1 Assertion Libraries

Assertion libraries contain components that perform checks for commonly used design properties. These properties include:

- Onehot checks
- Handshake checks
- State transition checks
- Checks for common components such as FIFOs and arbiters

Assertion libraries are convenient to use but are limited in the type of properties that they can check. As such, it is necessary to write additional assertions for properties not covered by a given assertion library. Assertion libraries are extensible. It is, therefore, recommended that new assertions defined for a design follow the same format as that of other assertions in the library so they can be reused.

OVL (Open Verification Library), developed by Accelera, provides a collection of 30+ verification modules. Tool vendors often provide more comprehensive assertion libraries which are a super-set of assertions defined in OVL.

Using assertion libraries such as OVL provides the following advantages:

- The library components are Verilog modules that have built-in assertions and coverage collection points. They can be instantiated in the same way as any other Verilog design module, which makes it easy for designers to adopt and get started with ABV.
- Assertions provided in the library can be used as examples for learning assertions and extending the library.
- The library components are highly parameterizable, so they can be reused in different design contexts.

16.5.1.1 Assertion Library Component Architecture

An assertion library component is modeled using a module and contains the following:

- Module declaration and port list
- Parameter declarations to help select the appropriate configuration
- Auxiliary HDL code to capture the variables required for verification
- SystemVerilog assertions that check for correct behavior
- Coverage statements (i.e., *covergroup* statements and *cover* directives)

The following example shows a SystemVerilog assertion library component:

```
Program 16.7: SystemVerilog assertion library component
1  :    module check_range(clk, reset_n, data, enable);
2  :
3  :        //List of parameters
4  :        parameter DATA_WIDTH = 32; //Default data WIDTH is taken as 32
5  :        parameter MAX_VALUE = {DATA_WIDTH{1'b1}};
6  :        parameter MIN_VALUE = 0;
7  :
8  :        //List of inputs signals
9  :        input clk;
10 :        input reset_n;
11 :        input [DATA_WIDTH-1:0] data;
12 :        input enable;
13 :
14 :        // auxiliary HDL code to capture variables required for cover collection
15 :        reg [DATA_WIDTH -1:0]   values_checked; //For covergroup implementation
16 :        always @ (posedge clk) begin
17 :            if(reset_n == 1'b0)
18 :                values_checked <= {DATA_WIDTH{1'b0}};
19 :            else if (enable)
20 :                values_checked <= data;
21 :        end
22 :
23 :        // SVA assertions
24 :        ial_range: assert property ( @(posedge clk)
25 :            (((reset_n == 1'b1) && enable) |->
26 :                ((data >= MIN_VALUE) && (data <= MAX_VALUE))) );
27 :
28 :        //The SVA cover directives
29 :        ial_cover_range_max_limit_reached : cover property ( @(posedge clk)
30 :            ((reset_n == 1'b1) && enable && (data == MAX_VALUE)) );
31 :
```

```
32  :    ial_cover_range_min_limit_reached : cover property ( @(posedge clk)
33  :        ((reset_n == 1'b1) && enable && (data == MIN_VALUE)) );
34  :
35  :    //Covergroup for values driven in "data"
36  :    covergroup ial_cg_type_range @(posedge (clk & enable));
37  :    ial_range_cover_values_checked: coverpoint values_checked {
38  :        bins value_bins[] = {[MIN_VALUE:MAX_VALUE]};
39  :    }
40  :    endgroup
41  :
42  :    //Covergroup instantiation
43  :    ial_cg_type_range ial_cg_range_cover_values_checked = new();
44  : endmodule
```

This assertion library component checks that a given data value is within the range provided by the parameters to this component. Lines 4–6 declare the parameters. Lines 14–21 include the auxiliary code needed to compute variable **values_checked** that is used to collect coverage values. Lines 24–26 check that the data value is within the expected range. Lines 28–33 collect coverage on when data value is equal to the maximum or the minimum allowed value. Lines 35–43 define and instantiate a *covergroup* to collect detailed coverage information on the value of the data input.

Assertion library components often include *ifdef* statements so that its behavior (e.g., whether or not to collect coverage) can be controlled by the user. These conditional parameters are, however, not shown in this example.

16.5.1.2 Using Assertion Library Components

Assertion library components are instantiated the same as any other modules in the design. Where to instantiate an assertion library component is discussed in section 16.4.6.

The following code segment shows an example of using the assertion library component shown in program 16.7:

```
Program 16.8: Using an assertion library component
1  :    module test;
2  :        bit clk=1;
3  :        logic [15:0] data=0;
4  :
5  :        initial for (int i = 0; i <= 8; i++) #1 clk = !clk ;
6  :        always @(posedge clk) data = data + 3;
7  :        check_range #(16, 10, 0) check_range (clk, 1'b1, data, 1'b1);
8  :    endmodule
```

Line 5 generates four **clk** pulses. Line 6 increments the value of variable **data** by **3** on each rising edge of **clk**. Line 7 instantiates the **check_range** assertion library component, requiring that the value of **data** remain between **0** and **10**, with **data** having **16** bits. In this example, the assertion will fail once the value of data is set to **12**.

16.5.2 Assertion-Based Protocol Checkers

Assertion-based protocol checkers use assertions to verify that a design interface follows its protocol properties. Building a complete and fully verified assertion-based protocol checker is not a trivial task, but if one is available, it provides significant benefits in carrying out the verification task. As such, assertion-based protocol checkers are best suited for popular and commonly used protocols such as PCI-Express, AHB, AXI, etc.

Assertion-based protocol checkers provide the following benefits:

- Complete verification of design adherence to protocol standards
- Complete, pre-verified set of assertions
- Cover checks for capturing interesting protocol scenarios
- Parameterizable data and address bus width
- Ease of use across formal, simulation, and acceleration environments

16.5.2.1 Assertion-Based Protocol Checker Architecture

The programming architecture of an assertion-based protocol checker is very similar to the one for assertion-based library components. The main difference, however, is that module ports in an assertion-based protocol checker correspond to the interface signals, and assertion and coverage points specified in the module correspond to a comprehensive set of protocol properties that the interface signals must follow.

An added complexity of building an assertion-based protocol checker is that such a component should be useful for checking the signal properties for all types of modules that can interact through the given protocol. For example, an ABPC for an AMBA bus should have assertions for both bus masters and slaves since during deployment, any of these devices may be represented by the DUV.

Figure 16.5 shows an example of a master/slave connection. Assume first that master is the DUV. During simulation, both the master and slave assertions provided by ABPC are evaluated and verified. In this case, slave assertions are environment assumptions that must be maintained and master assertions are design properties that must be verified. If slave is the DUV, then the situation is reversed, where slave assertions are design properties that must be verified and master assertions are environment assumptions that must be maintained.

In formal verification, only the DUV and ABPC are required to carry out the functional verification, since no test vectors need to be generated. If master is the DUV, then slave assertions are considered as constraints for the formal verification tool, which then verifies the master assertions. If slave is the DUV, then master assertions are considered as constraints for the formal verification tool, which then verifies the slave assertions.

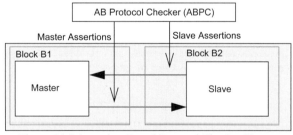

Figure 16.5 Assertion-Based Protocol Checker Usage

PART 7

Coverage Modeling and Measurement

CHAPTER 17

Coverage Collection Engine

The implementation of a coverage-driven verification environment is not possible without a coverage collection and analysis utility. Fundamentally, coverage collection is the process of storing values produced during the simulation runtime (i.e., signal values, or logical values representing complex objects such as transactions) and then using these stored values to decide whether or not relevant scenarios occurred during the simulation process. In its crudest form, coverage analysis can be done by dumping all signal value change information and then using this data to check for the occurrence of any target scenario. Even contemplating such a brute-force approach for a real sized design points immediately at challenges that must be addressed in a viable coverage collection and analysis utility:

- Storing all signal value change information is not practical for a real sized design with non-trivial behavior. As such, a coverage collection utility should include language constructs that provide concise, yet expressive mechanisms, for specifying the information that must be collected during the simulation runtime.
- Extracting relevant information from a set of stored values is a non-trivial task at best. As such, a coverage collection utility should include a coverage engine for analyzing and reporting coverage results extracted from the stored data.

SystemVerilog defines a set of powerful language constructs for specifying coverage information that should be collected. These constructs guide the underlying coverage collection engine to decide what values should be stored during simulation. This coverage engine and its accompanying analyzer are then used during a post-simulation phase to analyze, combine from multiple runs, summarize, and report coverage results. The coverage engine also provides a method-based interface for querying coverage results at simulation runtime. This feature allows coverage results to be used for guiding random scenario generation during simulation runtime.

The coverage engine in a SystemVerilog simulation tool must at least support the collection and reporting of constructs supported by the SystemVerilog language. The full set of features included in the associated coverage analysis and reporting tool does, however, vary among tool vendors. The effectiveness of a coverage analysis and reporting tool is affected by the following factors:

- Reporting utilities

- User interface
- Information, beyond those specified in the SystemVerilog program, that can be extracted from a coverage database (e.g., additional crosses, transitions, etc.)

The following steps are followed during coverage collection and analysis:

- Create a coverage plan derived from the verification plan
- Identify information that must be collected in order to enable the coverage analysis tool to extract the information required by the coverage plan
- Add coverage collection code to the verification environment so that information identified in the previous steps are collected during the simulation runtime
- After the completion of simulation, use a coverage analysis and reporting tool to report coverage results needed by the coverage plan

This chapter presents language constructs provided by SystemVerilog for implementing coverage collection. Steps for building a coverage plan and identifying the information that must be collected are discussed in chapter 18. Details of using coverage analysis and reporting engines is beyond the scope of this book and are described extensively in vendor specific operation manuals for these tools.

17.1 Coverage Collection Overview

In SystemVerilog coverage information can be collected for the value of an integral data object, transitions in the value of an integral data object, and simultaneous values of multiple integral data objects. A coverage group is the abstraction provided by SystemVerilog for specifying a set of data objects that are sampled at the same time. A *coverage group* implementation may include the following *coverage collection elements*:

- Point coverage
- Transition coverage
- Cross coverage

Point coverage provides information on how many times each possible value (e.g., **4**), or a value in a range of values (e.g., a number in the range **[2:12]**), of an integral variable (e.g., integer, logic, bit, etc.) was sampled during the simulation runtime. *Transition coverage* collects information on what sequence of values were sampled for an integral variable (e.g., how many times the value for an integer variable changed from **3** to **12** and then to **14**, or how many times the value for an integer variable changed from a value in the range **[12:99]** to a value in the range **[33:123]**). *Cross coverage* collects information on what simultaneous values were sampled for two or more integral variables (e.g., how many times two integer variables contained values **3** and **5** at the same time, or values in ranges **[2:13]** and **[33:132]** at the same time).

Conceptually, coverage collection is carried out by collecting information on how many times each possible value of a coverage element was sampled during the simulation process. Practically, however, storing information for each possible value of a coverage element leads to two problems:

- For some integral data types (e.g., 32-bit integer), it is not feasible to keep track of the number of times each value was sampled.
- In the majority of cases, treating each possible value of a variable separately doesn't provide any immediately useful information.

Consider a 32-bit address line in an address-mapped system bus where each peripheral responds to a specific address range. Ideally, full coverage of the address decoding logic requires that all possible address values are observed during the simulation runtime. Given this view, full coverage is defined as each address value having occurred at least once. In reality, however, achieving this ideal target is not possible because it is not practical to keep count of all observed address values, and more importantly, it is infeasible to generate all possible values of the address line within a reasonable time. These limitations make it impractical to define full coverage as each address line having been observed at least once.

SystemVerilog uses the concepts of _coverage bins_ and _coverage hits_ to facilitate the practical definition of what full coverage means for coverage group elements. In this approach, possible values for coverage elements (i.e., point, transition, cross) are grouped into bins and a required hit target is attached to each bin. Full coverage for a bin is defined as the number of sampled values falling within the range for that bin exceeding that bin's target hit value. Full coverage for a coverage point or cross is then defined as all of its bins being fully covered. This approach is further extended through weights and goals to derive a quantitative measure of coverage (see section 18.3).

The concepts of bins and hits can be used to define a practical definition for full coverage of the system-bus example outlined above. In this approach, a coverage point is defined as the value of the address line, coverage bins are defined to correspond to the address range for each peripheral. The hit requirement for each bin can be set either to 1 (if observing at least one address for each peripheral is judged to be a good test of correct operation of its decoding logic) or a number proportional to the size of the address space for that peripheral if more confidence is required. The actual decision of what weight value should be attached to each bin is subjective and depends on the judgement of the verification team.

Sampling events for coverage group elements can be defined using a number of different approaches. But not all values sampled for coverage elements in a coverage group are necessarily valid at every sampling event. For example, an address value falling in the range for a peripheral may not contribute to the overall coverage if that peripheral is disabled when that sample is observed. As such, SystemVerilog provides mechanisms for specifying when a sampled value for coverage elements and coverage bins should be included in the overall coverage calculations.

SystemVerilog provides additional features for controlling the definition, instantiation, initialization, and activation of coverage groups. Details of these facilities are described in the following sections.

17.2 Coverage Groups

In SystemVerilog, the *covergroup* construct is used to define a coverage group containing a set of interrelated coverage elements. All coverage elements included in a coverage group must share the same sampling event, even though the actual sampling of individual coverage elements may be disabled at a given sampling event.

Coverage groups are identified by the following properties:

- Covergroup name
- Coverage sampling event
- Formal arguments for customizing each instance of the covergroup
- Coverage elements
  - Includes coverage points and coverage crosses
  - Bin definitions for each coverage element
  - Transition coverage specified as bins for coverage points
- Covergroup customizations using covergroup options

SystemVerilog treats a coverage group definition as a user defined data type. This means that a coverage group object does not exist unless it is explicitly instantiated (except for coverage groups defined in classes, section 17.5). Multiple instances of a coverage group can be created by using the name of a *covergroup* definition. The following program shows a simple example of a coverage group definition and instantiation:

```
Program 17.1: Coverage Group Definition and Instantiation
1   :   module top;
2   :       bit reset, clk, sig_a, sig_b;
3   :
4   :       covergroup cg_ab @(posedge clk);
5   :           cp_a: coverpoint sig_a iff(!reset);
6   :           cp_b: coverpoint sig_b iff(reset);
7   :       endgroup
8   :
9   :       cp_ab cp_ab0 = new();
10  :   endmodule
```

This program shows the definition for a coverage group **cg_ab** that tracks values assigned to signals **sig_a** and **sig_b** during simulation runtime. The default clocking event for **cg_ab** is defined to be the positive edge of **clk**. Coverage group **cg_ab** contains two coverage points **cp_a** and **cp_b** which collect information for signals **sig_a** and **sig_b** respectively. Coverage points **cp_a** and **cp_b** are sampled only when **reset** is set to **0** and **1** respectively. In this configuration, coverage group **cg_ab** is activated at every positive edge of signal **clk** but the value of **sig_a** is sampled only if **reset** is set to **0**, and the value of **sig_b** is sampled only if **reset** is set to **1**. An instance of **cg_ab** is declared and created by calling its **new()** method in module **top** (line 9).

Coverage group sampling events and formal arguments are described in the following subsections. Details of coverage elements are described in the sections 17.3 and 17.4. Coverage options are described in section 17.6.

17.2.1 Coverage Group Activation

A coverage group is activated at every occurrence of its sampling event, if one is defined. A coverage group can also be activated procedurally by calling the coverage group predefined method *sample()* to activate an instance of a coverage group.

The sampling event for a coverage group can be in one of the following forms:

- Clocking event
- Block event expression

Clocking events are specified using the same notation used for defining the sampling event for other language constructs such as an *always* block (e.g., **@(posedge clk)**, **@(signal_a)**, **@(negedge clk or reset)**, etc.). A coverage group is activated immediately (i.e., its values are sampled) upon the occurrence of its sampling event.

SystemVerilog allows a coverage group instance to be stopped, restarted, or explicitly activated using procedural statements. This usage is shown in the following example:

```
Program 17.2: Using methods to explicitly control coverage group activation
1   :   module top;
2   :       bit sig_a, clk;
3   :
4   :       covergroup cg_aa @(posedge clk);
5   :           cp_a: coverpoint sig_a;
6   :       endgroup
7   :
8   :       cg_aa cg_aa0 = new();
9   :
10  :       initial begin
11  :           #10 cg_aa0.stop();
12  :           #10 sig_a = 10;
13  :           cg_aa0.sample();
14  :           #10 sig_a = 20;
15  :           cg_aa0.sample();
16  :           #10 cvr_a.start();
17  :       end
18  :   endmodule
```

In this example, the predefined *stop()* method of *covergroup* construct is used to stop the automatic activation of coverage group **cg_aa0** at time **10** (line 11). After this time, **cg_aa0** is not automatically activated when its sampling event (i.e., **(posedge clk)**) occurs. Coverage group **cg_aa0** is explicitly activated using the predefined *sample()* method (lines 13, 15). Automatic activation of **cg_aa0** is restarted again by calling its predefined *start()* method (line 16).

17.3 Coverage Points and Transitions

A *coverage point* is the fundamental unit of coverage collection as it defines the connection between the simulation environment and the coverage model. This means that all values brought into the coverage collection engine are sampled through a coverage point. These sampled values are then used to collect point, transition, and cross coverage information.

A coverage point is identified by the following properties:

- Label: Name given to the coverage point
- Source: Integral variable whose value, or expression whose result, is to be sampled
- Domain: Set of possible values for the coverage point source
- Guard expression: used for conditional activation of the coverage point
- Value bins: Coverage bins defining relevant value ranges
- Transition bins: Coverage bins defining relevant transitions between value ranges

The following program shows a simple example of using a coverage point in the definition of a coverage group:

```
Program 17.3: Coverage point source definition and its variations
1  :   module top;
2  :       bit reset, clk = 0;
3  :       bit [10:0] length, length1;
4  :
5  :       covergroup cg_length @(posedge clk);
6  :           cp_len: coverpoint length iff (!reset);
7  :           coverpoint length1 iff (!reset);
8  :           coverpoint (length+length1) iff (!reset);
9  :       endgroup
10 :
11 :       cg_length cvr_length = new;
12 :   endmodule
```

In this example, three coverage points are defined in coverage group **cg_length** (lines 6–8). A label can optionally be specified for a coverage point. For example, label **cp_len** is specified for the coverage point defined on line 6. If no label is specified and the coverage point source is a single variable, then the name of that variable is used as the label for that coverage point. For example, the label for coverage point defined on line 7 is **length1** and is taken from the variable that it samples. If no label is assigned to a coverage point and the coverage point source is an expression, then an automatically generated and tool specific label is specified implicitly for that coverage point (line 8). The label specified for a coverage point is used to call the predefined methods of that coverage point. It is also needed when specifying a cross coverage element that includes that coverage point.

A *coverage point source* is defined as the variable or expression whose result is sampled for that coverage point. A coverage point source can be a single integral variable or the result of an expression that produces an integral value. In the above example, coverage point **cp_len** (line 6) samples variable **length**, coverage point **length$_1$** (line 7) samples variable **length$_1$**, and the coverage point defined on line 8 samples the result of expression (**length+length$_1$**). A *coverage point domain* is defined as the set of all possible values for its source. For example, if the coverage point source is an enumerated type, then its domain is the set of all literals defined explicitly for that enumerated type. If the coverage point source is an M-bit integer, then its domain is the set of 2^M values that can be represented by that integer.

Each coverage point may include a *coverage point guard expression*. Upon occurrence of the sampling event for the containing coverage group, a value for the coverage point is sampled only if the sampling guard expression evaluates to true. In the above example, the coverage points defined on lines 6–8 are sampled if variable **reset** is set to zero (i.e., reset is inactive). Different sampling guard expressions may be defined for coverage points in the same coverage group. As such, the sampling time of each coverage point can independently be customized to conditions that make it relevant.

Values sampled for a coverage point are organized into coverage bins. Two types of bins can be defined for a coverage point: a value bin or a transition bin. A *coverage point value bin* identifies a range of values for the coverage point while a *coverage point transition bin* defines a set of transitions for the value of a coverage point. Value and transition bins are described in section 17.3.2.

17.3.1 Coverage Point Sampling Semantics

Generally speaking, a coverage point source is sampled when its containing coverage group is activated. This simplistic view of coverage collection may lead to problems with and/or limitations on sampled values. A problem may occur when a coverage group is activated multiple times in the same time-slot. A limitation may exist when sampled data should be taken from a specific scheduling region within a time-slot in which the coverage group is activated. This section describes techniques that allow better control over coverage group activation and sampling.

In a given time-slot, the sampled value of a coverage point depends on two factors:

- Scheduling region in which the coverage group is activated
- Scheduling region in which coverage point values are sampled

The activation time of a coverage group is well defined when a coverage group is activated explicitly (i.e., using *sample()* method) or by using a block event expression. In these cases, the activation time depends on sequential flow of program execution which is generally well defined and not susceptible to race conditions in which a code segment may be executed multiple times when only one pass was intended.

The situation is somewhat more complex when a clocking event expression is used for activating a coverage group. In such cases, activation of the coverage group depends on changes in signal values and events, and not on program execution flow. Given that a clocking event may be triggered multiple times in a given time-slot, using clocking event expressions may lead to a behavior where a coverage group is activated multiple times in the same time-slot. This behavior may or may not be useful depending on the intended purpose of coverage collection.

SystemVerilog provides a coverage type option (see section 17.6) for preventing a coverage group to be activated more than once during any one time-slot. The *strobe* option, if specified, forces a coverage group to be activated in the postponed region of the time-slot in which its sampling event was triggered. This activation will happen only once, even if the sampling event was triggered multiple times during that time-slot. The following example shows the use of this option along with a sampling event defined as a clocking event:

```
covergroup cg_a @(posedge clk);
    type_option.strobe = 1;
    cp_a: coverpoint sig_a iff(!reset);
endgroup
```

In summary, the number of times and the scheduling region where a coverage group is activated can be controlled by using the *strobe* option. When the strobe option is not used, the coverage group is activated once for each triggering of its event expression even if this happens multiple times in a time-slot. When the strobe option is used, the coverage group is activated only once at the end of the time-slot in which its event expression was triggered at least once.

In SystemVerilog, values sampled for a coverage point are tightly connected with the activation time of the containing coverage group. Essentially, sampled values are the value of the coverage point source at the time of activation. More fine-grained control of this behavior may, however, be needed, depending on the specific coverage collection requirements. Values sampled for coverage collection may need to be taken from any of the following regions of the current time-slot:

- Stable values before entering the current time-slot
- Values in the observed region of the current time-slot, resulting in stable values of sampled variables in the current time-slot before any property pass or fail code is executed
- Stable values at the end of the current time-slot

Using the *strobe* option results in a coverage group to be activated in the postponed region of the cycle in which its clocking event is activated. Given the default behavior of coverage collection in which variables are sampled at the time of activation, this behavior results in the sampled values to be taken from the postponed region of the current time-slot, yielding the final stable values of the sampled variable in the current time-slot.

Sampling stable values from preponed or the observed regions can be accomplished by using a clocking block. An example of this approach is shown in the following program:

```
Program 17.4: Using clocking blocks to control sampling time of coverage points
1  :   module top;
2  :       bit reset, clk = 0;
3  :       bit [10:0] length, length1;
4  :
5  :       clocking cb @(posedge clk);
6  :           input #1step preponed_length = length;
7  :           input #0 observed_length = length;
8  :       endclocking
9  :
10 :       covergroup cg_length @(posedge clk);
11 :           cp_pl: coverpoint cb.preponed_length iff (!reset);
12 :           cp_ol: coverpoint cb.observed_length iff (!reset);
13 :       endgroup
14 :
15 :       cg_length cg_length0 = new;
16 :   endmodule
```

In this program, reading the value of variable **cb.preponed_length** returns the value of variable **length** in the preponed region of the last time-slot in which clocking event (**posedge clk**) was triggered. Similarly, reading the value of variable **cb.observed_length** returns the value of variable **length** in the observed region of the last time-slot in which clocking event (**posedge clk**) was triggered. Collecting coverage on these variables (lines 11, 12) leads to the collected coverage to correspond to the values of variable **length** in the preponed and observed regions respectively.

17.3.2 Coverage Point Value and Transition Bins

SystemVerilog uses the concept of a coverage bin to group together values and transitions that need not be differentiated for coverage collection purposes. Obviously, the need for any differentiation is dictated by the coverage plan. As an example, consider a generic packet that has a valid size between **10** and **1000** bits. A crude coverage plan may only require coverage information on the number of short, valid, and long packets that were observed during the simulation process. This plan would require only three value bins, each covering ranges **[1:9]**, **[10:1000]**, and **[1001:MAX_VALUE]**, respectively. During the simulation runtime, the count attribute of the bin corresponding to each sampled value will be incremented (e.g., sampling a size of **8** results in incrementing the counter for the first bin).

Transition bins are also important for coverage collection purposes. For example, the coverage plan may require knowledge of how many times a short packet was followed by a valid packet and then by a short packet again. A transition bin is used to collect this type of coverage information. In this case, the transition bin is defined by three ranges of values consisting of **[1:9]**, then **[10:1000]** and then **[1:9]**. When any three consecutively sampled values of packet size fall into these consecutive ranges, then the count attribute of this transition bin is incremented.

Value and transition bins are described in the following subsections.

17.3.2.1 Coverage Point Value Bins

A value bin is identified by the following properties:

- Label: The name that identifies the value bin
- Domain: The set of values that define the bin
- Count: The number of times the sampled value is equal to any bin member
- Size: The number of values in bin domain
- Guard Expression: Used for conditional update of bin count

Consider the following example program:

```
Program 17.5: Coverage point bin definition constructs
1  :    module top;
2  :        bit length_is_relevant, reset=0, clk = 0;
3  :        bit [9:0] length;
4  :
5  :        covergroup cg_length @(posedge clk);
6  :            cp1: coverpoint length iff (!reset) {
7  :                bins bb1 = {[1:10], [8:12], [20:30], 34, 38, 34, [80:88]};
8  :                bins bb2[2] = {[111:120]} iff (length_is_relevant);
9  :                bins bb3[3] = {[111:120]} iff (length_is_relevant);
10 :                bins bb4[] = {[121:220]} iff (length_is_relevant);
11 :                bins bb5 = default;
12 :                bins bb6[] = default;
13 :            }
14 :            cp2: coverpoint length iff (!reset) {
15 :                bins begin_domain = {[$:10]};
16 :                bins end_domain = {[10:$]};
17 :                bins full_domain = {[$:$]};
18 :            }
19 :        endgroup
20 :
```

```
21  :          cg_length cg_ength0 = new(length, 34);
22  :      endmodule
```

This program shows the definition of coverage group **cg_length** which contains coverage point definitions cp_1 and cp_2. The following aspects of coverage point bin definition are highlighted in this example:

- Multiple value bins may be defined for each coverage point (lines 7–12).
- *Bin domain specification* (i.e., the syntactical representation of bin values) can be given using a mix of single values (e.g., **34, 38** on line 7) and/or ranges of values (e.g., **[1:10],[8:12]** on line 7).
- A bin domain specification may include duplicated values or overlapping ranges of values, leading to the same value being specified multiple times. All such multiply included values are assumed to have been specified only once. For example, the overlapping ranges **[1:10],[8:12]** on line 7 can be written equivalently as **[1:12]**. Also, note that for bin bb_1 (line 7), value **34** is assumed to have been specified only once even though it is included in its bin member specification twice.
- A *sized bin array* notation can be used to create a fixed number of bins for a range of values (line 8, 9). If the number of bins (**NB**) divides the number of values in bin domain specification (**NV**) evenly (i.e., **NV%NB=0**), then each bin will have (**NV/NB**) values in its domain. For example, bin definition on line 8 creates two bins ($bb_2[0]$ and $bb_2[1]$), whose members are defined by ranges **[111:115]** and **[116:120]** (having sizes **5** and **5**) respectively. If the number of bins does not divide the number of values evenly (i.e., **NV%NB>0**), then the remaining values are included in the last bin, which will then contain (**NB/NB + NV%NB**) domain values. For example, the bin definition on line 9 creates three bins $bb_3[0]$, $bb_3[1]$, and $bb_3[2]$, whose members are defined by ranges **[111:113]**, **[114:116]**, and **[117:120]** (having sizes **3**, **3**, and **4**), respectively. If **NB** is larger than **NV**, then one bin is created for each value.
- An *unsized bin array* notation can be used to create a bin array whose number of bins is derived from the number of values in the bin domain specification. In this case, one bin is created for each value included in the bin domain specification, with each bin having a domain size of **1**. The square bracket notation (i.e., "**[ ]**") is used for creating unsized bin arrays. For example, bin definition on line 10 creates **100** bins ($bb_4[0]$,...,$bb_4[99]$). each having a single member taken consecutively from the range **[121:220]**.
- A bin definition may optionally include a *bin guard expression*. The count attribute of a bin (or any of the bins in its bin array) is incremented only if the condition in its bin guard expression is satisfied.
- Bin domains for bins of the same coverage point may overlap. In this case, the count attribute of all bins that include the overlapping value are incremented if the overlapped value is sampled during coverage collection.
- The ***default*** keyword refers to all values in the domain of a coverage point that are not included in the domain of any of the bins specified for that coverage point. For example, the definition on line 11 defines a single bin bb_5 having as its members all values not already included in any of the other bin definitions for coverage point cp_1. The definition on line 12 defines a bin array bb_6 having one bin for every value not already included in any of the other bin definitions for coverage point cp_1.
- Keyword "**$**" can be used to refer to the beginning or end value of a coverage point

domain. As such, the full domain of a coverage point can be represented by range **[$;$]**. This notation is used in the above example to define bins describing a beginning range, an end range, and the full domain of variable **length** (lines 15–17).

SystemVerilog allows bins to be marked as illegal or irrelevant to coverage collection. _Illegal bins_ correspond to values in the coverage point domain that should not occur during the simulation process. _Ignored bins_ correspond to values that do not contribute to coverage collection and should be ignored for coverage collection purposes. The following program shows examples of illegal and ignore bin definitions:

```
Program 17.6: Illegal and ignore bins
1  :  module top;
2  :       bit length_is_relevant, reset=0, clk = 0;
3  :       bit [9:0] length;
4  :
5  :       covergroup cg_length @(posedge clk);
6  :            cp3: coverpoint length iff (!reset) {
7  :                 bins valid_bins[] = {[11:500]};
8  :                 illegal_bins nogood_bins = {[$:10]};
9  :                 ignore_bins nocare_bins = {[501:$]};
10 :            }
11 :       endgroup
12 :  endmodule
```

In this example, bins **nogood_bins** and **nocare_bins** are defined as illegal and ignored bins, respectively. A runtime error message is generated if a member of an illegal bin is sampled during the simulation runtime, even if that value is a member of another bin for the same coverage point. A value specified as a member of an ignored bin, is ignored in every bin having that value as a member. Also, keyword _default_ cannot be used to define the contents of an ignored bin.

Bins are automatically created for any coverage point that does not have any explicitly defined bins. In this case, an implicit sized bin array is created for the coverage point. The number of bins in this bin array is taken from the coverage group option **auto_bin_max**. Bin domain specification for this implicit bin definition is assumed to be the full domain of the coverage point (i.e., all possible values for the coverage point source). Given the bin array size and number of possible values for the coverage point, domain for each bin is decided according to the creation rule for sized bin arrays described earlier in this section. The automatic creation of bins is shown in the following example:

```
Program 17.7: Implicit bin definitions
1  :  module top;
2  :       bit length_is_relevant, reset=0, clk = 0;
3  :       bit [9:0] length;
4  :
5  :       covergroup cg_length @(posedge clk);
6  :            cp4: coverpoint length iff (!reset) {
7  :                 // The following implicit bin statement is assumed for cp4:
8  :                 // bins auto[option.auto_bin_max] = {[2:$]};
9  :                 illegal_bins nogood_bins = {0};
10 :                 ignore_bins nocare_bins = {1};
11 :            }
12 :
13 :            cp5: coverpoint length iff (!reset) {
14 :                 option.auto_bin_max = 3;
15 :            }
```

```
16  :          endgroup
17  :    endmodule
```

In this example, coverage point cp₄ has only illegal and ignore bins and no explicitly defined bins. In this case, an implicit bin creation statement (line 8) is used for creating the bins for cp₄. The number of bins is taken from option *auto_bin_max*, and the full domain of the coverage point, excluding the values indicated in the ignore and illegal bins, is divided between these bins forming the domain for each bin. The full domain of coverage point cp₄ is [0:1023] given that length is a 10-bit value. For an enumerated data type, the full domain of coverage point consists of the set of all literals for that enumerated type.

It is possible to modify the value for option *auto_bin_max* for each coverage point. This syntax is shown for coverage point cp₅ where the number of bins is set to 3.

17.3.2.2 Coverage Point Transition Bins

In SystemVerilog, value transition coverage for a data object is collected by defining transition bins for the coverage point that samples that data object. A *transition* is defined as the change of value from one sampling event to the next sampling event. A *transition set* represents a set of transitions (e.g., 1=>3, 1=>4). A transition set can be specified by giving ranges of values for the consecutive samples of a transition (e.g., {1,3}=>{4,5}). A *transition sequence* specifies changes in the value of a coverage point across multiple (two or more) sampling cycles. A *transition sequence set* represents a set of transition sequences. *Transition length* gives the number of cycles involved in a transition sequence. For example, the transition length of a transition is 2, while the transition length of a transition sequence may be 2 or more. Simple examples of these transitions are shown below:

```
Transition:                (12 => 14)
Transition Set:            ({[12:13],16} => {[14:16],18}) representing transitions:
                               12 => 14, 12 =>15, 12 =>16, 12 => 18,
                               13 => 14, 13 =>15, 13 =>16, 13 => 18,
                               16 => 14, 16 =>15, 16 =>16, 16 => 18,
Transition Sequence:       (13 => 14 => 15 => 16)
Transition Sequence Set:   ({[12:13]} => 14 => 15 => {[16:17]}) representing transition sequences:
                               12 => 14 => 15 => 16,
                               12 => 14 => 15 => 17,
                               13 => 14 => 15 => 16,
                               13 => 14 => 15 => 17
```

The values of a transition set or a transition sequence set at each cycle can be given using the same notation used for bin domain specification for value bins (i.e., using single value, a range value, using formal arguments, etc.).

SystemVerilog provides repeat operators for specifying transition sequence sets. These constructs include:

- Consecutive repeat operator
- Goto repeat operator
- Non-consecutive repeat operator

The behavior described by each operator is similar to those defined for sequence repeat operators (section 15.3.3). The following examples show the use of these repeat operators.

Abbreviation ATS (Any Transition Sequence) represents a transition sequence of any number of cycles and any values for each cycle.

Consecutive Repeat:	(12 [*3]) represents transition sequence: (12 => 12 => 12)
Goto Repeat:	(12 [-> 3]) Represents transition sequence: (ATS => 12 => ATS => 12 => ATS => 12)
Non-Consecutive Repeat:	(12 [= 3]) Represents transition sequence: (ATS => 12 => ATS => 12 => ATS => 12 => ATS)

A range of repeat values can be given for a repeat operator. Examples of these operators are shown below:

Consecutive Range Repeat:	12 [*2:3]) represents transition sequences: (12 => 12), (12 => 12 => 12)
Goto Range Repeat:	(12 [-> 2:3]) Represents transition sequences: (ATS => 12 => ATS => 12), (ATS => 12 => ATS => 12 => ATS => 12)
Non-Consecutive Range Repeat:	(12 [= 2:3]) Represents transition sequences: (ATS => 12 => ATS => 12 => ATS), (ATS => 12 => ATS => 12 => ATS => 12 => ATS)

A transition sequence may have a bounded or an unbounded length. Transition sequences that make use of **goto** repeat and non-consecutive repeat operators have an unbounded length since these transition sequences allow for any transition sequence of any length to come in between occurrence of their operands.

A transition bin is identified by the following properties:

- Label: The name that identifies the transition bin
- Domain: Transition sequences included in bin domain specification
- Count: The number of times a transition included in bin domain is observed during coverage collection
- Size: The number of transition sequences in bin domain
- Guard expression: Used for conditional update of bin count

Consider the following example program:

```
Program 17.8: Transition bin definitions
1    module top;
2        bit length_is_relevant, reset=0, clk = 0;
3        bit [9:0] length;
4
5        covergroup cg_length @(posedge clk);
6            cp_length: coverpoint length iff (!reset) {
7                bins tb1 = (10 => 20), ({11,12} => {21,22}) iff (length_is_relevant);
8                bins tb2 = ({[10:20],30} => {[40:50],60});
9                bins tb3[] = (12 [*2:3] => 30,40);
10               bins tb4 = (12 [=2:3] => 30,40);
11               bins tb5 = (12 [->2:3] => 30,40);
12               illegal_bins tb6 = ({[1000:$]} => {[$:$]} => {[1000:$]});
13               ignore_bins tb7 = ({[$:9]} => {[$:$]} => {[$:9]});
14               bins tb8 = default sequence;
15               // bins tb8[] = default sequence;   // illegal
16               // bins tb4 = (12 [=2:3] => {30,40}); // illegal
17               // bins tb5 = (12 [->2:3] => {30,40}); // illegal
18           }
19       endgroup
20   endmodule
```

This program shows the definition of coverage group **cg_length** containing coverage point **cp_length**. The following aspects of transition bin definition are highlighted in this example:

- Multiple transition bins may be defined for a coverage point (lines 7–14).
- *Transition bin domain specification* (i.e., the syntactical representation of bin transition sequences) can be given using a mix of single transitions (e.g., **10=>20** on line 7) and/or sets of transitions (e.g., **11,12=>21,22** on line 7).
- An *unsized bin array* notation can be used to create a bin array whose number of bins is derived from the number of transition sequences in the transition bin domain specification. In this case, one bin is created for each transition sequence included in the bin domain specification, with each bin having a size of **1**. The square bracket notation (i.e., "**[ ]**") is used for creating unsized bin arrays. For example, the bin definition on line 9 creates four bins (**tb$_3$[0]**,...,**tb$_3$[3]**), each having a single transition domain taken respectively from transition sequences (**12=> 12=> 30**), (**12=> 12=> 40**), (**12=> 12=> 12=> 30**), and (**12=> 12=> 12=> 40**).
- A transition bin definition may optionally include a *bin guard expression*. The count attribute of a bin (or any of the bins in its bin array) are incremented only if the condition in its guard expression is satisfied.
- Domains for transition bins specified for the same coverage point may overlap. In this case, the count attribute of all bins that include the overlapped transition sequence are incremented if the overlapped transition sequence is observed during coverage collection.
- The *default sequence* keyword refers to all transition sequences in the domain of a coverage point that are not included in a domain of any of the transition bins specified for that coverage point. The bin definition on line 14 defines a single bin **tb$_8$** having as its domain all transitions not already included in any of the other bin domains for coverage point **cp$_1$**. It is illegal to use this keyword with an unsized bin array definition (line 15).
- Unsized bin arrays cannot be used for unbounded length transition sequences (lines 16, 17).
- Illegal and ignore bins can also be specified for transition bins (lines 12, 13).

Transition and value bins described in this section provide a mechanism for collecting coverage on the value of a coverage point in one or across multiple sampling cycles. Cross coverage is used to collect information about the simultaneous values observed for two or more coverage points. Cross coverage is described in the next section.

17.4 Cross Coverage Elements

A *cross coverage* element collects information on simultaneous values (i.e., values at the same sampling event) of two or more coverage points. As such, cross coverage is used to collect information about the correlation between two or more variables or expression results.

Cross coverage description is identified by the following properties:

- Label: Name given to the cross coverage element

- Source: Coverage points whose combined conditions are monitored
- Guard expression: Used for conditional activation of the cross coverage
- Cross Domain: Cross product of value bins for all cross element sources (i.e., coverage points used in defining the cross element).
- Cross bins: bins defined as a subset of cross domain, specifying simultaneous values of coverage points that should be grouped.

The following program shows a simple example of using a cross coverage element in the definition of a coverage group:

```
Program 17.9: Cross coverage element definition
1  :   module top;
2  :       bit length_is_relevant, reset=0, clk = 0;
3  :       typedef enum {TOO_SHORT, SHORT, MEDIUM, LONG, TOO_LONG} length_t;
4  :       length_t length_A, length_B, length_C;
5  :
6  :       covergroup cg_length @(posedge clk);
7  :           cp_A: coverpoint length_A;
8  :           cp_B: coverpoint length_B;
9  :           xc_AB: cross cp_A, cp_B iff (!reset);
10 :           xc_AC: cross cp_A, length_C iff(!reset);
11 :       endgroup
12 :   endmodule
```

In this example, coverage group **cg_length** contains two coverage points **cp_A** and **cp_B**. Cross coverage element **xc_AB** is defined to collect coverage information on simultaneous values sampled for coverage points **cp_A** and **cp_B**. A cross coverage element must be defined in terms of coverage points. However, if a cross coverage is defined in terms of an integral variable, then an implicit coverage point is created for that variable and the cross coverage element is defined based on this implicitly defined coverage point. Cross coverage element **xc_AC** (line 10) is defined in terms of coverage point **cp_A** and variable **length_C**. In this case, an implicit coverage point is created for variable **length_C** which in turn is used in creating the cross coverage element **xc_AC**.

A cross coverage element may optionally include a *cross coverage guard expression* (lines 9, 10). A cross coverage element is evaluated if the expression for its guard expression evaluates to true. Otherwise, the cross coverage element is ignored.

A *cross coverage source* is a coverage point used in defining that cross coverage element. Sources of a cross coverage element must be from the same coverage group. It is illegal to define a cross coverage element whose sources are taken from different coverage groups.

Data collected for cross coverage elements is organized in terms of value bins of its source coverage points. This means that a cross coverage element does not keep track of its coverage point values but what value bins in these coverage points had a hit. *Cross domain* is the set of all bins in the cross product of bins for each cross element source. For example, if coverage point **cp_a** has bins ba_1, ba_2, and coverage point **cp_b** has bins bb_1, bb_2, then the cross domain for **xc_ab** (cross of **cp_a** and **cp_b**) is given by the set {(ba_1,bb_1), (ba_1,bb_2), (ba_2,bb_1), (ba_2,bb_2)}. Coverage point value bins marked either as illegal or ignore are not included in defining cross domain. A cross bin has a hit if all bins in its definition have a hit. For example, bin {ba_1,bb_1} is hit at a sampling event if both bins ba_1 and bb_1 have a hit in that

sampling event. SystemVerilog provides special constructs for defining bins for a cross element as a subset of bins in its domain. Cross coverage bins are described in the following
subsection.

17.4.1 Cross Coverage Bins

Cross coverage bins are defined in terms of value bins for coverage points used to define that
cross coverage element. In the absence of any bin definition, a cross coverage element will
implicitly include all bins in its domain. Consider the following example program:

```
Program 17.10: Cross coverage bin definition
1  :    module top;
2  :        bit length_is_relevant, reset=0, clk = 0;
3  :        bit [15:0] packet_length, link_speed;
4  :
5  :        covergroup cg_length_speed @(posedge clk);
6  :            cp_len: coverpoint packet_length {
7  :                ignore_bins way_too_short = {[$:2]};
8  :                bins too_short = {[3:10]};
9  :                bins short = {[11:200]};
10 :                bins regular[3] = {[201:800]};
11 :                bins long = {[801:1000]};
12 :                bins too_long = {[1001:$]};
13 :            }
14 :            cp_sp: coverpoint link_speed {
15 :                illegal_bins way_too_slow = {[$:2]};
16 :                bins too_slow = {[3:10]};
17 :                bins slow = {[11:100]};
18 :                bins average[3] = {[101:1000]};
19 :                bins fast = {[1001:10000]};
20 :                bins too_fast = {[10001:$]};
21 :            }
22 :            xc_length_speed: cross cp_len, cp_sp iff (!reset);
23 :        endgroup
24 :    endmodule
```

Coverage group **cg_length_speed** defines coverage points **cp_len** and **cp_sp**. These coverage points represent coverage information collected for the length of a packet and the
speed with which this packet was received (exact method of calculating this speed is not relevant to this context). Each coverage point includes a number of bin definitions that represent length and speed qualities that may be of interest for coverage collection purposes.
Cross coverage element **xc_length_speed** (line 20) is defined in terms of coverage points
cp_len and **cg_speed**. Given that no bins are explicitly defined for **xc_length_speed**, the full set
of bins in domain of cross **xc_length_speed** is implicitly created. The domain for cross element **xc_length_speed** is shown in figure 17.1, where all squares in this diagram correspond to
one cross bin for **xc_length_speed**. Note that value bins **way_too_slow** and **way_too_short** are
not included in this diagram, since they are marked as *illegal* and *ignore*, respectively. The
highlighted areas in this diagram show the grouping of individual bins into larger bins by
using special syntax introduced later in this section.

In this figure, every row corresponds to one value bin of coverage point **cp_len**, and
every column corresponds to one value bin of coverage point **cp_sp**. Every square in this grid
corresponds to a cross coverage bin for cross coverage element **xc_speed_length**.

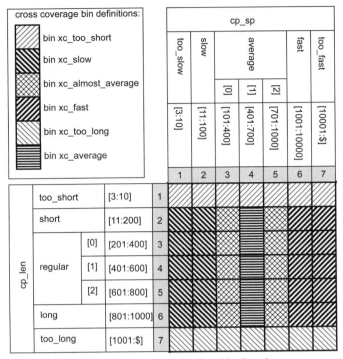

Figure 17.1 Cross Product Bin Creation

The grid in figure 17.1 shows the full domain of cross coverage element **xc_speed_length**. For a cross element composed of three coverage points, the figure would be drawn in three dimensions. SystemVerilog allows coverage bins for a cross coverage element to be defined as a subset of its domain. To that end, SystemVerilog provides special syntax for defining the desired subset. Specifying a subset for a two dimensional cross coverage element is described using the diagram in figure 17.1. Such specification for higher dimension cross coverage elements follows naturally from this discussion.

The following forms can be used to define any subset of bins in figure 17.1:

- All bins in a row (or a set of rows)
- All bins in a column (or a set of columns)
- All bins at the intersection of a row and a column (or a set of rows and columns)
- Any combination of the above forms

SystemVerilog provides the *binsof*, conjunction, and disjunction operators to define any of the subsets outlined above.

The *binsof* operator is used to select a subset of value bins for the bins of a coverage point (i.e., a number of rows or columns in figure 17.1). The syntax for this construct is:

binsof(bin_expression) intersect (range_expression)

Operator "*!*" can be used to negate the sense of selected bins so that bins specified using this notation are excluded from the set of selected bins. This operator can be applied to only a ***binsof*** construct. The *bin conjunction operator* "&&" is used to define the intersection of bins selected using the ***binsof*** construct (i.e., intersection of rows and columns in figure 17.1). The *bin disjunction operator* "||" is used to combine bins selected using the ***binsof*** and conjunction operators. Examples of bins selection using this syntax are shown in table 17.1.

Bin Selection Statement	Cross Coverage Bins Selected
binsof(cp_len)	rows 1,2,3,4,5,6,7
binsof(cp_len.too_short)	row 1
binsof(cp_len.regular[0])	row 3
binsof(cp_len.too_short) || binsof(cp_len.regular[1])	rows 1,4
binsof(cp_len.regular)	rows 3,4,5
binsof(cp_len.regular) intersect {[300:500]}	rows 3,4
!binsof(cp_len.regular)	rows 1,2,6,7
!binsof(cp_len.regular) || binsof(cp_len.regular[0])	rows 1,2,3,6,7
binsof(cp_sp.average)	columns 3,4,5
binsof(cp_len.too_short) && binsof(cp_sp.average)	intersection of row 1 and columns 3,4,5

Table 17.1: Coverage Point Bin Selection for Cross Coverage Bin Definition

The program below shows the definitions for cross coverage bins shown in figure 17.1.

```
Program 17.11:Cross coverage bin definition
              ⋮

1   :      xc_length_speed: cross cp_len, cp_sp iff (!reset) {
2   :          bins xc_too_short = binsof(cp_len.too_short)
3   :          bins xc_slow =
4   :              binsof(cp_sp) intersect {[3:100]} && (binsof(cp_len) intersect {[11:1000};
5   :          bins xc_almost_average =
6   :              binsof(cp_sp.average[0]) && (binsof(cp_len) intersect {[11:1000} ||
7   :              binsof(cp_sp.average[2]) && (binsof(cp_len) intersect {[11:1000};
8   :          bins xc_average =
9   :              binsof(cp_sp.average[1]) && (binsof(cp_len) intersect {[11:1000};
10  :          bins xc_fast = binsof(cp_sp.average) &&
11  :              binsof(cp_sp) intersect {[1001:$]} && (binsof(cp_len) intersect {[11:1000};
12  :          bins xc_too_long = binsof(cp_len.too_long)
13  :      };
              ⋮
```

Any of the bins defined in this program can be marked as ignore or illegal. In case of an overlap, the ignore and illegal settings take precedence in handling a sampled cross value.

17.5 Class-Based Coverage Collection

A coverage collection group can be embedded in a class declaration. This embedding is useful in that the coverage group can freely collect coverage on private and protected class members. In addition, each class instance can include a new instance of the coverage group allowing coverage information to be collected for each instance of a class object.

A coverage group included in a class is treated the same as other composite data objects that must be explicitly created (e.g., a class object). This behavior results in the following restrictions in dealing with coverage groups that are embedded inside class declarations:

- The name of a coverage group declared inside a class cannot be used for any other class member (data object or coverage group).
- A coverage group declaration inside a class is one and the same as declaring a pointer to that coverage group. As such, the name of that coverage group cannot be used to declare a new pointer to that coverage group. This is in contrast to using coverage groups in other blocks where the name of a coverage group declaration must be used as a data type to instantiate coverage groups of that type.
- A coverage group declared inside a class has to be explicitly allocated. Otherwise, no coverage group is created and no coverage is collected for that class.

The following program shows an example of coverage groups embedded in a class declaration:

```
Program 17.12: Coverage groups embedded in a class
1   :   module top;
2   :       class subpacket;
3   :           byte data;
4   :       endclass
5   :
6   :       class packet;
7   :           bit clk;
8   :           subpacket subp;
9   :           byte data;
10  :
11  :           covergroup cg_subp @(posedge clk);
12  :               cp1: coverpoint subp.data;
13  :           endgroup
14  :
15  :           covergroup cg_data @(posedge clk);
16  :               cp1: coverpoint data;
17  :           endgroup
18  :
19  :           function new();
20  :               cg_subp = new();
21  :               cg_data = new();
22  :           endfunction
23  :       endclass
24  :   endmodule
```

This program highlights the following aspects of embedding coverage groups inside a class declaration:

- Coverage groups **cg_subp** and **cg_data** are embedded inside class **packet**.
- Classes may contain multiple coverage group declarations.
- Each coverage group declaration is assumed to be an implicit creation of a pointer to a coverage group object. The actual coverage group must be allocated explicitly. In this example, coverage groups **cg_subp** and **cg_data** are allocated inside the class constructor (lines 20, 21).
- Names **cg_subp** and **cg_data** cannot be used for any other class member.

- Any variable referenced inside a coverage group declaration must be declared before the declaration of that coverage group. In the above example, class properties **clk**, **data** and **subp** are declared before coverage groups that reference these variables.

A class derived from a base class that includes a coverage group inherits that coverage group as well. It is possible to redefine the definition of that coverage group by using its name to define a new coverage group in the derived class. In this case, the coverage group in the parent class can still be accessed using the **super** keyword. This access is, however, allowed only for the immediate parent class of a derived class.

17.6 Coverage Options

A number of *coverage options* can be specified along with coverage constructs. These options can be specified at the following syntactical levels:

- Coverage groups
- Coverage points
- Cross coverage elements

In addition, options can be specified for a coverage group type or for each instance of that coverage group. Also, some options specified at the coverage group level imply defaults values for the same options at the coverage point or cross element levels, unless overridden at that level by providing a new value for that option.

Table 17.2 shows the complete list of all options allowed for coverage constructs. Column 2 gives the range of valid values for each option. Column 4 and 5 indicate if each option is available at the coverage group level as a type or instance option. Column 6 indicates whether an option specified at the coverage group level is considered a default value for coverage points and cross elements included in that coverage group. Columns 7, 8, 9 and 10 indicate whether each option is available as instance/type option for coverage point and cross elements, respectively.

17.7 Coverage Methods

SystemVerilog provides predefined methods that can be called for coverage constructs, as well as system tasks and functions used for managing the coverage database.

The following system tasks and functions are provided in SystemVerilog:

- *$set_coverage_db_name (db_name)*
- *$load_coverage_db (db_name)*
- *$get_coverage ()*

Task *$set_coverage_db_name* sets the name for the file that stores the collected coverage results. Task *$load_coverage_db* loads coverage information from the name passed as an

Option	Type	Description	Group			Point		Cross	
			Instance	Type	Is Default	Instance	Type	Instance	Type
1	2	3	4	5	6	7	8	9	10
name	string	Covergroup name	☑						
weight	int	Weight of each construct for grade calculation. Weight for type and instance are used for type and instance grading, respectively.	☑	☑		☑	☑	☑	☑
goal	0–100	Target coverage defined as a percentage.	☑	☑		☑	☑	☑	☑
comment	string	Text to include in the coverage report.	☑	☑		☑	☑	☑	☑
at_least	int	A bin must have at least this many hits before it is considered covered.	☑		☑	☑		☑	
auto_bin_max	int	Maximum number of automatically generated bins for coverage points.	☑		☑	☑			
cross_auto_bin_max	int	Maximum number of automatically generated bins for cross elements.	☑		☑			☑	
cross_num_print_missing	int	Number of missing (not covered) cross product bins that must be saved to the coverage database and printed in the coverage report.	☑		☑			☑	
detect_overlap	bool	Issue warning if bins defined for a coverage point include overlapped members.	☑		☑	☑			
per_instance	bool	Collect information for each instance of the coverage group.	☑						
strobe	0/1	Activate the coverage group only once at the end of the time-slot.		☑					

Table 17.2: Coverage Options

argument. Function *$get_coverage* returns a real number between **0** and **100**, giving a measure of overall coverage collected so far.

Predefined tasks and functions for coverage constructs are shown in table 17.3. In this table, columns 3, 4, and 5 indicate whether that method is defined at syntactical levels of coverage groups, coverage points, or cross elements, respectively.

17.8 Assertion-Based Coverage

Transition bins for coverage points provide a mechanism for collecting coverage on specific changes in value of variables and expressions. However, this approach is useful only for transitions that can be described with the limited sequence description constructs allowed for coverage transition bins. The *cover* variant of concurrent assertion statements provides a mechanism for collecting coverage on complex behaviors that can be specified using properties and sequences.

The syntax for this construct is as follows:

Method	Description	Group	Point	Cross
1	2	3	4	5
void sample()	Activate a coverage group	☑		
real get_coverage()	Returns type coverage grade	☑	☑	☑
real get_inst_coverage()	Returns instance coverage grade	☑	☑	☑
void set_inst_name(string)	Set the name for each coverage group instance	☑		
void start()	Starts collecting coverage information	☑	☑	☑
void stop()	Stops collecting coverage information	☑	☑	☑
real query()	Returns the cumulative coverage information (for the coverage group type as a whole)	☑	☑	☑
real inst_query()	Returns the per-instance coverage information for this instance	☑	☑	☑

Table 17.3: Predefined Coverage Tasks and Functions

```
[label] cover property (property_expression) [pass_statement];
[label] cover property (sequence_expression) [pass_statement];
```

The *cover* directive is used to include the results of evaluation of a sequence or property in coverage results. A pass statement can be specified for this statement, which is executed anytime the sequence succeeds or the property evaluates to true.

If the *cover* variant of assertion statement is used with a property expression, then coverage is collected on the following conditions:

- Number of times property evaluation is attempted
- Number of times the property succeeds
- Number of times property succeeds vacuously
- Number of times property fails

The pass statement is called for each success of the property expression.

If the cover variant of assertion statement is used with a sequence expression, then coverage is collected on the following conditions:

- Number of times sequence evaluation is attempted
- Number of times sequences match

The pass statement is called each time the sequence matches, but at most, once in each time-slot. Note that this behavior is different from the one for the *assert* statement where the pass statement is called only on the first match of the sequence expression and at most once in that time-slot. As an example, consider a sequence that when started at time **10**, produces matches at times **11** and **12**. With an *assert* statement on such a sequence, the pass statement is called only once, at time **11**, since sequence evaluation stops because of the implicit use the first match operator in a evaluating a property. With a *cover* statement on this sequence, the pass statement is called once at time **11** and once at time **12**.

CHAPTER 18

Coverage Planning, Implementation, and Analysis

Verification project productivity is not measured by the fact that verification progress is made, but rather by how fast such progress is made. Coverage collection provides the sense of direction necessary to guide a coverage-driven verification flow so that coverage progress is made at the fastest possible rate. Given the direct impact of coverage collection results on verification productivity, it is important to take the steps necessary for creating a well designed and executed coverage collection flow.

A coverage collection flow consists of the following iterative steps:

- Coverage design and implementation
- Coverage collection
- Coverage grading
- Coverage analysis

In the coverage design phase, a coverage plan is produced. This coverage plan outlines the types and quantity of information that must be collected in order to gain confidence in full execution of the verification plan. SystemVerilog provides a rich set of coverage collection constructs leading to choices in how coverage collection can be implemented. As such, an important part of coverage design phase is the decision of how to map coverage collection targets into an actual implementation. Coverage grading refers to deriving a quantitative measure from the set of data sampled during coverage collection. Coverage analysis provides a road map for using the coverage information collected so far to guide the following simulation and coverage execution steps.

Chapter 17 provides a detailed description of SystemVerilog constructs for coverage implementation. This chapter discusses coverage planning and execution phases and the implementation of this strategy using constructs described in chapter 17. Section 18.1 gives an example verification plan that is used as the source of examples discussed in this chapter. Section 18.2 describes how coverage collection targets identified from a verification plan are used to create a coverage implementation. Coverage grading and analysis are discussed in sections 18.3 and 18.4, respectively.

18.1 XBar Verification Plan

Figure 18.1 shows a pictorial view of the 4-port crossbar switch XBar introduced in section 12.2. The XBar communication protocol is also described in section 12.2. In the configuration shown in this figure, port **0** supports protocol **Proto_A**, port **1** supports protocol **Proto_B**, and ports **2** and **3** support both protocols **Proto_A** and **Proto_B**. In this configuration, a port can only initiate and respond to data requests that follow its supported protocol. Therefore, for example, the agent connected to port **0** can respond to any incoming data request following **Proto_A** and can initiate a data request to any port supporting **Proto_A** (i.e., ports **3** and **4**).

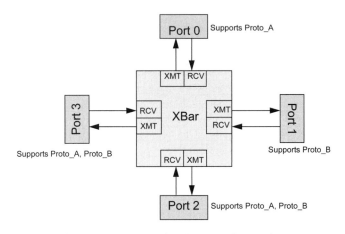

Figure 18.1 XBar Design Coverage Setup View

A verification plan contains two types of scenarios, as related to coverage collection:

- Scenarios whose occurrence must be confirmed by collecting coverage
- Scenarios whose occurrence can be assumed because of the occurrence of certain scenarios and the existence of environment checkers and monitors

For example, a beacon reply frame is always generated in response to a beacon request frame. If the verification environment contains a scoreboard checking that sending a beacon request frame from a source port to a destination port is followed by receiving a beacon reply frame from the destination port at the source port, then coverage information need only be collected for how many beacon request frames are sent from each source port to each destination port. For each generated beacon request frame, then the scoreboarding mechanism implies that beacon reply frames moving in the opposite direction were also generated.

A partial verification plan for this environment is shown in table 18.1. Note that this verification plan lists only scenarios relevant to coverage collection. The scenarios listed in this partial verification plan serve as examples for coverage implementation approaches described in the remainder of this chapter. This verification plan consists of four separate sections described in the following paragraphs.

	Scenario	Transfer	Src Port	Dest Port
TRANSFER ROUTING	Verify that each agent connected to an XBar transmit port responds correctly to beacon requests arriving at that port.	Beacon Request	0	1,2,3
			1	0,2,3
			2	0,1,3
			3	0,1,2
	Verify that each agent connected to an XBar transmit port responds correctly to data requests arriving at that port.	Data Request Protocol A	0	2,3
			2	0,3
			3	0,2
		Data Request Protocol B	1	2,3
			2	1,3
			3	1,2

	Scenario	Packet Kind Following Idle Time	Idle Time
IDLE TIMING	Verify that long idle time preceding a packet on the XBar receive port does not cause problems.	Data Request/Reply protocol A	0-100
			101-1000
		Data Request/Reply protocol B	0-333
			334-3333
		Beacon Request/Reply	0-555
			556-5555
	Verify that idle time before each packet should not exceed the maximum time allowed for that kind.	Data Request/Reply protocol A	>1000
		Data Request/Reply protocol B	> 3333
		Beacon Request/Reply	> 5555

	Scenario	XBar Receive Port Packet Kind Sequence		
		From Packet	To Packet	To Packet
RECEIVE PORT TRANSITIONS	Verify that for all legal packet sequences arriving at XBar receive ports, transfers formed by these packets are handled correctly by the switch and the destination agents	SOF	Data Request A Data Request B Data Reply A Data Reply B	----
		SOF	Beacon Request Beacon Reply	Data Request A Data Request B Data Reply A Data Reply B

	Scenario	XBar Transmit Port Packet Kind Sequence
TRANSMIT PORT TRANSITIONS	Verify that for packet sequences appearing at an XBar transmit port (listed on the right), these packets are handled correctly by the switch and the destination agents.	1, 2, or 3 consecutive SOF (one from each port)
		3 consecutive SOF followed by 2 Data Request A
		3 consecutive (SOF followed by Data Reply A)
		---list other interesting combinations as necessary----

Table 18.1: Partial Verification Plan for the XBar Design

The first section describes scenarios involving frames flowing between source and destination ports. Note that this listing does not include reply type transfers, since it is implicitly assumed that such transfers are generated in response to request type transfers and the automatic checking and scoreboarding mechanisms in the verification environment verify that the expected behavior for these transfer kinds is followed. Also note that the list of data request frames reflects the assumption that not all port agents support both protocols **proto_A** and **proto_B** (See figure 18.1 for protocols supported by each port agent).

The second section lists scenarios that are required for checking idle time behavior at each receive port of the XBar design. This section highlights the requirement that each group of packet kinds has a different maximum allowed idle time. Note also that the ranges of allowed delay values for each group is defined differently.

The third section lists the set of legal packet kind sequences that can be observed at any of the XBar receive ports. The list of legal transitions is derived from the set of guidelines described in the XBar communication protocol (section 14.1). All transitions starting with an **SOF** packet (e.g., **SOF** packet followed by another **SOF** packet) and not listed in the table are considered illegal and should not occur during the simulation process.

The fourth section lists "interesting" packet kind transitions at the transmit port of the XBar design. Note that at XBar transmit ports, the number of possible packet kind sequences is more than can efficiently be enumerated (unlike those at the XBar receive port). The reason is that packets may arrive from any of the other ports and hence the number of packet kinds and their possible orderings is a large number (e.g., an **SOF** packet followed by another **SOF** packet is possible at the transmit port of the XBar design, since these **SOF** packets may have arrived from different source ports).

The scenario categories shown in this table are used in the following sections to motivate the need for, and illustrate, different coverage implementation approaches.

18.2 Coverage Design

Coverage design is the process of creating a coverage plan whose implementation and execution provides information that is necessary for deciding whether or not all verification plan scenarios have occurred.

The structure and content of a coverage plan depends on the following issues:

- Glue logic that must be created between the verification environment and coverage collection constructs
- Choice of SystemVerilog constructs used in implementing the elements of a coverage plan

This interdependence essentially implies that a clear view of the final implementation of the coverage plan (not only what constructs but also what sampling events, and variables to be sampled and their timing) is required before details of a coverage plan can be laid down. The following subsections describe these issues. The ideas presented in this section are then used in section 18.3 to create the coverage plan for the XBar design.

18.2.1 Coverage Collection Glue Logic

A coverage tool can collect only the following types of information:

- Point coverage: How many times an integral variable (e.g., integer, logic, bit, etc.) held a specific value (e.g., 4), or a value in a specific range (e.g., a number between 2 and 12).
- Transition coverage: What was the sequence of values assigned to a single integral variable (e.g., how many times the value for an integer variable changed from 3 to 12 to 14, or how many times the value for an integer variable changed from a value in the range 12–99 to a value in the range 33–123 to a value in the range 144–188).
- Cross coverage: What simultaneous values were assigned to two or more integral variables (e.g., how many times two integer variables contained values 3 and 5 at the same time, or values in ranges 2–13 and 33–132 at the same time).

A coverage engine does not really understand or have any knowledge of composite data objects (e.g., packets) or multi-cycle behaviors (e.g., bus read cycle) that are usually the subject of coverage collection. This means that before coverage can be collected on any simulation related behavior, that behavior must be made identifiable through one of information types outlined above. For example, collecting coverage on how many times a system reset has occurred is straightforward, since it constitutes a point coverage where the number of positive edges for the reset signal are counted throughout the simulation process. Coverage collection for abstract behaviors is, however, more involved. Consider a memory read operation that takes place across multiple simulation cycles. Collecting coverage on the number of times that a memory read operation is performed for an address in the range 0x1112–0x1122, requires one or more integral values to be created for storing information about the latest bus operation type and its memory address. Only then can the required coverage information be collected by sampling these integral variables.

The following steps must be performed in making simulation behaviors identifiable to coverage collection:

- Collecting coverage on abstract data types, where each data item travels over multiple simulation cycles (e.g., a data packet).
- Synchronizing the sampling of two asynchronous (i.e., timing independent), yet verification-dependent behaviors (e.g., injection of a packet of type A at port 1 followed within 10 ns by injection of packet of type B at port 2).

Abstract data items, referred to in the first case, fall into two categories: 1) data items that are usually a part of the implementation of the verification environment (e.g., an XBar packet), and 2) data values that are specific only to coverage collection (e.g., time lapse between two events). In the first case, the verification environment has already been implemented using these abstract data items so building coverage specific glue logic, for these data items is not required. In the second case, special code must be added to the environment to make this information available to coverage collection. For example, in the XBar verification plan, it is not necessary to build special coverage related glue logic since the monitor attached to each port already extracts these packets in a form that can readily be used in coverage collection. In collecting coverage on scenarios related to idle times, however, a special coverage related variable must be added to store the idle time before each variable so that this idle time value can be sampled at the same time as coverage is collected on a packet.

The synchronization between two time-independent behaviors is a common requirement in implementing coverage collection. Consider a verification scenario for the XBar design whose activation requires that two beacon request transfers are initiated to the same port within 10 ns of each other. Collecting coverage on such conditions requires coverage glue logic to be added to the environment.

18.2.2 Cross Coverage Implementation Models

Once the necessary coverage glue logic is put in place, the required coverage information can be collected through coverage points, transitions, and crosses. The next step in building a coverage plan is to decide how to collect the required coverage information.

Coverage collection on a single variable is straightforward and can be implemented using coverage points. Collecting coverage on interdependent variables is, however, more involved. Multi-variable coverage implementation falls into one of the following coverage models:

- Muti-instance
- Hierarchical
- Multidimensional
- Multi-definitional

These implementation models are described in the following subsections.

18.2.2.1 Multi-Instance Coverage Models

A multi-instance coverage model uses multiple instances of the same coverage group definition to collect information on the same type of data from multiple places in the environment. SystemVerilog coverage constructs allow coverage information to be accessed for each instance (i.e., instance coverage) independently as well as collectively for all instances of the coverage group (i.e., type coverage).

Multi-instance implementation is best suited to cases where data to be observed originates or terminates in multiple places in the environment and there is interest in maintaining coverage information about each individual location as well as aggregate information on the data items targeted for coverage collection.

The verification plan for the XBar design requires that coverage be collected on packet types arriving at each receive port of the XBar design. A multi-instance model is a natural implementation choice for this coverage requirement since data objects to be sampled have the same format at all locations, and by using a multi-instance implementation, queries can be made on coverage values for each instance (how many packets of each type were observed at each port), as well as the aggregate results for all instances (how many packets of each type was observed at all ports).

The following example shows a multi-instance implementation of collecting coverage on the kinds of XBar packets observed at the XBar receive port.

Program 18.1: XBar receive monitor coverage collector

```
1  :    module top;
2  :        bit clk, reset;
3  :        typedef enum {INVALID, SOF, BEACON_REQ, BEACON_REPLY, DATA_REQ_A,
4  :                      DATA_REQ_B, DATA_REPLY_A, DATA_REPLY_B} packet_kind;
5  :
```

```
6   :       class xbar_packet;
7   :               rand bit [3:0] data;
8   :               rand bit [3:0] src_addr;
9   :               rand bit [3:0] dest_addr;
10  :               function packet_kind get_packet_kind(); // implementation not shown
11  :               endfunction
12  :       endclass
13  :
14  :       class xmt_monitor;
15  :               event col_coverage ;
16  :               rand xbar_packet pkt;
17  :               int port_num;
18  :
19  :               covergroup cg_xbar_packet @(col_coverage);
20  :                       option.per_instance = 1;
21  :                       pkind: coverpoint pkt.get_packet_kind() iff (!reset) {
22  :                               bins pkind_bins[] = {[$:$]};
23  :                               ignore_bins nocare_bins = {SOF, BEACON_REPLY,
24  :                                                          DATA_REPLY_A, DATA_REPLY_B};
25  :                               illegal_bins nogood_bins = {INVALID};
26  :                       }
27  :               endgroup
28  :
29  :               function new(int pnum);
30  :                       cg_xbar_packet = new();
31  :                       pkt = new();
32  :                       port_num = pnum;
33  :               endfunction
34  :       endclass
35  :
36  :       xmt_monitor mon0 = new(0); // monitor instance for port 0
37  :       xmt_monitor mon1 = new(1); // monitor instance for port 1
38  :       xmt_monitor mon2 = new(2); // monitor instance for port 2
39  :       xmt_monitor mon3 = new(3); // monitor instance for port 3
40  :   endmodule
```

The above implementation shows a generic description of the XBar packet (lines 6–12). This implementation includes a function declaration that extracts the packet kind from the content of the packet (lines 10–11). A simplified class-based implementation of an XBar receive port monitor is also shown (lines 14–34). For illustration purposes, all monitor instances are created in this top level example (lines 36–39). In the real environment, each monitor instance would exist in its appropriate verification component (see section 13.6).

The above implementation defines a coverage point based on the result of the packet kind returned by function **get_pkt_kind()**. One bin is created for each packet kind (line 22). An ignore bin is defined, reflecting the fact that only packets relevant to scenario creation should be tracked. Note that **SOF** packet kind is also placed in the ignore bin, since checkers in the environment guarantee that any packet of type **DATA_REQ_A** or **DATA_REQ_B** is preceded by an **SOF** packet. An illegal bin is also defined to include the **INVALID** packet kind. Note that instance based coverage collection is activated by using the appropriate option (line 20).

SystemVerilog coverage query functions allow coverage information to be collected for each monitor instance as well as for the coverage type as a whole. Instance coverage information for this example gives information on how many of each packet kind was observed at the port corresponding to that instance. Type coverage information for this example provides information on how many packets of each kind were observed at all receive ports.

In the next section, this example is extended to include a cross coverage element between packet type and its destination port. The result provided for this cross element is more interesting in that instance coverage information for this cross element provides information on how many packets of each kind were sent from the port associated to that instance to each destination port, and type coverage information on this cross element provides information of how many of each packet kind was received at each destination port from *all* source ports.

Multi-instance coverage implementation can be emulated through a cross coverage definition by introducing a variable corresponding to each location where a coverage group instance is placed. This approach, however, defeats the main advantage of an instance based implementation where coverage collection is viewed as tightly connected to structural blocks in the design and the verification environment.

18.2.2.2 Multidimensional Coverage Models

A multidimensional coverage model is used in cases where information must be collected on the relationship between multiple variables. The cross coverage element is the natural choice for implementing a multidimensional coverage requirement. The identifying feature of a multidimensional coverage model is that all bins obtained by creating the cross element may be relevant to coverage collection, subject to selective elimination of cross bins using illegal and ignore bins. This feature is in contrast to multi-definitional and hierarchical models (see sections 18.2.2.3 and 18.2.2.4), where bin definitions may change depending on specific cross combinations.

The following program shows the implementation of coverage collection on the relationship between packet kind and destination port in the XBar design.

```
Program 18.2:  Multidimensional coverage collection using cross coverage
                    ⋮
                    ⋮
1   :    covergroup cg_xbar_packet @(col_coverage);
2   :         option.per_instance = 1;
3   :         pkind: coverpoint pkt.get_packet_kind() iff (!reset) {
4   :              bins pkind_bins[] = {[$:$]};
5   :              ignore_bins nocare_bins = {SOF, BEACON_REPLY,
6   :                               DATA_REPLY_A, DATA_REPLY_B};
7   :              illegal_bins nogood_bins = {INVALID};
8   :         }
9   :         dest_addr: coverpoint pkt.dest_addr iff (!reset) {
10  :              bins dbins[] = {[$:$]};
11  :              illegal_bins nogood_bins = {[4:$]};
12  :         }
13  :         kind_cross_dest: cross pkind, dest_addr iff (!reset) {
14  :              bins breq[]   = binsof(pkind) intersect {BEACON_REQ};
15  :              bins dreq_A[] = binsof(pkind) intersect {DATA_REQ_A};
16  :              bins dreq_B[] = binsof(pkind) intersect {DATA_REQ_B};
17  :              illegal_bins nogood_bins =
18  :                   binsof(dest_addr.dbins[0]) and
19  :                        binsof(pkind.pkind_bins) intersect {DATA_REQ_B} or
20  :                   binsof(dest_addr.dbins[1]) and
21  :                        binsof(pkind.ptype_bins) intersect {DATA_REQ_A};
```

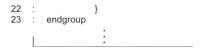

```
22  :                    }
23  :     endgroup
                  :
    |_____:_____
```

The implementation shown above is intended to replace the one shown in program 18.1. In this implementation, a coverage point corresponding to the destination address of each observed packet is added to the coverage group (lines 9–11). Appropriate definitions are used to define illegal bins (line 11), and to also define a bin array for this coverage point (line 10). Cross coverage element **kind_cross_dest**, defined using destination address and packet kind is also added to this coverage group (lines 13–21). The following observations hold about this implementation:

- The instance based coverage results for **kind_cross_dest** gives information on how many packets of each kind have been sent from the port corresponding to the given instance to each destination port. The type coverage result for **kind_cross_dest** gives information on how many packets of a given kind are sent from all ports to a given destination address.
- Bin array **breq** (line 14) contains four bins, one for each destination port. Each bin provides a count of how many **BEACON_REQ** packets have been sent to the destination address corresponding to that bin.
- Bin arrays **dreq_A** and **dreq_B** (lines 15, 16) each contain four bins, one for each destination port with each bin providing a count of how many **DATA_REQ_A** and **DATA_REQ_B** packets, respectively, have been sent to the destination address corresponding to that bin.
- Bins of **pkind** and **dest_addr** that are already marked as ignore or illegal in their definition (i.e., **pkind.nogood_bins**, **pkind.nocare_bins**, **dest_addr.nogood_bins**) are automatically excluded from consideration when forming the bins for their cross product. As such, it is not necessary to explicitly mark **kind_cross_dest** bins that include these bins as illegal or ignore.
- Illegal bin **kind_cross_dest.nogood_bins** is defined to include cases where the combination of valid values for **pkind** and **dest_addr** produce invalid combinations. This includes cases where a **DATA_REQ_A** packet is sent to port **1** and a **DATA_REQ_B** packet is sent to port **0**. In this notation (**binsof(dest_addr.dbins[0])**) selects **dest_addr** bin corresponding to port **0** and (**binsof(pkind.pkind_bins) intersect {DATA_REQ_B})** selects the bin of **pkind** that corresponds to **DATA_REQ_B** packet.

Table 18.2 shows a visual representation of the bin space for cross product element **kind_cross_dest**. Cross product bins excluded from the set of valid bins are marked in this table with the line number causing its exclusion. Bins not excluded on rows marked as **BEACON_REQ**, **DATA_REQ_A**, and **DATA_REQ_B** are form bin arrays **breq**, **dreq_A** and **dreq_B** respectively. Also note that the cross product space shown in this table is larger than the domain for cross product **kind_cross_dest** since it also shows rows corresponding to illegal and ignored bins of its coverage points, which are not included in the domain of a cross coverage element.

			dest_addr				nogood_bins
			dbins				
			0	1	2	3	4-15
pkind	nogood_bins	INVALID	line 7				line 11
	nocare_bins	SOF	line 5				
		BEACON_REPLY					
		DATA_REPLY_A					
		DATA_REPLY_B					
	pkind_bins	BEACON_REQ					
		DATA_REQ_A			line 18		
		DATA_REQ_B	line 20				

Legend: Valid Bin, Ignored Bin, Illegal Bin

Table 18.2: XBar Packet Kind vs. Destination Address Bin Space

18.2.2.3 Multi-Definitional Coverage Model

A multi-definitional coverage model is used in cases where the definition of ranges for one variable changes, depending on the value of another variable. For example, in the XBar idle-time requirements, the definition of idle time values changes according to the type of packet that interrupts the idle period. As shown in table 18.1, idle ranges for a **DATA_REQ_B** packet is defined as **{[0:333], [334:3333], [3334,$]}**, and idle ranges for a **BEACON_REQ** packet is defined as **{[0:555], [556:5555], [5556,$]}**. In such cases, a straight cross coverage element cannot be used to implement this coverage requirement. Multi-definitional coverage model is used to implement this special coverage collection requirement.

The strategy for implementing a muti-definitional coverage model is to first define a coverage point for each definition of the variables involved, followed by combining these coverage points to create a cross coverage element, and then excluding from the resulting cross coverage element all bins that represent illegal combinations of coverage point bins.

The following program shows the implementation of a multi-definitional model to implement the coverage collection requirement for the XBar idle-time scenarios.

Program 18.3: Multi-definitional coverage collection example

```
1  :   covergroup cg_xbar_packet @(col_coverage);
2  :       option.per_instance = 1;
3  :       idle_pkind: coverpoint pkt.get_packet_kind() iff (!reset) {
4  :           bins pkind_bins[] = {[$:$]};
5  :           ignore_bins nocare_bins = {SOF};
6  :           illegal_bins nogood_bins = {INVALID};
7  :       }
8  :       idle_Beacon : coverpoint idle_time iff (!reset) {
9  :           option weight = 0;
10 :           bins b1 = {[0:555]};
11 :           bins b2 = {[556:5555]};
12 :           bins b3 = {[5556:$]};
```

```
13  :      }
14  :      idle_Proto_A : coverpoint idle_time iff (!reset) {
15  :            option.weight = 0;
16  :            bins b1 = {[0:100]};
17  :            bins b2 = {[101:1000]};
18  :            bins b3 = {[1001:$]};
19  :      }
20  :      idle_Proto_B : coverpoint idle_time iff (!reset) {
21  :            option.weight = 0;
22  :            bins b1 = {[0:333]};
23  :            bins b2 = {[334:3333]};
24  :            bins b3 = {[3334:$]};
25  :      }
26  :      idle_cross_kind : cross idle_pkind, idle_Proto_A, idle_Proto_B, idle_Beacon {
27  :            bins beacon[] = binsof(idle_Beacon) and
28  :                            binsof(pkind) intersect {BEACON_REQ, BEACON_REPLY} ;
29  :            bins proto_A[] = binsof(idle_Proto_A) and
30  :                            binsof(pkind) intersect {DATA_REQ_A, DATA_REPLY_A} ;
31  :            bins proto_B[] = binsof(idle_Proto_B) and
32  :                            binsof(pkind) intersect {DATA_REQ_B, DATA_REPLY_B} ;
33  :            illegal_bins b_nogood[] = binsof(idle_Beacon.b3) and
34  :                            binsof(pkind) intersect {BEACON_REQ, BEACON_REPLY};
35  :            illegal_bins pA_nogood[] = binsof(idle_Proto_A.b3) and
36  :                            binsof(pkind) intersect {DATA_REQ_A, DATA_REPLY_A};
37  :            illegal_bins pB_nogood[] = binsof(idle_Proto_B.b3) and
38  :                            binsof(pkind) intersect {DATA_REQ_B, DATA_REPLY_B};
39  :            ignore_bins nocare_bins = default;
40  :      }
41  :      endgroup
                  :
                  :
```

The above implementation makes use of separate coverage point definitions **idle_beacon, idle_Proto_A, idle_Proto_B,** for each bin-grouping of idle time values. Even though it is possible to include all such bin definitions in one coverage point, using separate coverage points leads to a more compact cross coverage bin definition. The cross coverage element **idle_cross_kind,** is defined as a cross between coverage points **idle_pkind, idle_beacon, idle_Proto_A,** and **idle_Proto_B.** Bin arrays **idle_cross_kind.beacon, idle_cross_kind.proto_A,** and **idle_cross_kind.proto_B** are defined to hold the cross coverage information for idle time, depending on the packet type that ends the idle period. A default statement is used (line 39) to remove from consideration all cross bins that are not included in any of the explicitly defined bins.

In the above implementation, coverage points **idle_beacon, idle_Proto_A,** and **idle_Proto_B** do not contribute to coverage, as independent coverage points and their sampled values are relevant only when used in cross coverage element **idle_cross_kind.** As such, the weight for each of these coverage points is set to zero so that their definition does not affect the coverage grade (lines 9, 15, and 21).

Table 18.3 shows a visual representation of the bin space for cross coverage element **kind_cross_idle.** Illegal and ignored bins are marked in this view. Note that each of the bin arrays **beacon, proto_A,** and **proto_B** contains four bins, corresponding to those required by the verification plan.

			Idle Time								
			idle_beacon			idle_proto_A			idle_proto_B		
			b1	b2	b3	b1	b2	b3	b1	b2	b3
			0-555	556-5555	>5555	0-100	101-1000	>1000	0-333	334-3333	>3333
	nogood_bins	INVALID	line 6								
	nocare_bins	SOF	line 5								
idle_pkind	pkind_bins	BEACON_REQ	line 27		line 33						
		BEACON_REPLY									
		DATA_REQ_A				line 29		line 35			
		DATA_REPLY_A									
		DATA_REQ_B							line 31		line 37
		DATA_REPLY_B									

Valid Bin
Ignored Bin
Illegal Bin

Table 18.3: XBar Post-Idle Packet Kind vs. Idle Time Bin Space

18.2.2.4 Hierarchical Coverage Models

A hierarchical coverage model is used in cases where the collection of coverage information is dependent on status observed during simulation runtime. A hierarchical coverage model is a special case of multi-definitional coverage model where coverage collection is not relevant to all possible combinations of the crossed elements and is defined only for specific values.

In the XBar verification plan, ports **0** and **1** support only protocols **Proto_A** and **Proto_B** respectively. This means that the bins corresponding to packets for these protocols should be marked as illegal in their appropriate coverage collection instances on ports **0** and **1**.

The following program shows the implementation of this requirement using a simplified version of the approach used for a multi-definitional model:

```
Program 18.4: Hierarchical coverage collection example
                 ⋮

1   :   covergroup cg_xbar_packet @(col_coverage);
2   :       option.per_instance = 1;
3   :       pkind: coverpoint pkt.get_packet_kind() iff (!reset) {
4   :           bins pkind_bins[] = {[$:$]};
5   :           ignore_bins nocare_bins = {SOF,
6   :               BEACON_REPLY, DATA_REPLY_A, DATA_REPLY_B};
7   :           illegal_bins nogood_bins = {INVALID};
8   :       }
9   :       src_addr: coverpoint pkt.src_addr iff (!reset) {
10  :           option.weight = 0;
11  :           bins dbins[] = {[$:$]};
12  :           illegal_bins nogood_bins = {[4:$]};
13  :       }
```

```
14   :          kind_cross_src: cross pkind, src_addr iff (!reset) {
15   :              illegal_bins nogood_bins =
16   :                  binsof(src_addr.dbins[0]) and
17   :                      binsof(pkind.pkind_bins) intersect {DATA_REQ_B} or
18   :                  binsof(src_addr.dbins[1]) and
19   :                      binsof(pkind.ptype_bins) intersect {DATA_REQ_A};
20   :              }
21   :      endgroup
                    :
                    :
```

This implementation is similar to the multi-definitional model with the exception that only one coverage point **src_addr** is defined for the source address. Coverage point **src_addr** is then combined with coverage point **pkind** to form cross **kind_cross_src** (lines 14–20). Bin definition constructs are then used to define illegal combinations of packet and source address that should be excluded from the set of cross coverage bins.

An alternative approach for building a hierarchical coverage model is to use a cross coverage element and guard expressions for each bin of the cross coverage element.

18.2.3 Transition Coverage Implementation

In general, transition coverage is implemented as a set of bin definitions for the coverage point that samples the value whose transitions are to be covered. This approach works well for transitions that are simple to specify and depend on only a single variable. Using a coverage point to model transition coverage collection is, however, difficult for complicated transition sequences and not possible for transitions involving multiple variables without the use of glue logic.

The following program shows the implementation of the transition coverage requirements for the packet kind observed at the receive port of the XBar design:

```
Program 18.5:  Transition coverage collection
                    :
                    :
1    :   covergroup cg_xbar_packet @(col_coverage);
2    :       option.per_instance = 1;
3    :       pkind: coverpoint pkt.get_packet_kind() iff (!reset) {
4    :           bins trans_bin1[] =
5    :               {SOF} =>
6    :               {DATA_REQ_A,DATA_REQ_B,DATA_REPLY_A,DATA_REPLY_B};
7    :           bins trans_bin2[] =
8    :               {SOF} =>
9    :               {BEACON_REQ, BEACON_REPLY} =>
10   :               {DATA_REQ_A,DATA_REQ_B,DATA_REPLY_A,DATA_REPLY_B};
11   :           illegal_bins nogood_trans_bin = (SOF=>SOF);
12   :           bins remaining_trans_bin = default;
13   :           }
14   :       endgroup
                    :
                    :
```

Special transition bins **trans_bin$_1$** and **trans_bin$_2$** are defined to count the occurrence of transitions defined in the verification plan. In addition, **nogood_trans_bin** is defined to identify illegal transitions (line 11) and the remaining transitions are included in bin **remaining_trans_bin** (line 12). In this implementation, **trans_bin$_1$** bin array contains four bins and **trans_bin$_2$** bin array contains eight bins, corresponding to all possible transitions as allowed by their definition.

Defining complex transitions using coverage point bin definitions is not straightforward. In such cases, assertion-based coverage is a good alternative that allows the full power of sequence definition constructs to be used in collecting coverage on transitions of interest. The following program segment shows the implementation of coverage collection on transitions observed on the transmit port of the Xbar design (as required by the Xbar verification plan in table 18.1).

```
cover property (@(m0.col_coverage) ( m0.pkt.kind==SOF ##1 m0.pkt.kind==DATA_REQ_A) [*2]);
```

The drawback of using assertion-based coverage is that such assertions cannot be placed inside class declarations, and as such cannot be embedded inside class objects as coverage instances can be.

18.3 Coverage Grading

Coverage grading provides a quantitative measure of overall coverage progress. This quantitative measure is given as a percentage where full coverage corresponds to a grade of 100%. The overall coverage grade is computed recursively. First a grade is computed for each bin of cross elements and coverage points. The grade for each element is computed using the grade for its bins, the grade for each coverage group is computed using the grade for its elements, and the overall grade is computed using the grade for all coverage groups in the environment.

The coverage grade for each coverage construct is computed as a weighted sum of the coverage grade for its sub-elements. As such, it is possible to selectively emphasize specific coverage elements in the overall coverage grade by changing their weight option. The following equations are used for computing the grade for different coverage constructs. In the following equations, a coverage element is either a coverage point or a cross coverage element.

$$
\text{Grade(bin)} = \min\left(1.0, \frac{\text{Hits(bin)}}{\text{at\_least(bin)}}\right)
$$

$$
\text{Grade(element)} = \frac{\displaystyle\sum_{\text{all bins}} \text{Grade(bin)}}{\text{numberOfBins}}
$$

$$
\text{Grade(group)} = \frac{\displaystyle\sum_{\text{all elements}} \text{Weight(element)} \times \text{Grade(element)}}{\displaystyle\sum_{\text{all elements}} \text{Weight(element)}}
$$

$$Grade(global) = \frac{\sum\limits_{all\ groups} Weight(group) \times Grade(group)}{\sum\limits_{all\ groups} Weight(group)}$$

In above equations, only **Hit(bin)**, the number of hits for a bin, is extracted from the environment. All other values have default values which can be changed using specific options provided in SystemVerilog (see section 17.6).

The following steps are used to customize coverage grading:

- Define the minimum number of hits required for each bin using the "***at_least***" coverage option. A default value for this option can be set at the coverage group level. This default value will be used for all bins defined for elements of the coverage group. If necessary, this default value can be overridden for each coverage elements (i.e., coverage points and cross coverage elements).
- Specify a weight for each coverage point, cross coverage element, and coverage group. Note that different weights can be specified for type and instance coverage.
- Specify a goal for each coverage point, cross coverage element, and coverage group. Note that different goals can be specified for type and instance coverage.
- During simulation runtime, use the predefined method ***get_coverage()*** to get type coverage grade for a coverage point, a cross coverage element, or a coverage group.
- During simulation runtime, use the predefined method ***get_inst_coverage()*** to get instance coverage grade for a coverage point, a cross coverage element, or a coverage group.
- Alternatively, use a post-simulation coverage analysis tool to load and view the coverage results.

Coverage grades computed for each coverage construct can be used during the simulation runtime to guide the generation process towards the missing scenarios. Additionally, post-simulation coverage analysis can help improve the environment and/or change coverage goals to adapt to conditions observed during simulation. These considerations are discussed in the next section.

18.4 Coverage Analysis

Functional verification is an iterative process. This means that throughout the verification flow, all aspects of verification—including the verification plan, the verification environment, the coverage plan, and the coverage implementation and goals—will go through multiple rounds of changes and enhancements before verification is declared complete. The results of coverage collection provides the primary guidance in deciding how to proceed at each step of this process.

Each pass through this iterative process consists of these phases:

- Planning

- Execution
- Analysis
- Reaction

In the planning phase, coverage model is developed and implemented. In the execution phase, coverage information is collected. The execution phase consists of running the complete regression suite so that the contribution of all existing testcases to overall coverage progress is taken into account. The coverage engine handles the task of combining results from individual runs into a common coverage database. The result of coverage collection is studied in the analysis phase to decide what action should be taken in the reaction phase. The flowchart shown in figure 18.2 summarizes the steps taken in each phase.

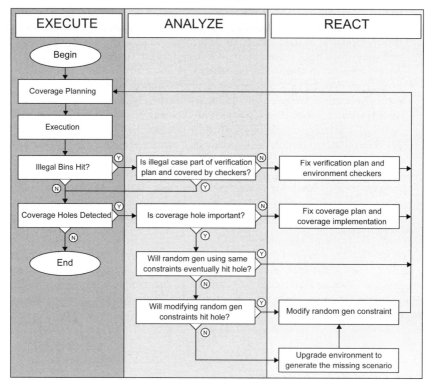

Figure 18.2 Coverage Execution, Analysis, and Reaction Flow

The first pass through the execution phase is started after the first version of the coverage plan is designed and implemented. The results of the execution phase indicates whether any illegal bins were hits and/or any coverage holes still exist. Illegal cases should ideally be detected by checkers and monitors in the environment. As such, if an illegal case is detected only as part of coverage collection, then either the verification plan should be enhanced to include this check or the monitors and checkers in the environment should be fixed to detect this condition as well.

A *coverage hole* is a bin that was not covered during the simulation runtime. It is possible that a coverage hole may not have been relevant to the overall verification progress and may have been marked as such because of a mistake in coverage design. If this is the case, then the coverage plan should be updated to either remove the bin that was not covered from coverage implementation or mark it as an ignored bin.

If a coverage hole is in fact relevant to achieving full coverage, then the random generation environment and its current constraints must be checked to decide whether continued simulation using the same setting is likely to create the condition that covers the coverage hole. No immediate action needs to be taken for such coverage holes.

If a coverage hole is not likely to be covered with continued simulation, then the current generation constraints must be examined to see whether modifying these random generation constraints can lead to the generation of the missing scenario. A new testcase should then be added to the verification environment with the new generation constraints.

If the missing scenario cannot be generated by modifying random generation constraints, then the verification environment must be enhanced to facilitate the creation of the missing scenario. For scenarios that are difficult to generate, it may be necessary to create a unit testcase.

Verification is declared complete when no illegal bins are hit during coverage collection and the global coverage grade exceeds the global coverage goal.

The flow shown in figure 18.2 handles one exception (i.e., illegal case, coverage hole) at a time. In practice, however, a number of simulation runs should be completed before this analysis is performed. In addition, during one pass through this flow, all or most illegal cases and coverage holes should be studied, and steps for dealing with them taken before new simulation runs are started.

PART 8

Appendices

Predefined Classes of the OVM Library

Type	Class Name	Parameters	Extends Class
	analysis_fifo	#(type T=int)	tlm_analysis_fifo
virtual	analysis_if	#(type T=int)	tlm_if_base
	default_report_server		
virtual	ovm_agent		ovm_threaded_component
	ovm_algorithmic_comparator	#(type BEFORE=int, type AFTER=int, type TRANSFORMER=int)	ovm_component
	ovm_analysis_export	#(type T=int)	ovm_port_base
	ovm_analysis_imp	#(type T=int, type IMP=int)	ovm_port_base
	ovm_analysis_port	#(type T=int)	ovm_port_base
	ovm_barrier		ovm_object
	ovm_barrier_pool		ovm_object
	ovm_blocking_get_export	#(type T=int)	ovm_port_base
	ovm_blocking_get_imp	#(type T=int, type IMP=int)	ovm_port_base
	ovm_blocking_get_peek_export	#(type T=int)	ovm_port_base
	ovm_blocking_get_peek_imp	#(type T=int, type IMP=int)	ovm_port_base
	ovm_blocking_get_peek_port	#(type T=int)	ovm_port_base
	ovm_blocking_get_port	#(type T=int)	ovm_port_base
	ovm_blocking_master_export	#(type REQ=int, type RSP=int)	ovm_port_base
	ovm_blocking_master_imp	#(type REQ=int, type RSP=int, type IMP=int, type REQ_IMP=IMP, type RSP_IMP=IMP)	ovm_port_base
	ovm_blocking_master_port	#(type REQ=int, type RSP=int)	ovm_port_base
	ovm_blocking_peek_export	#(type T=int)	ovm_port_base
	ovm_blocking_peek_imp	#(type T=int, type IMP=int)	ovm_port_base
	ovm_blocking_peek_port	#(type T=int)	ovm_port_base
	ovm_blocking_put_export	#(type T=int)	ovm_port_base
	ovm_blocking_put_imp	#(type T=int, type IMP=int)	ovm_port_base
	ovm_blocking_put_port	#(type T=int)	ovm_port_base
	ovm_blocking_slave_export	#(type REQ=int, type RSP=int)	ovm_port_base

Table A.1: OVM Predefined Classes

Type	Class Name	Parameters	Extends Class
	ovm_blocking_slave_imp	#(type REQ=int, type RSP=int, type IMP=int, type REQ_IMP=IMP, type RSP_IMP=IMP)	ovm_port_base
	ovm_blocking_slave_port	#(type REQ=int, type RSP=int)	ovm_port_base
	ovm_blocking_transport_export	#(type REQ=int, type RSP=int)	ovm_port_base
	ovm_blocking_transport_imp	#(type REQ=int, type RSP=int, type IMP=int)	ovm_port_base
	ovm_blocking_transport_port	#(type REQ=int, type RSP=int)	ovm_port_base
	ovm_built_in_clone	#(type T=int)	
	ovm_built_in_comp	#(type T=int)	
	ovm_built_in_converter	#(type T=int)	
	ovm_built_in_pair	#(type T1=int, type T2=T1)	ovm_transaction
	ovm_class_clone	#(type T=int)	
	ovm_class_comp	#(type T=int)	
	ovm_class_converter	#(type T=int)	
	ovm_class_pair	#(type T1=int, type T2=T1)	ovm_transaction
	ovm_comparer		
virtual	ovm_component		ovm_report_object
	ovm_component_registry	#(type T=ovm_component, string Tname="ovm_component")	ovm_object_wrapper
	ovm_config_setting		
	ovm_connector	#(type IF=int)	ovm_connector_base
virtual	ovm_connector_base		ovm_component
	ovm_copy_map		
virtual	ovm_driver		ovm_threaded_component
virtual	ovm_env		ovm_threaded_component
	ovm_event		ovm_object
	ovm_event_callback		ovm_object
	ovm_event_pool		ovm_object
	ovm_exhaustive_sequence		ovm_sequence
	ovm_factory		ovm_object
	ovm_factory_override		
	ovm_get_export	#(type T=int)	ovm_port_base
	ovm_get_imp	#(type T=int, type IMP=int)	ovm_port_base
	ovm_get_peek_export	#(type T=int)	ovm_port_base
	ovm_get_peek_imp	#(type T=int, type IMP=int)	ovm_port_base
	ovm_get_peek_port	#(type T=int)	ovm_port_base
	ovm_get_port	#(type T=int)	ovm_port_base
	ovm_hash	#(type T=int, I1=int, I2=int)	
	ovm_hier_printer_knobs		ovm_printer_knobs
	ovm_if_container	#(type IF=int)	
	ovm_in_order_built_in_comparator	#(type T=int)	ovm_in_order_comparator
	ovm_in_order_class_comparator	#(type T=int)	ovm_in_order_comparator
	ovm_in_order_comparator	#(type T=int, type comp_type=ovm_built_in_comp #(T), type convert=ovm_built_in_converter #(T), type pair_type=ovm_built_in_pair #(T))	ovm_threaded_component
	ovm_int_config_setting		ovm_config_setting

Table A.1: OVM Predefined Classes

Type	Class Name	Parameters	Extends Class
	ovm_line_printer		ovm_tree_printer
	ovm_master_export	#(type REQ=int, type RSP=int)	ovm_port_base
	ovm_master_imp	#(type REQ=int, type RSP=int, type IMP=int, type REQ_IMP=IMP, type RSP_IMP=IMP)	ovm_port_base
	ovm_master_port	#(type REQ=int, type RSP=int)	ovm_port_base
virtual	ovm_monitor		ovm_threaded_component
	ovm_nonblocking_get_export	#(type T=int)	ovm_port_base
	ovm_nonblocking_get_imp	#(type T=int, type IMP=int)	ovm_port_base
	ovm_nonblocking_get_peek_export	#(type T=int)	ovm_port_base
	ovm_nonblocking_get_peek_imp	#(type T=int, type IMP=int)	ovm_port_base
	ovm_nonblocking_get_peek_port	#(type T=int)	ovm_port_base
	ovm_nonblocking_get_port	#(type T=int)	ovm_port_base
	ovm_nonblocking_master_export	#(type REQ=int, type RSP=int)	ovm_port_base
	ovm_nonblocking_master_imp	#(type REQ=int, type RSP=int, type IMP=int, type REQ_IMP=IMP, type RSP_IMP=IMP)	ovm_port_base
	ovm_nonblocking_master_port	#(type REQ=int, type RSP=int)	ovm_port_base
	ovm_nonblocking_peek_export	#(type T=int)	ovm_port_base
	ovm_nonblocking_peek_imp	#(type T=int, type IMP=int)	ovm_port_base
	ovm_nonblocking_peek_port	#(type T=int)	ovm_port_base
	ovm_nonblocking_put_export	#(type T=int)	ovm_port_base
	ovm_nonblocking_put_imp	#(type T=int, type IMP=int)	ovm_port_base
	ovm_nonblocking_put_port	#(type T=int)	ovm_port_base
	ovm_nonblocking_slave_export	#(type REQ=int, type RSP=int)	ovm_port_base
	ovm_nonblocking_slave_imp	#(type REQ=int, type RSP=int, type IMP=int, type REQ_IMP=IMP, type RSP_IMP=IMP)	ovm_port_base
	ovm_nonblocking_slave_port	#(type REQ=int, type RSP=int)	ovm_port_base
	ovm_nonblocking_transport_export	#(type REQ=int, type RSP=int)	ovm_port_base
	ovm_nonblocking_transport_imp	#(type REQ=int, type RSP=int, type IMP=int)	ovm_port_base
	ovm_nonblocking_transport_port	#(type REQ=int, type RSP=int)	ovm_port_base
virtual	ovm_object		ovm_void
	ovm_object_config_setting		ovm_config_setting
	ovm_object_registry	#(type T=ovm_object, string Tname="ovm_object")	ovm_object_wrapper
virtual	ovm_object_wrapper		
	ovm_options_container		
	ovm_packer		
	ovm_peek_export	#(type T=int)	ovm_port_base
	ovm_peek_imp	#(type T=int, type IMP=int)	ovm_port_base
	ovm_peek_port	#(type T=int)	ovm_port_base
virtual	ovm_phase		
virtual	ovm_port_base	#(type IF=ovm_void)	ovm_port_base_base
virtual	ovm_port_base_base	#(type IF=ovm_report_object)	IF

Table A.1: OVM Predefined Classes

Type	Class Name	Parameters	Extends Class
	ovm_printer		
	ovm_printer_knobs		
	ovm_put_export	#(type T=int)	ovm_port_base
	ovm_put_imp	#(type T=int, type IMP=int)	ovm_port_base
	ovm_put_port	#(type T=int)	ovm_port_base
	ovm_random_sequence		ovm_sequence
	ovm_random_stimulus	#(type trans_type=ovm_transaction)	ovm_component
	ovm_recorder		
	ovm_report_global_server		
	ovm_report_handler		
virtual	ovm_report_object		ovm_object
	ovm_report_server		
	ovm_reporter		ovm_report_object
	ovm_req_rsp_driver	#(type REQ=ovm_sequence_item, type RSP=ovm_sequence_item)	ovm_driver
	ovm_req_rsp_sequence	#(type REQ=ovm_sequence_item, type RSP=ovm_sequence_item)	ovm_sequence
virtual	ovm_scenario	#(type REQ=ovm_sequence_item, type RSP=ovm_sequence_item)	ovm_scenario_base
	ovm_scenario_base		ovm_sequence_item
	ovm_scenario_controller	#(type REQ=ovm_sequence_item, type RSP=ovm_sequence_item)	ovm_scenario_controller_base
	ovm_scenario_controller_base		ovm_threaded_component
virtual	ovm_scenario_driver	#(type REQ=ovm_sequence_item, type RSP=ovm_sequence_item)	ovm_scenario_driver_base
	ovm_scenario_driver_base		ovm_threaded_component
virtual	ovm_scenario_driver_noparam		ovm_scenario_driver_base
virtual	ovm_scenario_noparam		ovm_scenario_base
	ovm_scope_stack		
virtual	ovm_scoreboard		ovm_threaded_component
	ovm_seed_map		
	ovm_seq_cons_if		ovm_component
	ovm_seq_item_cons_if		ovm_component
	ovm_seq_item_prod_if		ovm_component
	ovm_seq_prod_if		ovm_component
	ovm_sequence		ovm_sequence_item
	ovm_sequence_item		ovm_transaction
	ovm_sequencer		ovm_sequencer_base
virtual	ovm_sequencer_base		ovm_threaded_component
	ovm_simple_sequence		ovm_sequence
	ovm_slave_export	#(type REQ=int, type RSP=int)	ovm_port_base
	ovm_slave_imp	#(type REQ=int, type RSP=int, type IMP=int, type REQ_IMP=IMP, type RSP_IMP=IMP)	ovm_port_base
	ovm_slave_port	#(type REQ=int, type RSP=int)	ovm_port_base
	ovm_status_container		
	ovm_stimulus_scenario	#(type REQ=ovm_sequence_item)	ovm_scenario
	ovm_string_config_setting		ovm_config_setting
virtual	ovm_subscriber	#(type T=int)	ovm_component
	ovm_table_printer		ovm_printer

Table A.1: OVM Predefined Classes

Type	Class Name	Parameters	Extends Class
	ovm_table_printer_knobs		ovm_hier_printer_knobs
virtual	ovm_test		ovm_threaded_component
virtual	ovm_threaded_component		ovm_component
virtual	ovm_transaction		ovm_object
	ovm_transport_export	#(type REQ=int, type RSP=int)	ovm_port_base
	ovm_transport_imp	#(type REQ=int, type RSP=int, type IMP=int)	ovm_port_base
	ovm_transport_port	#(type REQ=int, type RSP=int)	ovm_port_base
	ovm_tree_printer		ovm_printer
	ovm_tree_printer_knobs		ovm_hier_printer_knobs
	ovm_virtual_sequencer		ovm_sequencer_base
	ovm_void		
	request_driver	#(type REQ=ovm_sequence_item, type RSP=ovm_sequence_item)	ovm_scenario_driver
	tlm_analysis_fifo	#(type T=int)	tlm_fifo
	tlm_b_get_export	#(type T1=int, type T2=int)	ovm_blocking_get_imp
	tlm_b_get_port	#(type T=int)	ovm_blocking_get_port
	tlm_b_put_export	#(type T1=int, type T2=int)	ovm_blocking_put_imp
	tlm_b_put_port	#(type T=int)	ovm_blocking_put_port
virtual	tlm_blocking_get_if	#(type T=int)	tlm_if_base
virtual	tlm_blocking_get_peek_if	#(type T=int)	tlm_if_base
virtual	tlm_blocking_master_if	#(type REQ=int, RSP=int)	tlm_if_base
virtual	tlm_blocking_peek_if	#(type T=int)	tlm_if_base
virtual	tlm_blocking_put_if	#(type T=int)	tlm_if_base
virtual	tlm_blocking_slave_if	#(type REQ=int, RSP=int)	tlm_if_base
virtual	tlm_blocking_slave_if	#(type REQ=int, RSP=int)	tlm_if_base
virtual	tlm_blocking_transport_if	#(type REQ=int, RSP=int)	tlm_if_base
	tlm_event		
	tlm_fifo	#(type T=int)	tlm_fifo_base
virtual	tlm_fifo_base	#(type T=int)	ovm_component
	tlm_get_export	#(type T1=int, type T2=int)	ovm_get_imp
virtual	tlm_get_if	#(type T=int)	tlm_if_base
virtual	tlm_get_peek_if	#(type T=int)	tlm_if_base
	tlm_get_port	#(type T=int)	ovm_get_port
virtual	tlm_if_base	#(type T1=int, type T2=int)	ovm_report_object
virtual	tlm_master_if	#(type REQ=int, RSP=int)	tlm_if_base
	tlm_nb_get_export	#(type T1=int, type T2=int)	ovm_nonblocking_get_imp
	tlm_nb_get_port	#(type T=int)	ovm_nonblocking_get_port
	tlm_nb_put_export	#(type T1=int, type T2=int)	ovm_nonblocking_put_imp
	tlm_nb_put_port	#(type T=int)	ovm_nonblocking_put_port
virtual	tlm_nonblocking_get_if	#(type T=int)	tlm_if_base
virtual	tlm_nonblocking_get_peek_if	#(type T=int)	tlm_if_base
virtual	tlm_nonblocking_master_if	#(type REQ=int, RSP=int)	tlm_if_base
virtual	tlm_nonblocking_peek_if	#(type T=int)	tlm_if_base
virtual	tlm_nonblocking_put_if	#(type T=int)	tlm_if_base
virtual	tlm_nonblocking_slave_if	#(type REQ=int, RSP=int)	tlm_if_base
virtual	tlm_nonblocking_transport_if	#(type REQ=int, RSP=int)	tlm_if_base

Table A.1: OVM Predefined Classes

Type	Class Name	Parameters	Extends Class
virtual	tlm_peek_if	#(type T=int)	tlm_if_base
	tlm_put_export	#(type T1=int, type T2=int)	ovm_put_imp
virtual	tlm_put_if	#(type T=int)	tlm_if_base
	tlm_put_port	#(type T=int)	ovm_put_port
	tlm_req_rsp_channel	#(type REQ=int, type RSP=int)	ovm_component
	tlm_scenario_fifo	#(type T=int)	tlm_fifo
	tlm_scenario_req_rsp_channel	#(type REQ=int, type RSP=int)	tlm_req_rsp_channel
virtual	tlm_slave_if	#(type REQ=int, type RSP=int)	tlm_if_base
	tlm_transport_channel	#(type REQ=int, type RSP=int)	tlm_req_rsp_channel
virtual	tlm_transport_if	#(type REQ=int, type RSP=int)	tlm_if_base

Table A.1: OVM Predefined Classes

SystemVerilog Reserved Keywords

alias	casex	do	event	illegal_bins
always	casez	edge	expect	import
always_comb	cell	else	export	incdir
always_ff	chandle	end	extends	include
always_latch	class	endcase	extern	initial
and	clocking	endclass	final	inout
assert	cmos	endclocking	first_match	input
assign	config	endconfig	for	inside
assume	const	endfunction	force	instance
automatic	constraint	endgenerate	foreach	int
before	context	endgroup	forever	integer
begin	continue	endinterface	fork	interface
bind	cover	endmodule	forkjoin	intersect
bins	covergroup	endpackage	function	join
binsof	coverpoint	endprimitive	generate	join_any
bit	cross	endprogram	genvar	join_none
break	deassign	endproperty	highz0	large
buf	default	endspecify	highz1	liblist
bufif0	defparam	endsequence	if	library
bufif1	design	endtable	iff	local
byte	disable	endtask	ifnone	localparam
case	dist	enum	ignore_bins	logic
Underlined keywords are new to SystemVerilog and not a part of Verilog				

longint	posedge	release	struct	typedef
macromodule	primitive	repeat	super	union
matches	priority	return	supply0	unique
medium	program	rnmos	supply1	unsigned
modport	property	rpmos	table	use
module	protected	rtran	tagged	var
nand	pull0	rtranif0	task	vectored
negedge	pull1	rtranif1	this	virtual
new	pulldown	scalared	throughout	void
nmos	pullup	sequence	time	wait
nor	pulsestyle_onevent	shortint	timeprecision	wait_order
noshowcancelled	pulsestyle_ondetect	shortreal	timeunit	wand
not	pure	showcancelled	tran	weak0
notif0	rand	signed	tranif0	weak1
notif1	randc	small	tranif1	while
null	randcase	solve	tri	wildcard
or	randsequence	specify	tri0	wire
output	rcmos	specparam	tri1	with
package	real	static	triand	within
packed	realtime	string	trior	wor
parameter	ref	strong0	trireg	xnor
pmos	reg	strong1	type	xor
Underlined keywords are new to SystemVerilog and not a part of Verilog				

Index